Third Edition

Methods of Educational and Social Science Research

THE LOGIC OF METHODS

David R. Krathwohl
Syracuse University

WAVELAND

PRESS, INC.

Long Grove, Illinois

For information about this book, contact:
    Waveland Press, Inc.
    4180 IL Route 83, Suite 101
    Long Grove, IL 60047-9580
    (847) 634-0081
    info@waveland.com
    www.waveland.com

7

To
Charles and Minnie
Marie, Sarah, and William
Helen Jean
Chris, David, Jim, Kate, Kristin, and Ruth
Abney, Becca, Elizabeth, Heather, Holly, Jamie, Keith, and Sarah
Harper and Katelyn
Six generations that have so greatly enriched my life

About the Author

David R. Krathwohl is Hannah Hammond Professor of Education Emeritus, School of Education, Syracuse University, where he also served as dean. In addition, he was on the faculty of the Unit on Evaluation of the Bureau of Research and Service of the University of Illinois—Urbana/Champaign, and he was a director and professor of the Bureau of Research at Michigan State University. A fellow of the Center for Advanced Study in the Behavioral Sciences, he was also a president of the American Educational Research Association, and of the Educational Psychology Division of the American Psychological Association. He is the author of *Social and Behavioral Science Research: A New Framework for Conceptualizing, Implementing, and Evaluating Research Studies, How to Write a Research Proposal* (3rd ed.); an author of Bloom's *Taxonomy of Educational Objectives, Handbook 1: Cognitive Domain*; senior author of the *Taxonomy's Handbook 2: Affective Domain*; and co-editor of *A Taxonomy for Learning, Teaching, and Assessing: A Revision of Bloom's "Taxonomy of Educational Objectives."*

Contents

SECTION II
FOUNDATIONAL RESEARCH SKILLS   81

SECTION III
FOUNDATIONAL RESEARCH CONCEPTS   131

SECTION V
THE CONTINUUM OF RESEARCH METHODS:
QUANTITATIVE SIDE   365

SECTION VII
THE LARGER CONTEXT OF RESEARCH   625

Preface

This is a *very extensively* revised edition, thanks in part to the fact that it was originally intended to be co-authored (more on that later) and we planned the revision from scratch. No chapter was untouched, and many changes resulted, some large in scale: new chapters, chapters being split, chapters moved, new and markedly improved graphics, an increased emphasis on the logic of the methods; and some smaller in scale, such as terminology and examples. And of course, as might be expected after a ten-year gap between editions, there was a massive updating of references with much new material originating from the World Wide Web and Internet.

As indicated by the substitution of the subtitle, *The Logic of Methods,* for the previous subtitle, *An Integrating Framework,* there is a considerably increased emphasis on the logic of research. This was always present in the tracing of findings to knowledge and in the chain of reasoning, but it is emphasized in several ways: The new chapter 11 (The Logic of Design) is part of the early sections that apply to both quantitative and qualitative research. It is summarized for qualitative research in Figure 12.3 (an unusual diagram worth studying), in Figure 13.2, and the steps described in chapter 15. The Logic of Statistical Inference is brought to the fore by separating it from the usual discussion of specific statistics (chapters 19 and 20).

A new chapter, The Reflective Researcher (chapter 27), calls researchers' attention to Schon's reflection-in-action and the larger picture of which their work is a part, suggesting that it may be strengthened by taking time to examine it from different perspectives.

The integrating framework of the second edition is as important as it was previously but has now been appropriately modified. Although the model of a study's supporting logic was always intended to apply to both quantitative and qualitative research, the terms in which it was described in previous editions seemed to some readers to be slanted toward quantitative research. This edition's terminology is more clearly neutral, thus reflecting the evenhanded treatment of the two orientations in the rest of the book.

Research methods have long lacked an integrating framework. The one provided in this book improves our understanding of the research process. It helps us to understand why research holds a special place in the knowledge-building process.

And it provides a structure around which can be built the details of method—criteria against which the goals of a study can be measured. Its logical chain of reasoning guides the presentation of findings where appropriate.

Many research texts involve the reader so much in the details of methods that it is difficult to maintain a holistic perspective on their knowledge-building contribution. Possibly you've experienced this in a statistics course, where learning a statistic, perhaps its derivation, uses up the class time, leaving almost none for the larger picture of its use. Some courses concentrate heavily on philosophical issues and assumptions, with attention to postpositivist, interpretivist, realist, and other positions. Their premise is that unless one understands how these issues undergird methods, the methods won't be used correctly.

There is a middle ground, however, one that leads to correctly understanding both the research methods and their role in the knowledge-building process. It is explored in this book, and it begins with understanding research's contribution to knowledge building as a social process through which findings transition into knowledge. This in turn allows us to deduce the various parts of a study's supporting logic. That logic, which is displayed in a graphic that is the frontispiece of this book, is used as an integrating base. Through developing an understanding of that model, one finds the logic of:

- a study's *chain of reasoning,*
- *Internal Integrity* and its relation to the chain,
- *External Generality* and its relation to the chain,
- *criteria to optimize* and their relation to the chain, and
- *constraints to observe* as they affect the chain.

In addition, there is emphasis on:

- the criteria for inferring causation,
- sampling and generalization,
- eliminating rival explanations, and
- analyzing data through data reduction.

As already noted, the chain of reasoning addresses:

- research design to infer causation (a separate chapter in this edition),
- the logical flow of information in qualitative studies, and
- the logic of statistical significance (a chapter now separate from the details of various individual statistics).

The integrating model, which appears as a graphic in the book's frontispiece, is developed along with supporting topics beginning with chapter 3. Individuals make knowing judgments about knowledge claims; these judgments then coalesce into a consensus around the proper interpretation of data, which, if the consensus remains unbroken from researcher to consumer, results in findings being accepted as knowledge. The presentation of knowledge claims as a chain of reasoning (chapter 4) facilitates our judgment of research reports. The chain also serves as a base for making explicit criteria for judgment that were previously only dimly sensed (chapters 7, 8, and 9). Where applicable, the model's graphic on a chapter's first page highlights the relevant part of the model for that chapter.

When you understand how a process works, that understanding is much less susceptible to memory decay. Learning these basic logic structures not only has the advantage of helping you to find and learn the fundamental aspects of method—it also provides a framework on which can be hung the various details of research method. Otherwise, learned separately and individually, they are easily forgotten. Such a framework facilitates retrieval of these details when the framework is activated. Thus, what students learn from this text is more likely to remain useful and be remembered long after the course is over than is the usual barrage of facts, vocabulary, and detail that constitute most courses.

IMPROVEMENTS TO THE THIRD EDITION

- The importance of understanding science as a social process is strengthened. References to this process occur throughout the text, but in particular:
  - — preceding the two contrasting examples of research in the first chapter.
  - — coming to the forefront in the first of two fundamental sections in the text, especially in chapter 3.
  - — closing the book in the final section with chapter 28. This chapter, by the way, is very popular; it evaluates the workings of social science and provides some perspective on it at the individual, peer, and societal level. Some instructors think its messages important enough to assign it early in their course, rather than at the end.

- Section IV, which covers the qualitative end of the research continuum, and Section V, which covers the quantitative end, are now discussed before the examples of areas that draw from both of them: evaluation, sample surveys, and history. This enables readers to familiarize themselves with the complete continuum before encountering those that draw on both orientations.

- As explained in a sidebar in chapter 7, the term *internal validity* is defined inconsistently across different texts and never did encompass all the aspects of causation. Problems with external validity stem from problems with internal validity. Hence, new names and more internally consistent definitions are employed. This edition is integrated not only by the chain of reasoning but also by the renamed and more clearly defined foundational concepts of *Internal Integrity* and *External Generality*.

- In chapter 6, a new and extensive example of the use of the computer in the literature search provides a model for students to adapt to their own search of the literature as well as summing up the points made in the chapter.

- *Conceptual analysis*, an important logic of analysis that was missing from the second edition, returns by request and now appears in chapter 13. Its explicit treatment is rare in methods texts but its logic is widely employed in both qualitative and quantitative methods.

- The pros and cons of using software in qualitative analysis are extensively discussed in chapter 15.

- Chapter summaries have been moved after the Opportunities for Additional Learning (application problems) and their answers (Key to Additional Learning Opportunities) with the intention of making these items a more integral part of the text material. The Application Exercises (ongoing in chapters 5 through 27), encourage students to work on the relevant aspects of their own problems as they proceed through the book so they emerge with a draft research proposal.

- Appendix A on writing a research proposal should continue to be helpful to doctoral students preparing dissertation proposals and masters students doing theses. It includes material on writing formats applicable to writing research reports.

GOALS OF THE TEXT

It helps to get there if you know where you're going, so the goals of this text are listed below. It is intended that readers should:

- Understand science as a social process through which findings become accepted as knowledge.

- Comprehend how the criteria for judging research flow from this process, and understand the implications of these criteria for how research is done and reported.

- Understand the fundamental logic underlying the major concepts of the methods discussed.

- Understand the model for a study's supporting logic as a useful conceptualization of this process for studies of causal relationships and processes and of their generalization—realizing, however, that the graphic does not necessarily describe the order of research stages (which, in actually doing a study, may differ).

- Conceptualize research methods along a continuum from which researchers may choose the most appropriate parts of method(s). At opposite ends are quantitative and qualitative approaches, with uses and adaptations of both approaches appearing in between (for example, sample survey research).

- Acquire the background needed to read, analyze, and understand research using a variety of approaches as well as the hallmarks necessary to evaluate each method.

- Use this background to capably pursue their own research projects, employing one or more research approaches or adaptations thereof to develop the best study feasible.

- Understand the concept of trade-offs in research and how each study typically is a compromise between the practical and the ideal.

- Understand that the responsibility for ethical research is fundamentally theirs, and that value choices are involved in research, beginning with the choice of problem.

Not all of these goals can be equally emphasized, nor can a text alone provide the necessary practice to develop any skill. It is intended, however, that each of the goals be achieved at some level.

INSTRUCTIONAL ASSISTANCE

Every chapter has a number of features to help you learn. Arranged in the order in which they may appear in a chapter:

- *Introductions* set the material to come in context for each chapter, describe the content of the chapter, and, where appropriate, locate its content within the complete model for a study's supporting logic illustrated in the frontispiece.

- *Summaries* appear after major points or sections. Processing the material as you read is especially important. To facilitate this, periodically try to summarize in writing the material you have read and compare your summaries with those placed throughout the text. Your summaries may be better than those provided, but where you find significant differences, reread the material to sort out and evaluate those differences. Such processing will help you integrate disparate facts and terminology into chunks and relate these chunks to other chunks; thus increasing the material's retention and usability.

- *Additional Reading* provides suggestions for more in-depth coverage of a topic or, perhaps, finding another presentation of a point or concept.

- *Important Terms and Concepts* appear at the end of each chapter. After you have finished reading a chapter, see if you can tell what each term means and why it is significant. If you miss some, check the index to determine where they are discussed. Many are in the glossary, particularly those not likely to be in your vocabulary or whose use here differs from common usage. Note, however, that terms appear in the list and are printed in **bold** type mainly when they are first defined in the text.

- *Opportunities for Additional Learning* (application problems) appear immediately after the important terms and concepts for each chapter. Try them and then check your answers against those given at the end of the chapter (in the *Key to Additional Learning Opportunities*). Again, your answers may be better than those given, but be sure you understand why Richard Kenny (who developed the majority of the problems for the book) and I gave the answers we did.

- *Application Exercises* begin with chapter 5, and their purpose is described on page 100. You are asked to choose a problem and then to develop it further by applying the content of each successive chapter. This not only helps you learn the material, but also (for doctoral students) it can result in a first draft of a proposal that can be developed into a dissertation. Many students in my courses have done so; it has helped to transform ABDs ("all but dissertation") students into doctorates. *Doctoral students should read the appendix on* Writing a Research Proposal *very early in the course as a source of advice and guidance, and then refer to it again periodically as their proposals develop.*

- *Chapter Summaries* supplement those within the chapters. Whereas the within-chapter summaries are more complete and detailed, the chapter summary highlights important material. Check it to see what, if anything, you missed.

- *A Look Ahead* at the end of each chapter helps you anticipate how the material you have just read ties into what comes next.

- Use the *Glossary* to refresh your understanding of familiar terms or to look up new ones. The glossary definition is often phrased differently than that in the text.
- For ease of reference, the frontispiece inside the front cover shows the components of the *model for a study's supporting logic*. Alternative graphic interpretations appear in Appendix B. Be sure to take a look at these; they may add to your understanding.

Additional Aids to Learning

Special features in many of the chapters highlight important aspects for researchers and for research consumers:

- *Hallmarks of methods.* How do you know when a research method has been used well? Or on what aspects to concentrate when you use it? All the chapters describing research methods have sections describing the hallmarks of quality so that you'll recognize good work when you see it (see chapters 14, 16, and 21–25). Like the guild hallmarks of the Middle Ages, they help ensure the excellence of the product. Hallmarks for the statistical chapters are best left for courses in that subject.

- *Tips* also appear in each chapter on research method. They provide researchers with pointers on using the method to create a stronger study. These suggestions add to the characteristics summarized for research consumers in the hallmarks section and, on occasion, tips and hallmarks are combined.

Much of the book is written in an informal style. As a student, Jim Ellsworth wrote to me, "it is intended to avoid the traditional 'droning lecture on paper' style exhibited by all too many authors" and to treat the reader "as a colleague, which is both appropriate and important for an upper-level text."

KEEPING THIS EDITION UP-TO-DATE

There are many URLs in this edition. In APA format these appear with the date they were last accessed so the reader will know when they were last known to be live links. We have omitted such dates, however, because all the URLs were accurate at the time we went to press. All URLs were live links as of September 18, 2008.

Thanks to the Internet, we can continue to communicate with you. As new developments arise, as statements in the book can be clarified, improved, or need replacement, as URLs change, or as we receive useful suggestions for instruction, we can put them on the Web. Check this Web site from time to time for useful postings regarding this edition: http://faculty.soe.syr.edu/drkrathw/

TO THE INSTRUCTOR

In this book I seek to legitimize a variety of routes to inquiry and cover each in some depth. Students need a broad understanding of methods—their logic, their strengths and weaknesses, and their complementarity. *Methodological purity*, in the sense that a field espouses only one way of doing research, is on the wane. Research at the margins of fields has stimulated the borrowing of methods. There is increased interest in qualitative methods and in mixed methods.

It is an exciting time to be teaching research methods; so many insights are developing. Even though we have greater perspective on what we are doing and why we do it, we do not yet have a consensus on a number of key methodology issues. Positivism is proclaimed dead but is clung to by many; talk of multiple realities confuses and leaves an uncomfortable feeling in those who argue there is only one world to discover. Qualitative researchers are seeking ways of working that will satisfy critics while at the same time maintaining flexibility and freedom. You face the same problem I did in writing this text: taking your students to the cutting edge, yet marking for them the boundary within which there is consensus.

ACKNOWLEDGMENTS

Alex Haley, author of *Roots*, says, "Whenever you see a turtle on top of a fence post, you know he had a lot of help getting there." I am, for sure, like that turtle! The first edition's lengthy list of acknowledgments makes clear the help necessary to produce a text such as this. Although there are many changes, this edition is built on the solid base of the first two, so my debt to those individuals continues in this one.

I especially appreciate Waveland Press both for continuing to keep the second edition in print and especially for the help of both my editor, Gayle Zawilla, who so ably guided the third edition through the publication process and improved my writing, and Deborah Underwood, who created graphics a quantum leap beyond those of the second edition.

Over and over again I turned to my graduate assistants, Nilay Yildirim, Kristen Evans Flint, and Jeremy Zhang, who made suggestions and tracked down difficult-to-find references, posted some information on the Web, and maintained the currency of the many URLs.

I thank Kastro M. Hamed, then at the University of Kansas, for his suggestion to portray the frontispiece as a flowchart or family tree (see Appendix B).

I am grateful to Richard Kenny for those Opportunities for Additional Learning that were carried over from previous editions, and to my sharp-eyed granddaughter, Sarah Krathwohl, who helped proofread.

About the Authorship

The first two editions had single authorship. For the third, I thought it desirable to bring in a partner for a number of personal reasons. Being impressed with the chapter by John Behrens and Mary Lee Smith (1996), I invited John, then at Arizona State University, to coauthor the third edition with me. John has a way of seeing things in a "big picture" perspective that is very helpful. We hit it off immediately and had frequent and long phone conversations, reviewing the second edition to see what needed to be changed. As I began the revision process, our discussions resulted in many ideas for improvement.

Fortunately for John, Cisco Systems also saw him for the intelligent, capable individual that he is, and they invited him to join them. John initially took leave but eventually left the university. As the demands of his new position grew, I had to settle for "with the assistance of." Therefore, if there are errors, I take responsibility. Let me know of them (my address appears below) and I'll correct them at the first possible opportunity. I wish John could have coauthored the book; it would have been even better. I am very grateful for his assistance; the book is considerably enhanced by his input.

David R. Krathwohl
IDDE
School of Education
Syracuse University
Syracuse, NY 13244-2340

The Nature of Research

This section helps you become comfortable with the nature of research and the variety of methods it employs. It explores how research findings assume the status of knowledge and the process that permits them to do so.

- Chapter 1 introduces you to the nature and goals of social and behavioral research. Starting off with two studies as examples, it helps you recognize that you already have a good knowledge base to build on.

- Chapter 2 shows the wide variety of methods that are employed in the social and behavioral sciences and how, given a problem, one chooses among them.

- Chapter 3 examines how the conclusions of a research study move from being merely findings to becoming accepted as knowledge.

- Chapter 4 describes a valuable general model of a study—the chain of reasoning— that we will use throughout the book.

Although this book opens with two research studies purposely chosen to illustrate contrasting research orientations, in the very next chapter we note there are other research approaches. Indeed, we explain that, while for purposes of explanation these two can be considered the end points of a continuum, there are research types in between, each with its own unique characteristics. This allows researchers to choose research approaches best suited to their problems and skills.

After examining some research basic knowledge and skills (Section II and III), both of the methods continuum's ends are explored in depth (Sections IV and V). Section VI describes in-between points: evaluation/action research, sample surveys, and history. In chapter 26, we come full circle by emphasizing that many problems are best investigated, and many researchers best served, by using a hybrid approach that appropriately combines parts of different research methods. Finally Section VII provides you with some perspective on the whole research process.

Two Research Approaches from a Continuum of Approaches

> We are a scientific civilisation; that means a civilisation in which knowledge and its integrity are crucial. Science is only a Latin word for knowledge.
> —Jacob Bronowski, *The Ascent of Man*
>
> I believe that human life is ours to study.... With a few exceptions, only students in our century have managed to hold it steadily in view ... without piety or the necessity to treat traditional issues. Only in modern times have university students been systematically trained to examine all levels of social life meticulously.
> —Erving Goffman, quoted in J. Lofland,
> *Analytic Ethnography: Features, Failings and Futures*

SOCIAL AND BEHAVIORAL SCIENCE: IMPORTANT BUT HISTORICALLY YOUNG

"Mom, why is Grandpa so suspicious of everyone these days? He seems always to feel that folks are trying to hide something from him, that they are out to get him. I'm sure not! And that stuff about not wanting him around, where did he get that idea? He used to be so easygoing! I don't understand what's going on!"

"I wish I knew, son, but I don't. I've noticed the change, too, and it's got me worried."

Zimbardo and associates (1981) thought they understood what was occurring in cases like this. They did an experiment to test their hunch. Researchers call such hunches that guide studies **hypotheses**. Research hypotheses are surmises that a particular relationship or condition exists. Their hypothesis was that individuals who are gradually growing deaf don't realize it. Deafness changes their perception of the world, which they interpret as increasingly hostile. Testing that hypothesis was an attempt to provide evidence supporting the experimenters' explanation of this phenomenon. Such testing is a common goal in research. Researchers call this confirmation process, the gathering of supporting evidence, **validation**. It is one of many important roles served by research.

The problems that accompany aging are only a few of the many such problems that have been speculated about since time began. How do you and I learn? Why do we act differently in a group from the way we act when we are alone? Why do we choose different ways to organize our governments, economies, and social groups? These fascinating questions have evoked many answers. Only in the twentieth century, however, did we begin to investigate social and behavioral questions by using systematic observation and measurement methods, standardized tests, sophisticated coding schemes for analyzing verbal and observational data, carefully constructed questionnaires, individual and group interview techniques, and large masses of data. Although our progress has become increasingly rapid in the past few decades as we have gained experience, many people believe it is still much too slow, especially if we consider the social problems that such research might relieve. One hope is that with improved methods and well-trained researchers, progress will accelerate. This book is intended as a step in that direction.

Your common sense will be a sound guide for most of what you will learn from this book. You don't believe it? The personal demonstration in the next section should ease any concerns you may have about your ability to master this material.

TWO ILLUSTRATIVE STUDIES

There is no better way to understand what is meant by "research" and to realize that social sciences use a variety of research methods than to start with examples of two contrasting but equally important methods of doing research. Although neither study is of recent origin, they were chosen as examples because they are good illustrations of their types. Further, although "hot" topics come and go, research methods change more slowly, so the methods illustrated are highly relevant. However, it is worth noting that their subject matter is still pertinent as well.

The first example:

• Uses quantitative research methods.

• Employs measures and statistics to describe phenomena.

• Is a tightly designed experiment in which events are controlled by the researcher.

• Employs deductive logic to predict the results from the proposed explanation (hypothesis).

• Validates an explanation and demonstrates a relationship.

The second example:

• Uses qualitative research methods.

• Employs verbal descriptions to portray phenomena.

• Consists of unstructured interviews in which subjects, expressing their own thoughts, explore the topic with the researcher.

• Employs inductive logic to find an explanation.

• Develops an explanation for a perceived relationship.

This chapter contrasts two methods of data collection and analysis, which, as you will see in chapter 2, can be viewed as the opposite ends of a continuum of research methods. It is true that quantitative and qualitative methods each have their own tradition, supporters, and literature, and so the distinction is useful for instructional purposes. For most of us, however, making too much of it can get in the way of seeing all methods as contributors to a panorama of tools. One selects from that panorama whatever best accomplishes one's research purposes.

Almost without regard to method, however, untrained readers show amazing skill in critiquing important aspects of a study. Training will make you sensitive to even more aspects and, most important, will give you a framework that will allow you to retain the important points in your memory. Read the following study critically, making notes on its strengths and weaknesses.

A Quantitative Experimental Study

Induced Hearing Deficit Generates Experimental Paranoia

Philip G. Zimbardo, Susan M. Andersen • Stanford University
Loren G. Kabat • State University of New York, Stony Brook

Abstract. The development of paranoid reactions was investigated in normal people experiencing a temporary loss of hearing. In a social setting, subjects made partially deaf by hypnotic suggestion, but kept unaware of the source of their deafness, became more paranoid as indicated on a variety of assessment measures. The results support a hypothesized cognitive-social mechanism for the clinically observed relationship between paranoia and deafness in the elderly.

1. Clinical observation has uncovered a relationship between deafness and psychopathology (1–3). In particular, when deafness occurs later in life and the hearing loss is relatively gradual, paranoid reactions are often observed (4–14). Delusions of persecution and other paranoid symptoms, first noted by Kraepelin (6) in 1915, seem especially prevalent among the hard-of-hearing elderly (7–9). Audiometric assessment of hospitalized, elderly patients (with age and other selection factors controlled statistically) has revealed a significantly greater degree of deafness among those diagnosed as paranoid than among those with affective disorders (10–12).

2. Maher (15) suggested that one process by which deafness may lead to paranoid reactions involves an initial lack of awareness of the hearing defect by the person, as well as by interacting with others. Paranoid thinking then emerges as a cognitive attempt to explain the perceptual anomaly (16) of not being able to hear what people in one's presence are apparently saying. Judging them to be whispering, one may ask, "about what?" or "why me?" Denial by others that they are whispering may be interpreted by the hard-of-hearing person as a lie since it is so clearly discrepant with observed evidence. Frustration and anger over such injustices may gradually result in a more profound expression of hostility.

3. Observers, without access to the perceptual data base of the person experiencing the hearing disorder, judge these responses to be bizarre instances of thought pathology. As a consequence, others may exclude the hard-of-hearing person, whose suspicious-

Source: "Induced Hearing Deficit Generates Experimental Paranoia" by Philip G. Zimbardo et al., 1981, *Science* (212), 1529–1531. Copyright © 1981 by the American Association for the Advancement of Science. Reprinted by permission. (Paragraph numbers added.)

ness and delusions about their alleged plots become upsetting (17). Over time, social relationships deteriorate, and the individual experiences both isolation and loss of the corrective social feedback essential for modifying false beliefs (18, 19). Within a self-validating, autistic system, delusions of persecution go unchecked (20). As such, they eventually become resistant to contrary information from any external source (21). In this analysis, paranoia is sometimes an end product of an initially rational search to explain a perceptual discontinuity, in this case, being deaf without knowing it.

4. We now report an experimental investigation of the development of paranoid reactions in normal subjects with a temporary functional loss of hearing. Across a variety of assessment measures, including standard personality tests, self-reports, and judgments of their behavior by others in the situation, these subjects became significantly more paranoid than did subjects in two control conditions. The effect was transient and limited to the test environment [by the specificity of the instructions, by extensive post-experimental interviews (debriefing procedures), and by the healthy "premorbid" status of each participant]. Nevertheless, qualitative observations and objective data offer support for the role of deafness-without-awareness as a causal factor in triggering paranoid reactions. Although the subjects were young and had normal hearing, these results have obvious bearing on a possible cognitive-social mechanism by which deafness may eventuate in paranoia among the middle-aged and elderly.

5. Participants were 18 college males selected from large introductory classes. In the selection process, each student (i) demonstrated that he was highly hypnotizable according to the Harvard Group Scale of Hypnotic Susceptibility (22) and the Stanford Scale of Hypnotic Susceptibility, form C (23); (ii) evidenced posthypnotic amnesia; (iii) passed a test of hypnotically induced partial deafness; (iv) scored within the normal range on measures of psychopathology; and (v) attended at least one of two hypnosis training sessions before the experiment.

6. Six participants were randomly assigned to the experimental treatment in which partial deafness, without awareness of its source, was hypnotically induced. The remaining participants were randomly assigned to one of two control groups. In one of these groups, partial deafness with awareness of its source was induced to demonstrate the importance of the knowledge that one's difficulty in understanding others is caused by deafness. In the other control group, a posthypnotic suggestion unrelated to deafness was experienced (a compulsion to scratch an itchy ear) along with amnesia for it, to establish whether merely carrying out a posthypnotic suggestion with amnesia might be sufficient to yield the predicted results. Taken together, these two groups provided controls for experimental demand characteristics, subject selection traits (hypnotic susceptibility), and the rational basis for the experienced sensory anomaly (24).

7. During group training sessions, each subject was instructed in self-hypnosis and completed consent and medical history forms, a number of Minnesota Multiphasic Personality Inventory (MMPI) scales (25), and our clinically derived paranoia scale (26). In the experimental session, subjects were hypnotized, after which they listened through earphones to deep relaxation music and then heard taped instructions for one of the three treatments. The use of coded tapes randomly selected in advance by one of the researchers (L.K.) made it possible for the hypnotist (P.Z.), experimenter (S.A.), observers, and confederates to be ignorant of the treatment assignment of the subjects. All subjects were given the suggestion to begin experiencing the changed state when they saw the posthypnotic cue ("FOCUS") projected on a viewing screen in the laboratory. In order to make the task socially realistic and to conceal the purpose of the experiment, each subject was led to believe he was participating, along with two others (who were confederates), in a study of the effects of hypnotic

training procedures on creative problem solving. Because of the hearing defect that subjects were to experience, all instructions and tasks were projected automatically by timed slides, the first of which was the post-hypnotic cue. While working on a preliminary anagram task, the two confederates engaged in a well-rehearsed, standard conversation designed to establish their commonality, to offer test probes for the subject's deafness, and to provide verbal content that might be misperceived as antagonistic. They recall a party they had both attended, laughed at an incident mentioned, made a funny face, and eventually decided to work together, finally asking the subject if he also wanted to work with them.

8. The instructions had previously suggested that group effort on such tasks is usually superior to solitary responding. The subject's behavior was videotaped, observed directly by two judges from behind a one-way mirror, and scored independently by the confederates immediately after the session. After this conversation, the three participants were asked to develop stories about pairs of people in ambiguous relationships [Thematic Apperception Test (TAT)]. On the first task, they had the option of working together or of working alone. Thus, an interdependence among confederates and the subject was created [important in the natural etiology of paranoia (17, 19, 21)], which centered around developing a common creative solution. On the second TAT task, participants had to work alone.

9. After these tasks were completed, each confederate was instructed by the slides to go to a different laboratory room while the subject stayed in the room to complete evaluation forms, including the MMPI and others. Extensive debriefing followed (27), and to remove any tension or confusion, each subject was rehypnotized by the experimenter and told to recall all the events experienced during the session. Subjects were reevaluated in a one-month follow-up.

10. Major results are summarized in Table 1, which presents group means and one-tailed

t-test values derived from a single a priori planned comparison that contrasted the experimental group with the two control groups taken together (28). This analysis followed standard analysis of variance tests. As predicted, the experience of being partially deaf, without being aware of its source, created significant changes in cognitive, emotional, and behavioral functioning. Compared with the control groups, subjects in the deafness-without-awareness treatment became more paranoid, as shown on an MMPI paranoia scale of Horn (25, p. 283) and on our clinically derived paranoia scale (26). Experimental subjects also had significantly elevated scores on the MMPI grandiosity scale of Watson and Klett (25, p. 287)—one aspect of paranoid thinking. Experimental subjects perceived themselves as more irritated, agitated, hostile, and unfriendly than control subjects did and were perceived as such by confederates ignorant of the treatment. When invited to work with confederates on the TAT task, only one of six experimental subjects elected to do so; in contrast, 9 of 12 control subjects preferred to affiliate ($z = 4.32, P < .001$).

11. The TAT stories generated by the subjects were assessed in two ways. Subjects' own ratings of the creativity of their stories indicated that experimental subjects judged their stories to be significantly less creative than did subjects in either of the control groups. Second, the stories were scored (reliably by two judges) for the extent to which subjects evaluated TAT characters. An evaluative-judgmental outlook toward other people is a hallmark of paranoia. The experimental subjects used significantly more evaluative language, both positive and negative (for example, right–wrong, good–bad) ($t = 2.86$, $P < .01$) than controls did. In addition, they differed significantly ($z = 5.00, P < .001$) from the controls in their greater use of positive evaluative language. Experimental subjects reported feeling no more suspicious than did control subjects. These last two findings weaken the possible criticism that the results were based simply on anger induced by the experimental manipulation.

12. Both groups experiencing a hearing deficit reported, as expected, that their hearing was not keen, but reported no other sensory difficulties. Those who were partially deaf without being aware of the source of the deafness did experience greater confusion, which is likely to have motivated an active search for an appropriate explanation. Over time, however, if their delusional systems were allowed to become more coherent and systematized, the paranoid reaction would be less likely to involve confusion. Ultimately, there is so much confidence in the proposed paranoid explanatory system that alternative scenarios are rejected.

13. Despite the artificiality of our laboratory procedure, functionally analogous predicaments occur in everyday life. People's hearing does deteriorate without their realizing it. Indeed, the onset of deafness among the elderly is sometimes actively denied because recognizing a hearing deficit may be tantamount to acknowledging a greater defect— old age. Perhaps self-deception about one's hearing deficit may even be sufficient, in some circumstances, to yield a similar response, namely, a search for a more personally acceptable alternative that finds fault in others rather than in oneself. When there is no social or cultural support for the chosen

Table 1   Mean Scores on Dependent Measures Distinguishing Experimental from Control Subjects

Dependent Measures	Deafness without Awareness (N = 6)	Deafness with Awareness (N = 6)	Posthypnotic Suggestions (N = 6)	t(15)	P
Paranoia measures*					
MMPI–Paranoia	1.50	.33	−.17	1.838	<.05
MMPI–Grandiosity	1.33	−.83	−1.00	1.922	<.05
Paranoia clinical interview form	.30	−.09	−.28	3.667	<.005
TAT					
Affective evaluation	83.35	16.65	33.50	2.858	<.01
Self-assessed creativity	42.83	68.33	73.33	3.436	<.005
Self-rated feelings					
Creative	34.17	55.83	65.83	2.493	<.05
Confused	73.33	39.17	35.00	2.521	<.05
Relaxed	43.33	81.67	78.33	2.855	<.01
Agitated	73.33	14.17	15.33	6.586	<.001
Irritated	70.00	25.00	7.00	6.000	<.001
Friendly	26.67	53.33	56.67	2.195	<.05
Hostile	38.33	13.33	13.33	2.047	<.05
Judges' ratings					
Confused	40.83	27.08	17.67	1.470	<.10
Relaxed	34.17	54.59	65.42	2.839	<.01
Agitated	51.25	24.59	13.75	3.107	<.005
Irritated	45.84	18.92	11.25	3.299	<.005
Friendly	23.34	48.34	65.00	3.385	<.005
Hostile	18.75	5.00	1.67	2.220	<.05

*These measures were taken before and after the experimental session; reported means represent difference scores (after minus before).

explanation and the actor is relatively power-less, others may judge him or her to be irra-tional and suffering from a mental disorder. Although our subjects were young and had normal hearing, these findings have obvious bearing on a possible cognitive-social mech-anism by which deafness may lead to para-noia among the middle-aged and elderly.

References and Notes

1. B. Pritzker, *Schweiz. Med. Wochenschr.* 7, 165 (1938).
2. F. Houston and A. B. Royse, *J. Ment. Sci.* 100, 990 (1954).
3. M. Vernon, *J. Speech Hear. Res.* 12, 541 (1969).
4. K. Z. Altshuler, *Am. J. Psychiatry* 127, 11 and 1521 (1971).
5. Personal communication from J. D. Rainer (14 July 1980), who has studied the psychiatric effects of deafness for the past 25 years at the New York State Psychiatric Institute.
6. E. Kraepelin, *Psychiatrie* 8, 1441 (1915).
7. D. W. K. Kay, *Br. J. Hosp. Med.* 8, 369 (1972).
8. F. Post, *Persistent Persecutory States of the Elderly* (Pergamon, London, 1966).
9. H. A. McCelland, M. Roth, H. Neubauer, R. F. Gar-side, Excerpta Med., *Int. Congr. Ser.* 4, 2955 (1968).
10. A. F. Cooper, R. F. Garside, D. W. K. Kay, *Br. J. Psychiatry* 129, 532 (1976).
11. A. F. Cooper, A. R. Curry, D. W. K. Kay, R. F. Garside, M. Roth, *Lancet* (1974-II, 7885) (1974).
12. A. F. Cooper and R. Porter, *J. Psychosom. Res.* 20, 107 (1976).
13. A. F. Cooper, *Br. J. Psychiatry* 129, 216 (1976).
14. D. W. K. Kay, A. F. Cooper, R. F. Garside, M. Roth, *ibid.* 129, 207 (1976).
15. B. Maher, in *Thought and Feeling*, H. London and R. E. Nisbett, Eds. (Aldine, Chicago, 1974), pp. 85–103.
16. G. Reed, *The Psychology of Anomalous Experience* (Houghton Mifflin, Boston, 1974).
17. E. M. Lemert, *Sociometry* 25, 2 (1962).
18. L. Festinger, *Hum. Relat.* 7, 117 (1954).
19. N. A. Cameron, in *Comprehensive Textbook of Psy-chiatry*, A. M. Freedman and H. I. Kaplan, Eds. (Williams & Wilkins, Baltimore, 1967), pp. 665–675.
20. A. Beck, in *Thought and Feeling*. H. London and R. E. Nisbett, Eds. (Aldine, Chicago, 1974), pp. 127–140.
21. W. W. Meisner, *The Paranoid Process* (Jason Aron-son, New York, 1978).
22. R. E. Shor and E. C. Orne, *Harvard Group Scale of Hypnotic Susceptibility, Form A* (Consulting Psy-chologists Press, Palo Alto, Calif., 1962).
23. A. M. Weitzenhoffer and E. R. Hilgard, *Stanford Hypnotic Susceptibility Scale, Form C* (Consulting Psychologists Press, Palo Alto, Calif., 1962).
24. A fuller presentation of procedures is available by request.
25. W. G. Dahlstrom, G. S. Welsh, L. F. Dahlstrom, *An MMPI Handbook*, vol. 2. *Research Applications* (Univ. of Minnesota Press, Minneapolis, 1975).
26. We derived this scale specifically for this study: it consisted of 15 self-declarative statements responded to on 7-point rating scales. The scale was drawn from a clinical study of paranoia (14).
27. L. Ross, M. R. Lepper, M. Hubbard, *J. Pers. Soc. Psychol.* 35, 817 (1977).
28. W. L. Hays, *Statistics for Psychologists* (Holt, Rine-hart & Winston, New York, 1965), p. 465.
29. This report is dedicated to Neal E. Miller as part of a commemoration by his former students of his inspired science teaching. We wish to acknowledge the expert and reliable research assistance of Harry Coin, Dave Willer, Bob Sick, James Glanzer, Jill Fonaas, Laurie Plautz, Lisa Carrol, and Sarah Gar-lan. We thank Joan Linsenmeier and David Rosen-han for critical editing of the manuscript.

Analysis

What did you think of this **quantitative research** study? Did you find in it things that concerned you? Were there things in it that you felt especially good about? When this study was discussed with several classes, students listed these strengths:

- There is an excellent explanation of the relationship of deafness to paranoia, both shown to be conditions of aging.

- Three different measures of paranoia were used just in case one might be consid-ered suspect by a reader.

- Hypnosis was cleverly employed to substitute available subjects for ones who could not ethically be used—the researchers just couldn't let elderly subjects go deaf and not tell them!

- There was an excellent use of groups to eliminate possible rival explanations. Post-hypnotic suggestion was eliminated as the cause because the group with the itchy ear did not show paranoia. The group that knew it was partly deaf showed that the phenomenon occurred only without knowledge of deafness. These two groups were like the experimental group in every way but the important one—they did not have unrecognized deafness. They are called "control groups" and permit the researcher to eliminate rival explanations; that is, they control for those explanations.

- Random assignment of the subjects to the groups meant that, on average, the groups were comparable in the relevant characteristics that might otherwise bias the experiment. For example, if one group were more anxious than the other, it might have performed differently. Even though anxiety was not measured and equated over the groups, random assignment would, on average, have equated that effect.

- None of the individuals who had contact with the subjects or who were responsible for making observations of the development of paranoia—hypnotist, researcher, observers, and confederates—knew to which treatment any given subject had been assigned. They couldn't have biased the results to come out "right" even if they had wanted to. In research terms, the observers were kept blind to the treatment.

- The first instructions to subjects were tape recordings; thus they were handled identically before being given different treatments. Later, instructions for different treatments given by automatically projected and timed slides served the same purpose without calling attention to the diminished hearing of two of the three groups.

- The confederates engaged in a well-rehearsed standard conversation so that all subjects were exposed to the same possibilities of misperceiving antagonistic parts of the "script."

- Subjects were extensively debriefed after the study to make sure that there were no negative consequences of their participation. They were followed up a month later to provide further reassurance that there were no lingering problems.

The students also listed the following weaknesses:

- Six persons in each group is a very small sample size.

- Only the subjects who were most susceptible to hypnosis were chosen. Such subjects might in some way be "different" and therefore bias the result.

- The subjects were not drawn from the population to which the results were to be generalized, the elderly; all were male and all were college students.

- The length of time the hypnotized condition existed was not given.

- Reliability and validity data were not given for the researchers' own "clinically derived" paranoia scale, so we cannot be certain that it is a valid instrument. By contrast, data on published instruments are publicly available. (They did give a reference, however, so we could presumably get such data.)

- Subjects knew it was an experimental setting and it was also an unusual one. They may have reacted accordingly.

- The researcher had to deceive the subjects.

- Hypnosis, an unusual procedure more associated with show business than with science, was used with no explanation or defense.
- There was no assurance that the paranoia created under the experimental conditions was the same as that affecting the elderly.
- Confederates had the opportunity to learn which subjects were partly deaf since their conversation included probes for the partial deafness to assure that it was maintained.

How did your lists compare? You might not have identified all the strengths and weaknesses. Remember that these lists are a compilation of the common responses across several classes. No doubt when you recognized an item not on your list, you said to yourself, "Oh, I should have put that down, too!" Remember that this is in fact a sophisticated behavioral science experiment in which many readers, without previous training in research methods, can either identify strengths and weaknesses or recognize them when pointed out. Furthermore, although these weaknesses and strengths were found in an experiment, most are relevant to other research methods as well.

This example suggests that you have a solid base of knowledge on which this book can build. That is not a surprise; Einhorn and Hogarth (1986) point out that in everyday life individuals use systematic rules for assessing cause as well as in science. We will further explore such rules in chapter 7.

Having examined a quantitative study, let's look at qualitative methodology. Although both quantitative and qualitative methods can be used to explore, quantitative methods are more often used to test an explanation. **Qualitative research** methods are particularly useful in constructing them. This is shown in our next study. Hoffmann-Riem (1986) studied how families who adopt a child construct "the sense of a common bond" that is perceived to exist in biologically related families. Although the report has been abridged for reproduction, nothing essential has been omitted.

A Qualitative Study

Adoptive Parenting and the Norm of Family Emotionality

Christa Hoffmann-Riem • University of Hamburg*

Abstract: This paper is concerned with the construction of "the sense of a common bond" in adoptive families.[1] First, I clarify how adoptive families construct this sense in relation to biological families. Second, by examining features of adoptive family life, I suggest a new way of understanding non-adoptive families. Presuppositions about "normal" family relationships dominate the start of adoptive family life. As seen from the actors' perspective, "emotional normalization" is a crucial indicator of successful adoptive family life. I outline how involuntarily childless couples try to accomplish normality when applying for a child, and how achieving the assumed normality of non-adoptive families continues after adoption.

*Note: I appreciate Shulamit Reinharz' careful editing, and thank her for helping me share some of my research findings with an American audience. Address correspondence to: Institut für Soziologie, Universität Hamburg, Sedanstrasse 19, 2000 Hamburg 13, West Germany.

Source: "Adoptive Parenting and the Norm of Family Emotionality" by Christa Hoffmann-Riem, 1986, *Qualitative Sociology*, *9*, pp. 162–177. Reprinted by permission. (Paragraph numbers added.)

*Methodological Assumptions and the
Technique of the Narrative Interview*

1. The fundamental processes which underlie the symbolic structuring of kinship and parenthood are usually invisible. Examining a special case (i.e., adoptive families) may help render these processes accessible if an appropriate method is used. Unfortunately, the sociological literature on adoption reflects the prevailing methodological orientation of the discipline, the pre-structuring of data collection by a set of hypotheses and their operationalization in a standard interview. The researcher who works with pre-structured categories will find only that which he or she has previously considered. An exception to this general trend is the work of David Kirk (1964) which draws on his own experiences as an adoptive father.

2. My study starts with the methodological assumption that basic structures of family life can be disclosed only if informants are given the opportunity to present their experiences in a manner I call "autonomous." Studies based on biographical documents like letters, e.g., Sorosky, Barron & Pannor (1979) or the detailed case study of an adoptive family (Huth, 1983) are the closest to my work. . . .

3. My research method, the "narrative interview," was drawn from the work of Fritz Schuetze (1977; see also Labov and Waletzky, 1967, and Kallmeyer and Schuetze, 1977), who recommends a strict division of the interview into two parts. The first or main part consists of the story told by the narrator without interruptions by the researcher; the second part consists of questions carefully put by the researcher in response to information already presented by the interviewee. . . .

4. My introductory question was formulated in the hopes of uncovering the whole history of the adoption, beginning with the decision to make an application for a child and ending with the development of their family life. After a number of introductory remarks emphasizing that the adoptive parents should tell their story the way they

wanted, they were asked: "Can you still remember what it was like when you applied for a child?" I did not select a specific beginning, e.g., involuntary childlessness, for a chain of adoption events. Rather, the couples began to recapitulate the beginning of their adoption story as they saw it (e.g., childlessness) or started with the process of application and then came to recognize that something was missing. This prompted them to return to that "missing link" in the chain (childlessness) in order to enable me to have a proper understanding of their story. I interviewed couples and generally, the adoptive parents gave a combined account as a couple rather than two separate accounts. On the average, telling the story took about two hours. All interviews were recorded on tape and transcribed verbatim.

Sampling

5. The selection of informants was guided by the idea that ability to communicate should have priority over the representativeness of the subjects. Representative sampling would have been possible only if I had been able to use the data of the adoption agency in Hamburg. I rejected this idea since it would have associated me with the agency and possibly revived negative experiences (e.g., dependency, control) or positive associations (e.g., getting a child). Fifteen couples who participated in regular discussion group meetings of adoptive parents were selected. Most members of these discussion groups were middle class, similar to most applicants for adoption. The procedures to define class membership and a comparison of class membership between the sample and a universe of applicants for one year are presented in detail elsewhere (Hoffmann-Riem [1984], pp. 17–19, 42–45, 314, 328). I had taken part in the meetings of one group for several months to get some insight into the social world of adoptive parents. I presented my research design to the members of another discussion group and asked them to support the project.[2] I legitimized my research by referring to the fact that I needed to know

more about the practical purposes, application process and the image of adoptive families. Almost all of the members were interested in participating as a means of informing the public (and the adoption agency) about adoptive family life. . . .

Data Interpretation

6. . . . My concern was not with the idiosyncrasies of a single case but with the commonalities of all the cases. To begin, I outlined the rough chronology of events reflected in the story: (1) the couple's motivation for adoption, (2) the process of applying for a child, (3) the development of the parent-child relationship. Since each of these categories contained a wealth of information, I further differentiated within them. First I sought the shared properties of all the cases. Then I used specific data from each of the interviews to illustrate variety. For example, to analyze the "motivation process" I first showed how the desire for a child is based on conceptions of the "normal" adult role. Then I examined more closely the alternatives to being a parent envisioned by childless couples, how the desire for a child is integrated into male and female role definitions, and how the prospective child is instrumentalized for the adult role.

7. I started by comparing cases that differed widely from one another ("strategy maximizing differences") in order to develop polar types. Then my analysis of the narratives in terms of their similarities allowed the range between the poles to be filled in.

8. My data interpretation is confined strictly to a reconstruction of what the research subjects themselves presented as their experiences. . . . I attempt to reflect the actor's perspective throughout the paper even if it is not explicitly stated in each sentence.

The Desire for a Child

9. On the basis of very detailed adoption stories, I came to recognize that the majority of data can be subsumed under the concept of "constructing normality." [This idea had not

been on my mind when I started the research.] . . . Before elaborating the adoptive parents' work to establish a "normal" parent-child relationship, I shall briefly outline the starting point of adoption—the desire for a child—as a chain of normalization processes.

10. The Federal Republic of Germany has the world's largest birth rate. Viewed against this background, narrative interviews with adoptive parents reveal that children are still very important in biographical planning for some West German adults. All the adoption stories begin with "We wanted a child." Considering the consequences of this desire, it is particularly worthy of note that no explanation is given. Seen from the narrator's perspective, no further clarification of the remark was necessary.

11. The motivational story preceding the decision to adopt is divided into sequences: a shift from what the couples defined as the "normal" starting point of marriage, to deviation and then, finally, to an attempt to reconstruct normality. Among these couples marriage was entered into with the aim of establishing a family. But like other couples, realization of the desire for a child was postponed until the household had been set up. As long as they practiced birth control, the couple experienced itself as being in harmony with the institutionalized pattern of the family life cycle. The unquestioned (or only slightly questioned) confidence in their joint reproductive ability made married life appear congruent with their own biographical planning for children. This enormous confidence paved the way for a crisis among these families and presumably the ten to fifteen per cent of married couples who unwillingly remain childless in West Germany.

12. Planning the transition from the phase of household establishment to the realization of a family is the step that progressively leads the couple away from feeling "normal." Biographical denormalization begins with the couple's first suspicions. When a certain level of fear is reached, medical help

is sought so that the plan of family establishment, once regarded as something they could achieve on their own, might be pursued. Many of the narratives express the suffering the couples endured during the medical procedures. They turned to the medical option in order to rescue their original biographical plans, yet it was that very system that forced them to recognize the impossibility or improbability of its realization. A sequence of short, temporally connected sentences provides an idea of the extent to which the narrators feel rushed as they go from doctor to doctor in an effort to prevent the threat of childlessness.

Adoptive Mother: We thought that we would like to have children.

Adoptive Father: And since that did not work although we were trying hard—my wife was under medical treatment and I went to see a doctor—, and since it was extremely improbable that we would get children of our own, we started to think of adoption. . . . But first we have been in the university clinics for a long treatment, and a very, very good and sensible doctor was in charge of us, and we submitted to a lot of treatment to get an own child and be it convulsively [sic]. You know, then they increase the doses of hormones you get from one treatment to the next, and finally we came to the point that if there would be a pregnancy the probability was one to ten for twins and one to hundred for triplets, and that was already a critical limit. . . . And my wife had to go to the clinic every day to be checked if there weren't any negative side-effects. And then we always had to get there at a special date dependent on the cycle, for example Sunday night at 10 or Sunday morning at 9.

Adoptive Mother: Yes, whenever ovulation was expected.

Adoptive Father: And the doctor rushed to the clinic to wait for the right moment. Believe me, I could write a book about all those events in the hospital.

Adoptive Mother: We were cared for very well, but finally we said to ourselves: Oh God, what are we doing here, why all this trouble?

13. Their "desperate" utilization of all the technological reproductive means available to them suggests that the definition of the family as a group of genealogically related persons is still firmly in place. It takes the couple a long time to accept the idea that being a "flesh and blood" relation is not the only way of constituting a family. Narrative interviews with adoptive parents reveal a great deal about the significance of kinship, i.e., the desire for establishing genealogical families who belong together. It takes the experience of missing parental autonomy and the suffering it causes to illustrate the way the biological family is an essential part of the normal biographical planning of many adults.

14. When medical procedures no longer justify the couples' hopes for a birth, the pattern of normality is redefined. The interviews reflect the couples' shift from being rushed to and fro to a new initiative of action: "And then we thought: let's adopt a child."

Adopting a Child:
From Strangeness to Familiarity

15. Adoption does not coincide with the actors' concept of a "normal" family. Therefore, once the adoption has been carried out the normality of parental role fulfillment has yet to be reached. One means for constructing "normal" parent-child relationships is through an emotional bond. The parents define this as something that has to be worked at. While waiting for a child the applicants experience a high degree of insecurity concerning their prospective roles as parents. Experiences as prospective adoptive parents are framed by suppositions concerning the "normal" case. For example, the anxious question: "Will I be able to love a child that is not my own?" crops up in several interviews. The question illustrates how prospective parents worry about the quality of their future family life. Since the principle of

biological filiation is violated, the parents fear that a quality constitutive of family life—the emotional bond—may also be adversely affected. The fact that prospective adoptive parents are so concerned about the affective bond shows how deeply the emotional parent-child relationship is accepted. When the principle of filiation is in effect, the emotional bond appears almost automatic.

16. When the status passage from applicant to parent is achieved, the emotional quality of the parent-child relationship becomes a point of overwhelming significance. This was reflected in every narrative interview. The conditions of developing an emotional relationship differ substantially: in some cases only a few moments or hours were needed for the couple to feel attracted to a baby; but in the case of an older child, it may take years to overcome the sense of unfamiliarity. The beginning of family life may be full of happiness or irritation. Even allowing for these differences, every narrative interview arrives at some kind of statement of relationship: "And then an intensive relationship (quickly/slowly) developed between myself and the child."

17. For adoptive parents this process signifies the attainment of a goal. It means conformity with a central norm of family life. However, the structure of the parents' narrative shows that this statement is not the final presentation of the relational quality. It is followed by another key statement which reveals how adoptive parents organize their experiences in relation to the "normal" case. In the majority of narrative interviews, the following sentiment is expressed: "It is as if it were our own child."

18. Since without any interviewer guidance the majority of adoptive parents recapitulate events using this endpoint, we can assume that it refers to highly relevant experiences of family life. I am suggesting that the "achieved relationship" brings adoptive parents in line with the "normal" case. Only by evaluating their own experiences in the "primary framework" of the biological family[3] can adoptive parents ensure that the new quality of their relationship is communicated without misunderstanding. "It is like one's own child"—that is how adoptive parents indicate to themselves and others that the normality of family life has been accomplished.

19. Almost every narrative reflects the point at which the adoptive parents no longer need to typify their boy or girl as an adopted child. Whereas for a short or a long period they may have observed an emotional distance between themselves and the child because of its adoption status, ultimately they experience an emotional identification. This is a turning point in symbolic interaction with the child—the turning point from adoptive child to child. One could call this turning point the moment of emotional normalization. Emotional normalization means overcoming the strangeness of a child that is my child to be. The case of adoption presents an interesting coincidence of "The Stranger" and "The Homecomer" (Schuetz, 1972). The problem of every stranger who has to approach a new social world is accentuated in the case of adoption because the adoption stranger is expected to become a familiar person. The stranger as the homecomer who has not been at home before—that is the frame in which the interview data could be analyzed. In the following section I will describe how the chances of overcoming strangeness differ enormously, depending on the age of the child. The baby is the homecomer with minor strangeness, whereas the older child is the stranger with minor homecoming properties. Consequently, quite different trajectories of emotional normalization shall be outlined here.

Emotional Normalization When Taking in a Baby

20. "I've grown so fond of the child so quickly" was commonly expressed during the twenty-one interviews done with parents who adopted a child younger than seven months. Their emotional bond with the child developed unburdened by the difficulties of its long "prehistory." Attachment evolved as a matter of course, as if the process had unfolded "automatically."

Adoptive Mother: . . . he was simply so tiny and so . . . and so in need of help that you automatically direct your affection toward the child and that happens . . . immediately. . . .[4]

Since the development of an emotional relationship is seen as occurring automatically, the narrative recapitulation of events does not usually involve long reflections on how the result was brought about. The new quality of the parent-child relationship is regarded as normal and the parents no longer analyze it from a reflexive distance ("I don't think about it any more"). Some see the declining preoccupation with one's own special status of family as evidence of unquestionably belonging together. In the words of Alfred Schuetz and Thomas Luckmann (1979), one could call this the development of a new "natural attitude."

21. The baby's physical dependence in itself produces an enormous density of parental interaction. Their involvement leads to a situation in which the child, at an extremely dependent life stage, quietly turns into the little being who seems familiar to them. His/her physical growth and first efforts to communicate reveal traces of their parental influence. A number of recent studies in developmental psychology have attempted to outline in detail the process of the emerging parent-child relationship. These investigations discovered a surprisingly wide-ranging repertoire of interactive behavior which a baby of only a few weeks can initiate and sustain (Stern, 1980; Schaffer, 1980). Smiling, movements of eyes, hands and feet, the turning of its head, and finally, the first prevocal sounds—these media of expression are the active bonding part of the child to which the parents react "automatically." They are what Stern (1980, p. 24) calls "infant-elicited behavior." In parental care the child unfolds its communicative abilities and radiates the charm of a small partner.

22. Adoptive parents of very young babies quickly come to believe that the principle of biological filiation is almost irrelevant for an emotional relationship. Here is an example:

Adoptive Father: What is it that really builds up the relationship? I'm not sure if it is really built up because the child has been /eh/ borne for nine months. Isn't it rather built up because /eh/ when it is still very small you have to feed it six times a day and to put on its nappies and to care for it and . . . you have to play with it and you observe its reactions to . . . to your own /eh/ remarks and aura . . . I think that /eh/ this is much more important than bearing the child for nine months during pregnancy. . . .

23. According to the narrative interviews, pregnancy and birth can be renounced as binding experiences if adoptive parents are able to utilize the plasticity of the child in its most formative developmental phase[5] and if they can superimpose social familiarity on biological strangeness. The turning point from adoptive child to child is then reached. This emotional normalization is reflected in almost every interview concerning a very young adopted child.

Adoptive Father: . . . We take it for granted that we feel this way,
Adoptive Mother: Yes, it's your own child, and that's it.
Adoptive Father: You adapt yourself to it; it's your own child.
Adoptive Mother: It is your own child, and that's it, it is . . . /eh/ now and again you also forget that it is adopted, it's incredible how much you forget.

Late Adoptions

24. The narratives concerning late adoptions make it clear that the trajectory of emotional normalization includes a process of self-communication, especially on the part of the adoptive mother. It may take months or years before so-called motherly emotions for the child are directly recognized as such, since attention initially focuses on coming to terms with other immediate problems. The narrative interviews relating to a late start in family life illustrate that emotionality is often not discovered in the ongoing interaction process but is grasped retrospectively.

To give an example: one adoptive mother infers from the sadness she feels when her daughter has to stay in hospital that the emotional bond must be more developed than she had assumed. The fact that her daughter shows a deeper attachment to her than she had expected reinforces the new feeling of belonging together. Another adoptive mother observes with relief that she now defends the child more against people outside of the family or that she has more sympathy for her child when it is ill or has been injured than she had in the beginning. It may take months or years before an adoptive mother is able to appreciate that she had "caught up with" the attitudes of biological parents.

Conclusion

25. The constitution of the adoptive family has been discussed in terms of the emotional work invested in parent-child relationships. The turning point from adoptive child to child is a source of relief and happiness, a sign of family authenticity. It is also a point of danger. Adoptive parents can indulge themselves in the feeling of normality to such an extent that they neglect to handle the structural difference characteristic of their family on a cognitive level. They may act as if they were the biological family, and reject the idea that they are not.[6]

26. Adoptive family life is family life with double parenthood. Emotional normalization is only a partial solution to the problems arising from the structural peculiarities of the adoptive family. Structuring the "awareness context" (Glaser & Strauss, 1965) towards the child and towards relatives, friends, and strangers is the work that remains after the emotional bond has been established.

27. Emotional normalization has been described as a process worked at by adoptive parents to minimize the difference between their own type of family and "normal" families. The process of overcoming strangeness in the adoptive family affords some insight into the conditions needed for the constitution of any family. The difficul-

ties in constructing family reality without the principle of filiation, and without a common history of early socialization suggest that the conditions of the "healthy" personality as outlined by Erikson must be understood in terms of specific types of families. The child has to experience certain interactive relationships and the parents must initiate and sustain them in order to establish familiarity. The greater the number of developmental phases that the child has gone through before the common history of the adoptive family, the more divergent are the systems of relevance of adoptive parents and child. Hence emotional normalization may not be established for a long time or at all.

28. This research may be useful for adoptive parents, applicant couples, and agencies who deal with adoptive family life. It should alert agencies to the different burdens they put on parents when placing a baby or a five-year-old child. Beyond the field of adoption, the findings might have some relevance for the growing number of step-parent–child relationships where familiarity also has to be accomplished. Finally, the concept of emotional normalization might contribute to an understanding not only of parent-child relationships but other types of family interactions as well.

Notes

1. A detailed analysis is presented in Hoffmann-Riem, Das adoptierte Kind—Familienleben mit doppelter Elternschaft (*The Adopted Child: Family Life with Double Parenthood*), Munich: Fink, 1984.
2. Twenty-three adoptive parents had adopted one child, four of them had also one biological child, two others had two or three biological children. Seven other adoptive parents had adopted two children, two of them also had one or two biological children. Among the eight cases with a combination of adoptive and biological children, there were only two where the adoptive child came first. For further information concerning the exact age see Hoffmann-Riem (1984), p. 327.
3. To use an analytical term of Goffman's (1974), the biological family is taken as a "primary framework" for determining the quality of relationship in the adoptive family.

4. All interview material is translated from German by the author.
5. One extreme statement about this dependency is Alfred Portmann's characterization of the dependence of the infant's first year as the prolongation of the fetal period ("extrauterines Fruhjahr"): A. Portmann, Die Biologie und das neue Bild vom Menschen, Bern, 1942, p. 21.
6. David Kirk conceptualized the adoptive family's alternatives as "rejection-of-difference" and "acknowledgment-of-difference" in his influential study *Shared Fate* (1964).

References

Arbeitsgruppe Bielefelder Soziologen (eds.) 1973 Alltagswissen, Interaktion und gesellschaftliche Wirklichkeit, Vol. 2. Rowohlt.

Douglas, Mary 1970 Natural Symbols: Explorations in Cosmology, London.

Glaser, Barney G., and Strauss, Anselm 1967 The Discovery of Grounded Theory, Chicago: Aldine.

Goffman, Erving 1959 The Presentation of Self in Everyday Life, Garden City: Doubleday.

Goffman, Erving 1974 Frame Analysis, New York.

Hoffmann-Riem, Christa 1980 "Die Sozialforschung einer interpretativen Soziologie—der Datengewinn. Kölner Zeitschrift für Soziologie und Sozialpsychologie, 22: 339–372.

Hoffmann-Riem, Christa 1984 Das adoptierte Kind— Familienleben mit doppelter Elternschaft, Munich: Fink.

Huth, Wolfgang 1983 Adoption und Familiendynamik, Frankfurt/Main: Fachbuchhändlung für Psychologie.

Kallmeyer, Werner, and Schuetze, Fritz 1977 "Zur Konstitution von Kommunikationsschemat der Sachverhaltsdarstellung." In: Dirk Wegner (ed.), Gesprächsanalysen, Hamburg.

Kirk, David 1964 Shared Fate, New York: Free Press.

Labov, William, and Waletzky, Joshua 1967 "Narrative Analysis: Oral Versions of Personal Experience." In: J. Helm (ed.), Essays on the Verbal and Visual Arts. Proceedings of the Annual Spring Meeting, Seattle. University of Washington Press.

Portmann, Alfred 1942 Die Biologie und das neue Bild vom Menschen, Bern.

Schaffer, Rudolph 1980 Mothering, Cambridge, Mass.: Harvard University Press.

Schuetz, Alfred 1972–3 Collected Papers, Vols. I and II. The Hague: Nijhoff.

Schuetz, Alfred, and Luckmann, Thomas 1979 Strukturen der Lebenswelt, Vol. 1. Frankfurt/Main: Suhrkamp.

Schuetze, Fritz 1977 "Die Tecknik des narrativen Interviews in Interaktionsfeldstudien." Arbeitsberichte und Forschungsmaterialien der Fakultät für Soziologie der Universität Bielefeld, 1: 1–62.

Sorosky, Arthur D., Baran, Annette, and Pannor, Reuben 1979 The Adoption Triangle, Garden City: Doubleday.

Stern, Daniel 1980 The First Relationship: Infant and Mother. Cambridge, Mass.: Harvard University Press.

Tyrell, Hartmann 1978 "Die Familie als 'Urinstitution': Neuerliche spekulative Überlegungen zu einer alten Frage." Kölner Zeitschrift für Soziologie und Sozialpsychologie, 30: 611–651.

Tyrell, Hartmann 1979 "Familie und gesellschaftliche Differenzierung." In: Helge Pross (ed.), Famile—wohin? Reinbeck: Rowohlt.

There are clearly distinct differences in the two methods, each with its own strengths and weaknesses.

Analysis

Finding the strengths and weaknesses in the qualitative study is this chapter's Opportunities for Additional Learning. Most chapters feature a section with this title at chapter's end; and they are an important part of the instruction offered by this book. It's a good idea to work them through, even if your instructor doesn't require you to do so. You will find that they highlight important aspects you may have missed or not understood in the chapter itself. Once you have constructed your answer to any given question, compare it with that listed in the Key to Additional Learning Opportunities section at the end of that chapter, but don't deprive yourself of important learning by reading the answer before trying to answer the problem.

DIFFERENT VIEWS OF A MODEL OF
SOCIAL AND BEHAVIORAL SCIENCE

What should a model of social and behavioral science look like? Would the model more closely resemble the Zimbardo study and its findings? That type of study seems similar to the natural sciences model of chemistry and physics. It helps us to work with those constructs such as paranoia that we can't directly sense through smell, taste, touch, or sight but are nevertheless useful to us in interacting with our world.

Or would it more closely resemble the descriptions of situations, neighborhoods, and communities of sociology and anthropology, like the description of the process of adoption of Hoffmann-Riem? Such studies have a greater affinity with the humanities. They help us to understand how different people make sense of their complex situations, and, as we see parallels to our own, are better able to cope with unfamiliar situations.

If you are like me, you ask, why do I have to choose? Both approaches have value in helping us understand our world. For that matter, it is only a step from the sociological and anthropological studies (which are classified as nonfiction in bookstores) to realistic fiction—the wonderful worlds created by authors out of their own and others' experiences. Although these accounts may or may not have really happened, they are realistic enough that they, too, can often help us understand our world through their characters who, with their particular sets of skills, dispositions, and personalities, solve problems and find their way through realistic, complex situations. Out of these too we find models we want to emulate as well as ones we want to avoid.

So, although we would probably not include fiction as a source of social science knowledge, most of us are not yet ready to confine the social sciences to any one model of what it ought to be. There are some who might try to do so, and others who at least would elevate one or another approach as higher, or better, or more important than the others. But we get useful knowledge of people and society from a variety of sources. Advocates of different points of view may disagree as to what kind of a social science we should strive for and support, yet most of us will be grateful for new knowledge, whatever its source.

And just as there are different perspectives on what model social science is, these two studies have shown that there are different approaches to research methods. Perspective helps one realize that research-method preferences are as old as history. Portraying the world in words began in ancient times. The Greeks described time with different words for these two orientations: *kairos*, designated time as what happened, as in "I had a good time"—what we would call a qualitative concept; and *chronos*, designated measured time—a quantitative concept.

For centuries the physical and biological sciences consisted largely of verbal discussions about nature—armchair science. As armchair speculation was replaced in these areas with systematic empirical and laboratory work, data became numbers and measures came to predominate. The social sciences, also initiated largely with verbal description, were late to engage in empirical research. With the expectation that the same results could be obtained, they sought to attain the status accorded the other sciences by mimicking their quantitative approach. Initially, research methods books in psychology and education consisted solely of quantitative methods; other methods were not considered "scientific" enough. And describing in numbers has tended to dominate the journal literature in psychology and education, though less so in sociology and anthropology.

Compared to that achieved in the natural sciences, however, there has been a slow growth of generalizable behavioral knowledge. This has been accompanied by increasing realization of just how complex behavior is, particularly social behavior. Contextual variables that could affect outcomes are so numerous that it is difficult to control for all of them. While describing in words may lack precision, abstracting in numbers and measures that describe only one aspect at a time may fail to capture inherent complexity and omit aspects that words can portray. Thus, interest in methods involving description in words—qualitative methods—has increased. (While description in words is a prime characteristic of qualitative methods, others are discussed in chapters 2 and 12.)

But, because studies can borrow methods and techniques from wherever they can find them to make the strongest case, each of these studies could have been pursued with the other tradition's methods—or, a combination of them; what is called a mixed-method study. Research is a creative act. Unless you prefer to do so, *you needn't confine your thinking about research to specific approaches. You can creatively combine the elements of methods in any way that makes the best sense for the study you want to do.* The only limits are your own imagination and the necessity of presenting your findings convincingly. The research question to be answered really determines your choices of appropriate method and design. So given that is the case, it makes the most sense for this book to provide you the opportunity to learn the fundamentals of each of these two basic traditions and how fields use them.

Before going further, this is a good place to make some important points:

- We present research methods in separate qualitative and quantitative sections because this grouping facilitates learning. The quantitative–qualitative continuum is presented and discussed in chapter 2.

- We encourage researchers to use multiple methods that strengthen studies by complementing each other and broadening their range. As just noted above, we advocate the use of whatever methods best suit researchers' purposes.

Some researchers, especially those using very complex methods that often involve sophisticated software, hone only those research skills and use no other method. The point of view presented in this book is not compatible with that of a relatively small group of qualitative researchers. They argue that the assumptions underlying qualitative research are incompatible with those of quantitative research and so should not be used in the same study—that mixed-method studies involve incompatible epistemological assumptions. This conflict is explored further in chapter 12 (pp. 242–245).

When you tried your skill at analyzing the two studies presented earlier in the chapter, you probably realized how much you already know about social and behavioral science research. Though you may have missed certain aspects on this first read-through, you no doubt were surprised at how many you recognized when they were pointed out. One function of this book is to provide an integrating framework that makes this kind of knowledge come more readily to mind.

IMPORTANT TERMS AND CONCEPTS

hypotheses   quantitative research
qualitative research   validation

OPPORTUNITIES FOR ADDITIONAL LEARNING

1. As you did for the Zimbardo study, critique the Hoffmann-Riem research and note its strengths and weaknesses. Compare your critique with that in the Key to Additional Learning Opportunities section below. As with the Zimbardo study, some, perhaps many, of the observations will match those in your own critique. Be sure to first write out your own answer to this and similar problems at the ends of chapters. Answering in your own mind and then reading the given answer does not provide as significant an encounter with the material to be learned as does writing the answer. Writing enforces clarity of thought.

2. We have noted that studies can be done different ways. Thus, Hoffmann-Riem might have used more of the methods used by Zimbardo and vice versa. To the extent that you can, think about how each study might have been done using techniques of the other.

KEY TO ADDITIONAL LEARNING OPPORTUNITIES

1. The following lists of strengths and weaknesses of the Hoffmann-Riem study were compiled from those of previous research classes who critiqued the study.

STRENGTHS

- The explanation makes sense; that is, the account that these couples experienced a progression from trying to have their own child to seeking a medical solution to adopting a child is plausible. Further, the explanation of the process of emotional normalization also has intuitive appeal—that once a child has been adopted, an emotional attachment develops similar to that of a biological family.

- The research was presented to the couples in a manner that would encourage cooperation, saying that the purpose was to inform the public (and adoption agencies) about adoptive life.

- The choice of couples from existing support groups aided communication. The researcher could safely assume that since these couples were accustomed to discussing their problems and experiences about adoption, they would more readily discuss them with an interviewer.

- Hoffmann-Riem recorded and transcribed the interviews. Recording could have a negative effect on an interview, but given the apparent cooperativeness of the subjects, it appears that it did not. Combined with the investigator's own observations, it provided an accurate and detailed record of each interview.

- The interviews were open-ended. In the first part, the couples were encouraged to "tell their story" without interruption. In the second part, Hoffmann-Riem used their comments to probe further. She was open to their accounts and did not attempt to lead or direct the discussion.

- The adoptive parents were interviewed as couples. This could be seen as both a strength and a weakness. Its strong point is that both members could fill in details, add to each other's comments, and so enrich the information.

- Hoffmann-Riem began the study with only a general idea of what she might discover. She was able to let the couples tell their stories and to let her conclusions develop inductively, to "emerge from the data." She was less likely to be blinded by her preconceptions and miss an important point.

- Her sample could be considered representative of adoptive parents in general as most were members of the middle class, the most common segment of West German society to adopt.

WEAKNESSES

- The data collected consisted entirely of narrative (words). There was no way to analyze it statistically. Another investigator could, presumably, interpret it differently.

- Since Hoffmann-Riem provides only small samples of her data, there is no way to verify her conclusions.

- There was no control on researcher expectancy effect, that is, no guarantee that Hoffmann-Riem was not leading or directing the interviews in some way (even subconsciously, perhaps) toward predetermined conclusions.

- The interview technique relied on self-reporting by the couples. The investigator had no real check on whether or not what they said was truly what they felt or believed. Further self-reports may limit information to whatever is comfortable or reflects favorably.

- The couples were interviewed together. A possible weakness in this approach is that an individual might dominate the interview or bias his/her spouse's answers. Separate interviews might provide different information.

- The sample could be viewed as unrepresentative because the couples were all members of a particular support group. Adoptive parents who participate in such groups may well have different attitudes from those who do not. Also, the support group itself could lead to changes in their views that would not otherwise have occurred.

- Fifteen couples is a small sample on which to base generalizations to all adoptive couples, although such sample sizes are not atypical in this kind of research. Further, the researcher drew the interviewees from only two support groups rather than sampling more such groups.

- Though Hoffmann-Riem did refer to prior research to justify her choice of methods, she might also have used prior research to help support her conclusions.

- Accuracy of translation is often a problem where two languages are involved. Perhaps this is not an issue in this instance because of the researcher's apparently excellent command of English. Back-translation into the original language by someone not familiar with the study permits comparison with the original statements for accuracy. This method is often used to check on the accuracy of a translation of a test or measuring instrument.

2. Either study could have used techniques that belong to the other approach or tradition. For example, following the measurement tradition based on a hunch that a widespread net of questions might turn up useful information about adoption, Hoffmann-Riem might have started by thinking up a lot of questions about the process of adoption. Then she would have her participants fill out a very general questionnaire about these various characteristics, seeking clusters of questions leading to scores that would begin to explain the adoption process—a quantitative approach. It would have missed the richness her quotations supplied.

Or, suppose that, instead of measures, Zimbardo's observers had interviewed the subjects to determine whether paranoia developed in the subject during social interaction. Then they wrote up case studies on each participant and analyzed this material for generalities. Such a study would still be designed around the preplanned testing of a hypothesis and a search for generalizable knowledge, characteristics we usually associate with the quantitative approach. But the analysis of verbatim transcripts is usually associated with the qualitative approach. It would have been much more difficult to characterize the approach of the study. Would the evidence have been as convincing as the statistics? Maybe, but maybe not. Each approach has its advantages.

SUMMARY

Your experience with the two studies you have just examined shows that you have a basic sense of what constitutes good research. What we need to do is to sharpen those skills and find a framework that will make such critiques easier and more comprehensive. Learning is like Velcro and without a framework you do not have a complete fastener.[1] This book will provide you with an undergirding of basic concepts in a framework that integrates many of them so they are better fastened. Then even as methods evolve you will be able to grasp and appreciate improvements readily as they occur. Further, you will be able to read research with an understanding and critical eye and, with careful study, can learn enough to begin to conduct your own research.

A Look Ahead

It is important to note that researchers do not have to choose between the two approaches illustrated in these examples. They may employ a hybrid, combining those aspects of each that best fit their research problem and match their skills, as well as adding other important aspects. The next chapter demonstrates some of this variety of possibilities as it develops a continuum of approaches anchored at the ends by quantitative and qualitative methods and then describes some of the diversity of other kinds of research, most of which are best characterized as being somewhere between the extremes.

Note

[1] Analogy adapted from Wurman (1989), p. 132.

2

The Variety of Research Methods

INTRODUCTION

Because our understanding of the world is constantly changing, approaches to research are also constantly changing. Therefore, researchers have many conceptual and information processing tools from which to choose. How does a researcher decide which methods to use to attack a problem? Some always use the same methods, perhaps because they have developed special related skills or have prior experience or background with them, or because the kinds of problems they work on call for these methods. Some are fixated on one or another method as the only "true" way to their kind of science, and this applies to both those doing quantitative experimental studies (like that of Zimbardo) as well as those doing qualitative studies (like that of Hoffmann-Riem). Let us approach this question under the assumption that the researcher is open to examining alternatives.

CHOOSING A RESEARCH METHOD

There is no standard way to decide which method to choose, but there are certain questions that researchers may consider. Let's explore them, beginning with the question, "How much is already known about the phenomenon of interest?" We might think of this as the maturity of knowledge surrounding the phenomenon, ranking it from very little to considerable.

Maturity of Knowledge

With little prior knowledge of a phenomenon, or even lack of clarity about what we are trying to understand, we begin by exploring and describing all that we are able to. Once a language and description give us a handle on the phenomenon of interest, we can move to successive stages of explanation, and possibly prediction. At the most advanced stages, prediction may be possible with increased precision and in multiple situations. So, regarding our problem we ask: "Where does the knowledge sought

stand on a continuum from *discovery* to *accepted as generally applicable knowledge?*"
In other words, is the intent of the researcher to:

- *describe* a situation to help others know what we are talking about, to perhaps understand what it is like, and vicariously to experience it;
- *explore* for an explanation of the phenomenon;
- *eliminate* rival explanations;
- on the basis of the explanation, *predict* with increasing precision what will occur in a new situation; or
- *determine generalizability*—that is, see in how wide a variety of situations the explanation seems to work?

For instance, were we starting out to explain why the elderly often present behavioral problems, we might begin at the exploration stage of the continuum. But Zimbardo's study in chapter 1 is beyond that—he has a clear idea of the phenomenon of interest and its components and a tentative explanation about how the components interact (one which may not only explain some elderly behavior but perhaps other behavior as well). Zimbardo is looking for a generalization like "perceptual discontinuities likely lead to paranoia." Working beyond the exploration stage has implications for method choice. It means that there is enough known to perhaps *preplan* the study—lay out the details of the study before it is carried out and data gathered.

Hoffmann-Riem chose to study the adoption process. Although "This idea had not been on my mind when I started this research" (p. 13 of chapter 1), early on she realized that normality was central to the adoption stories. However, while this provided a focus for the study, it did not move her very far up on the scale of knowledge maturity and left her exploring where and how this concept was involved. So her study begins with exploration and seeks an understanding and appropriate language to describe normality as well as an explanation of its role. Unlike the Zimbardo study that is tightly focused on a single phenomenon, Hoffmann-Riem's is less structured and is open to refinement in basic concepts and viewpoints. It is studying a process—that of adoption.

Another way of looking at this is that the Hoffmann-Riem type of research approach *ultimately* aims at depth of understanding of a process and the broad set of people's meanings that feed into it while the Zimbardo type, *ultimately*, aims at understanding a proposition, rule, or generalization.

So, the question of how much is already known about a topic of research begins to suggest directions for method choice. For instance, problems at the description and exploration level, like describing the adoption process and exploring explanations for it, typically fall into approaches like that used by Hoffmann-Riem. Corroborations of hunches (researchers call them **hypotheses**, statements about what is hypothetically true but needs to be substantiated) like that of Zimbardo's are done most often in an experiment, as his was. But the maturity of knowledge about the phenomenon does not definitively determine all aspects of method—for instance, description and exploration might also be done by a poll of a population, and testing of hypotheses can be accomplished without precise measures. So let's move on to other questions.

Can the phenomenon be "taken apart" for study, or should it be studied holistically?

Is it best studied by focusing on certain variables and their interaction (a dissecting analytic approach) or studied in its naturalistic completeness (a holistic approach)? Were we starting to study the behavior problems of the elderly without Zimbardo's hypothesis, we would have no way of knowing how to "take apart" this behavior, which aspects to concentrate on. We'd be unlikely to turn to hearing tests as a possibility. It is the hypothesis and a preexistent specific and operational language that permits us to "take apart" the phenomenon so as to focus on specific variables and their relationship.

Hoffmann-Riem, with an as-yet undifferentiated concept of normalization, has no basis for "taking apart" the phenomenon. Indeed, she realizes, as the parents-to-be exhaust the infertility clinics' efforts and turn to adoption, ultimately the concept of what is normal broadens to include adoption.

So, one of the essential differences between the two examples in chapter 1 is the extent of the researchers' prior understanding of the nature of what they were studying. That is, whether each phenomenon was studied in terms of predefined *variables* selected as those of importance, or studied as an emerging understanding of *process* in the complete, natural context in which it occurred.

In the Hoffmann-Riem approach, the researcher examines the process of how an adopting family establishes the sense of a common bond. The phenomenon is studied holistically in its natural setting. The researcher is not focusing on a single variable or a single behavioral outcome but rather is studying a process and developing a description of a previously unconsidered idea, that of *normalization* as it naturally occurs. The holistic approach is particularly well suited to studying process and developing understandings based on experiential narratives.

In contrast, the Zimbardo study asks if the unnoticed increasing deafness is the cause of the paranoia; the phenomenon is "taken apart" to focus on selected variables in a cause-and-effect relationship. The situation is simplified to examine a single kind of behavioral outcome—paranoia—resulting from the causative factors of unnoticed deafness in social situations. Although not always confined to the interaction of two or three variables, researchers utilizing this approach seek to simplify the interaction to relatively few variables so that it is clear which influences what.

Researchers use the term **independent variable** (or explanatory variable) to refer to something they believe may be a cause. It is a broad term. Besides including treatments (the hypnosis induced unaware deafness or itchy ear), or particular programs, teaching methods or kinds of curricula, the term encompasses potential causes such as social status or class, variables not under the control of the investigator.

If a cause is referred to as an independent variable, it follows that we would call the effect the **dependent variable** (or response variable). So, in the Zimbardo study, the appearance of paranoia (the response variable) depends on the presence of partial deafness and social interaction (the two explanatory variables, which together cause the paranoia).

If it is at all possible, manipulating the cause while studying a cause-and-effect relationship provides some of the strongest evidence for the causal linkage. Such purposeful manipulation is an important defining characteristic of an experiment—being able to show that an effect occurs when the cause is present and disappears when it is absent. The application of any potential cause controlled by an investigator is called a **treatment**. The investigator controls who receives what levels of treatment, under what circumstances, and when. In Zimbardo's study, the experimental treatment made the subjects temporarily deaf by telling them that while hypnotized they would not be able to hear well enough to understand the conversation around them. An alternative treatment resulted in an itchy ear. Experiments may have multiple treatments, as the Zimbardo study did, and may examine how the treatments interact with characteristics of the subjects and/or the conditions under which the study was carried out.

Because Hoffmann-Riem was trying to understand the general nature of the experience rather than testing for specific causes and effects, she took pains to disturb as little as possible the natural course of events. In retrospectively interviewing the parents after adoption, Hoffmann-Riem took care to let them tell their stories their own way, without influencing the flow or introducing a prior conceptualization in the discussion. This allowed the language of the phenomenon to emerge from the naturalistic language of the participants.

The question of whether a phenomenon must be studied holistically, together with the question of how much is known about it, begins to restrict the method possibilities. If the phenomenon can be taken apart and reduced to variables, then certain method alternatives are possible: measurement of selected variables, establishment of contrasting experimental and control groups, possibly a manipulated treatment. These alternatives are difficult if not impossible to implement in a holistic study of a phenomenon in a naturalistic setting, or in a study of a process with its complex interplay of relationships among context and persons over time. So, adding the nature of the phenomenon to the answers to the previous questions narrows the possibilities.

Is the phenomenon best described in numbers (e.g., measures), or with words?

Given answers to the previous questions, one might assume that the answer to this one has been predetermined. And to some extent, it has. However, presumably the behavioral problems of the elderly or the process of normalization could have been described using either measures or words. True, it would have been difficult to describe the process of normalization with measures without knowing how the concept itself changed over the various stages in the process, and without anticipating how the families defined normalization at the various stages. Moreover, at this stage of the research, Hoffmann-Riem did not have a finely formed understanding of the idea of *emotional normalization* but used this study to develop it. Whether she, or other researchers, would consider it a concept amenable to measurement, or whether it is too subtle to appropriately measure, would be a subsequent concern.

And even given Zimbardo's hypothesis, words instead of measures could have been used to examine the effects of the social interaction. The observers could have simply described the behavior they saw, and the participants could have been interviewed to determine how they reacted to the social interaction.

But the ability to describe complex situations in words and the precision conveyed by numbers are important factors in the choice. The two studies in chapter 1 differ markedly in their choice of approach. The Zimbardo study has a number of measures that lead to scores or rankings: the Harvard Group Scale of Hypnotic Susceptibility, the Stanford Scale of Hypnotic Susceptibility, the Minnesota Multiphasic Personality Inventory, the Thematic Apperception Test, and a clinically derived paranoia scale. Because Zimbardo had a very clear idea about the nature of the constructs to study, he thought he could study them individually; and because appropriate measures were available, he could provide numeric descriptions of the variables. So, as is typical of this approach to research, the various constructs involved (hypnotic susceptibility, paranoia) were translated into tests or scales that provided measures of them.

In contrast, in Hoffmann-Riem there are no measures; all description is in words. We have descriptions but no measures of the extent to which these parents consider it important to achieve a "normal" family relationship. Although there could have been, there is also no tally or count to indicate how well they succeeded, such as frequency counts of various key words like "adopting" and "normal family" in interviews. It is more difficult with words than it is with scores to discriminate one level from another, particularly if there are small differences. On the other hand, no numbers can eloquently convey *normality*, as do Hoffmann-Riem's quotations: "It is your own child, and that's it, . . . /eh/ now and again you also forget it is adopted, it's incredible how much you forget."

The choice of numbers or words tends to fall along the lines of the previous question—whether it can be taken apart—with holistic approaches tending to use words. Because measures assess only one dimension of a phenomenon, numeric assessments of holistic phenomena such as processes tend to be crude or piecemeal. But because it is difficult to distinguish levels with words (how bright is a "smart" person?), measures are preferred where precision is possible and desired. So, the question of how it is best described further narrows the possibilities.

Is the study best approached from the top and worked down, or from the bottom and built up?

This question asks whether the study is best implemented by starting with preconceptions and tracing out the implications, or by encountering the phenomenon without preconceptions and seeing what emerges. Finally, when combined with the answers to the previous questions, the top-down or bottom-up question decides the choice of general method. The two studies in chapter 1 typify these two approaches: Zimbardo is top-down and Hoffmann-Riem is bottom-up.

In this scheme, top-down begins with broad generalizations, bottom-up with specific information about the phenomenon. Zimbardo started from the top with a general idea about perceptual discontinuities that explained paranoia among deaf individuals, and he then worked down from that idea by looking for facts to test it. We think of such studies as *deductive*, starting with a proposed (hypothesized) explanation and deducing ways of testing it—a **preplanned study**. The deductive approach allows us, as Zimbardo did, to *preplan* the study and then carry it out. When working down, deduction and preplanning characterize this approach.

In contrast, Hoffmann-Riem started at the bottom, looking for information about how individuals understood adoption, and built up toward an explanation by finding what was common among the stories told to her about the reasons for adopting. Such an approach is *inductive*, starting with an exploration of a phenomenon, gradually finding a focus that leads to an understanding or explanation of what was focused on, and assembling common evidence over instances that leads to either further corroboration or results in modification of the explanation. The explorations of the inductive approach result in an **emergent study**, since the direction the study takes emerges as one proceeds. Working upward, the words *inductive* and *emergent* characterize this approach.

A CONTINUUM OF RESEARCH APPROACHES

As can be seen by how the Zimbardo and Hoffmann-Riem studies fit the above criteria, the conceptualization of the problem tends to lead the researcher to one approach over the other. Choosing the Zimbardo-type approach for one criterion leads to this same kind of approach in response to other criteria and vice versa.

Thus, corroborating an explanation, ability to take apart or simplify the phenomenon, describing in measures, a manipulatable treatment, and a top-down approach tend to go together. Researchers commonly characterize this approach as *quantitative*.

Similarly, describing or exploring for an explanation, a holistic approach, describing in words, and a bottom-up frame of reference form another type of approach to problems. This approach is characterized as *qualitative.*

It may be helpful as a teaching device to visualize these two traditions and their methods on a continuum. Notice that this is for teaching purposes only. This book emphasizes that one should borrow techniques from any point on the continuum appropriate to one's question.[1]

The characteristics of the end-points on the continuum are summarized in Table 2.1 and the continuum is displayed with typical studies in Figure 2.1. As noted earlier, some methods span the continuum and, depending on the particular configuration, can be considered either qualitative or quantitative. Survey research, as shown in Figure 2.1, is such a method. It can be either quantitative, as when one of the big polling organizations does preelection questionnaire studies of a political campaign, or qual-

Table 2.1   Characteristics Distinguishing the Ends of the Continuum, from Qualitative to Quantitative

Distinguishing Characteristics	Ends of the Continuum	
	Qualitative Approach	Quantitative Approach
1. Maturity of knowledge sought	explore, describe, explain	explain, corroborate, predict, explore generality
2. When the study design is finalized	inductive–emergent	deductive–preplanned
3. Primary form of data	words	measures and numbers
4. Composition of the study components	holistic (taken as a whole)	disassembled or taken apart

itative, as in group interviews of voters to understand what lies behind their choices. History, evaluation, and action research are areas where the methods also span the continuum and are considered in chapters 23–25. Further, as will be emphasized in chapter 26, quantitative and qualitative methods can be and often are combined in a single study with considerable benefit. Among other possibilities, such so-called "mixed-method" studies can combine the strengths of one method to counter the weaknesses of the other to corroborate a finding.

We can't emphasize enough that while it is useful to view quantitative and qualitative as broad categories at opposite ends of a methods continuum for the purposes of learning about them, for most of us the distinction is irrelevant to their use. We'll discuss some qualitative research exceptions in chapter 12. Viewing these research methods as a continuum makes clear that, for most of us, their characteristics are *not* entirely distinct from each other and that some characteristics can extend across the continuum. Consider that although we associate quantitative research with testing hypotheses and qualitative research with finding new ones, a rich tradition exists for the exploration and generation of hypotheses from quantitative data. It is called *exploratory data analysis* (Behrens, 1997; Behrens & Yu, 2003; Tukey, 1977). This approach focuses entirely on working with quantitative data, yet it addresses hypothesis generation and exploration rather than the most common emphasis, hypothesis testing (see chapter 19). Similarly, the characteristics of many mixed-methods studies span the continuum.

Figure 2.1   The quantitative–qualitative continuum.*

Qualitative	Quantitative and/or Qualitative	Quantitative
Case Study	*Sample Survey*	*Experiment*
Explore, describe, explain	Either	Explain, corroborate, predict, determine generality
Inductive-emergent, bottom-up	Either	Deductive-preplanned, top-down
Describe in words	Either	Describe in measures and numbers
Holistic approach	Either	Dissecting approach

*Notice the middle position for research that uses either approach or uses them in combination, such as with sample surveys.

THE NATURE OF SOCIAL SCIENCE KNOWLEDGE: AN ADDITIONAL FACTOR

Another factor that is extremely important for some researchers is their belief about what kind of social science is possible and desirable.[2] Most researchers have assumed that the natural sciences model is the ultimate goal of the social sciences. This assumption gets some affirmation from the increasing ability of the biological sciences to explain behavioral tendencies in terms of genetic markers or as the result of certain biological states or processes. Some wonder if the behavioral sciences may not eventually become largely biological.

While the remarkable similarities of identical twins, even those raised in dissimilar environments, attests to the power of genes, they still show differences reflective of their respective environments. The interaction of context and person is clearly complex. Add to this many random elements, the power of which has been suggested by chaos theory, and it is clear that predictability is not as certain as might be hoped for. Indeed, many behavioral researchers reject the natural sciences model as inapplicable to the social sciences and doubt that social science can ever reach the level of theory and predictability of some of the natural sciences. Many believe that all knowledge is at best local, confined to its original context with one making the best transfer to new situations one can, much as you do in applying the lessons of fiction to your own life. As might be anticipated, those expecting a natural-science type of social science are more likely to follow quantitative approaches and those oriented toward a local, context-oriented science likely favor qualitative approaches.

Like so many things, this is not an either/or choice; there are positions between fully accepting and rejecting the natural science model. For instance, Cronbach and Snow (1977) and Corno (2001) encourage us to look at aptitude by treatment **interactions**. These occur where person-dimension variables (e.g., aptitudes) are enhanced or degraded as they interact with the context-dimension variables (e.g., treatments) and, so, presumably are more predictable under those conditions.

House (2001) noted that qualitative studies, by seeking understanding of social behavior in context, take account of the possible causal factors and limit the alternative causal possibilities. He implies that this has led to a gradual broadening of what constitutes satisfactory evidence of causality. But as some researchers are broadening it, others are narrowing it—the federal government has established a What Works Clearinghouse (http://ies.ed.gov/ncee/wwc) in order to "help educators and education policy makers incorporate scientifically based research into their educational decisions." The Web site goes on to specify that "scientifically based research" is primarily experimental studies. This has been widely interpreted as putting other methodologies, such as qualitative, outside the circle of "good" research and has upset many researchers (e.g., see Howe, 2005). So what constitutes "good" research is a live topic, and House (2001) was correct when he labeled the topic of causation as "unfinished business."

UNDERSTANDING BOTH APPROACHES

Qualitative and quantitative researchers have developed criteria about:

- appropriate research methods to reach certain objectives,
- how to most appropriately collect and analyze the kind of data used in the research,
- the kinds of techniques that facilitate those analyses, and
- what constitutes good research when their methods are used.

Therefore, it makes the most sense to study the methods and criteria developed in each of these traditions separately. Then, understanding them, one can mix and match as appropriate to the demands of each particular study.

IMPORTANT TERMS AND CONCEPTS

dependent variable
emergent study
hypothesis
independent variable

interactions
preplanned study
treatment

SUMMARY

This book uses the continuum of methods to organize the presentation of the basics of the qualitative and quantitative traditions in separate sections (Sections III and IV). Emphasizing the continuum perspective, it then examines examples of research areas that make use of either or both of the traditions as appropriate: evaluations, sample surveys, and history. The intent is to illustrate the continuum well enough so that you can place other combinations in the context of what you have studied and can usefully combine elements as appropriate for whatever research you wish to do. Keep in mind, however, that what is important is:

- whether the research methods are appropriate to the purposes for which they are employed, and
- whether they were properly implemented.

Chapter 26 treats this topic in greater detail.

▶ Research is a creative act. Unless wedded to one or the other of the traditions, researchers should choose methods and techniques from either or both to imaginatively construct the strongest possible study, being sure to choose the most appropriate ones to achieve their goals, adapt them as needed, and use them properly.

▶ Qualitative and quantitative methods have their own traditions and their own criteria for what constitutes good research.

▶ Qualitative approaches are characterized by an inductive, bottom-up, emergent approach, beginning without structure but structuring the study as it proceeds, by exploring to find what is significant in the situation, by trying to understand and explain it, by working in a natural situation, and by describing in words. They are particularly well suited to studying complex processes.

▶ Quantitative approaches are characterized by a deductive, top-down approach with preplanning and structuring, by providing corroborative evidence for hypotheses and determining their generality, by describing in numbers, and by using measures. They are particularly well suited to studying the interaction of variables.

▶ Because each tradition has its own methods and criteria for what constitutes good research, it is best to learn the methods, techniques, and criteria in each, within their own context. Then one can mix and match as appropriate.

▶ To organize the research methods for learning purposes, we can structure a continuum of approaches from qualitative to quantitative, with studies that use methods from both traditions in a middle position.

A Look Ahead

We only rarely learn the history of the knowledge we are taught. But even when we study who did what when, even more rarely do we attend to the process whereby their research findings come to have the status we call knowledge. In the next chapter we not only examine that process, but in so doing we lay the basis for chapters 4, 7, 8, and 9.

Notes

[1] Ercikan and Roth (2006) also argue for an integrating point of view, suggesting research methods be viewed on a continuum of low-level to high-level inference.

[2] Philosophers concerned with the nature and validity of knowledge work in the field of epistemology. There are a number of epistemological points of view (e.g., see Crotty, 1999). Some recent orientations have emphasized feminist, minority, and economic equality aspects of epistemology.

3

From Findings to Knowledge

> What needs to be understood is how, scientifically, we come to know what we know.
> —Gerard Piel, *The Social Process of Science*
>
> I am tempted to say that we do not look for truth, but for knowledge. But I dislike this
> . . . for two reasons. First of all, we do look for truth, however we define it; it is what
> we find that is knowledge. And second, what we fail to find is not truth but certainty.
> —Jacob Bronowski, *The Identity of Man*

In the previous chapter we looked at how the choice of method depends on many things, including where we believe our problem stands in terms of certainty from discovery to acceptance as general knowledge. This chapter[1] describes the process by which the findings of an investigation move through various stages and come to be considered knowledge. It starts with a decision about the truth of a finding by the investigator and continues through a process of examination and communication by peers and editors. This leads to building **consensus** around a generalization, together with the proper interpretation of the research data that support it. This process differs from other ways that we come to know things, and it is a social process with norms that function as guides and standards.

Chapter 1 described two research articles that gave snapshots of the activities the researchers undertook. In this chapter, we will examine how those snapshots are just frames in a larger movie of how findings become knowledge. By discussing this process early in the book, we hope to instill recognition of the social nature of science and the place of scientific thinking in the modern world. You should come to understand:

- Why the characteristics of science are relevant to social and behavioral research methods.
- Why publication is so critical to the development of science.
- How science differs from other methods of knowing.
- The importance of answering the audience's questions so a consensus forms around the researcher's interpretation of the data.

An understanding of these critical issues will serve as the basis for the research criteria we will develop in later chapters as well as an understanding of a process that applies to research in *all* fields, not just the behavioral and social sciences.

INTRODUCTION

The processes of science are taking place around us all the time; they are as natural as breathing. We rarely give them a passing thought except, possibly, when there is a dispute about what scientific "facts" are true. Even in this instance, such as with the controversy over global warming, we typically focus on the issue rather than the processes. It is agreement on what is scientific, however, that allows consensus about what is good science and allows the creation of criteria by which a study will be judged.

Although there are occasional references to characteristics of social and behavioral science research or of natural science research, the overarching goal of this chapter is to describe how findings become knowledge and the norms of science in all science fields.

THE JOURNEY FROM FINDINGS TO KNOWLEDGE

We will use Kounin's research (1970) as our example of how research findings become knowledge. Kounin examined classroom practices to determine what teacher actions make a difference. If you've been in a classroom with an emotionally disturbed child, you know the havoc that such a child can produce; the learning process of the whole class can come to a standstill.

Kounin put boxes on tripods in classrooms, leaving them so the teacher and class became accustomed to them. Sometimes they contained a television camera to videotape classroom interaction, and sometimes they did not. Only Kounin knew. In this way, he gathered natural classroom reactions.

Kounin noticed that children diagnosed as emotionally disturbed acted up in certain teachers' classrooms but not in others'. Why? By videotaping teachers' classrooms where they often acted up as well as those where they did not, Kounin, Friesen, and Norton (1966) and later Kounin and Obradovic (1968) found several differences. Two of these differences they named momentum and smoothers. Momentum referred to keeping up the pace of instruction so that teaching was free from slowdowns—dwelling too long on a subject, nagging, giving overlaborious directions or comments. Smoothers referred to teachers who changed activities smoothly, as from art to mathematics. Pausing, looking around, and sensing the group's readiness for change characterized their behavior. In contrast, some teachers made changes whenever they felt the need, regardless of class readiness. Others did not follow through; they gave a transition direction and walked away to become immersed in something else, creating confusion. In examining classroom recitation sessions, Kounin found a significant relationship between deviancy and both slowdowns and nonsmoothing teacher behaviors.

How did this finding become accepted as knowledge? We can trace many steps in the publication records; others we must fill in.

1. First, there were the three researchers, Jacob Kounin and his assistants, Wallace Friesen and Evangeline Norton. Each brought a set of experiences, assumptions, tools, and understandings about past research and research methods to their investigation. They had to make many judgments about how to design and implement the study: what methods to use, what trade-offs to make, what were the biggest threats to drawing clear conclusions. In the end, each had to make a personal judgment that the most appropriate interpretation of the evidence showed consistent differences between classrooms of equally emotionally disturbed children. Where momentum was maintained and transitions were made smoothly, there was less behavior deviancy. Let's call their personal judgments *knowing judgments*. These findings were the beginning of the journey down the road to becoming knowledge. Such judgments will be made by individuals all through the rest of the journey, judgments about whether the researchers accept the interpretation of the evidence as the appropriate one.

2. It took a consensus of knowing judgments among Kounin, Friesen, and Norton for them to agree on the nature of their research report. They also had to come to a consensus regarding the nature of its communication. They would have to decide who was their primary target audience (psychologists or school teachers), how broadly they thought their claims would generalize, when their written account was ready for presentation or publication, and how technical to make the writing. These judgments about presentation of the findings facilitate the social communication that is essential to forming a consensus around the findings. Knowing is a personal judgment; for a finding to be accepted as knowledge requires a consensus of such judgments. Furthermore, such a consensus must exist at each judgment point on the path from initial investigator to research consumer; these steps are examined in items 3–15 below.

3. The steps at the next stage vary, depending on the researcher's situation. If colleagues work in the same or a closely related field, most researchers will share the report with them. If there are no close colleagues at their own institution, some send copies to professional friends at other institutions. At this or a later stage, some send copies to the **invisible college** in their field, a designation adopted by Garvey, Lin, and Nelson (1970) during their study of communication in psychology. It describes an informal (usually unorganized) cross-institutional group of colleagues who have a common research interest. Their mutual admiration for what the others have done, their concern at others' unintentional errors, and their goal to become the first to present new findings in a research area all drive a variety of informal means of communication.[2]

Because the publication process was (and still is) slow, invisible college members formed a mailing list of colleagues who might be interested in their research or who may have been helpful in the past. Each routinely sent copies of his or her research reports to this group, keeping them more up-to-date than readers who had to wait until the research findings appeared in a journal. Persons who were cited in an important way in an article may also have been sent copies so that they could see how their research had been built on. Sharing data and interpretation in these ways provided feedback that could either confirm or modify notions about the proper interpretation of any set of data. The questions that invisible college members asked were likely to be among the most penetrating to be faced, since having worked in the same field, they could anticipate potential weaknesses.

Although there is no record, we can assume that Kounin and associates had an invisible college network and mailed them copies of the report. Note that we are talking about research done around 1964. Invisible colleges now are more likely to do their communication by e-mail. They may have blogs, or a listserv (a forum) for the posting and discussion of problems in their work and for getting advice about how to proceed. Professional association-supported discussion groups (e.g., listservs) make the invisible colleges visible and accessible, since usually anyone can join these forums. They have broadened the definition of "colleague."

We can think of the ideas put forth in the written research report as radiating out like the rings resulting from an object dropped into a pond. As the wave moves out, it touches other researchers who will give feedback to the authors. The feedback might be general ("Good job") or very specific ("Did you transpose the numbers in row five of table 2?"). It might lead to additional collaboration, or, if the findings threaten existing viewpoints, to competing research. Both positive and negative reactions are welcome since they help the researchers think about what they have done, how they are thinking about it, and how to communicate their findings.

4. After receiving an initial round of responses, the authors probably decided to present their findings at an appropriate professional association meeting. They submitted an abstract of their report to the Program Committee of the American Educational Research Association (AERA) charged with selecting papers on classroom research for the annual convention. The abstract was sent to each member of the committee, who independently judged whether to schedule a presentation of the report. The committee members pooled their judgments and agreed to schedule the paper. Again, there was a consensus of knowing judgments that the proposed interpretation of the data seemed appropriate and contained potentially significant findings.

5. If, as we presume, the study was presented at the next AERA convention, a discussion period (in which findings and procedures could be questioned) followed the presentation. Informal discussions in the halls after the session would raise further questions. Again, these were colleagues knowledgeable in the field, respectful but tough critics. Their questions cued the researchers to points in the report that were of concern to their audience. Because Kounin and his researchers believed they could satisfactorily answer these questions, they maintained their belief that their interpretations were appropriate and took steps in future reports to ensure that the questions were answered.

In addition, persons who did not attend the AERA convention saw the title of the paper in the convention program and, if interested, wrote Kounin for a copy. We know that Kounin did send copies because this author received one on June 7, 1965, with Kounin's handwritten note "Unpublished as of 7 May, 1965." Although he didn't respond (not his research area), others probably reacted to the paper in writing, raising questions, making suggestions, and calling Kounin's attention to relevant research of which he may not have been aware.

6. Kounin and his colleagues submitted the paper, revised on the basis of the questions raised in previous airings, to the *Journal of Educational Psychology*. The authors' names as well as any other identifying information were stripped from the manuscript by Ray Kuhlen, the editor. He sent it to one of the journal's consulting editors (who knew the literature surrounding the study) and to a couple of other researchers (active in this area of research) whom he selected as competent and interested. These experts made knowing judgments that the findings held up under scrutiny, were interpreted appropriately, and constituted significant additions to the field. They recommended that the article be published, probably with some minor modifications to clarify procedure and interpretation. Because both authors and reviewers were kept blind to each other's identity, the presentation had to stand on its own, unsupported by the reputation of the researchers or their institution. Similarly, because their identities were protected, reviewers were free to give their candid judgment.

   Kuhlen carefully considered the readers' comments and his own reaction to the article. He had the authors make the few modifications needed and then scheduled it for publication. Consensus continued to form.

7. The paper was published in 1966 under the title "Managing Emotionally Disturbed Children in Regular Classrooms" in volume 57 of the *Journal of Educational Psychology*. The editor thought the article sufficiently important to make it the opening article of the issue.

8. The previous seven steps were also involved in a **replication** of the earlier study by Kounin and another assistant. Replication involves doing the study again. This time, they used 50 schools instead of 30 and videotaped full days of classroom activities rather than half-days. The findings were replicated; terminology and coding of activities were further clarified. This study was published in volume 2 of the *Journal of Special Education* as "Managing Emotionally Disturbed Children in Regular Classrooms: A Replication and Extension," by Kounin and Obradovic (1968). In social science research there is neither the tradition nor the funding for replication that seems to exist in the natural science fields. Unfortunately, even Kounin's own replication of his earlier study is not a common practice.

9. John Glavin and Herbert Quay were asked to write an article summarizing research on behavior disorders for the February 1969 issue of the *Review of Educational Research*. They read the Kounin studies and decided that those findings and their interpretations were sound enough that they should include them in their review. Their review was accepted and published.

10. The findings were now in a **secondary source**, removed from the initial evidence and dependent for acceptance on the reader's trust of the reviewers' judgments. Since individuals now would encounter the ideas of the study without the detailed argument and data, readers are likely to evaluate the conclusions by taking into account the authority and reputation of the author summarizing the work. By 1970, a dozen other authors had cited one or the other of the original articles in papers. The fact that the original findings had held up when the research was repeated was an important factor in their acceptance. Their confir-

mation by an investigator other than the original researcher, however, would have given even stronger confirmation.

11. In 1970, Kounin published a book that summarized the research to date: *Discipline and Group Management in Classrooms*. It began to take the place of the journal articles in citations by other researchers.

12. Robert Travers was charged with the responsibility of editing the second edition of the *Handbook of Research on Teaching* (1973). He asked Frank Hewett and Phillip Blake (1973), researchers who knew the literature, to write a chapter on teaching the emotionally disturbed. They included a section on classroom management and found the Glavin and Quay references to Kounin's work. They believed it of sufficient importance to read the original studies. They included a reference to the first study in their chapter, as did other chapter authors. In all, there were 20 references to this body of work. The new edition of the *Handbook* was published by Macmillan in 1973. The first edition had established it as an authoritative source; the second edition benefited from that reputation and rapidly became one, too.

13. Thomas Good and Jere Brophy (1977), leaders in the teaching research field, decided to write an educational psychology text. It was destined to become one of the most popular texts in the field. They had long known Kounin's work, since some of their own was based on it. They used the *Handbook* as a reference, and the many citations to Kounin's work strengthened their own impressions of its soundness and importance. They included his findings in their text, which was published as *Educational Psychology: A Realistic Approach*. Now thousands of students were exposed to the findings as knowledge.

14. Harold Mitzel was carefully chosen as editor for the massive task of preparing the fifth edition of the *Encyclopedia of Education Research*. On the advice of his board of editors, he asked Kevin Ryan to do an article on teacher characteristics. Ryan asked Debra Phillips to help, and they judged the Kounin work worthy of inclusion. The four-volume encyclopedia was published by the Free Press in 1982.

15. Subsequently, other writers of texts (e.g., encyclopedia articles, and advice to teachers to appear in *The Instructor* and similar journals) and articles aimed at parents in popular periodicals, women's magazines, and *Reader's Digest* all treated the findings as accepted knowledge. A consensus of knowing judgments extends all the way back to the first presentation of the study's results, which have now made the transition from findings to knowledge.

Compare this story with the stereotype of the lone scientist in a laboratory, antiseptically creating facts that are immediately accepted by a waiting public eager to be told the way the world really works. The true picture is one of a highly social process that is developed, controlled, and maintained by people.

Important Characteristics of the Journey

This story illustrates many aspects of the journey from findings to knowledge, from the initial findings of a research study to the acceptance of those findings as general knowledge.

1. The journey is a long one. Note the elapse of 16 years—seven years from initial publication to inclusion in the *Handbook of Research on Teaching* and another nine years from the *Handbook* to the *Encyclopedia of Educational Research*. Even in the beginning, time may seem to drag for the researchers and they need to balance short and long-term activities. Submission to AERA occurs in the summer, with presentation the following spring. Peer review of a journal submission may take anywhere from one to six months. In some fields, researchers choose the publication outlet with the shortest lag time.

2. The experts closest to the research make the initial decisions as to whether findings merit a claim as new knowledge. Probably nobody is in a better position to make this judgment than those who have done research in the area and who therefore know the problems to look for—likely rival explanations, weaknesses in methodology, and so on. Their reflective skepticism is critical to the start of the journey in that they must determine whether the conclusions were clear enough, the results positive enough, and the overall value of the study great enough to merit reporting. These experts make a data-based judgment based on the current theoretical worldview about the proper interpretation of the findings, which they then compare with the interpretation of the data by the original researchers.

   There is some risk in this situation insofar as the individuals who know the most about the research are also those with the greatest investment and therefore possibly the greatest bias (positive or negative). Nevertheless, the experience of the research community is that susceptibility to bias is overcome by the number of possible outlets and reviewers.

3. This process of judgment assumes that a negative result would not be published, an assumption that is probably true. In the early stages of the discovery–knowledge continuum, the discussion may not be about whether the results are negative or positive, but rather whether the endeavor was sufficiently well conceived to result in clear outcomes. Here, the feedback might be that the question being explored was not sufficiently clear, or that the method used was inconsistent with a clear conclusion.

   Not publishing negative findings, however, is not entirely foolish; editors know that there are myriad ways of getting negative results but relatively few ways of getting positive ones. Therefore, they are likely to publish only negative studies that definitively close off certain otherwise attractive directions that would waste other researchers' resources.

4. In their journey from colleague experts to lay audience, the judgments pass to persons increasingly removed from the knowledge and skills involved in the immediate focus of the research. Campbell (1988) has observed that the knowledge and skills of each individual regarding the phenomenon of concern overlap those of the previous person like the scales of a fish. Figure 3.1 illustrates this pattern using the **fish-scale analogy** to show the stages in process that we noted in the Kounin scenario. The arrowed line cuts across a cross-section of those who have successively made judgments regarding the findings—the original researchers, then specialists in the same field, then reviewers, and so on. The arrow points to a depiction of that cross-section across the bottom labeling the sequence of persons represented by the fish scales.

Figure 3.1   The fish-scale analogy of the transition of findings into knowledge.

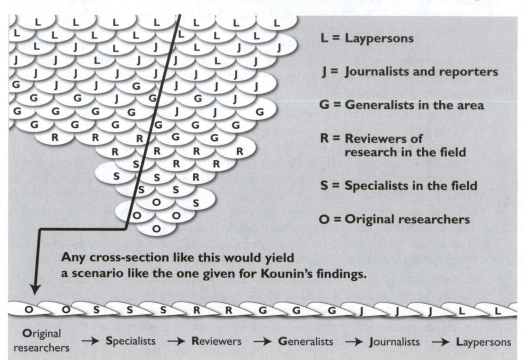

L = Laypersons

J = Journalists and reporters

G = Generalists in the area

R = Reviewers of
research in the field

S = Specialists in the field

O = Original researchers

**Any cross-section like this would yield
a scenario like the one given for Kounin's findings.**

Original
researchers → Specialists → Reviewers → Generalists → Journalists → Laypersons

We have traced only one path in the process, like the angled line in Figure 3.1. Unquestionably, other people were judging and using the Kounin results during the time frame we covered. They built on one another's work just as Kounin and colleagues did. These other researchers are portrayed in Figure 3.1 by all the other "fish scales" not intersected by the angled line. Although we often act like it is, no single research study is sufficient to result in knowledge. Knowledge requires an entire body of research—in our example, that of Kounin and the many who built on his work. The consensus spanning all these efforts results in the transition from research to knowledge.

5. Each individual who either makes or encounters a knowledge claim must make a personal judgment to accept the claim as knowledge; that is, each must make a knowing judgment. The initial knowing judgments are based on the most appropriate interpretation of the actual data and are made by the people with the best basis for forming that judgment. As the claim is passed to persons further removed from those initial judgments, except as an occasional person goes to the source documents, the acceptance of the claim as knowledge is based on trust in the expertise of all below them in the fish-scale network. As knowing judgments agree, a consensus is formed and the claim is accepted as knowledge.

Sometimes new developments in a field move so fast, or the communication patterns in a field are so slow, that it is difficult for a consensus to form around findings at the periphery of knowledge. Such a problem exists in medical and biological fields, where changes are rapid and researchers themselves may differ regarding what parts of the knowledge base are solid. The result is conflicting advice and critical comments about the research. Then experts lose credibility, and concern develops among practitioners and laypersons who would like to benefit from this knowledge. A technique of the National Institutes of Health (DeAngelis, 1988) is intended to speed up the process. Its "consensus conference" consists of a summarizing panel that evaluates the evidence and separates what they consider solid enough for practitioners to use from what is still experimental. In addition, journals such as the *New England Journal of Medicine* have made an effort to establish an "informal consensus view" in some fields. All these practices increase common recognition that science works by consensus.

6. While the most visible way to communicate is through published journal articles, there are a number of other methods of communicating research conceptualizations and findings. Scientific dialog occurs in written correspondence, in interactive oral presentations at conferences and in university research colloquia, in informal discussions following meetings, in books and chapters, and in other venues. These methods are further expanded by the use of the Internet, which allows rapid communication by e-mail and wide distribution through postings on the World Wide Web, blogs, and in listserv groups. An important part of the education of researchers is to learn to communicate effectively in these many modes.

IS KNOWLEDGE THE SAME AS TRUTH?

If knowledge is determined by a consensus of critical judgments, is it possible that such judgments could be wrong? That the truth lies elsewhere? Yes, of course. That gives us all an uncomfortable feeling we must live with. Reread the quotation from Bronowski on this chapter's opening page; this is the point he makes. As close as we come to "truth" with our available methods is to be adequately critical of a finding; we must listen carefully to all the arguments and then see if a consensus can be formed that the conclusion is warranted. Phillips (1992) notes that the great philosopher John Dewey, reluctant to use the term "truth," decided to replace it with "by 'warranted assertibility'" (p. 108), a considerably more descriptive term.

We tend to know this intellectually but ignore it most of the time. Trusting most new knowledge is essential; it just takes too much energy to question everything all the time. Only as questions are raised—for instance, about the truth of global warming—does questioning "what is true" come to the fore. Even then we often consider such questioning as a bothersome aberration, whereas we should view it as part of the normal process of science.

> ▶ Each individual making a knowledge claim or encountering such a claim must make a knowing judgment regarding the appropriate interpretation of the evidence. As a consensus of such knowing judgments forms, findings become accepted as knowledge.
>
> ▶ The development of knowledge results from the creation of a consensus around the interpretation of data in successively widening circles of decreasingly specialized persons.

Knowing Judgments in Everyday Life

Clearly, some results do not garner a consensus. Consider, for example, the controversy over whether there is a real crisis in the burning of fossil fuels. Many people are accepting findings in these areas as knowledge. However, some scientists are still uncertain whether these activities will result in a "greenhouse effect" and global warming or whether self-adjusting mechanisms are operating, making our concern unjustified. Until there is a consensus among the experts (acceptance as knowledge), it is unlikely that a crisis will be accepted widely enough that everyone will agree to appropriate action.

The picture is further complicated by the fact that there are different thresholds for acceptance as knowledge, depending on the seriousness of what is involved. Let us examine another way of considering this phenomenon.

Cronbach (1982) views the development of knowledge as one of **uncertainty reduction**. When our uncertainty about the proper interpretation of the data is high, we are unwilling to admit the research claim to the category "knowledge." When the evidence or the testimony of authorities sufficiently reduces our uncertainty below some threshold, we accept it as knowledge.

Conceiving that knowledge results from uncertainty reduction—or from its mirror image, the certainty with which we hold the knowledge—allows us to consider the matter of the certainty threshold for knowledge. This threshold varies with a matter's personal importance and relevance to our lives. For example, we may readily accept as true a claim that a certain individual has gone over Niagara Falls in a barrel because it means relatively little to us. However, a claim that a new chemical will facilitate weight loss without causing any bodily harm now or in the distant future may have a much higher threshold before the claim is accepted.

Furthermore, we make different knowing judgments in the various areas of our lives. We allow some sources of knowledge to push us over the threshold but reject others—we accept engineering specifications for the sizes of lumber for building a house, for instance, but we may reject advice to us as parents not to use physical punishment. The latter is an instance of behavioral science knowledge and points up the fact that despite the testimony of "experts" regarding the negative consequences of physical punishment, such "knowledge" is tested against our own experiences to see whether it "rings true."

Susan Haack, a philosopher who specializes in epistemology (the study of knowledge), describes

> the structure of evidence, to use an analogy I have long relied on, is more like a crossword puzzle than a mathematical proof. . . . Scientific inquiry is a deeply and unavoidably social enterprise; . . . so that scientists, in the plural, are like a bunch of people working, sometimes in cooperation with each other, sometimes in competition, on this or that part of a vast crossword—a vast crossword in which some entries were completed long ago by scientists long dead, some only last week; some are in almost-indelible ink, some in regular ink, some in pencil, some heavily, some faintly; and some are loudly contested, with rival teams offering rival solutions. (2001)

Much of natural science's "knowledge" is so complex that we have no basis for knowing when not to trust the experts. Such complexity, however, is much less true of social and behavioral science knowledge, which deals with everyday life—a special problem for social science researchers. Further, behavioral science findings that run counter to what our intuition tells us is true are difficult to accept unless the explanation supporting them is strong.

Research findings in the social sciences face this additional challenge. Once stated, findings are judged "obviously true" and therefore not worth having been researched. Taking this point of view, some members of Congress have called the whole social science enterprise a search for the obvious. Wong (1995), however, showed that what often seems "obvious and true" may not be. Studying twelve "durable, replicable and potent" (p. 505) findings from research on teaching, she found that experienced teachers were no more accurate than nonteachers and regarded "as obvious the majority of both the actual and the opposite findings." All participants selected the actual research finding "in only 4 out of 12 items" (p. 509).

Sample items: "Third graders learn more in reading groups when teachers ask a question first and then call a student's name" (opposite of finding) or "call a student's name first and then ask a question" (actual finding). "In Grades 1–9, students were found to get better scores on achievement tests in classes with more teacher control and less student freedom to select learning experiences" (actual finding) or "less teacher control and more student freedom to select learning experiences" (p. 511). Clearly the pervasive sense of what is obviously true is not always trustworthy. Research has an important role to play. Therefore, it is particularly important that social science researchers understand the process by which findings become knowledge so that they will design research that facilitates the process of consensus building.

> ▶ When experts disagree and cannot form a consensus, laypersons are leery about accepting research findings as knowledge.
>
> ▶ Each new bit of evidence contributes to our evaluation of the certainty with which a finding or an assertion is accepted as knowledge.
>
> ▶ The threshold at which point a finding or assertion crosses the border into the realm of knowledge varies, partly in accord with its personal importance to us.
>
> ▶ Social and behavioral science findings and assertions are tested against personal experience before being permitted to cross the threshold. This is not required of most natural science findings and assertions.

You should sense that to build a consensus around the findings of a study, it must satisfy a number of criteria that are widely accepted and understood by researchers. We will explore what those are more thoroughly in chapters 7–9. But first let us compare the knowledge gained from science with that from other sources.

DIFFERENT SOURCES OF KNOWLEDGE

Science is only one source of knowledge. Knowledge comes from a variety of sources, and we are constantly making knowing judgments about whether a source can be trusted, no matter whether the source is our eyes; our own past experience; some source of traditional wisdom like the Bible or Koran; or a person we respect as an authority because of training or status (e.g., clergy), specialized expertise (e.g., nuclear engineer, petroleum geologist, philosopher), or professional license (e.g., physician, dentist, lawyer, teacher, clinical psychologist, social worker). Because we use a variety of bases for making knowing judgments, it is worth examining the characteristics of other sources of knowledge to understand how science differs from them. Long ago Cohen and Nagel (1934) proposed a useful categorization—personal observation and experience, intuition, belief and tradition, authority, and science.

Personal Observation and Experience

Personal observation and experience is the source we trust the most. If you personally experience the maintenance of classroom order that results, as Kounin suggests, from making a smooth instead of an abrupt transition, you are likely to be convinced that this is reliable knowledge. Indeed, personal observation and experience constitute a particularly important source of knowledge. They are the raw stuff of science, for the personal experience of scientists is the basis both for claims to knowledge discovery and for ideas and hunches that lead to new knowledge.

A characteristic of personal experience is the need for us all, infant and adult alike, to find an order, or pattern, to our existence. Where there are no patterns, we impose them. Judson (1980) notes, "Beat of the traffic, pulse of the phone, the long cycles of the angle of the sun in the sky. Patterns, rhythms, we live by patterns" (p. 28). One of the most important things that researchers do is to find order and pattern in nature. As Judson further notes, "Patterns set up expectations. . . . To perceive a pattern means that we have already formed an idea of what's next" (p. 28)—a hypothesis. Guessing "what's next"—predicting—is one of the most important outcomes of knowing. If we can predict, we have the chance to change the outcomes for the better—to improve ourselves, to help others solve their problems, to have a better society.

Intuition

Intuition is sometimes used to describe our reaction to propositions so obviously true as to be self-evident; merely stating them is enough for their acceptance. Frequently, we infer such propositions from the world around us. It was accepted for centuries that the sun revolved around the earth because this appeared to be self-evident—along with the divine right of kings and the inferiority of different social groups. Accepting such propositions involves making a knowing judgment. Clearly, not all such propositions are true, however. It is threatening when any such proposition turns out to be false, because then we have no basis for knowing whether others equally obvious may be equally untrue. The use of intuition as a source may depend on the society and time period in which we live.

Belief and Tradition

As a source of knowledge, tradition confirms all those things that "have always been true." The wisdom of the Bible, Koran, and Talmud and the advice of a culture passed from generation to generation are examples. Traditional knowledge, especially of the religious kind, tends to be set forth by authorities who help interpret it. Knowing relies on a judgment of whether to accept the tradition and the authority.

For some individuals, religion and science address different parts of reality and work together symbiotically. For example, it is not uncommon for individuals to seek answers to questions about measurement of mental and physiological functioning through science, while relegating questions about the nature of life and what constitutes death to the realm of religion or some other tradition. On the other hand, some groups believe certain knowledge judgments are best understood by assent to long-standing traditions that cannot change.

The breadth of activities guided by tradition warrant some reflection. The types of clothes we wear, the styles of our homes and furniture, our choice of leisure activities, and many other aspects of our lives are by-products of tradition.

Authority

Authorities are, without question, the major source of our knowledge. Why? For one thing, we can personally experience only a small part of our world. For another, few propositions are self-evidently true. An **authority** is anyone we accept as being more knowledgeable than we are. Most professional persons earn their living as an authority in some area. Although authorities are generally accepted as experts only in their area of expertise, this distinction is not always made. Heroes and persons of prominence often voice opinions on public policy matters in which they have no special expertise. For most persons, and most decisions, the knowing judgment becomes one of whether or not to accept a particular source as an authority. Will you accept the previous sentence just because the author believes it, or will you seek additional basis for your belief or disbelief?

All authorities are not alike. At one end of a continuum are the arbitrary or dogmatic authorities, who assert that something is true by reason of their position or ability to enforce its truth. In the middle are authorities who are believable by virtue of their position, experience, and training. At the other end are reasoning authorities who, though they have a believable case and might also rest on the laurels of position, nevertheless indicate the basis for their judgment and present the case for all to judge.

Dogmatic authority is found in some traditions and religions—especially if there once was a rationale for a given truth, but it has long since disappeared. For instance, for many years the Soviet Union enforced Lysenkoism with dogmatic authority. (This was the theory that a plant or animal could genetically pass on to its progeny environmentally acquired characteristics.) Dogmatic authority generally regards challenges as threatening. If a challenge is permitted in one instance, where will it stop? Of course, should such an authority be successfully challenged, the halo of authority vanishes.

In the middle of the continuum we have the authority who is accepted by reason of education, experience, and especially past success. The past record is particularly important with respect to a current knowing judgment because it is one of the major bases for having been given the mantle of authority. Most licensed professionals, such as physicians, are in this category. Often they do not take the time to explain their decisions.

At the other end of the continuum is the **reasoning authority**, whose characteristics are much like those of the scientist, and they help make science the source of much accepted knowledge. Unlike the opinions of most authorities, however, every scientist's opinion is to be given equally serious consideration. Thus, when judging manuscripts, some editors routinely remove the authors' names so that reputation will not influence acceptance. Science does not always operate on this basis, however; we can surely think of many instances where the accepted opinions of senior scientists were wrong and impeded progress. The belief that the sun revolves around the earth was perpetuated by scientific authorities long after contrary evidence challenged it.

A distinguishing characteristic of reasoning authorities is the logical force of their arguments. Consider Kounin's assertion that the teacher's smoothing behavior aids in controlling emotionally disturbed children. It is more easily accepted when we understand that the teacher's behavior continuously directs the child's attention to external stimuli and away from the internal turmoil that would result in acting up.

Another characteristic of reasoning authorities is integrity: openness about what is not known, willingness to reveal weaknesses in the case, and a balanced presentation of the positive and negative sides of the case. This makes it less probable that something important and relevant is being hidden.

Challenges to the arguments of reasoning authority do not harm the authorities' expert status; in fact, such challenges are expected and welcomed. Only through challenge can the soundness of the case be tested. Furthermore, we can agree with such an authority in one instance where, in our judgment, the case holds up, yet we can disagree in another instance without rejecting the authority as a potential source of knowledge.

Of course, if a source is repeatedly found in error, there would seem to be some uncorrected problem in procedure or thinking. Unless the individual's integrity is challenged, however—as in faking data or being caught deliberately withholding knowledge that would affect its interpretation—any finding, no matter how unusual, is seriously considered by the reasoning authority. Typically the scientist is an example of a reasoning authority.

Science

We have already seen many of the important hallmarks of science: propositions are put forward based on systematic observation; the propositions are stated in a way that they can be disconfirmed; the observations and their interpretations are put forward in a public manner that fosters discussion and challenge; the observations can be replicated. All these aspects move ideas forward from the individual belief in the research toward the status of generally accepted knowledge. The conception of knowledge as reducing uncertainty has the advantage of allowing many knowledge levels between the extremes of "rejected" and "accepted." Not everything that crosses the threshold into the knowledge category is held with the same certainty. We may reluctantly accept fluoridation of our water but buy bottled drinking water to be on the safe side. Sometimes we accept something as knowledge but retain some uncertainty.

That is the way of science, including, of course, the social and behavioral sciences. All scientific knowledge, even the most basic, is held with a tinge of uncertainty—just enough that it could be replaced should more valid knowledge come to light. At times, multiple and competing theories may co-exist in an uncomfortable period of tension. Knowledge that is replicated and reconfirmed is held with considerable certainty—enough that we act on it as though it were unquestionably true.

Successful replication of research is considered essential in the natural sciences. Replication involves the repetition of a study, preferably by someone other than the original researcher and researched somewhat differently. If the same results are obtained by a different and improved study, they are considered confirmed or validated. Replication, especially using enhanced methods in new situations, is the ultimate validation.

Exact replication in the social and behavioral sciences is rare. In one common kind of replication, however, each successive researcher builds on the previous work. Should expectations fail to be confirmed, either the previous work was in some way invalid or the current researcher extended it incorrectly. If the researcher can find no fault in the extension study, a replication of the earlier work may be required.

As we have noted in the Kounin example, a finding must undergo the scrutiny of a host of **gatekeepers**—convention committees, editors, chapter authors, and so forth—to make the transition to knowledge. The researcher's interpretation of the evidence is repeatedly examined to make sure that it meets each gatekeeper's standards. This process of continual challenge, when combined with the tentativeness with which we hold all scientific knowledge, is relatively unique among the sources of knowledge. It allows knowledge to be changed as a natural part of the process without loss of the scientific community's status as an important source of knowledge.

Scientists understand the necessity of scrutiny, the tentativeness of knowledge, the importance of replication—the many steps to knowledge. However, the nature and length of the process is often not grasped by the public and by policy makers, who want concrete, correct answers and want them now! They frequently become impatient or do not recognize science as a social process in which networks of individuals assume responsible roles to make knowing judgments that coalesce into a consensus.

> ▶ Knowledge comes to us from many sources: personal observation and experience, intuition, belief and tradition, authorities, and science. Of these, only science and the reasoning authority routinely seek and survive testing and challenge. The others all have trouble handling the challenges.
>
> ▶ In the natural process of science, knowledge is routinely challenged and replaced. Challenging findings that were previously considered knowledge has less of an effect on science's status as an important knowledge source than it does on other sources.
>
> ▶ Replication, especially using improved research methods and new situations, is the ultimate validation of a proposition.

THE NORMS OF KNOWLEDGE PRODUCTION

Science is a social system in which individuals assume important responsibilities in various roles:

- Researchers design studies, carry them out, and interpret the results with integrity.
- Preliminary communications are passed around informal channels to help the researchers develop their communications in ways their colleagues understand.
- Journal, handbook, and encyclopedia editors; consulting editors; reviewers; and similarly trusted gatekeepers of knowledge dissemination ensure that studies selected for publication meet appropriate standards and that pertinent criticism of already published studies is disseminated so that an unwarranted consensus does not develop.
- Writers of reviews of research, textbooks, encyclopedias, and handbook entries carefully consider the results of studies and disseminate the deserving findings.

Each of these roles is governed by an informal but well-understood system of rules and norms. Although some are obvious, making them explicit describes the system and shows how it is maintained and its work is facilitated.

Merton (1968) described the norms of science as **universal standards** for everyone's knowledge claims (he called this *universalism*), **common ownership of information** (his term for this was *communism*, a far cry from its usual meaning), integrity in gathering and interpreting data (he referred to this as **disinterestedness**), and **organized skepticism** of all knowledge claims. These, of course, apply to the natural as well as the social sciences. Let's examine each norm in more detail.

Universal Standards for Knowledge Claims

As a neophyte researcher, you would not want your research to be judged by harsher standards than those of a respected colleague in your field. As a member of a minority, you would expect your work to be judged by a standard identical to that applied to everyone else. As a researcher at newly established East Snowshoe State, you should not expect different standards from those had you been employed by venerable and distinguished Oxford University. The quality of the work itself, rather than its author, sponsoring institution, or financial supporter, should be the focus of a judgment based on universal standards—standards that are the same for all.

Each field establishes norms for what is acceptable research. Over time, these norms are raised as more is learned and the general level of methodological sophistication of the field rises. At any one point in time, however, the standards that gatekeepers apply should be the same for everyone.

Common Ownership of Information

The belief that information is to be owned by all and shared freely—common ownership of information—is a norm subscribed to and maintained in academic and not-for-profit research settings. As we might expect, it is not always observed in the commercial sector since industrial research is often pursued for monetary advantage. Similarly, classified military research is beyond the reach of this norm. However, this is the norm for all the rest—the great bulk of science. Most major universities have rules forbidding sponsorship of research that cannot be freely published.

Thus, publication is not only a right of the researcher, *but also an obligation*. Researchers who dabble in research simply to satisfy their own curiosity and then do not publicly share their findings not only remove themselves from the social system of science, but they also are guilty of using for private curiosity resources that are expected to be used for the public good. The "publish or perish" rule of many universities is simply an enforcement of this norm.

This norm also requires that the data of a study be shared on request, once the original researchers have used the data for their purposes. The efforts of others who might want to analyze the data differently, for instance, should be facilitated in every way possible. The reasonableness of the norm is self-evident: It enables others to make sure that no errors were made in processing the data and that the most suitable methods were used to extract their appropriate interpretation.

Integrity in Gathering and Interpreting Data

Merton's disinterestedness is defined by Gove[3] (1976) as "not influenced by regard to personal advantage." That is to say, the researcher has integrity because he or she is disinterested in personal gain or advantage at the cost of method or findings. We all take for granted that researchers will gather and interpret data without regard to what they personally believe they should show. This disinterestedness is one of the norms to which we are most sensitive when it is violated. Thus, advertisers use presumably disinterested laboratories to provide the basis for claims like "Powder-Milk Biscuits give 4 out of 10 shy persons the will to do what needs to be done!"[4] We rely on the integrity of researchers to be as critical of their own behavior as would outside observers.

The pressures for success sometimes cause individuals to violate this norm. Indeed, no doubt some of us did so when our physics or psychology laboratory course required replication of famous experiments with a certain precision. Not realizing that these assignments were intended mainly to teach laboratory technique, we felt it necessary to generate fictitious data to meet the precision criteria. With pressure for exact results rather than acceptable laboratory technique, such class exercises can teach behavior that could disastrously end a career if carried over to later research where unsuspecting colleagues expect integrity.

Broad (1983) and Judson (2004) detail violations in both historical and recent times. These are instances where we know fraud did occur. No one knows how many uncaught cases there have been. Fortunately, the peer review process is in place in most settings where we seek to communicate a knowledge claim.[5] Both this process and studies that build on the findings of others are deterrents to fraud. The potential in active research areas for successful fraud seems small. Yet the possibility of any at all is unsettling, for the whole system is tarnished and loses credibility when just one member violates this norm.

Organized Skepticism

We have already described this norm in our detailing of the passage of Kounin's findings into knowledge. The editors, readers, and other gatekeepers show organized skepticism at work. Merton called this aspect one of the most necessary, and you can see how it makes science unique as a source of knowledge. Organized skepticism means that it is the responsibility of the community of scientists to be skeptical of each new knowledge claim, to test it, to try to think of reasons the claim might be false, and to think of rival explanations as plausible as the one advanced. Challenging new knowledge is sought in all science, instead of being avoided as in other knowledge sources.

Organized skepticism, however, cannot operate without the acceptance and observance of the other norms: The findings and the process by which data were obtained must be freely available—**common ownership of information**. Researchers must know that their work will be fairly and appropriately judged if they expose it to challenge—**universal standards**. We must assume integrity in gathering and interpreting the data if we are to accept the report at face value—**disinterestedness**. Given these conditions, organized skepticism can do its job of keeping an inappropriate consensus from forming and preventing invalid knowledge claims from reaching people who might otherwise unwittingly try to use them. The esteem in which scientific knowledge is held is testimony to the conscientiousness with which scientists voluntarily play their proper roles and make the system work.

In addition to Merton's norms, several principles that guide the development of science are worth noting:

- *Replication*, which we have already considered, is the ultimate validation of a finding.

- The *principle of parsimony* states that when there are several equally reasonable explanations for a phenomenon, we chose the simplest that accounts for the facts.

- The *preference for theory-based research* is another guiding principle. **Theory-based studies** help tie together disparate findings into an integrated explanation. Findings without a theory base float off alone, can become one of too many to track, and are unlikely to be as useful as those that can be found through their relation to an applicable theory.

Is Merton right about the norms of science? To Judson (2004), who wrote a book about fraud in science, "Merton's norms seem sadly naïve, idealistic, old-fashioned" (p. 35). This seems unduly harsh, but, as he goes on to explain, as originally formulated, they don't always fit today's society. And Judson is right—they are idealistic. But the fact of the matter is that, despite the instances of fraud that Judson describes, this book's author maintains that Merton's norms are ideals that are subscribed to and acted on to the extent feasible in today's society by the vast majority of scientists. We will look more carefully at each of them again in this book's final chapter as we consider how these ideals compare with reality in the larger system—the macrosystem—of science.

Suffice it to say at this juncture that it is clear from the historical record that science is by no means a perfect system. There is no way of ensuring that the norms of science prevent the knowledge of a given day from going astray. However, over time progress is made and wrongs are righted. This openness of science to self-correction is reassuring: The process will uncover errors. Further, much of its normative structure appears in one way or another in the codes of ethics of professional organizations. In this way we pass these ideals to new generations with an understanding of their vital roles. With the perspective you will gain from the last chapter of this text regarding how the norms work in today's society, you should be able to play your role more effectively, whatever it may turn out to be.

Merton found that the community of scientists observed certain norms or standards. These include:

▶ *Universalism*—The same standards apply equally to all, no one is exempted nor judged more harshly than anyone else.

▶ *Common ownership of information*—Information is owned by all and shared freely. Publication (or a substitute form of it) is a responsibility of the scientist.

▶ *Integrity in gathering and interpreting data*—Researchers are disinterested in personal gain or advantage at the cost of method or findings; they gather and interpret data without regard to what they personally believe they should show.

▶ *Organized skepticism*—It is the responsibility of the community of scientists to be skeptical of each new knowledge claim, to test it, to try to think of reasons the claim might be false, to think of rival explanations as plausible as the one advanced.

▶ Other principles are also observed, such as: acknowledging replication as the ultimate validation of a finding, choosing the simplest from among several equally reasonable explanations of a phenomenon (the principle of parsimony), and accepting theory-based research as the preferred method.

ETHICS

The previous discussion makes it clear that science is the result of a collaborative social enterprise with rules the participants are expected to follow. If there are rules, we might expect that the field of ethics would be an essential aspect of such an enterprise, as indeed it is. As Grunder (1986) points out,

> [W]hether you wish to become an ethicist . . . is not at issue. . . . You became one the minute you joined the profession. The only . . . issue now is whether you are going to be a good ethicist or a bad one. . . . You cannot use a human being [in a study] . . . without asking yourself, "Ought I to be doing this, in this way, to this person, at this time?" The moment the word "ought" is muttered, you have entered the realm of ethics. (p. xi)

In chapter 10 we will discuss at length the necessity of ethical standards and of obtaining the consent of those studied. (Because ethical concerns pervade many aspects of research, you will also find such discussion scattered throughout the book.)

ADDITIONAL READING

Campbell (1988); Cronbach (1982); Merton (1968); Phillips (1990, 1992)

IMPORTANT TERMS AND CONCEPTS

authority
common ownership of information
consensus
disinterestedness
dogmatic authority
fish-scale analogy
gatekeepers
invisible college

organized skepticism
reasoning authority
replication
secondary source
theory-based studies
uncertainty reduction
universal standards

OPPORTUNITIES FOR ADDITIONAL LEARNING

1. A Senate committee, concerned about safeguarding public funds spent on research grants, is questioning the scientific methods used by the grant recipients. The committee is convinced that the process is rife with cronyism and that researchers are not adequately critical of one another's work. The senators wonder if public money is being wasted on findings of questionable quality. How would you reply?

2. You have been studying the use of color in illustrations in school readers to heighten children's comprehension of text. Having established that children prefer color pictures to either black-and-white illustrations or none at all, you hypothesized that their inclusion would motivate students to pay more attention to the text and hence would increase comprehension. To your surprise, your results indicated that neither color nor black-and-white illustrations had any significant positive effect. Indeed, there was some evidence that color actually impeded understanding. What should you do with these findings? Should you submit them for publication?

3. As editor of a prominent journal in the field of information studies, you receive a paper from a psychologist who has been studying the psychological barriers that students develop to the use of computer-based information systems. This particular study focused on the on-line catalog system at the investigator's university. Should you consider publishing the study, even though the researcher is not in your field?

4. You are a junior researcher in the department of reading and are being considered for tenure this year. A senior member of your department is well known for his advocacy of the phonics approach for teaching young children to read. He is adamantly opposed to a contending theory, the whole-language approach, which is the fad at other universities. You do a comparative study that produces significant findings that lend credence to the latter approach and undermines his position. What should you do with your findings?

5. Powers, Fowles, Farnum, and Ramsey (1994) were concerned about the inequality of computer access. Their study examining the hypothesis that essays written on word processors would be graded more favorably than handwritten ones appeared in a reputable peer-reviewed journal. Assigning students the same topics, they collected two sets of essays, one written on word processors and another, handwritten. Each was also converted to its opposite format, and the papers were graded on a six-point scale by trained and experienced readers. Surprisingly, handwritten essays dropped from an average 3.6 to 3.0 when word-processed; word-processed-changed-to-handwritten scores rose slightly from 3.3 to 3.4. Replicating the study, the authors trained the readers to overlook the effect of mode of presentation, checked for differences in scoring the modes, used both modes in training, and double-spaced word-processed essays to make them look longer. The direction of effect was the same: handwritten-to-word-processed essays dropped from 3.5 to 3.2; word-pro-

cessed-to-handwritten essays increased from 3.5 to 3.7. It was noted that graders gave the benefit of the doubt to handwritten essays more often than to word-processed ones. Word-processed essays were longer (380 words versus 316), and length correlated with grades (.60). Poorer essays suffered more in word-processed format than in handwritten.

Now that you know about this study, you are given the option of word processing your next examination. Would you take it? Why or why not? Would you consider this finding as knowledge? Why or why not?

6. Make a list of a broad range of ideas you hold as knowledge from both personal and professional aspects of your life. For each one, consider the different sources of knowledge that led you to hold each idea as knowledge. Do you rely on different sources of knowing for different types of knowledge? What patterns can you see?

KEY TO ADDITIONAL LEARNING OPPORTUNITIES

1. Respond to the committee by describing the journey of findings to knowledge, explaining the thoroughness and professionalism with which research findings are examined by members of the field even before they are published. Explain that research findings are normally submitted for judgment first to colleagues at one's own institution and then to members of the invisible college, an informal interinstitutional group of colleagues with a common interest in the particular topic. In this way, the people most likely to know the potential weaknesses of the study are given a chance to respond to the methodology used and to the interpretation given to the results. They make a "knowing judgment" of the study. Any findings that progress further in the journey would have already been subjected to substantial scrutiny.

Given positive responses to this point, findings would likely be submitted for presentation at an appropriate professional association meeting. Abstracts submitted to convention program committees normally have the names removed and are submitted "blind" to committee members. Each paper is again judged by members of the field who pool their knowing judgments. Before a paper is scheduled, a consensus has been reached that the interpretation of the data seems appropriate and that the findings are significant. At the presentation itself and informally during the convention, the findings would again be questioned.

Finally, if the researcher is satisfied that all questions have been answered appropriately, the findings would likely be submitted to a professional journal for publication. Similar to the process used by the convention program committee, the paper would be submitted to a blind review by both a consulting editor and other experts in the field, and again subjected to knowing judgments. Only after these people are satisfied that the findings have been interpreted appropriately and are significant additions to the field is the paper published.

Although the findings may not yet be accepted by the field as knowledge, they have been subjected to a thorough and professional review process.

With regard to the charge of cronyism, you might point to Merton's standard of universalism at work in all these judgments.

2. You should attempt to disseminate your information. Negative findings may function to close off otherwise attractive research directions that would waste other researchers' resources. By submitting your findings either for presentation at a professional meeting or for publication, you put them up for peer review, allowing others in the field to judge their merit for themselves. In doing so, you are subscribing to Merton's principle of common ownership of information. This principle implies that publication is the obligation of any researcher participating in the social system of science who uses resources intended for the public good.

3. The functioning social system of science extends beyond the perceived boundaries of a particular field. This researcher would presumably be following the same norms of knowledge production as members of your field. Merton's universalism (universal standards for knowledge claims) applies to this case. That is, you should judge the quality of the work according to what is considered acceptable research for the methods commonly used in your field. While you, as editor, must use your judgment to filter out obviously inappropriate submissions, findings from another field may provide the members of your field with enlightening and useful knowledge that might not otherwise reach them. Thus you must make an initial knowing judgment based on the nature of the study, not the identity of the investigator and, if appropriate, allow the findings to be judged on their merits by putting the study through your review process.

4. Although you are in a politically sensitive situation, you should submit your findings to the peer-review process and share your information with others in the field. As in the study on color illustrations in problem 2, Merton's principle applies: Ownership of the data is shared, and you have an obligation to disseminate your results. Perhaps your first step is to seek the feedback of this particular researcher concerning your interpretation of the findings. He will likely be one of your most severe critics and may help confirm or modify your analysis. You may also wish to provide copies of the study to other members of the department or friends at other institutions to garner their reactions. After seeking such informal feedback and making any appropriate modifications, you should submit your findings for presentation at a professional meeting or for publication. You should allow the community to judge the merits of the study.

5. Here we face the question of knowledge that has personal consequences versus knowledge that does not. Taking the latter first, would these findings generally be considered knowledge? Since the findings appeared in a peer-reviewed journal, we can trust that expert review assures these conclusions reasonably follow from the data. Given that the study is well done, is that enough to make them knowledge—especially when the findings are counterintuitive? We are more willing to accept findings as knowledge when the findings are replicated in additional studies. There is no evidence that these have been. Further, since we require counterintuitive findings to meet a higher standard before they are accepted as knowledge, it seems likely that these findings would be only very tentatively accepted until replicated. However, the explanation that handwritten material was given the benefit of the doubt does explain away some of the counterintuitiveness of the findings. This often occurs when a problem is better understood; what appears initially as counterintuitive turns out not to be.

   Should you use word processing for your examination? Here you must make a knowing judgment to guide your own behavior. Each of us might make the decision differently, depending on how much trust we put in the study. Some would be so bothered by the counterintuitive nature of the findings that they would still choose to use word processing. For myself, since the study appears to be a sound one, and, assuming I can compose as well in handwriting as with a word processor, answering in handwriting will not hurt and may increase the score, so it would be the safest course.

6. Different individuals hold different ideas as knowledge, depending on the background they have. Researchers should be aware of the ideas they hold as knowledge and the justifications or bases they have for holding them.

SUMMARY

In research, we continually make knowing judgments as to whether a knowledge claim is an appropriate interpretation of the evidence. As others agree with these judgments a consensus forms, and findings become knowledge. A network of individuals extends from those closest to research to the lay public, with decreasing levels of expertise in judging the evidence directly. The individuals at each level, as appropriate, either judge the evidence themselves or determine whether to accept the judgment of others closer to research in the network. Individuals are leery of accepting research findings on which experts cannot form a consensus.

We can also consider each new piece of evidence as increasing or decreasing our uncertainty about a knowledge claim. The threshold at which a finding or assertion becomes knowledge varies, partly in relation to its personal importance to us. Although it is not possible to test many natural science assertions, social and behavioral knowledge claims are typically checked against our own personal experience.

There are a variety of knowledge sources: personal observations and experience, intuition, belief and tradition, authority (dogmatic and reasoning), and science. Science and reasoning authority invite challenges to knowledge assertions to ensure their validity. The development of knowledge reveals science as a social system of individuals in roles of important responsibility governed by well-understood rules and norms. Merton (1968) has suggested that at least four norms are essential: (1) that the same standards be used in judging knowledge claims for all individuals regardless of status, personal characteristics, institutional affiliations, or other considerations; (2) that information be understood as owned by all and freely shared; (3) that there be absolute integrity in gathering and interpreting data; and (4) that it is the responsibility of the community of scientists to be skeptical of all new claims, to test them, to try to think of reasons why they may be false, and to seek rival explanations as plausible as the ones advanced.

In addition to norms, certain principles direct the progress of science. Replication reduces the uncertainty surrounding any finding by showing that it is not dependent on the circumstances, method, or investigator of the original study. Replication

Different Viewpoints on Knowledge

As far as it goes, this chapter's account of science would currently be widely accepted, and it provides a sufficient base for developing the model of Internal Integrity and External Generality and other criteria for judging research used in this book (see the frontispiece). However, it skims the surface of a variety of philosophy-of-science issues raised by persons who identify themselves as postmodernists, postpositivists, realists, and many others. There is not space, nor is this book the place, to go into this discussion. However, to give you a flavor, some dissenters argue that researchers have largely sought consensus among elitist, Eurocentric males to determine accepted knowledge. This bias has marginalized less developed countries, female voices, and minority voices. Furthermore, since all science is affected by the culture and context in which it is produced, objectivity is impossible. Some, like Bereiter (1994), seek to rescue science by suggesting that all that counts is that we can sense progress as, through open discussion, we achieve a consensus within the context in which we are working.

Intrigued? Read further: Bernstein, 1986; Carr & Kemmis, 1986; Freire, 1970; Habermas, 1984; and Phillips, 1987, 1992, 1994, and 2000 (with Burbules).

is the ultimate validation of any finding. Where multiple explanations are advanced for a phenomenon, use the simplest one—the principle of parsimony. Basing studies in theory is critical to making science an integrated network tying together disparate findings. Merton's norms assume ethical scientific behavior.

A Look Ahead

It seems reasonable that the social process of evaluating knowledge claims described in this chapter should have evolved standards and criteria to help us process the many published studies. An analysis of that processing reveals those standards and criteria and shows them as parts in a structure through which studies make their way to being considered knowledge. Further, this structure can be used to guide construction of new studies. Chapters 4 through 11 present the results of that analysis.

To get an overview of that structure at this point in the text, let's start with any completed study and then successively reveal the criteria and judgments to which it was subjected. Figure 3.2 is a graphical presentation of such as analysis.

Starting at the top, the study is represented by "Any Research Study." Below it, we note that the study is constrained to observe certain limits, represented by the hands pressing on their three labels:

1. What resources could be mustered to do it,

2. What the institutions and persons involved in the study would allow to be done in the study, and

3. What the ethical standards of the field would permit.

Within these constraints, we judge whether the study seems to have optimally made judgments and trade-offs:

1. In allocating resources to the various stages of the study (e.g., developing needed new measures, extending the sample).

2. In the balancing of Internal Integrity against External Generality (e.g., allocating resources to show the variables are causally linked or related in a process versus showing that the linkage has generality beyond the persons, places, and study configuration used in this study).

3. In designing and doing the study so that it would gain credibility with the intended audience (e.g., using a random instead of a convenience sample, using well-known instead or obscure measures).

Because these judgments all affect how the study is done, this is reflected in the chain of reasoning through which the results of the study are presented. The successive links in the chain of reasoning depend on its prior links (e.g., the development of the study out of past work, its translation into a design, the delineation of the parts of the design, etc.). The write-up often appears as a logical chain with links ordered as those in the graphic, but when presented in a different order, the information called for by these links appears somewhere in the presentation.

We also examine the judgments described in the boxes on both sides of the chain. They make up:

• *Internal Integrity* —The judgments that firmly link cause to effect, or variables in a process and provide it conceptual (e.g., the translation from problem statement to

Figure 3.2   An analysis of the criteria and judgments through which a study passes on the way to be ready for publication.

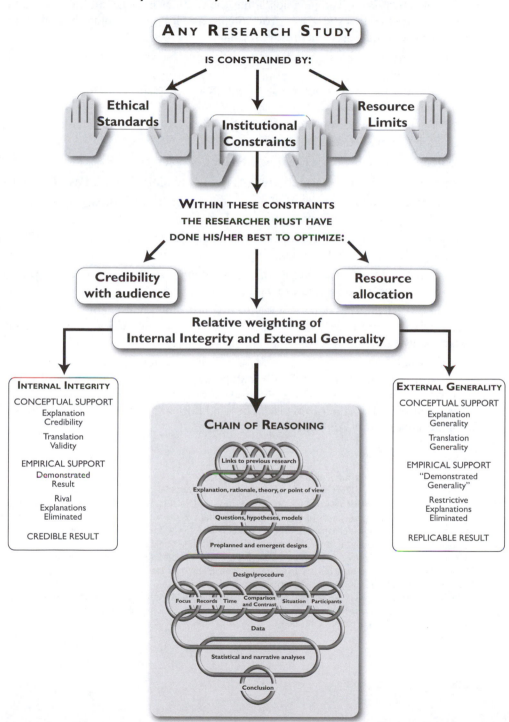

sample, situation, and measure choice) and empirical support (e.g., affirming data and eliminating rival explanations).

• *External Generality* —The judgments that the findings have generality beyond the circumstances of this study and provide conceptual (e.g., sampling broadly), and empirical support (e.g., sampling appropriately).

Both reveal the judgments that help us to determine the validity of the study's claim to being knowledge.

In contrast to the way one reads the graphic, succeeding chapters take up the parts described in Figure 3.2 in detail, starting with the bottom parts and working up:

• The logical structure through which the study is presented (chapter 4, The Research Chain of Reasoning);

• Problem finding (chapter 5, Creating Research Problems);

• Relating the problem to past research (chapter 6, Finding Links to Past Research);

• The criteria by which the claim of cause and effect (or of process) is established (chapter 7, Causal Inference and Internal Integrity);

• The criteria by which the generality of that claim extends beyond the circumstances of this study (chapter 8, Sampling, Representation, and External Generality);

• The trade-offs and limits within which the study must be developed (chapter 9, Optimizing Trade-Offs within Limits);

• Chapter 10 (Ethical Standards and Legal Constraints) and chapter 11 (Showing Relationships through Design), the last chapters of this section, more carefully examine two parts of the above.

This whole structure is presented in a slightly different graphic form in the book's frontispiece, which additionally juxtaposes the judgments making up Internal Integrity and External Generality alongside those links in the chain of reasoning from which they draw their evidence. Three additional graphical interpretations of this material appear in Appendix B.

Notes

[1] This chapter is adapted from Krathwohl (1988), chapter 11.

[2] This book owes much to Lee Cronbach's membership in an invisible college concerned with how knowledge develops. Professor Cronbach generously shared its files with me, putting me in contact with the mainstream and saving me hours of searching. As important as prepublication copies of articles was his correspondence. It indicated openness about certain conceptions that could be only dimly discerned in publications, encouraging signs for work contrary to established dogma.

[3] Gove, as editor of *Webster's International Dictionary*, is an example of an authority being accepted as a source of knowledge because of background, experience, and training.

[4] Adapted from Garrison Keillor's radio broadcasts.

[5] The lack of peer review on the Internet and the problem of how to provide it has been a serious concern of those using this means to communicate research results. In response to this concern, peer-reviewed electronic journals have been established.

chapter

4

The Research Chain of Reasoning

> A chain is only as strong as its weakest link.
>
> —old proverb

This chapter describes the way evidence is organized in the presentation of the results of studies concerned with generalities. In contrast to purely descriptive studies, the results of these studies (e.g., rules, principles, theories) are expected to apply to other situations. They generally follow a logic that assembles data in support of one or more conclusions. It is that organizing logic that forms the basis for the structure presented in this chapter. In chapter 3, it was suggested that if many individuals are making judgments about studies, ways must develop that facilitate the judging process—an integrating framework or model for the presentation of such studies. This chapter describes such a framework and explores some of its implications for designing and critiquing research studies. Like the previous chapter, the framework applies not only to social and behavioral science research but also to generalizable science research.

INTRODUCTION

Several federal reviewers are chatting about journal articles submitted as final reports for projects that they had funded:

> "I had a hard time with that last one. She started right off describing her data, and it was only later that I learned how and where she had gathered it. In the end, she had answered all my questions, but I guess I have a set of customary expectations about how a report of research should be written. I'm surprised this journal permitted such a deviation."
>
> "Move over—I have the same expectation; there are a lot of us in that 'rut.' I must say, though, yours was an exception; the last one I reviewed was a dream—everything was there, and in good logical order."
>
> "The report is the one thing for which we don't provide a standard federal form. I guess it is so the researchers are free to write their report in any way that

makes sense to them. Sometimes I wish we did enforce a particular sequence or outline, especially for reports that are not in journal article form. It would make them easier and faster to read and critique."

"Whoa! Come on, now, you don't really believe we need another form, do you? There is more than enough bureaucratic regulation around here! Give them some freedom!"

"Okay, I'll grant you that we don't want to stifle creativity. But most journals create expectations in their readers and authors that certain parts of the research will be reported in a particular order. I think we should too. It makes such good logical sense to build one's case that way."

"Yes, and if there are headings, one knows just where to look for certain items."

"Sure, but even without headings, the organization of the write-up provides an orderly sequence so that readers can follow the argument and find what they need."

This conversation simply reinforces the fact that science is a social process; the researcher is communicating with an audience to present the study properly and to convey how carefully it was done. Similarly, the reader or reviewer is trying to follow, raising and answering questions as the report is read, judging whether it supports the claim of new generalizable knowledge that is being asserted. It is not surprising, therefore, that a fairly standard form or sequence of presentation has evolved. The standard has been informal—that is, accepted by authors rather than being required by journals. But some journals rarely seem to depart from it, so researchers conform in order to enhance chances of publication. This standard form is exemplified by the Zimbardo article reprinted in chapter 1. Although that particular journal saves space by eliminating headings used by many journals, the article is organized in typical sequence.

LINKS IN THE CHAIN

Articles that present a research-based **generalization** are typically presented as logical arguments. The sequence of article sections corresponds to what we might think of as a prototypical or model **chain of reasoning** that applies to any such article. Even when the usual sequence is not followed, all the links in the chain are required to make a logical case. A representation of these links in the chain of reasoning appears in Figure 4.1.

The chain-of-reasoning model applies differently to preplanned and emergent studies:

- In **preplanned studies,** the researcher develops the study's design once the question, hypothesis or model is decided upon, and that determines the links of the chain that follow. Therefore, it is easy for researchers to write up the study following the links in the chain sequentially. (In reality, there may be false starts and loops back to earlier links that are usually omitted from the report.)

- In **emergent studies**, as the name implies, the design of the study emerges as the focus of the study is successively clarified. The events and process in an emergent study often don't occur in the sequences represented in the chain, and this is often reflected in writing the report. However, the information conveyed by the links in the chain is usually included somewhere in the presentation of the study.

Figure 4.1   The links in the chain of reasoning in the presentation of a study.

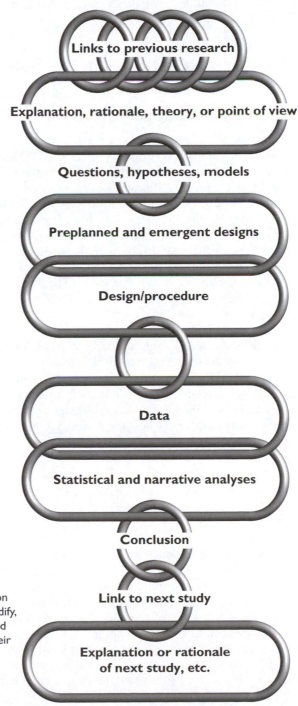

Links to previous research

Explanation, rationale, theory, or point of view

Questions, hypotheses, models

Preplanned and emergent designs

Design/procedure

Data

Statistical and narrative analyses

Conclusion

Next study that builds on this one to confirm, modify, or negate its findings, and increase or decrease their generality.

Link to next study

Explanation or rationale of next study, etc.

Because of this difference, it is easier to explain the nature of the links in the chain by initially using preplanned studies, with the Zimbardo study as an illustration. Then in the section that follows, we do the same with emergent studies, using the Hoffmann-Riem study as an example.

THE CHAIN OF REASONING IN PREPLANNED STUDIES

Let's look at the links in order, starting at the top of the chain.

Explanation, Rationale, Theory, or Point of View

In Figure 4.1, previous work on the topic is represented by the combination of the small links at the top of the figure labeled "links to previous research." The large link running through them represents the **explanation, rationale, theory,** or **point of view** that is drawn from this past work.

Turn back to the Zimbardo article on page 5. How does it begin? The first three paragraphs describe the rationale underlying the causal relationship that the study is intended to demonstrate. The first paragraph begins with a discussion of previous research, showing that psychopathology, especially paranoia, has been clinically observed to accompany deafness. In the second paragraph, a mechanism is suggested as to why there might be a relationship. The third paragraph indicates how a psychopathological response could be reinforced and maintained. All paragraphs draw heavily on previous work.

The explanation, rationale, theory, or point of view underlying a hypothesized relationship is usually laid out at the beginning of an article, as is done here. It is important as the basis for understanding and interpreting the rest of the presentation. As an explanation, it indicates how a relationship works. A rationale indicates the basis for thinking that it works this way. A theory indicates how this relationship fits into a larger scheme of previous knowledge and how these variables relate to others. A point of view indicates how the researcher views this relationship and compares or contrasts it with the views of others. Studies usually have one or more of these; Zimbardo has only an explanation and rationale. In building this section of the study, the researcher draws on previous relevant work, selectively citing it to indicate that the idea is not a "bolt from the blue" but is in fact solidly based on what has gone before.

Questions, Hypotheses, Models

Building on the explanation, rationale, theory, or point of view is the next link, that of **questions, hypotheses, models**. In the Zimbardo case, the previous research cited in the first two paragraphs lays the basis for the hypothesis. It appears at the end of the third paragraph: "In this analysis, paranoia. . . ." It is a hypothesis because it goes beyond merely stating a question. It tells us where to look and what to look for—the development of paranoia. We don't know how much paranoia or exactly how it is related to a certain amount of deafness, so we can't make a precise prediction. Such a prediction requires that you know even more about the phenomenon.

When one can link all, or a great many, of the variables in the situation and can make a more precise prediction, one has a model. With increasing prior knowledge we have successively:

- a question,
- a hypothesis that something will happen,
- that it will occur in a certain direction,
- that it will be of a certain size as well as in a particular direction, and
- that, in addition, it is related to a chain of events and/or variables—a model.

Once one of these is chosen, the study is then devoted to informing us whether what has been conjectured fits the facts. In Zimbardo's case, there is enough previous research to suggest that there is a relationship between unrealized deafness and paranoia but not enough to make a precise prediction or build a model. Doing so depends on how much basis the previous research gives us for anticipating what will happen.

Adapting the Presentation Format to the Researcher's Purposes

The fourth paragraph is a summary of the rest of the article. Its placement here is evidence that the chain of reasoning format need not be followed slavishly and rigidly. Each author adapts the format to the requirements of the readers. In this case, this article appeared in a journal that is devoted primarily to biological and physical science reports. Those who aren't social scientists might be interested enough to read a few paragraphs but are not likely to read the whole article. Thus, placing the summary early, right after the rationale and hypothesis, is savvy writing. It summarizes what will be found and serves as a possible motivator to read the rest of the article. Such a paragraph is not part of the usual structure but rather illustrates its adaptation for this particular audience.

A Word about Preplanned vs. Emergent Designs

At this point in the chain (if not already decided at the study's outset) choices made in the previous steps have begun to move the study in the direction of either a preplanned or an emergent study. The Zimbardo study, with a hypothesis that lends itself to an analysis of the effect of individual variables, is clearly headed in the direction of a preplanned study—in this case, a well-planned one. As noted in chapter 2, this is typical of studies beginning with a hypothesis or model. For now we continue to focus on the preplanned Zimbardo study, and we will take up the chain's relation to emergent studies in the chapter's next major section.

Design in Preplanned Studies

Zimbardo's is a carefully reasoned experimental design intended to demonstrate the effect at the same time that it removes particularly relevant rival explanations from consideration. After stating the expected relationship in the third paragraph, in succeeding paragraphs Zimbardo begins laying out the design by describing how the study was carried out. Implementing the study means translating the various aspects of the presumed relationship into aspects that dramatize it, so to speak. A playwright, having described a plot as "Lillyann falls in love with Joe," must then write a script that translates that into a scene where individuals move to certain places at certain times, say certain things that convey love, and so on. Similarly, in this study the researcher must translate such terms as paranoia, deafness, and perceptual discontinuity. But that is not all that has to be translated.

The six facets of design.   There are six aspects we should look for when we examine the translation of the hypothesis link into a study. Together these constitute the research design of the study. Their place in the chain is indicated in Figure 4.1 by the unlabeled link between "Design/Procedure" and "Data." In Figure 4.1 they are shown as a single link, but in reality they are a set of six links lined up behind each other and viewed from the front end so that the other five are hidden behind the first one. Figure 4.2 shows the six spread out in a side view and Figure 4.3 labels each of the links: **Focus, Records, Time, Comparison and Contrast, Situation,** and **Participants**.

Figure 4.2   Detail of the links in the chain of reasoning between Design/Procedure and Data.

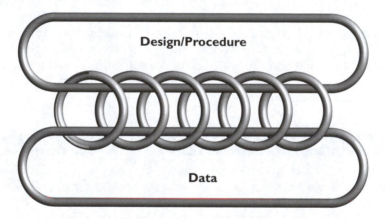

Figure 4.3   The connecting links in the chain of reasoning between Design/Procedure and Data.

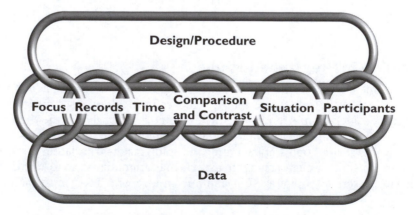

These links correspond to the five Ws and an H that all journalists learn to include in a story: who, when, where, what, why, and how. A useful mnemonic borrowed from Rudyard Kipling helps us remember the six links joining Design/Procedure with Data:

> I kept six honest serving men
> They taught me all I knew:
> Their names are What and Why and When
> And How and Where and Who.

For research application, this ditty can be translated as follows:

- *Focus. What* is being studied? (What was focused on among the things that occurred—e.g., a process, causes, experimental and control treatments, main and side effects?)

- *Records. Why* do you think something of interest occurred? (What records are there of what occurred that provide data to be analyzed—e.g., the measures and their scores, the observations, the interviews? See also the section on measures as operational definitions, p. 404 of chapter 18.)

- *Time. When* did things occur or were they to occur? (The procedure—How was the researchers' and participants' time scheduled? What schedules actually were followed? How were decisions made about how time was used?)

- *Comparison and contrast. How* will you know when something is changed? And what and how much change occurred? (In preplanned studies: What similarities and differences are there over the time or among the groups studied? In emergent studies: What are the common attributes across individuals, groups, times, or situations? How did they change?)

- *Situation. Where* is the study site?

- *Participants. Who* is being studied?

In the Zimbardo study, paragraphs 5 through 9 translate the hypothesis into the six facets of design in Figure 4.3.

The whole of the fifth paragraph is devoted to the *Who (Participants)*. The *Where (Situation)* is implied rather than specified, and it is clearly a laboratory, presumably at the author's institution. The *Focus* (or *What*) of the study, the hypothesized cause and effect, is described in the sixth paragraph. In experiments, as in this case, the cause is usually an administered treatment. Part of the *How*, the *Comparison and Contrast* by which the effect was sensed, is also described in that paragraph. Comparing and contrasting the effects highlights similarities or differences over time or across groups. In this instance, by randomly assigning participants to the three different treatments, Zimbardo was able to measure differences in the treatments' effects. It also, as we shall see, rules out rival explanations.

Evidence of the *Why* you think something occurred was provided by the *Records*, the observations and measures that are described in the seventh and eighth paragraphs. Note that Zimbardo used multiple measures of paranoia so that even if we have concerns about one of them, it's hard to argue that all three might be wrong. These paragraphs also have extensive description of the *When* (*Time*—when what was done to whom) and *How* it was done (the *Procedure*). Thus, we can see that all the important information regarding the design and structure of the study is presented in this midsection of the article. Here the concepts in the explanation that were pulled together into a hypothesis are translated into actions. These are the basis for gathering the data for analysis.

Data, Analysis, and Conclusion

The next links in the chain are labeled Data, Statistical and Narrative Analysis, and Conclusion. The data derived from the study, if quantitative, are subjected to statistical analysis; and if qualitative (in words), to narrative analysis. In either case, some kind of conclusion or summary is drawn. In Zimbardo, the data of the study are presented in the tenth and eleventh paragraphs and the accompanying table. The statistical and narrative analysis of the data show that the hypothesized relationship is demonstrated across all the measures and observations. This claim in turn leads to the last link in the chain of reasoning for this particular study, the conclusion. This appears as the last paragraph of the article, paragraph 13. There the authors note that despite the artificiality of the laboratory procedure, the rationale is sound and the findings have a bearing on the problems of the elderly.

The Next Study

The last two links shown in Figure 4.1 actually belong to the next study that builds on this one. The two studies will be connected by one of those links-to-previous-research rings like those at the top of the figure. The new study would use the findings from Zimbardo to support some further explanation of this or a related phenomenon.

In summary, the chain of reasoning begins with links to the results of previous studies that are used to build an explanation, rationale, or point of view. Depending on how much previous knowledge we find, we draw from it a question, hypothesis, or model. This in turn we translate into a design or procedure that can be described in terms of choices of: focus, records, time, contrast and comparison, situations, and participants. The design and procedure guides us in the collection of data, which permits us to demonstrate a relationship by means of data analysis. Future researchers may in turn pick up the demonstration of the relationship and conclusion in a new study.

THE CHAIN OF REASONING IN EMERGENT STUDIES

It is easy to see how the chain applies to preplanned studies, in which the six links in the chain at the design stage can be nearly fully described from the outset. But in emergent studies using an inductive method, whatever design develops is the result of an emergent procedure, not preplanning. Hence, that link in the chain is labeled Design/Procedure. Does the chain of reasoning also apply to the Hoffmann-Riem study in chapter 1, for instance? Yes, but only if the study presents one or more generalizations. That is, the study is setting forth findings that are expected to be true in samples of persons and situations beyond those studied.

Some qualitative studies, however, are almost entirely descriptive—for instance, a **case study** of a person, group, or culture. An example of the latter is William Foote in Whyte's *Street Corner Society,* which describes Boston's North End gangs. The intent of such studies may be to give you an insight into a particular corner of the world, or a community you are unlikely otherwise to encounter. Their intent, as per Geertz (1973), is "not to codify abstract regularities but to make thick description, not to generalize across cases but to generalize within them." These studies are primarily efforts to understand a person, group, or situation. Such studies:

- may or may not build on previous research;
- have a question only in the sense of focusing on some phenomenon or process;
- usually present only selected data (that is often the extent of the analysis); and
- draw no conclusions.

Obviously, such studies need not follow the chain pattern.

However, studies that arrive at a generalization, even though carried out inductively, can be and usually are presented deductively. Hoffmann-Riem is an example of this; she clearly expects her findings to be useful to other individuals who adopt children. Sometimes the details of procedure, design, and analysis are put in a methodological appendix—one can adapt the presentation to one's audience.

Frequently, the links of the chain are all present but not necessarily in the order shown in Figure 4.1. This makes the chain more difficult to discern than it is in the Zimbardo study. Frequently the write-up tells the story of the study. Figure 4.4 diagrams the pattern of many emergent studies as they relate to the chain of reasoning, including Hoffmann-Riem.

As shown in Figure 4.4, emergent studies frequently start with curiosity about (or observations of) an individual, a group, and/or one or more situations. As one's observations are analyzed they lead to some kind of focus, perhaps rather fuzzily at first. This focus becomes clearer as explanations emerge from the data. As shown in the diagram, often the researcher goes through several cycles with trial analyses, modified or new foci, possibly new data, and sometimes searching for conditions that help rule out rival explanations.

Hoffmann-Riem begins with an interest in the "fundamental processes which underlie the symbolic structuring of kinship and parenthood" (paragraph 1). For the first *Data* ring in Figure 4.4 she has her own background of experiences and her studies of kinship in sociology. As she analyzes this knowledge, she realizes these processes are usually invisible and resolves to work in that field. She rejects the preplanned structured questionnaire approach as likely to "find only that which he or she has previously considered." Instead she favors allowing her respondents to tell their stories uninterrupted (the results of her analysis of what she already knows in the field). She indicates in paragraph 4 that she narrowed her research from the structuring of parenthood to an interest in "the whole history of the adoption, beginning with the decision to make an application for a child and ending with the development of their family life" (the *Focus* ring in Figure 4.4 leading to her questions that structure her interviews).

For data, she gets a sample of participants (described in paragraph 5) to tell their stories, beginning her interviews with "Can you still remember what it was like when you applied for a child?" (the second *Data* ring in Figure 4.4). The interviewed couples are the *Participants* and the process of adoption the *Situation*.

This leads to analyses of the data and the emergence of important common characteristics of the phenomenon. This process is described in paragraphs 6–8. Sometimes, as shown in the diagram, this leads to additional data gathering—for instance,

Figure 4.4 **Diagram of a qualitative study showing the steps that relate to the chain of reasoning in the study's write-up.**

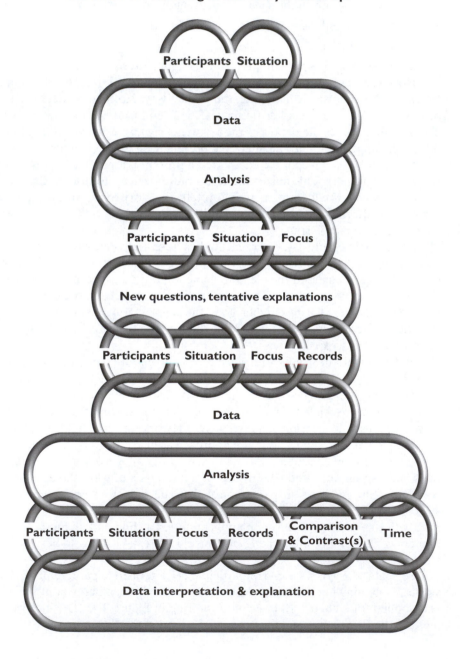

to create groups of participants whose input contrasts with a proposed explanation. Hoffmann-Riem found this unnecessary. But, with the analyses, the other six parallel links between *Design/Procedure* and *Data* in Figure 4.3 emerge. For instance, paragraphs 1 through 4 deal with data collection methods and procedure, including the *Time* and *Records* links. The *Comparison-and-Contrast* link is described in paragraph 7. As is typically true of qualitative research, there is no manipulated treatment. Instead, in place of treatment, the *Focus* link is concerned with the study of a naturally occurring process—the desire for a child, adoption, and normalization. In this manner all the links at the *Design/Procedure* stage are covered.

The other links in the chain are covered as well. Paragraph 6 deals with the Analysis. Paragraph 9 is an early statement of her conclusion, which, of course, is also reflected in the section headed Conclusion (paragraphs 25 to the end). More analysis and its results are described in paragraphs 9 through 24, which present the context and the process of adoption with relevant quotations from the data to make her points come alive. These paragraphs give a reality to the data that it would lack if using only numbers. She discusses various adoption stages and situations (paragraphs 8–23). Where appropriate, as in paragraphs 19 and 21, there are references to relevant previous literature. Clearly, the case has been built with all the parts of the chain being present but without necessarily following the Figure 4.1 chain sequence in doing the study. However, note that the published report in significant measure follows the chain's sequence, as is generally true of emergent studies setting forth a generalization.

USING THE CHAIN OF REASONING IN STUDY DESIGN

Any published study makes the choices in the chain of reasoning seem easy and obvious, like looking through binoculars focused on a particular phenomenon. But have you turned the binoculars around and looked through the other end? You will see far more—the phenomenon of interest is embedded in a whole distracting context. So it is in developing a study. Consider the example shown in Figure 4.5.

As shown in Figure 4.5, past research literature suggests that there are naturally occurring zones of activity in the classroom that are normally occupied by high achievers. The rationale for the study that grows out of this literature is that perhaps this phenomenon could be turned into a treatment for students who are achieving poorly by seating them where high achievers normally sit. That in turn leads to the hypothesis to be tested in the study, that putting students in the action zone has the intended effect on their achievement.

Figure 4.6 is an attempt to portray the context in which the researcher works. In the next links of the chain she is required to select among the many combinations of alternatives for translating this simple hypothesis into choices for the design. Although merely sampling the possibilities, the figure gives an idea of the decisions involved in choosing a design. We will describe the bases for choosing in later chapters on specific methods.

The chosen design in Figure 4.7 suggests a set of reasonable alternatives that might have been combined into a study. The study would involve at least two sections in the same college course to which students have been randomly assigned. The

Figure 4.5   The first links in the chain of reasoning of a classroom-seating placement study showing the results of a literature search (adapted from Krathwohl, 1985).

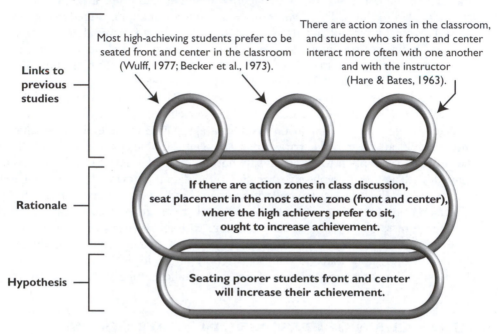

Links to previous studies

Most high-achieving students prefer to be seated front and center in the classroom (Wulff, 1977; Becker et al., 1973).

There are action zones in the classroom, and students who sit front and center interact more often with one another and with the instructor (Hare & Bates, 1963).

Rationale

If there are action zones in class discussion, seat placement in the most active zone (front and center), where the high achievers prefer to sit, ought to increase achievement.

Hypothesis

Seating poorer students front and center will increase their achievement.

Figure 4.6   Design choices in the classroom seating placement study (adapted from Krathwohl, 1985).

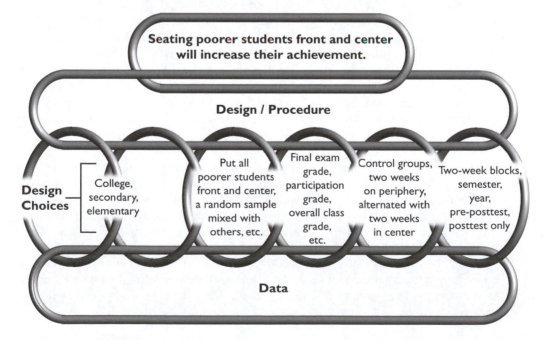

Seating poorer students front and center will increase their achievement.

Design / Procedure

Design Choices

College, secondary, elementary

Put all poorer students front and center, a random sample mixed with others, etc.

Final exam grade, participation grade, overall class grade, etc.

Control groups, two weeks on periphery, alternated with two weeks in center

Two-week blocks, semester, year, pre-posttest, posttest only

Data

poorer students will be randomly assigned to seating in the control group, and mixed with other students front and center in the experimental group. The final examination will be given at the end of the semester.

Figure 4.7   The chosen design in the classroom seating placement study (adapted from Krathwohl, 1985).

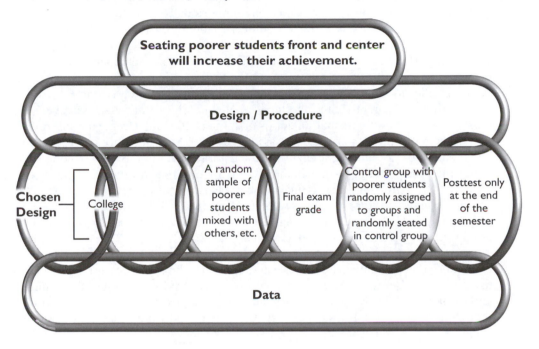

FOUR USEFUL CHARACTERISTICS OF THE CHAIN ANALOGY

If the chain of reasoning were made of metal, it would have four physical properties that, by analogy, are helpful in understanding the use of the chain of reasoning in research (Krathwohl, 1985). Let's examine them.

A chain is only as strong as its weakest link.

Just as a metal chain breaks at the weakest link, so does the argument for a research conclusion. To the extent that any part of the argument can be faulted, the whole chain is weakened, and readers are less likely to accept the conclusion. With a serious fault, the chain fails and the conclusion is rejected. For example, if we were convinced that the paranoia of the elderly is different from that produced in the college men in the Zimbardo study, then the choice-of-participants link is weakened. If we consider this to be a serious problem, the conclusion would be rejected.

All links in the chain should be equally strong.

A second characteristic of a metal chain, which is derived from the first, is that ideally all links in the chain should be adequately and equally strong. This is typical of a metal chain; a set of strong links is not interrupted by a small, thin link. It makes little sense that one link in the chain is thick enough to anchor a building in a hurricane and others are as thin as a decorative gold necklace. Basically, this characteristic of the chain is concerned with the appropriate allocation of resources to assure all aspects undergirding the conclusion are adequately supported. Thus, there would have been little point in allocating considerable resources to the *Records* link as Zimbardo did— he used three measures of paranoia—if he had developed the hypnotic technique only to the point where deafness was irregularly and unpredictably maintained. Better that he reassigned some resources from measures to improving the hypnotic technique. Resource allocation should ensure that all the links are adequately strong.

In whose judgment should the links be adequately strong? As researcher, you must satisfy your own personal standards first, but others will accept your interpretation of the data only if their standards are met as well. Your audience makes the final judgment; you are building a chain intended to achieve a consensus among them about the interpretation of the findings. Anticipating the thresholds of their standards may be a problem, but it is unavoidable. Learning these standards is part of the socialization process that maintains science. Many things influence the standards: the judgments made by panels awarding research grants, journal and convention program referees, editors—and, of course, books like this.

A problem occurs when your personal priorities about what to strengthen differ from those that you anticipate others will require and the resources are not sufficient to satisfy both. Because resources are always limited, **trade-offs** are usually required, and completely satisfying all parties may not be possible. Zimbardo obviously thought a laboratory study was preferable to a field study in a retirement home. He traded positives for negatives:

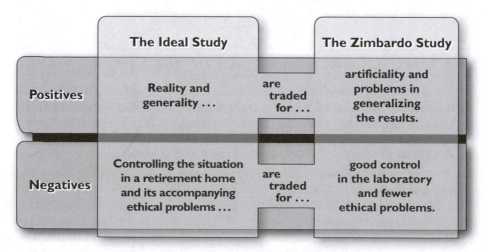

We try as best we can to find the choice that optimizes satisfaction for all.

Many trade-offs are hidden in the research process. This is the first trade-off we have encountered. There will be others, however, and you should look for them. Because researchers differ about trade-off solutions, we often have to consider more than one "right" way to do a study, an unanticipated characteristic of science. It makes many people uncomfortable; indeed, some argue that there is always only one best way to do a study—a position you may find difficult to support. But such arguments are also a part of the social process, one that seems to work itself out as efforts are made to replicate or build on studies and create consensus about a particular generalization.

Each link in the chain is determined by the link before it.

The steps leading to the conclusion must be logically linked together. Each link depends on the preceding one. The explanation or rationale is built on previous research. The question, hypothesis, or model grows out of that rationale or explanation. Because the extent of knowledge about the problem determines whether a *question, hypothesis, or model* is formulated, that link is dependent on the prior one.

The next link, the *design/procedure* of the study, is a translation of the preceding link into the operations that constitute the study and that result in the following link, the collection of *data*. What can be shown from *analysis* of the data, the next link, depends on the design choices and available data. *Analysis* in turn leads to the final link, *conclusion*, which is clearly dependent on how the analysis of the data turned out.

It is the way each step advances the argument for the conclusion that sets boundaries for the next; each step is shaped by the argument to that point. Thus, being aware of the desired breadth for the lower links, we need to build in sufficient breadth in the earlier ones. If Zimbardo wishes to generalize his conclusions to the elderly and sees the use of college students as narrowing the range of his conclusions, then he must make a different choice of participants in the earlier links.

Where links share the load, one may be made stronger to compensate for weakness in another.

This last characteristic of the chain is not quite as obvious as the previous ones. Although it rarely occurs with metal chains, it is important in research. Each of the links shares the load where several horizontal links across the chain's breadth together connect the links above and below them. Therefore, a weak link can remain if another of the horizontal links is made stronger. In the research chain of reasoning, this situation occurs at the design level. At that level, all six links join the design to the *Data* link.

Zimbardo used this principle in his study; hypnosis is a weak treatment in the sense that it will not work with some individuals. For them, the posthypnotic suggestion might not have been effective. He strengthened the *Participants* link by choosing participants who were especially susceptible to hypnosis, thereby making that treatment stronger.

ADDITIONAL READING

For an earlier explanation, see Krathwohl (1985).

IMPORTANT TERMS AND CONCEPTS

case study
chain of reasoning
emergent study
explanation/rationale/theory/point of view
generalizations
preplanned study
question/hypothesis/model

research design and its six facets:
1. focus
2. records
3. time
4. comparison and contrast
5. situation
6. participants
trade-offs

OPPORTUNITIES FOR ADDITIONAL LEARNING

The following paragraphs summarize a 1987 study by Dr. David Jonassen of the University of Colorado in which he set out to verify *pattern notes* as a method to assess an individual's cognitive structure. Jonassen began his article with a brief discussion of instructional design theory. He noted that such theory had traditionally been based on experience with programmed learning and behavioral task analysis. But it was slowly giving way to cognitive theory, which assumes that knowing is a process based on the experience of constructing our individual cognitive structures. Thus, the purpose of instruction is to build the best of these structures in the learner. Instructional design theory provides techniques to determine the learner's cognitive structure and to organize content to fit it. The problem was to find a feasible procedure for mapping cognitive structure.

Jonassen proceeded to describe the available methods, dismissing most for reasons ranging from being too limited to being too difficult. His solution was "pattern notes," a form of spatial word-association task first developed as a technique for taking notes during a lecture. The student placed the topic of the lecture in the middle of the page and then added related concepts around it. Lines were drawn between concepts to indicate relationships. This simple technique, he noted, depicted the relationships between concepts associated with each other. They should, he reasoned, represent cognitive structure.

The purpose of the study was to verify this hypothesis. To do so, Jonassen proposed to compare a learner's pattern notes to a free-word association task on the same topic. The free-word association technique was, in his assessment, the most valid and reliable of the available methods for assessing the learner's cognitive structure. However, it requires the use of sophisticated statistical analysis. Relationships were measured by counting the number of common links between concepts—whether the lines from one concept to another in the pattern note corresponded to the response when one or the other concept was the stimulus in free-word association.

Jonassen used both measures to assess the cognitive structures for Newtonian mechanics of 24 high school students. All were members of an advanced elective physics course and were presumed to be motivated and capable. The first part of the study was carried out on three separate days over a period of a week. The students were first administered the word-association task. The order of concepts presented in each test was random for each student. The following week, they were taught how to construct pattern notes and finally were asked to construct one note for each of the concepts presented during the first test. Analysis of the data showed a significant relationship between the two measures, indicating that they could use pattern notes to assess cognitive structure as it was represented by free-word association. In his concluding section, Jonassen then provided a number of suggestions for the use of pattern notes in instructional design.

1. Explain whether or not this summary of Jonassen's work follows the research chain of reasoning.

2. What do you consider the weak links to be in his argument?

3. For any weak links, indicate if Jonassen compensated by making other links stronger.

KEY TO ADDITIONAL LEARNING OPPORTUNITIES

1. Jonassen did follow the chain of reasoning, but with a slight twist. He began with a rationale for the study and a statement of the problem rather than with conclusions from previous research studies. He described traditional instructional design theory first and then described how it was changing as a result of a new theory, cognitive psychology. His rationale, though, was based on prior research. Once he had stated his problem—to find a feasible procedure for mapping cognitive structure—he explored the research, examining the available techniques. Only then did he offer a hypothesis—that pattern notes would provide a practical technique for mapping cognitive structure—and it, too, was based on previous research.

The next step was to translate his hypothesis into a research design. The *who*, 24 high school students in an advanced physics class; the *where*, in the high school classroom; and the *when*, over three separate school days, are clearly specified. To demonstrate *what* effect occurred, that pattern notes measure cognitive structure, Jonassen again returned to the literature to find a method to measure cognitive structure. He chose free-word association, a technique that he thought was the most valid and reliable measure of cognitive structure available. A high relationship between the scores on the free-word association task and on the pattern notes would demonstrate how he knew that the effect had occurred. Perhaps the most difficult task was to demonstrate *why* the effect happened—in this case, why pattern notes (and free-word association) could be said to measure cognitive structure. This he did by means of a theoretical assumption—that the relationship between two concepts can be determined by their links in free-word association or in the notes. The *why*, then, was shown by counting the corresponding links between the concepts produced by the students in pattern notes and by free-word association. Although not indicated in our summary, both the experimental and the analysis procedures were described in some detail. The relationship was demonstrated statistically, and the conclusion, that pattern notes were a valid measure of cognitive structure, was based on the analysis of the data. Jonassen concluded his report by relating the pattern note technique to instructional design theory and thus provided the link on which future studies could be built.

2. Possibly the weakest link is Jonassen's assertion that cognitive structure can be represented by the number of references of one concept to another. It is a means of inferring what cannot be observed directly. We must accept his argument that this is true in order to believe that cognitive structure was actually being measured.

We may also consider his choice of sample a weak link. First, it was quite small (24 students). However, a small sample under the right circumstances can be used to demonstrate an effect. (Know statistics? See power analysis, pp. 449–454.)

Second, the effect may have resulted from the characteristics of this one sample. The class was advanced, and the students were probably more capable than average, so maybe intelligence accounted for the relationship. Further, it was quite a uniform group; it did not have the variability of a group representative of that grade. This might not have been a weakness since it was necessary that each student have a well-developed cognitive structure in this subject to provide something to measure. The researcher's purpose was to demonstrate that pattern notes could be used to measure cognitive structure, not necessarily to show that the technique worked for all learners. The study would surely require replication with samples having different characteristics before we could accept the technique as widely useful.

Finally, we could advance a rival explanation, that of the added motivation that results from the special attention of being part of an experiment (often called the Hawthorne effect). The experiment was carried out in the students' own classroom, however, which would probably dampen any such effect.

3. Not that you can tell from this summary. In the article, Jonassen (1987) strengthened the *Observation and Measurement* link for assessing cognitive structure by basing the technique solidly in theory and prior research. He indicated considerable theoretical and research support for it.

SUMMARY

Studies setting forth a generalization are expected to supply certain information that allows readers to assess the study and make a knowing judgment of whether to accept the interpretation of the evidence being advanced. Most of these studies, though not all, follow a standard sequence in presenting the findings of their research. If they do not follow the sequence, they nevertheless include the same information.

The case for a generalization is usually presented (or can be arranged) in a sequence that forms a chain of reasoning. A universal or prototypical model of such a chain of reasoning has been herein presented that contains the essential elements. Such a model begins with an explanation, rationale, theory, or point of view that is linked to or grows out of prior research studies and writing. The generalization being studied flows from this explanation, rationale, theory, or point of view.

The stronger the previous evidence, the more detailed in its development, the more comprehensive in its breadth, then the stronger the explanation, rationale, theory, or point of view, and in turn, the stronger the links that flow from it. With the most prior knowledge, we can pose a model that links many variables. With less prior knowledge, we may still be able to make a reasonably precise prediction of how large an effect will occur, as well as where and when it will happen. With still less, we may have a hypothesis that describes the direction things may take and how they are related. With the least prior knowledge, a question focuses our attention on certain aspects of the phenomenon of interest that presumably have potential for guiding the research.

The question, hypothesis, or model is translated into the design of the study. The result is the choices of participants (who), situation (where), focus (what), records (why), comparison and contrast (how), and time (when). These choices determine how to gather data that demonstrate whatever relationship is being studied. These data are analyzed, and a conclusion is drawn to represent the most appropriate interpretation of the data.

The chain-of-reasoning model is analogous to a metal chain and has four of the same properties:

1. Because an argument is only as strong as its weakest link, a chain of reasoning is only as viable as its weakest part.

2. Links at all levels of the chain should be adequately strong, ideally equally so. This is a matter of allocating resources so that one doesn't spend time and resources on a link that should have been devoted to a weaker one. At the design/procedure level, it is the combined strength of the six links that equals the strength of each of the prior links.

3. The nature of each prior link in the chain constrains the nature of successive links.

4. Since all six links at the design/procedure level "help carry the load," weak links may be made up for if one or more of the other six links is strengthened.

   Note: Research is often messy, not done in the neat sequential chain's steps; the latter are the report's organization of the information.

A Look Ahead

With the next section, we examine in some detail the top links of the chain of reasoning: finding a research problem in chapter 5 and relating it to the body of literature from which we will build forward in chapter 6.

We can infer from the chain of reasoning what evidence must be present in the report of a good study. But what criteria do we apply to that evidence? It should now be clear that, in making the knowing judgments involved in forming a consensus, audiences use criteria to assess links in the chain of reasoning. We will consider these criteria in chapters 7 through 9.

section

II

Foundational Research Skills

In this section we begin supplying the knowledge, insights, and skills to enhance your ability to handle various parts of the chain of reasoning, beginning with the top links of the chain. Foundational to any study is starting with a good problem. You'll need to know about the marvelous array of reference works that you may use to find your problem and then build on what has already been researched.

• Chapter 5 discusses the criteria of a good problem and gives problem finding suggestions. Some persons seem particularly adept at selecting important overlooked problems—clearly more than a matter of mere luck. We will explore a number of suggestions regarding the process of finding, conceptualizing, and creating a research problem that may strengthen your skill in this critical area.

• Chapter 6 explains the characteristics of a good literature search and the means for doing one. It discusses: relating your study to previous research and thought, the tremendous breadth of available resources, the different kinds of indexes, how to find where the cataloger put it, how the nature of your problem determines where to start, and how to organize the search.

Links to previous research

Explanation, rationale, theory, or point of view

Questions, hypotheses, models

Preplanned and emergent designs

Design/procedure

Focus   Records   Time   Comparison and Contrast   Situation   Participants

Data

Statistical analysis and/or narrative analysis

Conclusion

Link to next study

Explanation or rationale of next study, etc.

5

Creating Research Problems

> A question well-stated is half solved!
>
> —Anonymous
>
> We need theories to live by. A theory is an intellectual armature which allows only certain facts in. . . . We will all die of word pollution if we allow our minds to become empirical dustbowls where every fact is as salient as any other. . . . What I must learn to do is to ask the right questions. And that, it seems to me, must come from having some working theories about what's important.
>
> —Warren Bennis, as quoted in R. S. Wurman (1989)

Where the central topic of a chapter focuses on a part of the framework illustrated in the frontispiece, the chapter's opening page will locate that section in the framework by highlighting it, as does this chapter's opening graphic.

INTRODUCTION

Developing a problem statement is critical because it sets the course for the study, yet it is also difficult for many of us. In this chapter, we explore the criteria of a good problem and problem development methods that biographies and literature suggest have been successful.

THE PROBLEM OF THE PROBLEM[1]

Not only is the choice of problem the most important decision each researcher makes, it is also a real gamble! There is no certain way of telling at the outset whether the investment of time, energy, and resources will yield any return—with luck, a reputation can be made. Is it luck, however, that some persons are known as good researchers? No more so than that some people can make an honest living from the stock market, generally win at cards, or beat the odds at a racetrack. What research there is on problem finding suggests that some individuals are consistently better at it than others (Getzels, 1982). All of us know individuals who are particularly creative; I have known some from whom I got a good idea whenever I talked with them. But Osborn and others involved with industrial training have data that suggest everyone's creativity can be increased (Osborn, 1959; Parnes, 1967).

Past studies have shown that relatively few researchers account for the bulk of useful work: 10% of scientists account for more than 50% of published research, and 10% of published research accounts for 40% of the citations in books and articles (Pletz, 1965; Price, 1975). There is little reason to believe the current situation differs. Often we will find that someone has researched a phenomenon that we had noticed but had never thought to do research on it ourselves. Clearly, some individuals improve their odds for success by transforming thought into action. Modifying such behaviors as well as learning some of the behaviors that enhance problem-finding capacity will improve research capabilities.

How can we facilitate a creative process that by definition defies formulas or routine processes? First, we can understand how findings become knowledge to give us some idea of how an individual study can navigate the gates to acceptance. This was the intent of chapter 3. Next, we can describe the criteria of good problems so that when one appears, you will recognize it. We can note some problem types not amenable to research methods. Finally, we can describe behavior and activities characteristic of productive researchers and suggest some creativity enhancement techniques. You choose among these the ones you think may be personally effective. These topics outline this chapter.

Before we begin, let's reemphasize the fact that, as we noted at the close of chapter 3, we are ethicists whether or not we elect to be. As such, we have an ethical responsibility to consider the consequences of whatever problem we choose.

PROBLEM FINDING AND RESEARCH METHOD

Some persons recognize a problem, define it well, gather data, analyze them, and write them up, following each of these steps in sequence. Research is typically visualized this way, a stance usually associated with quantitative methods. It involves considerable investment in problem finding, problem redefinition, and the literature search (the latter being the topic of the next chapter). As we previously noted, other researchers immerse themselves in a situation of interest and let the research project emerge as they explore what is there, an inductive approach usually associated with qualitative research. In fact, however, we can adapt either approach to any method. With qualitative work, we can begin data collection as soon as we identify what might be called an *orienting question*—one that focuses and directs our attention. In the Hoffmann-Riem study in chapter 1, the problem began as "how parents viewed adoption" and ended up as "how adoptive parents normalized their lives."

Novice researchers often concentrate on method before they are clear on what the problem is. To a certain extent, working on method can help formulate the problem if you don't go too far before you clarify the problem. For most of us, however, research method follows problem definition. Once we know what to study and how we want to do it, we adapt method of investigation and problem to one another until we personally feel comfortable. Often this involves a combination rather than a single method.

For example, Mike, a part-time doctoral student, is also a school administrator whose school board has been bargaining with his teachers. The teachers want the same pay as a nearby richer district. If he could show that meeting their demand would not cause budget defeat in the annual budget referendum, the board could give the raise and everyone would be happier. If it would cause failure, that knowledge would give the board a bargaining chip of value. This gets him interested in being able to predict the outcome of such budget referendums.

However, initially worried that the problem is too big for a dissertation, he begins talking about this problem to other students and his adviser. Someone suggests looking at the impact of taxpayer burden on such votes. While a smaller problem, he realizes that a given tax rate does not translate into an equal burden for rich and poor districts—it isn't the reality of the amount, it is the way it is perceived that counts. Worse yet, burden is only one of many handles on the problem. For some defeats, the main factor was how voters felt about the superintendent; for others it was the total tax burden, not just that of the schools. It becomes clear that he must first understand the major aspects of the problem. What can he do?

As we have seen in previous chapters, the focus of a research endeavor does not exist on its own but rather is an idea embedded in previous understandings and language. Accordingly, Mike looks at the existing research literature in the general area. But there is not a lot on predicting budget approvals. Further, his state law is relatively unique in requiring school district voters to approve the school budget annually, further narrowing interest in his problem. He turns to the closest related literature, bond issue referendums. He begins to develop a list of variables involved in these studies. Can he translate these directly to his problem? Bond issues commit for 20 to 30 years, not just the next year. Though most variables seem applicable to both problems, he finds he must think carefully about each one.

Mike begins to list the variables but is bedeviled by questions. How complete is his list? Shall he look for others? Seek evidence about which are really crucial? Find which ones others believe to be critical? Try them out to see if they predict current referendums? Each option takes him down a different road.

Suppose that he wishes to better understand budget defeats, getting a complete roster of variables and their interrelationships. That might involve qualitative research, and interviews with individuals who can tell him stories about budget defeats and their perceptions about what caused them.

Suppose Mike thinks that he has a rather complete list, and he would like to find which ones experienced superintendents think are crucial. Survey research of this group with a questionnaire might help him both add variables and point to the important ones.

If he believes he knows the crucial variables, he might use statistics to set up an equation to determine how accurately he can predict some actual school referendums. He would need to find or construct measures of the variables and learn something about quantitative correlational prediction techniques.

Alternatively, he might compare pairs of districts where his understanding of the problems suggests a particular variable is likely to cause defeat in both districts. Intervening in one of them, he can see if he can sufficiently ameliorate its effect—an experimental approach. If he can, then he has not only a method of predicting referenda but also a way of doing something about them. This is where he ultimately would like to be.

Of course, if Mike is wrong about having a good list, or in identifying the key variables, then neither of the latter studies is going to show positive results; they mainly would tell him he was on the wrong track and may help discern why. But there are millions of variables that are not relevant to the problem, and he must find the few that are. Finding these is fastest with a good understanding of the process, facilitated by either qualitative and/or survey research.

Notice how research method follows from how well you understand your problem and what you want to get from it. Don't freeze into method too early. Good problem homesteading requires a nice balance between staying open with respect to focus and method until you understand your problem well enough to proceed further, and making the necessary choices that allow you to make progress toward doing and finishing the research.

The names *problem finding* or *homesteading* suggest that it is a one-time process—a problem that, once defined, does not change. Nothing could be further from the truth. *Problem creating* is a better term. In qualitative methods, problem finding is usually expected to be a continuous process in which the possibility of **redefinition** continues even through data analysis. Although a less frequent expectation, redefinition also can occur with quantitative methods if something new and interesting shows up in data analysis. Indeed, the whole focus of the problem can shift, sometimes to a phenomenon quite different from the original one. With either approach, such redefinition often doesn't appear in the study's report, which is written as though the final choice were always the focus of investigation. (The reader is more interested in the case you present than in how you came upon it. Publication space is at too great a premium to include the whole story of every research.)

Yet when it occurs, reformulation is an important part of the research process. After all, only as complete data collection informs us sufficiently about the phenomenon do we understand the important questions to ask.

> ▶ Problem finding and the redefinition of the problem and its focus are continuing processes.
>
> ▶ In the typical case using quantitative methods, a clear conception of the problem emerges before data gathering, whereas in one using qualitative methods, it sometimes does not occur until the data analysis stage.
>
> ▶ Novice researchers often focus too tightly on method before they clarify the problem—not realizing they can use exploratory or validating approaches with either quantitative or qualitative methods.

CRITERIA OF A GOOD PROBLEM

A good problem is (1) of interest, (2) embedded in theory, (3) likely to have impact, (4) original in some aspect, and (5) feasible—within your conceptual, resource, ethical, and institutional limits. Below are additional criteria from Teplin's tongue-in-cheek suggestions (Youngstrom, 1990, p. 7):

- *The Goldilocks test:* Is the research question so broad it's untenable, so narrow it's dull—or is it just right?

- *The five-year test:* A five-year-old should be able to understand the purpose of the project.

- *The persimmon test:* Can you state the purpose of your study in 25 words or less?

- *The blood test:* People other than your blood relatives should want to read the research results.

Interest: A Necessary but Not Sufficient Condition

For most researchers, interest is the prime qualification, for it provides the motivation to work on the problem. As one doctoral student put it: "It's your baby, so it better be one you can love when you are up with it at night!" (Grant, 1986). Professors' files are full of projects that failed this test, and the many doctoral ABD (all but dissertation) candidates are further testimony to its importance. Clearly, it is one necessary condition; the other is feasibility. Besides these two, however, a problem should have as many of the following characteristics as possible: a basis in theory, some impact in its field, and some originality and creativity.

Basis in Theory

An isolated study typically has little impact. However, when a study contributes to explanations or significant ideas, when it modifies, contradicts, or extends them in some way, it multiplies its impact. As it affects the network of previous findings, it becomes embedded with those ideas and shares in their implications and effects. Problems that either build new rationale and theory or affect previous work are less likely to get lost. The power of Skinner to sway people to behaviorism lay not in his individual studies of learning, though these were important in building the base. Rather it lay in the rationale he built around these findings, a rationale that had important implications for explaining much of human activity. In fact, he even used the theory to suggest how language develops (Skinner, 1957).

What is meant by theory? Simply put, it means an explanation of behavior that makes good logical sense and either is consistent with the research and explanations that preceded it or convincingly negates or modifies them. Discussion of what constitutes good theory could fill the rest of this book. Although social scientists and educators don't have the kind of grand and precise theories that natural scientists have, theories help them find the significant variables, unify a variety of findings, assimilate them into a cohesive and interrelated body, and locate points where research is needed. Good problems are strengthened when they relate to theory.

When choosing or developing theory, be guided by what Yvonna Lincoln, in a speech at the American Educational Research Association convention, called the Coco Chanel principle: "Simple is always elegant, ultimately timeless and usually in fashion. Parsimony is prettier!" When choosing among explanations, choose the simplest that adequately covers the data.

Some Impact in Its Field

Beyond interest and feasibility, the criterion most researchers consider important is impact. Cronbach (1982) describes impact with the term leverage: "Leverage refers to the influence that reducing a particular uncertainty has on decisions. . . . [It] is directly visible in the response of the community to the evidence" (p. 226). A social worker, concerned that supervisors instead of social workers themselves determined the content of their in-service training, decides she will experimentally show the relative effectiveness of the two orientations. If she ignores the realities of administrators' responsibility and their role perceptions, however, she is likely to have little impact—leverage—in changing the situation. Predicting impact requires an accurate understanding of the dynamics of the situation and answers to such questions as: "Why hasn't it changed?" and "What would it take to change it?"

Originality and Creativity

A good problem reflects some of the originality and creativity of its author. As Morris Klein says: "I think that in research you want to satisfy your own ego. You want to know you did it before the other fellow" (Rosner & Abt, 1970, p. 99). Yet the hard fact of the matter is that we all stand on each other's shoulders. The competitive spirit provides a useful drive, but it gets in the way when it blinds us to our dependence on others. Graduate students often refuse problems they did not invent—perhaps one suggested by their major professor—in a kind of **second adolescence**." They want to be independent and show they can do things on their own (Krathwohl, 1988). Researchers can make problems theirs by adding just enough of their own thinking to another's problem to get an "investment" in it. None of us starts from scratch; it is important to find that middle gound.

Feasibility

A good problem is feasible; that is (1) it lends itself to investigation with the instruments and techniques that are either available or can be assembled; (2) it is within the capability of the investigator's available or acquirable experience and skills; and (3) it can be accomplished within whatever social, ethical, and resource limits must be observed. As a criterion feasibility is obviously critical, yet in their zeal, novice investigators often believe that the only way to have impact is to choose a topic well beyond their capacity in terms of size, complexity, or required skills. This also is part of the second adolescence phenomenon—"I can do it, don't tell me I must cut it down, don't demean me that way!" Unless such advice is viewed from the perspective of someone seeking to help, it can be incorrectly perceived.

Social, Ethical, Institutional, and Resource Limitations

All studies must be done within limits, for example:

- The research time and/or effort required may not be tolerated by a busy clinic.
- Having a control group without treatment may not be permitted by those who insist on receiving the experimental treatment as well.
- The potential for harm or unpleasantness in prying into people's value structures, political affiliations, or sex lives may not be justified by the value of the information gained.
- The cost to investigate the number of subjects required to do a study well may be beyond the resources of the investigator.

Prime considerations are what an institution will allow, what a community deems appropriate, and what ethical constraints one's profession places on research (see chapter 10, p. 206). In addition, there are the limits on our own time, funds, and energy, which, though somewhat flexible, have boundaries that we must find and observe. Feasibility is important, both in not being overly intimidated by apparent limitations and in acknowledging realities.

Ask yourself these questions about your problem:

▶ Is it of sufficient interest that I will continue to be motivated throughout the study to its completion?

▶ Is it embedded in theory so that it is part of a network of propositions and explanations?

▶ Will it have some impact on the field?

▶ Has it an element of originality and creativity about it?

▶ Is it feasible in terms of my acquired or acquirable knowledge and skills, as well as being within my social, ethical, institutional, and resource limitations?

Choosing a Researchable Question

Be sure your problem is researchable; not all are. The most common nonresearchable problems deal with what ought to be done—children *ought* to be able to read the classics by the sixth grade, clients *should* be permitted to find their own solutions in therapy. Notice the italicized value judgments: ought and should. Research cannot directly affirm or deny a value proposition. It can show what will happen if sixth graders try to read the classics or evaluate the success of a program in doing so. Others can use those consequences to make the "ought" decisions.

▶ Research can help a decision maker determine the implications of something that is desirable or desired, but it can never determine what ought to be. That is a value judgment.

SUCCESS-ENHANCING PROBLEM-FINDING BEHAVIORS

The behaviors characteristic of productive researchers in the following sections are drawn from the autobiographies of researchers, from observation, and from studies of problem finding and creativity. They have been organized somewhat sequentially, but many should be used continuously or repeatedly revisited. These stages are consistent with the empirical work of Klahr (2002), who provided extensive data to support his view that scientific discovery is really about problem solving. Work in expert–novice differences and general problem solving led him to articulate a model with steps for searching the hypothesis space, testing hypotheses, and evaluating evidence. For this chapter, we focus on the first and last of these, which require that one (1) build a knowledge base with possible explanations to work from; (2) work the knowledge base to identify patterns, generating ideas, questions, and hypotheses; (3) try out some combination of logical analysis or empirical data; (4) get feedback from others; and (5) keep going, repeating earlier steps as needed.

Build a deep knowledge base from which to work.

Experts are different from novices in several ways. First of all, they have more knowledge than novices. This gives them a base from which to recognize more patterns and possibilities and put things together differently. Here are some ideas to build a knowledge base from which to launch your problem generating and formulating.

Fill your mind with the best relevant material.   One of the most profitable ways to find a good problem is to fill your mind with the best relevant material from your area of interest. Have you had the experience of learning a new word that you thought was rare? Once you learned it, you were surprised at how often you heard it thereafter! It must have been there before. Research is no different; as Pasteur said, "Discovery favors the prepared mind." Fleming's discovery of penicillin was accidental, but his prior work prepared him to recognize the breakthrough when it appeared. He noticed that his bacterial cultures seemed not to grow where there was mold and wondered why this occurred. No doubt this had happened to other investigators. Fleming, however, being curious and having worked intensely with bacterial cultures, asked why. Acting on that query made a discovery worthy of a Nobel Prize.

Delve into what is already known about a phenomenon.   Immerse yourself in the literature and explore each of its important facets. If this search does not suggest the desired research problem, you will be sufficiently familiar with the area that when the unusual appears, you can recognize and act on it—like solving a jigsaw puzzle, where you have in mind the shape of a missing piece.

Read the writings of the seminal minds in your field.   Studies show that productive scientists read deeply into the historical background of their problems. In addition, they read the original versions of literature by the **seminal minds** in the field, not digests. Often, those researchers had already sensed something that was not well understood in their time. In other instances, they took a problem as far as they could, but you could now take it further. Reading such accounts against the background of more recent work often gives a new perspective and meaning. For instance, Campbell and Stanley (1963), who made important contributions to understanding social science experimentation, start with a tribute to what was then a 40-year-old book by McCall (1923). He described concepts they built on, setting them in a new and broader context.

You can sometimes stimulate ideas by reading the works of individuals with a creative turn of mind. They model the perceptiveness and fresh way of seeing that characterize inventive researchers. For example, the work of Milgram, Sabini, and Silver (1992) is full of provocative questions of this kind. Ask faculty about comparable individuals with your interests.

Read actively and anticipate the author.   One of the most important skills to develop is **active reading**. Anticipate where the material is going; project the argument that is being fashioned instead of passively following it. We process what we read more thoroughly if we underline or make marginal comments. This practice reduces reading speed and allows time to think ahead to where the argument leads. As we foresee what is coming, we will often find that the author zigs where our thoughts have zagged. Why the zig? Here is a question worth pondering. Our zag might have been a more profitable course to follow. Many new leads are discovered by active reading.

Reread material.   The mind can focus on only a few things at a time. Put aside those authors who seem to have the best grasp of your area and let them grow "cold." Then read them after they are again fresh to you; focus on different things than when you read them the first time, look for things you missed.

Actively search for inconsistencies in the argument.   Look for gaps where existing ideas do not adequately account for the phenomenon. This step may call for revision of existing explanations or even for new ones. For example, Merton (1959) notes that regularities in cultural behavior are typically thought to result from prescriptions by cultural norms. However, he notes, "Men have higher suicide rates than women, for example, even when the cultural norms do not invite males to put an end to themselves" (p. xxiii). Apparently, regularities can result from something besides cultural norms, and the concept of cultural norms must be reworked to account for this anomaly; Merton has suggested an interesting topic.

Challenge assumptions.   When reading past research, examine the assumptions on which the arguments are based. Are they reasonable? Could you make less restrictive ones? What would be the result if you change the assumptions? Would such changes lead to different consequences? Consider the problem of the mentally disabled. If you assume that they learn essentially as does everyone else but more slowly, given sufficient time and motivation they could achieve normally. The consequences of this view are to give the individuals more time, to isolate them in classes where the competition is less intense, and to motivate them to achieve.

A different assumption is that the conceptual structures into which the mentally disabled fit what they learn are not the complex ones that others use. This assumption leads to the search for simplified conceptual structures they can learn—structures that will allow their learning to approximate that of more normal children. This is but one example of how different assumptions result in quite different consequences, in this instance for remediation, each of which could be tested for their validity. (See the Opportunities for Additional Learning at the end of this chapter for other examples.) Try different assumptions to see where they lead.

Keep a log of your ideas.   Your brain is excellent at generating ideas, but recalling them is often very context dependent. To support your memory keep a running journal of ideas and activities—a diary or **log of ideas** related to your research, study, and exploration. Review the log periodically to refresh its best possibilities in your mind. Old ideas may have new meaning in the light of something you have read since their formation. New techniques, instruments, and models often suggest possibilities and extensions of past research. Other languages and cultures often hold possibilities that await discovery and development.

Employ a format that you are likely to use. If a small paper journal is most comfortable because of its size and the fact that it is "always on," use that. Some may keep a small paper journal yet transfer information to a computer as well. To prevent insights from being lost, be sure to make backups if the journal is electronic.

Organize the material you have read.   In the preface we noted that internal processing is important. Such processing results in *chunking* material into meaningful collections. The networking of these chunks makes connections that bring new material to mind. The "chunks" of experts are larger and more complex than those of novices. Some writers and artists seem to have learned this process intuitively, since they often spend large amounts of time practicing and rehearsing their material before producing a masterpiece. For instance, before he began a novel, Sinclair Lewis developed notebooks that described his characters and their complete setting—their personalities, what they wore, even maps of the community and floor plans of the buildings. Did he refer to the notebooks when writing? We don't know, but advance rehearsal chunked this material so effectively that he probably had little need; he could just let his characters interact; their characteristics, and those of the situation they were in, came almost automatically to mind. Similarly, before Andrew Wyeth painted his Helga pictures, he discarded sketch after sketch on the floor, even walking on them. They were chunks transferred to his mind for use in later drawings. Charles Darwin carefully indexed the books he read and organized the material into portfolios that he consulted at the beginning of each new project (Steiner, 1984).

Everyone uses chunks in their problem solving; however, the best writers and thinkers find that it takes work and time to build those chunks and their relational network. Maybe this is one of the differences between the greats and the not-so-greats: the willingness to do the work that is involved in building and relating the chunks that go into a masterwork.

Work your knowledge base for patterns: Generate ideas, questions, and hypotheses.

As you are creating a rich landscape in your mind of ideas, connections, and possibilities, you are ready to start formulating ideas, looking for patterns and generating questions and hypotheses. Sometimes this happens naturally in the previous stage, sometimes it takes additional effort and focus. Here are some ideas to help promote this kind of thinking.

Organize material into suggestive patterns. There are many arbitrary ways of organizing material into suggestive patterns; one set of steps outlined by Allen (1962) was extended by Zwicky (1969). First, you put all the material onto small cards, spreading them out without order and reading them to transfer the material to your unconscious mind. Next, you work on something else for awhile. Then you organize the cards into groups and organize the groups into mega-groups, each with a title, continuing until you have seven or fewer mega-groups. Finally, you examine the interrelations of these groups and their components.

Having such a model to follow may have value in that all the possible options are touched. Elstein, Shulman, and Sprafka (1978, 1990) have shown that having a model, or *heuristic*, to follow increases effectiveness in medical problem solving. Computer software is available that helps one organize material and suggests relationships. Do an Internet search on "creativity software" (see the addendum to this chapter).

"When you run onto something interesting, drop everything else and study it" (Skinner, 1959, p. 363). Since often the most significant findings turn up when we are pursuing something else, it is advice worth considering. This quotation is one of a series of principles about research that the highly inventive researcher B. F. Skinner (who founded a science of behavior) draws from studying his own research. He described how, while concentrating on a rat's learning, he treated the jamming of the food dispenser as a defect, which caused him to discard data. Then he realized that the record he was getting showed the extinction of learning. He says, "I can easily recall the excitement." His tale makes fascinating reading as he illustrates this meandering "disorderly and accidental process" of science, so different from the stereotype of scientific method. Indeed, Skinner notes:

> [T]he. . . scientist is puzzled and often dismayed when he discovers how his behavior has been reconstructed in the formal analyses of scientific method. . . . It is a mistake to identify scientific practice with the formalized constructions of statistics and scientific method. These disciplines have their place. . . . They offer a method of science but not, as is so often implied, the method. (p. 260)

As indicated repeatedly in this text, the logical process described in the chain of reasoning—similar in many ways to what is often ascribed to scientific method—describes the way research is usually reported, *not* necessarily the way it is done! Don't be concerned if your trail of investigation zigs and zags. A direct approach is not the only way to do research, and many of the world's most significant discoveries were serendipitous findings.

Look for new ways to tease the problem apart. Psychologist Daniel Kahneman (as found in Getzels, 1982) suggests a trick for questions about behavior that he claims derives from Lewinian psychology. Instead of asking, "Why does a person behave this way?" he asks, "Why doesn't he behave otherwise?" Instead of asking why a person is hostile in a particular setting, he asks, "Why isn't he more hostile?" "Why isn't he less hostile?" The kinds of answers made available by this reformulation are radically different from those derived from "Why is he hostile?" It may be much easier to remove the factors driving him to greater hostility uncovered by the question "Why isn't he less hostile?" than to manipulate forces intended to suppress the hostile behavior. Sometimes it also helps consciously to switch the focus of attention from the end result to the process of getting there. Guns don't get used up in violent acts, but bullets do. Maybe it would be easier and more effective to control ammunition than to control guns.

Another way of teasing the problem apart is to look for concepts that have not been effective in differentiating important aspects of a phenomenon. Merton (1959) notes that current concepts may have taken research as far as it will stretch. To go further we need new differentiations. For example, at one time self-concept was conceived as a single entity. Later, researchers came to realize that each of us has different self-concepts in different situations. Our self-concept of ability describes how capable we believe ourselves to be in solving academic problems, and this may be further differentiated into self-concepts of capability in different subject matter. The term "self-concept" has become highly differentiated, with several books delineating these different meanings (e.g., Wylie, 1979).

Break your mind-set.   We have all been exposed to problems that require us to think about them differently in order to solve them. Remember the game of passing the scissors? One person passes a pair of scissors to another, saying, "I'm passing it to you crossed" or "I'm passing it to you uncrossed." Players unfamiliar with the game are puzzled; no matter how they position the scissors, they can do it correctly only by accident, if at all. They are concentrating on the scissors. Only when they realize that "crossed" or "uncrossed" refers to the position of the person's legs when the scissors are passed do they break the mind-set of concentrating on the scissors. Breaking the mind-set, viewing an area or a problem differently, is often the secret to an important piece of research. The next several tips are often useful mind-set–breaking tools.

Harness the unconscious.   There comes a point when we have read enough to have a flavor of the literature, but new approaches have not suggested themselves. Here it is well to recognize that our minds do not always do their best work when we are consciously tackling a problem. William Safire gives the first rule of holes: "When you are in a hole, stop digging!" It is time for the unconscious mind to take over. Read Raudsepp's (1977) recitation of the testimony of the greats on this score:

> Dostoevsky found that he could dream up his immortal, moving stories and characters while doodling. Brahms found that ideas came effortlessly only when he approached a state of deep daydreaming. And César Frank is said to have walked around with a dreamlike gaze while composing, seemingly unaware of his surroundings.
>
> John Dewey stated, "I do not think it can be denied that an element of reverie, of approach to a state of dream, enters in the creation of a work of art. . . . Indeed, it is safe to say that creative conceptions . . . come only to persons who are relaxed to the point of reverie."
>
> Thomas Alva Edison also knew the value of "half-waking states." Whenever confronted with what seemed an insurmountable hitch defying all efforts, he would stretch out on his workshop couch and let fantasies flood his mind. (pp. 27–28)

Poincaré (1913) concluded that the unconscious mind collates and sorts random possibilities among pertinent variables at a rate that defies the efforts of the conscious mind.

We must all find our own best means of commanding the muse, but **harnessing the unconscious** as an important resource is too rarely emphasized. Some people are helped by daydreaming, a reverie in which the mind floats over the problem, reject-ing no possibilities. Some adopt a kind of half-awake, half-asleep posture. Still others get their best ideas at night and keep paper and pencil at hand to record ideas imme-diately, lest they be unable to retrieve their thoughts upon becoming fully awake. Whatever your means, *use the unconscious; it is one of the most powerful tools of cre-ativity available*. Then be prepared to record the results. Nothing is more frustrating than to have grasped a solution you are positive you'll remember, only to find it has subsequently slipped away.

Reduce the censorship of ideas.   The process of **brainstorming** involves admit-ting possibilities for examination that would normally be rejected by typical problem-solving processes. Popularized by Osborn (1959), it consists of assembling a group of people to attack a problem with certain basic rules of interaction: Renounce criti-cism, avoid interrupting, listen, respect differing points of view, welcome freewheel-ing ideas, seek quantity but avoid repetition, inject humor, and try to combine and improve previous suggestions. Once considered a fad, over time this technique has proven itself. Although it can lead to time-consuming consideration of impossible suggestions, it may free individuals to consider desirable ones that otherwise would have been discarded. Thinking of analogies—even far-fetched ones, such as "How is this phenomenon like an animal?"—have shown results. Once the bulk of the ideas has emerged, select the best for further development and sometimes, in turn, as the focus of further brainstorming sessions.

Move up the causal chain if the problem focus proves elusive.   Recall the story of the battle that was lost for want of a nail: For want of a nail the shoe was lost, for want of a shoe the horse was lost, for want of a horse, the rider was lost, and so forth. It demonstrates how everything is part of a causal chain. If you are interested in an area but have difficulty pinning down a problem, it sometimes helps to move to ear-lier links in the causal chain. For example, a researcher concerned with the in-service training of teachers wonders what to study. Move up the causal chain: Why do teach-ers seek training in the first place? For social contact with other teachers? Improved pay? Chances for leadership? These may be interesting possibilities.

Abelson (1995) found a formula in Tesser (1990) that takes a hypothesis a level deeper: State the hypothesis, then its opposite, and then find a way of reconciling the two. For example, an outstanding performance by someone produces jealousy in those close to him. But the opposite can also be demonstrated, whereby an excellent performance arouses pride in close others, a "basking in reflected glory" (Cialdini et al., 1976). The resolution of this contradiction is that what is at stake is the mainte-nance of self-esteem (Abelson, 1995).

Identify your most productive working conditions.   Become aware of the condi-tions that make you productive. For instance, you probably have an optimal level of motivation. At a higher level, you may be unable to stay focused long enough to per-ceive patterns. Administrators in particular are inclined to think that if a little moti-vation is good, more must be better. This is not necessarily so.

Where and when you work can be important. Find a place without too many dis-tractions. Many productive writers set aside a regular time for writing, continuing with provisional tries even when they are blocked. Some rent a hotel room, having meals sent up until they finish.

Patterns of writing are particularly likely to be unique to each person. Outlining used to be considered a necessity by many English teachers. Neil Simon, the famous playwright, was advised to try it:

> I . . . tried to make it go that way. It wouldn't! I did it 20 times! That is not the way to write a play . . . because that is not the way life is. You don't know what the end is going to be so you don't twist and push it. It just carries you along, somehow, predetermined by your character. (Rosner & Abt, 1970, p. 363)

Clearly, outlining was not for him, and it may not be for others. There is, however, some pattern that is better for each of us, and we must find it.

Try out some ideas.

After building a rich knowledge base from which to generate ideas, and going through an idea generation phase without too much constraint, it's time to begin testing and playing with the possibilities from the previous work.

Formulate the problem as a written statement.   Setting down your thoughts as a **written problem statement** is clarifying and organizing. As Merton (1959) puts it, try formulating questions that register your "dimly felt sense of ignorance" (p. xxvi). Writing enforces a discipline that helps articulate half-formed ideas. Something happens between the formation of an idea and its appearance on paper, a latency that somehow results in the clarification and untangling of our thinking. Writing helps bring unconscious processing to light as articulated synthesized statements—what we all are seeking! When we are reading widely, we cram the ideas into our memory, often without checking against what is already there; even contradictory material may exist side by side. Writing makes us confront these internal inconsistencies and assemble relationships.

Sometimes continued writing pays off. Listen to Albert Schweitzer in a translation of his autobiography:

> For months I lived in a continual state of mental agitation. Without the least success, I concentrated—even during my daily work at the hospital—on the real nature of affirmation of life and of ethics and on the question of what they have in common. . . . I saw the concept that I wanted to attain before me, but I could not . . . formulate it. While in this mental condition I had to undertake a long journey on the river. . . . Slowly we crept upstream. . . . Lost in thought I sat on the deck of the barge, struggling. . . . *I covered sheet after sheet with disconnected sentences merely to keep myself concentrated on the problem*. . . . Late on the third day, . . . there flashed upon my mind, unforeseen and unsought, the phrase, "reverence for life." The iron door yielded. The path in the thicket became visible. (Schweitzer, 1990, p. 155; italics added)

Particularly striking in this passage is the italicized sentence. It is so typical of good writers that even when they are blocked, they persist with provisional tries in order to formulate what they are seeking. Schweitzer "covered sheet after sheet with disconnected sentences" until he succeeded.

Slowing the writing process may help with difficult formulation. I can use a keyboard when I know what I want to write, but I must write with a pen when I'm struggling. As a last resort, a fountain pen seems to work better than a ballpoint. Each method takes progressively longer to form the words on paper. I can hold longer internal discussions with myself about what comes next, do a memory search for the right concept or word, and still put it down without unduly interrupting my flow of thought. This flow is important. Poor writers are often so involved with grammar, spelling, or even word formation that they have difficulty remembering where their sentences are going.

Try your ideas in simple form before starting a complex investigation.   When computers were still rarities, ideas that would have required writing expensive software were often tested for feasibility and problems by having humans play the role of computer in a paper simulation. Valenstein (1994) relates how Richard Jung missed discovering how the cortex of the brain received orientation information because he was warned against doing sloppy research. So he spent two years constructing a machine capable of presenting stimuli and recording the responses. Meanwhile, two other researchers, who received the Nobel Prize for their work, "made their discoveries by simply waving objects in front of cats" (p. 142). Try ideas in simplified form.

Don't close the problem definition too quickly.   Getzels and Csikszentmihalyi (1976) found the most creative solutions to be those of artists who kept problems open longer. They suggest that solutions must be discovered by interaction with the elements that constitute it—mucking around in the problem. Superficial solutions are also likelier to be rejected if closure is delayed.

Get feedback: Explain your ideas to other people.   Explaining ideas to someone else—ideally an uninformed but intelligent observer—is similar to writing. It is said that the best way to learn something is to teach it. Furthermore, an intelligent observer can often do better than we can for ourselves, especially if we are too close to whatever we are working on. Scheerer (1963), for example, assigned subjects randomly as observers and workers. The workers were to solve a problem that required use of a missing piece of string. A string that they could use was present but in the form of a hanger for a wall calendar. Only half the workers—but all of the observers—broke the mind-set of the string as hanger and solved the problem. Talking with others may also restore a sense of excitement.

Talk to specialists in the field.   Experts who have worked in a field for a long time build their conceptions of it from their experiences. Researchers comparing the problem solving of experts and novices note little difference in strategies but find a significant difference in the repertory of experiences organized in long-term memory. Chase and Simon's (1973) study of chess players nicely illustrates this point. Grand masters and masters were asked to reconstruct the positions of 22 chess pieces after viewing them for five seconds. When the positions were those from actual games, experts could place 81% of them without error, whereas novices could correctly position only 33%. When pieces were arranged at random, however, experts were no better than novices. Experts apparently identified patterns as games they had learned or experienced instead of memorizing the position of individual pieces. Note the specificity of their knowledge: Their capabilities would not apply to another sort of subject matter. Since research on expert–novice differences suggests these long-term memory patterns are subject-matter specific, choose an expert in your field to talk to.

Assess experts' reactions carefully, however. Some persons discourage ideas that didn't originate with them. Others, for whatever reason, may fail to grasp your problem and react superficially. With these caveats in mind, you will find that experts can be extremely valuable and save you much time, especially by helping you avoid false and unproductive leads.

Test your ideas on the Internet.   Increasingly, graduate students are asking for help with their problems on Internet forums. We tend to think of colleagues as those at our institution, but we must broaden our horizons. Highly competent colleagues—not only on our continent but also around the world—monitor these bulletin boards. Several emeritus professors, who apparently miss teaching, regularly respond to requests for help with sage advice on a listserv I regularly read. Most professional organizations have established such forums; contact them for information. Ask your professors for Web sites worth monitoring in regard to your problem area, and then join the online conversation.

Discard entries to a problem as soon as they no longer fit.   When the development of a human fetus is monitored, there is always considerable surprise that it seems to go through all the developmental stages of a previous evolution—for example, developing useless gills that then atrophy and become something else. As a problem statement develops, the structure of its introductory statement tends to grow, retaining the problem's developmental history and repeating useless aspects that no longer contribute to the current problem. Its structure is useful to us in that it retraces our thinking and gets us into the problem, but sometimes much of it is simply excess baggage. Other people can usually see this more easily than we can. It also is more apparent after the passage of time. The sooner we trim away this excess material, the stronger and more clearly we can develop the problem.

Some individuals find themselves rewriting the introduction to their problem every time they leave the work for a period of time. Not only is this likely to result in an introduction that needs to be trimmed, but it also tends to be unproductive labor. Write those sections you are ready to write rather than writing linearly from beginning to end; you are less likely to become blocked.

Rather than leaving the work at a point where a section is complete, stop at a point that cries out for completion and you know what you plan to do next. It will be easier to continue at that point.

Keep going.

While in a previous section we encouraged you to know the "first rule of holes," it is also important to keep going. All individuals who move from novice to expert experience failure, and some experience failure frequently. Edison was especially famous for tenacious approaches to problem solving, even sending a team of materials scientists around the world in a multi-year quest to look for appropriate filament for light bulbs, testing any possible material they could lay their hands on (Israel, 1998).

Early in his career, John Behrens commented about the large body of work created by a colleague, who responded by pointing out that he had amassed a large corpus simply by doing a steady amount each year. No unachievable Herculean effort was required, only persistence.

Having trouble formulating your problem? Use the suggestions in the previous material as a checklist.

ADDITIONAL READING

A wiki site (a Web site to which anybody can add material) on creativity and innovation techniques exists at The Creative Education Foundation's Creative Problem Solving Institute (CPSI) at http://www.mycoted.com/CPSI. The section on creativity techniques may be of special interest. Getzels (1982) provides a helpful combination of speculation and data; Leong and Pfaltzgraff (2005) includes a useful chapter on finding a research topic in a very useful book; Meehl (1974), an argument for theory in social science research and some examples; and Merton (1959), still relevant advice from one of the greats in sociology.

IMPORTANT TERMS AND CONCEPTS

active reading
brainstorming
harnessing the unconscious
log of ideas

redefinition
second adolescence
seminal minds
written problem statement

OPPORTUNITIES FOR ADDITIONAL LEARNING

1. Johnson (1978), drawing upon the theories of Carl Jung (1923), theorized that a person's psychological style is defined by how he or she makes decisions. He developed a two-dimensional decision-making scheme based on the way information is gathered (systematically or spontaneously) and on the way data are analyzed; that is, internally (the individual needs to think about it first) or externally (the individual needs to discuss it with someone). From this, Johnson surmised that individuals could be classified into four personality types: spontaneous external, spontaneous internal, systematic external, and systematic internal. If you were interested in researching psychological styles, how could you use Johnson's theory to develop a research problem?

2. Assume that you are a graduate student in educational psychology interested in "intelligence." You have read widely on the topic and know that over the years a number of theories have been advanced about its nature. These include such concepts as Thurstone's seven primary mental abilities; Spearman's g, or general intelligence factor; Guilford's structure of intellect model; and the idea of fluid versus crystallized intelligence championed by Cattell and Horn. To which of these should you look as the potential source of a research question?

3. A master's degree student in nursing is interested in the care of brain-injured patients. She has focused on a disorder called unilateral neglect, which leaves a patient unaware of one side of his or her body. The student wishes to investigate the degree to which such patients could carry out ordinary activities of daily living and what the implications would be for their nursing care. How might she proceed?

4. A doctoral student in the field of educational technology is working with an advisor who has gained international recognition for his instructional model for selecting and sequencing

content. The student has identified a set of motivational strategies to add to the model and is considering their verification in an instructional setting as her dissertation topic. However, the student wonders if this topic is sufficiently original, since she did not develop the original model. What would be your advice to her?

APPLICATION EXERCISE

Beginning with this chapter, it is suggested that you choose a topic or problem that interests you and use it throughout the rest of the book to gain familiarity with the content of each chapter. Find a topic that you may be willing to stay with. Try some of the techniques described in this chapter to stimulate your creativity. Actively read some of the references found for your topic (the material in the next chapter will help you find references). See whether there is a member of the invisible college in your institution, at a nearby institution, or on the Internet who will correspond with you. Get together with a small group and brainstorm. Have one person in the group play the role of observer to help you reflect on the process, and make sure you follow the rules. Have this person summarize progress every 10 minutes or so or when there is a good breaking point and have her point out any breeches of the rules. Try the card sorting suggested on page 93. Read extensively and fill your mind with material; then concentrate on something else for a while and see what develops. Even if all this is effective, also try working at your project by yourself, filling a sheet of paper with ideas or whatever comes to mind to keep you engaged with the problem. Experimenting with these different approaches will help you learn what works best for you.

By applying the content of this and each succeeding chapter to your topic, you can easily end up with a proposal for a study that has been subjected to analysis from the standpoint of the foundational skills and concepts of research and has been thought about in relation to various research methods. You will know which skills were applicable and useful for your project. You'll have compared the potential of the various research methods for it. What process could better strengthen your proposal for a research study than that?

Many doctoral students in the two-semester course in which this book was pioneered came out of it with proposals ready to go to their committee for final refinement. It gave them a big start on their doctoral program and helped save them from the aforementioned ABD status. By doing these application exercises and using the suggestions in the Appendix and/or *How to Prepare a Dissertation Proposal* (Krathwohl & Smith, 2005), you can similarly benefit.

KEY TO ADDITIONAL LEARNING OPPORTUNITIES

1. Do you find these assumptions believable, or do you find yourself questioning them? One approach would be to challenge Johnson's assumptions. Examine their basis. Is there an alternate explanation that comes to mind? Are these personality types stable aspects of an individual's personality, or are they a function of the particular situation? If they are based on exhibited behavior, is there another way of explaining that behavior?

   Conversely, you may find these assumptions appealing. Note that they have a basis in established theory. Jung is a seminal writer; review Jung's theory rather than relying on Johnson's interpretation. However, you may be able to come up with a way of extending, validating, or applying these conclusions. Coscarelli and Stonewater (1979), for instance, suggested that these personality types could be useful in a model of consultation to help determine the best way to work with a client.

2. All have potential. You could apply the criteria of a good problem here. First, which of the approaches interests you, makes most sense to you, perhaps gets you excited? Do any of them suggest a question to you immediately? Second, all of them are embedded in theory,

but is one developing a stronger network than the others? Does it seem to fit better into our developing knowledge base? Third, in terms of impact, which of them appears to be the most current? Exploring a problem based on a theory of prevailing interest in one's field is more likely to produce findings that have an impact than exploring one based on a theory that has been replaced or discarded. Fourth, which allows you to be creative? Do any of them lend themselves to analysis by a new technique, instrument, or model? This is one way to revive an older theory and still have impact.

3. She should begin, of course, by immersing herself in the literature of this topic. It would be worth her while to talk to anyone available to her who has experience or expertise with this disorder. These experts may be able to answer questions about such matters as certainty of diagnosis, spontaneous recovery, and length of disorder. She should learn the best current explanation of the disorder and how well it is embedded in the network of theory that explains it and similar problems. Then she may turn to the problems of feasibility: Will patients with this disorder be available to her and, if so, in sufficient number to conduct a study? How would she evaluate how well they carry out the activities of daily living? Knowing that this is of concern in special education and with the developmentally disabled, she might look for scales in those fields that could be applied here.

4. You should advise her to proceed with her question. If her adviser's model is indeed well recognized, she is in effect embedding her problem in current theory. She is more likely— particularly as a novice—to have an impact on her field in this way than to produce a more original but isolated study. Second, by adding her own touch to the model and providing an interesting and possibly useful extension to it, she has demonstrated originality.

SUMMARY

Choice of problem is the most important decision a researcher makes. Good problems are interesting enough to motivate you to carry them to completion, are typically embedded in theory, are likely to have some impact on the field, have an element of originality or creativity about them, and are feasible. Although feasibility in terms of personal skills often stretches further than you might initially think, the problem must be researchable within the ethical and institutional limits and the resources available. Research cannot affirm or deny a value judgment. It can only show the consequences of a given value position or, through polling, find the support for or against it. This may be helpful to decision makers in determining policy.

Although some researchers are better at problem finding than others, you can learn the necessary skills. Discovery favors the prepared mind. Reading actively, reading widely, reading the seminal minds in the field, talking to specialists, challenging assumptions, looking for new ways to tease the problem apart, and departing from conventional ways of looking at it—in short, filling the mind with the grist that allows the unconscious to sort matters and organize thoughts—all are highly conducive to finding new research ideas.

In addition, you can use techniques to enhance creativity, such as those that organize material into suggestive patterns and reduce the censorship of ideas (brainstorming). Formulate the problem as a written statement and/or explain it to someone else. Learn your most productive working conditions. When having trouble focusing, trace your problem back to earlier links in the causal chain. Don't finalize the problem definition too quickly.

A Look Ahead

Obviously, one of the most important sources of material to develop a "prepared mind" is the work of others. For this we need library skills, to which we turn in the next chapter.

In subsequent chapters you will encounter many URLs (the "http://" addresses of Web sites). As we mentioned in the preface, in APA format these should appear with the date they were last accessed, so the reader will know when they were last known to be live links. We have omitted such dates, however, because all the URLs were current at the last typeset draft prior to publishing (September 18, 2008). Thanks to the Internet, we can continue to communicate with you. As URLs change and newer references and research methods develop, we can inform you on the Web. Check this Web site (http://www.faculty.soe.syr.edu/drkrathw/) from time to time for these useful postings.

Note

[1] This is also the title of an excellent chapter by Getzels (1982); he is one of the few people who have done research on problem finding and formulation.

CHAPTER ADDENDUM: PATTERN NOTES

Please reread the first two paragraphs of the Additional Learning Opportunity on page 76, which introduces Jonassen's pattern notes. Especially for those of you who are visual learners, this is a way of helping you organize and diagram what you have learned. Figure 5.1 is an example of a pattern note for this chapter. As you trace the lines and their titles, you will be reminded of the chapter contents and the inter-relationships among its parts.

This was a student's way of organizing what he learned from the chapter. The intent of this addendum is to suggest that you experiment with it to see if you find it helpful and useful in future study. Use it in studying the next chapters. Because this is a general example, it does not contain references to personal experience or prior learning as a pattern note should, in order to tie what you are currently learning to your past personal and academic experiences. Adding such references to your pattern notes will make them more meaningful and the learning more permanent.

Because personal prior experiences differ, there clearly could be many ways to pattern-note this chapter; it depends on how you relate the material to what you already know. So, maps may differ significantly from person to person, though sections may be similar. Given differences in prior learning, one can argue that there is no right way to pattern-note a chapter. Some persons have suggested that the more successful the teacher, the more closely a student's pattern note will resemble the instructor's.

The process of making the map is what is important: organizing your thoughts, relating parts of the chapter to other parts, and integrating the new into your prior learning. The product, the pattern note itself, then serves as shorthand for what one has learned and is useful in reviewing the material. In a meta-analysis (see chapter 22, p. 520), concept mapping was found more effective than reading texts, attending lectures, or participating in class discussions. It was slightly more effective than writing summaries and outlines, but the size of the differences in effect sizes was small and possibly unreliable (Nesbit & Adesope, 2006).

Concept mapping is a similar process done a bit differently. Free software for all computer operating systems to produce concept maps, as well as a concept map used to explain concept maps, is available from the Institute for Human and Machine Cognition (http://cmap.ihmc.us/).

Figure 5.1 **A pattern note showing a student's understanding of the relationships of the topics in this chapter.**

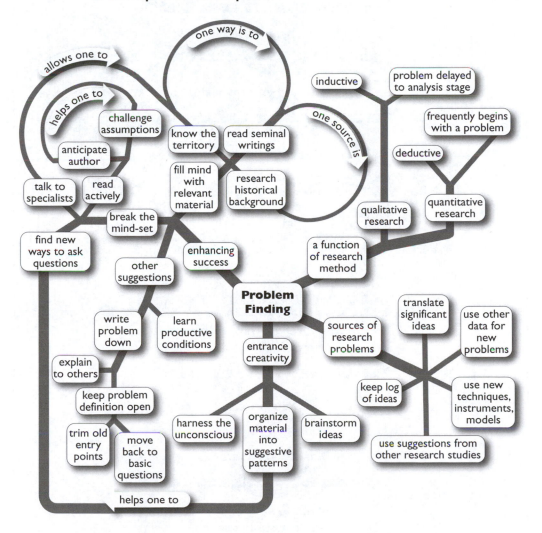

Links to previous research

Explanation, rationale, theory, or point of view

Questions, hypotheses, models

Preplanned and emergent designs

Design/procedure

Focus   Records   Time   Comparison and Contrast   Situation   Participants

Data

Statistical analysis and/or narrative analysis

Conclusion

Link to next study

Explanation or rationale of next study, etc.

6

Finding Links to Past Research
The Literature Search and Literature Review

> If no use is made of the labors of past ages, the world must remain always in the infancy of knowledge.
>
> —Cicero, *De Oratore II*
>
> One of the diseases of this age is the multiplicity of books; they doth so overcharge the world that it is not able to digest the abundance of idle matter that is every day hatched and brought forth into the world.
>
> —Barnaby Rich, 1613 (in De Solla Price, *Little Science, Big Science*)
>
> The longer we look back, the farther we can look forward.
>
> —Winston Churchill (in Coyne, *Dobzhansky Revisited*)

HOW TO READ THIS CHAPTER

The conventional way to read this chapter is to start at the beginning and read straight through. There is also an unconventional way, made possible by the section beginning on page 120, "A Literature Search Example," which serves as a detailed chapter summary. It illustrates how all the various sources of information in Figure 6.1 (p. 110) flow into a literature search (your computer and the Internet, your institution's faculty, and your institution's library—both the physical facility and its virtual browsable collection of online reference works and subscription accessible journal and book archives). It extracts most of the substance of the chapter and adds some tips on computer use. You can go back into the chapter for more detail as you need it.

To help you decide, here is the chapter's organization:

- The function of the literature search in a research study (p. 106)
- Overall map of information sources (p. 110)
- Search actions at successive problem-development stages (p. 109)
- Types of information sources (p. 113)
- Types of indexes (p. 119)
- A literature search example (including tips on computer use) (p. 120)
- Tips for writing the literature review (p. 127)

Whatever you decide, first read the next three sections: The Functions of the Literature Search (p. 106), The Dissertation's Literature Review: Two Points of View (p. 108), and The Literature Search in Emergent Studies (p. 109).

INTRODUCTION

This is a time of transition for libraries. As their online virtual collections grow, unneeded paper copies can be removed from the shelves to warehouses or even to regional collections. This opens up valuable shelf space—always at a premium. Because libraries differ in how far along they are in this process, this chapter straddles the fence, providing enough information in instances where paper copies are still in use yet providing information on the online versions as well.

THE FUNCTIONS OF THE LITERATURE SEARCH

The literature search is the phase in which most individuals develop their research question and formulate the major direction of their study. We enter with an area of interest, an *orienting question*, a hunch about something worth pursuing—like a newspaper reporter's "sniff." This focuses our attention, directs us to sources of information, and permits us to determine whether there is indeed something worth delving into. We leave our literature search with at least a more definitive notion about the area, its important variables, how they are interrelated, what the good questions are, and what research methods have been used. Sometimes a hypothesis emerges. Even better, if the literature base is solid enough, we may be able to make a prediction or create an explanatory model of the interrelations of variables. At a minimum, by exploring the literature we move a long way down the road in the development of our research focus. At best, we can fully formulate our research problem.

Often, however, our simple orienting question doesn't prepare us for the complexity of the problem shown by the literature. Consider this example:

> When learning to swim, is it better to learn the Australian crawl as a whole or to master all the parts—arm strokes, breathing, flutter kick—and then put them together? The literature refers to this process as part–whole learning and shows there is more than one part–whole method. We learn, for instance, among other possibilities, we can alternate practicing a new part and integrating it into the

whole, or we can start with a part and then add successive parts until the whole is achieved. The problem has taken on a new complexity. Furthermore, the studies use these methods under different conditions of practice—massed in a single session or large, concentrated blocks or distributed over time. Distribution of practice is a concomitant variable that affects learning strategy; a second complexity has been added.

Thus, although a first function of the literature search is to define the problem, it is only one of several. The following list shows how critical the literature search can be to problem and research-method formulation. The literature search:

1. *Helps define and refine the problem.*
   - Identifies which facets of the phenomenon are important (in the case of the example above, patterns of practice as well as learning strategy)
   - Suggests the nature of the relationship among the variables (whether massed or distributed practice facilitates part–whole learning)
   - Provides the basis for reducing the problem to feasible proportions (if investigating all the part–whole strategies seems too much)

2. *Shows us the research frontier.* The literature search helps us to determine how far previous research has come. (Part–whole learning and distribution of practice were the key factors; what additional factors will your study investigate?) Finding the frontier allows you to place your study in perspective when compared with the work of others—showing how it fills a gap and advances what has already been done. You shouldn't automatically assume that the newest work has advanced the field. Read in historical depth; the frontier may not have been advanced much by the latest efforts.

3. *Relates the problem to the network of theory, rationales, and previous explanations that already exists in the area.* This results as we trace the path of past research all the way to the newest studies—the frontier. Context is important because when research findings are isolated facts, they don't much advance our understanding of how things work. It is the networked knowledge that allows us to transfer findings to new situations and to improve the way we deal with the world. For example, a new explanation of how massed versus distributed practice affects learning in general might suggest how the various swimming methods would be affected by the explanation and how distribution of practice might be still further improved.

4. *Finds research methods and designs worth considering, problems to avoid, and new refinements to methods.* (Weren't there some clever designs in previous investigations that you could use in yours?) You can glean valuable ideas for data analysis from others' experiences. Studying distinctions in methods may suggest why study outcomes differ; the phenomenon may be more amenable to exploration with one method than with another. Furthermore, this literature may include potentially useful instruments and measures and provide data on their validity; experimental instruments for hard-to-measure characteristics appear earliest in research studies.

Look at the retrieval of knowledge on a cost-benefit basis, in effect substituting relatively cheap literature-search time for the costs of rediscovering it with new research. The more economically we can find how far previous investigators advanced a topic, the more resources are available to "stand on their shoulders" and advance the field.

This list of functions reinforces how crucial the literature search is. Despite the massive increase in publications over the past decades, new retrieval methods and index types have made access easier. This chapter introduces you to the tools and methods that make retrievability possible.

The literature search:

▶ helps define and refine the problem;

▶ shows how far previous research has come;

▶ relates the problem to the network of theory, rationales, and previous explanations; and

▶ finds research methods and designs worth considering, problems to avoid, and new refinements to method.

THE DISSERTATION'S LITERATURE REVIEW: TWO POINTS OF VIEW

The literature search forms the basis for the review and analysis. The search should be wide enough to assure you have uncovered the important pieces of research bearing on your problem. There are two schools of thought with respect to writing the review, however. The first of these holds that it should cover all the literature on the problem that can be found in the field, excluding only the really marginal material. Such a review is similar to those found in journals devoted to reviews—*Psychology Reviews* and *Review of Educational Research*, for example. The focus of the review is on summarizing the findings of this literature and showing how it bears on the problem. Some advisors expect their students to include such a review in their dissertation.

The other point of view held by advisors is that the literature review should be narrowed to focus on the particular problem chosen for the dissertation. From this viewpoint, in writing the literature review the researcher should:

• provide a coherent, integrated, and critical examination of the best, *selected* relevant literature.

• appropriately critique and comment on these selected studies.

• explain how this literature (1) modified and sharpened the problem's focus, (2) shaped how the problem is investigated, (3) tied the problem to the network of other work and theory in the field, and (4) makes clear that this problem "stands on its shoulders" and advances the field.

• show an increased understanding of the problem as a result of prior work.

Certainly, before either writing the review of literature or doing the search (since it likely affects how you analyze the literature), you will want to determine which of these points of view is closest to what you intend.

THE LITERATURE SEARCH IN EMERGENT STUDIES

Many researchers, especially those who use qualitative or inductive methods, expect their problem focus to emerge as they do their study. Therefore, to consult the literature too early will burden them with other people's perceptions rather than allowing them to form their own. Their problems in this regard are discussed in chapter 12.

In the remainder of this chapter, we'll assume that researchers are entering the literature search with only an orienting question and thus will discuss tools and skills that can help. However, this material will also serve those doing a literature search late in their study.

ENTRY POINTS FOR DIFFERENT STAGES OF PROBLEM DEVELOPMENT

The following discussion suggests different entry points that depend on how concretely and specifically you are able to conceptualize and state your research problem. Listed in successive order, beginning with the most general stage, is a review of the purpose of the search at that stage and the sources to consult. Figure 6.1 on the following page is a map of the various knowledge sources available and the ways in which they are interrelated.

In Figure 6.1 there are four major sources of information: your computer and its access to the Internet, your faculty, and your institution's library—both physical and virtual. Study of how each diagrammed source leads to other information will suggest actions to take as you proceed in a literature search. For example, it suggests that faculties at institutions other than your own are available as sources of information and advice through the many forums, blogs, and listservs.

The circled numbers within the figure are referred to in the discussion below and in the example near the end of the chapter.

A General Problem Area

Purpose: To get an overview of the area and find the important sources of information in an area.

Information Sources: Overviews are provided by encyclopedias, handbooks, and reviews of research in the area, including Wikipedia (www.en.wikipedia.org/). Because entries on wikis are editable by anyone, anytime, regardless of expertise, it can be very useful as an introduction but rarely as a definitive reference. Area guides to reference books, such as Reed and Baxter's (2003) *Library Use: A Handbook for Psychology*, can be found by an online search with "reference guide (subject)"; use a meta-search engine like Dogpile (http://www.dogpile.com) or Clusty (http://www.clusty.com; use the result clusters in the left column to narrow your search). ①

Academic OneFile is a very broad subscription database consisting of full-text articles from a very wide variety of areas. Search it to find possibilities not yet considered; often we may not be aware of certain wide ramifications that might apply to our area of interest.

Figure 6.1   The various sources of information available for a literature search and how each leads to other sources.

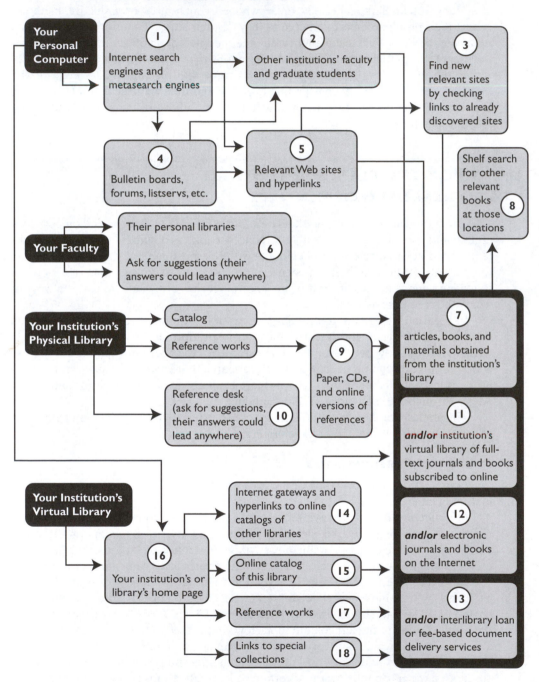

A Specific Problem Area

Purpose: To learn what research has been done, what terminology is being used, where the frontier is, what keywords to pursue in journal literature, and whether there are dissertations of others in the area.

Information Sources: A library's subject index or online catalog for relevant bibliographies, books, and other materials. ⑮ ⑭ (Find one centrally relevant book; try clicking on its call number to bring up the list of books shelved with this one; browse! ⑧ Or do a call-number catalog search—a virtual way to search the library shelves.)

Consult compilations such as handbooks (*Handbook of Research on Teaching, Handbook of Social Psychology*), research reviews (*Annual Review of Anthropology, Annual Review of Psychology, Annual Review of Sociology, Review of Educational Research*), and encyclopedias (*Encyclopedia of Educational Research, Encyclopedia of Psychology*). ⑦

Dissertations can be searched at the ProQuest Web site: ①
http://www.proquest.com/products_umi/dissertations/
Electronic dissertations are also available at the Networked Digital Library of Theses and Dissertations (NDLTD): http://www.ndltd.org/ ③

Find the various search terms relevant to the area in a thesaurus. For instance, the *Thesaurus of Psychological Index Terms* (American Psychological Association, 2004) covers a lot of social science (online in a subscription database; look for the *Thesaurus* under advanced search). For other thesauri, see the section on Types of Indexes later in this chapter. ⑦

A Specific Problem

Purpose: To identify the major aspects of the topic and prolific writers in the area, find recent research, learn how terminology is changing, identify new fields related to the problem, explore current methodological approaches, and find the current frontier.

Information Sources: Narrowed to a specific problem, we can go directly to relevant entries in indexing and abstracting services: ⑪ *Psychological Abstracts* (online as *PsycInfo*), Sociological Abstracts (*Sociological Abstracts Online*), SocINDEX, ERIC, and *Dissertation Abstracts International.*

Once one has found some of the key references related to the problem, one can see who has built on them by consulting *Social Science Citation Index, Science Citation Index*, and *Arts and Humanities Citation Index* (all in *Web of Science*). ⑦ ⑪

Cambridge University Library provides a list of electronic journals, including a social science category broken down into subcategories. The Communication of Research Special Interest Group of the American Educational Research Association (AERA) also maintains a list of education-related journals online. ⑫ For others, an Internet search of "electronic journals (subject)" will find useful leads. ①

• *Cambridge University Library list*   http://sfx7.exlibrisgroup.com/cambridge/az

• *AERA list*   http://aera-cr.asu.edu/ejournals/

Finding Research Studies Basic to the Problem

Purpose: To find the authors most cited in an area of work and the basic references to which other authors in the field refer; and to trace the path of historical development of an area all the way back to the first author(s) cited in an area, who cited this initial work, and who, in turn, cited that work, and so on.

Information Sources: The three citation indexes: *Social Science Citation Index, Science Citation Index,* and *Arts and Humanities Citation Index* (see p. 123. These may be found in the *Web of Science*). ⑦ ⑪

The Latest Published and Currently Ongoing Research

Purpose: To locate the most recent work in an area, including ongoing projects.

Information Sources: For the latest published work, *Current Contents: Social and Behavioral Science* (a spin-off of the citation indexes) reproduces the tables of contents from the major journals, clustering them in sections such as political science, sociology, psychology, education, and special education. A keyword index exists for each issue. ⑦ ⑪

For ongoing research, visit the http://USA.gov Web site ("Government Made Easy") and click on the Benefits and Grants link. For National Science Foundation (http://nsf.gov) grants, click on awards in the Behavioral and Cognitive Science Division or the Social and Economic Sciences Division. For private funding, visit the *Journal of Philanthropy* Web site.

• *Behavior and Cognitive Science Division*   http://nsf.gov/div/index.jsp?div=BCS

• *Social and Economic Sciences Division*   http://nsf.gov/div/index.jsp?div=SES

• *Journal of Philanthropy*   http://www.philanthropy.com

Convention programs of professional associations, where research is often reported before publication, are often posted online and increasingly are searchable. ① Such papers are also listed in the *Index to Social Science and Humanities Proceedings*. ERIC solicits papers from professional association meetings for inclusion in its collection and so may have research before it is in journals. Your faculty will know relevant professional associations and have access to membership directories and convention programs. Write to project directors working in the area; e-mail addresses are often in convention programs or membership directories.

Don't overlook listservs, blogs, and forums, and the so-called invisible colleges—networks of communication with persons of similar interest (see chapter 3, p. 37). CataList is a subscription database of over 53,000 listservs open to the public. Professional associations often maintain listservs not open to the public; ask your faculty about them. Many professional associations have graduate student memberships that make you eligible to join the list. ⑥

ORGANIZING THE SEARCH

How organized should your search be? Most people begin by yanking at a corner of the problem—an aspect of it that interests them—like a loose thread on a sweater, tugging on it to unravel the garment. This technique often works; problems can usually be approached from a variety of directions. It is certainly difficult to organize a search for something you don't know much about. Thus, before researchers organize, they usually engage in a period of broad exploration. Most important at this juncture is being flexible enough to recognize potentially profitable byways and side issues. Sometimes these turn out to be more important than what we set out to pursue.

To be sure you have found the boundaries of your topic (if you haven't done so earlier), before sitting down to organize, conduct a computer search based on a careful consultation of relevant thesauri or dictionaries. Both activities, however, are much more useful earlier than as clean-up activities.

Nevertheless, there comes a point in the process where you will need to stop, get some perspective on what you have done, and carry out an organized search from that point on. It may come earlier than you anticipate. The only way to know is to take a few minutes every so often to reflect on what you have done, to consider where you are going, and to estimate further requirements for learning the dimensions and nature of the sought-for body of literature (see also chapter 27, p. 629). You will intuitively sense when you have arrived at this point of organization because you will have become comfortable with what you have learned, findings begin to repeat, and expectations of new surprises have diminished. Then, plan your future reference acquisition pattern, deciding what to cover heavily and what more lightly. Ways of organizing the search are described in the example at the end of the chapter.

We have been considering literature searches in which the summary and analysis of the literature is done purely in descriptive verbal terms. Increasingly, these are accompanied or sometimes replaced by what have been termed **meta-analyses**, in which the quantitative findings of studies of a given phenomena are summarized in quantitative terms. This process is described in chapter 22.

Types of Information Sources

In the sections that follow we consider the variety of information sources available in more detail, taking up the sources one at a time and also discussing their delivery.

The Internet

The Internet has created a new knowledge industry, and Google and various other search engines have changed the way we search the knowledge base. Instead of consulting bound volumes that indexed and abstracted the literature, we either use them online or use what we know to find what we want in a search engine. Many times we don't need an abstracting service such as *Psychological Abstracts* or *Sociological Abstracts*; the search engine takes us right to the original document. Once there, we can either read its abstract (if it has one) and scan it to decide if it is worth reading, or possibly use computer software to summarize the article for us. What a change!

The wide variety of Web sites maintained by libraries, faculty, and various other centers and institutions contain online syllabi, archives, conference proceedings, online journals, full-text reproductions of journals, and books. Google Books (http://books.google.com) is a project that aims to scan and digitize all the books in the world and is working with the largest libraries to do so. Thus, it is obvious that the World Wide Web is where computer-literate searchers likely first turn for information. Cooper (1985), in an early study of the sources used by professional reviewers, found **computer searches** yielded the most references. Short of using the references from previous reviews of the area, they yielded references with the greatest centrality and significance.

Internet Terminology for Online Research

The *Internet* is a network of interconnected computers that employ languages (or protocols—for example, FTP or file transfer protocol) for e-mail, instant messaging, and accessing the World Wide Web. The Web uses HTTP (hypertext transport protocol) to exchange information between computers. A *browser*—e.g., Internet Explorer, Netscape, Safari, or Firefox—interprets HTML code (hypertext markup language, the programming language that specifies hypertext *links* between related objects and documents), with the result being a nicely formatted page on your computer screen. It utilizes URLs (uniform resource locators) to identify sources of HTML. Each URL is a unique address for a file accessible on the Internet (or Web *page*—sometimes one of many URLs that comprise a Web *site*). Web sites often grow and reorganize so that the original URL leads to different material or to a dead link. DOIs (digital object identifiers) avoid this problem by permanently assigning a unique number that leads to the target electronic intellectual property, even if the URL changes. DOIs are coming into use in some science areas.

What to do when the URL doesn't work? Try successively eliminating parts of the URL starting at the end, for example:

http://www.lib.berkeley.edu/TeachingLib/Guides/Internet/
http://www.lib.berkeley.edu/TeachingLib/Guides/

If this doesn't work, http://www.lib.berkeley.edu/ takes you back to the home Web site where you may be able to find what you are seeking; reorganization of Web sites is common. Alternatively, put the URL or its topic into a search engine. Google will show you similar sites and sites that link to it.

Search Engines

Search engines make searching easy. The names and URLs of the more commonly used ones are: Google (http://google.com), AltaVista (http://altavista.com), Ask (http://ask.com), and Yahoo (http://yahoo.com). Search engines don't run out to search the Internet for each query. Their software involves webcrawlers that create an index (**database**), and an algorithm that matches your request to the database. Engines differ, therefore, in both their databases and how they interpret your search.

Meta-search engines. Meta-search engines simultaneously engage multiple engines. A 2005 study by meta-search engine Dogpile highlighted engine differences. Only 1.1% of the first-page results were common to four leading search engines and 11% to two (Google, Yahoo, MSN, and Ask). Overlap was greater if one included full results, but still two-thirds were unique to one engine (Dogpile, 2005). Their study argues for using meta-search engines such as Dogpile (http://www.dogpile.com) and All the Web (http://www.alltheweb.com). You can compare the results of your search at Google and Yahoo at: http://www.googleguy.de/google-yahoo/. Some meta-search engines, such as Clusty (http://clusty.com), also cluster the results to eliminate meanings other than the one intended (e.g., a search for "saturn" will cluster results separately for the planet and the automobile) and give the number of leads in each cluster.

Specialty search engines.   There are many specialty search engines that index only those parts of the Internet relevant to their topic. They return a better wheat-to-chaff ratio, so winnowing is easier. For lists see http://webquest.sdsu.edu/searching/specialized.html or query general-purpose search engines (e.g., "sociology search engine").

Google Scholar (http://scholar.google.com) is particularly useful to academics. It indexes peer-reviewed papers, theses, books, preprints, abstracts, and technical reports from broad areas of research as well as the publications of professional societies, preprint repositories, and universities. Google has gained access to password-protected sites of a range of academic publishers, so as to include at least an abstract in its index. In cases where university libraries have site subscriptions, students and faculty will be able to access the full articles. The advanced search option in Google and AltaVista can limit the search to a given domain such as .edu, or .org (e.g., using searchedu.com searches only .edu sites). Certain search engines (e.g., Ask) are programmed to answer searches posed, not as the usual key words, but as questions (e.g., What causes attention deficit disorder?).

The invisible Web.   Sites not identified by crawlers are part of the invisible Web, estimated at several times larger than the indexed Web. It includes those sites not referred to by an index; those located behind a password or firewall, requiring visitors to register or pay a fee; and those that are interactive (e.g., sites that respond to a query; such sites have a question mark in the URL). Efforts have been made to catalog these types of pages. See, for example, http://www.robertlackie.com/invisible/.

What computer searches can do that hand searches can't.   Computer searches are especially helpful in the following circumstances:

- *When what you are seeking is not likely to be included in the title but would probably appear in the abstract.* The indexes to abstracting and indexing services generally are confined to the title and keywords of an article, but computer searches will additionally search the abstract and may index the full document. Thus, every term in an abstract is an indexing term, so we can search for methodological details (e.g., stratified sample, analysis of variance) or instruments or measures (e.g., Minnesota Multiphasic Inventory). Often, looking at the keywords assigned to relevant entries suggests additional searches.

- *When your search words have a single stem (e.g., psychology, psychiatry, or psychological, each of which would require a separate search).* A single computer search using a truncated term like psych+ would allow the searcher to find all forms of the word.

- *When you wish to find references best identified by a combination of two or more descriptors or index terms (e.g., personality typology).* This process can be difficult and very time consuming in a search on paper, requiring two or more separate searches and a comparison to find common ones or to find a heading with the proper subheads. For a computer this is a simple task.

- *When a search over a period of years must be pursued in individual printed volumes.* Databases nearly always search across all years available.

- *When you wish to copy index entries, abstracts, or all or part of an online article.* They can be easily printed from the computer. Sometimes you can copy and paste into a word processor or send them to yourself via e-mail.

- *When you seek a particular title or the work of a specific author but do not have information on the journal or date of publication.* This information is easily available from an online abstracting or indexing database and often from a search engine. (Note that, until the references have been converted to database form, searches involving older references must still be done from paper volumes.)

- *When a topic is too new to have a descriptor in an index but may be mentioned by a key phrase or term in a title or abstract.*

- *When a hand search might be constricted because of time or energy problems.* A computer search likely will use less time and energy and enlarge your horizons.

   Maximizing relevant responses from search engines.   Finding that "just right" set of search terms with minimal effort is a matter of knowing how to phrase your search and use symbols that specify what you want.

- Connecting search terms with "and" returns only matches that contain *all* the terms, whether or not they are adjacent. Most search engines assume that queries of two or more words are linked by "and."

- If search terms must be adjacent in matches, enclose them in quotation marks.

- Using "or" gives matches containing any one of the search terms. It returns the most responses.

- Placing "not" before a search term excludes returns that contain it.

- Most searches are not case sensitive (e.g., saturn and SaTuRn will return the same results). To make capitalization count, use an advanced search.

- Most search engines drop common and short words (where, when, the, a, to) from the search. To include them, use quotation marks or an advanced search.

   Google includes other useful symbols, some of which may apply when using other search engines, or they may have an alternative:

- Inserting a tilde (~) in front of a term allows you to include synonyms and plurals in the search. This broadens the search so that, for instance, the query "~car" searches cars, auto, automobile, vehicle, BMW, and so on. (The tilde is the farthest left key in the top regular row of the keyboard, plus the shift key.)

- A minus sign preceding a term excludes responses that contain the term.

- Substitute the wild card * for whole words which you don't know that are missing (this works for whole words only; for a partial word or letter, use ~). This is useful for facts or quotations (e.g., to find the unknown names of three of the seven dwarfs in Snow White, type: dopey sneezy doc sleepy ***).

- Add "+site:" with edu, org, net, or com to limit the search to URLs with that suffix (e.g., +site:edu will likely turn up more academic responses). Similarly, "–site" excludes sites with that suffix (e.g., –site:com eliminates booksellers and commercial sites and may be useful in academic searches).

To learn the tricks of a particular search engine, input "(name of search engine) search help" in the search engine (e.g., altavista search help).

Books

The front end of the university library, formerly considered as just the card catalog, has become a virtual online library that augments and in some ways replaces certain library services. As university libraries computerized their catalogs, they put them online and added links to catalogs at other universities and to OCLC (Online Computer Library Center). OCLC and its offspring, http://worldcat.org, is a combined online catalog that covers the holdings of over 9,000 research institutions worldwide, including the Library of Congress. It indicates close-by libraries for visits or obtaining books by interlibrary loan. Students at institutions without such links can access other university libraries through each institution's home Web site. ⑪ Thus, as noted in Figure 6.1, libraries at other institutions are increasingly available electronically. ⑭ ⑱

If you are a shelf browser, you'll appreciate a good cataloger who lets you find the books on a topic all in one place. You need only find the call number of one book on the topic to have access to other books on the same topic. That can be tremendously valuable because you can browse books you didn't know existed and books more recent than the one that brought you there. ⑧ To test whether a given call number is worth going to the shelves, do a call-number search in the online catalog and skim the titles. For Library of Congress cataloging, enter just the first letter(s) and the number immediately following.

Guides to Reference Works

A general source of information on reference works can be especially valuable to those new to a field, not only in helping locate indexes but also in pointing out the variety of handbooks, bibliographies, review sources, and other access points. ⑨ The most general of these, and the one used by general reference librarians, is *Guide to Reference Books* (Balay, 1996, often referred to as "Winchell" for its original author). Another general reference is Hillard's (2000) *Where to Find What: A Handbook to Reference Service.*

Reed and Baxter's *Library Use: A Handbook for Psychology* (3rd ed., 2003) covers psychology's widest boundaries as well as parts of bordering social science fields. It provides detailed information on how to access such commonly used reference works as *Psychological Abstracts, Sociological Abstracts,* and *Social Science Citation Index* (in *Web of Science*). Freed, Hess, and Ryan's (2002) third chapter, which lists nearly 200 "Where do I go to find . . ." questions with answers, is a gem for education queries. Some general guides to reference works in specific fields are:

Aby, S. H. (1997). *Sociology: A guide to reference and information sources* (2nd ed.). Englewood, CO: Libraries Unlimited.

Freed, M. N., Hess, R. K., & Ryan, J. M. (2002). *The educators' desk reference (EDR)* (2nd ed.). Westport, CT: Praeger.

Reed, J., & Baxter, P. M. (2003). *Library use: A handbook for psychology* (3rd ed.). Washington, DC: American Psychological Association.

Roberts, A. R., & Greene, G. J. (2002). *Social workers' desk reference.* New York: Oxford University Press.

Women's studies database: bibliography. University of Maryland, Women's Studies Program (http://www.mith2.umd.edu/WomensStudies/Bibliographies/).

The Internet virtual libraries include psychology, economics, sociology, women's studies, and social sciences. Each is subdivided into topics that provide access to Web sites dealing with aspects of the subject matter. Access the virtual libraries at http://vlib.org.

In any search engine try "(subject of interest) bibliography" with and without the quotation marks.

Reviews of Research

New work integrated with, or building on, the old is included in reviews of research. You can find such reviews in annual review books and research review journals. A committee of relevant specialists usually puts together the annuals, allocating space to cover the topics of an area according to the importance and extent of recent work. Reviewers evaluate this material and place it in context of previous research in a way valuable to the novice. Two useful annual review sources are:

• Annual Reviews, Inc. publishes annual reviews in anthropology, psychology, and sociology (e.g., *Annual Review of Anthropology*), as well as a number of other areas such as medicine and the biological and physical sciences.

• *Review of Research in Education* is published annually by the American Educational Research Association.

In addition, many professional associations publish yearbooks that serve the same purpose. For example, the National Society for the Study of Education publishes several yearbooks each year, each providing an examination of a particular topic. There are also a variety of journals devoted to reviews, such as *American Sociological Review, Psychological Review, Review of Educational Research,* and *Sociological Review*. To find others, use a search engine, inputting "(subject) review journal." ⑨ ⑪

Review journals and books, handbooks, and encyclopedias are considered **secondary sources** because they give someone's opinion about what the research said; they do not usually reproduce the original research. Therefore, especially when you have doubts about the conclusions of a review or summary or wish additional detail, consult the original source. Access to original research is facilitated by indexing and abstracting services.

Journal Indexing and Abstracting Services

Research reports are typically found in journals. Exceptions are large reports that become a monograph or a book, as when researchers summarize their work—for instance, the Kounin example in chapter 3. Journals are also where you will find the most recent work and can spot emerging topics. ⑦ ⑪ This literature is accessible through a variety of indexing and abstracting services, with many specialized compilations available for nooks and crannies (e.g., *Language and Language Behavior Abstracts, Physical Education/Sports Index, College Student Personnel Abstracts*). Again, search engines will show those that are in your interest area: "(subject) research abstracts."

Abstracting and indexing services compiled into computer-searchable form are referred to as databases and usually include multiyear volumes. The database form sometimes has a different but related name (and may contain additional material). For instance, *Psychological Abstracts* as a database is titled *PsycInfo*. Currently available databases are listed in the *Gale Directory of Online Databases* (Nolan, 1983–present). ⑰

Most abstracting and indexing services cover only journal articles, but there are exceptions. *PsychBOOKS* has included books and book chapters since 1987.

Open Access Publications

The ease of access to publications provided by the Internet, the high costs of publishing, and the fact that much of the editorial work of journals is provided as a service by the profession all have contributed to the movement to open journals to Internet access and to publishing online, either in institutional or disciplinary archives or in online journals. This movement was given impetus at a meeting called by the Open Society Institute in December of 2001. The purpose of the meeting was to accelerate progress in the international effort to make research articles in all academic fields freely available on the Internet. The resulting Budapest Open Access Initiative signed by those attending has since attracted many individual and organizational signers. While open access is slow in being adopted by organizations and publishers who are afraid they will lose revenue, it has gained many adherents, as evidenced by the *Directory of Open Access Journals'* current listing of 1,142 journals (Anthropology–43, Education–181, Psychology–68, Social Sciences–110, Sociology–59). Many are searchable at the article level so that one can search the collection of journals across all fields by keyword and author (http://www.doaj.org).

Document and Book Delivery Services

The first place to turn for materials that are not available at your library is its interlibrary loan department. Not only books but also photocopied articles can be obtained that way and they are likely to have access to commercial services as well. However, fee-required document delivery services can supplement interlibrary loan. The Document Solution® (http://www.isinet.com/products/docdelivery/ids/) supplies full text articles from almost anywhere. Articles in journals published by the American Psychological Association are available from their Full-Text Document Delivery Service (http://www.apa.org/psycinfo/fulltext.html).

TYPES OF INDEXES

Two kinds of subject indexes you should be familiar with are controlled vocabulary indexes and keyword indexes. **Controlled vocabulary** subject indexing resembles a book index but uses a controlled vocabulary because library catalogers, or reference works such as *Psychological Abstracts*, can't use a set of terms one year and another the next. Without a standard set of terms you wouldn't know what to search across years. Although in book cataloging most large libraries use *Library of Congress Subject Headings (LCSH)*, there is no single listing that other references follow. Each may publish a thesaurus or list—for example, *Thesaurus of Psychological Index Terms* (in *PsycInfo*, online in a subscription database; look under advanced search); *Thesaurus of ERIC Descriptors* (available as a tab in searches at http://www.eric.ed.gov/); *Medical Subject Headings (MeSH)* (http://www.nlm.nih.gov/mesh/); *Thesaurus for Sociological Abstracts* (online in a subscription database; look under the tab search tools).

Controlled vocabularies are conceptually based, hierarchical structures that start with main headings and then subdivide to account for specialties within them. They are often published as a list or thesaurus; consulting them is like getting an aerial view of a maze to save time over the trial-and-error method.

Keyword indexes are alphabetical lists of terms used to describe aspects deemed important and likely to be the subject of searches by people familiar with the material. Each item has more access points because typically it will have more keywords than "see also" index entries. The differences between the two types are summarized in Table 6.1.

Table 6.1   A Comparison of Controlled Vocabulary with Keyword Methods of Subject Matter Cataloging and Indexing

Controlled Vocabulary Cataloging and Indexing	Keyword Cataloging and Indexing
A periodically updated standard set of terms usually published as a dictionary or thesaurus.	Keywords are those most descriptive of important components and are the search terms that readers are likely to use.
Consistent in the use of the standard set of terms over time, but each system has its own term set.	Other than using words based on their standard meaning, no special efforts are made to maintain consistency.
New terms are incorporated only after they are considered established.	New terms show up immediately; keeps up with field's jargon; requires knowing the current jargon.
PsycInfo, *Sociological Abstracts*, and *ERIC* add descriptors where adequate description requires it.	As many key terms as are needed can be assigned.
Based on a conceptualization of the field; usually hierarchical; new terms often subdivide broader terms.	No structure.
Structure reflects historical roots; subjects lodged together may be no longer considered closely related (e.g., psychology and philosophy).	Lacking structure, terms do not show relationships among fields; finding related material requires knowing comparable terms.
Professional indexer or cataloger assigns classification.	Abstractor, indexer, and very often, author, assign keywords. Web site authors list invisible keywords for browsers; add software metatags for search engines.
Likely to feature only one or two subject entries besides author and title.	Likely to feature more entries than controlled vocabulary.

A Literature Search Example (Including Tips on Computer Use)

Those who like to learn by example will especially welcome this section of the chapter. It describes how a student, Liz Howard, went about her literature search. In doing so, it illustrates the many routes one can take and the variety of tools that are available to harvest the available material on a topic. The illustrations both summarize the chapter's literature search suggestions and move them from abstract to concrete. They also demonstrate how the computer has opened new pathways for searching while making the search easier and more effective.

Let's revisit Figure 6.1 (replicated here as Figure 6.2 on the following page). The figure displays four starting points from which a search can be initiated—your computer, your faculty, your university's physical library, and your university library's virtual library—but it also shows that you can start at any of these points and follow a variety of paths to uncover new information and new leads. The circled numbers in the figure match those in the following material, indicating the location in the diagram of the various literature search events. Working back and forth between the figure and the text will provide a useful perspective on all the possibilities as the description proceeds.

The Search Process

From her own personal experience, Liz Howard was convinced that students learned better when she showed enthusiasm for the subjects she was teaching. She thought that there was probably evidence for this generalization in the literature, but, more than that, she wondered if showing enthusiasm was a teachable skill. Too many of her colleagues seemed to show little. If they had been taught to show enthusiasm during their student teaching, might they now be more successful teachers? Was there any research on this? Where to start?

Liz turned to her institution's online virtual library ⑯ because she had picked up a pamphlet earlier that explained how to access the library's Web site from her off-campus computer. Her university's library made a large number of online databases available to its students through its subscription to Academic OneFile. ⑰ So she tapped into it from home, using her student number and name to gain access. She had been advised that it was an interesting place to start—it is such a broad base of material in so many fields that it might turn up some interesting things.

How about searching "teacher enthusiasm"? On opening OneFile, Liz saw she could do a Basic Search, Subject Guide Search, Publication Search, or Advanced Search. She thought she'd like something more than a basic search, but she wasn't ready for an advanced one and didn't know what publications to search, so she tried the Subject Guide Search. Searching "teacher enthusiasm" brought her a long list of terms related to her topic, including the number of entries in the database for each one. Teacher Education seemed appropriate and had over 5,000 entries. Under its heading were clickable "Subdivisions" and "Related Subjects." Clicking on Subdivisions showed her a similar list but with a refined list of descriptors and fewer entries for each. Evaluation had 162 entries and Research had 164. Clicking on them brought Liz to titles of individual articles she could skim for relevance, and while a bit over 300 is a large group, it was a skimable number. She printed them out to peruse while she tried another way to approach the topic while still at the computer.

How about using one of the search engines like AltaVista on the Internet from her home computer? Liz found that AltaVista turned up 1.7 million responses for the term *enthusiasm* and 2,750 for *teacher enthusiasm*, 2.5 million responses for *motivation*, and over 1,500 for *motivating students*. Too many responses! Maybe she should

Figure 6.2   How sources of information lead to other potential sources.

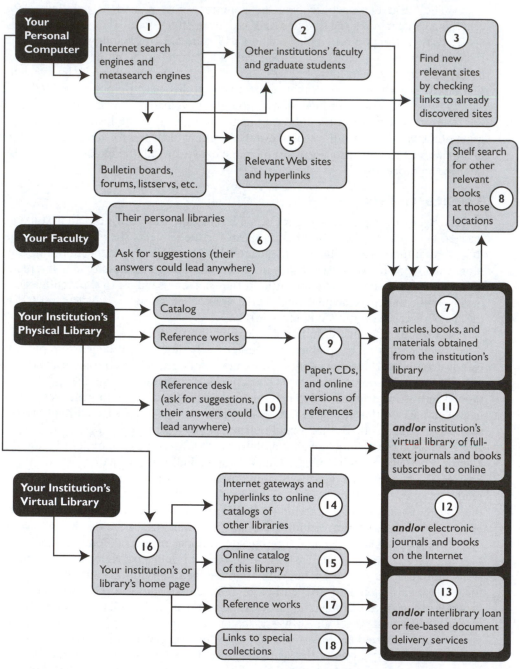

have started by asking whether teacher enthusiasm does indeed result in higher student achievement. So she put the following double-barreled term into AltaVista: "teacher enthusiasm" and "student achievement." ① The quotation marks assured that the words they enclosed would be adjacent, not in separate places. Being connected by "and" assured that both phrases would be present in a response. Liz still got large, but manageable, results: 175 responses. (She might have obtained different results if she had tried other search engines like Yahoo or Google, or a meta-search engine that sends the search to multiple search engines like Dogpile or Clusty.)

She clicked on the first response because it was presumably the most relevant. Although not research itself, the article titled "Teacher Enthusiasm in Upper Grades" included references to four journal articles, three dealing with the relation of enthusiasm to achievement. ⑤ The fourth, a 1983 article by Bettencourt, Gillett, and Gall, was research on the effect of enthusiasm training! Right on target, Liz thought, how lucky! Now she had relevant leads. She could look up the Bettencourt article and see whom they cited to get an idea of who was interested in this area prior to 1983 (actually probably 1981, given the typically approximate two-year lag for the publication process). Their references would provide still more leads. Once researchers have relevant literature as a starting point, they can work backward by examining the work on which they built (e.g., the references in the Bettencourt article), and forward by finding studies that built on these studies.

How did Liz search forward? When she wondered aloud to her faculty adviser as to who might have built on Bettencourt, ⑥ he suggested consulting a citation index, in this instance the *Social Science Citation Index* (in *Web of Science*). There she could see who cited her starting-point literature and thus possibly built further research on it.

Liz again turned to her institution's online virtual library. ⑯ She tapped into it from home but found that the citation indexes were not available. She called the library's reference desk ⑩ about this and learned that because *Social Science Citation Index* was an expensive subscription, her library did not subscribe online. Not having heard of **citation indexing**, she was glad to find a tutorial to *Web of Science* online (http://scientific.thompsonreuters.com/tutorials/wos7/). Her library did provide Social Science Citation Index in CD and paper format, so Liz went to the library to access it on CD. ⑨ She would have had to go there anyway to consult the copy of the *American Educational Research Journal* in which the Bettencourt article appeared. ⑦

As Liz thought about what she was finding, she wondered if her search shouldn't be wider than those references linked to the Bettencourt article. Shouldn't she do a book and article search, maybe including electronic journals? She decided to start with an article search; if there were relevant books too, the article search might turn them up in the citations. Since her library made databases available online, Liz could easily do a search of the journal literature from her home computer. ⑰ That way, she wouldn't have to go to the library to wait her turn at a computer for the library's CDs, nor access paper copies that typically cover only a year or at most five years. In contrast, online versions typically compile results across all the years for which digital data is available.

For Liz's topic, the librarian at the reference desk ⑩ recommended starting with *PsycInfo*, one of *FirstSearch*'s databases. ⑰ Her search of its database turned up a number of relevant articles. One of these articles was available in full text from the database *WilsonSelectPlus*, ⑪ to which her university subscribed as part of *First-Search's* databases. This saved a trip to the library. It looked like an important article in a journal that her library did not subscribe to, so she ordered a copy from the inter-library loan office on her library's Web site. ⑬ Later, she got an e-mail that she could pick up a photocopy of the article at the circulation desk.

Liz had noticed an entry that read "More like this" on the *FirstSearch* record of the important journal article. ⑰ Clicking on it opened a form where she could refine her search by checking several of the search terms offered. This led her to several additional relevant journal articles. ⑦ Once she got into the literature, she found that there were a variety of paths to search. She'd searched conventionally published journals; what about those published only in online electronic journals? She input *directories "electronic journals"* (note the quotation marks that went around only "electronic journals") at Google. ①

How did Liz know to put her query to Google in quotes? The reference librarian had mentioned to her that the best way to learn to use Google was to read Nancy Blachman's *Google Guide* (http://googleguide.com). In particular she read the sec-tion on interpreting queries that explained how to use Google's symbols to ensure her query was correctly understood. She noted that although there was a directory listed for the Association of Research Libraries, she couldn't find it on the site. There were lists in particular fields, like psychology (http://psych.hanover.edu/Krantz/journal.html) and other fields, but she didn't see an overall list. She thought that strange but then had an inspiration. She tried *list "electronic journals."* Lo and behold, there it was—an a-to-z list (http://sfx7.exlibrisgroup.com/cambridge/az). Liz thought to herself, that just shows how important it is to try a variation of the original search when it doesn't yield what was wanted.

Since the above sources were online, Liz could copy and paste from them into her notes, saving the retyping labor. However, while she might copy and paste com-plex material such as data or other material difficult to summarize, when she found highly relevant articles that she could epitomize, she summarized instead of copying and pasting them. This was because she remembered the research of Katayama, Shambaugh, and Edmonds (2004), whose title read "Why Keying-in the Notes May Lead to Higher Knowledge Transfer." She found that she remembered the material better, and it was more readily accessible in her mind when she created a note instead of cutting and pasting.

As Liz had hoped, the e-journal literature had turned up a book that appeared to be of interest. A check of her library's online catalog ⑮ showed her that it was not checked out, so she went in to pick it up. ⑦ While at the library, she also looked at the other books that were shelved in the same vicinity. ⑧ Shelf searches often turn up surprises—new books just shelved and old ones still relevant, although no longer much cited. Particularly competent past writers often had a unique perspective on the field or a different approach that could be helpful to present-day researchers. Reading such eminent thinkers is often worthwhile.

Checking the shelves drew Liz's attention to gaps where books were checked out. Now that she knew the relevant call numbers, she could also do a shelf search from her home computer. ⑮ In doing this, she discovered what looked to be a particularly relevant book that was already charged out; she placed a recall on it from her computer so she would be notified by e-mail when it was available. Although she didn't do so, Liz realized that she also could have done a shelf search of the online catalogs of other nearby universities Ⓖ with different collections. Incidentally, when she mentioned to her advisor that she had to wait for the book to be recalled, he told her that he had it and loaned it to her from his personal library. ⑥

Clearly, Liz mused, there are multiple paths to following up leads; what is another one? Once she had the first names of the Bettencourt article authors (too many false responses with just first-name initials) Liz put them in a search engine to see if they had Web sites. ① One, Meredith D. Gall, ⑤ did turn up, and the vita on his Web site listed his publications. In addition to the article he wrote with Bettencourt, the only other relevant item was a 1980 presentation to an American Educational Research Association convention. Apparently Gall did not continue research in this field. But where might Liz find the 1980 convention presentation? She called the reference desk ⑩ and was told that convention presentations having to do with education are often included in the Education Resources Information Center (ERIC) (http://eric.ed.gov/search), a compilation of abstracts and full texts of education research and materials supported by the federal government. ⑪ It can be searched by author, title, and subject. A search of the ERIC database for the paper failed because the government switched vendors and some of the old material was not in the database.

Liz also could have checked *Current Contents, Social and Behavioral Sciences* edition, which also lists convention proceedings, abstracts, and program listings. ⑨ But since that would not yield the complete text, she decided to contact the author through his Web site and ask if he had a copy he could send her. He was glad to e-mail her a copy and glad that she had asked.

At that moment, Liz heard her kitchen timer ring. She had set it at the suggestion of Mary Ellen Bates, who does searches for a living (http://batesinfo.com). Ms. Bates advises setting the timer for 15 minutes when starting a search project. When it goes off, stop, assess where you have been, and decide whether you are still on the most profitable course. Liz did so and decided that she now knew the terms that would turn up references of interest. So she decided to try a meta-search engine that queries several search engines at once (i.e., Dogpile). ① Clusty, another meta-search engine, clusters responses. It presents a list of topics representing clusters of common responses—particularly useful if there are multiple interpretations of a search term, some of which are irrelevant. Since her query required more than one term to describe what she wanted (and to assure all three terms were present in every response), Liz placed plus signs between them (e.g., enthusiasm+teacher+training). (If she had wanted the three words to show up as an exact phrase, she would have put them in quotation marks instead of joining with plus signs.)

She turned up a number of relevant sites to check. ⑤ When she found relevant references on the sites, she copied and pasted the entries into bibliographic software (input "bibliographic software" in a search engine to find them; they are proprietary but most have student prices). The software would save her time by formatting them into proper APA or MLA format. In still another way of following up leads, having found one faculty member's Web site with particularly relevant work, Liz checked to see what sites were linked to Bobbi Kerlin, another relevant Web site. By placing http://link: followed by any Web site's address (its URL) in Google (e.g., http://link:kerlins.net/bobbi/), ③ she obtained a list of Web sites linked to Kerlin, some of which touched on her research topic.

The URL for one site turned up a "404 not found" message; Liz trimmed successive pieces from the complex URL (e.g., from [http://www.ualberta.ca/~jrnorris/qda.html] she trimmed to [http://www.ualberta.ca/~jrnorris] and then to [http://www.ualberta.ca]) until she found one that worked. From there she was able to trace the new location of the one she originally sought.

Liz noted that this author had also been an officer in an interest group of the American Educational Research Association. Using the search engine Yahoo she found the association's Web site ① and, from there, the interest group's Web site. ⑤ It indicated that the group sponsored a listserv. ④ A listserv records free-floating e-mail conversations on topics contributors raise for discussion. Liz had to register to become a member of the listserv. She received an e-mail of directions for participating and also for accessing the archives. She searched the archives of the previous discussions and found some interesting material on her topic. She also noted which persons actively contributed to the site on her topic and searched for their Web sites and publications. She also noted that it was not uncommon for graduate students to ask for assistance on this Web site—references on a topic, useful software, and technical assistance. She filed that away in the back of her mind for future use. ②

Organizing the Notes

One of the difficult problems of an extensive literature search is keeping track of interrelated points in your notes. Liz had taken a lot of notes, and it was time to organize them. Using a word processor's table function (or she could have used a spreadsheet program), she entered her notes in the first column of a table made up of four or more columns. She placed the source of each note in the second column. She confined each note to a single aspect of her topic. Thus, a note might be a phrase, a sentence, several sentences, a paragraph, and so on. Each note occupied a row so she might use many successive rows to include all the notes on a single source. In the third column she put a descriptor of the most relevant aspect—a keyword or code that described the note. Since there may be other relevant characteristics (e.g., grade level, gender, etc.) she put those in a fourth column. Depending on the study, she might need more than just two descriptors and thus more columns. She used a separate column for each type of descriptor. For example, for a 1975 dissertation by Mary Collins her first descriptor was "effect size," which indicated the study had such data, and her second descriptor indicated it had a control group—both important characteristics of this study.

DESCRIPTIVE NOTE	SOURCE	1ST KEYWORD	2ND KEYWORD
1975 study of enthusiasm training	Collins	Effect size	Control group

If Liz performed a meta-analysis of relevant studies, she could sort her notes to find those with effect sizes and also those with control groups. To sort her notes this way, she used the sort function in the table menu. She first did an alphabetical sort to bring together the rows for the same secondary descriptor, and then similarly sorted on the primary descriptors. This moved notes with the same descriptors into successive rows. Considering how she might outline her material brought to her attention the areas where the notes were thin and those where they were ample. This would provide a road map to guide her in further literature searching. For an online description of the use of a word processor, see "Categorizing, Coding, and Manipulating Qualitative Data Using the WordPerfect® Word Processor" by John H. Carney, Joseph F. Joiner, and Helen Tragou (http://www.nova.edu/ssss/QR/QR3-1/carney.html).

As indicated in the example above, Liz generated a lot of notes; this is typical. She used software with which she was familiar that did the job, but in a somewhat awkward manner. She traded off awkwardness for the time required to learn new software. If the notes are really voluminous, however, it may be worth learning specialized software. For instance, Liz could have used qualitative analysis software (see the discussion beginning on p. 315. Free downloadable demonstration software allows you to try out coding notes, interrelating codes, and organizing them. Student prices reduce the cost.) There are several examples that show how to use them; di Gregorio (2003) used Nvivo for her literature search. Look under "Training Tasters" (http://www.sdgassociates.com/mainframe.html).

Another way to organize is to make concept maps or pattern notes, described and illustrated at the end of the previous chapter. They involve using a type of flowchart to indicate how the various concepts involved in a problem relate to each other.

Tips for Writing the Review of the Literature

Whether verbal or numerical, an integrative review of the literature around unifying frameworks, theories, or explanations is the goal.
Keep these suggestions in mind:

- Aim for a coherent, integrated, critical examination of selected relevant literature.

- Relate the problem to the network of theory and explanations already existing in the field whenever possible.

- Show how this study fits with and "stands on the shoulders" of previous work.

- Read some **original sources**, not just secondary sources; especially do not depend on just one secondary source. Read in depth to the cutting edge and backward in time. Include seminal sources, deep thinkers who really grasp the field.

- Look for technical and design flaws to avoid and for innovations you may use.

- Use a thesaurus or a search-term dictionary. It forces you to think your search strategy through and teaches the standardized terminology of the field. It adds to your search terms the descriptors used in highly relevant publications.

- Record each entry immediately in whatever bibliographic style you plan to use; then you'll know you have all the required information. (Software is available to assist in this task—e.g., EndNote, ProCite, Reference Manager; most libraries have the major citation style guides online in the reference category.)

- Be sure to label photocopies with the source when it is not in the heading or footer.

- Do a computer search of the journal literature.

(continued)

- Check sources of current information to find others working on your problem. Search the Internet, the citation indexes, *Current Contents: Social and Behavioral Sciences*, the subject indexes of the programs of recent relevant professional association meetings.
- Actively think about, argue with, praise, and otherwise react to your reading—do so with colleagues as well as yourself.

Avoid errors such as these:

- Aiming for comprehensiveness instead of discussing the best articles that bear on the topic.
- Merely citing previous work instead of relating it to the problem with an explanation of its contribution.
- Accepting the methods of others uncritically instead of being appropriately critical or laudatory of aspects that deserve comment.
- Providing a loose collection of citations and miscellaneous facts that show coverage but little understanding.

ADDITIONAL READING

See Reed and Baxter (2003) for psychological topics and those at all related; Freed, Hess, and Ryan (2002) for education related topics; and White (1994) for an excellent chapter on social sciences in general.

For scales to judge the quality of a literature review, see Boote and Beile (2005).

For links to useful information sites, see The Extreme Searcher's Web Page; click on *here* in "Click here for links to the sites covered in the second edition" (http://www.extremesearcher.com).

For Web searching see Calishain (2005), or for specific questions search the archives of her daily newsletter (http://www.researchbuzz.com/new_users.shtml).

For reviews of Web-searching books, see Sherman (2005), or do a search for "Web searching book reviews."

Hart's (2001) book is more about the construction of the literature review—even to the inclusion of instruction in logic—than about the nuts and bolts.

IMPORTANT TERMS AND CONCEPTS

citation indexing	keyword indexes
computer searches	meta-analysis
controlled vocabulary	original sources
cross-references	secondary sources
database	

OPPORTUNITIES FOR ADDITIONAL LEARNING

1. You are beginning an examination of how instruction in learning strategies will affect the achievement of high school students in history. You are seeking an overview of research on learning strategies and key authors in this area. Where might you start, both to better define the research questions and to answer these questions?

2. A colleague has referred you to articles by Wittrock and Jonassen for your topic of generative strategies in learning. How might you go about finding more on the topic and exploring the work of these researchers?

3. You are studying the use of the new whole-language approach in elementary basal readers. How might a computer search make this review of the literature easier to complete?

4. Designing instruction to accommodate different learning styles has gained attention in recent years. How might you sample recent research in the field to determine the history and future direction of learning-style-based instruction?

5. A project to teach senior adults the use of computers is being developed in the local school district. You are going to be studying how effective the chosen methods of instruction are with these learners. Why might you do a literature review first? Why not?

APPLICATION EXERCISE

Continuing the exercise begun in chapter 5, take your chosen topic, and using Figure 6.1 choose the most relevant entry point. To gain familiarity with the reference works at upper and lower entry points, perhaps choose more than one point, pretending that you know more or less than you do. Consult the various general and specific sources listed. Be sure to include the use of such references as a citation index, *Current Contents: Social and Behavioral Sciences*, and at least one journal index or abstract source such as *Psychological Abstracts*. Do an online search. As you work, consult the general suggestions at the end of the chapter.

KEY TO ADDITIONAL LEARNING OPPORTUNITIES

1. Search-engine searches might lead you to encyclopedias and handbooks with relevant material that might help you determine what terminology is used for this topic, gain an overview, and pick out keywords and authors. The information on keywords and authors might then be used to access the journal indexes and abstracts. Descriptors or keywords (or both) may be used, depending on the index. If an online virtual library is available, these might be used for a more comprehensive search once the terms have been determined. Indexing and abstracting services can provide an overview of current research, help locate review articles, identify authors who appear frequently, and show various aspects of a topic. Once key authors and works are found, *Social Science Citation Index* (SSCI) (in *Web of Science*) could be used to determine who has cited these authors and thus possibly contributed to furthering the directions of this research.

2. To trace the works of the authors, you could search some of the major indexes by author to locate all their works (or their Web sites, if they have one). Then you might check the citation index of SSCI to determine who has cited their works on generative strategies. This could lead you to more recent work on the topic.

   It would also be useful to locate review articles that deal with learning and specifically touch on generative strategies. This would help situate the topic on a conceptual map and lead you to other sources that might contain information on the topic or be related to it.

   To find still more on this topic, you would probably first check the thesauri for **cross-reference** terms that are broader, narrower, related to, or used for "generative learning strategies." If "generative learning strategies" or its parts were not used in the major indexes with thesauri, keyword searching would be the next step. This is possible in SSCI, ERIC, and *PsycInfo*. When relevant articles appear, look at the descriptors or subject headings used to index those articles for further leads to search. References in the articles themselves are usually relevant to the topic and provide additional avenues to follow.

3. Computerized searching makes it easier to search for terms such as "whole-language approach" that are not descriptors or subject headings. This is especially true for new terms or specific topics that might be subsumed in larger concepts. It also allows the search to combine more than one concept in a search. For example, the search in this case could look for articles that are about whole language, about basals, and about the elementary level all at the same time. This is a great time-saver. If the whole-language approach were a recent idea in the literature, this computerized search would also help identify the appropriate indexing terms. It would point out the major authors in the field and reveal the research frontier on the topic.

4. Encyclopedias, handbooks, and the online catalog will give you a start in tracing the history of the field of learning-style-based instruction. Bibliographies on the topic, located through the online catalog or through *Bibliographic Index Plus*, may also be useful. Articles on the topic can be found in ERIC and *PsycInfo*. You could use the large number of journal indexing and abstracting services to locate articles and then narrow the topic to something workable. Use *Dissertation Abstracts International* to find dissertations.

5. A literature review before the study begins would provide background on senior adult learners and methods of instruction in computer use. It could point out which methodologies work and which ones don't. It could help determine the variables, relationships, and confounding factors in other such studies. In addition, it would show the state of research on the topic.

However, some researchers might argue that such a literature review done before the study might bias the observations through preconceived notions of what should happen. If the treatment and the sample are already set, it might predispose the researcher to expect certain results based on prior research. They prefer to search the literature after they have "mucked around" in data or observations on their own to better define what they are looking for.

*   *   *

The section "A Literature Search Example" (earlier in this chapter) provides a more complete summary of the chapter than could be provided here.

A Look Ahead

Your literature search will have suggested how your variables are related—in most instances, causally. Although we take causality for granted, it is nevertheless worth examining to see on what basis one can reasonably infer it—the topic of the next chapter.

III

Foundational Research Concepts

To build a firm foundation for studying research, regardless of method, you need to understand some underlying basic concepts. They provide the supporting structure and the criteria to be met for research to be accepted as contributing to knowledge.

- Chapter 7 discusses causation and the criteria used to show it. Chapter 4's chain of reasoning forms the basis for the presentation of findings that support causation. Criteria flowing from the chain, the study's Internal Integrity, link its variables in a causal relationship or link variables in a process.

- Chapter 8 discusses generality. If variables are related causally or in a process, how generalizable is that relationship? Because sampling is the basis for generalizing from one context to others—its External Generality—this chapter describes the principles of sampling and their pervasive application to the links in the chain of reasoning.

- Chapter 9 examines additional criteria and constraints applied to studies. We optimize each study for these three criteria: (1) the credibility we build with our audience, (2) the balance of Internal Integrity and External Generality, and (3) the allocation of resources. And we do so within these three constraints: (1) our resource limits, (2) what institutions will allow, and (3) what is ethically permissible.

- Chapter 10 considers in more detail how we determine what is ethically permissible. It describes the safeguards that the federal government has erected to protect human subjects and the codes of conduct that professional societies have developed to guide researchers.

- Chapter 11 describes the logic of design. We design studies so that they logically allow us to infer relations, determine their nature, and exclude rival explanations.

The criteria and constraints that flow from the chain of reasoning combine into a model that will prove useful over and over again in conceptualizing, implementing, and evaluating research studies. For that reason, its diagram is on the inside front cover of this text for easy reference.

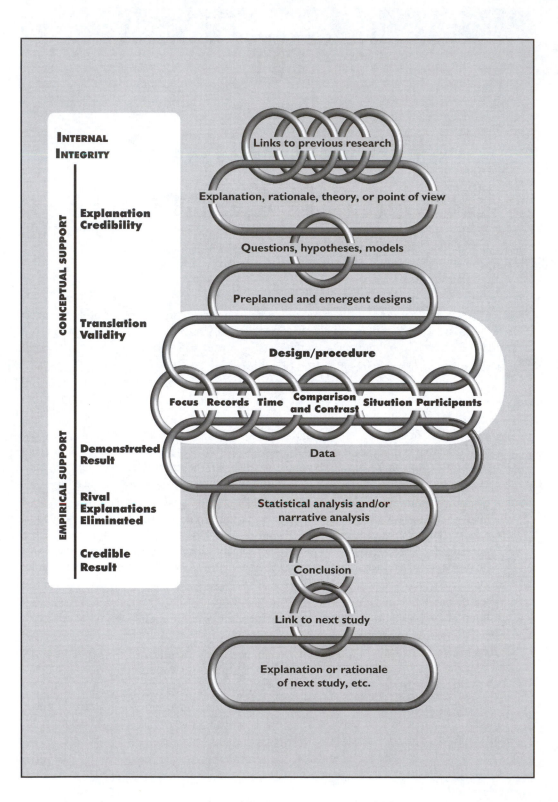

7

Causal Inference and Internal Integrity

> Rags make paper, paper makes money, money makes banks, banks make loans, loans make poverty, poverty makes rags.
>
> —Anonymous
>
> For want of a nail the shoe was lost, for want of a shoe the horse was lost, for want of a horse the rider was lost. . . . For want of a nail, the battle was lost!
>
> —George Herbert (1593–1633)

The review of literature discussed in the previous chapter will most likely provide you with the question that sparks your study, or provides the basis for a proposed rationale, hypothesis, or model to be studied. In many cases you will be investigating not only whether variables are related, but also whether they are *causally* related. This chapter is about causation and what judgments allow us to infer it from the evidence internal to the study—its Internal Integrity. A parallel set of judgments allows an inference of how broadly the relationship applies, its generality external to the circumstances of this study—its **External Generality.** That is the topic of the next chapter.

As we saw in chapter 3, audiences make knowing judgments about the proper interpretation of data; hence, findings are usually presented as a logical chain of reasoning. This and the following chapter also show how these judgments are derived from the links in that chain.

INTRODUCTION

The term *cause* is often used very loosely. Such usage frequently hides at least three sets of complexities: (1) different understandings of what is meant by the term, (2) different perceptions of the nature of the world and their implications for what a social science can be, and (3) the variety of complex as well as simple causal patterns to consider. This chapter will both sensitize you to these different understandings and examine common patterns.

However, the term *cause* is not always appropriate. Consider the temperature and pressure of a gas, for example. Either can be considered cause or effect in different contexts, and the language of causality does not adequately describe the relationship. Similarly, it is problematical to ask whether stress is a cause of failure to succeed, or failure to succeed is a cause of stress. Although discussed in the context of causality, Internal Integrity and External Generality apply more broadly than causal relationships; they work equally well with any cyclical, interactive, and reversible relationships, or especially with processes in which either variable can be considered the cause or the effect. We can apply these concepts to determine the existence, extent, and nature of relationships and their generality.

ASSOCIATION AND CAUSALITY

The fact that things vary together and thus are apparently related doesn't mean that the relationship is necessarily causal, in the sense that changes in one caused the other to change. Many relationships are associations, resulting from the fact that both are influenced by one or more variables. Yet we often incorrectly impute causality where the evidence is sufficient only to establish association. Consider, for instance, this headline:

SCHOOLWORK UNDERMINED BY TV, CALIFORNIA SURVEY SHOWS

We've all been taught to always read the small print under the headline. While the headline says television viewing caused poor schoolwork, the article itself interprets the evidence more cautiously:

> The more a student watches television, the worse he does in school. . . . No conclusions were drawn as to why television watching seems to go hand in hand with lower reading, writing and math test scores. (*Report on Educational Research*, November 26, 1980)

The author was careful to walk the fine line between *association* and *causation*; instead of ascribing causation he said they merely go "hand in hand." Indeed, the fact that they vary together could be explained by the fact that poorer students prefer watching exciting TV to struggling with difficult and often unrewarding schoolwork. This is but one example of the care we must use with the concept of causation. Some people consider the conceptual difficulties of using the term *cause* so serious that they believe its use should be abandoned. We cannot do justice to that volume of literature here, but we can alert you to some of the common complexities that may suggest some directions to explore.

COMPLEXITIES IN THE CONCEPT OF CAUSE

An important complexity is that whenever we use the term *cause,* without realizing it we are emphasizing a part of a causal history. Consider that a car stops with the gas gauge at empty. Did it stop because it ran out of gas? That seems to be the immediate cause. But perhaps the real cause was the driver's lack of attention to the gas gauge or the fact that the driver never learned regular habits of maintenance and the necessity of allocating time for them. Perhaps, even more basically, because his parents always took care of the maintenance tasks, he never learned to be responsible for them. Each is a step back toward a more "fundamental" cause, and each is part of the **causal chain**. *Use of the term* cause *always means selecting the part of a causal chain that is the most appropriate for a particular inquiry.*

Which Is the Cause in the Causal Chain?

Sometimes cause is defined as the last link that completes the causal chain—a football player flops into an antique chair; it comes apart, depositing him abruptly and painfully on the floor. He is perceived as the "cause" of the chair's demise. But in reality, he is but the last link in a years-long causal chain as the glue changed to powder, the sockets dried out, the wood shrank, innumerable individuals of varying weights sat in it and loosened the joints, and so on.

We often attribute cause to the last link in the causal chain because it is the most immediate and obvious. There are many choices, however: the part that is most immediate in time, most important, most able to be remedied, most fundamental, the part without which the event would not have occurred (the necessary part). As Lewis (1983) notes, one cause may be salient in a particular context, another in a different context. By selectively choosing from a causal history, he argues, we "explain" an action. That is, explaining an occurrence means giving some information about its causal history. Thus, we can describe the causal chain for a particular situation—as one of the chapter's opening quotes traces the chain from the missing horseshoe nail to the lost battle. But more usefully, we can describe a chain that generalizes across situations. That is what we do when we set forth a hypothesis or theory—for example, economic theory. "Lowering interest rates increases business activity" describes not just one causal situation but a whole host of them. It is a proposition that has *generality*, and it is a kind that we seek in building a social science.

Solving problems is sometimes easier when we view them from the perspective of a causal chain. This approach can reveal where intervention will affect subsequent events. For example, the threat of acquired immune deficiency syndrome (AIDS) may be combated at an early link in the chain through education for sexual abstinence. At a later link, we could promote the use of condoms or make sterile needles available to drug users who might otherwise share them. At a still later link, we could seek a drug that will attack the virus. Of these, we might consider the earliest, the least expensive, the most likely to succeed, and the most socially acceptable. Examination of the causal chain suggests where to break the cause-and-effect relationship.

Causes as Inferences

Assuming we continue to use the term *cause*, a continuing puzzle for philosophers has been to determine what conditions permit its use. David Hume (1902 [1748]), for instance, advanced the commonsense criteria: (1) cause and effect occur close together in time, (2) the cause always appears before the effect, and (3) the cause is present whenever the effect is observed. However, we can think of exceptions to the first condition:

the association of smoking with cancer or emphysema. The effects of smoking are cumulative rather then immediate. As for the second condition, when a racquet hits the tennis ball, what precedes what? This condition may be improved by changing it to "the effect did not begin before the cause began," but the change does not solve all the problems.

Some people have argued that we should find the **necessary** and **sufficient conditions** for a phenomenon. Sufficient conditions are all those conditions in the presence of which the effect will occur. But without trying all the possible causes, we would never know whether we had missed a sufficient condition—there may still be one we hadn't tried. So we say that causal relationships are always inferred, never proven.

We say that causation is an inference for still another reason, a prime one: We never directly sense a causal connection. A billiard ball hits another and bounces away; we do not directly "see" the causal connection. The compression of the billiard ball material seems a reasonable explanation. Maybe oxygen atoms on the surface repel the balls. We must infer the most reasonable explanation from the circumstances; the attribution of causation is always an inference on our part.

Validated Causal Propositions Escape Disconfirmation

Popper (1959) points out that even though causal propositions and theories cannot be proven, they can be tested. Indeed, he argues that our major responsibility is to try to falsify such relationships by posing hypotheses about them and try to prove them false—finding instances in which, although expected to do so, they do not hold. As he puts it, "man proposes, nature disposes." Theories and propositions are never proved; they merely escape **disconfirmation**. As noted in chapter 3, Cronbach (1982) views this process of escaping disconfirmation as one of "reducing uncertainty." Of course, once they have escaped disconfirmation enough times—the self-correcting nature of science—we consider them part of that structure we call "knowledge."

▶ Any explanation selects some part of the causal chain to highlight.

▶ The term *cause* is often used to designate the last link that completes the chain but there are many other possibilities: the most important, the most remediable, a necessary part, and so forth.

▶ Problem solving is often facilitated by considering not just the endpoint but also significant portions of the causal chain.

▶ Defined as the necessary and sufficient conditions for an effect to appear, causation is always an inference. Like all inferences, it can never be proved; there is always the possibility of a nonconforming case, as yet undiscovered.

▶ Each successful test in which propositions and hypotheses escape disconfirmation reduces uncertainty as findings move toward becoming accepted knowledge.

COMPLEXITIES IN OUR CONCEPTION OF SOCIAL SCIENCE

The notion of universal causation, that every event has a cause, implies a very mechanistic conception of the world. Popper (1972) conceived of a **clocklike world** of *determinism*, like that of an old clock with numerous gears. Turning one gear generates a response in other gears. The physical sciences are often perceived this way; able to make precise predictions in specific situations.

Popper contrasts this with a **cloudlike world**—the normative behavior exhibited by a swarm of gnats in summer or a flock of birds flying south for the winter. A bird or a gnat strays only a certain distance from the center of the flock or swarm, returning when it becomes an outlier. In contrast to the clocklike world, predictions in this cloudlike world are probabilistic rather than exact—what would be typical, somewhat atypical, or highly atypical. With the assumption of such loose coupling of events, it is clearly more difficult to find causal relations. Yet, the cloudlike world model seems to fit social and behavioral phenomena more closely than does the clocklike one.

Some experts have argued that social science involves such complex interactions that it may never be predictable (Cronbach, 1975). They do not expect a science of rules, laws, and propositions like those in the physical sciences. But, Phillips (1987) notes, there are interactions in the physical sciences as well:

> Processes in the natural world in essence are arenas where a host of forces interact, and scientists cannot make accurate predictions because of the ensuing complexities. (Consider weather forecasting.) But this does not mean that theories are either unattainable, or useless when they are found. . . . The situation in social science research undoubtedly is of similar complexity. (pp. 55–56)

A very complex, loosely coupled world probably calls for equally complex explanations.

> ▶ What we perceive as effects may often actually be causes or parts of a causal chain. Put another way, any effect is likely also to be a cause of some future event.
>
> ▶ Effects often have more than one cause, and this results in complex causal patterns. Such causal patterns may involve large portions of the causal chain.

EVIDENCE OF CAUSATION

Now that we have examined some of the complexities of defining cause, on what basis can we infer causation? We can answer this question on two levels: (1) by describing the evidence that permits the inference of causation, and (2) by describing the situational patterns that facilitate drawing the inference of causation (the "comparison and contrast" link in the chain of reasoning).

You may have noticed that we have limited our discussion to studies involving generalizations. What is a **generalization**? Basically, it is a statement of a relationship between two or more variables that has generality; that is, it applies to persons, places, times, measures, and research procedures other than those involved in the original study. These two aspects, causality and generality, suggest that two separate concerns of any research are (1) whether a cause-and-effect relationship exists between the constructs in the particular constellation of circumstances studied, and (2) whether that relationship has any generality beyond those circumstances.

Internal Integrity describes the judgments involved in determining the first of these. In similar fashion, the evidence permitting inference of generality is described by External Generality. Both include evidence that provide conceptual support (evidence based on reasoning) and empirical support (evidence based on data), and this evidence is subject to a set of five judgments in the case of Internal Integrity and similarly five parallel judgments of External Generality.

> ▶ Internal Integrity refers to whether the evidence of a study supports the existence of a causal relationship between its variables or among the variables in a process.
>
> ▶ External Generality refers to whether that relationship generalizes beyond the characteristics of the study in which it was found.
>
> ▶ External Generality and Internal Integrity are characteristics of an entire chain of reasoning supporting a generalization.

INTERNAL INTEGRITY

Internal Integrity is the power of a study to create a consensus around the judgment of how tightly its variables are linked in a causal relationship. A lawyer would say "it makes the case" for the process or the relation(s) between the variables involved. When the study involves processes where variables are interactive and it doesn't make sense to call one a cause and another an effect, as many social variables are, Internal Integrity is determined by how tightly the evidence interlinks the variables. We are trying to answer the questions in the minds of research consumers about the strength of the evidence linking the variables. Zimbardo carefully designed his study cited in chapter 1 to have strong Internal Integrity. Most readers agree with the study's conclusion that the evidence causally linked paranoia to a lack of awareness of developing deafness. (Whether this linkage has generality is a separate judgment.)

Internal Integrity is composed of five judgments (discussed in detail in the following sections) that provide it with:

- *Conceptual support.* **Explanation credibility**—the reasonableness of the explanation or rationale for the relationship (e.g., disruptive behavior occurs with perceptions of personal rejection, which are less likely in a warm classroom climate) and **translation validity**—the validity with which the cause and effect concepts are translated into measures or observations (e.g., valid observation scales for disruptive behavior and classroom climate are available).

- *Empirical support.* **Demonstrated result**—the expected result did occur (e.g., as anticipated, the amount of disruptive behavior was negatively related to warmth of classroom climate) and **rival explanations eliminated**—any explanations other than that of the original one were ruled out (e.g., although classroom climate observations would likely be affected by disruptive behavior, observations on days with such behavior were included in estimates of warmth).

This leads to a summing up: the **credible result**—an overall determination of the Internal Integrity of a study considering the combined strength of the conceptual and empirical support, together with the consistency of these findings with previous research (e.g., prior findings and the prior four judgments are consistent in supporting a causal connection between a warm classroom climate and lower levels of disruptive behavior).

A study with Internal Integrity, based on judgments of conceptual support, empirical support, and credible result, supports an inference linking the concepts of the study in a causal relationship or the variables in a process as tightly linked.

Let's examine more closely the five judgments that make up Internal Integrity, starting with the two that constitute the conceptual support.

Conceptual Support

Initial conceptual support for Internal Integrity is what links the empirical support—the data—to the concepts being studied. It involves clarifying the constructs used to describe a relationship; embedding them in an explanation, theory, or rationale; and translating them into operational definitions for use in the study. Judgments of how well these steps are done are typically the first appraisals made of a study and tend to color one's view of the empirical support. If they are not favorable (e.g., a scale used to assess warmth of classroom climate that includes only teacher/pupil interactions, ignoring pupil/pupil interactions, will provide inadequate warmth data), conclusions must reflect that limitation.

Because it allows us to anticipate what to expect, conceptual support also helps us discriminate a chance result that has no reasonable explanation from one that makes sense because it has conceptual support. (For example, although the teachers with the warmest classrooms all have birthdays in the first three months of the year, this has no conceptual support as an explanation and therefore is likely a chance result.)

Conceptual Support: (1) Explanation Credibility

What was the first thing that struck you about the Zimbardo study? It probably was the rationale for proposing that paranoia might be related to the chain of events that begins when elderly persons do not realize their hearing is gradually disappearing. They no longer understand what is occurring in a previously comfortable social context. They become angry and confused and perceive the environment as hostile. This explanation is well presented; it makes the study interesting and the results plausible. The hypothesis sets the stage for the rest of the study: "Paranoia is sometimes an end product of an initially rational search to explain a perceptual discontinuity, in this case, being deaf without knowing it."

This first judgment of whether a study has *explanation credibility* is critical. If the explanation is plausible, we are willing to pursue the rest of the study to see whether the proposed relationship is borne out by the data. If it is not, we may only reluctantly pursue it. Einhorn and Hogarth (1986) note that if we do not perceive a reasonable causal link—perhaps we think it a coincidence—we may still refuse to attribute causality in spite of the evidence. Certainly, we will read it exceedingly critically, since it will need to meet a very high standard of evidence to be persuasive. Note that one of the strengths of the Zimbardo study was its explanation credibility; it is often the first item students list as a strength.

> ▶ Explanation credibility is a judgment of the credibility of the rationale of a study—its plausibility built as it is on previous research and thought. It involves discussion and definition of the constructs involved in the study, and explanation of their interrelationships expressed as a question, hypothesis, prediction, or model.

Conceptual Support: (2) Translation Validity

What is the next thing that attracts your attention as you read the Zimbardo article? After ending the explanation with the statement of the expected relationship, the hypothesis, Zimbardo begins an extensive description of how the study was carried out. This translates the various aspects of hypothesized relationship into the choices that form the design of the study—a translation of the "five Ws and an H" of chapter 4 (what, why, when, where, who, and how).

The hypothesis defines perceptual discontinuity as "in this case, being deaf without knowing it." But that only takes us part way; the terms need *operational definitions*. We have to operationalize the terms *perceptual discontinuity*, *paranoia*, and *deafness* so that we will recognize valid representations of them in the study—valid in the sense of being true to their meaning in the hypothesis. The decision of how well the operationalizations are done is a judgment of their *translation validity*. What does translation validity mean in the Zimbardo article? To see, we shall have to examine the translations of each of the six links of the design. In addition to the ditty of the six serving men that appeared in chapter 4, for an easy way to remember the rings see note 3, page 157.

Focus. *What* is being studied? What was the focus among the things that were created or occurred (e.g., processes, causes, experimental and control treatments, main effects, and side effects)? The focus of the Zimbardo study is the creation of a perceptual discontinuity—the cause, and its effect—paranoia. In an experiment the cause is called a *treatment*, and in this instance the treatment is a sequence of three events: (1) the hypnosis of the participants, (2) one of three alternative posthypnotic suggestions, and (3) the social situation, which called the participants' attention to the sensory anomaly and resulted in efforts to explain it. Each of these phases must be operationally defined.

Although we are told that the participants were trained in self-hypnosis and heard "deep-relaxing" music, we are never told exactly how the hypnosis was accomplished. Zimbardo expects us to trust him that this was done well and properly. The posthypnotic suggestions were operationally defined by tape recordings randomly assigned to the participants. The social interaction leading to the discovery of the sensory anomaly and perceptual discontinuity—the effect—was operationally defined as the role playing of a "well-rehearsed standard conversation" by two confederates. Note the efforts to standardize all contact with the participants by using audio tapes and rehearsed conversation, so that each participant experienced as nearly as possible the same situation and treatment. We will refer to this standardization later in discussing the fourth judgment of Internal Integrity: rival explanations eliminated.

Because unrecognized partial deafness is essential to the study, and the experimenters couldn't intentionally make people truly partially deaf, the use of hypnosis to create this condition temporarily is a clever solution—provided that we accept hypnosis as capable of creating the condition (which some readers may not, thus rejecting the study).

Note that the treatment in this case was administered in a laboratory-type situation. But treatments are sometimes given under natural conditions, as in a study of the effects of intentionally varied housing designs (for example, the effect on security and privacy when residents can enter their apartments directly in contrast to when all must first pass through a single door to reach their apartments) or naturally occurring conditions (e.g., studying the effect of these configurations in existing housing).

The complexities of representing a treatment are considered in chapter 21. Here, suffice it to note that the treatment chosen for a study should faithfully represent at least one appropriate version of the reasonably likely treatment variations.

Records. *Why* do you think something of interest occurred? (What records are there of what occurred that provide data to be analyzed—e.g., the measures and their scores, the observations, the interviews?) The records of the effect are to show that when the cause is present, the effect appears. The effect, paranoia, must be defined operationally. The measure of a concept is referred to as its **operational definition** because the operations performed in measuring it determine what the data represent. For instance, the answers to the problems on an intelligence test become what is meant by "intelligence" for that study.

In addition to using observations, Zimbardo operationalized by employing both a well-known and a less-known test. His well-known measure was the Minnesota Multiphasic Personality Inventory (MMPI), a commonly used clinical tool. The less-known instrument was a clinically derived paranoia scale that had been used for an earlier study. Two unseen judges served as observers and rated the social interaction in all three groups for paranoid behavior. Note that three different types of measures of paranoia were used, possibly to assure the audience that paranoia really did occur. Readers can choose whichever measure they trust most; all showed the effect.

Surely, one of the three indicators should be acceptable as a measure of paranoia to the readers among whom Zimbardo hopes to form a consensus; but there is another reason for using multiple measures. When all give the same result, we are additionally sure of it. A surveyor establishes a particular location not with one measurement but by **triangulation**—that is, using two or more sightings from different angles. (More on triangulation in chapter 13.) Known as the **multimeasure-multimethod procedure**, such triangulation ensures that the result is neither dependent on the peculiar characteristics of a single measure nor on a particular measurement method. In the Zimbardo case, with multimeasures we find that each of three different, imperfect measures indicates the same effect—triangulation support for the fact that the effect did occur. Multimethod in this instance refers to two different ways of gathering data: the two measures (MMPI and paranoia scale), and observation by the observers. Both should, and did, give us similar results.

In making a judgment regarding translation validity we are asking for evidence of **construct validity**—that is, whether the operational definitions were valid measures of the construct(s) described in explanation credibility. In most cases one looks for empirical support on which we can base the judgment, but we also make a conceptual judgment about the fit of the measures to what is intended. If tests are used, we expect evidence of test validity and/or reliability relevant to their intended use; if observation scales are employed, we require evidence of confirmability/objectivity; and, if two or more raters are used, interrater reliability. (For validity of tests see chapter 18, observation see chapter 16, and reliability among judges and observers see chapter 18).

An aside regarding terminology: The problems involved in using the term *validity* are discussed in the addendum to this chapter. In the case of translation validity, however, its use was intentional to call attention to the important work in the field of tests and measurement and its relevance for translation validity.

Time.   *When* were things to occur and/or when did they occur? (In a preplanned study, *when* was what done to whom—*when* were treatment, measures, and/or observations and their analysis scheduled to be done to participants? *When* were they actually done? In an emergent study, *when* was data gathering—observations, interviews, etc.—and analysis done?) The "when" is the description of the study's steps; it defines the operations involved in procedure. In a preplanned study—an experiment—the procedure includes who received what treatment, when and how they received it, who was observed and measured, and where this was done.

Note that besides ensuring comparable experiences for individuals among the three groups, the standardized procedure was designed such that the investigator, accomplices, and observers were not privy to the participants' treatment assignment; they were given by tape recordings delivered through headphones. As well, judges were "blind" as far as what to expect from a subject.

Comparison and contrast.   *How* will you know when something is changed, and *how* much change occurred? (In preplanned studies, *how* much difference was there over the time of the study or among the groups studied? *How* did they change? In emergent studies: Where there are common attributes or behaviors across individuals, groups, times, or situations, *how* did they change?) Sensing the particular effect of interest or the changes that resulted from treatment is the "how."

A useful way to show that a relationship exists is to demonstrate that the effect is present when the cause is also present and absent when the cause is absent. We could compare participants with themselves before and after treatment conditions or compare treated with untreated comparable groups. The Zimbardo study used the comparable groups condition, assigning participants to three treatment groups at random so that they would be comparable. Two of the groups were alike in that both involved partial deafness, but they differed in knowledge of the deafness. The aware group would expect and understand the sensory deficit. The researchers used a third group with a different posthypnotic suggestion (itchy ear with amnesia) to eliminate the rival explanation that posthypnotic suggestion itself caused the effect.

Discussions of the criteria for determining causality have involved some of the best philosophic minds over the centuries and are too extensive to recapitulate. Note, however, that the above design is one of many we use to show causation. In addition to Hume's three criteria covered earlier—the cause (A) always precedes or is contemporaneous with effect (B); A is always present when B occurs; and a plausible mechanism links them—we often infer causation when

- with increases or decreases in A, B increases or decreases (possibly inversely);
- B never occurs before A;
- a pattern of change in A is reflected in B;
- everything present that is not A does not result in B, so the cause lies in A;
- a baseline change in B is changed by the presence of A.

The point is that the comparison-and-contrast link must include such conditions to infer causation. They are embodied in experimental designs used in quantitative research, and in the logic used in qualitative research when selecting data that links variables.

Situation.   *Where* is the study site located, and what are its characteristics? For Internal Integrity purposes any situation to which the question, hypothesis, prediction, or model would apply is appropriate. You may have decided that the substitution of the laboratory situation for a social situation involving elderly persons was a weakness of the Zimbardo study. Consider, however, whether features of the normal social situation omitted in the laboratory are essential to the relationship expressed in the hypothesis. All that is important is that the situation be one in which the phenomenon can be displayed—a situation where there can be social interplay allowing individuals to discover that they can't understand the conversation but not realize they are growing deaf. The laboratory meets these conditions. Furthermore, by bringing the study into the laboratory, the social situation could be controlled so that it was almost identical for each of the participants.

Participants.   *Who* is being studied? Participants are the "who," the individuals chosen to be studied. As in the case of situation, for Internal Integrity purposes the participants can be anyone to whom the question, hypothesis, prediction, or model applies. And also as with situation, you probably considered the use of college students in place of the elderly in Zimbardo's study as a weakness of the study—the translation validity was weak. The study's rationale leads us to believe that the subjects should be a sample from among the elderly. Although the origin of the study was a problem of the elderly, the hypothesis is more general, stating that "paranoia results from a rational search to explain a perceptual discontinuity." It applies to *anyone* experiencing a perceptual discontinuity of *any* kind. For example, the proposition might apply to persons with Alzheimer's disease who cannot remember from moment to moment even that they have a memory problem. Often someone will refer to something that occurred earlier that the affected individuals don't believe occurred. If they still trust their own senses more than they trust those of other people, they would come to distrust others and view the world as hostile.

The experimenters could not ethically test elderly participants' hearing and then stand by, allowing them to misinterpret their social world. A necessary condition for Internal Integrity in terms of choice of participants is simply that they be an example of participants to whom the hypothesis would apply; college students meet this criterion.

Three links in the chain of reasoning—comparison and contrast, time, and records—are critical aspects of design where causation is to be inferred. They provide important cues to causation:

- Precedence of cause before effect (or at least contiguity of cause with effect);
- Indicators of change from some base state to a new one as the presumed result of one or more intervening causative agents; and
- With a change in the state of the cause, there is a congruent pattern of change in the effect.

When the effect is delayed rather than contiguous, a strong, plausible explanation is required for the delay.

If you review the list of strengths and weaknesses on pages 9–11 of chapter 1, you will notice that many of them are concerned with translation validity. Without valid translation of the hypothesis, question, prediction, or model into the actual steps in a study, we do a different study from the intended one. If the gap in translation is serious, the evidence that is provided may be totally irrelevant. Translation validity is a second critical judgment contributing to conceptual evidence of Internal Integrity.

> ▶ Translation validity is a judgment of the validity with which the meaning of the terms in the question, hypothesis, prediction, or model, as described in the study's explanation or rationale, are translated in operations in the study—that is, operationalized. It is the second judgment providing conceptual evidence of Internal Integrity.

Initial Empirical Support: (3) Demonstrated Result

What evidence contributes to the judgment of a strongly demonstrated result? Data showing these four attributes:

- authenticity of the evidence,
- precedence of cause,
- presence of effect, and
- congruence of explanation and evidence.

Let's examine each of these attributes more closely.

Authenticity of evidence. Although authenticity is important in any study, it is of particular concern in historical studies. It asks the question, "Is the evidence what it purports to be?" If we claim that the moldering notebook in our library is Napoleon's diary, we must have convincing evidence that it is. We assume that scores on a test were the achievement of a certain individual. Can we be sure that someone else did not take the test in that person's stead or help that person with it? If the test was a take-home, this claim is not assured. Thus, *authenticity of evidence* is a legitimate concern we must be prepared to address if we are to accept the evidence as authentic.

Precedence of cause.   Cause is temporally antecedent to, or concomitant with, effect; never the reverse. If a person is nervous and smokes cigarettes, does the smoking cause the nervousness? Only if we have evidence that smoking started before or at the same time as the nervousness can we show *precedence of cause*. Precedence, obvious in laboratory experiments, is more difficult to establish definitively in natural situations. Often, because we don't know until later what causal factor we should have been attending to, it may not be in our records.

Presence of effect.   With an experimental treatment, we are sure there was an intended cause, but was there an effect? We need no statistical test to know that penicillin is effective; however, most behavioral science effects are not so obvious. Even an effect in the proper direction may be a chance deviation caused by sampling or other error. If there are quantitative measures, we can use inferential statistics to minimize the likelihood that a chance deviation is mistaken for *presence of an effect.* This assumes, however, that the correct statistics were used, were properly interpreted, and were sensitive enough to show a significant treatment result if one occurred. Cook and Campbell (1979) refer to these latter characteristics as *statistical conclusion validity*.

Congruence of explanation and evidence.   Astronomy is not an experimental science, yet we consider it a strong one. Why? Its explanations prove to be good predictors; there is *congruence of explanation and evidence*. Einhorn and Hogarth (1986) note that we typically expect both contiguity of cause and effect and congruity of the effect to the cause. By congruity we mean, for instance, that a large cause would be expected to provide a large effect and a small cause a small one. When there are both contiguity and congruence, causation is often inferred even in the presence of little conceptual support, if we can eliminate rival explanations. When either contiguity or congruence is lacking, and especially when both are, strong conceptual support is required for the inference to be made. But when explanations lead to an effect that appears as expected (for example, inferring causality of pregnancy from intercourse where both contiguity and congruence are lacking), this is usually judged potent evidence of causality.

Evidence for causality is most impressive when:

- *The effect follows a detailed prediction.* For example, one can accurately predict when the effect will appear, how it will do so, in what strength in relation to that of the effect, and so on. These are very convincing aspects of astronomy; astronomers tell us where to look, when, and for what magnitude of heavenly body. Although there are few instances in the behavioral sciences where we can make such precise predictions, we can aspire to do so. The principle is sound.

- *The effect follows the pattern of a manipulated cause.* This cause-and-effect pattern is probably the most compelling evidence of all. The more complex the causal pattern, the stronger the evidence for causality. Would we not be convinced that a strong causal link exists between food coloring and emotionally disturbed behavior if we can show that the behavior appears when the coloring is in food eaten? Disappears when absent? Is greater when more coloring is added? Less frequent with less? That such behavior parallels even a random pattern of coloring devised by an independent observer?

Let's examine the Zimbardo study for these four conditions. Much of the responsibility for *authenticity of evidence* rests with the researcher. As will be noted in chapter 28, such trust is occasionally misplaced, but most researchers do not consider trust a problem. There is certainly no reason to mistrust Zimbardo and his associates;

he is an established researcher, and the article appeared in a respected journal with careful peer review and high standards.

Precedence of cause is easy to determine in an experiment such as Zimbardo's since the procedure used assures it.

The next condition is that *an effect is found.* In a quantitative study we use inferential statistics, as Zimbardo did. Without explaining the two columns on the right of Table 1 on page 8, the differences in the mean (average) scores of the groups in the first three columns of the table are apparent. Thus, for the moment, we can accept the researchers' interpretation of these statistics as showing that the paranoia of the treated group exceeded that of the other groups on all the measures.

Was the effect congruent with the explanation or rationale and its translation into a hypothesis, prediction, or model? Clearly, in Zimbardo's case it was. All four conditions were met, and we have a demonstrated result.

> ▶ A demonstrated result appears when the evidence is authentic, there was precedence (or concomitance) of cause, and an effect occurred as was expected in terms of the relationship described by the hypothesis, prediction, or model.

More Empirical Support: (4) Rival Explanations Eliminated

Returning to Zimbardo, so far the study has met our criteria: The paranoia appeared when and where expected. But is there any other reasonable explanation for its appearance? There are nearly always a variety of possible rival explanations, some realistic, some far fetched. It is the responsibility of the researcher to anticipate any rival explanations that the audience might consider reasonable and to build the design of the study to render them implausible. *Rival explanations eliminated* is a judgment of whether there are equally plausible rival explanations that account for the data as well as the proposed explanation, or whether these can be ruled out or rendered implausible.

A common way of eliminating rival explanations is to be sure that the alternative possible causative factors are present both when the treatment is present and when it is not. If the effect occurs only when the treatment is present, regardless of the presence or absence of the rival factor, then the rival is not the cause. The treatment and nontreatment groups must be comparable with respect to all possible rival explanations or a factor that differs might be a rival explanation. In the Zimbardo study, the researchers ruled out rival explanations in several ways.

There were two nontreatment groups: one of them partially deaf, the other with an itchy ear. The intent was to rule out posthypnotic suggestion as a cause of paranoia. If it had been the cause, the itchy ear group would have had as high an incidence of paranoia as the deafness groups. It didn't.

Random assignment of the participants to the groups plus random assignment of the groups to treatment prevented the researcher from ensuring that the group most favorable to the hypothesis received the treatment. Furthermore, after the tapes for the treatment instructions were played in their headphones, the groups were exposed to exactly the same procedure. The posthypnotic suggestion and all succeeding directions were given by slides so that the two partially deaf groups would not be disadvantaged. The confederates conducted a "well-rehearsed standard conversation" for all the groups. This made unlikely the possibility that the social interaction situation for the groups might have varied and therefore might have been the cause of the difference in paranoia. Finally—and this is a critical feature—no one having contact with the participants knew to which of the three groups subjects belonged. In research terms, the judges were kept *blind*—they could not have favored the experimental group even if they wanted to.

Clearly, the researchers tried to anticipate many of the possible plausible rival explanations and eliminated them in their design of the study. Note that the design of the study is the prime protection against these rivals, and the study ideally should be designed so that they are eliminated.

Einhorn and Hogarth (1986) explain that the inference of causation depends on the context of the study; the study's explanation, rationale, point of view, or theory describes this context. The study focuses us on the part of the causal chain involved in the phenomenon, delineating it as the "figure" from its background context including the rest of the causal chain. It is important to examine these for rival explanations of the event (e.g., if we are studying disruptive behavior in relation to classroom "warmth," then research into the causes of disruptive behavior and of classroom warmth might hold rival explanations we should consider in our study).

> ▶ For the projected explanation or rationale to be accepted, all reasonable rival or alternative explanations of the data must be eliminated. *Rival explanations eliminated* contributes to empirical support by judging whether all such reasonable alternative explanations have been ruled out.

The Final Judgment: (5) Credible Result

Credible result is the final judgment that sums the previous evidence, both conceptual and empirical. It includes an examination of external evidence to see whether this study is consistent with earlier studies. (This assumes, of course, that they don't all have the same flaws or, should that occur, that the researcher is capable of spotting them.) It reflects the degree of confidence with which we can infer that the proper interpretation of the evidence links the variables in a causal relationship or in a process.

In the Zimbardo study, the four earlier judgments are all positive: the conceptual support of explanation credibility and translation validity, and the empirical support of demonstrated result and rival explanations eliminated. The evidence is consistent with the literature, and there is no directly comparable study, so we have a credible result. We conclude that the study's conclusion has strong Internal Integrity.

Note, however, that in a study with multiple conclusions, each conclusion must be examined for Internal Integrity and External Generality. These judgments bear on the conclusions and the claims for them, rather than on the study itself. But clearly, the design of the study structures what claims can and cannot be made.

> ▶ Credible result is a judgment that sums up the four earlier judgments and asks whether, in terms of external prior evidence, we support the study's conclusion. It is a judgment of the extent to which the uncertainty regarding the existence of the causal relationship has been removed.

INTERNAL INTEGRITY AND THE CHAIN OF REASONING

The five successive judgments of Internal Integrity draw their evidence from the successive links of the chain of reasoning. Showing them in relation to the chain is instructive and provides an easy way to remember them, as we can see in Figure 7.1. Each of the judgments in Internal Integrity can be placed alongside a certain part of the chain of reasoning where we find evidence used in making that judgment.

Figure 7.1   The judgments of Internal Integrity superimposed on the chain of reasoning.

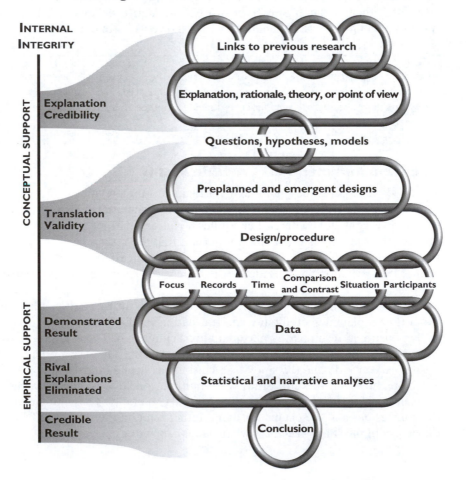

Internal Integrity and External Generality as Uncertainty Reduction

Just as knowledge is better viewed as a reduction in uncertainty (instead of an all-or-none, true-or-false matter), so is Internal Integrity. In this instance, we are reducing our uncertainty that the relationship exists in the circumstances in which it was investigated. The better the study meets the criteria of Internal Integrity, the greater the reduction in uncertainty.

In a similar vein, External Generality, discussed in the next chapter, is also a reduction in the uncertainty that the relationship generalizes beyond the circumstances in which it was studied.

Additional Reading

Many useful treatments of causation go beyond this discussion. Examples are Ellsworth (1977) in psychology, Köbben (1973) in anthropology, and Hage and Meeker (1988) in sociology. Chapter 1 of Cook and Campbell (1979) is a clear and readable summarization of the progression of philosophical positions. Guba and Lincoln (1982) similarly summarize them and argue for abandonment of causation in favor of "plausible explanations," a construct especially congruent with qualitative positions. See also the early sections of Messick (1989). A careful discussion of causality appears in Shadish, Cook, and Campbell (2002). See also Schneider, Carnoy, Kilpatrick, Schmidt, and Shavelson (2007).

For treatments of internal validity (which is related to, but not the same as, Internal Integrity—see the addendum to this chapter [pp. 153–157] for the difference) see Brinberg and McGrath (1985), Campbell and Stanley (1963), Cook and Campbell (1979), Cronbach (1982), Krathwohl (1985), and Kruglanski and Kroy (1976).

Important Terms and Concepts

authenticity of evidence	External Generality
causal chain	generality/generalization
clocklike world	Internal Integrity
cloudlike world	multimeasure-multimethod procedure
comparison and contrast	operational definition
congruence of explanation and evidence	precedence of cause
construct validity	presence of an effect
credible result	rival explanations eliminated
demonstrated result	translation validity
disconfirmation	triangulation
explanation credibility	

Opportunities for Additional Learning

1. Considering the definition of causation given in this chapter, how would you comment on the age-old question, "Which comes first, the chicken or the egg?"

2. Assume you are an elementary school teacher conducting an interview with the parents of a student who has consistently demonstrated low achievement. They claim that the "real" reason for their child's performance is that he is "lazy." How would you answer them?

3. Bernard Weiner's attribution theory (1972, 1980a, 1980b) identifies several "causes" to which individuals "attribute" (use to explain) success or failure, including ability, effort, task difficulty, luck, mood, illness, and help from others. Each of these causes, Weiner asserts, shows the presence or absence of three properties: (1) stability (consistency of the attribution over time, as with luck versus ability), (2) controllability (degree to which the cause is under the person's control, such as mood versus illness), and (3) locus of control (whether the cause has an origin internal or external to the person, as in effort versus task difficulty). These are all factors in an individual's understanding of an outcome. Thus future behavior is determined by a person's perception of these causes. Are these factors truly causes, or are some of them effects? How does this theory fit the definition of causation outlined in this chapter?

4. You are an educational researcher who is interested in the effect of cognitive styles on learning. It is your conviction that independent of ability, some individuals tend to be impulsive in their approach to learning activities while others are more reflective. You set up an experimental study to determine whether these styles exist. What conceptual support can you provide to show the validity of your idea?

5. You are a psychologist with a deep interest in the age-old practice of astrology. You suspect that there may be some validity to the belief that an astrological sign determines aspects of personality. Consequently, you decide to try to show that people who are born under the sign of Taurus tend to be more stubborn than others. What conceptual support can you provide for the relationship?

6. Internal Integrity applies to qualitative studies as well as to studies like Zimbardo's; indeed, it is of concern wherever a generalization is developed. Use the Hoffmann-Riem study to illustrate the judgments to be made with respect to Internal Integrity as the Zimbardo study was used in the text.

Compare your answers with those following the Application Exercise.

APPLICATION EXERCISE

Where does your selected problem fall in the causal chain? What part of the chain have you chosen? The most important part? The most recent? The most easily explored? What pattern of causation do you expect to find? Might others apply? After considering the various causation possibilities, have you changed your mind about what to expect?

Consider the Internal Integrity of your problem. Do you have a strong explanation or rationale so that it has explanation credibility? Although the translation of the study into operational terms has yet to come, what problems, if any, do you sense there might be with translation validity? Although demonstrated result will have to await the gathering of data, can you think of rival explanations that might be as plausible as your intended explanation? While you'll be more aware of common rival explanations to watch for after studying the research methods of Sections IV and V, what reasonable alternatives might you anticipate now? Have you checked the other research evidence regarding your problem? Do you expect yours to be consistent with it? If not, are you attempting to refute prior work?

KEY TO ADDITIONAL LEARNING OPPORTUNITIES

1. Needless to say, the question does not refer to any specific chicken or any particular egg but to chickens and eggs in general. It addresses the problem of precedence of cause and is an example of what appears to be a simple causal pattern that has been, with tongue in cheek, turned around. Did there have to be a chicken egg from which the first chicken hatched? If so, where did the egg come from? Which was the "cause" and which was the "effect"? Was the egg the cause, by hatching the first chicken (the effect), or was the first chicken the cause, laying the first chicken egg (the effect)? The saying is an example in popular terms of the fact that everything is part of a causal chain, and we use this saying in nonresearch problems to make the causal chain salient.

2. Your answer would naturally depend on the specific circumstances: the particular student, his instructional history, his environment, and so on. You would likely emphasize that patterns leading to low achievement are never simple and that there might be rival explanations. In effect, there is a causal history to the student's behavior, and its pattern should be explored. Maybe the causes are multiple and affect each other in complex ways. What, for example, is the home situation? Have the parents encouraged or discouraged learning? What is the student's perceived or measured ability level? Has he in the past made an effort but not succeeded? Is he now achieving at his ability level? Is he learning disabled? What is his medical condition? All are possible explanations for, or factors involved in, his behavior, some of which may be more important than others. It is likely that the cause is some constellation of these factors and not one simple answer (such as "The student is lazy").

3. The causes are probably best explained as all being part of a causal chain in a multiple-cause pattern. Some will be real and some perceived. Not all will be present in any one circumstance, but some group of them will act one on the other, or in concert to affect an individual's understanding of a situation. Consequently, they will influence that person's choice of behavior in that situation or in similar ones in the future. Take an individual who normally does poorly on exams and believes he is a poor student. He may prepare well for a test and be successful. Yet instead of identifying the cause of his success as his ability or his effort (or both), he may attribute it to conditions such as luck or the exam being "easy." He might then choose to depend on luck the next time rather than believing in his ability and therefore preparing for the exam. In each case, multiple factors or causes, both real and perceived, produce a behavior.

4. First, consider explanation credibility. Is your rationale plausible? In this case, it makes good sense intuitively that some people respond quickly to situations while others prefer to take their time and ponder. It is especially apparent in exam situations. Is there existing research evidence that might help explain the idea? In fact, these categories *did* grow out of research into analytic versus global reasoning. Kagen and colleagues (1964) developed a categorization test (the Conceptual Style Test) to compare the concepts. As a side product of their research, they found that children who adopted an analytic reasoning style took significantly longer to answer the test questions than those who gave relational answers. It led the researchers to wonder whether the tendency to delay responses was a stable characteristic of certain individuals. Their explanatory evidence, then, had its roots in prior research.

Second, consider translation validity. How well have you operationalized this explanation? What is your hypothesis here, and how have you designed your study? Kagen and colleagues (1964) operationalized the concept of "impulsiveness–reflectiveness" by stating it as a tendency to delay a response to a task. Because the hypothesis involved time, it was easily measurable. Furthermore, so was the individual's error rate. Kagen and associates developed another test, the Matching Figures Test, consisting of sets of very similar pictures in which the task was to pick out the ones that match exactly. Time and error scores were kept. Individuals were classified as above or below average on each score. An impulsive person would be quick (below average on time) but would make many errors, while a reflective person would be slow (above average on time) with few errors. The researchers appear to have soundly operationalized their construct. That other researchers corroborated their studies gives evidence of this.

5. The evidence for this concept may not be as easy to provide as for impulsiveness–reflectiveness! Again, consider explanation credibility. To some people, the relationship between signs of the zodiac and personality is intuitively obvious; witness the popularity of astrology columns in many newspapers. To others, the idea of any relationship between personality and star patterns is inherently ridiculous. To the first group, the explanation is plausible, but to the second, it will be a hard sell! You will have to provide strong empirical support. Is there any research evidence to support the idea?

   Think about translation validity. How would you operationalize this concept? Members of the sign of Taurus are indicated by birth date. But you will need a convincing measure of stubbornness. If you do find or develop such a test, you may be able to sense an effect—that is, demonstrate that a relationship exists. Even so, you will have a problem eliminating rival explanations. For example, how will you show that the zodiac and not the season of the year causes the relationship? Personality issues are extremely complex, and so are the influences on them.

6. To determine the Internal Integrity of Hoffmann-Riem we will have to consider the five judgments that contribute to it: explanation credibility, translation validity, demonstrated result, rival explanations eliminated, and credible result.

   Explanation credibility—Is her explanation credible? Definitely, it makes good sense that adoptive parents would want the same relationship with their child as biological parents have with their own children. Hoffmann-Riem elaborates on this theme with quotations such as the one of the father who had "quickly come to believe that the principle of biological affiliation is almost irrelevant for an emotional relationship." The explanation she presents, together with her description of the process by which normalization develops, is entirely credible.

   Translation validity—The term she uses, "normalization," seems entirely appropriate to the process she is describing, and she includes sufficient quotations and description of the process that one has a good grasp both of what the concept of what normalization is, and of how it is operationalized in her data. This close correspondence of concept and operational definition is typical of qualitative studies where the concept, in this instance normalization, has been developed inductively out of the data.

   Demonstrated result—She provides evidence in her quotations that normalization occurs. There seems no reason to doubt the statements of the parents.

   Rival explanations eliminated—She is silent on this point. We don't know whether she looked for any, nor are there any clues as to what such rivals might be. As a reader, I had none to suggest.

   Credible result—She does not give any indication that others have studied this problem, and unless this was one's specialty, one couldn't be expected to know whether these data are consistent with previous literature. However, given what evidence we have, and assuming her study is not contradicted by other work, the study would appear to have strong Internal Integrity.

Summary

This chapter has focused on some of the complexities in the concept of causation and on the criteria for inferring causation. Any statement of causation emphasizes a part of a causal chain that leads to the effect. Understanding this relationship helps to draw attention to the rest of the causal chain, which may be more amenable to study or control. Use of the term *causation* tends to imply that the world has a mechanical, clocklike nature. Some persons see a cloudlike conception that yields predictions only in terms of probabilities or odds as more compatible with a social science. Added to these complexities are the many possible causal patterns that should be considered, including multiple causation.

Internal Integrity and External Generality are two major criteria by which studies are judged. Internal Integrity is a judgment of how strongly the appropriate interpretation of the evidence links the variables in a causal relationship (or process) in the circumstances in which it was studied. External Generality is a judgment of how strongly the evidence supports the generality of the relationship beyond the circumstances in which it was studied.

Internal Integrity consists of five judgments: two of conceptual support (explanation credibility and translation validity), two of empirical support (demonstrated result and rival explanations eliminated), and a final summary judgment (credible result).

The Internal Integrity/External Generality framework described in this and the preceding chapters seems to capture the decision-making process involved in giving assurance of a generalizable causal relationship. As discussed in the addendum to this chapter, it builds upon and goes beyond the Campbell-Stanley-Cook-Shadish formulations and avoids some of their problems. It comprehensively incorporates relevant judgments and fits researchers' expectations. It provides a sequential set of criteria to help evaluate the design adequacy of preplanned studies and to guide the evolving decisions of an emergent study. It takes into account the many major decisions that must be made regarding the credibility of a claim of causality and of generality for a proposition—the many bases that must be touched to convince audiences of one's conclusions. Its judgments are broadly relevant to studies of generalizable causal relationships, including those where the supporting evidence is qualitative in nature.

A Look Ahead

External Generality consists of a set of judgments parallel to those of Internal Integrity. Because in generalizing we are extrapolating from the sample of evidence on hand, we will consider External Generality in the context of sampling. These are the subjects of chapter 8.

We will further explore how the logic described in this chapter plays out for qualitative research in chapters 15 and 16 and in experimentation in chapter 21.

Chapter Addendum:
Internal Integrity and Internal Validity

Because you will find the terms internal and external validity in studies (after all, they have been around for over 40 years), you may wonder why this text substitutes the terms Internal Integrity and External Generality for them. This addendum explains this intentional substitution. In short, today there are so many meanings to the term *validity* that determining which one is intended has become a problem. Furthermore, the definitions of internal validity and the expectations created by the name "internal validity" do not match the original definition and can be "fixed." Such fixes, in turn, change external validity, so the terms are given new but related names that, it is hoped, are an improvement.

The Many Validities and Social Science Terminology

Unlike the physical sciences where terminology appears to standardize easily, it appears that social sciences terminology jells more slowly. And for a variety of reasons, sometimes it doesn't. In using terms, additional useful distinctions come to light, and somebody tries to add them to the original definitions. This has happened to the term *validity*, which, so far as I can tell, originally meant that a valid test measured what it was intended to. But then it became modified by the kind of evidence used (construct validity, content validity, predictive validity, etc.). Others pointed to the fact that rather than an indelible characteristic of the test, it was a characteristic of the usage that was involved. Further, Messick (1995) noted that the consequences of test usages also should also be considered part of validity. Validity came in many flavors.

The unsettled (and unsettling) usage of the term internal validity.   Terms standardize most easily when the distinctions involved in their definition "cleave nature at the joints"—that is, when the distinctions follow logically from the names used. When the expected meaning does not follow from the term's name, its meaning takes longer to standardize, if it ever does.

This excursion into terminology is an outgrowth of the original definitions of internal and external validity that did not "cleave nature at a joint." One expected that internal validity dealt with the relation of constructs, not just of measures. But as originally defined it referred only to the measures, and only in that particular study's context. Further definitions and clarifications followed. Campbell and Stanley's (1963) original definitions were split into four validities, two concerned with causation (internal validity and statistical conclusion validity), and two with generality (external validity and construct validity) (Cook & Campbell, 1979). Then the concept of local molar validity was advanced (Campbell, 1986). The most recent formulation in Shadish, Campbell, and Cook (2002) continues the four validity types of Cook and Campbell essentially unchanged. However, statistical conclusion validity is extended "to consider the role of effect sizes in experiments" (p. 38). Construct validity is extended to include persons and setting as well as higher-order constructs, and external validity is extended to include treatments and observations.[1]

Although some textbooks follow the original definitions, internal validity in particular has been defined differently in different textbooks.[2] The current situation seems little changed; internal validity often appears to be reduced to the elimination of rival explanations and to using the terms *variable* and *treatment*, without specifying their reference as constructs or as operationalizations.

When told that the study links cause with effect because of its strong internal validity, one naturally assumes it is the *concepts* the study represents—not the particular operational definitions that are linked. However, internal validity, as originally defined by Campbell and Stanley (1963) and continued through later formulations, linked only the particular operational definitions used in the study. Cronbach (1982) notes,

"Campbell's writings make internal validity a property of trivial, past-tense, and local statements" (p. 137). Cook (1991) noted that Cronbach and Campbell, "two great theorists of social science method, use the same label, external validity, but imbue it with different meanings that are . . . partially contradictory in that Cronbach's internal validity seems equivalent to Campbell's external validity!" (pp. 130–131). The linking of the operational definitions with the constructs was a judgment of construct validity. Kruglanski and Kroy (1976) referred to Campbell's placement of construct validity with external validity as a "misclassification of validity types." To emphasize that their internal validity was restricted to linking the measures used, Campbell (1986) proposed renaming it "local molar causal validity." Shadish, Cook, and Campbell (2002) note that "local" referred to the constructs as operationalized; and "molar" underscored that treatments, though studied as entities, are nearly always complex packages.

Although these terms originated in a discussion of experimentation, writers concerned with qualitative research have redefined these concepts in qualitative terms (e.g., Lincoln, 2001; Lincoln & Guba, 1986; Miles & Huberman, 1994). One also finds varying interpretation of these terms in the literatures of psychology, sociology, political science, anthropology, and medicine. Even within the experimental communities in these disciplines, variations in interpretation create a range of conceptions—and often miscommunications, which poses a sizable problem for advancing scientific language.

Internal Integrity aligns meaning and expectations.   Why the resistance to the original formulation? A prime problem has been already noted; internal validity's definition is contrary to our expectation. Because typically research is explained in terms that extend beyond the immediate setting, we expect validity statements to causally link the constructs, not just operationalizations. The second problem is that the original definitions separate construct validity from internal validity by putting it with external validity when it is really a necessary part of internal validity. A third problem is that the original definitions are not complete—not taking into account all the evidence that goes into the decision to accept the findings as causally linked. For all these reasons, this book uses the term *Internal Integrity* in place of internal validity with new definitions for it and uses *External Generality* in place of external validity, again with adjustments in the definition.

The concept of Internal Integrity developed in this chapter addresses those problems noted in the preceding paragraph. In particular it addresses the first problem of aligning the meaning of Internal Integrity with expectations by causally relating the constructs of the study. When we say that it "cleaves nature at a joint," we mean that it is not limited to the study's particular operationalizations of them, and refers to the construct.

Construct validity should be part of the judgment of Internal Integrity.   Evidence of construct validity allows inference from the operationalization to the construct that it represents, so Campbell-Stanley-Cook-Shadish pair it with external validity. But Internal Integrity requires construct validity as part of translation validity, one of its five judgments. This assures that the constructs are translated properly into operationalizations. Indeed, there are several reasons for construct validity's inclusion in Internal Integrity.

First, the goal of most studies is to causally link constructs. Success depends on Internal Integrity. Construct validity is required to link the operationalizations of a study to the constructs.

Second, in most instances, assurance of Internal Integrity is the first concern. If the data also support External Generality, then so much the better. Cronbach (1982) notes there are instances where external validity is primary (e.g., "This classroom practice seems to work! We need to show some success, so let's try it in other settings. If it works there also, let's find out why it does."). But typically our first concern is causality. When construct validity is paired with external validity, as in the Campbell-Stanley-Cook-Shadish formulations, it is relegated to secondary importance.

Third, the various Campbell-Stanley-Cook-Shadish formulations for judgments of external validity confound two kinds of inferences. To judge external validity requires:

• *Inferences based on empirical evidence of construct validity.* Except for instances of so-called "face validity," construct validity is based on data.

• *Inferences based on apparent similarities to other persons, places, times, and ways of conducting the study.* Typically lacking empirical evidence, these are inferential leaps based on speculation that sufficiently similar conditions exist in these instances so that similar results might be expected to apply.

To say that both types of inferences are bases for external validities' generalization actually masks their different logics. For most studies, empirical evidence is available to determine how well the operationalizations represent constructs—for instance, correlations with other measures. When these evidence-based judgments are lumped with judgments based on speculative similarities in external validity, they provide an inappropriate aura of solidity to external validity. Including the data-supported inference of construct validity in translation validity has the happy consequence that it separates these two kinds of inferences. As just indicated, it puts the data-supported evidence in Internal Integrity. It leaves the speculative inferences of construct validity concerning the similarity to persons, places, times, and study methods in the realm of External Generality.

You may be asking yourself: What about qualitative studies in which empirical correlation evidence of construct validity doesn't exist? In such cases, we must judge from "thick description"—that is, excerpts from interviews and observations that the researcher provides as examples of the construct. Yes, this is also a judgment of similarity, but it is not speculative; it is an inference from empirical behavioral evidence to the construct's conventional definition, a grounded task.

Moving construct validity into the realm of Internal Integrity, however, requires emphasizing another rival explanation that must be eliminated, that of unreliable or invalid measurement, or of biased or inadequate observation.

Internal Integrity includes additional evidence used in the judgment of causality. In addition to the changes in the reformulation of internal and external validity, if we want to include all the evidence used in judging causality, we must be aware that some evidence is missing from the original Campbell-Stanley-Cook-Shadish formulations but is included in Internal Integrity. The first is conceptual evidence—explanation credibility, the explanation and rationale that provides the logical basis for expecting a causal relationship and tells us what to expect. Although sometimes missing, when an explanation is available—and it usually is—it forms an important part of the logical chain.

Neither does the Campbell-Stanley-Cook-Shadish formulations include the last judgment of Internal Integrity: consideration of the external evidence in credible result. Is the other evidence bearing on the phenomenon consistent with the evidence of this study? If not, why not? These are important parts of Internal Integrity and influence how a study is viewed.

> ▶ The term internal validity is used differently in various texts and studies. To eliminate the problems leading to its different definitions, this text defines Internal Integrity as a replacement.
>
> ▶ Internal Integrity causally links concepts, whereas internal validity links only the operational definitions in the Campbell-Stanley-Cook-Shadish formulations.
>
> ▶ In Internal Integrity, the empirical-evidence inference from the data-to-concept aspect of construct validity is subsumed under translation validity, and the speculative inferences regarding the generality of the construct remain in External Generality.
>
> ▶ The judgments of explanation credibility and credible result that contribute to Internal Integrity bring important evidence to support causality that is not considered in the Campbell-Stanley-Cook-Shadish formulations.

Differences between External Generality and External Validity

The differences between External Generality and the Campbell-Stanley-Cook-Shadish formulations of external validity parallel those between Internal Integrity and internal validity. As in the latter instance, External Generality adds two judgments not found in the Campbell-Stanley-Cook-Shadish formulations—explanation generality and replicable result. Further, as indicated in the discussion of "records" under "translation validity," the construct validity judgment in the Campbell-Stanley-Cook-Shadish formulations is split into two parts: the judgment of the accuracy with which the operational definition reflects the construct is part of translation validity in Internal Integrity. The extent to which that operational definition would generalize to other persons, places, and research methods is part of translation generality in External Generality.

* * *

It is a slow process to gain acceptance for new frameworks and even more difficult when usages of the same terms vary widely. The framework described herein, by clarifying and encompassing the judgments involved in conferring causality and generality, is intended to provide a solid basis for such judgments until new formulations provide further improvements.

Notes

[1] For still other frameworks, see Brinberg and McGrath (1985) and especially Cronbach (1982).

[2] This was noted in Krathwohl (1985) and recently reconfirmed by a survey of recent texts by the author.

[3] An easy way to remember the six rings of the design in order is to remember the word "Forectsp," (pronounced "forec-teaspoon"—expanding the cooking abbreviation "tsp"). Remember also that the single "c" stands for three c's, the last letter of rec for Records and the first letters of Comparison and Contrast. Expanding to 3 c's and adding capitalization gives us "FoRecCCTSP," using the first letters of all six rings—Focus, Records, Comparison and Contrast, Time, Situation, and Participants—Fo-Rec-CC-T-S-P.

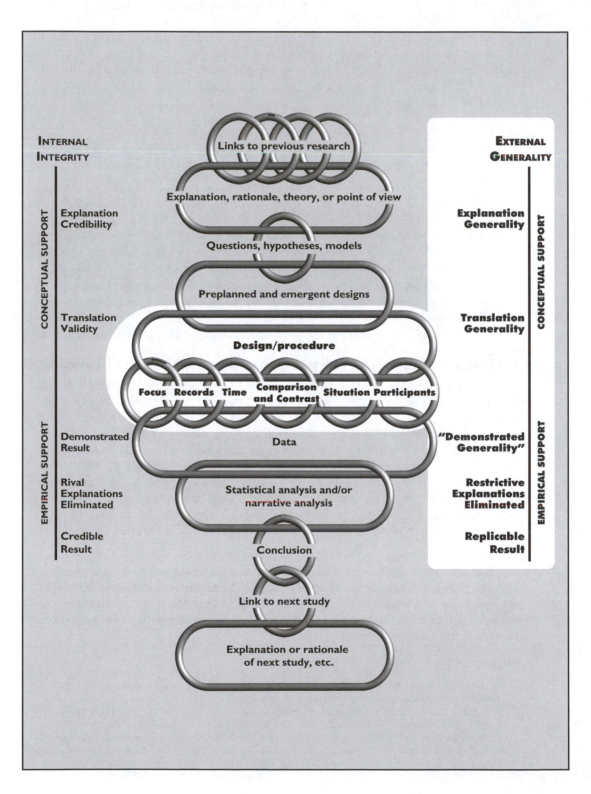

8

Sampling, Representation, and External Generality

Sampling is ever present throughout the chain of reasoning. Obviously it is of concern in the selection of a **sample** of participants. Wherever we use a subset to represent the larger whole, we are sampling. Indeed, the design of the study itself is a sample of the possible designs that could have been employed. Unrepresentativeness limits generality of the findings, sometimes severely. The judgments through which we infer how widely a relationship applies—its generality—are described by the *External Generality* of a study. These judgments are external in the sense that the generality being considered is that beyond the circumstances in which the study was done.

This chapter describes the general principles of sampling, shows how they are used, and since sampling is basic to the inference of generality, describes the judgments of the evidence used to infer External Generality.

INTRODUCTION

We intuitively apply sampling principles in our everyday lives, unconsciously approximating various sampling methods. From the slice we cut off, we judge whether the whole roast is done; from our neighbor's experience with a particular car, we judge whether that model provides reliable transportation. We are continually making the intuitive leap from a sample to the population, or universe, making judgments on the basis of incomplete information. Our essential decisions are of this nature: whether to attend a college on the basis of a brief guided tour, which house or apartment to rent or buy on the basis of a short visit, which job to take after brief interviews. We continually gather information from specific instances and generalize to new ones on the basis of their belonging to a common population of instances. In doing so, we treat information as a representative sample. Thus, sampling is continually present in our lives.

However, the sampling described above tends to be haphazard, sometimes even biased, instead of methodical. Unfortunately, we often find out too late that the sample we chose was not representative—the neighbor's car was used mainly on long rather than on short trips, the apartment looks dreary at night compared with the daylight visit, the college's guided tour presented only the best side of the college. Systematically applying sampling principles has the advantage of giving greater assurance of representativeness.

Just as in daily life, sampling is everywhere in research. Some instances such as those involved in polling and sample surveys differ from those involved in historical studies and qualitative work, but the principles of sampling are the same in all instances. Wherever our research points to a generalization, the question is: "What is its generality to persons, places, times, and events beyond the situation in which it was researched?"

The inference of **generality** is derived from the relationship between what is studied and that piece of the world of which it is a component and of which it is therefore representative. The piece of the world to which we wish to generalize, in sampling, we refer to as the **population** or universe. Populations and universes are made up of units. In social science research the units are usually people or behaviors, and it is these we sample. Because we can only interact with small parts of our world at any given time, we are continually sampling and, on the basis of what we can see or otherwise sense, make judgments about the rest that we cannot sense directly.

> ▶ Sampling procedures are ways of selecting a small number of units from a population to enable researchers to make reliable inferences about the nature of the population to which the units belong.

Sampling is used in public opinion and consumer polling to make inferences about how citizens will vote on Election Day or how consumers will react to a new product or television program. Sampling is used in qualitative research in the selection of interviewees or persons to observe. Sampling is involved in all six facets of design choice in experimentation. Its use to find *participants* and *situations* is obvious. Its use in measurement and other *records* is less obvious but nevertheless important (see chapter 18). So, sampling is universal to the methods and is an important tool.

PRINCIPLES OF SAMPLING

As a child, each of us may recall reaching into a cookie jar so high on a shelf we couldn't see into it. If we wanted to know the contents, we didn't necessarily take the top cookies but reached in, mixed them up, and then drew out a few cookies. We intuitively knew that we could judge from the handful we had withdrawn the freshness or staleness of the cookies we could not see or smell (*the inferential leap from sample to population*).

Further, we understood that the larger the sample of cookies we drew, the more certain we could be in any conclusion we might draw about the rest of the cookies (*certainty of the inference increases with sample size*).

We also intuitively understood that if the first cookie was stale, as was the second, the third, and even the fourth, there was very little or no variation in freshness. Thus, even with that small a sample, we inferred the jar contained stale cookies. (*Where there is very little variation among the units of the population, a small sample will do. If the units are all identical, a sample of one tells the nature of the population!*) However, if the first were quite fresh, the second stale, the third in between, and the fourth on the stale side, we would have a hard time judging the average freshness from a small sample. (*All things being equal, a larger sample is required to judge the nature of a highly variable population than of one that is homogeneous.*)

Suppose we think the chocolate cookies are larger than the molasses ones in the jar but we aren't sure. How many cookies do we need to examine to find out? It depends. Let's say chocolate cookies vary one from another by as much as half an inch because of different baking conditions, and so do molasses cookies. In our cookie jar the typical chocolate cookie is two inches larger than the molasses, a difference easy to see even given the half-inch variability due to baking conditions. But there is another cookie jar over at a friend's house, and the difference between the chocolate and molasses cookies there is only half an inch. Remember, the normal variation in baking conditions also causes differences of half an inch. This could mask the difference between chocolate and molasses, especially in a small sample that might accidentally consist of a bunch of big ones or small ones. In a large sample, differences in baking conditions will average out over both the chocolate and molasses cookies such that the average difference in size of the two kinds will be apparent. (*A larger sample is required when a difference we are trying to sense—or estimate—is masked by the normal variation in the sample.*)

Let's stop for a moment and recapitulate what we intuitively know: We are interested in generalizing from a sample to some target we shall call a population or universe. In our example, the cookies in the jar were the population about which we wished to infer freshness. As the cookie tale illustrates, sample and target need not be individuals. Although we generally think of populations as consisting of individuals, the terms *population* and *universe* can apply to anything; these words are very broadly used in research. For example, we sample not only individuals but also universes of situations, of instruments, of possible treatments or variables, of possible designs and procedures—each is a realm to be sampled.

In the Zimbardo study, the college student sample represented the population of persons who might develop paranoia with an unrecognized sensory deficit. The laboratory interaction was representative of social situations. The measures of paranoia were a sample of possible instruments from the universe of measures of paranoia. Each choice stood for, or represented, a target population of persons or a universe of situations or instruments and was intended to allow us to generalize to it. Although there were good reasons for the particular choices made for the study, other choices presumably would have been acceptable. Said in another way, the choices made for that or any study are made from larger sets of alternatives. Other choices presumably could be made from those sets of individuals, situations, measures, and procedures and provide us with the same results. In other words, the study would replicate if it had generality.

Required sample size is related to four factors. A larger sample is necessary if:

▶ Greater certainty is required of the inferential leap from sample to population. (We want to be absolutely sure the cookies are fresh!)

▶ We desire to be more precise about the exact nature of the target population. (We want to know very accurately how fresh they are.)

▶ Many units in the sample vary from one another on the characteristic of interest— being heterogeneous rather than homogeneous. (Because the small sample varies in freshness, it is hard to know just how fresh the cookies are on average.)

▶ The effect to be sensed is small, relative to the normal variation among the sampling units. (The variation in cookie size due to normal baking conditions is large in relation to the difference in size between two kinds of cookies.)

The first two principles in the summary above make good intuitive sense. We might do a quick pilot study with a few cases, but we intuitively know that it will only approximate the results of a larger study. Our faith in the results of the former cannot be as great as it would be in the results of the latter. If we want to know the average height of men very precisely, although we might be able to approximate it to the nearest inch with a sample of 20 or so, we can sense intuitively that a much larger sample is required to know it to the nearest hundredth of an inch.

The third principle also seems intuitively true. When the population varies considerably with respect to a characteristic, the cases in any sample will typically vary widely on that characteristic as well. However, a small sample might contain only cases at one extreme of that characteristic (stale cookies). Because of the variability we wouldn't know whether the whole population was stale or whether by chance that sample of cookies contained mainly stale cookies and those in the population were mainly fresh. Only with a larger sample is the chance factor minimized.

According to the fourth principle, the sample size is frequently increased to ensure that a study's positive result won't be missed. This is called *increasing the sensitivity or power of a study*. The waves left behind by a speeding boat are easy to follow for long distances when the water has few waves but are difficult to see even a short distance behind the boat in a storm. When the normal variability among units of a population is large and the effect we are looking for is small by comparison, normal variability may mask consistent differences.

Consider again our friend's chocolate and molasses cookies, remembering that in the population, on average, the chocolate cookies are half an inch larger. Remember too that variation in baking conditions can also create differences of half an inch. A small sample might, by chance, consist of a combination of undersized (normally larger) chocolate cookies baked under unfavorable conditions and oversized (normally smaller) molasses cookies baked under favorable conditions. Inferring the relative sizes of the cookies in the population from this small sample, we might judge them equal—no difference in size. With a sample of 1,000 cookies, however, favorable and unfavorable baking conditions would average out, and the average size of molasses cookies would be almost the same from sample to sample. So too would a larger sample stabilize the average size of the typically larger chocolate cookies. As a result, any sample of chocolate cookies would have a larger average size than any sample of molasses cookies. The difference is no longer masked by the variations between samples when the samples are large and the averages therefore have little variation.

These principles govern sampling of all kinds. Indeed, it is through the use of these principles that different probability methods of sampling are devised. We will refresh our memory of them as we study the various sampling methods.

PROBABILITY AND NONPROBABILITY SAMPLING

Sampling methods are typically divided into probability and nonprobability techniques. **Probability sampling** enables us to make inferences about characteristics of the population—for example, its average value, its variability across the population, and the margin of error in these statistics. In announcing polling results, for example, "Johnson received 42% of the straw poll" is usually followed by something like "the poll has a margin of error of 3.2 points." The latter figure is computed using inferential statistics which, based on sampling, allow us to estimate probabilities.

All probability samples involve random sampling of units from the population at some stage in the sampling process ("We didn't necessarily take the top cookies but reached in, *mixed them up, and then drew out* . . ."). It is from this process that statisticians can construct a probability model. That model allows the construction of statistics that give us probabilities such as those in the Zimbardo study—for example, ($t =$ 2.86, $P < .01$) and ($z = 5.00$, $P < .001$). P refers to probability values that come from these inferential statistics, as do such statements as "significant at the 5% level." Inferential statistics are the topic of chapter 19.

If probability samples involve random sampling at some stage in the sampling process, it follows that **nonprobability sampling** does not. For example, the panels used in rating television programs' audience size are not random samples but meet the profile of typical TV-viewing families. They may indeed be representative of such families but, because random sampling did not enter into their choice, they are not probability samples.

We noted that sampling pervaded all six links at the design level of the chain of reasoning. Where employed, random sampling is usually confined to the *participants* link and occasionally the *situation* link (e.g., sampling schools or communities). Nonprobability methods are typically used for the selection of measures, forms of treatments, designs, procedures, and other aspects of the study design. For example, in the choice of treatment that involves the teaching of outlining in English composition, we would intentionally choose a teaching method selected to be representative of possible ways of teaching outlining rather than choosing by random sampling. Furthermore, additional criteria such as ease of use and popularity might additionally make nonrandom sampling appropriate.

PROBABILITY SAMPLING PROCEDURES

Sampling procedures allow us to substitute the study of some of its units for a study of all the units of the population. The list of units from which we draw the sample in any sampling procedure is called the **sampling frame.** For a survey of teacher morale in a school district, the sampling frame might be a list of all the teachers in the district. The population would be the teachers in the district, and from the data obtained on our sample we would infer the morale of the teachers in the district. A city directory, a faculty directory, a telephone book, and a club or church membership list are all examples of sampling frames. At some point in the sampling procedure, probability samples must have a list of the units from which they intend to sample—a sampling frame.

Problems of nonrepresentativeness can usually be traced to some inadequacy of the sampling frame. A famous case is the *Literary Digest* poll, which had experienced considerable success in predicting presidential elections using telephone books as a proxy for voter rolls. In 1931, their prediction of Herbert Hoover as winner was wrong by a wide margin. Franklin D. Roosevelt's win was missed because their sampling frame excluded the many less well-to-do Democratic voters who could not afford telephones. (See Kish, 1965, for a discussion of frame problems.)

Simple Random Sampling

The basic method on which all other methods of probability sampling are built is simple **random sampling**, because all probability methods involve it at some stage in the process. Simple random sampling requires that each unit of the population have an equal chance of being selected. A more precise definition is that all possible samples of a given size have an equal opportunity of being selected.

The definition makes it clear that the choice of any unit is independent of the choice of any other. Recall that before we drew a cookie, we mixed the cookies. That was to ensure that every unit had an equal chance at each drawing. Note that randomness is provided by the process by which we drew the sample.

How do we obtain a random sample in research? The first task is to define the population and the sampling unit. The population is that group from which the sample is to be chosen and of which the sample is to be representative. Put another way, the population is the group to which we would expect the results of our study to generalize. For simple random sampling, the sampling frame and the population are the same.

Although we may have a conceptual notion about what the target population should be, it is the translation of this conceptual notion into a sampling frame that makes the concept real and is the determiner of the generality. Suppose a university faculty member, concerned that her students do not seem to be applying themselves to their doctoral studies as they once did, hypothesizes that they are working full- or part-time while also trying to be students. She suggests surveying students regarding their employment status while working for a doctoral degree. Sounds straightforward, doesn't it?

But what is the sampling frame? All students, both part-time and full-time? If only full-time students, what defines a full-time student? Those taking nine hours of credit? Aren't graduate assistants who take only six credit hours considered full-time students? In some cases, to exclude graduate assistants would exclude whole departments. But, since graduate assistants are not supposed to be also employed outside the university, including them artificially lowers the averages for everyone. However we answer these questions, the definition of "full-time graduate student" determines the sampling frame and the population. The population definition clearly is a critical question in designing studies.

Disjunction between the sampling frame and the target population of generalization is a common problem of simple random sampling. If we want to generalize to all college students, how representative of the target population is one university? The generality we can ascribe to the data of a study always depends on the study's operational definition of the population and an inferential leap from it to the target population.

Sampling unit.   As might be expected from the chain of reasoning, the unit used in stating the problem is usually the same as the unit used in the hypothesis, in sampling, in analysis, and in stating the conclusion. In the morale survey of a school district cited above, the individual teachers in the district would be the sampling unit. But the choice of unit is less clear when we make comparisons between aggregated units. For instance, when we test a new curriculum in a school, we are not interested in how well, as individuals, Johnny did with the new and Rebecca with the old, but in how well Johnny's class did in comparison with Rebecca's. Is our sampling unit here students or classes?

Ordinarily, the rule to follow is that the **sampling unit** is the smallest unit receiving the treatment. In a typical curriculum study this would be the class, since all students experience the same treatment together rather than independently. Some studies examine both class and individual effects and require that attention be paid to achieving a representative sample at both levels.

How to choose units.   Typically, having numbered the units in the sampling frame, we use those numbers to choose the sample. This method can also involve using the page number, column number, and location in the column as a set of numbers to designate each person in a paged list. In a 20-page, two-column, 25-names-per-column directory, this would be a randomly selected five-digit number. Presumably, as is done with many lotteries, we could enter the numbers on slips and then have someone who is blindfolded draw the required number of slips. Partly because of the labor and especially because of the difficulty of ensuring that the slips are really thoroughly mixed, we more often use computer software to generate random numbers (see http://random.org, a Web site that offers true random numbers to anyone on the Internet) or a table of random numbers (e.g., RAND Corporation, 1969). Use any arbitrary rule as long as it provides an equal chance for any number to be chosen. For example, if a sample of 60 is wanted out of a sampling frame containing 423 units, arbitrarily pick a starting place in an output of random numbers. Examine each successive set of three numbers, accepting as a sample member those under 424, discarding those 424 and up.

Representativeness and bias.   Why is so much emphasis placed on randomness? It avoids **bias** by ensuring that all relevant population characteristics have an equal chance of being represented in our sample. Bias has many possible causes. Without guidance from a table of random numbers, interviewers sampling individuals in a shopping mall may choose more men than women or more well-dressed than shabbily dressed people because of unconscious personal preferences. This would clearly bias the sample.

A nice thing about a genuine random sample is that it will, on average, represent *all* characteristics of the population, especially with large samples. Thus, we are protected even from characteristics that we were not aware could affect the study. What does that protection mean in practice? Well, let us suppose that we are interested in how well a new curriculum will fare with the average youngster in a school district. A random sample will, on the average, give us a group that has not only the same average intelligence level as the students in the district but also the same motivation level and attitude toward whatever subject we are working with—all characteristics that might affect our study. The same average length of fingernails and shoe size are characteristics that probably will not affect our study—but exposure to and interest in TV programs are characteristics that might, although we may not have considered them in advance.

Sample size—How big is big enough?   Notice that we have always hedged by saying "on average" and "with large samples." How big is big enough? The answer depends on the four principles of sampling we considered earlier: How precise do we want to be? How sure do we want to be of our answer? How much variation is there in what we are studying? How small an effect do we want to sense in contrast to the normal variation in the sample units? If we can answer these questions, there are statistical formulas that will tell us how large a sample is required (as we will see in chapter 19). *This is the only way we can determine the minimum needed sample size.* Conventional wisdom, such as "thirty cases are enough," doesn't do it.

Stratified Sampling

There are other things we can do to ensure representativeness besides increasing sample size. For example, we can use **stratified sampling**. Recall that a smaller sample will do the job of a larger one when the units are homogeneous. Stratified sampling uses that principle.

Because researchers want to do what they can to assure representativeness, stratified sampling is more common than simple random sampling. Suppose that when we eat some cookies, we notice—maybe because they help retain moisture—that the number of raisins in the cookie is an approximate guide to its freshness. Suppose further that the baker, afraid she might run out of raisins, started by using slightly fewer (but about the same number of) raisins than the recipe called for in each cookie batch. Later, realizing she had underestimated her stock, she grew more and more generous with the amount of raisins used in each batch.

Several weeks later we want to find the batch's freshness. Since each jar was filled from a single cookie sheet, although the average number of raisins per cookie differs from jar to jar, the number of raisins per cookie within each jar is pretty much the same—homogeneous. Therefore, the batches' freshness can be represented by a smaller random sample of cookies from each jar than if each had the full range of variation.

This is the process of stratified random sampling: we classify the units in the sampling frame (the cookies) into strata (the jars) on the basis of a characteristic (order of baking sequence and, therefore, number of raisins) that, if not properly represented in the sample, might bias our inferences. This reduces the variability of that characteristic in each stratum. Randomly sampling from each stratum gives us representativeness with a smaller sample size (or, using the same size, allows us to be more exact in our estimation of the population characteristic and surer of that estimate).

Proportional stratified sampling.   This is the most common form of stratified sampling. Consider the determination of overall mathematics achievement in a junior high school. To ensure proper representation of each grade, we make each grade a stratum and randomly sample within each one—the proportion taken being determined by the size of desired sample in relation to the size of the school. For a sample of 40 from a school of 197, 20% of each stratum would be taken.

Stratification on more than one variable.   We may stratify on more than one characteristic at a time, for instance, stratifying on gender in addition to grade to ensure proper representation of boys and girls. In a multi-cultural neighborhood, we might additionally stratify as African American, Hispanic, Asian, and other minority children as shown in Table 8.1, which illustrates three-way stratification on the basis of minority, grade, and gender for a mathematics achievement study of a junior high school. The numbers in the boxes indicate the number of students in that cell from which a random sample of pupils would be drawn. With a total of 197 students in the table, to obtain a sample of 50 we would randomly select 25% of the students in each cell, alternately rounding 50% up or down.

Table 8.1   Stratification on Multiple Variables

Minority	African American			Hispanic			Asian			Other		
Grade	6	7	8	6	7	8	6	7	8	6	7	8
Boys	1	7	7	4	3	6	2	3	1	7	8	6
Girls	3	9	8	6	1	5	2	1	1	9	9	6

Unless the stratifying variables are independent of each other, we gain little by stratifying on more than one characteristic. For example, since at one time most women were not given advanced education, gender and highest level of education were not independent and stratifying on gender achieved most of the advantage of also classifying on education. With the equal education of women this is no longer true, and the additional stratification is justified. It is rare, however, that more than a triple stratification is advantageous.

Intentional oversampling.   How does one handle situations like that in Table 8.1 where many cells are less than four? With small cell sizes, some groups might not even be present in a small sample. With only one case in each cell, seventh- and eighth-grade Asian girls and eighth-grade Asian boys would be rounded down to zero and would not be included. A 25% sample taking all the Asians in Table 8.1 would be only three students. **Oversampling**—taking extra cases, perhaps everyone from those cells—permits us to study these groups separately and then combine them by appropriately weighting them. Taking 10 Asians would constitute 20% of the sample, but this overrepresentation would allow accurate characterization of them. However, when the average achievement of the school is determined, Asians are weighted 10/197 when combined with the rest of the strata, or about 5%, their correct proportion in the school.

When to stratify.   You should stratify when a bias threat is serious (as, for instance, an unrepresentative religion sample would be in studying the abortion issue) or whenever you can do so easily. By randomly sampling within strata, you do no worse than simple random sampling although you lose the extra time and energy involved. If the stratifying variable turns out not to be biasing, stratifying gains mainly peace of mind—not an unimportant aspect. By the luck of the draw ten pennies will come up all heads once in 1,024 tosses, but if that one time is your sample it is little consolation that your sample is unusual. It is best to ensure representativeness through stratifying if you either have or can easily obtain the accurate information you need.

Advantages and Disadvantages of Simple Random and Stratified Sampling

Table 8.2 summarizes the advantages and disadvantages of simple random and stratified sampling. Note that where considerable information about a population is available one should use stratified sampling to take advantage of it; simple random sampling doesn't. However, where no information is available, random sampling will obtain, on average, a representative sample of every characteristic of the sample.

Systematic Sampling

One of the most commonly used and simplest sampling patterns is **systematic sampling**. Although not really simple random sampling, this method can approximate it. To draw a sample of 50 from a sampling frame of 500 names, we would take every tenth name instead of bothering with a random number table. If the characteristic on which the sampling frame is ordered could be considered a stratifying variable in the study, systematic sampling will have the effect of stratification. Suppose the sampling frame lists individuals in order of their learning ability. A systematic sample of the top 10% would be comparable to a proportionate random sample of the top 10% stratum. The same is true for the middle and lowest groups, which would thus represent the sampling frame just as if we had done proportionate stratified sampling. Another advantage is that in an alphabetized list of names, this approach will avoid repeat sampling from the same family.

When using systematic sampling, however, we should be sure there is no periodicity in the sampling frame that is related to what we are investigating. Let's suppose we take every tenth name, and every tenth room in a list of dormitory rooms is a corner room. Being preferred suites, these are assigned to student floor leaders. Then, depending on where we start in the sampling frame, we may have either all corner rooms or no corner rooms—neither a representative sample. Such a sample would make considerable difference in a study of the social life of students. Table 8.3 summarizes the advantages and disadvantages of systematic sampling.

Table 8.2   Advantages and Disadvantages of Random and Stratified Sampling

	Description	Advantages	Disadvantages
Simple Random Sampling	• Assigns each population member a unique number; selects members using a random number table.	• Requires minimum knowledge of population in advance. • Is free of possible classification errors. • Makes it easy to analyze data and compute statistics.	• Does not make use of knowledge of population that researcher may have. • Results in larger errors for same sample size than stratified sampling does. • Requires identifying and in some studies traveling to units over whole population area.
Proportional Stratified Sampling	• Sorts units of population into groups (strata) on basis of the characteristic(s) to be properly represented in the sample, characteristics that, if improperly represented, might result in incorrect inferences. • Randomly selects from each stratum cases equal in number to the ratio of that stratum's size to the population or sampling frame.	• Ensures representativeness of whatever characteristic is used to classify units. • Depending on how closely the stratifying variable is related to the variable being studied, there will be greater homogeneity in each stratum so each can be represented with fewer cases. • Compared with simple random sampling, fewer cases yield equal accuracy. If size is retained, we gain greater accuracy and confidence in the estimates.	• Requires accurate information on proportion of population in each stratum, or error is increased. • If information for classification is not available, may make it costly to obtain and prepare lists. • Risks improper classification of individuals in strata due to clerical error or poor measurement.

Table 8.3   Advantages and Disadvantages of Systematic Sampling

Description	Advantages	Disadvantages
• Uses the natural order of the sampling frame, selecting every nth item beginning at some random point and cycling through the list; the value of n is the ratio of the desired size of sample to the size of the sampling frame.	• Very simple to draw a sample. • If a population list is ordered with a variable related to what is being studied, it has the effect of stratification on that variable.	• May result in nonrepresentativeness if n is related to a periodic ordering in the population listing. • If the stratification effect is not taken into account, certain statistics will yield estimates of accuracy that are too low.

Cluster Sampling

We noted in Table 8.2 that if the selected units were scattered over large distances and we wished to contact them personally, random sampling would create significant travel problems. Researchers use **cluster sampling** to solve these problems by dropping a grid over a map to divide the area into geographic units, and then randomly select units. We may use all the cases in a unit (which may be a block or several blocks), or randomly sample within it. We may do multiple-stage sampling. For example, after cluster sampling, we would stratify within each cluster on a relevant variable and randomly sample within each strata—cluster followed by stratified and then random sampling.

Cluster sampling has the advantage not only of reducing travel but also of requiring complete sampling frames only for the selected clusters. Because both travel and compilation of sampling frames can be costly, cluster sampling is widely used for studies involving interviewing.

You may ask, "Since people live in relatively homogeneous neighborhoods, how can a few units be representative of the whole city?" Unless the selected units cover all neighborhood types, such lack of representation can be a problem. Indeed, the error in estimating population values is likely to be greater with cluster than with random or stratified sampling for the same size sample. Researchers often use multistage to ensure appropriate sampling of neighborhood types, stratifying within clusters on a significant characteristic such as socioeconomic class.

Clusters need not be geographical areas. Depending on what we are studying and how we define the population, we may use classrooms, schools, or other institutions as clusters. The nature of any already existing unit, however, may result from factors that make it nonrepresentative for our study (for example, problem students are given to the new teacher, parents choose neighborhoods for its better schools, occupations attract persons with certain skills and values). Users of cluster sampling must be fully aware of its potential difficulties. Table 8.4 summarizes the advantages and disadvantages of cluster sampling.

Table 8.4   Advantages and Disadvantages of Cluster Sampling

Description	Advantages	Disadvantages
• Uses as sampling unit a natural grouping (e.g., classrooms) or arbitrary grouping (e.g., a grid of squares placed over a city map); take a random sample of units and then either all individuals or a random sample of individuals in each unit.	• Reduces travel if clusters are used for in-person contact (e.g., interviews). • Sampling frames need be constructed only for units used in sample. • Permits studies of individual clusters and comparison of clusters. • Follow-ups can use other persons within a cluster if cluster was sampled, or other clusters can be used.	• May result in larger error in estimating population values than other probability sampling methods. • Requires each member of population be assigned uniquely to a cluster (thus, for example, if clusters are families, where should children born out of wedlock be assigned?); otherwise may omit or duplicate cases.

NONPROBABILITY SAMPLING

Nonprobability sampling methods do *not* include random sampling at some stage in the process. Because of their convenience, they are very common. Undoubtedly, the most common is the grab or convenience sample, using whatever individuals are available: the researcher interviews the first 100 persons encountered in a shopping mall, the graduate student uses students in an introductory course, the radio station invites callers to phone in votes.

How representative are such subjects? Short of taking a probability sample, there is no way to know. Clearly, the nature of situations, the constraints of time, and the characteristics of individuals predisposing them to act in certain ways all lead to a selective effect. For example, what kinds of individuals take the trouble to call the television station to praise it for a certain program? Or to complain? The kinds of persons entering a mall vary, depending on whether it is morning (when homemakers, preschool children, and retirees are likely to predominate) or lunch hour (when workers join in). Certain kinds of persons choose occupations that make them available to public access; others prefer to deal with things instead of people. These are all likely to be groups with characteristics that set them apart from random samples.

Because use of any nonprobability sampling procedure immediately raises questions regarding the representativeness of the sample, it is the responsibility of the investigator to provide the best possible answer. This usually involves comparing pertinent demographic characteristics of the sample to those of the community or population to which the researcher intends to generalize. To lessen such questions, nonprobability sampling methods often have some carefully considered base. Judgmental or purposive samples and quota samples are two such types.

> ▶ Nonprobability samples are those that do *not* involve random sampling at some stage in the process.

Judgmental and Purposive Sampling

Judgmental sampling uses the experience and wisdom of the researcher to select a sample representative of the population. In **judgmental sampling**, the researcher selects individuals presumed to be typical of segments of the population who as a group will provide a representative panorama of the population.

How good are judgmental samples in representing the population? In one sense, they are as good as the researcher's knowledge of the population. In another, the answer is a pragmatic one; if the researcher is able to consistently extract accurate new information from them, they are useful. However, conditions often change and if the researcher doesn't change the sample appropriately, inaccurate information can result. For instance, what judgmental samples of television program ratings would you use, given the increasing trend of releasing recently aired programs on the Internet? Only a genuine probability sample protects against such changes. The fact that researchers have continued to produce beneficial information from judgmental samples accounts for their continued use.

Purposive sampling is most often used in qualitative research to select those individuals or behaviors that will better inform the researcher regarding the current focus of the investigation. It is common in qualitative research and sometimes evaluation. Researchers might chose individuals to interview or observe who have information, perspective, social contacts, or whatever the researchers need next. Such individuals may or may not be representative of the group to whom one wishes to generalize. For example, after picking their initial sample and drawing some conclusions with that group, qualitative researchers often test the robustness of those conclusions by deliberately choosing individuals who will put their ideas to the test. Such sampling strengthens the logic of the method and, when done properly, is a good test of the findings.

Similarly, researchers may sample extreme or deviant cases, either to see how far a generalization extends or to view the problem in an extreme light with the hope of finding some clue about more normal cases. Sometimes, anticipating audience questions, researchers sample cases that if not included might cast doubt on the conclusions of the study.

Quota Sampling

This sampling method requires prior knowledge of the characteristics related as stratifying variables to whatever we are studying. A nonprobability form of stratification, **quota sampling** requires that we establish quotas for characteristics of individuals to ensure that they are distributed in the sample as they are in the population. For example, knowing the community's gender ratio and the proportion of each racial group and religion helps the researcher establish quotas for each of these variables to ensure that the sample has those characteristics. This assumes, of course, that providing an accurate representation of these variables assures sufficient representativeness with respect to whatever we are studying.

Fitting the sample to quotas often requires obtaining the respondent's profile at the interview's outset and proceeding only if he or she fits an open quota. Alternatively, the interviewer can gather data regardless of fit, and, provided that all quotas are sufficiently covered, weight the results so as to represent each group's responses in a proportion appropriate for the population.

Despite the appealing logic of the method, the individuals in any quota are simply a convenience sample of that group. Unless properly supervised, interviewers will seek out busy areas to easily fill their quotas—shopping malls, entertainment areas, terminals and depots, and so forth. Depending on the problem, oversampling the kinds of individuals who collect in such places could result in a biased study. Even when properly instructed, interviewers are likely to avoid less desirable situations—upper floors where there is no elevator, dilapidated buildings, and so on. Clearly nonrepresentative samples can occur many ways. Still, quota sampling is a favorite of pollsters who, with experience, have learned to avoid some of its problems.

Chain–Referral Sampling

This sampling method (also called *snowball sampling* and *referential sampling*) is used to find members of a group not otherwise visibly identified. Suppose we wished to learn the names of influential members of the state legislature lobbying community. Although we could identify the members of the lobbying group, we would not know which were influential; indeed, such individuals might not be visibly identified within that group. Using **chain-referral sampling,** we start with a powerful state legislature member and ask the names of the most influential lobbyists as well as others in a position to give an opinion. Interviewing the latter, in turn, might lead to other individuals whom they think would know; and so we continue until we come full circle, getting names of persons already identified. This method has been used to identify members of crime groups and others engaged in covert activities. (For additional reading see Biernacki & Waldorf, 1981.)

> ◗ Whenever nonprobability samples are used, the representativeness of the sample is a prime question in the reader's mind.
>
> ◗ Judgmental, purposive, and quota sampling all involve some conception of characteristics of the target population (often based on demographic data) that could critically influence what is being studied. Judgmental and quota sampling are used by pollsters who select their samples to fit the appropriate profile of these characteristics. Qualitative researchers use purposive sampling to explore their problems, test their hypotheses, and/or show generality.
>
> ◗ Chain-referral sampling is used to discover the members of a group of individuals not otherwise easily identified by starting with someone in the know and asking for referrals to other knowledgeable individuals.

Sequential Sampling

Starting with an initial batch of cases, data from successive samples is cumulatively analyzed in **sequential sampling** to determine if the needed statistical precision has been met. If not, sampling is continued until it is. (*Statistical precision* refers to estimating desired population statistics, such as the average income of the sample, with a predetermined accuracy, such as to the nearest $1,000. The procedure for doing this involves developing a *confidence interval*, a concept discussed in chapters 18 and 19.) Sequential sampling is used in field samples where whatever is being studied is not continually changing, and the study itself has not caused an increased awareness of the topic, thereby biasing further data collection. Increasingly used in telephone polls, population values are cumulatively computed as interviewee responses are entered, and interviewing is stopped when the desired accuracy is reached.

Sequential sampling can be used with any of the probability or nonprobability sampling methods. It is of particular advantage when we know how precisely we wish to estimate the population characteristics but do not know the variability of the population. The work of qualitative researchers may be considered as a kind of sequential sampling as they continue to observe and/or interview until they stop getting fresh insights or having new useful experiences.

> ◗ Sequential sampling involves gathering additional data in successive waves until some criterion of adequacy is met. It can save resources but assumes that the units do not change during the sampling process.

EXTERNAL GENERALITY

When we make a judgment of how broadly and strongly the appropriate interpretation of the evidence supports the generalization of the causal relationship beyond the circumstances in which it was studied, we are determining the study's **External Generality**. Put another way, it is the power of a study to create a consensus among research consumers about the appropriate interpretation of the study's evidence regarding the generality of the study's conclusions. As with Internal Integrity, the judgment of generality is based on evidence gathered in anticipation of questions in the minds of the study's research consumers.

Just as knowledge is better viewed as a reduction in uncertainty, so are Internal Integrity and External Generality. Internal Integrity reduces our uncertainty that the relationship exists in the circumstances in which it was investigated; External Generality reduces our uncertainty that the relationship generalizes in certain ways beyond the circumstances in which it was studied.

By now it must be clear that generality depends on what the study's sample can be presumed to represent—that is, its relation to the populations of persons, situations, forms of treatments, measures of constructs, and other things to which the researcher intends to generalize. However, it is the judgment of the "gatekeepers to dissemination" that determines the likely useful generality of the findings. On what basis do these gatekeepers make the judgment of generality? A series of five sequential judgments make up External Generality. The judgments are parallel to those of which Internal Integrity is composed; each is similar in name and content.

Again, we have both conceptual and empirical evidence and a wrap-up judgment, this time of generality. The conceptual evidence consists of two judgments: The first is a judgment of the generality claimed, implied, or inferred from the explanation—**explanation generality**. The second is the extent to which the generality claimed, implied, or inferred is operationalized in the choices made in the design of the study—**translation generality**. The empirical evidence consists of the two judgments: **"demonstrated generality"** (the quotation marks are intentional and explained in the detailed discussion that follows) and the elimination of **restrictive explanations (conditions)**. Finally, a judgment is made whether there is a **replicable result** (a criterion suggested by Cronbach, 1982). The evidence is summed up to gauge the strength of the study's External Generality. Figure 8.1 places these criteria with their parallels in Internal Integrity on the chain of reasoning.

> ▶ External Generality is a judgment of how broadly and strongly the appropriate interpretation of the evidence supports the generalization of the causal relationship beyond the circumstances in which it was studied. It involves judgments of conceptual evidence, empirical evidence, and a credible result.

Relation of External Generality to Internal Integrity

Some of the judgments of External Generality depend on those of Internal Integrity. For example, if the explanation makes little sense and therefore lacks

Figure 8.1   The judgments of External Generality and Internal Integrity as they relate to the chain of reasoning.

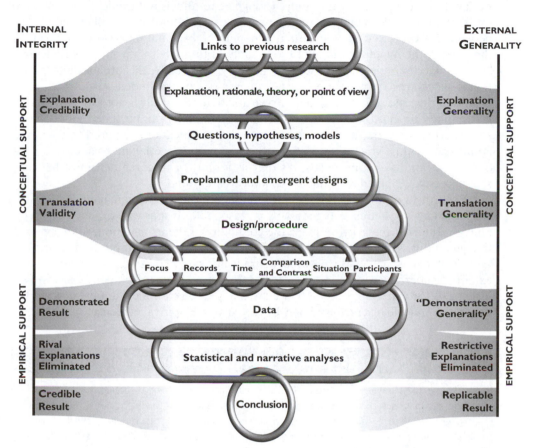

explanation credibility, explanation generality is typically irrelevant. Similarly, if the translation into the operations of the study is unsatisfactory (translation validity), it makes little sense to be concerned with translation generality. If there is no effect and no demonstrated result, there can be no "demonstrated generality." Some of the rival explanations that were not eliminated may restrict the generality of the findings and may therefore be involved in the judgment of whether restrictive explanations were eliminated. Finally, of course, if we do not have a credible result, we can hardly expect it to replicate; thus, replicable result is affected.

In addition, strengthening Internal Integrity is often done at the expense of External Generality—for instance, moving the study into a laboratory. Balancing the demands of the two is discussed in the next chapter, chapter 9.

Let's return to the Zimbardo study to illustrate how we would make the five judgments of External Generality.

Initial Conceptual Evidence: (1) Explanation Generality

Explanation generality is a judgment of the generality stated or implied in the explanation or rationale of the study. Though generality is not explicitly described in the Zimbardo study, by implication the hypothesis is intended to apply to all elderly people. However, as we noted earlier, although the explanation is stated in terms of the elderly, the hypothesis is stated so broadly as to apply to anyone experiencing a "perceptual discontinuity" or "sensory anomaly." Certainly, this broader interpretation is necessary to make sense of data gathered on college students.

As in this case, often the generality we attribute to a study is not explicitly stated; it is implied or must be inferred. After all, explanations can be stated more simply and clearly if they are not cluttered with all the qualifications required to detail the boundaries within which they hold. Furthermore, many explanations start out without qualifications—as universals. It's only as a body of research develops that they are successively limited as boundary conditions are found.

Regardless of whether clearly stated, implied, or inferred, explanation generality is a judgment of whether that generality is reasonable. Just as with explanation credibility, in Internal Integrity we judge the credibility of the explanation, so in explanation generality we judge the credibility of the claimed, implied, or inferred generality. If it seems reasonable, we proceed to translation generality to see whether that extent of generality was operationalized in the study. If we reject, doubt, or can find little basis for expecting generality, we are likely to be extremely critical of a study's generality and will be convinced only by very strong empirical evidence.

Strong Empirical Evidence without Conceptual Explanations

There are studies with little rationale that do present strong evidence. For example, some researchers devise studies with only the loosest rationale for why they might uncover predictive relationships and then seek them—like the medical clinician who tries all kinds of plants as he or she looks for one with therapeutic properties. Such studies have created highly successful predictive instruments such as the Strong-Campbell Interest Inventory and the Minnesota Multiphasic Personality Inventory (MMPI). Even though we can't conceptually explain why they do so, such instruments have proven to have wide "demonstrated generality" and have been shown to work in a broad range of situations. The Strong-Campbell, for instance, can usefully predict vocational success in a number of fields, and the MMPI is heavily used in clinical psychology as an aid in diagnosing mental illnesses in a wide variety of patients. Even for such uses the search to provide explanation credibility continues as clinicians seek explanations for why the instruments work.

▶ Explanation generality is a judgment of the plausibility of the generality that is claimed, implied, or inferred for the relationship.

More Conceptual Evidence: (2) Translation Generality

The *determination of generality is always an inference*. It is a leap of faith to generalize from any given instance to others like it. That leap is clearly much safer if the instances in which it was demonstrated are representative of the target to which the leap is to be made. That is the importance of translation generality. Both translation validity and translation generality are concerned with accuracy of translation into operational terms. The former is concerned with the accuracy of translation of question, hypothesis, or model into choices at the design level; the latter, with whether the breadth of generality claimed, implied, or inferred is represented in those choices. Are the choices representative of the targets to which the researcher wishes the study to generalize—the individuals, situations, treatment versions, alternative instruments, alternative research procedures, times, and so on?

Usually, the question, hypothesis, or model stemming from an explanation is but one instance out of the breadth of expected generality. A test of the proposition "frustration leads to aggression" might be to study crowded elevators, but such a focus would not validate the extent of generality. That would require evidence from a variety of kinds of individuals, situations, and so on. Clearly, we should make design choices from within the populations to which we hope to generalize; however, in addition, these choices ought to be representative of them. Let's look at the six facets in which we make design choices.

Focus.   In some instances, the treatment is carefully standardized for all participants. This is particularly true of the Zimbardo study; directions were administered mechanically with slide projectors or electronically with tape recordings. Standardization was achieved in the social interaction by carefully training and rehearsing the confederates. Such standardization is typical where the goal is knowledge of whether the causal relation exists. Standardization is very important for Internal Integrity because it eliminates the rival explanation that differences in treatment application were in some way involved in producing the effect. Standardization that requires unusual situations or equipment may restrict the generality to similar situations or equipment.

Representativeness with respect to treatment involves including that variability in the definition of the treatment. Where we are interested in the useful application of a treatment, there is likely to be variability in its application among the persons using it, the way it is applied, the equipment used, the circumstances preceding application, the application situation, and so on. For example, in studying a particular way of increasing classroom learning, different teachers might apply the method in their own ways.

One aspect of the definition of treatment is how the treatment will be mastered by the people who apply it. If it is to have useful generality, it should be mastered as it would be in normal practice. For example, if the new classroom procedure is to be mastered from a teacher's guide, learning from the guide alone is an essential aspect of the treatment. If, however, teachers would typically be given extra help and explanation, either by a supervisor or by in-service training classes, then either or both should be a part of treatment.

Another aspect of treatment definition is determining appropriate treatment variability for generality. Internal Integrity requires maintaining treatment fidelity—

that is, how much variation can be tolerated and still have the intended treatment. External Generality is concerned with representation of the likely variability of application in practice. For example, Rowe (1974) noted that as the time that a teacher waits for a student's response increases, classroom discussion changes toward more considered responses, more student-to-student interchange, higher-level thinking, and so on. Treatment fidelity for Internal Integrity would involve defining the range within which wait-time should be increased (too long and discussion drags) and monitoring teachers to ensure it is maintained. Translation generality would involve assuring there was a representative variety of wait times within this range appropriate to typical teachers.

Records.   How representative of all possible valid measures and instruments are the chosen measures or observation instruments? Could we substitute others for them without changing the results, or is there something unique about them? For example, is the measure affected by the way it is administered—paper and pencil, interview, observation? Might we get substantively different results if the information were gathered in a different way? In the Zimbardo study, the key factor to be measured was the development of paranoia. The researchers used three measures of paranoia and two data modes (tests and observation). Fortunately, all of them showed the effect. If they had not, the researchers would have been faced with the difficult problem of deciding and justifying which measure of paranoia had the greatest validity and seeking a reason for the disparate results.

Time.   We seldom consider time as a factor in designing a study from which we wish to infer generality. However, Cronbach (1975) points out that some generalizations decay, especially as the culture changes. Child-rearing patterns effective in one decade may not generalize to a later one. This decay can be a serious problem for the behavioral sciences, which are often seen as progressing by assembling findings over time into larger generalities. Cronbach notes:

> The trouble . . . is that we cannot store up generalizations . . . for ultimate assembly into a network. It is as if we needed a gross of dry cells to power an engine and could only make one a month. The energy would leak out of the first cells before we have half a battery completed. So it is with the potency of our generalization. (p. 123)

We are left with the uncomfortable feeling that our generalizations are becoming less valid even as we are discovering them—which may indeed be the case. Where a social or cultural aspect is undergoing rapid change (for example, the role of women in the past half-century), knowledge about it may not generalize to a future time. Thus, where possible the circumstances of a study should anticipate those of future time to which it is expected to generalize.

Comparison and contrast.   These aspects of design also need to be representative of the kinds of designs and procedures that would allow generalization. For example, the Zimbardo study used a straightforward design comparing experimental and control groups. Except for the fact that the subjects were hypnotized, there was nothing about the way the treatment, measures, and observations were carried out that would prevent generalizing the results. The use of hypnosis, however, is a condition of the experiment that is in no way implied by the hypothesis and might limit generality. Suppose we considered hypnosis only a parlor trick or believed that easily hypnotized people are different from others. Then the results would be atypical of the population to which the study is intended to generalize.

Situations and participants.   These two aspects of design are considered together since they are often linked in research studies. Kruglanski and Kroy (1976) make the point that when a particular group is the target of generalization, a representative sample is the only appropriate set of subjects. Consider studies of how well the Scholastic Aptitude Test predicts college success. A study of students from a particular high school would not be sufficient; a cross section of the variety of high schools represented in a typical freshman class would be needed. Cook and Campbell (1979) note that using a sample of convenience (usually college undergraduates in a required course) may save time and energy. But there is a trade-off—a question nearly always exists as to whether the sample really is representative of the larger universe it is intended to represent.

The same advice applies to situations. Bracht and Glass (1968) use the term ecological validity to describe whether the choice of situation is representative of the situations to which generalization is intended.

By contrast, in instances where a proposition is universally applicable we can use anyone and any situation except where subject or situational characteristics might be biased in support of (or against) the proposition. Goldstein and Arms (1971), for example, hypothesized that watching aggressive athletic contests increases hostility and aggressiveness. They tested their hypothesis with spectators at a football contest. Suppose there were reasons to believe that their proposition might be more applicable to sports-minded individuals than to the population at large. Then, as designed, the study is a weaker demonstration of generality than, for example, one using a sample of shoppers at a mall.

In the Zimbardo study, the hypothesis seems intended to be universal—that is, intended to apply to all people who are unaware of their sensory deficit. Therefore, college students are as good as any other subjects unless something about them is particularly favorable (or unfavorable) to the hypothesis. Although they were a subgroup of such students who were particularly susceptible to hypnosis, it is hard to see how this characteristic has any bearing on their developing paranoia in the instance in which they did.

> ▶ Translation generality is a judgment of the extent to which the generality claimed, implied, or inferred in the study is represented in the operational choices of its design.

Initial Empirical Evidence: (3) "Demonstrated Generality"

In a study where the data showed generality in the instances where it should have and did not where it should not have, we say the study has **"demonstrated generality."** In the Zimbardo study, paranoia was highest in the group that was partially deaf but did not know it and, on most measures, was considerably higher than in the other groups. This finding is, of course, just what the explanation called for.

Why is "demonstrated generality" in quotation marks? To call attention to the logical impossibility of demonstrating generality in all the instances where it is intended to apply. No matter how exhaustively we research it, there is always the possibility it will not hold in an instance that has not yet been tested. Instead, we make an inferential leap from the sample to instances to which it should generalize. The quotation marks reinforce that it is an inference, not a certainty.

> ▶ "Demonstrated generality" is a judgment of the extent to which the relationship appeared in all the instances of the study in which it would be expected to do so and did not where it shouldn't.
>
> ▶ There is always an inferential leap from the particular instances in which the relationship is demonstrated to those to which it is intended to generalize.
>
> ▶ "Demonstrated generality" is in quotation marks because generality can never completely be demonstrated. There is always some untested instance in which, presumably, it might not hold.

More Empirical Evidence:
(4) Restrictive Explanations (Conditions) Eliminated

The conditions of a study under which a relationship is demonstrated may include conditions that are atypical of those to which it is intended to generalize. A study that fails to be representative of the targets to which it is to generalize has restricted generality unless those restrictive explanations (conditions) are eliminated. For example, suppose that teachers in a learning study were given extra assistance in interpreting the manual for administering the treatment. Therefore, generality could only be reasonably extended to similar situations where that same assistance was available. We couldn't be sure from the study's data that the manual alone would be effective in conveying the essentials of the treatment, even though that was the study's intention.

Why Restrictive Explanations (Conditions)?

Rival explanations of Internal Integrity became restrictive conditions in External Generality (Dr. Jason Millman pointed this out to me). To keep the names parallel, they are called restrictive explanations (conditions). They are conditions that provide explanations for restricting the generality to the particular conditions under which the relationship was demonstrated.

Such restrictions are more common than might be anticipated. For example, if a study was completed with volunteers, their extra motivation might be necessary to make the treatment effective. If the subjects know they are part of an experiment, their desire to please the researcher or to do well might also be an important factor. A test given to determine pretreatment status might cue students as to what to attend to in treatment. The most appropriate generalization of data is to situations similar to those in which the data were gathered.

Thus, this judgment looks backward to the way in which generality was translated into the study and looks forward to the intended generality of the conclusion. It places such restrictions on the latter as are necessary in view of the special conditions under which the data were gathered; or, if the study is still being designed, the researcher seeks to eliminate conditions that might be restrictive.

> ▶ Restrictive explanations (conditions) that were part of the study but would not be part of the target of generalization must be eliminated for the inferential leap to the target to be confidently made.

The Final Judgment: (5) Replicable Result

Assuming the previous four judgments are positive, we come to the final judgment, replicable result. The heart of External Generality is replicability: Would the results be reproducible in the target instances to which we intend to generalize—the subjects, situations, treatment forms or formats, measures, study designs, procedures, and times? Do we have a replicable result? Of course, we can never be sure unless we actually do a study under each of those instances, and that is an impossibility. So the final judgment of External Generality is a thought experiment about the reproducibility of the results under this variety of conditions. We can use comparable studies to facilitate this judgment, if they exist.

Would the Zimbardo study replicate with the elderly, with subjects less susceptible to hypnosis, in a different laboratory, in a field situation rather than laboratory, with different measures of paranoia, or with observations of individuals suspected of growing deaf in a home for the elderly? These are the kinds of questions this last judgment requires. If you can find no reason that the study would not replicate in those circumstances and the four prior judgments are positive, then the External Generality is strong.

Of course, this fifth decision of the sequence is dependent on the previous four: (1) the explanation must specify or imply a reasonable generality, (2) this generality must be represented in the choices for the study's design, (3) the result must appear with the generality expected in those choices or not appear where it shouldn't, and (4) the conditions of the study must be without restrictive explanations—that is, conditions that are atypical of the targets to which we hope to generalize.

Assuming four positive previous judgments, replicable result is the final judgment of External Generality. It is a judgment of the extent to which the results of this study could be replicated in the target conditions to which it is intended to generalize.

ADDITIONAL READING

See Appendix B for its third graphic that brings together all the questions to be answered in making the judgments of Internal Integrity and External Generality. See Jaeger (1984) and Kish (1965) for discussions of sampling. Bracht and Glass (1968), Campbell and Stanley (1963), Cook and Campbell (1979), and Shadish, Cook, and Campbell (2002) all discuss external validity. Kruglanski and Kroy (1976) and Cronbach (1982) critique the Campbell and Stanley version of validities. Brinberg and McGrath (1985) propose a different set of validities. Krathwohl (1985) is an earlier and fuller treatment of the validities proposed in this and the previous chapter.

IMPORTANT TERMS AND CONCEPTS

bias	purposive sampling
chain-referral sampling	quota sampling
cluster sampling	random sampling
"demonstrated generality"	replicable result
explanation generality	restrictive explanations (conditions) eliminated
External Generality	sample
generality	sampling frame
judgmental sampling	sampling unit
nonprobability sampling	sequential sampling
oversampling	stratified sampling
population	systematic sampling
probability sampling	translation generality
proportional stratified sampling	

OPPORTUNITIES FOR ADDITIONAL LEARNING

1. A researcher wants a simple random sample of 150 students from the population of all sixth-grade pupils who attend private schools in Syracuse, New York. The total population is just over 900 pupils. What steps should the researcher use to get the sample?

2. Mary Wayne, doctoral student, wants to study the effect of post-instruction summaries on high school student achievement. She will use the Liverpool school district's high school, which has about 3,000 students (grades 10–12). She wants a representative sample of about 300 cases by grade level (10, 11, and 12), gender (male and female), and three different levels of reading ability (low, medium, and high). (a) What method of sampling should she use and why? (b) What steps should she take in selecting her sample?

3. The manager of a food company wants to test the effectiveness of a new product before marketing it in California. He plans to administer a questionnaire and interview 75 persons individually. What sampling method should he use, and what criteria would influence his decision?

4. The English faculty at Luce University wanted to offer its introductory writing course, using distance-learning methods, to adults who could not come to campus. In collaboration with the computer applications department, the English department produced a computer-based writing course that could be offered off campus without the need for an instructor. Field tests were conducted with first-year on-campus students, to whom the writing course was also normally offered. Those following the computer-based course showed significant improvements in writing scores as compared with those taking the equivalent course taught by an instructor. Proceeding from these results, the department decided to offer the course off campus in computer-based form. Was this the correct decision?

5. Criminologists conducted a five-year study of a boot-camp-style correctional program for young offenders (age 20 or younger) at minimum-security institutions. Participation in the program was voluntary. "Graduates" of the program exhibited an extremely low incidence

of recidivism (repeat offenses). The researchers were extremely enthusiastic about the results of their study and thought the program would work as well if applied to any offender of any age throughout the country. Was this enthusiasm warranted?

6. External Generality applies to qualitative studies as well as to studies like Zimbardo's; indeed, it is of concern wherever a generalization is developed. Use the Hoffmann-Riem study to illustrate the judgments entering into External Generality as the Zimbardo study was used in the text.

Compare your answers with those following the Application Exercise.

APPLICATION EXERCISE

Using the topic you have chosen to follow throughout the book, think about the generality you'd like your work to have. Then consider the kind of sample that would permit inference of that kind of generality. In addition, think about how you might apply each of the different kinds of sampling to your problem. Include both probability and nonprobability sampling processes. You may want to reconsider your original choice after examining some of the other sampling possibilities.

Consider External Generality as well. What generality do you intend for your study? Are you examining a universal proposition, or is it bounded in some way in its applicability? What are those limits? Will the translation of your concepts plumb the boundaries of the generality you intend the study to have? Can your design choices be changed such that the generality is increased? What restrictive conditions do you see in your study as now planned that might limit generality? Would you expect your study to replicate with different design choices? If not, would better design choices allow it to replicate?

KEY TO ADDITIONAL LEARNING OPPORTUNITIES

1. (a) Obtain a list of the names and addresses of all private elementary school principals in the city of Syracuse from the Superintendent of Schools. (b) Contact each principal by mail and request a roster of sixth-grade pupils enrolled in that school. (c) Number the 900+ names on the lists, continuing across schools from 1 into the 900s. (d) Use the output of the random number generator of a computer to create a sequence of random numbers. Draw the desired sample from that list by doing the following: Select a starting point randomly in the random number output and, using the following numbers in sets of 3, select 150 sets, skipping any number higher than the highest number assigned to a name. These 150 sets designate the names of your sample.

2. (a) To assure representativeness of the three variables (grade, gender, and reading ability), she might use proportional stratified sampling. This will also represent the subgroups of each of these three variables in their correct proportion in the high school. (b) The steps in the proportional stratified sampling are as follows: (i) Get the names, sex, and reading ability test scores of the high school students from the principal of the Liverpool High School. (ii) List the students by grade level. This yields students in the equivalent of three cells. (iii) Divide the students within each grade list into male or female. The three cells are now divided into six. (iv) Set dividing points for low, medium, and high scores on the reading ability test. Divide students within each of the six cells into high, medium, and low groups using the dividing points from reading test scores. This yields 18 cells. The cells will not have equal numbers because: the classes may be of unequal size, girls may be more numerous than boys, and the scores determining low, middle, and high reading ability will not nec-

essarily divide the whole group into equal thirds, let alone those in a cell. (v) Since there are about 3,000 students in the schools and we want a sample of about 300, we can take 10% of each cell. We can use a computer-generated set of random numbers to select a random sample from each of the 18 cells. Alternatively and easier, since the list of names within each cell is not likely to be ordered in any way that is related to our study, taking every tenth name will likely give us a random sample (this is systematic sampling).

3. He should use cluster sampling. The state of California is so large that one researcher cannot cover every city, area, street, and block. Traveling and interviewing are expensive and time consuming.

4. No. There is a problem here both with translation generality and with whether all restrictive explanations (conditions) have been eliminated. The faculty members cannot be certain that the significant findings would replicate with the adult population to whom the course would be offered. Are the learning needs of adults and undergraduates the same? For example, most adult students are likely to be taking the course for an applied purpose that is quite different from undergraduates' term paper needs. They'll react differently to program exercises. Further, the undergraduate students may be more experienced or comfortable with composing on computers.

   In addition, the conditions of the study do not appear to be sufficiently similar to those under which the course would be offered. Since the field test was conducted on campus, it seems likely that assistance from instructors, both with the subject matter and with use of the computers, was available to students. Further, knowledgeable peers were available to consult if there were problems, some being especially valuable because they had previously taken the course. Any such assistance could very well be quite significant and could account for the findings. This is a restrictive condition with strong implications for "stand-alone" (without human intervention) computer-based instruction. The faculty should have repeated the study with more representative participants in more representative learning conditions.

5. No. Again there are problems with translation generality and with whether all explanations (conditions) have been eliminated. One translation generality problem is that these inmates had volunteered for the program and therefore probably already had a willing attitude. They may well have been in the process of "going straight" anyway, and this program only served to shorten their prison terms. Furthermore, there is a restrictive condition. The program may have taken them out of an environment (prison) that could otherwise have negatively affected them and therefore contributed to recidivism. If conducted in the prisons, it might not be as effective.

   Further, these offenders were from a very specific population (translation generality again). They were young offenders (20 years or under) who had committed less violent crimes. The investigators have no way of knowing if the technique would work with older, more "hardened" inmates or with the more violent. The study may hold promise, but it needs replication.

6. We must examine the evidence contributing to the five judgments making up External Generality: explanation generality, translation generality, "demonstrated generality," restrictive explanations (conditions) eliminated, and replicable result.

   Explanation generality—It is clear from this statement in her concluding section, "This research may be useful for adoptive parents, applicant couples, and agencies who deal with adoptive family life," that Hoffmann-Riem intends for this study to have wide generality. One might say that her generalization is intended to be universally applicable to adopting couples. Therefore judgment of the study's External Generality is very relevant.

   Translation generality—Clearly she can't sample from all the "adoptive parents, applicant couples, and agencies" to which she expects the results to be useful. What she can do is to study a typical sample to which it should be applicable and show that the generalization does indeed hold. She does so by choosing a discussion group of adoptive parents, a convenient but purposive sample. In her discussion of sampling, she notes that the members of such groups are "middle class, similar to most applicants for adoption." She also refers to a comparison she presented elsewhere that shows the similarity in makeup of her group to a year's data on the characteristics of applicants for adoption. Both of these pieces of evidence are intended to show that the sample she used is like applicants for adoption generally. Readers must judge for themselves whether this evidence is strong enough for them to believe this group is typical of adopters.

"Demonstrated generality"—As indicated in the discussion of explanation generality, one can't really demonstrate generality. There may always be some untried instance in which the generalization doesn't hold, hence the quotation marks. However, does it hold with a group in which it would be expected to? Hoffmann-Riem indicates that it does and provides participant quotations to back up the claim.

Restrictive explanations (conditions) eliminated—Since the data were gathered under the very conditions to which the generalization would be expected to apply, there are no restrictive conditions.

Replicable result—I know of no other studies that bear on the questions studied; neither apparently did Hoffmann-Riem. So the remaining question is whether one would expect the same findings in replications of the study done different ways, with other participants, with other situations, and so on. Probably, of these, the main question mark is over the participants—whether the individuals (and the sample drawn from them) who attend these discussion groups are typical of adoptive parents. Hoffmann-Riem obviously thinks that they are. She indicates she has data indicating the parents in this group are like adoption applicants over a previous year. Whether one would judge the results as replicable is a thought experiment; I am inclined to think they would. All five judgments are positive; thus, the study has strong External Generality.

SUMMARY

Sampling procedures are ways of selecting a small number of units from a population to enable researchers to make reliable inferences about the nature of the population to which the units belong. Four basic principles underlie sampling. A larger sample is required: (1) whenever we require greater certainty in the inferential leap from sample to population, (2) whenever we desire to estimate the characteristics of the population more precisely, (3) the greater the variability of the population in those characteristics, and (4) the smaller the effect to be sensed relative to the normal variability of the population.

All probability samples involve random sampling at some point in the process. Random samples require that each possible sample from a population be equally likely to be drawn. Probability samples allow us to estimate the population characteristics with specified accuracy and certainty. Random, stratified, systematic, and cluster sampling are all probability sampling methods. Often they are combined in a multistage process. Their characteristics, advantages, and disadvantages are summarized in the chapter's tables.

Convenience and grab samples are nonprobability samples and are popular because of their ease of use. Judgmental or purposive samples rely on the researcher's knowledge of population characteristics to sample appropriately. Nonprobability samples are usually justified by showing the samples fit certain demographic characteristics of the target population. Such characteristics form the basis for quota sampling, which is commonly used in surveys, especially telephone interviewing.

The generality that can be attributed to a study is a function of the quality of the sampling process. When well done, sampling makes the inferential leap from sample to population less tenuous. Not all studies depend on sampling for generality, only those that are intended to apply to a particular target population. Propositions that are assumed to be universal—that is, to apply to everyone—can be studied with convenience samples. Such samples are, of course, only one demonstration of universality; we may want additional evidence.

External Generality is a judgment of how broadly and strongly the appropriate interpretation of the evidence supports the generalization of the causal relationship or process beyond the circumstances in which it was studied. It is the power of a study to create a consensus among research consumers about the appropriate interpretation of the study's evidence regarding the generality of the study's conclusions. Like Internal Integrity, External Generality consists of two kinds of conceptual evidence, explanation generality and translation generality; two kinds of empirical evidence, "demonstrated generality" and restrictive explanations (conditions) eliminated; and a final summary judgment, replicable result.

A Look Ahead

It is already apparent that still other characteristics affect how we build a consensus and that other criteria apply to the links in the chain of reasoning. In the next chapter, we examine these other characteristics. In chapters 18 and 19, we shall discuss how the basic principles of sampling are used in measurement and in statistics.

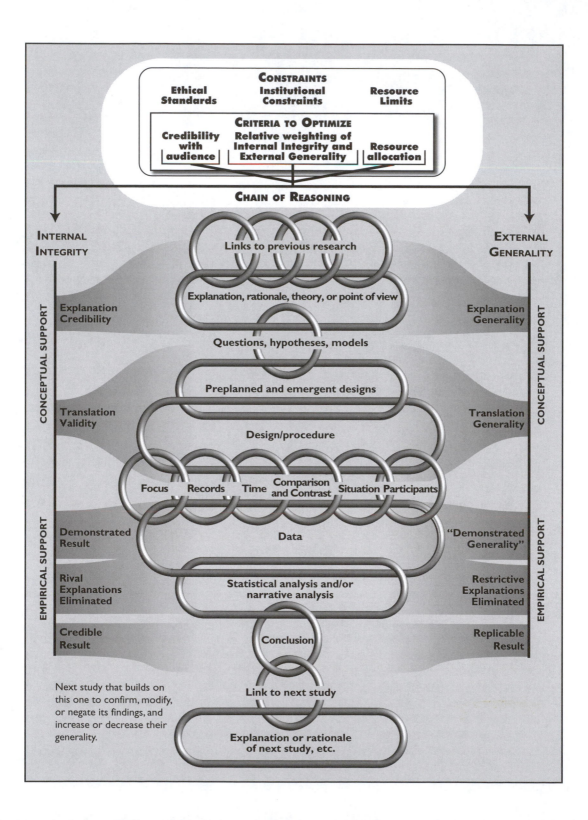

CONSTRAINTS

Ethical
Standards

Institutional
Constraints

Resource
Limits

CRITERIA TO OPTIMIZE

Credibility
with
audience

Relative weighting of
Internal Integrity and
External Generality

Resource
allocation

CHAIN OF REASONING

INTERNAL
INTEGRITY

EXTERNAL
GENERALITY

Links to previous research

CONCEPTUAL SUPPORT

Explanation
Credibility

Explanation, rationale, theory, or point of view

Explanation
Generality

CONCEPTUAL SUPPORT

Questions, hypotheses, models

Translation
Validity

Preplanned and emergent designs

Translation
Generality

Design/procedure

Focus   Records   Time   Comparison
and Contrast   Situation   Participants

EMPIRICAL SUPPORT

Demonstrated
Result

Data

"Demonstrated
Generality"

EMPIRICAL SUPPORT

Rival
Explanations
Eliminated

Statistical analysis and/or
narrative analysis

Restrictive
Explanations
Eliminated

Credible
Result

Conclusion

Replicable
Result

Next study that builds on
this one to confirm, modify,
or negate its findings, and
increase or decrease their
generality.

Link to next study

Explanation or rationale
of next study, etc.

Optimizing Trade-Offs
within Limits

In addition to building a strong chain of reasoning and meeting the requirements of Internal Integrity and External Generality, every study must work within three limits and must optimize three aspects of each study through trade-offs among them. This chapter discusses the impact on decisions and judgments of these added aspects to the model of the chain of reasoning.

INTRODUCTION

The three limits imposed on every study are:

1. **Ethical standards**—what ethically can be done,
2. **Institutional constraints**—what an institution will permit to be done in the name of research, especially when its primary goal is service to clients, and
3. **Resource limits**—although the available resources can sometimes be increased, they are always limited, usually too much so.

The three criteria to be optimized are:

1. **Audience credibility**—balancing the requirements of the study's design with those of building credibility with the audience. Researchers must elicit credence not only from the gatekeepers to the study's publication or presentation, but also from the audience of relevant readers and reviewers after release to the public.
2. **Relative weighting of Internal Integrity and External Generality** to meet the goals of the study. That is, appropriately weighting the demands of Internal Integrity with those of External Generality. Internal Integrity is usually strengthened at a cost to External Generality, and vice versa.
3. **Resource allocation**—balancing the allocation of available resources among the various demands of each aspect of the study (i.e., each judgment of internal credibility and of External Generality) so each can be satisfactorily accomplished. The research report

shows only the *results* of resource allocation, not the *process*. Differences in researchers' allocations of personal time, energy, and attention often explain how they arrive at different design strategies for the same problem. Resource allocation can be an important determiner of problem formulation and of the choice of alternatives in design. Readers, however, are typically unaware of such considerations and constraints.

These three criteria need to be optimized because, to the extent the resource limit is fixed and additional resources are unavailable, they are part of a zero-sum game. Resources spent on one part of the study limit what is available for another. Furthermore, optimizing these aspects for one audience will not necessarily do so for another; researchers must keep their principal audiences in mind. Figure 9.1 adds all these aspects to the model we have been discussing and shows the complete framework of criteria and constraints.

The top box encloses the three constraints that each study must observe; the box below it, the three criteria each study endeavors to optimize.

WHY SETTLE FOR OPTIMIZATION?

In chapters 7 and 8, we discussed Internal Integrity and External Generality as though, if the proper choices were made as the study evolved or was designed, each could be raised to an entirely satisfactory level. Given sufficient resources and a tractable problem, we could build a rationale that would be credible. As a result, it would get a satisfactory translation of the hypothesis with protection against both rival and restricting explanations, attaining considerable strength in both simultaneously. However, Internal Integrity is usually bought at the expense of External Generality, and vice versa. Greater control gained by complex designs or by taking the study into the laboratory typically results in decreased generality. Using widely dispersed and different participant groups, situations, and times to gain generality results in poorer control of the study, the greater likelihood of there being a rival explanation to the phenomenon, and thus weaker Internal Integrity. Furthermore, resources expended in pursuit of increased External Generality are not available for strengthening Internal Integrity, or the reverse. Therefore, because resources are always finite and are usually less than we would ideally like, we optimize to gain the goals of our study.

Audience credibility also faces an optimization problem. Credibility with whom? Who are all the relevant audiences? Can we simultaneously build credibility with all of them? Must we not choose one or a few and find the optimal choices for them? And unless we have all the resources we could ask for (a rare occurrence), the optimization problem is obvious. All we can do is optimize the design for our purposes and intended audiences.

Simon (1992) suggests that where problem solving is complex—as it certainly is in designing a research study—and since optimizing requires the impossible task of considering all the possibilities, we *satisfice* instead of optimize. We find a solution that at least partially meets (satisfices) our criteria. This is probably a more accurate description of our attempts to optimize; although we set out to optimize, we end up satisficing. With this introduction to the idea of optimization, we can understand it in greater depth as we look at each criterion.

Figure 9.1   The complete framework, including constraints to observe and criteria to optimize.

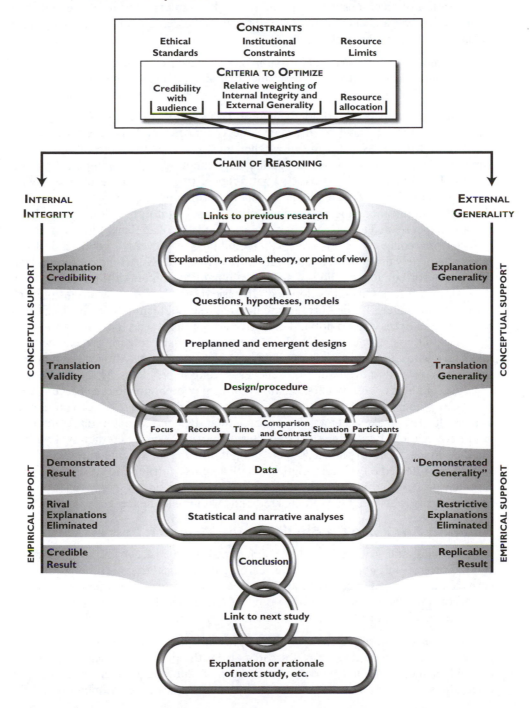

Audience Credibility

Creation of a consensus around the researcher's interpretation of the evidence requires that the audience attribute credibility to the researcher. Cronbach (1982) ingeniously phrased the problem this way:

> Validity depends . . . on the way a conclusion is stated and communicated. Validity is subjective rather than objective: the plausibility of the conclusion is what counts. And plausibility, to twist a cliché, lies in the ear of the beholder. (p. 108)

Audience credibility is in part a judgment of the integrity of the researcher in carrying out the study, especially for the many aspects not described in the report.

To build that consensus, the researcher must consider the expectations of the audience at each study stage: designing, implementing, and communicating the results. The audience may consist of gatekeepers (e.g., committee members who select presentations for professional association programs, readers who review proposals for publication and/or funding, and journal editors), fellow researchers, researchers in related areas, and practitioners interested in applying the results.

Ignoring concerns about audience credibility may prevent a good study from being adequately disseminated if the gatekeepers reject it. Even if they accept it, lack of concern for building credibility with the ultimate consumers of the research may delay or prevent consensus development. In basic research, if such a consensus is not formed immediately, it may form belatedly when the field is ready for it. In applied research, audiences who do not understand or accept the research will not apply it.

Credibility is a function of both (1) substance—what steps the researcher has taken to ensure that the study is credible, and (2) presentation—how clear it is that the author is forthright about the weaknesses and/or problems of the study. For example, qualitative researchers, arguing that it may be impossible to prevent personal viewpoints from affecting their work, seek to be as self-aware of such influences as possible. They make that awareness part of their data and take it into account during interpretation. But taking such steps is only part of ensuring credibility. Readers must be made aware of the steps they took, and of the viewpoints and biases that might have affected their interpretations. Both actions contribute to credibility in the research process and adequately communicating those steps in a way that conveys one's integrity is essential to building credibility with the audience.

Building Audience Credibility in the Research Process

We build audience credibility by conducting ourselves according to the highest code of professional conduct as well as learning the particular expectations and concerns of our main audiences. A good place to learn the latter is at professional association conventions, where questions posed at the close of a presentation indicate audience concerns. In addition, here are a few suggestions:

Build on knowledge the audience has already accepted.   Remember the use of hypnosis in the Zimbardo study? To readers from the physical sciences, hypnosis is probably a stage trick, not based on solid accepted knowledge. Such readers might reject the study as soon as they encounter hypnosis in the report. Zimbardo and his associates assumed that the audience they wished to reach, behavioral scientists, would not find it objectionable and thus did not bother justifying its use.

Policy studies are sometimes designed to show the generality of a finding—studies with considerable External Generality. That is fine if you are less concerned with whether the mechanism worked than how it did so (see the Head Start example later in the chapter). But when you are trying to understand what is going on, particularly in basic research, you should make sure that the earlier work on which you are building had strong Internal Integrity or that the lack of it has been taken into account.

Avoid the weaknesses of previous studies. The audience members most likely to knowledgeably criticize your work are the real and self-perceived experts in your research area. If you are familiar with their past and current work, you will be able to convey how your study builds on their past literature and avoids its errors. You may make some mistakes of your own, but repeating theirs damages your professional credibility. If there isn't a better way to do the study, make that point explicitly to avoid inappropriate conclusions about your competence.

Use accepted techniques and measures. All things being equal, use accepted methods, measures, definitions, terminology, and knowledge. The audience's familiarity with conventional methods facilitates communication. It results in readers who feel more capable of judging the study and have more confidence in that judgment.

Using standard methods permits the audience to readily find the hallmarks of excellence it has come to associate with particular approaches. In a questionnaire study, for instance, they will look for that special effort to obtain a sample of nonrespondents' replies to show that they were like those of respondents and that the respondents were not atypical.

To reach lay or practitioner audiences, use common terminology with few technical terms. Using instruments that appear valid may be particularly important.

Justify use of the nonstandard. Whenever researchers depart from the accepted, they carry the burden of proof. Pioneering a new method, coining new terms, and developing a new instrument all require making it "self-evident" to the audience that these were appropriate. (I followed this advice when I explained the reasons for the new terms and External Generality in the addendum to chapter 7!) Usually, these new versions require comparison with the standard choices to demonstrate their advantages. In some instances, we must first teach the hallmarks of excellence for an innovation used in a study.

Sometimes an accepted instrument is not quite "on target" for a construct; perhaps a less well-known one measures it more precisely. We trade ready acceptance of the standard measure for a better measure, but we must exert the extra effort to educate the audience about its merits. This is just one of the many trade-off decisions in research and is part of the optimizing process.

Audiences generally willing to trust findings in a field other than their own may not allow them to generalize to theirs. Credibility with each new audience may require repeating previous studies in circumstances relevant to them. For example, language laboratories had to be shown to work with each of the foreign languages, and programmed instruction and educational television with each different subject matter. We have learned the importance of demonstrating effectiveness in each new field from county agricultural extension agents, who learned the effectiveness of demonstrating new seed corn in each county to convince farmers it will work for them (further discussed on pp. 645–647).

Credibility with the audience is enhanced by several actions taken in the research process:

▶ building on knowledge that the audience has already accepted;

▶ demonstrating familiarity with the relevant literature;

▶ avoiding the weaknesses of previous similar studies;

▶ using accepted research techniques, measures, definitions, and terminology; and

▶ justifying the use of any nonstandard or controversial aspects and educating the audience to their appropriateness.

Building Audience Credibility in the Presentation of Findings

You are the most essential audience with whom credibility must be built. Maintaining your integrity as a scientist and a scholar is a first priority. Do you recall Merton's norm of disinterestedness (see p. 51)? This does not refer to a lack of motivation. Rather than a lack of interest it means that, insofar as they are able, researchers prevent their personal expectations, hopes, and aspirations from influencing how they gather, analyze, and interpret their data. The integrity conveyed when a study is presented is a reflection of your own. (True, it is possible for individuals to succeed in playing the role of a person of integrity when in fact they are not, but few researchers appear to be accomplished liars.) Integrity may require paying attention to such things as building a chain of reasoning only as strong as the data permit and not using a sales pitch (e.g., "this superbly chosen sample") to increase its apparent strength beyond what is warranted. Scientists are chided for showboating, and such work tends to be suspect.

Once an audience discovers something it thinks it should have been told and wasn't, audience credibility is weakened. That the audience may be wrong in its perception makes no difference. The line between a solid and appropriate presentation that takes full advantage of the strengths of the study without concealing its weaknesses and one that exploits its strengths and underplays its weaknesses may be a fine one. But it is a boundary that must be found and observed. Erring on the conservative side may delay proper recognition of a knowledge claim, but it is generally considered the lesser of the evils.

Is there a role that the researcher can adopt? The researcher's task is more akin to that of a judge writing a decision than to that of a lawyer trying to make a case. Having come to a decision, the judge prepares a document that, while recognizing the cons, presents the strongest possible argument for the pros, explaining how and why the conclusion was reached. Similarly the researcher, having made a knowing judgment about the proper interpretation of the data, prepares the case. He or she reports it in such a way that we can carefully examine the argument, and it does not depend for its appeal on the eloquence of the writer (Cronbach & Suppes, 1969). In preparing that decision, both judge and researcher must consider the expectations of the audience and what concerns its members are likely to have.

The foregoing should make clear that building credibility with the audience has nothing to do with hiding a study's weaknesses, misconstruing the data, or overgeneralizing. Protection of the progress of science is reason enough for a credible stance, which reflects on one's professional competence as well.

Credibility with the audience is important to acceptance of a study's findings. It involves presenting the findings in ways that:

▶ provide the kinds of evidence expected by the audience,

▶ answer the audience's questions and allay its concerns,

▶ appropriately reflect the study's strengths and weaknesses, and

▶ convey the integrity of the researcher.

RELATIVE WEIGHTING OF INTERNAL INTEGRITY AND EXTERNAL GENERALITY

Ideally, studies have enough Internal Integrity to create a consensus that a relationship exists and enough External Generality to show appropriate generality. Preferably, both are optimized. Actions taken to strengthen Internal Integrity, however, tend to weaken External Generality. Thus, for each study the researchers must decide how to achieve the optimum relative weighting of Internal Integrity and External Generality to reach the goals of the study.

For example, to strengthen Internal Integrity, we tend to narrow the scope of the question studied. This permits us easily to observe the phenomenon under controlled conditions, possibly even laboratory conditions. Its artificiality shrinks External Generality. Bronfenbrenner (1977) described the efforts to strengthen the Internal Integrity of developmental psychology studies as resulting in "the science of strange behavior of children in strange situations with strange adults for the briefest possible time" (p. 513).

Internal Integrity is usually stressed in the early studies to ensure that a relationship does indeed exist. Once established, however, interest turns to how broadly it applies, and emphasis shifts from Internal Integrity to External Generality.

However, some policy studies that determine whether a given program or policy works place the initial emphasis on External Generality. Is it valid across a variety of persons, places, and times? Take, for example, the Head Start studies of preschool programs for underprivileged children throughout the United States. They evaluated programs with every possible range of activity, cultural backgrounds, regions of the country, and school milieus. The initial studies showed no advantage to the program, so studies seeking the "effective ingredient" were delayed. More carefully designed later studies showed the expected gains both in Head Start (Royce, Lazar, & Darlington, 1983) and similar programs (Schweinhart & Weikart, 1985). They had strong

External Generality—change occurred widely. Typically, findings that a treatment worked in a variety of situations (that is, had generality) would be followed with tight Internal Integrity studies to determine the cause.

Limited resources may restrict the size of the sample or the number of sites we can study; as a result, External Generality must often be constrained. By contrast, there are a wide variety of design choices for determining that a relationship exists. Thus, comparatively, studies emphasizing Internal Integrity are typically less expensive.

The relative importance of Internal Integrity and External Generality varies with the disposition of persons to try something new. Some individuals are innovators, risk takers, early adopters, persons on the "cutting edge." They eagerly try out findings of studies with Internal Integrity before much evidence of External Generality is available. Others that are more conservative require External Generality evidence before accepting a finding as useful to them—late adopters.

Similarly, the nature of the decision influences which validity we emphasize. Suppose the decision requires a good bit of investment of resources (time, effort, money) with a relatively small return. In that case, to be sure it will work in a new instance we seek evidence of External Generality. This may be one of the reasons expensive curriculum packages had to be shown to work before they were adopted. If little investment may yield big potential payoffs, trials in a variety of situations may not be as important, because individuals are more willing to risk the investment.

Thus, the emphasis on Internal Integrity or External Generality can be affected by such factors as whether (1) it is a basic or applied study, (2) it requires a large investment, (3) the ratio of potential payoff to costs is large or small, and (4) the researchers are risk takers. This may seem like a lot to bear in mind, but successful researchers manage to balance Internal Integrity and External Generality so as to meet their own and others' requirements.

> ▶ Because strengthening Internal Integrity usually diminishes External Generality, each study must find the proper balance for its purposes. Basic research usually emphasizes Internal Integrity; certain applied research and policy studies may initially emphasize External Generality.

RESOURCE ALLOCATION

We have already noted that the myriad of choices involved in building a design means that researchers may differ as to the ideal. In fact, within a given method there may be alternative "best" choices leading to different resource allocations. What is the ideal design? Even if we construct what we consider to be a good design, others might construct a better one according to their view of appropriate resource allocations.

When you read a study, you see only the final choices that were made in problem creation, design formulation, data gathering, analysis, and interpretation of findings. Resource allocation is concerned with decisions about investment of researcher (and staff) time, energy, and other resources. Decisions regarding resource allocation are based on such questions as: How much time should be devoted to problem conceptualization? Study design? Data gathering? Analysis? Interpretation? What will be required to procure research space, equipment, measuring instruments, and so on? Resource allocation also contributes to the determination of the relative emphasis of Internal Integrity and External Generality.

We noted an earlier instance of resource allocation when discussing the chain analogy. When we say that "a chain is only as strong as its weakest link," we draw the conclusion that all the links should be of approximately the same strength (chapter 4). That conclusion is a prime criterion of good resource allocation. It makes no sense to concentrate resources on one link when weakness in another might weaken or destroy the argument. Let's examine how resource allocation decisions affect the links.

Question Choice and Formulation

There is considerable testimony on the contribution of problem formulation to problem solution. Getzels (1982) quotes Einstein:

> The formulation of a problem is often more essential than its solution, which may be merely a matter of mathematical or experimental skill. To raise new questions, new possibilities, to regard old questions from a new angle, requires creative imagination and marks real advance in science. (Einstein & Infeld, 1938, p. 92)

Getzels notes that this idea is reinforced by Wertheimer (1945): "Often in great discoveries the most important thing is that a certain question is found. Envisaging, putting the productive question, is often a more important, . . . a greater achievement, than the solution of a set of questions" (p. 123).

Although question choice and formulation are intertwined, the choice often precedes formulation. Given an "itch one wants to scratch," can we find a satisfactory formulation? Clearly, some questions lend themselves easily to investigation. Others, such as Zimbardo's problem in chapter 1, are difficult—we couldn't let aged people grow gradually deaf and do nothing about it. Only by reformulating it to substitute temporary deafness through hypnosis of college students did Zimbardo make it tractable.

Once found, the answer is obvious, as in Zimbardo's case, but troublesome aspects often become apparent only during our search for a satisfactory formulation. For example, we would expect that the more we spend in educating students, the better the education should be. However, many problems appear when trying to unravel per-pupil expenditure figures—differences in salary schedules, determinants of salary increments, costs of space and maintenance, and so on.

Zimbardo doesn't state how long it took to come up with their reformulation of the basic question. The general problem for researchers is to decide at what point to stop and proceed with the study. Frequently, researchers are concerned they stopped too soon. It is possible that further work could result in a more important problem or a better-formulated one—the reason why this criterion is optimized instead of being completely fulfilled. Researchers reformulate until some inner criterion of optimality is satisfied and then proceed, never knowing what might have been missed.

Other Links in the Chain of Reasoning

In a fashion similar to the analysis of the problem formulation link, the researcher must consider each successive link in the chain. How can we best design this study? What method or combination of methods should be used? What sample of subjects? What situations? What treatment or independent variable? The questions are legion.

Mostly, we allocate resources in accordance with the difficulty of finding a satisfactory choice. If an appropriate measure is not available, we must allocate resources for the construction of a new one. If the initial design does not rule out certain important rival explanations, we develop a new design. Designs are often reformulated several times before a satisfactory one is found.

Readers rarely realize that the final design may have been but one of a number that were explored. Remember how long a trip seems the first time you make it? Retracing the route, without the wrong turns and byways, is so much shorter. Readers of a study see it in the latter way, not as it looked to the researcher the first time through. Thus, although you can judge the allocation of resources in the study's report, it very often does not show the total allocation pattern.

> ▶ Resource allocation is the hidden decision making that determines the relative strength of the various parts of a study. Although confined within resource limits, what is available may be allocated in many ways. The researcher's task is to optimize the allocation to fit the problem, goal, and audience.

LIMITS AND CONSTRAINTS

Limits and constraints are our final set of considerations: (1) What can ethically be done? (2) What research will an institution allow? and (3) What are the resource limits?

Ethical Standards

Because of its importance, we shall devote all of chapter 10 to the question of ethics and discuss additional aspects as required throughout the book. It suffices here to note that professional societies have developed codes of ethics. Human subject protection committees (and similar committees for animals) are established by institutions to see that ethical standards are observed by their researchers and determine whether the potential worth of knowledge gained justifies whatever discomfort or suffering may be incurred.

Institutional Constraints

Researchers who do studies in institutional settings find research a secondary consideration to whatever activity achieves the service goals for which the institution was established. Such institutional constraints limit what the institution will allow the researcher to do, especially if a study interferes with an institutional schedule or interrupts essential activities. For example, only a limited amount of time can be taken from classroom teaching or asked of a patient receiving therapy.

Institutions try to maintain "business as usual" come what may. So when institutions allow their schedules to be disrupted by research, it is unusual. Yet, limits are rarely so fixed that researchers cannot negotiate exceptions for the right project. But such disruptions bear testimony to some combination of the negotiating skill of the investigator, the perceived value of the research, and/or the atypicality of an institution for allowing such disruption. The last, of course, weakens the generality of those findings in which the nature of the institution is an important factor.

Access is especially difficult when controversial topics are probed or when a study could reflect unfavorably on the institution. Administrators often grant access for study of what they perceive as a desirable development only to find it reported unfavorably. Rist (1977), for example, observed the integration of African American children bused to previously all-white schools in Portland, Oregon—a program of which the administration was proud. He pointed out, however, that integration meant assimilation to the point that African American culture was devalued. The school administration was offended.

Similar incidents make administrators reluctant to approve researcher requests that appear more interested in revealing unfortunate conditions than in protecting the institution. Each highly critical report, as its controversy spreads, probably raises barriers to similar studies. A no-win situation sometimes develops, and the researcher must decide who shall be harmed instead of avoiding harm altogether. Taylor (1977), for example, found that institutional attendants drank beer to the point where it interfered with their duties to the patients. Yet he did not report this, rationalizing that the impact of the study on the institutionalization problem as a whole was more important than remedying this instance of impropriety.

Whether and how to "blow the whistle" on such social problems are also ethical dilemmas for the researcher. The researcher believes that society should know about such conditions, yet such revelations may undermine support for the institution and deny what help is now given to people who need it. In addition, the professional careers of persons who cooperated may be damaged. Although some people might argue that if they created the conditions, they deserve to suffer the consequences, this reasoning in no way enhances the researcher's access. Researchers come to be perceived by the authorities as meddlers unsympathetic to administrative complexities and lacking real understanding of the problems. Such perceptions interfere with the study of social problems needing correction, and the institutions most needing study sometimes become inaccessible.

The foregoing discussion has assumed that the researcher is approaching the institution as an outsider seeking permission. Many take the position that research, and especially evaluations (see chapter 23), should be a collaborative affair between the researcher and the institution's personnel and/or administrators. In the case of *action research* (also in chapter 23), the institutional personnel who will be the research users do the research themselves. Rather than a situation in which constraints are externally imposed by an administrator, in these latter instances the situation becomes one of researcher and institutional personnel mutually seeking to determine what institutional limits are appropriate.

> ▶ Institutional constraints typically prevent researchers from engaging in activities that may interfere with their ongoing routine or may reflect unfavorably on the institution, its performance, or its personnel. Such constraints have serious implications for what social problems researchers can investigate.
>
> ▶ Where the research or evaluation studies are done collaboratively, as in action research, the institutional limits are not externally imposed but internally determined by the researchers.

Resource Limits

Resources are rarely sufficient for all we hope to do. We think of the main resources as our time and energy as investigators. Graduate students writing dissertations tend to think of these as relatively unlimited—they simply put in whatever it takes. Nevertheless, these resources are limited in a practical sense. Time expended on a study must be evaluated in terms of its alternative uses, what economists call its *marginal utility* or *opportunity cost* (e.g., working to earn money instead of spending that time on more dissertation development). Hence, the real costs are rarely included in the researcher's decision making. Keeping a study in the perspective of alternative important activities and alternative research projects allows us to assign more reasonable limits to it.

Resource limits are often fixed by the available staff, equipment, instruments, and the like as well as by money—a grant or budget. Given positive results, however, we can sometimes find new resources, and limits may not be as fixed as we tend to regard them. Nonetheless, expanding such limits takes time and energy and is usually far from certain. Thus, deciding to seek additional funds is itself part of the resource allocation process. Note also that seeking funding may subject you to the requirements of a sponsor. These can bring many changes to such areas as the focus of the study, the relative importance of various audiences, and the time schedule for completion—all factors that you must view in terms of the study's importance in the larger picture of: the needs of your discipline or profession, your responsibility to society, and your career.

With some experience, you will discover that the same study can be built in a variety of sizes. This realization suggests that a resource limit may not be a bad thing because many alternative formulations of a study can be made to fit within it. However, different study goals—for example, large and impressive studies for Congress and lay audiences, smaller studies done to very high standards for professional audiences—suggest that there are guidelines for resource size. Optimal size for a study is determined by such variables as the need for sufficient sensitivity to show the relationship, size for representativeness and generality, and impressiveness for uncertainty reduction. This also suggests that there may be a minimal level below which the study may not have the intended effect—a study too small to reduce the uncertainty of a nonprofessional audience or too small to sense an effect, even if it should occur (more on the latter point in chapter 19).

Resource limits clearly determine the constraints within which resource allocation can take place. Because the latter is one of the essential tasks of a researcher, resource limits can be a determining factor of research quality.

> ▶ Resource limits set the boundaries on resource allocation. There is considerable flexibility in the design of studies. Studies of a given problem can be built to different sizes to fit particular goals or designed in alternative ways to fit a resource limit.
>
> ▶ Resource limits imposed on a given problem often reflect its relative importance in the larger scheme of knowledge development.
>
> ▶ There is probably both an optimal and a minimal size for a study based on the expectations of the audience, the size required to sense the expected effect, and the generality intended.

ADDITIONAL READING

If you did not refer to Appendix B of this book for the previous chapter, do so for this one. It contains three alternate renderings of this framework that are helpful in understanding it. The first shows the framework in a larger context of the population of studies. The second shows the relationships of the various terms to those larger terms they belong to. The third places all the questions to be answered in the judgments of Internal Integrity and External Generality in a single graphic for easy reference. See Krathwohl (1985) for an earlier version of the framework.

IMPORTANT TERMS AND CONCEPTS

audience credibility
ethical standards
institutional constraints
relative weighting of Internal Integrity
  and External Generality

resource allocation
resource limits

OPPORTUNITIES FOR ADDITIONAL LEARNING

1. Reread the summary of Jonassen's study of pattern notes (p. 76). His purpose was to verify this technique as a simple, practical means of assessing a learner's cognitive structure. What has he done to build audience credibility?

2. You are a researcher who is interested in the value of laboratory experience in chemistry. You want to test a newly developed lab technique for teaching titration to high school students in comparison with the program in current use. The equipment is rather expensive but would probably be worth the cost if it could be shown to considerably improve on present methods. You are considering whether or not to bring groups of students to the university's chemistry laboratory, where you can randomly assign them to one or the other approach. You have the support of local school officials and can bus in several classes. Considering Internal Integrity and External Generality, what would be the advantages and disadvantages of doing so?

3. Reread the description of the study on impulsiveness-reflectiveness by Kagen and associates in the answer to problem 4 on page 151. Note that the concept was developed during research on analytic versus global reasoning. From the information available, what choices did these investigators appear to make in terms of resource allocation?

4. Psychologist Sarah Ellenova compared the learning that resulted from student-generated questions about a text passage with that resulting from questions intended to enhance learning inserted by the author. She sought to carry out her study in several elementary schools in the local school system but was granted permission to do so by only one group. It was the sixth-grade class at the University Elementary School, a laboratory school run jointly by the university and the school board. It was, she was told, the only school properly set up to allow such research without unnecessarily disrupting school routines. How could these institutional constraints affect her study?

Compare your answers with those following the Application Exercise.

APPLICATION EXERCISE

What constraints do you think you might encounter with your problem? Do you anticipate ethical problems? If so, you may want to jump ahead to chapter 10. Will institutions be reluctant to let you in to gather data? What might you do to lessen such problems? Entry is often a problem; we'll consider that further in chapter 12. Do you anticipate insufficient resources of some kind? If you need additional monetary resources, see the Web sites listed below. What balance of Internal Integrity and External Generality do you anticipate? Is yours closer to basic research or applied research? Do you anticipate any particular problems with audience credibility at this point in your problem's development? You may want to think about this issue again after you have chosen a research method. As for resource allocation, as your plans for your study firm up, consider doing a work plan. Put "work plan timeline" or "Gantt chart" into a search engine for references.

- *National Science Foundation:* http://www.nsf.gov/dir/index.isp?org=SBE
- *National Institutes of Health:* http://grants.nih.gov/grants/guide
- For education: http://ies.ed.gov/funding
- For private funding: http://www.philanthropy.com/ (the *Chronicle of Philanthropy* Web site)

KEY TO ADDITIONAL LEARNING OPPORTUNITIES

1. First, Jonassen built his study on knowledge that the audience had already accepted. He began his article with a discussion of existing instructional design theory and pointed out what he thought was missing. He next compared the various techniques available for assessing cognitive structure and, on the basis of that information, presented his rationale for choosing to use pattern notes instead. Part of this explanation showed why he believed the existing methods were not appropriate. Thus, he also attempted to avoid the weaknesses of previous similar studies.

   Second, he used an existing, accepted technique, free word association, to validate pattern notes as an assessment method. It was, he noted, the most valid and reliable method available for assessing a learner's cognitive structure.

2. You want to demonstrate that the new approach is more effective than the current one—Internal Integrity—but you would also like to show that this is true with other such groups and in other situations—External Generality. Conducting the study in the laboratory would allow you tight control of most variables and would probably help to strengthen Internal Integrity. Most important, you would be able to use such methods as the random assignment of students to either treatment and the standardization of your instructions to eliminate rival hypotheses. It is, however, an artificial situation (for these students) and not one

in which the approach will normally be used. That in itself could account for a demonstrated effect.

Demonstrating the relationship through a study conducted in the schools—in the natural environment—would certainly improve External Generality. The new approach could be shown to be superior in the situation in which it would normally be used, but it would be hard to standardize your treatments. Furthermore, random assignment of students to the two approaches (presumably dooming one to inferior learning) could be unacceptable for ethical or administrative reasons. You would generally be less able to guarantee the equivalence of your samples, and it would be more difficult to eliminate rival explanations.

In this case, however, it is probably essential to know whether the procedure works, even under good conditions, before devoting resources for a more expensive program in a broader trial. So you may wish to emphasize Internal Integrity first and conduct your study under the more carefully controlled university conditions.

3. Resource allocation reflects the hidden decisions that a researcher makes, such as what question to choose, how to formulate it, and where to invest time and energy. Perhaps the most obvious (and important) choice that Kagen and colleagues made was that of the question. They were originally studying other concepts when they noticed the tendency of analytic individuals to take longer to respond to questions. It led them to wonder whether this was a stable trait and made them want to investigate it.

    Once they had chosen this question, the study's formulation was fairly easy: Measure the time taken to complete questions or problems and the error rate in doing so. They also had to invest considerable effort in the development and validation of a new measure, their Matching Figures Test, before they could actually test for the concepts in question.

4. They could strongly affect the generalizability of any results she might obtain. Although perhaps not totally a laboratory situation, such a school probably would not be representative of the other schools in the district. We would expect more (and more varied) visitors than in a typical school. It would likely be staffed with enthusiastic and capable teachers who had agreed to work in a more public atmosphere and to be equipped with extra resources and paraphernalia for research, such as two-way mirrors.

    All of this could contribute to an unusual atmosphere in the school, perhaps allowing for more highly motivated students than would be found in an average school. It is probable that the school would be the site of a variety of experimental programs. Further, if such a school were located in a residential district near the university, we might also find a higher proportion of children from professional families who might be expected to be, on average, more capable than those in a typical school.

SUMMARY

Although it is apparent that Internal Integrity and External Generality are important characteristics of a research study, other characteristics also shape it. One, audience credibility, is a function of how well the design, implementation, and report of a study anticipates the concerns of gatekeepers and its main audiences and alleviates those concerns. It provides evidence of the integrity of the researcher and builds trust by using standard procedures, explaining the merits of nonstandard ones, and supplying an understanding of why the researcher made what may appear to be dubious or controversial design or procedure choices.

A second characteristic is the relative weighting of Internal Integrity and External Generality such that the evidence sufficiently supports the existence of the relationship and appropriately indicates its intended generality.

A third characteristic, resource allocation, is apparent in the complex process of allocating time, energy, and funds during the designing, implementing, and reporting of research. However, only the final product of the process appears in the research report. Ideally, it permits the intended balance of Internal Integrity and External Generality to be achieved and the links in the chain of reasoning to be appropriately strengthened.

There are many ways in which each of the three criteria may be satisfied. Fulfilling one may be at the expense of another. Furthermore, there may be differences among researchers concerning the optimal level to be achieved on each criterion. Therefore, these criteria are optimized for each study rather than being fully satisfied.

This optimization must be achieved within: (1) the ethical standards prescribed by each discipline for the protection of both humans and animals; (2) the constraints of each institution that protects their operations in the face of research requirements; and (3) the limits on the investigator's personal time and energy as well as on the resources available from the institution, a research grant, or a contract.

A Look Ahead

This chapter noted the importance of understanding and abiding by the constraints imposed by ethical standards. Chapter 10 expands further on the nature of these standards; how they have come about; and the role of the federal government, institutions, and professional associations in developing them and seeing that they are observed.

chapter 10

Ethical Standards and Legal Constraints

> The scientific research enterprise is built on a foundation of trust. . . . To maintain that trust . . . more attention must be given to the mechanisms that sustain and transmit the values . . . associated with ethical scientific conduct. In the past, scientists learned [them] . . . by working with senior scientists. . . . That tradition . . . is no longer sufficient.
> —B. Alberts & K. Shine, "Scientists and the Integrity of Research"

Ethical standards, one of the three constraints on research discussed in chapter 9, has two aspects: (1) the legal and institutional constraints designed to protect the people from whom data are gathered, and (2) the responsibility of the individual researcher for proper conduct above and beyond legalities. The former, covered by U.S. federal regulations, ensures that the researcher's institution provides adequate safeguards for the protection of human participants in all federally funded research. Most institutions require that these regulations be met for all research, even unfunded studies, by both faculty and graduate students.

The latter, the responsibility of the individual researcher, goes beyond the legal framework and is typically detailed in the codes of conduct of professional associations. Associations are involved because widely publicized ethical breaches not only tarnish the perpetrator but also affect the work of other researchers. Ethical violations that occur in the privacy of a professional office are almost impossible to police. Trust, integrity, and voluntary compliance are the cornerstones that make these ethical standards work.

In addition, this chapter discusses the ethical problems involved in research question selection, confidentiality and privacy, decisions in the field, data ownership, and relations with the institutional review board. Analyzing and reporting data with integrity are the topics of chapter 28, which is concerned with whether and how well science works.

INTRODUCTION

Although published professional standards in psychology were formulated in 1951 (American Psychological Association, 1951), emphasis on the protection of human subjects arose primarily as a result of government intervention. Before that, many members of the professions were concerned by studies that, although they made important points, did so by deceiving the participants. Milgram's (1963) study was one that provoked an early outcry. In his experiment, a first participant in a cubicle thought he was helping a second in an adjoining cubicle to learn. The first participant did so by applying electric shocks to the second at the request of the investigator. When asked to do so, the first participant moved a lever, presumably increasing the shocks into what was labeled as the "danger" level even after hearing a groan and then silence from the person presumably receiving them. Individuals were informed during debriefing after the study was concluded that no shocks were given and that the other person was a confederate.

Milgram thought the study important in that it showed that ordinary persons could be made to do extraordinary things under certain circumstances. As Sieber and Stanley (1988) noted, blind obedience to authority is "more contextual and less characterological than most [people] have assumed" (p. 52). Milgram believed his evidence was relevant to the questions involved in the Nuremberg trials of Nazi officials as war criminals, when they claimed they were merely following orders. What a furor this interpretation created! People questioned whether the circumstances were comparable to those in Nazi Germany. It gave prominence to the issue of whether the value of the information gained was worth the discomfort of participants requested to do such awful things. (Milgram [1974] notes, incidentally, that there were no objections to his study until the results were known. This raises the interesting question of how many of the criticisms resulted because the conclusions ran counter to what people wanted to believe.)

A second issue involved the protection of participants. Neither had they asked to have such distasteful knowledge of themselves, nor did they realize they were going to receive it. It could be very disturbing to realize that one was capable of such behavior. Whether deception of participants resulting in self-knowledge and stress is conscionable is at issue.

How does one decide? A 1979 report of the National Commission for the Protection of Human Subjects of Biomedical and Behavioral Research posited three principles:

> *Respect for persons* involves a recognition of the personal dignity and autonomy of individuals, and special protection of those persons with diminished autonomy. *Beneficence* entails an obligation to protect persons from harm by maximizing anticipated benefits and minimizing possible risks of harm. *Justice* requires that the benefits and burdens of research be distributed fairly. (Penslar, 2001)

These three, sometimes conflicting principles are embodied in regulations shared by 17 different federal agencies and offices (Pritchard, 2002). As an example of the conflict between *respect for persons* (the right not to participate) and *justice* (equitable research benefits and burdens), Pritchard suggests "a study of the educational circumstances of young children poorly served by the current school systems, many of whose parents are embarrassed by, suspicious of, or simply uninterested in having their children participate in research of any kind" (p. 9). We noted earlier the importance of judgment in determining knowledge; so too is judgment required in determining the ethicality of research. However, where knowledge judgments are based on evidence, judgments of proposed research must be formed around anticipations of what is likely to occur as well as the value of likely results. These factors compound the complexity of the judgments to be made.

How do we translate *respect*, *beneficence*, and *justice* into research decisions? Two groups, the federal government and professional associations, have stepped into the breach. We shall first examine the federal apparatus for the protection of participants and then consider the codes of conduct established by professional associations.

LEGAL AND INSTITUTIONAL PROTECTION OF PARTICIPANTS

Two U.S. federal laws provide for regulation in ethical matters: the Family Educational Rights and Privacy Act[1] and the National Research Act 93-348 of 1974. The requirements of the latter are in Code of Federal Regulations, Title 45, Part 46, or 45CFR46, as it is usually referred to (online at http://www.hhs.gov/ohrp/humansubjects/guidance/statute.htm). It provides for what are known as **institutional review boards** (**IRBs**, sometimes also called Human-Subjects Research Review Boards), which must approve projects forwarded for funding consideration. Technically the IRBs are responsible only for research funded by the U.S. Department of Health and Human Services (HHS), but Grunder (1983) found that 96% of institutions have been applying the regulations to all research, whether funded by HHS or not.

Institutional Review Boards

The membership of an IRB is specifically prescribed in the regulations:

- It must have at least five members.
- It may not consist of all men or all women.
- It must include at least one nonscientist (examples given are lawyers, ethicists, clergy).
- It must include one person not affiliated either with the institution or with part of the immediate family of persons affiliated with it.
- Persons with a conflict of interest are to be excluded except to provide information.
- Persons with competency in special relevant areas may be invited to assist in the review but may not vote.
- If the board regularly reviews research involving a vulnerable category of participants (such as the developmentally disabled), the IRB must include one or more individuals "who are primarily concerned with the welfare of these subjects" (Sec. 46–107).

Approval is by majority vote. These boards not only have the responsibility of approving research plans, but they also may suspend or terminate approval of research that is not being conducted in accordance with the IRB's requirements or in which unexpected serious harm occurs. Adequate documentation of all IRB meetings and actions is required.

The criteria for IRB approval focus on the safety of participants and include a lengthy discussion of informed consent:

- Risks to participants are to be minimized; that is, the risks of harm must be "not greater, considering probability and magnitude, than those ordinarily encountered in daily life or during the performance of routine physical or psychological examinations or tests" (Sec. 46–103).

- "Risks are reasonable in relation to anticipated benefits, if any, to subjects, and the importance of the knowledge that may reasonably result" (Sec. 46–111). Note that this statement makes the IRB specifically responsible for evaluating the trade-off—for deciding how much risk this knowledge is worth.

- "Selection of subjects is equitable" (Sec. 46–111); that is, for example, that friends are not put at less risk or have greater potential benefits than strangers.

- Adequate provision is made for monitoring the safety of participants, where appropriate.

As Grunder (1986) notes, the IRB is "a work of bureaucratic genius," a reasonably satisfactory solution to a complicated problem to which no solution will be lauded by everyone. It transfers the responsibility from the government to the institution but specifies what the institution must do to comply. Thus, there is no "ethical FBI," as he puts it, to check out rumors; "no army of investigators lurking around thousands of laboratories" (p. 7). It solves the problem of where and among whom to obtain a consensus by specifying the board as the place where agreement must be found and by reducing "consensus" to a majority. It provides guidelines, leaving it to the board to interpret them and to decide when a rule is violated. The penalty for violation is the removal of eligibility for all future research moneys involving human subjects for the researcher and the institution—a severe penalty for a research institution.

The work of IRBs has become of such importance that a search of the Internet turns up much discussion and their own journal, *IRB: A Review of Human Subject Research* (online at http://www.thehastingscenter.org/publications/irb/irb.asp).

> ▶ Institutional review boards bear the responsibility for determining whether projects involving human subjects are ethically permissible and, if there are ethical questions, for deciding whether the potential knowledge that is gained is worth the potential risk that is involved.

> ▶ Although established under federal regulations for funded projects, IRBs are used for other such research conducted at most institutions—regardless of funding sources.

INFORMED CONSENT

A key part of work with human subjects is obtaining **informed consent**. It is especially important where:

- There is any possibility of risk.
- Minors are involved.
- Privacy may be invaded.
- Potentially distasteful self-knowledge may result from participation.

Similar to other topics in the values arena, there is more to the issue of informed consent than meets the eye. Who can give informed consent? A jailed prisoner? A psychotic? A developmentally disabled person? What constitutes "giving sufficient information"? How do we know when a person really understands and so can provide informed acquiescence? Certain safeguards have been put in place, and a number of aids have been developed.

To gain consent, a form is accompanied by a verbal explanation that indicates the individual has been given information regarding the study, understands what he or she is committing to, and has received answers to all questions. Two copies must be signed and dated by the participant. The verbal presentation should give the information needed to make an informed decision. A reasonable opportunity must be given to the participants to decide whether to participate. Those not signing should be dismissed courteously. The participant retains one of the two signed and dated copies.

Contents of the Consent Form

What must the consent form contain? These are its minimum requirements:

- Information as to who is doing the study, as well as its nature, purpose, procedures, hazards, risks, inconveniences, and benefits. If therapeutic in nature, information must include the alternative treatments that could be chosen and the duration, and identification of any experimental procedures.
- Availability of compensation and treatment if an injury should occur in cases of more than minimal risk.
- The extent, if any, to which confidentiality of records identifying the participant will be maintained.
- The name of the contact person to whom to address questions or report an injury.
- Notification that participation is voluntary and that refusal to participate or discontinue participation will be without penalty or loss of benefits to which the person is otherwise entitled.

In some instances, where appropriate, it should also reveal the following information:

- The fact that some risks are unforeseeable.
- The investigator's right to ask a participant to leave the study (usually the criteria for termination are given to show that this is not arbitrary).
- The promise that participants will continue to be informed as information develops that may bear on participation.
- Additional costs to the participant resulting from participation.
- The consequences of withdrawal and the procedure for orderly termination of participation.
- The approximate number of participants.

The consent form must be written so that its reading level makes it understandable to the participants. Readability formulas, available in word processing software, can be used to achieve this. Stanley, Sieber, and Melton (1987) note studies that indicate, in general, the risk disclosure required by the consent process has had only a minimal influence on decision making with regard to medical procedures. This finding seems consistent with the few available psychological studies as well.

A generic consent form is available at Syracuse University's IRB Web site (http://orip.syr.edu/IRBInstructions.php). It specifies the required information so the investigator can replace the bold text with the project details.

Altering or Waiving the Consent Process

The decision to alter or waive the consent process can be made only by an IRB. Its criteria are that the research does not involve greater than minimum risk, the rights or welfare of the participants will not be adversely affected, the research could not otherwise be done, and the participants will be debriefed. Consent documentation can be waived if the consent form links the individual to data that, if made public, could be harmful to the subject. For example, in a study of drug dealers, merely being identified as part of such a study might be considered the basis for subpoenaing the data to search for an illegal act. Humphreys (1975) makes fascinating reading on this latter problem. He studied an illegal act, homosexual behavior in public places. He identified participants through their license plate numbers, tracked them down, and interviewed them. Realizing later that he could not protect his data from subpoena, he destroyed them. This problem is further discussed later in this chapter.

Obtaining Consent When the Individual Is Incapable of Giving It

Can freely given informed consent be obtained from children, prisoners, persons with mental disabilities, and the elderly? Each is a special case. With children, informed consent must be obtained from one parent or legal guardian. In addition, assent—agreement to take part in the procedures—must also be sought from the child, and the IRB must determine if the child is capable of giving assent. The definition of a child is determined by state instead of federal statutes, because the age of legal majority varies from state to state.

Prisoner consent must not involve procedures that would compare too favorably against normal prison conditions, thereby serving as an enticement. Risks must be comparable to those of nonprisoner volunteers. The selection of participants must be fair. Participation must have no effect on parole decisions, and participants must be so informed.

Procedures for working with mentally disabled persons and the elderly are not addressed by the regulations. Grunder (1986) strongly suggests using a professional who regularly works with the population in question and has no ties to the project. This person can attest that consent procedures were followed; that consent or assent was obtained during a period when the participant was lucid; and that if assent is not within the realm of capability, the lack of objection may be enough if minimal risk is involved. In cases that involve more than minimal risk but are still beneficial to the participant, approval from a court of appropriate jurisdiction should be sought.

> ◗ Voluntary signed consent is good protection when individuals are participants in a study, but it is especially important if there is any potential risk, if minors are involved, if privacy may be invaded, or if potentially distasteful self-knowledge may be gained. Special procedures must be used when individuals are unable to give consent because of such circumstances as incapacity, lack of freedom to make decisions, or status as a minor.

CODES OF ETHICS FROM PROFESSIONAL ASSOCIATIONS

Most associations in the professions have developed a set of ethical standards or **code of ethics** for their field and, in some cases, casebooks that show their application. Typical of the standards is *Ethical Principles of Psychologists and Code of Conduct* (2002), which contains a section on research and publication. These standards include discussions of the meaning of beneficence, integrity and justice, expanding these to include sections on "Fidelity and Responsibility" and "Respect for People's Rights and Dignity." However, they also contain sections specifically dealing with informed consent for recording voices and images, dispensing with informed consent, offering inducements, deception, and debriefing. Access them at: http://www.apa.org/ethics/code2002.html#8

Other associations' codes of ethics are also found online:

• The American Educational Research Association (contains a particularly useful section on "Responsibilities to the Field")
http://www.aera.net/ (click on "About AERA" and "Research Ethics"

• The American Anthropological Association
http://www.aaanet.org/committees/ethics/ethcode.htm

• The American Sociological Association (has useful sections on "Planning and Implementation" and "Unanticipated Research Opportunities")
http://www.asanet.org/cs/root/leftnav/ethics/code_of_ethics_table_of_contents

In addition to ethical standards, associations have formulated standards for particular fields of work, such as standardized testing (see chapter 18) and evaluation (see chapter 23). Although without legal standing, these carefully crafted statements are often cited as expert opinion. They have therefore come to have marked influence.

> ◗ Professional associations have developed codes of ethics and standards for the guidance of both the lay public and members of their professions. Although without legal standing, they are sometimes cited in legal cases.

COLLABORATION WITH RESEARCH PARTICIPANTS

There is increasing interest in making research collaborative. Collaboration may be impractical in some studies, for instance, where knowledge of a treatment would have its own effect. But collaboration comes easily for qualitative researchers who consider those whom they study as informants. Although such collaboration is less frequent among quantitative researchers, they also can often design their projects (including the identification and solution of ethical problems) by working with their participants. Such a stance educates those brought into the collaboration and gives them increased feelings of self-worth. It motivates them to work with the researcher both to find the best solutions to problems and to perform well as participants. The topic of collaborative research is discussed as a part of evaluation and action research in chapter 23.

The concern for collaboration with those one is researching is only part of the larger concern about the social consequences of research. This concern comes up again in the chapter on the report of a qualitative study (pp. 344–357) and still again in regard to the effects of testing—especially high-stakes testing such as that required for a diploma or degree, for the closing of a not-up-to-standard school, or for employment.

COMMON ETHICAL CONCERNS

Ethical decision-making concerns common to all researchers include problem choice, data confidentiality and personal privacy, ethical decisions in the field, consent on the Internet, and ownership of the data. Let's consider each of these concerns below.

Problem Choice

Ethical decision making begins with the choice of problem and how it can be investigated as is made clear in the excerpt on page 53. Some researchers choose to forgo pursuit of a problem rather than violate their sense of what is right. It is the responsibility of the researcher to try to anticipate the ethical aspects of each new study as part of the decision to pursue it.

Some topics cannot be studied without **deception of participants**. Examples are studies of entrance procedures to college to determine the effect of racial and sexual identification, the effects of subliminal messages, or the effects of certain drugs. The Zimbardo study in chapter 1 is such an example. IRBs do approve such studies from time to time.

Why do some persons categorically reject such procedures? Baumrind (1985), summarizing the arguments from different points of view, notes that such approvals fail to take into account long-range costs that are "unknown and therefore easy for investigators and review boards to dismiss" (p. 167). Decreased trust of others is one such cost. Debriefed participants have been found to be less inclined to trust experimenters to tell the truth (Fillenbaum, 1966). That same distrust rubs off on the rest of the profession. Baumrind (1985) also sees the practice as deteriorating the researcher's "ethical sensibilities and integrity." She argues that the continued use of such practices becomes self-defeating. As enough participants are made suspicious, naiveté becomes a variable, and Page (1973) showed that naive participants generally behave differently from suspicious ones.

Further, it is difficult to obtain evidence regarding the absence of harm to participants that is acceptable to opponents of deception. For instance, Milgram (1974, 1977, 1992) argues that he adequately debriefed his participants. In a one-year follow-up, 80% said they were glad to have taken part, and less than 1% of his participants regretted it. Patton (1977), however, argues that the evidence comes from "destructively obedient" individuals; that is, we could hardly expect them to say otherwise. Furthermore, Baumrind (1985) notes that when queried about the study, such participants need to deny that they have allowed themselves "to be treated as objects, and . . . [therefore] most will say that they were glad to have been subjects" (p. 169). In the face of such arguments, it is difficult to gather evidence acceptable to people who oppose the practice.

There are clearly strong arguments against using deception, and IRBs no doubt carefully weigh any proposal for its rare use. Careful **debriefing** by a skilled professional certainly is one condition. Using the experience to educate the participants may help overcome the negative aspects.

> ▶ Certain research topics cannot be pursued without deception. Some people believe that they should be excluded from the research agenda.

Data Confidentiality and Personal Privacy

Confidentiality and privacy are often mistakenly assumed to relate to the same concern. **Confidentiality** refers to control of access to information; **privacy** refers to a person's interest in controlling boundaries between self and others (Sieber & Stanley, 1988). Anonymity, a related concept, refers to researchers' not knowing the identity of participants or at least not being able to link data with specific persons. In most research, ensuring confidentiality of data is just plain good practice.

Because social science researchers have no general immunity from subpoena like doctors or lawyers, they must gather data in such a way that anonymity is ensured from the outset. Researchers can also use various means that do not violate confidentiality to link data or to gather responses to sensitive questions (see p. 590). Sometimes a neutral third party can receive the data, remove the identifiers, and pass the data on to the researcher. Placing the keys with a neutral person in another country is sometimes suggested. Immunity from subpoena can be granted by the U.S. Department of Health and Human Services and the Department of Justice for certain kinds of projects. In short, there are enough ways of handling this situation that the problem more often stems from inadequate attention to solutions than from a lack of them.

Confidentiality of information from school records is within the jurisdiction of the U.S. Family Educational Rights and Privacy Act, also known as the **Buckley Amendment**. This act requires that before information may be gathered from school records, a waiver must be obtained from the parent or guardian or, if over 18 years of age, the student. It indicates what records will be disclosed, the purpose of the disclosure, and the persons to whom disclosure will be made. School personnel with legitimate educational interests are exempt, as well as organizations conducting studies for local or state agencies for the purpose of developing and validating tests, administering student aid programs, or improving instruction. The local institution is the final judge of what constitutes "improving instruction." Data so gathered must be reported so that individuals cannot be identified and destroyed when the study is completed.

▶ Confidentiality of data must be maintained so that individuals or institutions cannot be identified in ways that may be harmful or invite undesirable comparisons.

▶ Unless a special exemption is obtained from the U.S. Department of Health and Human Services or the Department of Justice, social science investigators have no immunity from subpoena. Special steps must be taken from the outset of data collection to make sure that participants are not at risk.

Ethical Decisions in the Field

Perplexing ethical decisions are often encountered in the course of field research. Although specifically discussed in the context of qualitative research in chapters 13 and 14, they can occur with any method anywhere. Researchers encountering such problems usually have to make their decisions on the spot, without the opportunity to consult others or an IRB. When an illegal act, incompetence, or serious mistake is observed (such as an error by an incompetent surgeon), should the researcher report it? At a minimum, reporting such incidents usually results in termination of the project. Therefore, some researchers believe that revealing the overall problem so it can be corrected is the better solution. This was Bosk's decision (1979) after observing surgical errors.

The administrator who wishes to control the flow of information from the study creates a special problem. Such a desire may seem unreasonable from a researcher's point of view, but because unfavorable reports may cost the administrator's job, this is not an illogical request. Researchers with the attitude that administrators with something to hide ought to lose their job will find it more difficult to gain entry. Once again, individuals' rights as human beings, society's needs for protection, and the scientist's freedom to provide the free flow of information (which is the lifeblood of science) come into conflict. Many investigators prefer not to use a site rather than submitting to censorship or obtaining the data through deception.

▶ Entry to field situations, especially where a negative report may reflect on the people giving such access, can cause serious ethical dilemmas, especially when the public's right to know is also involved.

Consent on the Internet

Research on the Internet is still finding its ethical base. Clearly, the same concerns apply as with offline research, but how? Because individuals can easily assume roles, research dependent on self-identification of age, gender, or other characteristics is often suspect. Research on chat rooms, support groups, and other online communities are another grey area. Are they public property? Can persons be quoted out of context? How would one get permission? Because chat room participants often depend on an established sense of community, published research on their behavior can poison that atmosphere. Is the knowledge likely to be found worth disturbing these groups? Will obtrusive observing distort typical behavior? These and other questions are addressed online in "Ethical decision-making and Internet research" by Ess and the Association of Internet Researchers (2002). For a discussion of ethics in qualitative research see Eysenbach and Till (2001).

Research Ownership

At least two ethical issues arise with respect to research ownership: availability of the data to others for secondary analysis, and apportionment of credit on publication. The rules are clear for each of these areas. With regard to the availability of the data, concern over possible fraud (see chapter 28) makes it important for researchers to retain rather than discard it so that others can check their findings. Anonymity can be compromised, however, if individuals try to check on the way data were collected or to follow up on cases. Nelkin (1984) cites cases where federal granting agencies claimed and were granted access to data that researchers obtained under the promise of confidentiality. Ownership of data and maintenance of confidentiality should be agreed on at the time a grant is negotiated.

Who should get credit on publication? Various situations are discussed quite thoroughly in Section III of the *Ethical Standards of the American Educational Research Association* (AERA, 2002). But its main principles are that all persons making a "creative contribution to the generation of an intellectual product are entitled to be listed as authors," and that authorship order should reflect that contribution. Other associations have similar statements.

> ▶ The right of outsiders to obtain data for secondary analysis may pose a dilemma for the investigator who has promised confidentiality to participants.
>
> ▶ Publication credit should be given in direct proportion to contribution to the project.

RESEARCHER RESPONSIBILITY TO THE INSTITUTIONAL REVIEW BOARD

Although it is the IRB's responsibility to make the final decision, the board depends on the researcher to present the case. This responsibility can create a dilemma for the researchers, who must anticipate the negative consequences as well as the positive side of each new study. It is easy to see the IRB as the enemy to be thrust aside. But the attitude everyone must take is not much different from the impartial attitude that researchers assume, insofar as they can, in assessing data on which they have invested their time, their resources, and sometimes their reputations. As Koshland (1990) notes:

> Scientists are the servants of society, not its masters, and we should remain so. . . . It is our special responsibility to spell out the disadvantages as well as the advantages of a new discovery as far as we can. What is good for science is not necessarily good for the country. . . .

> As architects of change, we have occasionally oversold the product, implying that it will bring unmixed good, not acknowledging that a scientific advance is a Pandora's box with detriments or abuses as well as benefits. By confessing that we are not omniscient we may lose some awe and admiration, but we will gain in understanding and rapport. (p. 9)

If an IRB turns down your proposal, try to understand their position. Simple adjustments in the research plan will often take care of the matter. In other instances, counterarguments can and should be expressed. Before a counteroffensive is launched, however, careful listening, genuine understanding, and a real attempt to view the situation from both sides are essential to keeping this decision process working as it should.

ADDITIONAL READING

The papers of the interdisciplinary Social and Behavioral Sciences Working Group on Human Research Protections examine and suggest ways to enhance such protection are online at http://www.aera.net/AboutAERA/default.aspx?menu_id=90&id=669. Before submitting, many universities ask you use their IRB checklist. Find examples by searching "IRB checklist."

For examples of ethical problems in the field and qualitative research, see Lee-Treweek and Linkogle (2000) and Van den Hoonaard (2002).

For experiences of a qualitative researcher with an IRB, see Milne (2005). Mazur (2007), despite the focus on medical research, usefully discusses issues in the IRB system.

Koshland (1990) further discusses the issues mentioned in this chapter's quotations—the relation between science and society. Bersoff (2003) discusses ethical conflict in psychology and devotes a chapter to problems in academia, research, and supervision. Barnett and Johnson (2008) is a pocket guide to the American Psychological Association's standards.

IMPORTANT TERMS AND CONCEPTS

Buckley Amendment
code of ethics
confidentiality
debriefing

deception of participants
informed consent
institutional review boards (IRBs)
privacy

OPPORTUNITIES FOR ADDITIONAL LEARNING

1. An educational sociologist was interested in determining if there was a relationship between teachers' socioeconomic backgrounds and their job performance. She decided to begin with an exploratory approach using several qualitative research techniques, including classroom observation, interviews, and document analysis. She met with a local school superintendent to negotiate entry to the schools and permission to interview teachers. The superintendent agreed to arrange for her to meet several school principals and, in the meantime, provided her with copies of various documents from the personnel files of teachers in the district. Is there an ethical problem here? If so, for whom?

2. A cognitive psychologist wanted to study the effect of modeling behavior on school-aged children's willingness to persist in a task. To do so, he chose a task, solving a wooden puzzle, and developed two videotapes to provide a model. The first showed a child of comparable age as the participant solving the puzzle easily (a positive model); the second featured a child having great difficulty, becoming frustrated, and not finishing the puzzle (a negative

model). Each videotape was also accompanied by one of three audio messages explaining what to do in the task and stating whether or not the child would succeed. One message was positive, one neutral, and one negative. Combining each audio message with each video-tape provided six treatments. Having designed the experiment, the psychologist approached the local school authorities for permission to carry it out with local school children in grades 5 and 6. He received permission from the superintendent of schools and from the principal of a particular school. Need he have done more?

3. A team of social psychologists wished to investigate the cognitive processes underlying the concept of altruism. They decided to conduct a field experiment to study the phenomenon under "natural" conditions. This was carried out in an urban subway to determine whether assistance to an ill passenger would be affected by the severity of the problem (blood or no blood). A passenger (member of the experimental team) with a cane would collapse in a subway car. In some cases, blood would trickle from his mouth. The responses of the partic-ipants (regular, unsuspecting passengers) were observed and timed. If no regular passen-gers came to his aid within a specified time period, a helper, disguised, for example, as a clergyman, would assist the victim and help him off at the next station. What ethical issue was involved with this experiment?

4. Daniels (1983) used participant observation to study wealthy women involved in charity organizations. She gained acceptance into the group and, in particular, developed a close friendship with some of the women (her key informants), who were aware that she was engaged in research. This relationship involved such activities as frequent lunches together and the exchange of gifts. As the study wound down, the investigator found herself bored with the friendship and wished to terminate it. In effect, it no longer served a research pur-pose. Is it ethical for a researcher to have developed such a friendship?

Compare your answers with those following the Application Exercise.

APPLICATION EXERCISE

Consider what problems of informed consent you might have with your proposed project. Will you be collecting data from individuals from whom informed consent can be obtained, or will you need to contact parents or guardians? Is there a problem in terms of confidentiality? Will you be the only one seeing the data? Can you ensure that no one else will have access to it? Is there any reason you can't destroy identifying information shortly after the data are col-lected? As a better alternative, can you collect data without identifying information and still get the participants' cooperation?

Are you collecting data about which there might be a privacy question? If so, how will you handle it?

Does your institution require that both federally and nonfederally sponsored grants be approved by its institutional review board? If so, do you know the procedure? You might get one of the board's forms now and fill it out for your project. See what potential problems it brings to mind.

If you plan to do the project with others, have you tentatively decided how you will allo-cate credit and authorship?

KEY TO ADDITIONAL LEARNING OPPORTUNITIES

1. There is a possible invasion of privacy here with legal implications that should concern both the investigator and the superintendent. It involves these issues: gaining access to data,

ownership of data, and obtaining consent. It appears that the superintendent released information from confidential files without the permission of the teachers involved. Since the consent of particular teachers was not sought or obtained, the question becomes one of ownership of the data. Were the data contained in the files the sole property of the school system, in which case the superintendent may have been within his rights, or was this a case of joint ownership? Without seeking the involvement and permission of the teachers, both the superintendent and the investigator could be leaving themselves open to possible litigation. Their best course of action would have been to obtain consent before the release of the information.

Since she intends to observe the teachers, she will also need the permission of their principals, and she will want to obtain the teacher's consent as well.

2. Yes, the institutional review board should have required him to obtain the consent of each child's parent or guardian and also of the children themselves. Furthermore, since his experiment seems likely to produce psychological discomfort in at least some of the participants, in obtaining consent from the parents he would have to make clear the possible negative consequences and the expected effect of the debriefing. He would have the responsibility to make clear the nature of the treatment to the children.

3. This controversial experiment was conducted as described by Piliavin and Piliavin (1972). It clearly involved deception and also likely invoked considerable anxiety on the part of participants who were not given the opportunity to consent to the treatment. It was actually quickly terminated because of dramatic participant reactions and the possible danger to them as well as a result of harassment from subway police. The research was inspired by the highly publicized attack and murder of a young woman in broad daylight, observed by a number of people who did nothing to help. The research problem thus appeared to have significant social value (the gain). It was conducted surreptitiously to create a "natural" situation and allow "valid," interpretable results. The cost was to the participants who had not consented, may have experienced negative effects, and certainly gained no direct benefit (other than perhaps the satisfaction of assisting a fellow citizen).

4. The question of ethics in the study by Daniels (1983) focuses on deception. There does not appear to be any serious breach of ethics. The respondents were informed that Daniels was conducting a research study and had consented to participate. The question the investigator asked was whether or not she had deceived these women by appearing to have developed a friendship and then letting it gradually lapse as the study wound down. Because friendships usually have a basis in some common interest and because the investigator was not otherwise involved in these charities, this may well have been the natural course of events. Nevertheless, qualitative investigators view the persons they study as informants who should not be harmed as a result of study. The very fact that the investigator is raising the question is indicative of this responsibility. She would no doubt want to take steps to assure that her informants' sense of self-worth was not harmed as she slowly terminated the relationship.

SUMMARY

Ethical principles to guide the work of the researcher have been established by the federal government and by professional associations. The government has entrusted the enforcement of these principles to institutional review boards (IRBs), which must be established at institutions seeking federal funds for research involving humans. In most institutions, these boards must approve all such research, not just that which is federally supported. IRBs are responsible for holding participants harmless, both physically and psychically. They also enforce specific rules regarding eliciting informed consent from participants and protecting the confidentiality of data and the privacy of participants. Researchers must also observe federal specifications protecting the privacy of information obtained from school records.

In addition, through the publication of ethical standards, professional associations have sought voluntary compliance in research areas not covered by federal regulation as well as in such fields as testing, evaluation, and personnel selection.

Despite these standards, there is concern over possible fraud in science. Do scientists live up to the standards set for them? Can their work be trusted? These concerns raise questions as to whether the whole system works. Those questions are addressed in chapter 28.

A Look Ahead

The final chapter in this foundational research concepts section examines logic that is basic to social and behavioral research, that is, logic's use to design studies to infer causation.

Note

[1] P.L. 93-380, Title V, Sec. 513 (b)(2)(i), 88 Stat. 574; 34 CFR Part 99. Regulations similar to those for humans exist to protect animals used in research.

Links to previous research

Explanation, rationale, theory, or point of view

Questions, hypotheses, models

Preplanned and emergent designs

Design/procedure

Focus   Records   Time   Comparison and Contrast   Situation   Participants

Data

Statistical analysis and/or narrative analysis

Conclusion

Link to next study

Explanation or rationale of next study, etc.

11

Showing Relationships through Design
Design's Logic

> Despite the creative use of experimental design features from the seventeenth century onward, it was not until the past century or so that experimental design notions became systematized.
>
> —Thomas D. Cook & Donald T. Campbell,
> *Quasi-Experimentation*

Both the studies in chapter 1, which represent different research approaches, related a cause (Zimbardo: a perceptual discontinuity; Hoffmann-Riem: a desire for normality) to an effect (Zimbardo: paranoia; Hoffmann-Riem: adoption). How were they able to convince readers? Regardless of whether the study is of preplanned or emergent orientation, or whether it is pursued through a quantitative or qualitative approach, the design of a study allows us to determine whether relationships among variables exist, what kind of relationships they are, and what allows us to exclude rival explanations of the phenomenon. In short, without Mill's logic to show causation, explained in this chapter, researchers would be unable to advance a credible explanation of a phenomenon. So the logic of design is an important component of any study.

INTRODUCTION

As applicd to a research study, the term *design* describes the art of arranging the evidence gathered, or planning for the gathering of that evidence, so that a convincing chain of reasoning is constructed. The term design applies to experimental studies where the conditions for evidence collection are so designed as to provide for:

- the use of the logic of one of Mill's methods (agreement, differences, concomitant variation, and residuals—discussed in the following sections).

- all reasonable rival explanations for the appearance of the phenomenon or process to be ruled out. You may be saying to yourself, "That seems reasonable with a pre-planned study, but is it true with an emergent one, particularly one in which researchers are 'following their noses' to what is important?" Good question! Design isn't a factor where the study is simply a descriptive report of persons, situations, or phenomena without an attempt at an explanation intended to apply beyond that situation. But when a report of a study is so organized as to present a generalizable explanation, then some kind of comparison or contrast—with previous behavior, with other persons or groups—occurs. The choice of that comparison or contrast is the element of design.

In a qualitative study, design may or may not initially guide data collection. For instance, the researcher often gathers a body of qualitative data and only then discovers a relationship in it. Design then enters as the researcher selectively chooses from the body of data those instances that show the relationship—a phenomenon or process that repeatedly occurs under specified circumstances (the method of agreement or method of concomitant variation). And design even more amply enters if the researcher, gathering further data, then steers the collection procedures to comparable instances where the phenomenon did not appear and should not because the specified aspects were not present (the method of differences). Indeed, such researchers often go on to collect evidence where rival explanatory factors are present but either the phenomenon or process did not appear or was of a different kind—eliminating rival explanations. So, although we more often associate design with experimentation, the term *design* is widely applicable to describe the logic associated with

- the use of design to build a convincing argument from *empirical evidence* (*demonstrated result*) that a specific phenomenon or process occurs in the presence of one or more conditions (e.g., in the Zimbardo study, paranoia in the presence of a sensory discontinuity, or, in the Hoffmann-Riem study, a desire for normality in the case of couples adopting children). However, in some instances the design may influence decisions strengthening conceptual evidence (*explanation credibility* and *translation validity*), as when Zimbardo used three measures of paranoia to convincingly assure that it occurred. But design is crucial to a demonstrated result.

- the use of design to *eliminate relevant rival explanations* of the phenomenon or process (the use of taped directions, different posthypnotic suggestions to the groups, the rehearsed interplay of the confederates, etc.).

- a summing of the above evidence and comparison with evidence from earlier studies to determine how strongly one can infer that the study's evidence links the variables in the phenomenon or process as a *credible result* of the study.

> ▶ Design is the critical element both in providing a demonstrated result and in eliminating rival explanations of the phenomenon being studied.

DESIGNING STUDIES TO FACILITATE THE INFERENCE OF CAUSATION

In 1843, John Stuart Mill elaborated on Sir Francis Bacon's recommendations for discovering causes in a series of what he called "canons," since he believed they were fundamental rules for proving causation. We now realize that they are not methods of proof; indeed, they are really impossible conditions. However, although their conditions cannot be completely fulfilled, they describe the logic we use to infer causation. Mill called them the methods of agreement, of differences, of concomitant variation, and of residuals.

The Method of Agreement

Mill (1868) formulated the **method of agreement** thus: "If two or more instances of the phenomenon under investigation have only one circumstance in common, the circumstance in which alone all the instances agree, is the cause (or effect) of the given phenomenon" (p. 428). It is extremely rare, of course, that phenomena, especially social phenomena, have only one aspect in common. Yet, by confining ourselves to reasonable possibilities, this is a commonly used logic for finding potential causes. To return to the Kounin example in chapter 3, Kounin noted that smooth transitions by teachers were a common characteristic of classrooms where disturbed children were not acting out. Although it wasn't proof, it was suggestive of a causal relationship.

The method of agreement is often used with observation and descriptive case studies. It is the logic that underlies qualitative methods (chapters 12–16), and is exemplified in the Hoffmann-Riem study in chapter 1 (where the common attribute across different adopting families was seeking "normalization").

The negative form of the method of agreement is also useful: Nothing can be the cause of a phenomenon that is not a common circumstance in all instances of the phenomenon. This method eliminates potential causes that were not present where the effect occurred. However, like the banning of carcinogens in food where presence is a matter of degree, it is sometimes difficult to define what we mean by "presence."

Assuming we have control of the situation, as in preplanned studies, we can design the study to use the method of agreement, identifying varied instances that all differ from each other but show that when a particular effect is present, there is a particular cause as well. *Meta-analysis*, a method of combining the results of a variety of quantitative studies of the same phenomenon, is an extension of the method of agreement by, for instance, tabulating the studies that confirm or disconfirm a particular relationship (see chapter 22). (Those readers already familiar with statistics may realize that the method of agreement underlies the use of such statistics as Chi-square and the run test, both of which compare the incidence or appearance of non-randomness of a phenomenon or condition with chance.)

In naturalistic settings and emergent studies where we do not control the situation, we select from our data repeated instances showing the relationship or instances where they vary together.

> ▶ The method of agreement is used to infer causation where, over a variety of instances in which the effect occurred, there is one—and *only* one—aspect in common.
>
> ▶ The negative form of the method of agreement is also useful: nothing can be the cause of a phenomenon that is not a common circumstance in all instances of the phenomenon.

The Method of Differences

The **method of differences** combines the method of agreement with its negative form and is the logic used in experiments. In practice, this calls for two groups as alike as possible, one of which (the *experimental group*) is exposed to the experimental variable (the treatment); the other (the *control group*) is not. If the effect shows only in the experimental group—and, because in all other respects the groups are alike, there is no other plausible explanation than the treatment is the cause—we infer causation. Experimentation is probably the most strongly accepted evidence of causation.

The method of differences also requires an impossible condition—namely, two identical situations. In reality, no two individuals are identical nor is anyone identical from moment to moment. Attaining sufficient functional equivalence for the logic to be effective is one of the most important aspects of experimental design. Many reasons for nonequivalence give rise to a variety of rival explanations to the treatment. We'll examine them in chapter 21.

Except when events arrange themselves as a natural experiment, the method is mainly used in preplanned studies. Rarely is a treatment introduced in an emergent study. Where the constructs can be adequately translated into measures, quantitative methods are typically used; but where they are not—for instance, to measure creativity—mixed-method designs involving qualitative and quantitative methods are used to assess constructs. Qualitative studies frequently test the explanations in contrasting situations or groups where they ought to hold, as well as those where they ought not. For instance, had Hoffmann-Riem gathered data from couples visiting today's fertility clinics, she would have expected them to express the same desire for normalization as the parents interviewed in her study. But one would less likely expect such expressions from childless couples interviewed before fertility clinics existed.

> ▶ The method of differences is used to infer causation where two or more groups are alike in all respects except that, following the introduction of the presumed cause in one or more of them, the effect appears in those and only those.

The variety-of-difference designs.   Although the comparison of treatment groups with control groups (or the pre- and posttreatment testing of individuals) is what initially comes to mind in considering method-of-difference designs, there are many possibilities. For instance, we can compare an individual's present behavior with future behavior. Alternatively, this can be compared with that of past individuals as shown by test norms. Or we can compare people in natural situations or groups especially designed for the study. One can choose individuals particularly likely to show the effects of treatment, if there are any. We can describe such possibilities in a decision tree like the one in Figure 11.1. The tree suggests alternatives that might be considered in a particular study.

Similarly, one may instead, or in addition, contrast different levels of treatment, different ways of physically administering the treatment, different patterns of timing the administration of the treatment, as well as different patterns of who got what treatment and when. Or one can vary the situation or setting, providing different settings for different treatments as well as different settings for various timing of treatments. As you can see, depending on what is being studied, the number of possibilities

Figure 11.1   **A decision tree of possible alternatives in the chain of reasoning's "comparison and contrast" link involving participants.**

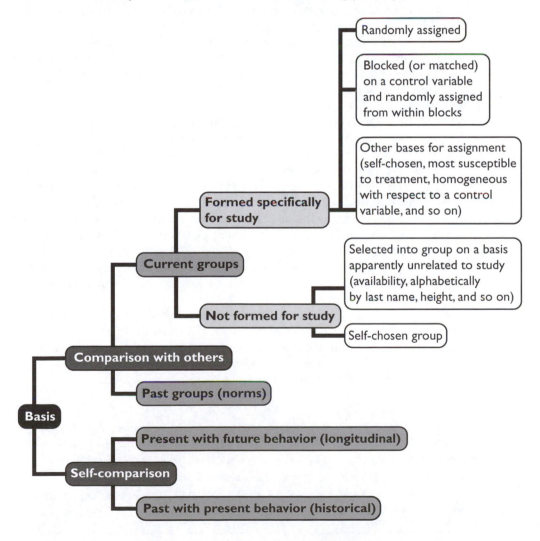

is large. The question being studied will guide you. (Those familiar with statistics will realize that the method of differences underlies statistics such as the *t* test, analysis of variance, analysis of covariance, and multiple analysis of variance.)

The Method of Concomitant Variation

This method is often used when it isn't possible to manipulate situations experimentally. The **method of concomitant variation** asks whether cause and effect vary together in some regular way. Unfortunately, however, two things may vary together because of a common link in their causal chain. A colleague of mine, Silas Halperin, uses as an illustration a plot of average reading level at each elementary school grade to average weight at that grade. It is true that sixth graders both weigh more and read better than the first graders, but would overfeeding first-graders improve their reading capacity? Of course not! Both vary with a third variable, growth over time. So one must be wary of assuming causation when varying together might be the effect of a third variable.

The method of concomitant variation is widely used in prediction studies—such as finding variables to predict learning (e.g., SAT) or job success (e.g., a sample of their work). The results are then used to guide college admissions or hiring. The method of concomitant variation can usually also help rule out causes that do not vary with the effect.

Much of the scouring of demographic data for clues for useful concomitances is based on either the method of difference or method of concomitant variation (e.g., to find what foods have desirable health effects—Italians on a Mediterranean diet have less . . .). These are after-the-fact natural experiments (see p. 507). Using the method of difference, individuals are put into categories (e.g., healthy and unhealthy) and their data scanned to find consistent differences between the categories; or the data are ranked according to some variable (e.g., from very healthy to very unhealthy) and the data searched for variables that show similar or inverse rankings—concomitant variation. (Readers familiar with statistics will realize that the method of concomitant variation underlies the use of statistics such as the Pearson product-moment correlation coefficient, rank correlation, multiple correlation, and structural equation modeling—also called causal modeling.)

As with the method of difference, depending on what is being studied there can be many different possible variations of the cause. For example, treatment variations may include greater strength or duration of cause and how it is applied. The physical setting under which the treatment is administered may be varied through a range of conditions (e.g., temperature, silence or noisiness, etc.).

> ▶ The method of concomitant variation is used to infer causation where a change in one variable is accompanied by a similar change in another variable (or its exact opposite).
>
> ▶ It is especially useful in inferring causation where the cause is under the control of the researcher and the effect can be shown to follow manipulation of the cause.
>
> ▶ It is also useful where experimentation is not possible, but one must be wary that the covariation is not the result of both variables being affected by a third variable.

The Method of Residuals

This method, more often used in natural science research, is rare in behavioral science research. The **method of residuals** asks us to account for as much of the situation as we can on the basis of prior work, and the cause is to be found in the residue not accounted for. This method is regularly used in troubleshooting. A mechanic working on a stalled car pulls a wire from a spark plug to test for failure of the high-voltage electric system. If it passes that test, then the culprit is another system—carburetor, fuel pump, timing, and so on. The mechanic then checks these in order of their likelihood of failure.

Clearly, the method of residuals works best in a well-explored system of limited scope. In comparison with the natural sciences, problems in the behavioral sciences tend to have fuzzy boundaries, broad scope, and less firm knowledge about constituent parts that would permit their elimination.

> ▶ The method of residuals locates the cause in the residue remaining after prior work has eliminated as much of the rest of the situation as a possible cause.
>
> ▶ It is less useful in the realm of social and behavioral sciences with its less firm knowledge, broad scope, and the fuzzy boundaries of its generalizations.

STRENGTHENING MILL'S METHODS

Combining the Methods

Mill's methods assume a single cause; they are not as successful in cases of multiple causation. This flaw is especially obvious with the method of residuals, as many car owners have discovered the hard way. By itself, a weak spark plug or a bad fuel mixture might not cause engine failure; together they may do so. A mechanic looking for a single cause might pass over individually adequate contributors to a multiple-cause problem.

As in the example of the multiple causes of engine failure, Mill's methods are often stronger when they are used in combination. The method of concomitant variation combined with the method of differences can show not only that the effect occurred, but also that it was related to strength of cause. For example, suppose we place food coloring in increasing concentration in a series of batches of processed food. We can show that presence of the food coloring only above a certain level causes hyperactivity in children (the method of differences). But then, by showing that the degree of hyperactivity corresponds to the level of concentration above the critical level (the method of concomitant variation) we have very strong evidence of a causal relation.

Evidence that Links Cause Convincingly to Effect

An essential task of design is to link cause to effect. What kinds of evidence can one provide that convincingly does this? Here are four types of evidence:

1. Use a theory or a rationale to predict the appearance of the effect in as much detail as possible. Indicate when it will appear, how strongly, how long it will last, and so on. Design the study to show the agreement of prediction and results.

2. Design the study to make the difference between untreated and treated conditions as large as feasible. If there is a treatment (a cause under the control of the investigator), maximize the treatment effect (discussed on pp. 483–484).

3. Show that the effect follows only the cause.

4. Vary the treatment, and demonstrate that the effect has the same pattern.

The first kind of evidence is not confined to experimentation. Astronomy is not an experimental science. An astronomer can tell you, however, that the sun's massive sun spot display will result in a disruption in world communications at a particular time. The disruption occurs. It is an impressive display of evidence of the cause-and-effect linkage. In similar fashion, let's theorize that having skipped a developmental task in choosing a vocation, even individuals who were initially happy with their professional choice will become discontent after a period of about ten years. Comparing the satisfaction of those individuals about ten years into their chosen occupation who can recall having completed that developmental task to others at the same career point who did not will confirm the prediction. The more detailed we can make our predictions, the more compelling will be the evidence for the expected relationship when our prediction comes true. Using a theory or a rationale to predict the effect in as detailed a fashion as possible is an important way of strengthening the evidence. Qualitative researchers use this technique when, having found a presumed cause-and-effect relationship in one circumstance, they predict what they will find in a similar one.

The second kind of evidence, showing a large effect, is not uncommon in the natural sciences but is rarer in the social sciences. Dramatic results from trials of a medical drug or procedure are front-page news. Because dramatic effects are uncommon in the social sciences, however, we design studies with sensitivity sufficient to sense weak effects. (However, see the Rosenthal [1994] reference on p. 522 [chapter 28]. Do we expect too much in the social sciences?)

The third kind of evidence comes from a condition of cause-and-effect relationships—the effect occurs with or follows the cause. Experiments have an advantage in those instances in which the treatment is administered, since the effect should appear only with the administration of treatment.

The fourth kind of evidence, showing congruence in pattern of cause and effect, is the most convincing if the cause can be manipulated. There are so many ways to change the causal pattern: frequency, strength, and duration of treatment application in steps just large enough to produce measurable results; or in increasing steps (a single unit of strength, twice as strong, three times, and so forth); or in rapidly accelerating fashion (twice as strong, four times as strong, 16 times, 256 times). We can cluster treatment administration between testing intervals and change the pattern of clustering and length of intervals. We can use a random pattern of administration, possibly dictated on the spur of the moment by an independent third party. The more complex the pattern, the more likely it is that chance is ruled out as an explanation. Such patterns, when accompanied by a similar pattern in the effect, will convincingly link cause to effect.

Studies involving learning or other effects that change the individual or that do not rapidly decay can present special problems, since the "off" period may show little or no loss. The amount of forgetting may not be measurable during the short period of the study. To overcome this, we may use strongly contrasting treatment levels—more practice problems or increased contact time—that are different enough to be reflected in the effect. We should remember, however, there are sometimes learning "plateaus" that do not immediately respond to either strength of treatment or extent of practice.

Replication of a study provides its ultimate validation. This is especially true when combining studies of the same phenomenon that use different designs and methods. They rule out the possibility that a particular design or method influenced the results, and they yield stronger evidence than single studies. Meta-analysis (discussed in chapter 22), a way of quantitatively combining studies, is a strong method of providing evidence for causal propositions. Furthermore, depending on what evidence is available, a meta-analysis can explore the nature of the causal relation, show how it is affected by other variables, and determine where evidence is needed for more complete understanding.

ELIMINATION OF RIVAL EXPLANATIONS

Throughout the book so far, the elimination of explanations other than the intended one has been described as an important part of the logic of showing causation. Are there common rivals that we should watch out for? Can each study have rivals that are unique to it? The answer is yes to both of these questions, but the description of those rivals is best left to the research methods in which they are most likely to be encountered. Thus, fuller treatment of rival explanations in qualitative methods is given in chapter 15, and in quantitative methods in chapter 21 on experimentation.

Chapter 21 also discusses experimental control, another topic relevant to the elimination of rival explanations. Although primarily relevant to experimentation, this section may be useful in some other studies as well. To maximize your understanding, it is suggested that you at least acquaint yourself with this material now (pp. 484–486).

ADDITIONAL READING

For an excellent discussion of what is required to show causation, a critique of the randomized controlled trial design (RCT), and a discussion of other ways besides RCT of showing causation, see Scriven (2008). For a detailed model of what is involved in design, see Reichardt (2006). Also for designs and for a good treatment of causation, see Shadish, Cook, and Campbell (2002).

IMPORTANT TERMS AND CONCEPTS

meta-analysis	method of differences
method of agreement	method of residuals
method of concomitant variation	rival explanations

OPPORTUNITIES FOR ADDITIONAL LEARNING

1. You are a psychologist with a deep interest in the age-old practice of astrology. You suspect that there may be some validity to the belief that astrological sign determines aspects of personality. Consequently, you decide to try to show that people who are born under the sign of Taurus tend to be more stubborn than others. You considered this problem in chapter 7 in a different context. Here we ask you to consider how this problem might be approached from the method of agreement and the method of differences.

2. Could you use the method of concomitant variation on the above problem?

3. Does watching violence on television in the early elementary grades result in aggression in the students' everyday behavior? Is the method of concomitant variation applicable to this problem? If so, how?

   Compare your answers with those following the Application Exercise.

APPLICATION EXERCISE

Consider how the problem you have chosen might be explored by the method of differences and the method of concomitant variation. In what way does your literature review use the method of agreement?

KEY TO ADDITIONAL LEARNING OPPORTUNITIES

1. You would find a convenience sample of boys (such as a tenth-grade high school class) that, so far as you can tell, was not likely to have been selected on the basis of stubbornness. Finding all the boys born under the sign of Taurus, you could ask the teachers to write a brief paragraph describing the boys' dominant traits. Using the method of agreement, you would search all of those descriptions for adjectives related to stubbornness.

   Using the method of differences, you could ask for similar descriptions of boys in the rest of the class and compare the average frequency of references to stubbornness in the two groups to see if the incidence in the Taurus group is greater. If you repeated this experiment over a variety of other classes to determine whether the same result occurred, you would be using the method of agreement on those results.

   Note that this is not an experiment in the sense that the cause is under the control of the experimenter; it isn't. It is an after-the-fact design (discussed in chapter 21), so one will need to assure readers that there is no causal linkage to a third variable affecting both stubbornness as a trait and being born under the sign of Taurus. However, readers who believe that there might be such a variable, even though unknown in exact nature, would be unlikely to be convinced by negative findings with the methods above.

2. Because one is either born under the sign of Taurus or one isn't, there are no in-between gradations that would provide support for the *dose effect*—stronger treatment, stronger effect. However, there are ways of estimating the relationship between a dichotomous variable (Taurus or non-Taurus) and amount of stubbornness that might provide some evidence.

3. Yes, it is applicable, but one would need to find a way of defining and measuring television viewing time, violence on television, and aggressive behavior. Then one would need to combine the first two measures and relate the result to the measure of aggressive behavior. Time watching television is the easiest of the three, and there are scales available in the literature for the other two. Combining the time and violence measures is a weighting prob-

lem that involves estimating which is more important. One could provide the reader with the results of several weightings: heavily weighting time, heavily weighting violence, and weighting them equally.

SUMMARY

The caveats of this chapter are well worth bearing in mind along with the possible complexities of inferring causation. However, it is evident that we can and do construct strong evidence for causal relationships, and our methods of doing so are continuously improving.

- Comparison and contrast is a key link in the chain of reasoning for inferring causation.
- The logic described by John Stuart Mill is used in our research methods and is embodied in the *comparison and contrast* link. Mill proposed:
  1. the method of agreement (used in case studies and in historical studies),
  2. the method of difference (used in experimental studies),
  3. the method of concomitant variation (used in predictive studies and in studies examining data gathered after an event has occurred, after-the-fact natural experiments), and
  4. the method of residuals.
- We approximate Mill's conditions as closely as possible, add such conditions as we can to strengthen the logic, and often combine the methods to support our inferences.
- A particularly convincing design linking cause and effect manipulates the cause in a complex manner that could not be easily duplicated by chance and then shows that the effect follows the cause pattern.
- New methods are improving our bases for inferring causation. For example, meta-analysis quantitatively combines the findings of studies and provides strong evidence for causation.

A Look Ahead

The concepts covered in this and the previous four chapters that make up this section will be referenced wherever they are relevant in the next sections on methods of research. The first, Section IV, discusses qualitative research. Chapter 12 addresses the characteristics of qualitative methods, and chapters 13–16 cover successive aspects of doing qualitative studies.

The Continuum of Research Methods
Qualitative Side

This section describes qualitative research methods. They are particularly useful in establishing how individuals understand their world, in showing how individuals' perceptions and intentions in situations determine their behavior, in exploring phenomena to find explanations, and in providing concrete and detailed illustrations of phenomena. They have become the focus of extensive interest and debate for a variety of reasons—dissatisfaction with the pace of progress with quantitative methods, rethinking positivist philosophy, and as an alternative to quantitative methods and statistics, among others.

- Chapter 12 introduces this research, showing the variety of qualitative approaches. It describes the advantages of these methods, their use with quantitative methods, and an overview of the qualitative research process.

- Chapter 13 discusses fieldwork including entry, participant observation, fieldnoting (with examples), the beginnings of analysis, and ethical problems encountered in data gathering.

- Chapter 14 discusses a second major source of qualitative data—interviews. It describes the different types of interviews (including nondirective), choice of interviewees, and multiple interviewees.

- Chapter 15 concentrates on data analysis with extensive discussions of coding, including starting points. It describes the advantages and concerns that flow from using specialized qualitative analysis software. Also explained are audit trails, as well as factors that may bias analysis.

- Chapter 16 addresses the research report with considerable emphasis on what constitutes quality qualitative research and on the qualitative equivalents of Internal Integrity and External Generality. Report format, organization, content, and style are discussed.

Qualitative Research Methods

> If one wishes to understand the term holy water, one should not study the properties of the water, but rather the assumptions and beliefs of the people who use it. That is, holy water derives its meaning from those who attribute a special essence to it.
>
> —Thomas S. Sasz, *Ceremonial Chemistry*
>
> Reality is in the eye of the beholder.
>
> —Miguel de Cervantes Saavedra, *Don Quixote*

This chapter provides basic background for understanding qualitative methods. Initial exploration of the strengths of qualitative methods leads to an examination of the kinds of studies in which they may be particularly helpful. Because researchers use these procedures with different emphases and orientations, a brief description of some of them follows. Singled out for special attention is the one noted in chapter 2 that views qualitative as a point of view inseparable from method. In contrast, this book, in taking the pragmatic view of using whatever technique is required by a study, concentrates on the use and usefulness of its methods.

Noted also is that the literature search, which precedes problem identification in quantitative, may follow in qualitative because many qualitative workers inductively develop their research problem. And the variety of data that qualitative researchers gather, such as observation, interview, archival material, documents, photographs, and artifacts, is noted as well. A graphic displaying the flow of data through the qualitative process of gathering, processing, analysis, and interpretation ties it all together at chapter's end.

INTRODUCTION

We begin with discussion of the research continuum at the qualitative end for two reasons: First, qualitative methods build on the well-practiced verbal descriptive skills and the techniques for selecting and categorizing information that you have used in writing term papers and reports. Therefore, you come to qualitative methods with extensive and relevant experience and skill. Don't assume, however, that qualitative methods are a breeze compared with quantitative ones. As you will see, both require skill, and qualitative methods are extremely labor intensive. It is difficult to appreciate this fact thoroughly until you are confronted with the usual mountain of material that you must organize, analyze, digest, and interpret.

Second, familiarity with qualitative procedures is useful even if a researcher chooses to specialize in quantitative methodology. Adding qualitative data to a quantitative study can help keep quantitative researchers close to participants so they learn what lies behind the numbers—information crucial to their proper interpretation.

The characteristics associated with qualitative procedures were already described in broad strokes in chapter 2:

- oriented toward exploring, describing, and explaining;
- inductive and emergent in approach;
- dealing with words;
- holistic in orientation;
- not using treatments; and
- concern with local knowledge and with perceived and constructed reality.

Qualitative researchers typically view participants they observe or interview as collaborators or teachers from whom they learn.[1]

ADVANTAGES OF QUALITATIVE PROCEDURES

Qualitative procedures are ideal for exploring complex phenomena about which there is little knowledge. Becker's (1963) qualitative work in *The Outsiders*, for instance, showed how labeling people made them outsiders from the surrounding culture with serious consequences. This early study probably influenced the movement for inclusiveness of the handicapped in education. Through exploration, qualitative methods teach us how to understand a phenomenon. For example, Borman and O'Reilly (1987), studying children's social roles in kindergarten, discovered that boys' speech used to establish same-sex friendships was quite different from girls'. In asserting their status as friends, girls made no attempt to "conceal their 'goofs' and scribbles" whereas "among boys, declarations of competence and extraordinary accomplishments in exploits such as running footraces . . . served the same purposes as the revelation of inadequacies" by girls (p. 63). Such differences, revealed by the qualitative method's inductive approach, would have had to be recognized and hypothesized if a quantitative approach were used.

Even when much is already known, however, some qualitative researchers intentionally approach phenomena without consulting prior work so that they come to the problem afresh. For well-studied problems, such an approach may be fruitless unless, through careful attention to some significant aspect that others had taken for granted, or through viewing from a new angle, they find a way to make a contribution. But, regardless of method, researchers always risk wasting time; there is no sure payoff when venturing beyond present knowledge—research is an adventure!

Stake (1995) described the intent of qualitative research as "not necessarily to map and conquer the world but to sophisticate the beholding of it." By sophisticate, he means qualities that humanize problems; that holistically portray complex, interactive phenomena; that show how others perceive their world; and that provide handholds on difficult problems.

Where Qualitative Approaches Might Be Most Useful[2]

These capabilities suggest that qualitative procedures may be useful when humanizing the problem is required to:

- make people, problems, and situations "come alive"; portray phenomena in context.
- attach emotions and feelings to phenomena—sometimes also faces and their accompanying personages, even their situation, context, and accompanying emotional and social climate and milieu.
- describe complex personal and interpersonal phenomena that would be impossible to portray with quantitative research's single dimensional scales.
- provide examples that put "meat" on statistical "bones."

An inductive rather than a deductive approach is required:

- when research is lacking in an area and one must emphasize discovery rather than corroboration of hypotheses. The focus and design of the study is not preplanned; it develops as work proceeds; it is an emergent study.
- because the nature of a program or process is sufficiently diffuse that goals are best discerned in the research process rather than determined beforehand.
- when research progress in an area has plateaued and you are seeking a new perspective for a fresh start or are attempting to find something that was overlooked in previous work.
- when help is needed to find a "handle" on a problem without obvious starting places.

Information provided by quantitative methods is inadequate because:

- the problem involves complex interactivity and feedback loops/systems.
- the process does not have quantitatively identifiable outcomes.
- the focus of study is mainly on a process and its internal dynamics or its strengths and weaknesses rather than on its product or effect; you want to understand the process of local causality in depth.
- detailed, in-depth information is sought (e.g., on the implementation or quality of a program or process) as well as a description with many nuances and details.
- you want to start in an open fashion rather than with someone else's conceptualizations. Developed instruments come with preset categories.
- you are interested in the diversity among, the idiosyncrasies of, and the unique qualities of persons or processes (in contrast to comparing them on standard measures).

- the administration of standardized instruments (questionnaires, tests) would be obtrusive or impossible in contrast to observations and informal interviews, or there isn't enough time to set up and administer tests.
- no valid standardized instrument is available; it isn't worth the effort, it is too difficult to build one, or there isn't time to do so.
- a holistic picture of phenomena will restore perspective on the problem.
- a well-grounded explanation of a phenomenon is needed.
- there are too few cases or too little data to handle the problem quantitatively.
- there may be unexpected consequences or side effects.
- a side effect may become more important than the intended main effect.

An insider's view is needed because:

- you need to "get inside" others to view the world as they perceive it (this is the anthropologist's *emic perspective*—see the sidebar on p. 243).
- you believe that the perceptions of the participants differ from those of outside observers in such a way as to explain their behavior.
- you and/or your audience prefer a qualitative orientation.

Note that in many of the above situations, a combination of qualitative and quantitative methods in the same study will further strengthen it (a *mixed-methods study*, see chapter 26).

Some problems cry out for a qualitative approach. For example, Allen and St. George (2001) sought to improve domestic violence therapy. They decided on qualitative analysis of interviews with couples who had undergone it. Consider these aspects, selected from the list above, that make qualitative methods a good fit for their study: (1) the emphasis on discovery, (2) study of a complex interpersonal process, (3) involvement of interactivity and feedback loops, (4) lack of a good instrument, and (5) the need to get inside and view therapy as the participants perceive it. The qualitative vignettes used to illuminate aspects of Allen and St. George's research portray a reality about domestic violence and therapy that would be difficult to achieve with just the numbers and statistics of quantitative methods.

Qualitative methods require skillful interpretation of the data. In fact—although we don't generally make the connection—like historians, qualitative researchers are judged by how insightfully they analyze their data, how well they present their interpretations, and how carefully and tightly they relate them to their information base. Turn to page 605 and read the first two paragraphs on interpretive history, as these paragraphs apply equally well to qualitative research in general.

Stake (1995) sees qualitative work as primarily providing explanations—explaining how an effect is related to a cause. Although much quantitative work also does this, Stake contrasts this kind of explanation with understanding. Qualitative research is especially helpful when it provides us with someone's perceptions of a situation that permit us to understand his or her behavior. For another example, much has been made of how so-called culturally deprived children see the world as hopeless. But when, through qualitative research, a study reveals in detail the hopes, fears, dreams, and nightmares of a few cases, that general statement takes on new meaning. Stake means that besides understanding, the research provides an emotional acceptance and an empathic feeling toward the individual in an especially effective manner.

The qualitative study, with its real-life context and stories, may be particularly effective in communicating with practitioners who can identify with the examples portrayed. Along these lines, Hargreaves (1996, p. 110) contrasts academic knowledge with that of practicing professionals like clinicians, teachers, social workers, librarians, journalists, and so forth, as follows:

Academic Knowledge	Practicing Professional's Knowledge
generalized	content-specific
propositional in form	metaphorical, narrative, story-based in form
rational	rational but also moral and emotional
public	interpersonal or private
theoretical	practical

The characteristics of academic knowledge in the left-hand column are those of the scientific knowledge that both quantitative and qualitative academic researchers generally seek. Note how much better, however, the practicing professional's knowledge's characteristics match the case study produced by qualitative methods. Such compatibility suggests that the qualitative case study may be particularly effective in communicating with practitioners.

Other Considerations in Choice of Research Method

A comparison of qualitative methods with quantitative methods is analogous to the difference between essay questions and multiple-choice ones. Because there are always many ways of interpreting and answering essay questions, you collect the data first and do the scoring and analysis later. In contrast, you decide on the correct answer and the alternatives of multiple-choice questions at the outset; thus, the scoring is a clerical rather than a judgmental task. Quantitative studies, like multiple-choice tests, are largely planned beforehand; carefully designed data collection and the pattern of analysis, like multiple-choice scoring, follows from the plan. Qualitative research, like an essay examination, typically involves much less structured collection of data and an analysis stage where judgments are made. Each method involves precious research time, either in quantitative study planning and design or in qualitative data gathering and analysis—there is no getting around it.

Novice researchers often choose to do a qualitative study—for instance, for a dissertation—because it looks easier than learning all those statistics for a quantitative study. Or perhaps they have a math phobia and feel more comfortable with words as data. But qualitative research requires skill as well. It takes a special ability to organize and reduce the incredible detail amassed in qualitative research to a significant finding. Some researchers gather drawers of data and are unable to find a way to pull it together meaningfully. Qualitative procedures require much time-consuming, hands-on attention.

However, choice of method is less and less a matter of easier and harder. Computer programs now do the computation and solve the equations of quantitative research. Furthermore, statistics can be learned conceptually at a verbal level without going through algebraic derivations. Computer programs similarly facilitate qualitative data analysis. The truth is that appropriately disciplined procedures must be learned for the proper use of any research method. Choice should depend on:

- which approach is most appropriate for your problem,
- which best fits your personal problem-solving style,
- whether you prefer (or are better at) working with people or with things,
- your ability to "pass" in fieldwork (e.g., to be one of the group studied),
- your flexibility and tolerance for ambiguity, and
- your commitment to accepting the discipline of whichever process you choose.

In some instances, qualitative methods stand alone; in others, they are usefully combined with other methods, often supplementing quantitative methods. All methods have strengths and weaknesses; the researcher's task is to learn when and where to capitalize on strengths and avoid weaknesses. This and the next four chapters present qualitative research as an approach to gathering and analyzing data that seeks to anticipate and allay the concerns of the researcher's audience that might impair acceptance of the findings.

> ▶ Qualitative methods use familiar techniques for handling verbal material that make situations "come alive"; they keep the investigator close to the data and markedly facilitate understanding of the phenomenon being studied. They also can be usefully combined with all other research methods.

THE VARIETY OF QUALITATIVE APPROACHES

Adherents of qualitative research distinguish many variants. Figure 12.1 from Wolcott cleverly illustrates some of them as a family tree with many branches. Some have bewildering names like human ethnology, micro-ethnography, ethnomethodology; others are more easily interpreted like community study, investigative journalism, and content analysis. Some are labeled in terms of what is studied: culture, communities. For an explanation of many of these terms, see: http://onlineqda.hud.ac.uk/methodologies.php.

At the base of the trunk, we find that all are rooted in the skills involved in experiencing, inquiring into, and examining everyday life. Major parts of the trunk designate sources of data: observation, interviews, archives. While Wolcott's tree is an interesting and useful portrayal, others might organize the field differently and/or include other terms from the field, such as naturalistic methods, content analysis, case studies, responsive evaluation, feminist or minority orientations, or symbolic interaction. The point is that qualitative methods, as such, lend themselves to a variety of uses. Applicable to diverse phenomena, they can even be used by individuals with differing views of how the world works (though, as we'll see, some of the latter believe they shouldn't be).

Examining, for example, how ethnography, ethology, ethnology, ethnomethodology, phenomenology, and connoisseurship differ from each other might be an interesting exercise but it also is a complex way of learning qualitative methods. To give a flavor of the variations, however, let's examine two of them: ethnography and symbolic interaction.

Figure 12.1   **"Family Tree" of different approaches to qualitative methods.**

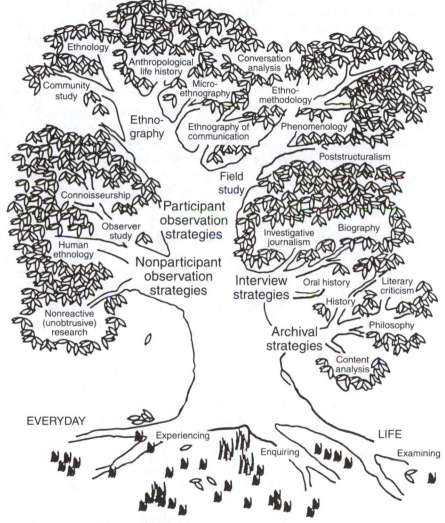

From "Posturing in Qualitative Inquiry" by Harry F. Wolcott, in M. D. LeCompte, W. L. Millroy, and J. Preissle (Eds.), *The Handbook of Qualitative Research in Education*, pp. 3–52. Copyright © 1992 by Academic Press and Harry F. Wolcott. Reprinted with permission of Elsevier Science & Technology Books.

Ethnography

Social scientists with an anthropological orientation typically call their work *ethnography*. Their research emphasizes the role of culture in influencing behavior. They study the meaning of shared patterns for behavior, and they trace how culture evolves. Physical aspects of the surroundings and the behavior of others are interpreted in terms of cultural standards. Some analyze particular cultures, comparing and contrasting them. Examples are the famous work of Margaret Mead, who studied child rearing in Samoa and popularized her conclusions as well as those of fellow anthropologists who challenged her findings.

"Researchers in this tradition say that an ethnography succeeds if it teaches readers how to behave appropriately in the cultural setting, whether it is among families in a black community (Stack, 1974), in the school principal's office (Wolcott, 1973), or in the kindergarten class (Florio, 1978)" (Bogdan & Biklen, 2007, p. 30).

Such researchers constantly engage in self-reflection, called **reflexivity** in the qualitative literature. It refers to awareness of the personal factors that might affect the observer's view of phenomena—their interests, values, and self-perception in that context (e.g., the likely self-reflections an upper-class Caucasian woman might experience when interviewing African American males in their neighborhood). They introspect to determine how their observations and perceptions might be affected; they include such reflection in their report as well as try to correct it for such tendencies.

Symbolic Interaction—A Different Epistemology

Do you recall as a child wondering whether the world that you perceived around you was real? Did you ever consider that maybe it was somehow set up for you—like Catherine the Great of Russia, for whom her staff set up false-front villages as she traveled down a river, taking them apart and reassembling them downstream? If so, you were pondering the question of what is true knowledge and how to separate it from false, a problem that has engaged philosophers' minds for centuries. This is the field of **epistemology**.

Without going too deeply into it, we can note that in chapter 2 we discussed two epistemological positions. We noted that most scientists assume that there is a real world out there to be plumbed and discovered, and that what becomes knowledge is the result of a social process of corroboration and judgment that something is true. Social science research has proceeded on these bases for some time, examining relationships and looking for causal links that had generality over situations and persons. Perhaps we should have identified this as the **positivist** epistemological position in chapter 2, but it is not too late to do so, especially now that we will have something we can contrast it with.

That "something" is the view of some qualitative researchers who hold symbolic interactionist or **phenomenological points of view**. Although not denying the role of culture, they emphasize the meanings persons attach to others and to the things that surround them—*symbolic interaction*. That is, people act according to the meaning they attribute to things and persons; their reality is socially constructed. From this viewpoint, to reach a full understanding of the purpose of a person's behavior it is necessary to see the world through their eyes. (See, for example, Pifer's [2000] "Getting in trouble: The meaning of school for 'problem' children.") As Bogdan and Biklen (2007) note:

> People act not, however, according to what the school is supposed to be . . . but rather according to how they see it. For some students, high school is primarily a

place to meet friends; . . . for most, it is a place to get grades and amass credits so they can graduate. . . . The way students define schools determines their actions, although the rules and the credit system may set certain limits and impose certain costs, and thus affect their behavior. (p. 28)

We might add (as Bogdan and Biklen do) that the students' actions are also a result of how they see themselves: Seeing themselves as individuals who succeed or fail in such settings strongly influences their behavior as well.

From this point of view, there is only a perceived reality; therefore, multiple interpretations of a situation can be experienced by different persons, and knowledge is local and situation specific rather than generalizable. And because social phenomena are interactive, a researcher couldn't tell which is cause and which is effect. This perspective explains many actions that are inexplicable from a strictly external point of view, and therefore it is an important one. It strongly affects what data are gathered and how they are interpreted. These views challenge key aspects of the positivist epistemological orientation.

These researchers argue that through our experiences, we construct a view of the world that determines how we act. Each new piece of information is integrated into one's existing knowledge structure, and one's perception is affected by that structure. Researchers immerse themselves in the social milieu of their participants in order to determine how they understand the world around them—the *emic* perspective—that is, how they perceive their local setting and culture and how they see themselves in it. Investigators are studying the meaning-making process, asking, "What would it be like to be one of *them*?" This knowledge is a *social construction*, a joint product of the culture and the meanings assigned by the individual. (So also, however, is quantitative interpretation a joint product with one's culture. See the example of volume as the pitch of a sound on p. 402. What characteristics of a phenomenon are attended to, and how they are measured, are social constructions. Such measures are so much a part of our culture that we often consider them as natural, as though that were the only way to view them.)

What else must we add to the characteristics of qualitative research listed in Table 2.1 (p. 30) to distinguish the symbolic interactionist point of view? Additionally, the researchers themselves are typically the principal instrument of data collection. This means they adopt a role that goes beyond that of the uninvolved observer,

Etic and Emic Perspectives

Contrast the **emic** perspective with the anthropologist's **etic** perspective—that is, how it looks to the outside observer. As we will note later in the chapter, many qualitative researchers stress the internally perceived world's emic perspective, whereas quantitative researchers are seen as emphasizing the outside observer's etic. The latter seek to describe the world in an objective way—there is a reality "out there" that they are trying to describe. Objectivity refers to description that other observers of the same events agree is accurate. In comparison, when describing thoughts and perceptions and supplying their interpretation of them in providing an emic perspective, qualitative researchers may present different interpretations of the same phenomenon.

because entering the world of another requires emotional as well as cognitive involvement—*empathy*.

These researchers assert that there can be multiple correct views of a situation. How can this be so? Phillips (1992) notes that societies construct their own meaning, an observation we make again in chapter 18. For example, the Eskimos believe there are 14 kinds of snow; we refer to only one. Are they right and are we wrong? According to the philosopher Popper (1972), each of us assumes a physical and a social world, and their nature at any given time reflects the level of our understanding of these worlds.

Because people perceive things differently, various researchers may properly advance their own interpretations of a situation without trying to reconcile the differences. For instance, as Glesne and Peshkin (1992) note, both Redfield and Lewis studied the Mexican village of Tepoztlan with different results. Redfield argued his hidden question was, "What do these people enjoy?" whereas Lewis's was, "What do these people suffer from?" As Redfield (1995) notes, "we must recognize that the personal interests and values of the investigator influence . . . the study" (p. 136).

Researchers who adopt this point of view will not typically use tests and measures. If they did, they would certainly first plumb what a person's perceptions are. Only then might they be able to select a matching measure that could capture these perceptions as a way of gathering additional data.

Although symbolic interactionists are concerned with self-reflection and reflexivity, among feminist and minority researchers it often goes beyond that—to being aware of what effect the research is intended to create, that is, its social and political implications. For instance, Lather (1991, p. 71 as found in Maher, 1991) notes that the purpose of feminist research is "to correct both the invisibility and distortion of female experience." Where quantitative researchers focus primarily on contributing to knowledge, many qualitative researchers argue that they should be much more aware of the effects their roles create.

Whereas researchers may use qualitative methods without embracing all these characteristics, for those who argue that qualitative method is inseparable from its underlying epistemological position, these aspects form a unitary outlook from which certain important research implications follow. These individuals would not engage in research that combines qualitative and quantitative methods and would argue that others should refrain as well. Because of the various underlying epistemological assumptions it makes no sense to design mixed-method studies.

At this point in time, those arguing for the symbolic interactionist point of view are a minority of researchers, even among those who use qualitative methods. Building a social science from research findings that are local and context bound is currently outside the mainstream of research. For development of the position that knowledge is local and social science generalizations are limited in scope, see Geertz (2000).

▶ For qualitative researchers of the symbolic interactionist tradition, qualitative research methods and epistemological point of view are inseparable. This point of view involves understanding how people perceive their world, make meaning of it, and act on that information. Holistic study of natural settings is sought, and researchers adopt an empathic stance toward those studied. Research findings tend to be local and context bound. Multiple interpretations of a situation may be quite acceptable if various researchers perceive the situation differently. They view the epistemological basis of quantitative methods as incompatible with their own epistemology and would therefore not engage in studies that mix quantitative and qualitative methods.

▶ Qualitative methods can, however, be used without adopting all aspects of the symbolic interactionist point of view.

▶ Qualitative methods as data gathering and analysis tools are useful and important to understand, even for those whose main research method will be quantitative.

COMBINING QUALITATIVE *AND* QUANTITATIVE RESEARCH

Because the majority of researchers using qualitative methods do not share the epistemological concerns discussed above, most are not constrained from using both qualitative and quantitative methods in the same study. Indeed, as is described in chapter 26, there is increasing use of multiple and mixed-method studies. Furthermore, findings from studies of the brain's reaction to perceptions and the real thing suggest there is reason to do so.

The importance of perception in determining behavior has received an important boost by findings from functional magnetic resonance imaging (fMRI). It has long been known that sugar pills, when perceived as if they were medicine (i.e., placebos), often cure the patient. But only recently have brain scans shown us that the areas that react to the medicine are the same as those that react to the placebo. The brain has the same reaction to perception as it does to the medicine itself.

For those of us who argue that there is a real world out there to be discovered, this puts perception in the same category as other sensed reality from sight, sound, touch, and smell. It puts a more positive slant on those who argue that what we deal with are perceptions of reality rather than reality itself, and it moves us all into the same tent. It confirms the importance of perception as a determiner of behavior, and it implies that inclusion of the perception of participants may be an important additional variable to take into account in many quantitative studies. And that, in turn, suggests that mixed-method studies using qualitative methods to tap perception will more likely be profitable than pursuing one method alone. Most social scientists are oriented toward seeking generalizable knowledge using any and all of the techniques that will further this aim. This pragmatic approach is pursued in chapter 26 on mixed methods.

LOCATING AND DEVELOPING A QUALITATIVE FOCUS

For the researcher with a clear idea of a research problem, the approaches of examining the literature and proceeding to develop a research design discussed in chapters 5 and 6 are similar in both quantitative and qualitative methods. Many qualitative methodologists, however, stress letting a foreshadowed problem develop inductively, immediately beginning to gather data in an area of interest with considerable openness and looseness of design. They immerse themselves in the situation to see what emerges. Researchers say they are instructed by the phenomenon as to what is important rather than imposing some framework that determines importance. This **emergent approach** requires selecting an area of interest and engaging it in whatever way is available and appropriate—for example, observation, interviewing, reading records, examining artifacts. As a glimmer of an idea emerges, the researcher works at developing it.

When to Turn to the Literature for Help

Those using the emergent approach believe that consulting the literature too early will burden them with other people's perceptions; they don't want to miss what the naive eye might see. You come fresh into a situation only once; therefore, do the literature search after you have been exposed to the situation and have begun to form your own notions about what is important, how things are related to each other, the general context, and what explanations you can advance. Then, with a much-sharpened notion of your study, you ask how others have understood it in the literature in contrast to your own understanding. With this approach, you begin the literature search with quite a different background from that of others just starting to define their problem.

But immersing yourself to see what emerges can lead to collecting data on everything—to initial diffuseness of effort, to breadth rather than depth of data, and often, for novices, to bewilderment: What details to attend to and record? How to limit the study? The admonitions of openness and looseness of design are indeed appropriate for experienced researchers studying complex problems with reasonably adequate resources. (It seems there never are enough; a study always consumes whatever resources are available and needs still more "for a solid completion" or to "round it out.") Examples exist in which novices handle these conditions successfully. In general, however, especially when studying a structured phenomenon that has been the subject of prior work, novices may find that too open a design pursued too deeply will result in little new "pay dirt." Such individuals would do well either to cut their losses early if little appears or to try a more focused and structured approach to a part of the subject that has not been well explored.

Fetterman (1989) is right on target: The researcher "enters the field with an open mind, not an empty head." Past experience may suggest that there is more here than meets the eye. As Miles and Huberman (1994) point out, in most studies:

> Something is known conceptually about the phenomenon, but not enough to house a theory. The researcher has an idea of the parts of the phenomenon that are not well understood and knows where to look for these things. And the researcher usually has some initial ideas about how to gather the information. (p. 17)

These hunches begin to structure the approach to data gathering and make choices easier about where, from whom, and how to gather data.

So, as with many aspects of qualitative methods, researchers differ about how much preparation to do before data collection. Wax and Wax (1980) note that reading about the situation the researcher intends to enter

> is a mark of respect to the hosts, as it demonstrates that one considers their affairs of sufficient importance to learn whatever one can about them before formal introduction. Preparation is also a mark of respect to the scholars who have studied the community in the past. (p. 6)

But doesn't this impose a framework that may alter your view of the situation? Wax and Wax note: "True, when one enters the field, one may be hampered by inaccurate ideas gained from prior studies, [but] the researcher will always be entering with some freight of expectations. It is better that these be grounded in past scholarship" (p. 6). Given these differences of opinion, you must decide when to consult the literature for yourself in terms of your style of working, your problem, and especially in terms of your ability to maintain openness to new perceptions.

When to Write the Problem Statement

Most individuals know why they choose a particular phenomenon to study and what they hope to find, even when they use an open qualitative approach. They may not want to make that reason explicit for fear of appearing to slant the study to fit their predilections. In fact, qualitative researchers pride themselves on recognizing and making explicit potential sources of bias, and they have more control over those that are made apparent.

On this basis, it makes sense to formulate the best possible statement of your study as early as you can. This does not mean that it won't change with further data collection—certainly you must be open to that possibility. But the formulation of the problem will help clarify your thoughts and feelings about the direction of your effort. You'll have an initial gut feeling that "No, that isn't quite right; it will do for now but I've got to . . ." Or, "That doesn't capture what I'm looking for. Maybe I should . . ." When the ellipses in those statements are filled in, they begin to chart directions for the study that can lead to boundaries and a clearer focus.

The very act of seeking a focus and verbalizing that focus keeps you working at conceptualizing the problem—it is facilitating. My colleague, Sari Biklen, tells her students to keep trying to express the problem or purpose of the study in a single sentence. Others suggest trying out titles for the study. Gradually, you will be able to develop a problem statement and rationale for the study. It may even be possible to embed the study in some kind of an explanation or theory. Clearly, the closer you can get to an explanation, the better. Whether that is best done near the outset or later depends on how open to change you can be once you have a tentative formulation. Yin (1984) notes:

> When Christopher Columbus went to Queen Isabella to ask for support for his "exploration" of the New World, he had to have some reasons for asking for three ships (why not one? why not five?), and he had some rationale for going westward (why not north? why not south?). He also had some criteria for recognizing the

New World when he actually encountered it. In short, his exploration began with some rationale and direction, even if his initial assumptions might later have been proved wrong. This same degree of rationale and direction should underlie even an exploratory case study. (p. 30)

WAYS OF GENERATING QUALITATIVE DATA

Although observation and interviewing are the major qualitative data-gathering methods, qualitative researchers, especially historians, frequently analyze diaries and other personal as well as official records and artifacts. Similar to quantitative data, qualitative data may be gathered from situations as diverse as the human imagination permits. To illustrate the many ways that qualitative data may be gathered, suppose we are studying—as did Bogdan, Brown, and Foster (1982)—communication between hospital staff and parents in a neonatal ward where extremely premature infants hover between life and death. Once we have identified a problem of communication between staff and parents, we might begin *observation* of their interaction, asking to sit in as *researcher–observer* on their conferences. Or, since this may seem intrusive, we might simply take the role of a nurse or staff member but participate neutrally in such discussions as we try to fix in memory what went on—*participant observation.*

Alternatively, if it can be arranged, conferences might be held where staff and parents can be unobtrusively observed, perhaps through a two-way mirror—*concealed observation*. Such observation without parental consent should be cleared with the institutional review board (or IRB; see chapter 10).

Such observations may be supplemented by informal *interviews* or, as we close in on particular data that we need, by structured interviews. We might interview small groups of staff and parents about the problem of communicating the right amount of hope and pessimism to parents—*group interviews, focus groups*. The group setting gives them the chance to discuss and react to one another's ideas, possibly expressing ideas and reactions that we as researchers might not have asked about, and stimulating thoughts that might not have come up in individual interviews.

We might also use *projective techniques* to gather data, showing pictures taken of parent-staff conferences in the ward and asking other parents and staff to describe what was going on. The pictures should be somewhat ambiguous to allow the respondents to bring their own typical and most salient interpretations to the scene.

Using a more *structured stimulus*, we might put phrases on 3- by 5-inch cards describing what was going on in the ward, ask both parents and staff to sort the cards into piles, and then ask them to describe the piles and explain why they placed each card there. Like the pictures, this technique allows the respondents to project whatever organizing schemes are most salient in their minds, schemes that may or may not be readily apparent from their actions. We then compare the parents' sorting results with the staff's sorting results.

We might use the **stimulated recall method**, which involves video recording the actions we wish to learn about—in this instance, parent–staff conferences. We would then play the video in which they were involved to each of the parents and staff individually. During this replay, we ask them to stop at points they think were significant, tell what they were thinking at that time, and describe why those points were significant. We might also stop the video at additional points that we think were significant and ask what was going through their minds at those points.

Note that these are all ways of eliciting how individuals perceive situations and what organizing frameworks come readily to their minds to make sense of them. We can either video record responses or describe them in handwritten notes, kept as close to verbatim as possible. If we have a categorizing and coding scheme, we can tally responses directly into it.

Thus, there are a variety of ways of generating qualitative data. Some come out of the sociological and anthropological traditions, in which interviewing and observation are central; others are closer to psychological traditions, in which reactions to tests and specially designed stimuli are more central. Because chapter 13 deals with fieldwork, we will examine observation as a means of gathering data more closely there.

> ▶ Qualitative data may be gathered in as many ways as the researcher's creativity permits. Although the most widely used sources are observation and interviewing, the analysis of records, documents, photos, and videos is also common. In addition to observation and interviewing in the sociological tradition, methods of eliciting individual responses to specially designed stimuli, as in psychology, may be useful.

OVERVIEW OF THE QUALITATIVE PROCESS

Figure 12.2 on the following page is a simplified overview of the typical interactivity among the various major steps in qualitative research. The feedback loop at the top and right side of the graphic—describing, gathering data, sampling, analyzing, organizing, and interpreting—is the primary ongoing effort for many qualitative researchers. As the feedback arrows suggest, once some data are gathered, these steps are all engaged and interact simultaneously in an immediate and continuous process. Some researchers, however, do not get involved in analysis until all the data have been gathered and then go back to fill holes. Note that, in this overview pattern, the nature of the expected final report interacts with each of the steps from the very beginning, each step affecting what will be included, and being affected in turn by what is needed to make a convincing and effective report. Self-reflection (reflexivity), the researcher's examination of selective and biasing factors that might affect each of the steps (the gray background), is continuously active as an encounter with new situations in one aspect brings to mind concerns that may also affect others.

Figure 12.3 (on p. 251) presents the interacting process of Figure 12.2 in greater detail. It more completely specifies the activities at each of these steps, including many suggestions that enhance study quality that are described in the following chapters. It illustrates the simultaneous pursuit of three streams (the columns) of data gathering, data analysis, and report development; the continuous data reduction through the steps; and the merging of the streams of activities in the closing steps of the study. The steadily narrowing arrows in the background portray data re-

Figure 12.2 A simplified overview of the various major steps of qualitative research.

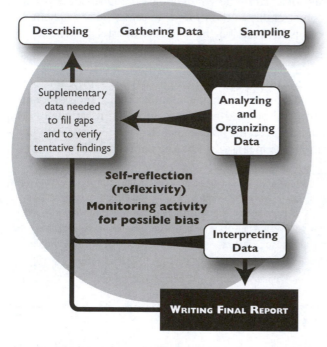

duction to increasingly relevant data. The self-reflection (reflexivity) shown in Figure 12.2 is clearly present in these processes but is omitted in 12.3 to avoid adding complexity. The major steps of the study are arranged down the left side of the graphic as though they are completed in order, when in fact many of them will be going on at the same time in different parts of the study.

The columns are not separated by lines, indicating their openness to being affected by and to affect activity in the other columns. Cross-stream transfers of information occur throughout the process—especially in the maze of arrows depicting the coding process where successive steps alternate between the data and analysis streams, as data are coded and winnowed and codes are developed and refined. The researcher's focus transfers:

- from the data stream to analysis in order to separate those data that are at the study's center from those at the periphery;

- from the analysis stream back to data gathering, having been informed of data needs by gaps found in coding;

- from the report stream to both data and analysis streams regarding information needed to flesh out and test emerging conclusions (this is present at all stages, but arrows were omitted for the sake of simplification); and

- from data and analysis streams to the report stream for summarization, narrative, and/or chain-of-reasoning construction.

The data and analysis streams become increasingly interdependent as data determine the direction of analysis, which, in turn, determines what new data to gather. Both increasingly converge into the report stream in the closing steps of the study. This pattern has the advantage of being able to note and correct deficiencies in data collection before leaving the field, and successive data collecting and analysis efforts can be kept maximally effective as the researcher increasingly focuses on the emerging problem. Putting aside material for the study's report from the start as shown at upper right keeps this ultimate goal an ever-present priority.

Figure 12.3   Representation of the steps in a qualitative study (after Carney, 1990 and Miles & Huberman, 1994).

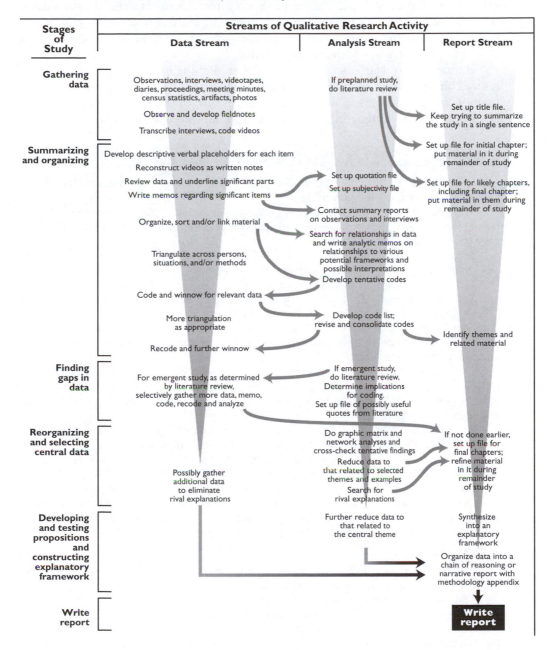

Data Reduction

In summary, the process is basically one of data reduction: Masses of data are gathered in the early steps. These are reduced to relevant material in the middle steps. Selective additions are made to round out the body of work in the middle and late steps. And the ultimate data reduction—the abstraction of the data into a descriptive final report—is the closing activity.

Return to this figure as you read the material in the next chapters, where unfamiliar concepts like *quotation file* and *subjectivity file* are explained so that the diagram increasingly comes to life. By using this picture of the whole process, you can keep what you are reading in perspective and see how each activity fits.

ADDITIONAL READING*

Crabtree and Miller (1999a, pp. 26–30) and Madill and Gough (2008) describe the different branches illustrated in Figure 12.1.

The following studies have methodological discussions that illustrate the process of qualitative research. Most gathered data by participant observation. Any will give a feel for the process; choose one in a topic of interest:

Medical situations: Becker (1961); Bosk (1979).

Academic situations: Becker, Geer, and Hughes (1968).

Cooperative education, a phenomenological study: Groenewald (2004).

Special populations: Blee (2002); Bluebond-Langer (1980); Humphreys (1975); Rubin (1976); Schneider and Conrad (1985); Venkatesh (2008).

Social communities: Liebow (1967); Lynd and Lynd (1929)—old, but appendix discusses use of multiple sources of data, including observation, documents, interviews, statistics, and questionnaires; Whyte (1993).

Other useful discussions of methods are: Bogdan and Biklen (2007); Denzin and Lincoln (2000); Glaser and Strauss (1967); Janesick (1998); Johnson (1975); LeCompte, Millroy, and Preissle (1992); Miles and Huberman (1994); Strauss (1987); Strauss and Corbin (1998); and Taylor and Bogdan (1998).

See Creswell (1998) or Lancy (1993) regarding different qualitative traditions; Stake (1995) regarding case studies. Schwandt (2001) is a dictionary of qualitative terms.

Aids to doing qualitative research dissertations: Heath (1997), the proposal outline; Piantanida and Garman (1999), the process from start to finish; Biklen and Casella (2007).

Longitudinal qualitative research: Although it emphasizes the qualitative approach, Saldaña (2003) is a useful guide for any longitudinal project. His original field is theatre, but "I realized that playwrights and qualitative researchers write for the same purpose: To create a unique, insightful and engaging text about the human condition" (p. x).

Useful Internet sites:

QUALRS-L (Qualitative Research for the Human Sciences listserv). Its archives are at: http://www.listserv.uga.edu/archives/qualrs-1.html

Text analysis information: http://www.textanalysis.info/

The *Qualitative Report*'s list of resources on the Internet: http://www.nova.edu/ssss/QR/

Besides links to other qualitative sites and to the Qualitative Research Web Ring, Bobbi Kerlin's site provides access to her own writing: http://www.kerlins.net/bobbi/research/qualresearch/

The Open Directory Project lists a large number of qualitative research sites, many quite relevant: http://www.dmoz.org/Science/Social_Sciences/Methodology/Qualitative

*My thanks to my colleague Dr. Steven Taylor for many of these suggestions.

IMPORTANT TERMS AND CONCEPTS

emergent approach	phenomenological point of view
emic	positivism/positivist epistemology
epistemology	reflexivity
etic	stimulated recall method

OPPORTUNITIES FOR ADDITIONAL LEARNING

1. The use of the library in elementary school tends to be highly variable, with some teachers making much use of it and others, little. The superintendent wonders whether or not to use some funds available for instructional improvement to strengthen the library. To help make up her mind, she asks you for an evaluation of its services to instruction. A colleague who is committed to the quantitative tradition of research suggests you do a study largely consisting of tabulations of services to show how much the library is used. Another suggests a mix of qualitative and quantitative methods. Still another suggests you adopt the symbolic interactionist point of view and gather solely qualitative data. What would be your choice, and how would you justify it?

2. Professor James Oxford wants to validate the proposition that students in the ninth grade learn more with tight teacher control of learning experiences than when they are allowed to select their own. He plans to use qualitative methods when a colleague warns him that these are inappropriate for validating propositions. Professor Oxford turns to you for advice. What would you tell him?

3. Dr. Penelope Wilgren is interested in gender differences in preschool play. She is planning to gather qualitative data from a pre-kindergarten day-care center with all-day observation over the course of a week. She will then do an analysis of it. A colleague suggests that she would be better off analyzing it while she is gathering it. Any advice for her?

Compare your answers with those following the Application Exercise.

APPLICATION EXERCISE

How might you pursue your problem with qualitative methods? Is there some facet of it they might uniquely fit, provide new insight into, or tell you whether your study is proceeding as expected?

For this and the following four chapters, some of you may wish to choose a different problem better suited to qualitative methods; feel free to do so.

KEY TO ADDITIONAL LEARNING OPPORTUNITIES

1. Your answer will depend on whether you think qualitative and quantitative methods can be combined, whether you would be willing to adopt the symbolic interactionist point of view for a study, and what data would be most useful and convincing to the audience for the study (the superintendent).

Quantitative data only—It is true that quantitative data would be very useful in providing statistics about how much the library is used, but it would not necessarily show how that use contributed to instruction. A researcher might compare the achievement scores of the classes of teachers who were heavy versus light users. However, without additional evidence he or she couldn't necessarily attribute those differences to library use; there would be too many rival explanations.

Quantitative and qualitative data—Although some researchers who adopt the symbolic interactionist point of view might not accept the mixing of the two methods in the same study, most qualitative researchers see them as complementary. From this viewpoint, a combination of quantitative and qualitative data would not only provide data on the extent of library use, but also provide details about how the library was used and provide a basis for interpreting the value of the numbers. Is heavy usage indicative of reading for pleasure or instructional use, for instance?

Qualitative data gathered from a symbolic interactionist point of view—If you adopt the symbolic interactionist point of view, you would explain that it involves understanding how the library is perceived by the people being studied and how they act on that information. Therefore, you would be interested in what the library means to the librarian, the teachers who do and don't use it, and the students who do and don't use it. Probably you would interview the librarian and a sample of students and of teachers. Because the superintendent is interested in the library's impact on instructional improvement, your questions would bear on this relationship.

Credibility with the audience—An important factor guiding the kind of study to do and what kind of data to gather is, "What evidence will be most convincing to the superintendent?" Depending on what kind of data the superintendent typically relies on for solving problems like this, one might want to take that into account in one's choice.

2. I would have told him, first of all, that one never "validates" a proposition as absolutely true, as described in chapter 4; one gathers evidence to corroborate it, and each positive finding increases the certainty that it is true. At some point there is a broad enough consensus about the interpretation of these findings that the proposition is accepted as knowledge and people act on it as such.

Then I would have commented that, although it is more common to use qualitative methods to explore rather than to provide confirmatory evidence, they can be used in the latter role. However, Professor Oxford needs to ask himself what he is expecting to accomplish and who his audience is. If he seeks to contribute to publications where quantitative learning studies on this subject are being published, then the sheer quantity of observations that would be expected in order to build a case that would gain a consensus among editors, reviewers, and readers would likely be prohibitive. Such a case might be much better achieved by using achievement tests and gathering data from a large number of students in classrooms with differing levels of teacher control and student freedom.

Incidentally, this generalization that achievement tests scores would be higher with teacher control than with student control of learning experiences was one of the findings that Wong (1995) used in looking at the obviousness of social science findings. Achievement was higher with greater teacher control and less student freedom, but, when asked to predict the outcome of the study, this finding was not obvious to either teachers or nonteachers.

On the other hand, were Professor Oxford interested in showing that "learning more" meant more than test score "achievement," he would probably be looking at a much wider range of outcomes than simply higher scores on achievement tests. When students were allowed to choose their own learning experiences, for example, changes in motivation to learn, interest in new fields, and so forth might be expected. Qualitative methods would easily permit the recording of a variety of such changes. Interpreting the statement as "learning" instead of "change in test score" is probably what many had in mind when they predicted greater student freedom would have the more positive outcome.

As Wong's study showed, however, this finding is not obvious; it doesn't unmistakably "ring true," a usual test of such statements. Therefore, Professor Oxford may also want to consider the intended audience and the evidence that audience is most likely to accept. If the intended audience were teachers and practitioners, they would probably find qualitative findings and their accompanying examples especially convincing if they could identify with the examples in terms of their own experience. This by no means is intended to convey that when communicating to practitioners one must always use qualitative methods; generalities supported by quantitative evidence that "ring true" are also likely to be convincing. It is when the findings are less obvious that use of evidence that fits the pattern of communication of the audience is more likely to be effective.

3. Dr. Wilgren already has the focus of her observations in mind; she is looking for differences in play patterns of boys and girls. So, her study is exploratory in the sense of looking for where these differences exist, but it is targeted in knowing what activities are the focus of data collection. The latter makes it more feasible to gather the data in a condensed period of time. In gathering all her data before analyzing it, she is assuming that she will have carefully observed those instances that display differences. However, were she to analyze her data as she collected it, as suggested in Figures 12.2 and 12.3, she would spot the types of instances where such differences typically occur. Then, using purposive sampling, she could concentrate further data gathering on obtaining many such examples as well as seeking their broadest instances to determine the limits of generality.

The flow of the process depicted in figures 12.2 and 12.3 must always take into account, however, the reality of circumstances. If she does not have enough time and energy to do analysis during a concentrated period of observation, why not spread observations out to allow interim time for analysis? As suggested in the discussion of sequential sampling in chapter 8, this might be a good solution if the situation is relatively stable and one could return to the field to take up approximately where one left off. However, if it were the beginning of the school year and boys and girls were learning to play with one another, Dr. Wilgren might decide to continuously observe so she would not miss this period of adaptation. This is an example of the on-the-spot decisions fieldworkers must make in adapting their pattern of work to specific situations.

SUMMARY

Qualitative methods are especially useful for exploring a phenomenon, for understanding it, and for translating that understanding into theory. These methods humanize situations and make them come alive. They are particularly useful in describing multidimensional, complex interpersonal interaction in cases where the limited focus of quantitative measures would be inadequate. They are especially useful in studying processes. Their case descriptions communicate well to practitioners.

Although qualitative methods build on verbal skills, they require skillful interpretation of data. Qualitative researchers are judged by how insightfully they interpret the data and present their findings and by how well their interpretation fits their data. Qualitative research is extremely labor intensive. Appropriately disciplined procedures must be learned with any method, and qualitative research is no exception.

There are a variety of approaches to qualitative methods: ethnography, ethnomethodology, naturalistic methods, and so forth. One of these approaches, phenomenology, adopts a different epistemological point of view from positivism, the mainstay of the past. It seeks to understand the world as individuals perceive it. Whereas other persons might see a situation as conducive to growth, an individual who is the subject of study may see it as stifling. It is the individual's own perception and what impact this perception has on his or her actions that is the focus of the symbolic interactionist point of view. Although some adherents see qualitative methods and this point of view as one and the same, many more distinguish them from one another and use qualitative methods without necessarily adopting the epistemological point of view.

Although observation and interview are two of the main methods of gathering qualitative data, diaries, personal records, official documents, photos, videos, and artifacts can serve as alternate sources.

A Look Ahead

The next four chapters discuss in sequence: (13) fieldwork and observation, (14) interviewing, (15) data analysis, and (16) drawing conclusions and reporting. It may seem, therefore, that these activities must follow one another sequentially. You may already have noted that this isn't the case from your study of figures 12.2 and 12.3 where, for example, analysis and final report issues are worked at from the very beginning.

Qualitative researchers adapt their method to fit their problem with issues such as: gaining entry, securing acceptance, purposive sampling, data analysis, and ethics, all of which continue to be revisited throughout a study. In the linear presentation to which books are confined, it is difficult to do justice to this simultaneous processing of different aspects of the study. So, while the text will remind you from time to time of the holistic nature of the process, it will help if you bear figures 12.2 and 12.3 in mind as you read the material in the following chapters.

Note

[1] Are qualitative methods influencing quantitative? The 2001 edition of the American Psychological Association's *Publication Manual* recommends that the term *participants* replace *subjects*, which was used in earlier editions. "Participant implies a more active, voluntary role in research . . . : [replacing subject] involves . . . ideological change" (Madigan, Linton, & Johnson, 1996, p. 654).

[2] Some points adapted from Patton, 1980, pp. 88–89.

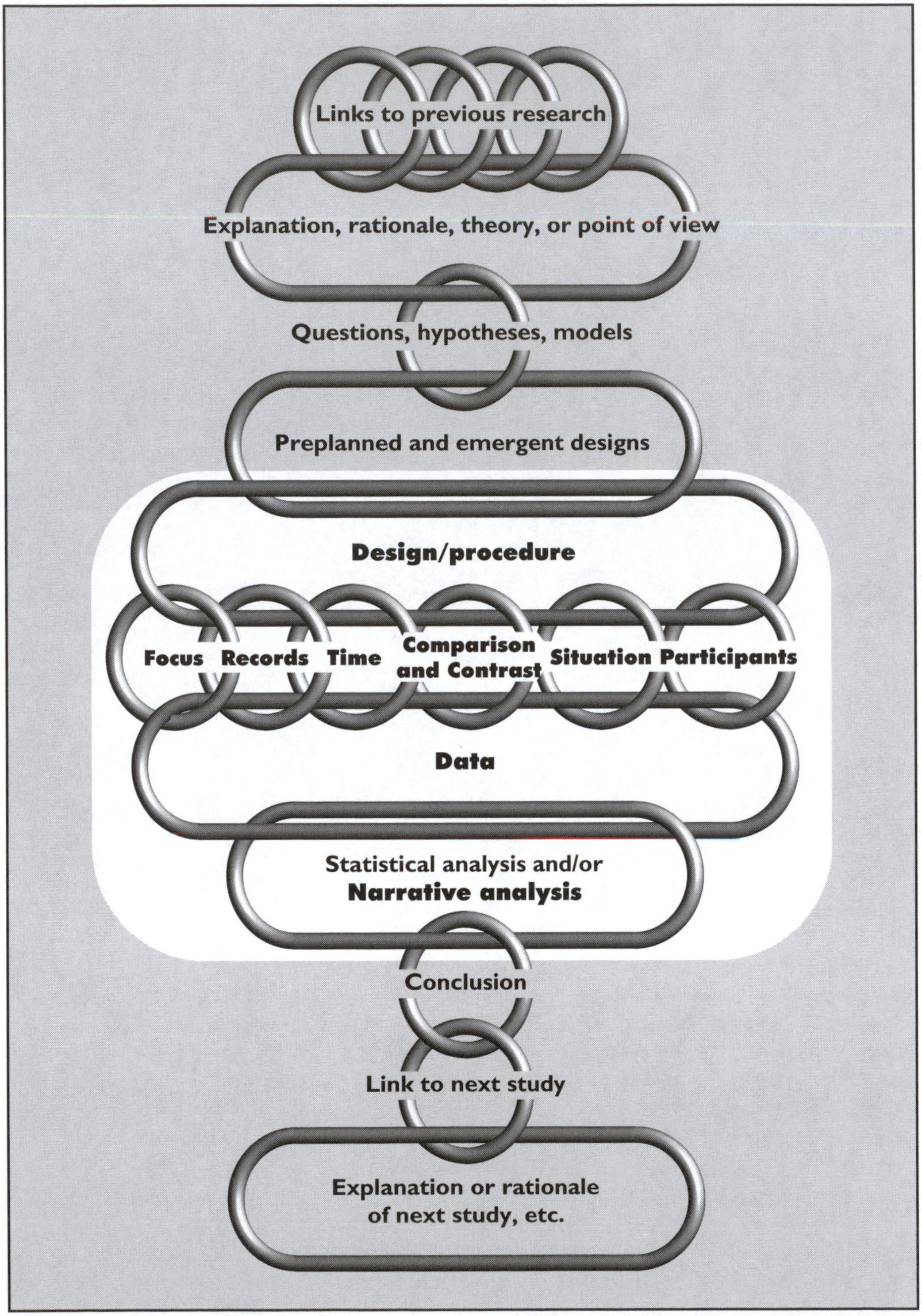

Links to previous research

Explanation, rationale, theory, or point of view

Questions, hypotheses, models

Preplanned and emergent designs

Design/procedure

Focus Records Time Comparison and Contrast Situation Participants

Data

Statistical analysis and/or
Narrative analysis

Conclusion

Link to next study

Explanation or rationale
of next study, etc.

chapter

13

Fieldwork and Observation

> Unfortunately, events do not come with labels on them. . . . Such labels must be imposed. . . . Until they have been, a scientist has nothing to work with.
>
> —G. A. Miller, *Spontaneous Apprentices*
>
> To be perceptive, we must . . . recognize the role . . . bias plays in everything. . . . Once we acknowledge that our perceptions are selective, we can allow the point of view to enrich our experience with information. When we know that Monet's eyesight . . . approached near-blindness as he got older, we can begin to understand his water lily paintings.
>
> —R. S. Wurman, *Information Anxiety*

Most of this chapter's content applies to any kind of data gathering, but, you don't just do fieldwork; you do it in a context—observing, interviewing, video or audio recording, and/or gathering documents. Therefore, this chapter describes the tasks of fieldwork in the context of observation. So, bear in mind that "observer" really refers to any fieldworker. The chapter has two tasks: (1) to discuss observation, how it is done, its possibilities and its problems; and (2) to describe the tasks of fieldwork, both in general and in particular observation.

INTRODUCTION

Fieldworkers are faced with many tasks beyond first deciding how best to gather data:

- if by observation, choosing how best to observe;
- gaining entry;
- finding a way to preserve the naturalness of the situation while gathering data and securing acceptance;
- on the basis of successive visits, deciding which persons, activities, situations, events, documents, pictures, and so forth to sample and which informants to query;

- capturing what is significant in descriptive **fieldnotes**;
- writing memos that form the basis for coding and analysis and for eliminating rival explanations;
- analyzing data as it is accumulated;
- developing constructs that help reduce the mass of detail to what is important;
- using emerging hunches to guide further data collection;
- triangulating to assure accuracy;
- testing explanations;
- resolving ethical dilemmas on the spot; and
- deciding how much fieldwork is enough.

When listed in the abstract so many operations may seem overwhelming, yet most fieldworkers find themselves capable of handling these requirements as they arise and, with practice, becoming skilled at them. They form the topics of this chapter and are taken up in the order described above.

WAYS OF OBSERVING

Observation is like a flashlight: It reveals only where it is directed. Indeed, observers are judged by whether they are sensitive enough to capture the critical aspects of what is occurring, how well they can make sense of these aspects, and how accurately their explanations fit the data.

A central problem of observation is that individuals typically behave differently when conscious of being studied, often exhibiting more socially approved behavior or acting in accord with perceived expectations. But there are exceptions, such as resentful experimental school pupils who are tired of being observed and may purposely act atypically. Indeed, it is often hard to predict how individuals will react to observation; we just know that they usually do, at least initially.

Covert observation, in which the individual is not aware of being observed, is one way of solving the problem. A more common solution is to reduce obtrusiveness by having the observer participate as one of the group—**participant observation**. With extended contact, it is usually assumed that reaction to an observer diminishes. We can construct a continuum of observation techniques from a combination of the dimensions: obtrusiveness, fidelity, and secretiveness. Obtrusiveness in the sense that the natural situation is least disturbed, fidelity in the sense of "ability-to-get-what-is-really-happening" in the situation, and secretiveness in the sense that there is no attempt to hide the observation. In the following, we discuss positions on the continuum beginning with the least obtrusive, best able to get what is going on, and most to hide—the top section of the continuum in Figure 13.1.

Covert Participant Observation

The most difficult of all the observation roles is **covert participant observation**. There is a constant tension between the mental vigilance needed to stay in character and the effort to relax so the role seems natural. The former is physically exhausting,

Figure 13.1   Observation methods placed on a continuum of obtrusiveness (adapted from Bouchard, 1976).

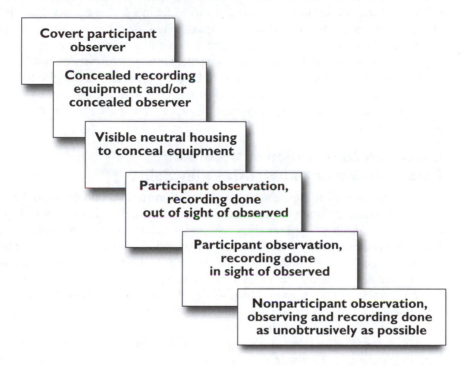

yet the latter—too much naturalness—runs the risk of "going native." How exhausting is it? Sullivan, Queen, and Patrick's (1958) covert observer of basic military training lost 35 pounds, presumably from role tension.

There are other difficulties as well. Reconstruction of events over a long time period between debriefings can be a problem. If a group is small and the behavior of the participants is neither routine nor prescribed, the observer's role may affect what the group does. To maintain a natural role, covert observers may initiate action, thus causing group outcomes different from those without their presence.

Inquiries are limited to those consistent with the observer's role. Questions may be too personal, too prying, or too naive (Ornstein & Phillips, 1978). Interpersonal relationships must be consistent with one's role. A teacher would not be expected to spend too much time with the school superintendent. Certain records may be inaccessible as well.

Cultural background, age, sex, race, appearance, manner of speaking, physical build, family situation, and other relatively unchangeable characteristics may preclude not just covert but any kind of participant observation in certain groups. Age, for instance, precludes participation roles by senior professors in any kind of youth situation.

Of course, there are problems if the ruse is discovered and the questionable ethics of spying are brought to light. Negotiated entry is already difficult enough for non-covert observers. It is not made easier with publicized academic prying. Like research fraud (discussed further in chapter 28), it reflects on the rest of us who did not transgress.

On the positive side, however, participants gain access to behavior uninhibited by the presence of an outsider—behavior to which no one else could be privy. How else could a researcher record how a mental, penal, or other institution looks to an inmate; how the army feels to a recruit; or how certain religious, fraternal, and political groups view their world? Further, as participants, researchers do not have to rely on marginal and often atypical persons to be their informants. Despite these advantages, this method of observation is rarely used because of the difficulties involved, as well as the dilemma of whether to report illegal or unethical behavior (discussed later in the chapter).

Concealed Observation or Recording from a Hidden or Unobtrusive Viewpoint

In institutional settings, **concealed observation** (the second position down in the continuum) from behind two-way mirrors or from some hidden or unobtrusive location is often feasible. Experimental schools associated with universities frequently have such observation rooms. Teachers and students are usually informed when they are "on stage," and permission of the students' parents is usually obtained. With nothing visible to remind them that they are being observed, behavior usually returns to what appears to be normal. Because the ability of the human ear to follow one conversation when several are occurring has yet to be duplicated in video recording, the sound track for such observations may not always be understandable.

Unobtrusive placement of the equipment, the third position down in the continuum in Figure 13.1, eliminates the need for a special room and is probably as effective. Kounin (1970), for instance, placed empty boxes in the classroom that might be interpreted as concealing cameras; left in place, they came to be regarded as part of the furniture. Equipment was installed in the boxes when the room was empty. Tracking, close-ups, and perspective views require additional equipment. Audio recording alone produces voluminous records that are expensive and often difficult to transcribe. They also miss nonverbal cues.

Unconcealed Participant Observation

The role of an active onlooker (the fourth and fifth positions down the continuum in Figure 13.1) is preferred by most observers. Although the observation is obvious, the fact that the researcher is acting as a participant at some level reduces the obtrusiveness. At the same time, it instructs the researcher as to what it is like to be in the situation. *Unconcealed participant observation* allows the researcher access to important places and people while remaining "in character." With a high level of participation (the fourth position on the continuum), note taking may have to be done on the side, but with less engagement (the fifth position) it is often done openly.

Nonparticipant Observation

The most obtrusive of the roles, **nonparticipant observation** (the sixth and bottom position in Figure 13.1), nevertheless provides the researcher with the freedom to concentrate entirely on observation and on the significance of what is occurring. Just as it is difficult for an observer to sustain an unnatural role, however, so too is it difficult for those observed to maintain "on-stage" behavior over a long period of time. Thus, even under obvious surveillance, those observed usually relax into more normal behavior over time.

Some people might argue that without participation we are unable to appreciate fully the affective reactions of participants, but there is little evidence that this is the case. Good observers train themselves to be as sensitive as possible. They cultivate a combination of empathy and detachment—the former so that they can understand, the latter so that they can record and place in perspective what they are observing. Hughes (1971) has noted that a person who is of a culture, but feels not wholly a part of it, often is a good observer of that culture.

Awareness of observation changes the behavior of the people being observed. Efforts to avoid this effect result in a continuum of observation roles:

▶ Covert observation provides exceptional access to the observed's point of view and to other unobservable behavior. It may involve complications if the ruse is discovered or if illegal or unethical behavior is observed or participated in.

▶ Concealed observation is usually made known to those being observed, but they grow accustomed to it more rapidly in the absence of a constant visual reminder.

▶ Unconcealed participant observation makes the observer less obtrusive because he or she becomes a member of the group. It also informs the observer what being a group member is like.

▶ Nonparticipant observation requires a longer time period before accommodation by those being observed returns to natural behavior (if it ever entirely does), but it also allows the observer to concentrate on the observation process.

INITIAL STEPS IN OBSERVATION

Gaining Entry

Fieldworkers seek a way of **gaining entry** that conveys they can be trusted. Often they seek the help of a friend or colleague who either is a part of the setting or is trusted by those within it. The process is often complex. The experience of Bosk (1979), who studied surgeons' errors, is an example. Bosk's department provided a letter of introduction. He started with a surgeon he had met at a party who, as supervisor of residents, was a **gatekeeper**—someone with authority to give permission for entry to the desired field of observation. Although the surgeon expressed enthusiasm about Bosk's proposed fieldwork, he also feared his sponsorship would be a "kiss of death." He felt that Bosk needed to talk to the residents directly and be seen as his own person: "I learned . . . there was no instant access for the fieldworker." When sent to the chief resident, Bosk was not sure whether he was being given assistance or the runaround. The chief resident said he also approved of Bosk's research project, but he needed to check with his supervisors prior to granting access. "Gaining my initial entrée was a multistage diplomatic problem," Bosk explained. "Each action was a test, and access was the result of continual testing and retesting. Entrée was not something negotiated once and then over and done with . . . but a continuous process" (p. 194).

Bosk is absolutely correct! Entrance and acceptance are continuous processes. Researchers not only are making an entrance with each new person and situation, they also are seeking acceptance to gain access to the data or situation they choose to study.

Bosk's experience is not uncommon, nor is his paranoia about possibly being given the runaround. Respondents may not like granting access but fear being labeled "against research and progress." They may refer the request to others in the hope that someone will find a legitimate objection. Organizations that might gain favorable publicity are much easier to access than those wary of criticism. The latter, however, are more often desired as subjects of study.

Sometimes one can enter a secure area of an organization and use trust established there to enter less accessible parts. This strategy is advantageous for researchers who do not know all they will ultimately want to observe.

Administrators often ask for something in exchange for access. They want a report on some subordinates or an evaluation of "how we are doing." They may want to exercise some control over the project or the report, to see fieldnotes, to view the draft and make suggestions, to rule certain aspects of their operation "off limits," or perhaps even to approve the report's release. Such requirements create difficult situations that may violate academic freedom and might possibly abrogate the necessary confidentiality of informants. Clearly, the fewer restrictive conditions the better. Some argue for renegotiating once the initial fear has been replaced by trust. Although this tactic may be successful, it may be better to use another site.

For many researchers, especially new ones, entering the field is an anxiety-producing experience. Ely (1991)[1] quotes Hillary:

> A cold shudder hit . . . the selfsame shyness which helped make me an attentive observer . . . could sabotage . . . my efforts to place myself. . . . What is this terror . . . all about? . . . Among my fellow classmates, the sense of angst and inertia . . . is all too common. . . . I think this feeling comes from human self-doubts and fear of rejection. . . . So? So you could be refused! So what's so devastating about that? The trouble is that this rational line doesn't really reach what these fears may be all about. (pp. 17–18)

Experienced researchers suggest you acknowledge such fears and then work through or around them. Writing **memos** about your feelings or keeping a log of them are helpful in this regard. Hillary further states:

> The first and most important thing to do, I found, was to confront my feelings . . . via the log, where . . . researchers record what they plan and feel about their experiences. . . . Here is a "safe-place," a haven where feelings, fears, doubts, suspicions, intuitions all have an honored place. . . . [It] gets them "up front," and gives them a reality and sense that they are perfectly legitimate and human. (Ely, 1991, p. 18)

Students are often tempted to study situations where they already have entry, or that are familiar to them. There is a saying that the intent of qualitative researchers is "to make the strange familiar and the familiar strange"—that is, looking at a familiar situation as though they were a stranger, or trying to learn what is going on by emptying themselves of their presuppositions. In a familiar situation this is difficult to do, not only because of previous experiences but also because others may not accept your new role.

A principal who decides to observe in the rooms of her teachers may be doing so as a student practicing for a research course. But, to the teacher, she is still the school principal and she cannot escape that role—especially when principals are involved in teacher competency evaluations. At least initially, choose a different context from what you usually encounter every day. There will be less of a problem of "making the familiar strange," and you can concentrate on "making the strange familiar."

▶ Find a way of gaining entry that will convey your trustworthiness.

▶ Negotiating entry is a continuous process that must be repeated at each level in the organization.

▶ It may be best to enter where those observed feel comfortable about being observed; then, having established trust, move to other initially less accessible areas.

▶ Writing in fieldnotes about discomfort in seeking entry or observing helps to objectify these feelings; it places them "out there" where they can more easily be seen as expected and normal.

▶ Gaining entry to institutions requires the approval of administrators who may impose conditions on the process or ask for something in exchange. This can be a serious problem.

▶ Choosing a situation because prior familiarity makes entry problems minimal but may result in problems in making the "familiar strange," especially when the familiar includes the baggage of past experience and expectations regarding your role.

Securing Acceptance

To quote Bosk (1979) again, "Access—being allowed in the scene—is one thing, but approval and trust . . . is quite another. Just like access, cooperation . . . is earned again and again when the fieldworker shows that he or she is trustworthy" (p. 194). In part, the act of participating demonstrates researcher approval of what is going on; in return, **acceptance** of the researcher is expected. Sometimes this means doing menial tasks, as when Bosk was asked to open bandage packages or retrieve charts. Acceptance may be enhanced when the researcher's professional knowledge is used to assist, as when Rist (1977) was asked to comment on classroom situations while observing the integration of black children bused out of inner-city schools.

The observer as participant must maintain close rapport with all from whom information is sought while maintaining sufficient psychological distance so as not to be identified with one adversarial group. Wax (1971) appropriately calls this *instrumental membership* and notes that host and researcher jointly construct a suitable role. Sometimes it helps if the observer simply explains that a researcher is not supposed to take sides. The observed may understand, even though they will believe that, as Ornstein and Phillips (1978) put it, "'deep down' he or she is on our 'side.'"

Acceptance does not necessarily mean acting like the rest of the group. Whyte (1993) tried using some of the obscenities he heard all around him. Conversation stopped, and one of the members said, "Bill, you're not supposed to talk like that. That doesn't sound like you" (p. 304). Patton (1987) points out that the ideal is not necessarily full participation, but *"that degree of participation which will yield the most meaningful data given the characteristics of the participants, the nature of questions to be studied, and the sociopolitical context of the setting"* (p. 76, emphasis in the original).

Even though access to public places requires no permission, acceptance in the sense of appropriate behavior—that is, suitable lack of eye contact, studied lack of interest in others, and careful management of physical contact—is important (Hammersley & Atkinson, 1995). Loitering so as to observe may need to be explained (collecting for a charity, passing out advertising material) and otherwise carefully managed (leaving the site at random times).

> ▶ Administrative approval of entry does not guarantee acceptance; indeed, it may delay it. Acceptance, like entry, is a continuous process and must be negotiated anew at each level and with each new informant.

DATA GATHERING

Most observers start at the same place, a first phase of trying to find what is significant in a situation. In that initial stage, the researcher is like a sponge, soaking up all that is around and listening intently. Interviewing is open ended, and sometimes just observing is best. Starting with a broad focus can be very confusing to the newcomer—there is so much to attend to! One of Ely's (1991) students, Belén Matías, observing in a classroom put this very well:

> There are so many things going on at the same time! My head is spinning. What should I write in my log? What should I leave out? And to top it all, . . . the minute I write . . . I'm disconnected from what's happening. . . . If I'm the instrument, I need to be sent to the repair shop. (p. 48)

Before you despair, just jot down as much as you can. Even things that don't seem significant at first may later turn out to be important. Gradually, it will become apparent what is relevant, and what your focus will be. This is not to say that the whole process is automatic; you will have to think about what you have observed in the time between observations. Try to understand what is happening, and what is significant about it for your purposes. As you work at that (and it does take work!), you will find yourself more interested in certain aspects than in others, and the focus will emerge from those. Here is an example, again from one of Ely's students, Marcia Kropf:

> As I reread my log entries each week, it became increasingly clear that, because . . . of my own fascination with people, my topic had changed! I no longer noted, in explicit detail, the computer programming functions being explored and how students gained insight into how they worked. Instead, I was describing in great detail when students came to class, how they behaved when they entered the

room, where they stood, what they said and to whom, and how they were greeted.... I did not develop insights into how students learn computer programming.... I did, however, learn a great deal about how students can be invited to participate in a class. (p. 55)

Recall the six rings in the chain of reasoning and their relation to the journalist mantra of finding the "who, what, where, when, why, and how" of any situation. Many researchers (Bogdewic, 1999; Goetz & LeCompte, 1984; Strauss & Corbin, 1998) suggest that these are useful questions to bear in mind when doing fieldwork. Consider how using these questions might have broadened and perhaps led to new questions in the Hoffmann-Riem study in the first chapter. *Who* is doing the adopting? What are their characteristics? *What* kinds of adoptions are occurring? What is being said about them? *Where* is this happening? Are there norms or characteristics of the community that affect it—many same-age families having children? *When* does it occur? At what time of life? *Why* does it occur? What triggers it—failed infertility treatments, miscarriages? What keeps it going—contact with mothers of young children? What slows it down—problems of new mothers? What accelerates it—birthdays after 40? What stops it—bureaucratic red tape? *How* does it occur? What are the steps involved? How are they perceived? How do they affect the adoption process? How do couples feel about the process? These questions provide a framework for gathering data and can also serve as an early structure for organizing it. Drawing a map of the situation serves both to help you find the best situation for observation and to locate individuals and objects in space for later reference.

But Whyte (1993) notes that we must "learn when to question and when not to question as well as what questions to ask" (p. 303). For example, conversation stopped when Whyte remarked to a gambler who was telling the group about his operations, "I suppose the cops were all paid off?" His friend Doc commented the next day that he should go easy on all the who, what, why, and when stuff or people would clam up. If he'd just hang around long enough, he would learn the answers without asking. Whyte declares, "I found this was true. As I sat and listened, I learned the answers to questions that I would not even have had the sense to ask" (p. 303). Apropos of the same point is this beautiful quotation from Huxley (1982, as found in Worthen & Sanders, 1987):

> The best way to find things out is not to ask questions at all. If you fire off a question, it is like firing off a gun—bang it goes, and everything takes flight and runs for shelter. But if you sit quite still and pretend not to be looking, all the little facts will come and peek round your feet, situations will venture forth from thickets and intentions will creep out and sun themselves on a stone: and if you are very patient, you will see and understand a great deal more than a man with a gun does. (p. 138)

It is important to remember that no matter how unobtrusive you try to remain, your merely having entered the situation may have changed it. Ely (1991) notes an instance in which a teacher-friend who had invited the observer into his classroom became increasingly defensive and argumentative. Discussing this situation with other student researchers, one of them remarked, "That is because you have introduced the reflective mode into that room. No matter how unobtrusive and nonjudgmental your presence, it is *heightening his own awareness of what he is doing*" (p. 196, emphasis added). Few are entirely comfortable with their performances, and when they become reflective their behavior is likely to change.

While unobtrusiveness is the rule for participant observation, Harrington (2002) notes there are exceptions that can strengthen a study. She gives as an example Schwalbe's (1996) study of the men's movement, a reaction to the feminist movement. Participant observing over a three-year period, Schwalbe became a movement insider and intentionally on occasion, in Harrington's words, a "critic and provocateur." In doing so, she points out that he discovered individuals appreciated his taking this role, which allowed them to be more freely critical. Harrington notes that this enabled "Schwalbe to present the men's movement in all its texture and complexity—not [as] a monolith. . . . These shadings lend authenticity and credibility to . . . [the] account" (p. 57). Like all rules, there are instances where they should be broken.

Over the course of a study, researchers may consult a variety of documents—transcripts and minutes of meetings, court proceedings, diaries, letters, questionnaire responses, census statistics, photos and so forth. They also look for artifacts—pieces of art, choices of furniture, items on desks or tables, available equipment. In short, they will seek any evidence that will be helpful in extending and deepening their understanding.

Learning to Observe

Ely (1991) quotes one of her students: "Well, thank heavens! I've finally come to an easy part in this. Participant observation is a snap," and continues, "Well, it isn't . . . [as if] an attitude of curiosity and a heightened attention are required in order to attend to those very details that most of us filter out automatically in day-to-day life" (p. 42). Van Maanen (2002) quotes Sherlock Holmes as saying, "The world is full of obvious things . . . which nobody will ever see" (p. 165). Spradley (1980) lists six "dos" that distinguish the participant observer from a participant:

• Watch yourself as well as watching others.
• Try to become explicitly aware of what others take for granted.
• Look beyond the immediate focus of your activity—use a "wide-angle lens."
• Try to experience the situation simultaneously as both an insider and an outsider.[2]
• Be introspective as you watch.
• Keep a record, not only of what you see but also of how you experience the situation, and mark the latter in such a way that you can separate what you see occurring from how you experience it.

The last, separating observations from reactions, is important. Reactions in the context of greater experience may lead you to perceive the same events differently. You must then sort out the more appropriate interpretation.

Information-Processing Limitations

In an article discussing the mind's cognitive limitations as they affect qualitative data gathering, Sadler (1981) lists a number that are research supported, of which two critical ones are listed below. Knowing these limitations is the first step toward disciplining their effect.

Data overload.   Research suggests that most individuals are able to keep only about seven things in their mind at one time. The mind can beat this limit by "chunking" things as we routinely do—we don't see four legs and a top; we see a table. When many aspects of a situation must be considered at once, however, observers may be fooling themselves in thinking that they are attending to more of the information than they really are. When others are also observing, comparing perceptions may help identify overload situations.

First impressions.   We know that first impressions are important, something that has also been confirmed in research. For instance, research with regard to physical stimuli in situations where individuals must estimate size indicates that estimations can be manipulated by the first stimuli they receive. First impressions tend to be enduring, perhaps because after the first piece of knowledge is retained, the second piece constitutes only half our knowledge base; the next increases the base only 33%, the next 25%, and so on. Because each new piece is a smaller part of the base, it may be more difficult for it to markedly affect the whole. If we are aware of this problem, later efforts to distinguish and then verify early impressions become important.

The Multiple Demands of Participant Observation

As you may have already sensed, the role of the participant observer is complex. Trying to monitor all aspects from the very beginning may easily swamp the neophyte observer. As Winne (1995) indicates, monitoring one's own thoughts and behavior reduces the mental resources available to observe and select significant aspects from the situation one is observing. (Remember the limitations noted above.) As greater comfort in observing develops, attending and noting become routinized and resources are freed for examining one's own behavior for relational and bias problems. Novices should probably build their repertoire of observation behaviors gradually over successive sessions. Transferability of repertoire probably varies with both the nature of the situation and the skills of the observer, but it appears that for many observers there may be a period of adjustment in each new situation.

> ▶ Gradually build up a repertoire of observation skills.
>
> ▶ Observe and record what you are doing and thinking as you observe others.
>
> ▶ Try to keep everything in a larger perspective as an outsider would. At the same time, empathically try to sense how those in the situation are experiencing it.
>
> ▶ Learn when to question.
>
> ▶ Be aware of data overload.
>
> ▶ Double-check first impressions.

Informants

As noted earlier, qualitative researchers treat those being observed as individuals to learn from—an egalitarian perspective that contrasts with the term *subjects,* formerly universally used in experimentation. Qualitative researchers see this as more than a difference in designation, involving a change in attitude that has implications for how we interact with those we observe and how we treat the data we obtain from them.

Bouchard (1976) distinguishes between respondents and informants. **Informants** are selected for their sensitivity, knowledge, and insights into their situation, their willingness to talk about it, and their ability to help gain access to new situations. **Respondents** are random or systematic samples and may be considered replicable. Bouchard warns that it is important to distinguish between data from informants (especially whose reasons for informing may influence what they say) and data from respondents. (Since typically, obtaining information from informants basically involves interviewing, much of the next chapter's advice applies here as well.)

Persons who have less stake in the system (and thus are less defensive about it) are particularly sensitive informants, as are those who view it from a standpoint different from those of more central players. Examples are persons who come from another culture, social class, or community and who can contrast their impressions with their previous experience. Newcomers and individuals with a new role or status are especially likely to note things that others might take for granted, having left one role but not yet being comfortable in the other. However, beware of their viewing their new situation in terms of their old role.

Other informant types may similarly have hidden agendas: rebels or malcontents welcome the opportunity to "get things off their chest." Former insiders who have lost power usually eagerly share views of current insiders, most likely negatively. Flattered by the attention, some say whatever they think the observer wants to hear. Persons too well entrenched to worry about repercussions from communicating with outsiders may be harder to tap; they have the least to gain—unless they magnify their own roles in past actions.

Although we intend to represent a situation as viewed by its participants, we often wind up with what Sieber (1973) calls an **elite bias**, an overweighting of the elite in the selection of informants and in the interpretation of data. Sieber notes that there are many reasons for this. Elites are likely to be more articulate and give the impression of being better informed. The observer is careful to keep on the good side of those who are gatekeepers. Sieber discovered this type of bias when he tried to predict the results of a survey he had given teachers. "It became obvious . . . that I had unwittingly adopted the elites' version of reality. For example, I overestimated the extent to which teachers felt that the administration accepted criticism" (p. 1353).

The most desirable informant is the "natural" (Bouchard, 1976); he or she has a perspective on the situation and is able to communicate it. Whyte's (1993) "Doc" is the prototype of such individuals. Doc had a perspective not only on his situation but also on the role that Whyte should play in the community. He steered Whyte to situations and introduced him to persons who were helpful in the study. Every researcher should be so lucky!

The main caveat with informants is a continual concern with the questions: "Why are these persons willing to talk to me? What point of view are they using?" Whereas only you can answer these questions satisfactorily, only you will be able to determine the extent to which you must discount the information. Interviewing in front of others who can correct misstatements facilitates identifying informant bias. Don't assume informants will necessarily confront misstatements at the time; provide private opportunities later. In addition, you might let the informants know that you are also gathering data from others. This not only helps you determine consistency but also likely makes them more careful about their statements. Remember too, that these are not independent cases but instead a social network whose members will be interacting with each other after you have left the scene; they must protect themselves. With much at stake, they may get together, compare notes, and possibly align their stories or otherwise misguide you.

> ▶ Informants help the observers to understand the views of the people being observed, introduce them to new individuals and situations, and may teach the observer how to behave unobtrusively.
>
> ▶ Such cooperation may not be without its price. Therefore, observers must ask themselves, "Why is this person talking to me and being so helpful?"
>
> ▶ Informants are often new and/or marginal persons who have less stake in the status quo or are not constrained by it. Because they may be atypical, their information must be appropriately discounted ("taken with a grain of salt").

Inferring Cognitive and Affective Processes

Qualitative methods are particularly useful in studying cognitive and affective processes that cannot be directly observed but must be inferred from overt behavior. Indeed, inferring from careful observation is often the first method of studying such behavior. Sometimes such observation can be augmented by careful analysis of behavior in video recordings, especially nonverbal reactions.

A second approach involves *retrospection*—reviewing the situation and behavior with the respondent, asking her to describe what was going on in her mind. Such review can be enhanced by **stimulated recall**, described in the previous chapter (p. 248). Still another way is to have the respondents think out loud, reporting on their thoughts as the process takes place. Review of a recording of the think-aloud session in stimulated recall mode can show where their processes were slowed or otherwise changed by having to think aloud.

FIELDNOTES AND ANNOTATIONS

Fieldnotes and logs are the observer's records of what has been observed; they should begin as soon as the project gets underway. Notes on the initial contacts with gatekeepers as you seek access should be part of the record. They may shed light on something that occurred later, but without your notes you would have missed the connection. Rile's term *thick description* aptly captures the character of fieldnotes (in Geertz, 1973).

Typically, fieldnotes are a chronological account. They may include relevant incidents from outside the formal observation process as well—comments elicited at a party, reflections from an informant encountered later, and so on. They may include diagrams showing the relative positions of the participants, furniture, and the like. To adequately convey the context, they typically include the room and its furnishings, as well as physical characteristics, dress, and mannerisms of the participants. Conversation is quoted insofar as possible, including gestures, accents, and facial expressions. Observer actions are recorded as well.

Try to capture the language used as it shows how people define one another. Taylor (1977, pp. 117–138), for example, studied a mental institution and found that the attendants categorized patients in terms of their interaction with staff (e.g., troublemakers, spoilers, vegetables, runaways, headbangers). Such terms suggested the attendants' attitudes, which could then be confirmed or modified by further observation.

Inexperienced observers tend to summarize what went on. Experienced ones jot down detail, especially what they think may later be important and give the "feel" of the situation. Ely's (1991) student Donna Flynn wrote in her log:

> Thinking back to Nurse's Training, a great deal of emphasis was placed on clear, concise . . . recording. . . . During our first field observation/informal interview my tendency would have been to log "E told me about her day as substitute teacher." Instead I had to learn to log: "E said: 'You'll never guess what I did yesterday. I subbed for a first grade class, and boy, was I wiped out at the end of the day. . . .'" All this was logged so that I could retain the flavor of her day and how she saw it and felt about it. (p. 70)

Because description involves selecting aspects to emphasize, include in fieldnotes the observer's

- reflections on the processes of selecting what was important to capture;
- behavior in the situation (comfort, obtrusiveness, apparent impact on others, treatment by others);
- ideas or hypotheses explaining what was occurring;
- problems in observing, recording, or coding; and
- suggestions for the next steps and from whence they were derived, and so on.

Label these remarks *O.C.* for "observer comment" and indent, box, or put on new pages as personal memos so that opinion is isolated from fact. But embed them in the fieldnotes so that they can be tied to the time and context.

Write up your observations as soon after the field trip as possible—certainly within 24 hours. "Forgetting begins as soon as the experience ends" (Ely, 1991, p. 79). Experienced observers suggest not talking about sessions with others before writing to avoid changing emphases as a result of the discussion. Although you can strengthen your memory by rehearsing what you have seen, such rehearsal will tend to be selective and likely lead to reflection on the events. This may change your first impressions; record them separately.

Limit the length of your observation period. Ninety minutes is more than enough for most observers. Novices are typically concerned about remembering the conversations or being able to re-create them from notes. Ely's (1991) student Laura Berns writes that, worried about missing significant activity, she did not take extensive notes. Then, when writing, she feared being unable to make sense of them. "Fortunately that fear turned out to be groundless . . . for those few notes were in fact sufficient to jog my memory, to bring back a wealth of detailed data—often more than I could conveniently manage. Later, comments of fellow students confirmed my experience" (p. 72). Berns found following her notes easy:

> There is no need to agonize over the best order, as you can whiz along, putting first what came first in time and continuing chronologically to the end. In addition, you don't have to be concerned about how many t's in inputting because such polished details are unimportant in a text intended for your eyes only. (p. 74)

Novices are always amazed at how lengthy the notes become. Laura Berns again comments, "I routinely found that an hour of observation generated ten or more pages of log, an experience shared by many others in the course. . . . I found myself crossing the street to avoid conversations with [her observees] . . . because a pleasant five-minute chat meant adding five more pages" (p. 75).

An Example of Fieldnotes

Box 13.1 on the following page gives an example of fieldnotes. Only about one-fifth of the full set of fieldnotes is reproduced. An excellent example, the notes include an accidental contact at a party long after the observation that led to an insightful observer comment.

Note the wealth of detail—thick description! Not knowing ahead of time what will be significant, the observer records what he was wearing as well as the attire of the important others being observed. Persons entering and leaving the school help establish the atmosphere, as do the notes about who was in the halls doing what and the observer's interaction with the students there. The use of a map of the classroom shows the relationships of students, teacher, teacher's aide, and observers. Further, note that every attempt was made to record the conversation verbatim. There is even a note that a quotation may not be exact because the observer was embarrassed about coming in late.

Note also the many observer comments marked *O.C.* They include introspection by the observer about his feelings, explanations of the teacher's comments, evaluative observations (unsupervised halls), and questions to check up on later—material set off from the factual observations themselves yet important to understanding those observations.

▶ Fieldnotes are the observer's record of observations. They can be made while in the field, if this can be done unobtrusively and without changing the behavior of those observed. Otherwise, they must be completed as soon as possible after leaving the field.

▶ Good fieldnotes include as much verbatim conversation as possible, as well as notes regarding context.

▶ Comments, inferences, and judgments are kept separate from observations, preferably as observer comments or as memos.

Box 13.1   An example of fieldnotes.

March 24, 1980
Joe McCloud
11:00 AM to 12:30 PM
Westwood High
6th Set of Notes

The Fourth-Period Class in Marge's Room

I arrived at Westwood High at five minutes to eleven, the time Marge told me her fourth period started. I was dressed as usual: sport shirt, chino pants, and a Woolrich parka. The fourth period is the only time during the day when all the students who are in the "neurologically impaired/learning disability" program, better known as "Marge's program," come together. During the other periods, certain students in the program, two or three or four at most, come to her room for help with the work they are getting in other regular high school classes.

It was a warm fortyish, promise of a spring day. There was a police patrol wagon, the kind that has benches in the back that are used for large busts, parked in the back of the big parking lot that is in front of the school. No one was sitting in it and I never heard its reason for being there. In the circular drive in front of the school was parked a United States Army car. It had insignias on the side and was a khaki color. As I walked from my car, a balding fortyish man in an Army uniform came out of the building and went to the car and sat down. Four boys and a girl also walked out of the school. All were white. They had on old dungarees [jeans] and colored stenciled t-shirts with spring jackets over them. One of the boys, the tallest of the four, called out, "oink, oink, oink." This was done as he sighted the police vehicle in the back.

> O.C.: This was strange to me in that I didn't think that the kids were into "the police as pigs." Somehow I associated that with another time, the early 1970s. I'm going to have to come to grips with the assumptions I have about high school due to my own experience. Sometimes I feel like Westwood is entirely different from my high school and yet this police car incident reminded me of mine.

Classes were changing when I walked down the halls. As usual there was the boy with girl standing here and there by the lockers. There were three couples that I saw. There was the occasional shout. There were no teachers outside the doors.

> O.C.: The halls generally seem to be relatively unsupervised during class changes.

Two African American girls I remember walking down the hall together. They were tall and thin and had their hair elaborately braided with beads all through them. I stopped by the office to tell Mr. Talbot's (the principal) secretary that I was in the building. She gave me a warm smile.

> O.C.: I feel quite comfortable in the school now. Somehow I feel like I belong. As I walk down the halls some teachers say hello. I have been going out of my way to say hello to kids that I pass. Twice I've been in a stare-down with kids passing in the hall. Saying, "How ya' doin'?" seems to disalarm them.

I walked into Marge's class and she was standing in the front of the room with more people than I had ever seen in the room save for her homeroom which is right after second period. She looked like she was talking to the class or was just about to start. She was dressed as she had been on my other visits—clean, neat, well-dressed but casual. Today she had on a striped blazer, a white blouse and dark slacks. She looked up at me, smiled and said: "Oh, I have a lot more people here now than the last time."

O.C.: This was in reference to my other visits during other periods where there are only a few students. She seems self-conscious about having such a small group of students to be responsible for. Perhaps she compares herself with the regular teachers who have classes of thirty or so.

There were two women in their late twenties sitting in the room. There was only one chair left. Marge said to me something like: "We have two visitors from the central office today. One is a vocational counselor and the other is a physical therapist," but I don't remember if those were the words. I felt embarrassed coming in late. I sat down in the only chair available next to one of the women from the central office. They had on skirts and carried their pocketbooks, much more dressed up than the teachers I've seen. They sat there and observed.

Below is the seating arrangement of the class today:

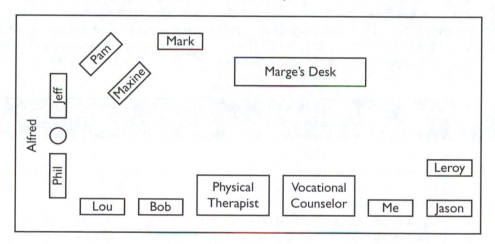

Alfred (Mr. Armstrong, the teacher's aide) walked around but when he stood in one place, it was over by Phil and Jeff. Marge walked about near her desk during her talk which started by saying to the class: "Now remember, tomorrow is a field trip to the Rollway Company. We all meet in the usual place, by the bus, in front of the main entrance at 8:30. Mrs. Sharp wanted me to tell you that the tour of Rollway is not specifically for you. It's not like the trip to G.M. They took you to places where you were likely to be able to get jobs. Here, it's just a general tour that everybody goes on. Many of the jobs that you will see are not for you. Some are just for people with engineering degrees. You'd better wear comfortable shoes because you may be walking for two or three hours." Maxine and Mark said: "Ooh," in protest to the walking.

She paused and said in a demanding voice: "OK, any questions? You are all going to be there. (Pause) I want you to take a blank card and write down some questions so you have things to ask at the plant." She began passing out cards and at this point Jason, who was sitting next to me made a tutting sound of disgust, and said: "We got to do this?" Marge said: "I know this is too easy for you, Jason." This was said in a sarcastic way but not like a strong put down.

O.C.: It was like sarcasm between two people who know each other well. Marge has known many of these kids for a few years. I have to explore the implications of that for her relations with them.

Memos

Miles and Huberman (1984) note that we become so fascinated with the flood of particulars that we "forget to think, to make deeper and more general sense of what is happening, to begin to explain it in a conceptually coherent way" (p. 69). Thinking is carrying on a conversation with oneself, and memos are records of those conversations. Date memos to audit progress. Strauss (1987) argues that memoing should take precedence over coding or data recording so that the ideas will not be lost. He suggests that if we do not have time to memo on the spot, to make at least a note to write the memo, and then set aside time for memoing as well as coding and analysis. In addition, if we write titles on memos, it makes them easier to code later and highlights their generality. Label hunches and intuitive guesses to avoid later confusion with suppositions linked to evidence. Add modifying commentary as analysis progresses. Box 13.2 is an example of a memo from a study of educational innovations in Miles and Huberman (1984). The researchers note that this memo pulls data from many sites and reformulates them around the issue of career patterns.

Box 13.2   An integrating memo showing the kinds of musing that leads to new hypotheses and guides future data collection.

Memo: Career patterns 2/22/80

In a general sense, people are riding the innovations in a state of transition; they are on their way *from* somewhere *to* somewhere *via* the project. . . .

Where could people be going? They could be going

—*up:* from a classroom to a supervisory or administrative role or to a higher administration slot. Innovations are a lot faster than waiting for someone *else* to move on or going back for a *degree*. They get you visibility and good positioning. If it gets institutionalized, you get institutionalized with it in a new role. Also, they're less brutal than getting promotions by doing in the person above you and more convenient than having to move away to move up.

—*away:* from teaching by easing into a part-time or more flexible job. These projects tend to be marginal, loosely administered (although Tindale [one of the schools] is contrary), transition-easing. They also can allow for permutations, as in the up-and-away pattern Cary may be following at Plummet.

—*in:* the remedial programs are less choosy about formal credentials. They provide access to civil services like education to people with weird backgrounds. Aides can get positioned to become certified teachers; people from business or the arts can come into a marginal or experimental universe and ease gradually into a more formal role incumbency.

It is especially worth keeping track, as we dictate and code, of where these people have come from and where they are, or think they are, on their way to. I suggest we ask each informant:

—a little more directly, *why* he/she is doing this, in terms of roles and role changes.

—what he/she expects to be doing in 2–3 years.

—if he/she has a sense of being in a transitional period.

From M. B. Miles & A. M. Huberman, *Qualitative Data Analysis: An Expanded Source Book* (2nd ed.), p. 73. Copyright © 1994. Reprinted by permission of Sage Publications.

Because the writing of this memo occurred partway through the data collection, it affected subsequent collection and suggested specific means of doing so.

Memos are the basis for analysis and for further data-gathering directions. Steinmetz (Ely, 1991) writes a memo (at a minimum) after every three sets of fieldnotes, finding that unless she does so, too much data accumulates and "we experience input overload and the uneasy realization that we are floundering because we haven't given ourselves the direction we need" (p. 80).

Some researchers suggest you keep trying to title your study, retitling as you narrow the focus. The more you learn about your situation, the more possibilities you see in it, the more fascinating leads to follow. Intentionally focusing your efforts is usually essential to gathering data in depth.

Memos should also serve another purpose, that of reflecting on one's impact on the situation, and vice versa—the impact on the research of situation, of observing, of developing friendships, and on one's self. For example, this quotation from Shulamit Reinharz (Gergen & Gergen, 2000, p. 1028) reflected on the effect of his multiple selves over the course of his research:

> I trace the way I referred to myself during the course of the year. . . . At first, the most obvious "difference" with the [other group] members is what defines myself. . . . After that, more layers are unpeeled. As these different layers are uncovered, people get to know me in different ways, which leads to their telling me different things. This in turn allows me to know them in different ways.

Some researchers keep a **reflexivity** journal consisting of self-reflective memos on these issues. Symon (2002) suggests that researchers be aware of their purpose: "It is one thing to recount your personal experience and another to reflect on your motivation for interpretation of the data or the wider political context of which the research process is a part" (p. 177). Such memos help one to gain perspective on data validity, which we discuss next.

▶ Memos are used to integrate thoughts, to record hunches, facilitate the gradual development of an explanation or theory, and suggest future directions.

▶ Memos should also reflect on one's impact on the situation being observed, the impact of the research on oneself, the implications for both of these on the research itself, and one's intent in doing the research. Some researchers keep a separate reflexivity journal consisting of these self-reflective memos.

ANALYSIS IN THE CONTEXT OF DATA GATHERING

A substantial portion of each qualitative study is spent in data gathering: getting the study's target to emerge and focusing data gathering around it. As you sift the data and are able to better identify your target, you concentrate your observations and inquiries on a purposive sample that includes individuals, documents, situations, events, processes, times, and other aspects that can further develop your understanding. Strauss (1987) and others refer to this as theoretical sampling to indicate that the choice of the next subjects and situations is designed to develop and extend theory. Data analysis begun in the field reveals data gaps that guide purposive sampling.

The implication in this discussion of purposive sampling is that such sampling is of different persons or sites. But the same principles of purposive sampling also extend to sampling the behavior of individuals over time. Thus, we may observe particular individuals at set time intervals, or when certain behaviors occur. Or, for instance, we may sample the classroom behavior every so many minutes or seconds, recording verbal descriptions or tallying it, as Flanders's (1970) interaction analysis does.

Not all researchers begin analysis in the field, some do fieldwork simply to describe some situation or process; they produce a narrative with little formal analysis other than ordering their notes to tell a story. Some enter the field with codes predetermined from theorizing and previous research, applying them as they gather data. Some immerse themselves in the data as it is gathered, inductively developing an explanation. Some wait to begin analysis on leaving the field (e.g., Strauss & Corbin, 1998). We begin discussing analysis in this chapter but continue doing so in greater depth in chapter 15.

The Constant Comparison Method

As its name implies, a common analysis pattern—**constant comparison**—intertwines data gathering and analysis from the outset. In overview, it involves successively gathering data, analyzing it, using that analysis to guide more data gathering, analyzing that, and so on until additional effort brings no new learning and researchers are satisfied with their understanding (e.g., Bogdan & Biklen, 2007).

In more detail, it involves coding each item in the fieldnotes in terms of the dimension or concept of which it is an indicator. Then, you seek new indicators of these concepts until the same kinds of instances are found repeatedly and the concept is well identified—a concept called **saturation**. Commonalties in the data lead first to a description as concepts are linked with other concepts, then to an explanation or theory of the phenomenon. You compare this explanation with new data from the field, trying to find where it is applicable and where it is not—seeking key examples. Where the explanation should apply but does not, as in adjusting an ill-fitting dress or suit, we move back and forth between checking and modifying until the proposed explanation accounts for the data. If we are stumped by cases that are not covered, we go back to these or similar cases for additional information that permits appropriate adjustment to accommodate them. This is a funnel-like process as the range of new informants and situations is increasingly narrowed to focus on ones that will add to and test previous formulations. (Although using different terminology, this is basically an application of the process of conceptual analysis described in the sidebar on p. 279.)

For example, Gouldner (1954) found that workers in a factory never talked back to supervisors, did what they were told to do, adhered to a rigid schedule, and left repairs to maintenance workers even though this practice meant interrupting production. He considered these factors to be evidence of the construct "bureaucratization." (Note that whereas the quantitative researcher might build a scale to be administered to workers to measure bureaucratization, Gouldner inferred it from the many indicators of the concept across the cases observed. This process contributes

Conceptual Analysis: A General Method for Defining a Concept*

Some physical features of the world—like pencil, clock, clouds, thunder, and dog—have direct referents we can see and touch; they stand out almost begging for names. Other features—like joy, sadness, intelligence, and role—have no direct physical referent. They have to be *cut out,* as it were. These covert aspects of experience are named by the constructs of science.

—after May Brodbeck

The constant comparison process described in this chapter is but one example of a more general method called **conceptual analysis** that was devised by philosophers for defining a **concept** or **construct**. Generalizing from the constant comparison application, you can see that it consists of identifying key examples that characterize the heart of the concept being defined—**model examples**—and then of finding borderline and contrary examples that delineate the concept's boundaries. To these categories, we might add related and invented cases (Green, 1971, p. 211). Let's try an example.

Consider *creativity*: It is a concept—one can't see, smell, or touch *creativity* itself. What might be a model example? How about that a student creates a work of art different from art done by that of other persons? Green (1971) notes: "The study of model examples should yield some initial formulation of the necessary, if not sufficient, conditions that must be satisfied if any example is to be a genuine case of the concept" (p. 208). What would seem to be the defining characteristics of this model case? They appear to be that the work is new in the sense that it is different from what anyone has done before.

Contrary cases test those conditions. Can we think of contrary cases where the work is different from art done by that of other persons? Suppose that the work of art were to be carved from a piece of foamglass, a problem common to art classes. If a student's sculpture were unique in this class but often duplicated in previous classes, would it still be creative? This points out that the uniqueness of the creation must be judged by a standard that goes beyond a comparison with other work of the moment.

What about **borderline cases**? Suppose the work of art resembles, but is not quite the same as, previous work by this student—it is a variation on that same theme. If the student's original work was unique, is this variation also to be considered original? If it must be different, how much so? Clearly, we must make a judgment—a judgment with which others may not agree. We have come to one borderline of the term *creativity*.

What about **related cases**? Are there related terms that throw light on the nature of *creativity*? What about *imaginative*? Is a person who is creative also imaginative, and vice versa? When we refer to someone as imaginative, we think of that person as demonstrating repeated and varied instances of imagination, not just one. Come to think of it, that is true of saying that a person is creative. One instance won't do; *creativity* is shown by repeated acts—in different circumstances, in a variety of situations. This related case reveals other defining characteristics of *creativity,* repeated acts, varied circumstances, and fields of endeavor.

Finally, we come to **invented cases**. Sometimes it helps to release all the normal restraints. What would the world be like if suddenly a special virus, to which their *creativity* made them susceptible, wiped out all the highly creative people? What would happen? Behaviors that had been learned would continue. Individuals could learn those behaviors from others. But once those were learned by all survivors, no new behaviors would occur. Hence, creative acts go beyond what one has specifically already learned.

(continued)

So this example of conceptual analysis has led us to three defining characteristics of a creative person: (1) the person engages in acts unique in terms of both his or her own and others' experiences (the standard for uniqueness is a matter of judgment), (2) such acts occur with sufficient frequency and variety that we can say that they characterize the person's behavior, and (3) they go beyond what the individual has learned earlier.

Figure 13.2 shows in diagram form the relation of the different cases to the concept to be defined.

Figure 13.2   A diagram displaying the relation of the stages in conceptual analysis to the concept to be defined.

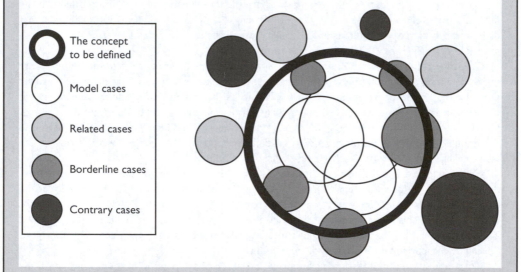

Because conceptual analysis is a useful way of distinguishing what a concept means and how it relates to its operationalization, it has been employed in a number of fields. We meet it in this chapter in the constant comparison method (see Figure 13.3 on p. 282). We also find it used in the discussion of qualitative data validity. It appears still again in chapter 18 in *construct validity*, where Cronbach and Suppes (1955) used it to determine the validity of a test or other instrument. For more on this method, see Machado and Silva (2007); from a philosophical standpoint, see Green (1971) or Wilson (1971).

*In the field of content analysis, the term "conceptual analysis" denotes coding a text for concepts and analyzing their relative frequency; "relational analysis" denotes analyzing the relationships among a text's concepts.

▶ Conceptual analysis is highly useful whenever you want to clarify a concept or construct's meaning, develop a concept or construct, or show the relation between a concept or construct and its operational definition.

substantially to the translation validity facet of Internal Integrity; it links the concept firmly to those indicators that emerge from this process.)

Once core concepts and explanations (e.g., bureaucratization) are well developed—densified with detail and example—the funnel is reversed to broaden sample choice. You then try to find borderline and contrary cases that show the limits of the explanation and determine the generality of the theory. This step may lead to the choice of new sites to study and a comparison of findings at the new sites with those of the old in a cross-site comparison.

Gouldner continued his research by selecting a contrasting work site—a mine—and focusing his attention on the same indicators. He found that workers stood up to their supervisors, made repairs themselves, rotated jobs, and had no factory-like schedules. In fact, the track-laying gang was given only general instructions about where to work, and the supervisor then asked them how long it might take. Gouldner considered these behaviors to be indicators of a lack of "bureaucratization," concluding that the red tape was greater in the factory than in the mine (Gouldner, 1954, in Ornstein & Phillips, 1978, p. 361). With both positive and negative examples helping to define the construct, he then focused on "bureaucratization's" effects.

Finally, you leave the field as a result of having arrived at saturation—that is, when new observations cease to add much insight to that already gained.

Through this process you gradually develop an understanding of the phenomenon, as well as a theory or explanation that is grounded in observations—you have what Glaser and Strauss (1967) termed **grounded theory**. Note the role of emerging explanation, or theory, in controlling the direction of the study and therefore directing purposive sampling. Extreme cases may be selected to help illuminate aspects more difficult to discern in run-of-the-mill examples. Cases are chosen to "flesh out" descriptions, densify theory conceptualization, and test and extend the formulations. Cases especially suitable for these purposes are those with which your audience can identify, and which have aspects that suggest their generality (Patton, 1980). Patton also notes that cases may be chosen because your audience would expect those cases to be included. While these cases may or may not contribute to the constant comparison or analytic induction process, they may be important to an acceptance of the study's findings by your chosen audience (optimizing audience credibility).

Figure 13.3 on the following page graphically portrays the constant comparative process from its start box at the upper left, following the solid lines to the write-up box at the bottom right. Researchers initially cycle through the activities in the upper-left circle labeled *Explanation Development* as many times as necessary to formulate an explanation or rationale for the phenomenon. With each cycle they are constantly comparing proposed hypotheses about what is significant and what is going on with the data, successively modifying their hypotheses to fit. This cycle of formulation goes on along with observing, interviewing, and gathering artifacts and records. Researchers consider what is happening and write memos—their hypotheses, suggestions for whom or what to observe or ask about next time, what is significant and what is less so, and how they are reacting to the process.

This material guides researchers to their next actions, and to further refinement until they are no longer learning anything new. Then they exit the cycle to the top right, where the label *Explanation Emerges* appears. With a firm enough idea about

Figure 13.3   The process of developing and testing hypotheses and explanations in the constant comparison method* (adapted from Gladwin, 1989).

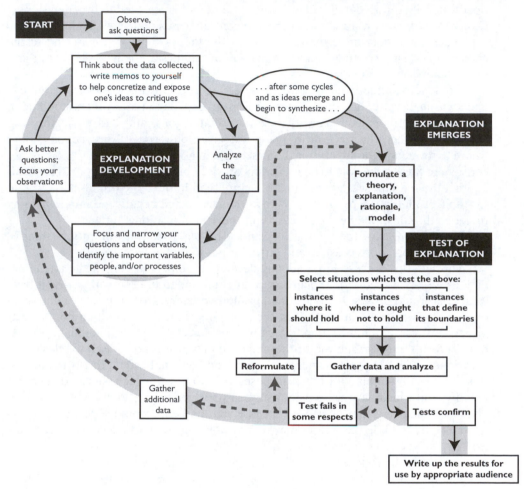

START → Observe, ask questions

Think about the data collected, write memos to yourself to help concretize and expose one's ideas to critiques

. . . after some cycles and as ideas emerge and begin to synthesize . . .

EXPLANATION EMERGES

Ask better questions; focus your observations

EXPLANATION DEVELOPMENT

Analyze the data

Formulate a theory, explanation, rationale, model

TEST OF EXPLANATION

Focus and narrow your questions and observations, identify the important variables, people, and/or processes

Select situations which test the above:

instances where it should hold   instances where it ought not to hold   instances that define its boundaries

Reformulate   Gather data and analyze

Gather additional data

Test fails in some respects   Tests confirm

Write up the results for use by appropriate audience

*An application of the conceptual analysis process is described in the sidebar, page 279, to developing explanations.

what is going on (its significance and explanation), in order to test it, researchers then follow the steps leading (they hope) to corroboration and write-up—the part of the figure labeled *Test of Explanation*. Should confirmation fail, however, as the dotted lines show (beginning in the lower right of the figure), the process leads either to further explanation development in order to determine what was wrong (the dotted line to the circle at the upper left), or to a reformulation with sufficient modification that it ought now to fit the data (the dotted line to *Explanation Emerges*). Then they test the new explanation and either corroborate it or repeat the cycle of reformulation.

The process just described is one example of the efforts to increase the credibility of qualitative methods through descriptive procedures that improve and discipline the process without restricting it to a set formula. Glaser and Strauss's (1967) guidelines for analytic induction to develop grounded theory had considerable impact. Such efforts have been joined by others, including Bogdan and Biklen (2007), Guba and Lincoln (1986), Levine (1985), Miles and Huberman (1994), Strauss (1987), and Strauss and Corbin (1998). These efforts have been facilitated by the development of qualitative data analysis software. However, some are concerned by these efforts. Consider this quotation from Wolcott (1995, p. 11):

> By all means the move to increase the general research sophistication . . . should be encouraged. But at the same time, it would be tragic to lose what some converts call "soft," "unscientific," or "fuzzy" research. Much of the world we seek to understand has just those characteristics, including our own involvement in it as researchers.

▶ Most formulations begin as the observer—like a "sponge"—listens intently and observes open endedly.

▶ With the constant comparison method, as the target emerges, so do explanatory hunches that guide the further selection of cases and observations.

▶ Purposive sampling is used to find cases that extend and densify understanding, test an explanation, find the limits of its generality, and ensure the validity of information.

▶ Hunches are tested on new cases, modified as needed to fit, further tested, further detailed and related to other hunches, further modified and retested, and so on, until saturation is reached—the point at which further efforts add little or nothing.

▶ The intent of the constant comparison process is to develop an understanding and explanation grounded in and accounting for the observations—that is, grounded theory.

▶ Practitioners of qualitative research continue to provide discipline to their methods without restricting them to a formula.

Gathering Data to Infer Causation

The logic of Mill's methods, which are described in chapter 11 (pp. 223–227), is applicable wherever qualitative researchers seek to establish cause-and-effect relationships. Mill's method of differences uses the presence and absence of a cause to infer a causal relationship. Usually unwilling to intervene to create contrasting experimental conditions, qualitative researchers must wait for such natural conditions to occur. They purposively sample situations where appropriate presence and absence conditions might occur, a so-called "natural experiment."

Alternatively, especially where studies are mainly descriptive, using the *method of agreement* they infer causation from repeated instances. Precise identification of the cause and effect may be an iterative process, with observations to rule out alternative causes in similar situations where the effect did not appear. For more on design issues, review chapter 11 and see chapter 21.

> ▶ Qualitative researchers seeking to show cause-and-effect relations use Mill's methods for inferring causation.
>
> ▶ Use of Mill's method of differences requires waiting for conditions to form a "natural experiment."

DATA VALIDITY

Explanations are only as good as the data on which they are based; therefore, validity must be attended to as data is gathered. We will discuss this further in the following chapters, but aspects particularly integral to fieldwork are noted here; representativeness is one of them (Miles & Huberman, 1994). We assume what we are seeing is typical, but is it? For example, only a few board members took part in a meeting's discussion. Therefore, you examine previous minutes to determine whether this is typical. Basically, this is a purposive sampling problem. Taking larger samples contributes to representativeness as well as, from the outset, sampling people and characteristics you know are important.

Unless you consciously attend to weighting sources of data, each tends to be regarded as good as the next. We know, however, that some sources are much more reliable than others. Data gathered in informal situations and from those comfortable with us are usually more representative. Some individuals have a perspective on what is going on that others lack. Reflect your judgments about the trustworthiness of sources in memos. Such judgments may change as you reflect on a source's consistency over time. Consciously take these facts into account in synthesizing findings.

Extreme Cases, Outliers, and Surprise Findings

Whether dealing with qualitative or quantitative data, extreme cases, outliers, and surprise findings can be a problem (more on quantitative outliers on p. 388). We love data that support our ideas and hate data that do not. Our initial tendency to ignore such instances would be a mistake; we need to find the cause of such deviations. They may indeed highlight some aspect that's not very visible with run-of-the-mill cases. For example, research shows that students learn more rapidly if they read aloud around a circle than they do if the teacher calls on them at random. However, we occasionally find a reading circle where this is not true. Should we ignore it and be satisfied that it generally works, or should we find out why it sometimes doesn't? In the latter case we find that with sufficient reading skill, silently rehearsing the paragraph prior to one's turn is no longer necessary; the generalization applies only to beginning readers. Outliers may have a simple explanation (the individual was tired); while the explanation does not affect the findings, explaining the outlier away satisfies the audience. Or outliers may show the explanation's generality or limits. Outliers usually lead to modification rather than negation of ideas. Outliers may affect important parts of External Generality—explanation generality, translation generality, and "demonstrated generality."

Triangulation

Bias is inevitable, observed historian Barbara Tuchman (1981, in Miles & Huberman, 1994):

> [It] . . . is to be expected. . . . Even if an event is not controversial, it will have been seen and remembered from different angles of view by different observers. . . . As the lion in Aesop said to the Man, "There are many statues of men slaying lions, but if only the lions were sculptors there might be a different set of statues." (p. 19)

Triangulation uses purposive sampling to determine the validity of data and bias. The concept of triangulation is borrowed from surveying. A property boundary can be established by simply measuring in the right direction from an established point, but it is more accurately found by using two established points as the base of a triangle to establish a third. The term has come to apply to any means of providing additional data to reinforce a finding where the new data are independent of the original set. Further, since data are subject to various errors, Guba and Lincoln (1986) compare it to a fisherman who uses multiple nets, each with some rips and tears. When used together, the holes of one net are covered by intact sections of others.

Denzin (1978) outlined three useful types of triangulation: (1) data triangulation, using multiple sources of data across time, space, and persons; (2) investigator triangulation, using multiple investigators; and (3) method triangulation, using multiple methods. He validly argues for triangulating data across all three source types—time, space, and persons. For example, a finding that a school board's meeting procedures appear to discourage minority parents from presenting their concerns should be checked not only at more than one meeting but also with more than one set of parents, and perhaps with regard to more than one issue. This is similar to sampling to establish the borderline generality of a finding—External Generality.

Data triangulation, the most common of the three, involves the use of two or more sources to establish factual accuracy. Thus, we confirm an informant's recall of a meeting by checking the secretary's minutes. Data triangulation can involve many different sources. You compare for consistency: differently phrased questions getting at the same point, present observations with past records, verbal responses with actual behavior, solitary behavior with that constrained by the presence of others, nonverbal with verbal, volunteered responses with called-upon answers (the latter may have an element of "polite agreement"). Triangulation may be particularly important where you seek the covert meaning of a situation that differs from the expressed meaning.

Investigator triangulation refers to obtaining accounts from different investigators of the same phenomenon. Thus, we might compare the reports of two observers of a teacher's lesson for similarities. (In quantitative research this is referred to as *objectivity* [see p. 419], also discussed in chapter 16.) But, because observers may focus on different things, multiple observers will likely also add richness and depth to the observations.

Method triangulation uses different methods to assess the same aspect of a phenomenon. The possibilities are endless and depend on the problem: minutes of meetings, interoffice memos, letters, excerpts from student records or portfolios, personnel records, test scores, performance appraisals, psychologist and teacher reports. Leinhardt (1989) used a variety of methods to compare novice and expert teachers: She observed, video recorded, transcribed the videos, interviewed each teacher before and after each lesson, and did stimulated recall interviews in which she asked teachers to comment on videos of their lessons.

Although triangulation is intended to provide support for a finding, Mathison (1988) suggests that the result can be inconsistency or contradiction. As in the discussion of outliers above, the search for an inconsistency's explanation frequently leads to new insights. In tracking teachers' activities with a new curriculum, Mathison noted that teachers reported including mathematical activities in unplanned times of the day, but triangulation corroboration found only 14 instances in 200 classroom observations. The discrepancy turned up the fact that there was almost no unplanned time.

Taylor and Bogdan (1998) suggest that we discount the value of the information not only in terms of consistency over sources but also in terms of such questions as these: Was it volunteered or solicited? (Just asking a question may make salient a point usually ignored.) Who was present? (People often reveal things when authority figures are not present.) Was it established through direct observation or hearsay? Finally, in regard to others' research, who paid for it?

Perhaps the best advice is this: "Triangulation is not so much a tactic as a way of life. If you self-consciously set out to collect and double-check findings, using multiple sources and modes of evidence, the verification process will largely be built into the data collection as you go" (Miles & Huberman, 1994, p. 267).

> ▶ Triangulation is the process of using more than one source to confirm information: confirming data from different sources, confirming observations from different observers, and confirming information with different data-collection methods. It should become a "way of life."
>
> ▶ With the discovery of disconfirming information, seeking reasons for the contradiction frequently points to directions for extending or modifying explanations instead of discarding them.

The labor intensity of qualitative research makes multisite studies rare, but choosing a contrasting site can helpfully bring characteristics of interest into stark relief. Studying the socialization of new assistant professors at a research-oriented university in contrast with that in a small college will highlight differences in values, collegiality, and responsibilities to the organization that might otherwise be missed. Because evidence from multiple sites strengthens External Generality, studies advancing a generality for consideration often add other site data.

ETHICS

Because the observer faces more problems in the field with less support than most other researchers, it is important to discuss the issue of ethics in addition to its coverage in chapter 10. Observers make on-the-spot ethical decisions without the help of human-subject protection committees or advisors; they may witness illegal acts that should be reported. Should the researcher's own sense of justice be substituted for whatever is the normal corrective course in the situation being observed? Bosk (1979), for instance, confronted the question of his responsibility to the patient and her relatives when he witnessed a nursing or medical error. He decided that he would let the system handle these cases; his disclosure of the entire system would be more effective than "tilting at windmills in one or two select cases" (p. 200). Unless lives are in danger, this is a fairly common ethical choice: ignoring the transgressions of individuals while making public those of the institution and its administration. The latter are perceived as the real culprits in need of reform. This is not to imply that such a decision is improper, but, if made, the socially easier choice coincides with achieving the desired effect. Remember, immunity from subpoena is not generally extended to scientists.

All observers encounter the problem of ambiguity in interpersonal relationships. Along these lines, P. Cusick (personal communication, July 28, 1980) writes:

> In every study I've done, I've . . . found people . . . with whom I could relate on a personal level . . . and [used them] to help with understanding how people really behave in the organization. All that is fine and according to the book. . . . The problem is that when one joins a small, normative unit he agrees to abide by an ethical agreement . . . and he has to internalize those ethical constraints. [The result is] when writing the study I was constrained by all the . . . internalized constraints that I took from those small affective groups. . . . I never felt it quite so strongly before, but prior studies had been of adolescents, not adults like myself. One doesn't tell tales on or even take a dispassionate view of his friends. . . . The argot of "informants" . . . etc. is one that denies affective relation. . . . All that research talk is just a little too glib and quick. It's a paradox of course; affective involvement is essential to the study's success, but involvement places a whole set of (from a researcher's perspective) irrational constraints on the process.

Some of the stress resulting from making private information public can be reduced by reviewing the report with those studied prior to releasing it, and then deciding what to release (called **peer review**).

- ▶ Ethical problems are inevitable in some qualitative research, and many ethical decisions must be made on the spot without the support of committee discussion or ethicists.

- ▶ The betrayal of the bond of intimate friendship with informants, which occurs when the report is made public, is always a problem; it may be helped by peer review.

- ▶ Serious ethical problems arise when observations include acts that are either legally or morally reportable to authorities. To report them at the least interrupts, and more probably terminates, the study. The serious consequences of not doing so must also be faced but sometimes seem justified by the study's likely impact.

- ▶ Researchers and their data are not immune from subpoena. Therefore, data that might harmfully identify individuals should probably either not be collected or be quickly destroyed.

LEAVING THE FIELD

When do you have enough data to leave the field? Patton (1980) comments: "The moment you cease observing, pack your bags, and leave the field, you will get a remarkably clear insight about that one critical activity you should have observed . . . but didn't" (p. 195). That fear causes concern for beginners, and sometimes for experienced researchers as well. The usual advice is that you will intuitively know when to stop collecting data, since you will find that you are learning nothing new. True, you will find such a point. However, the anxious researcher, wanting not to miss anything, sometimes feels a compulsion to continue. Ely (1991) tells of leaving for a tropical island on a sabbatical. After several months analyzing her data, she still had a nagging feeling that she might not have done all she should. So she packed up, returned, and gathered more interviews—only to find the new data confirmed her earlier work. Whether doing quantitative or qualitative work, research is the search for the unknown. The real pay dirt *may* be just around the corner; nobody can be assured it isn't. But we can put more trust in our initial instinct.

Tips on Observation

Following are helpful suggestions based on the experience of seasoned observers:

1. Write up the notes as soon as possible; you will remember more than expected. Writing notes may require triple or quadruple the time spent observing; allow for it. Dictation is faster than writing but requires a certain amount of skill. Dictated notes will likely be more copious and more organized. Software like *Soundscriber*[3] (free), and *Media Player* can facilitate your notes transcription. With adequate training to your manner of speaking, software programs like *Via Voice* and *Dragon Naturally Speaking* may sufficiently and accurately transcribe for you.

2. Rehearse every 10–15 minutes what you have seen; this refreshes your memory (but may selectively change recall). Play back scenes in your mind; try to visualize what your write-up of the scene will look like.

3. Talking about your observation before you record it may change the importance you attach to certain events—possibly change the way you remember them (Bogdan & Biklen, 2007). Record, then discuss, and then add separate notes regarding changed impressions or recollections.

4. When something significant happens that you can't immediately record, change something inconspicuous that will help you remember to record it—Sari Biklen suggests moving a ring to the other hand or turning your wristwatch around.

5. Focus on the opening and closing of conversation; you can fill in the rest later. Include contextual factors.

6. Get down key words and phrases, outline what went on, and then go back and fill in. Develop a set of abbreviations appropriate to the study.

7. Draw a diagram, not only to give the picture but also to trace your own movements.

8. Ask, "Why is this person telling me this?" Be sensitive to both others' and your own impact on the situation.

9. Ask not only why someone is doing something but also why the person is not doing something else!

10. Remember that actions and expressed attitudes may differ, as may verbal and non-verbal reactions. What someone does not say may be significant, too.

11. Don't be so intent on recording data that you forget to be human; share feelings and personal experiences. But also try to keep track of the effect of that sharing on the behavior being observed and on your own feelings toward the situation.

12. Memoing is one of your most important field activities. Don't slight it—it is the beginning of analysis.

13. Separate inferences and interpretation from observations with observer comments and memos. Keep track of your hunches. Write them in the notes with *O.C.* before them to designate them as observer comments, and enclose them in parentheses to set them off from the narrative flow.

14. Memos should also reflect on one's impact on the field as well as the field's impact on one's self, and the effect of both on the research process and on interpretation.

15. Zoom out occasionally to make sure you haven't lost sight of the larger picture (Lancy, 2001).

16. When you begin by gathering data broadly, work at consciously narrowing the focus of your study.

ADDITIONAL READING

For useful general references see Ely (1991); Denzin and Lincoln (2000); Miles and Huberman (1994); Hammersley and Atkinson (1995). Strauss (1987) illustrates different types of memos with 16 pages of memos from a project on the impact of medical technology on hospitals. He usefully comments on their intent and actual effect (pp. 111–127). Persons planning on doing participatory observation in a covert role may find of interest Mitchell's (1994) exploration of the topic.

Those interested in life histories, ethnographies, and autobiographies may be interested in Casey (1995). See Edwards and Lampert (1993) about making a written record of a conversation or video with references to a variety of speakers, their intonation, loudness variations, and so on. See Emerson, Fretz, and Shaw (1995) regarding fieldnotes. Kidder (1981) has a useful discussion of negative case analysis. Wolcott (1995) is a chatty discussion of fieldwork and reporting as an art. Webb et al. (1981) discuss unobtrusive ways of gathering data. Feldman, Bell, and Berger (2003) explore gaining entry along with case study examples. Insider reflections by 18 established scholars on what a qualitative research study was really like shows how it is done (deMarrais, 1998).

For useful examples and commentary on qualitative research, see *The Qualitative Report,* an online journal (http://www.nova.edu/ssss.QR).

IMPORTANT TERMS AND CONCEPTS

acceptance	informants
borderline examples/cases	invented cases
concealed observation	memos
concept	model examples
conceptual analysis	nonparticipant observation
constant comparison method	participant observation
construct	peer review
contrary examples/cases	reflexivity
covert participant observation	related cases
elite bias	respondent
fieldnotes	saturation
gaining entry	stimulated recall
gatekeeper	triangulation
grounded theory	

OPPORTUNITIES FOR ADDITIONAL LEARNING

1. You wish to conduct a study at an inner-city high school located in a low socioeconomic district. You are aware that the community and the school have well-documented problems with juvenile crime and truancy. You want to engage in participant observation at the school in order to investigate how the youths who attend it view their schooling experience. How will you go about establishing your study? What problems might you encounter, and how will you overcome them?

2. Assume that you have gained entry to the school in problem 1 and have succeeded in conducting observations for several months. Many students have taken you into their confidence and have begun to accept you as one of them. You then observe that one of these students is selling cocaine to other students. What do you do?

3. You wish to study preschool children (aged 3 to 4 years) at a local nursery school. To understand how they interpret their experience, you decide to observe them over the period of the school year. On the continuum of obtrusiveness, which method would provide you with the most informative data?

4. Your study of children's use of computers has led you to some interesting conclusions. From your observations in two classes—one of first graders and one of third graders—it appears that a number of elementary-aged children view computers as something alive or, at least, as an entity with psychological characteristics. This has caused you to reflect upon the question of animism. You wonder whether their apparent attitude is peculiar to these classes or to this school, or whether these conclusions are generalizable to other children of this age group. How will you go about extending the study using qualitative methods?

5. You live in Columbus, Ohio, a city with a large Greek immigrant population. As a researcher in the field of nursing, you are interested in the topic of folk health in immigrant populations. In particular, you wish to study the Greek folk-healing tradition, which practices matiasma, the beliefs surrounding the prevention, diagnosis, and treatment of the "evil eye." You wonder about the extent of this practice and how to take it into account as a nurse working with these people. Why might you incorporate both quantitative and qualitative research methodologies into such a study?

Compare your answers with those following the Application Exercise.

If you pursue your research project with qualitative methods, what problems of access do you expect, if any? How will you record what occurred? Are there persons who you think might serve as particularly useful informants? Where will you look for them? What memos will you write to yourself regarding your feelings about the project and your entry into it? What problems do you anticipate in writing up your fieldnotes? Will you be able to do so right away? If not, how will you manage? What other sources of data might be available to provide triangulation of some of your findings? What ethical problems, if any, do you anticipate?

KEY TO ADDITIONAL LEARNING OPPORTUNITIES

1. Your problem is the one faced by all investigators who wish to engage in participant observation. You have the dual task of gaining entry and securing acceptance.

   Gaining entry. You need to find a way to enter that conveys the message, "I am to be trusted." Your first step will probably be to secure the approval of the school administration—possibly of the school superintendent—or begin the process of approval with a member of the school board. In one such study of students at a junior high school, the researcher, Everhart (1977), was able to legitimize his presence at the school through his role as evaluator for a government agency. Even so, the school administration resisted his entry for several weeks. The administrator with whom you are dealing may also impose conditions on your study or demand some sort of favor in return for the privilege. You must be careful that such conditions neither violate academic freedom nor abrogate the confidentiality of your informants. In Everhart's case, the school principal set the parameters for the study by limiting it to students (that is, excluding teachers) and by insisting that the researcher's role be one of observer and not *confidant*. Everhart was restricted to specific classes and limited interviewing. Fortunately, he was able to renegotiate these conditions once on site for a couple of months, but researchers should not count on being able to do so.

   Securing acceptance. Once you are on site, you will have to gain approval and trust—in this case, of the students. Simultaneously, you must remain enough of an outsider to avoid the constraints on the behaviors the group expects of its members. Everhart slowly developed the role of friend to his respondents. He did so by first developing an explanation of his presence (he was a writer there to do a story about what students did in junior high) that made sense to them and indicated that his presence was legitimate. He was then able to present himself as a friend, both by spending a considerable amount of time with the students and by reducing his contact with the adults. In time, he became so well accepted by the students that he was able to become an ex-officio member of certain groups in the school.

2. This is an example of an ethical dilemma to which the answer may not be as clear-cut as it first appears. It is a no-win situation that is frequently encountered in this kind of research. Reporting the people involved to the authorities may well identify you as a part of the authority structure and disrupt any special relationships that you have developed, thus terminating your study. Conversely, you may endanger yourself and your study by becoming party to a criminal act. A fairly common choice is to ignore such transgressions in favor of completing the study and letting the natural corrective forces of society come into play. You should understand, however, that unlike an attorney you are not in a privileged position. You cannot protect the anonymity of your informants or subjects. Furthermore, once published, your information is public knowledge. Your notes can be subpoenaed by a court of law.

3. Depending on the equipment available, you might consider two possibilities:

   a. *Covert nonparticipant observation*. If done from behind two-way mirrors it allows observation of "natural" actions. However, it limits action to special rooms and/or the range of equipment. It will provide behavioral and descriptive data but will not afford you the opportunity to gather explanations from the children's point of view.

   b. *Participant observation*. Within this role is a continuum of possible researcher behaviors. At one end, you may make it clear that you are conducting research and make it obvious by means of low interaction with your subjects. At the other extreme, you may observe covertly. You could adopt an authority role within the situation, such as being a teacher (covert observation), or try to become a part of the situation (with minimal explanation—at least to the children). Some researchers conducting such studies have gone so far as pretending to be one of the children, playing with them as if they were a child. Perhaps the most common approach within this tradition, however, is to adopt the friendship role, maintaining your status as an adult but eschewing a position of authority. By adopting this role, you would be able to minimize your influence on the situation and to develop trusting relationships in which you are able to ask the children for their own explanations.

4. Your first step would be to conduct further observations in other classes in the same school and, if possible, at the same grade levels as those you have already studied. Develop your understanding and densify it with detail and example. Test your understanding with negative instances, borderline cases, and key examples. Extend your observations to other grade levels within the school. Once the concept becomes saturated (the same kinds of instances are being found repeatedly) within the school, reverse the funnel and broaden your sample choice to gather new data. First, include other similar schools (in terms of age level, socioeconomic status, exposure to computers, etc.). Then move on to less similar schools until you are no longer able to discover new instances of your theory. Continue this process until you develop a solid understanding of the phenomenon—in this example, how children interpret their interactions with computers.

5. Such a study was carried out by Tripp-Reimer (1983) in Columbus with the intent of identifying the extent of such beliefs across the generations in order to help plan health care. She used the qualitative methods of semi-structured interviews and participant observation in the Greek community in order to establish baseline data concerning the description of matiasma. The descriptions she obtained allowed her to develop categories indicating levels of belief in matiasma and levels of knowledge of the practice.

   Tripp-Reimer also used a questionnaire to quantify the distribution of these beliefs and practices within the population. It was devised to elicit demographic and social characteristics of the population, including sex, age, and generation.

SUMMARY

The tips on observation already summarize many points in the chapter. In addition, however, we discussed the problem of gaining entry, the constant comparison analysis process, the interaction with informants and covert processes, data validity concerns, and ethics.

Gaining entry does not guarantee acceptance. It is convenient to start at the top of the administrative ladder, but that sometimes makes acceptance more difficult at lower hierarchy levels. Regardless of strong administrative support, acceptance must be won from each group. Gaining entry and winning such acceptance are not one-time efforts but rather are continual processes activated with each new situation and change of personnel.

Analysis and data gathering are intertwined in the process of constant comparison analysis, in which data are coded shortly after gathering. These data show where concepts and constructs that inform explanation are developing and therefore suggest the purposive sampling needed to flesh them out. Additional examples of developing constructs are sought until no more can be learned from them; negative and borderline examples then serve to delineate their boundaries and generality. Constant comparison analysis is one application of a more general method that is also used elsewhere in this book. That method, conceptual analysis, is described in the sidebar on page 279.

Informants can help you view the situation from the inside, but you must always ask yourself, "Why is this person telling me this?" and appropriately discount it. When you are interested in what persons are thinking, stimulated recall may be useful.

Maintaining data validity is a state of mind for the careful worker, who in addition uses triangulation for quality assurance. Triangulation judges the comparability of different sources of data, different observers, or different methods of data collection of the same events. Such multiple perspectives also may lead to new insights.

Fieldworkers must make off-the-cuff ethical decisions when they encounter professional errors, illegal acts, or improper decisions. In some instances, not reporting is itself an illegal act, but reporting may end the study and require observers to accuse persons who placed their trust in them. Fieldworkers must decide whether to let the system take its normal corrective course or to "blow the whistle." Neither alternative is without problems.

A Look Ahead

Because interviewing skill is often called upon in fieldwork, those skills are explored in the next chapter. Questionnaires, often employed with interviews, are discussed in chapter 24 on Survey Research and Questionnaires.

Notes

[1] Excerpts in this chapter taken from *Doing Qualitative Research: Circles in Circles* by Margot Ely et al. (copyright © 1991) are reprinted by permission of the author and Taylor & Francis Books, U.K.

[2] Accumulating evidence of the existence of *mirror neurons* in primates and humans indicates that the same brain regions involved in an action or feeling become active when we watch another person experiencing that action or feeling (Jaffe, 2007). Possibly, this is the basis for empathy.

[3] Available for download at http://www.personal.umich.edu/~ebreck/sscriber.html.

Links to previous research

Explanation, rationale, theory, or point of view

Questions, hypotheses, models

Preplanned and emergent designs

Design/procedure

Focus   Records   Time   Comparison and Contrast   Situation   Participants

Data

Statistical analysis and/or narrative analysis

Conclusion

Link to next study

Explanation or rationale of next study, etc.

14

Interviewing

[Any response] is only in part a function of . . . the questions. It is also a function of the social interaction of the interview, of the interviewer's appearance, of the respondent's fear of similar strangers, such as bill collectors.
—Donald T. Campbell, *Definitional versus Multiple Operationism*

Interviews are a prime qualitative data-collecting tool that serve the purposes of qualitative method, and also those of sample surveys. Much of what is in this chapter applies equally well to sample survey method, the topic of chapter 24. Be sure to read some of what is covered there, especially the formulation of questions. Were this book on the Internet, these chapters would be full of hyperlinks tying the two chapters together.

We tend to think of interviewing as straightforward, question-and-answer conversation between two individuals directed by the interviewer. But interviews vary, depending on whether the researcher is simply exploring, verifying a hypothesis, or determining the limits of its generality. However, of the number of available choices, those listed below are particularly important:

- structuring the interviewer role on-the-spot as opposed to predetermined questioning by the interviewer
- structuring the respondent role by asking his or her choice of predetermined responses versus recording their free responses verbatim
- recording responses verbatim in contrast to categorizing in predetermined response codes
- focusing the interview narrowly and deeply versus broadly and less deeply; go-with-the-flow versus focused versus exploratory
- nonprobability, convenience, or purposive sampling in contrast to probability, random, or stratified sampling
- true purpose, given the respondent, in contrast to concealing with a false purpose

- uses and types of rapport builders, prompts, and responses (nondirective, directive)
- determining the number of interviewers and respondents: one on one, two on one, and so forth
- determining the location of the interview: normal context or special circumstances

Let's explore these options in the following material.

INTRODUCTION

Qualitative researchers often gather data by interview; interviews and observations interact—observations provide meanings to the interviews, and interviews suggest things to look at or attach new meanings to the observations. Interviews are particularly useful in the following pursuits:

- exploring, probing, and searching for what is especially significant about a person or situation (e.g., how would you describe your advisor–advisee situation?)
- determining how individuals perceive their situation: its meaning to them, what is especially significant about it, what might be significant to others but is less important to them, how it came to be what it is, how they think it will be changed in the future (Tell me about your advisor, and how you came to choose her. How did your adversarial situation arise? How do you now perceive her? How do others perceive her? How do those perceptions affect your relationship to her?)
- identifying the cause in causal relationships (What do you believe really lies behind this adversarial relation?)
- finding explanations for discrepancies between observed and expected effects (I'd expect you to be very disturbed about this situation, but you don't seem to be. Why?)
- finding explanations for deviations from common behaviors by individuals or subgroups (Many students would be seeking another advisor. Tell me your thoughts about that possibility.)
- providing clues to the processes and mechanisms called into play by the situation (What factors do you think contributed to your situation? Milieu? Personal characteristics? What?)
- making sure the respondent correctly understands what was asked (I've described this situation as adversarial. How else might you describe it?)
- following up incomplete or nonresponsive answers (Tell me more about the latter. I'm not sure I understand you correctly. Are you saying that . . . ?)
- getting responses from individuals who might not respond to or might not understand a questionnaire

These are some of the obvious reasons to interview; you'll undoubtedly think of others. It is the major means of tapping thought processes to gain knowledge of a person's perceptions, feelings, or emotions, or to study complex individual or social behavior.

Structuring Interviewer and Respondent Roles

Interviewer and respondent roles can be structured beforehand to suit the interviewer's purposes. For instance, in order of increasing structure, the interviewer may be given: no structure (responsibility for on-the-spot formulation of questions covering any content, in any order, and in whatever form seems appropriate), a little structure (advance choice of general areas to cover), more structure (specific information to obtain), or still more structure (an interview schedule to follow). Similarly, respondents' answers may be recorded verbatim, may be summarized, or may be coded into given alternative responses. Respondents may be asked which of a set of responses best represents their answers to the question. The structure of respondent answers roughly parallels the interview structure.

Strictly speaking, no interview is unstructured. Even if it is simply an exploratory interview, researchers always enter with at least a focus of interest, or sometimes a list of issues to be covered in a free-flowing conversation. Each rejoinder follows the lead of the previous response, as interviewers gently bend the conversation so as to cover the topics in which they perceive there may be useful information. The columns of Table 14.1 on the following page contrast the implications of lack of interview structure with those of high structure. Obviously, this is a continuum with many positions between the extremes.

Reflecting on the skill required with less structure, Ely's (1991) student, Ewa Iracka, says:

> There were times when I used to . . . [think] Barbara Walters, the alleged interviewer of all time, . . . was overpaid. After all, she would merely sit comfortably in a lovely setting and glibly and effortlessly ask poignant questions that would elicit informative and sometimes sensational replies. Anyone can do that. After having indulged in this communication art form for the first time, [I realize] . . . perhaps I had judged Barbara Walters too harshly.[1] (pp. 63–64)

Clearly, more structure is appropriate for a preplanned research study than an emergent one. The ultimate structure is a standardized interview with even clarifications, prompts, and elaborations built into the interview plan and interviewers trained in their questionnaire administration to minimize interviewer effects and interview time. Structuring both respondent and interviewer roles facilitates larger-scale data gathering.

Obviously, the unstructured end of the continuum is closer to the qualitative tradition concerned with the respondent's view of the world; interviewing allows us "to enter the other person's perspective" (Patton, 1987, p. 109). The interview is seen as a negotiated dialogue to which both parties actively contribute, blurring the distinction between interviewer and respondent (Fontana, 2002).

The contrast makes clear that the researcher must choose among many trade-offs such as: the division of professional time between gathering interview data and its analysis, between using that time to analyze open-end responses, or to devise closed-end questions that get meaningful responses, and between selecting skilled interviewers or training unskilled ones.

Table 14.1   Comparison of Extremes in Interview Structure

Relatively Unstructured Interview	Structured Interview
Requires a researcher–interviewer who can point the interview in directions that may be rewarding. Questions are adapted to the immediate situation and individual differences so as to increase rapport.	The interviewer may be a clerk with good social skills who can comfortably follow a script while recording answers with check marks on well-designed forms.
The nature of the sample may not be predetermined but may unfold as each interview suggests where leads may next appear. Unless the interviewer is exploring the characteristics of some particular group, emphasis is not on generality but on understanding.	The nature of the sample will be carefully predetermined to reflect an emphasis on generality to a target population; it will be representative of the widest types within the population.
Compilation of data is labor intensive and results in extensive records.	Compilation of the data is easy and, if computer-assisted telephone interviewing (CATI) is used, results may be continuously compiled as the interview is conducted.
Analysis of the data requires professional skill to catch "pay dirt."	With preplanning, most of the analysis can be carried out by a technician.
Professional expertise is required to catch unexpected findings in data collection, context, etc., as well as analysis. Often the most exciting part of the research, this aspect requires professional time regardless of how the data are collected.	Same as relatively unstructured interview.
The profitability of such interviews depends directly on the skill in interviewing, the "nose for pay dirt," and the keen recognition of insights.	The profitability of such interviews depends on skill in anticipating where "pay dirt" lies during interview development and doing sufficient pretesting of the interview.

Content of the Interview

Patton (1987, pp. 118–119) notes there are six basic kinds of questions that can be asked of people, and they can be used with any topic. These are questions about

- *experience/behavior*—actions the interviewer would have observed if present;
- *opinion/belief*—people's thoughts about the interview's target(s) revealing "goals, intentions, desires, and values";
- *feelings*—emotional responses to the target(s);
- *knowledge*—facts about the target(s);
- *senses*—what is seen, heard, tasted, touched, or smelled (the "stimuli" to which the respondent is subject); and
- *background/demographics*—location of the respondent relative to others.

This typology of questions may be suggestive when framing an interview schedule. Patton (1987) further notes that each may be asked about the past, present, and future. An experienced interviewer, Patton finds the sequence of the above topics a useful ordering for schedules. (See also the section on querying sensitive topics in chapter 24.)

The Focused Interview

Exploratory and emergent studies start by searching broad areas to find what is significant. As the study progresses, questioning focuses on increasingly narrow areas, probing in some depth for detail. An interview format that encompasses both ends of this structure in a single interview, allowing exploration and targeted information gathering in the same sitting, is the **focused interview** (Merton, Fiske, & Kendall, 1956, 1990).

The focused interview begins with broad questions and with nondirective responses (discussed in the section after next), then moves to semi-structured questions, and finally to structured ones. The last section tests the researcher's ideas about what was significant and its effects. For example, in a voting literature study the researcher might ask early in the interview: "What did you think of the brochure?" But toward the end, the questions are quite structured. Early interview material provides focus for the structured parts so that the questions are continually evolving—for example, having learned that fear of being an outsider was an important reaction: "Did the cartoon on the back page that showed neighbors poking fun at the protesting nonvoter make you want to prevent that from happening to you?" Later questions corroborate insights from early ones.

> ▌ Interviews can range from being highly structured to relatively unstructured.
>
> ▌ Unstructured interviews are useful for exploring issues. They must be conducted by skilled personnel and analyzed by professionals. The nature of the sample may be progressively determined as responses suggest new leads.
>
> ▌ Highly structured interviews can be used with less skilled personnel and are easier to analyze than less structured interviews. They require professional time in planning, devising, and pretesting. When they are used for measuring the responses of a population, the nature of the sample is generally carefully specified.
>
> ▌ Focused interviews can combine exploration and structure, starting broadly and then narrowing.

Using Rapport Builders

No interview succeeds unless the interviewer builds a relationship with the respondent in which both are comfortable talking with one another. The ability to develop rapport at the same time one gets the information desired is one of the most important skills of an interviewer. The initial experience of Ely's (1991) student, Ewa Iracka, is not uncommon: "My first interview can be compared to taking a puppy for a walk. In the attempt to make the respondent feel comfortable, I wound up being led everywhere except for where I had intended to go" (p. 64). Studying men who were primary caregivers of their children, another of Ely's (1991) students, Steve Spitz, found it important to adapt to the interviewee:

> During the next few interviews I was reminded of the never-ending variability among people. Not every participant was as open and articulate as Barry. Ira, for example, was much harder to get to know. . . . In the end it became a matter of . . . adapting the questions and probes to each participant's style. . . . My experience with Ira . . . heightened my sensitivity to each participant's unique style. (p. 68)

The rhythm of questioning, taking turns speaking so that the flow is natural and sustained, is important to develop. Various things can throw you off—a waiter drops a tray of dishes, or you are prepared for one person and find that another was substituted. Ely's (1991) student, Patricia Thornton, remarks: "Interviews suffered because I was busy trying to regain my equilibrium and switch gears . . . to ask appropriate questions for that [unexpected] person" (p. 63).

Avoid questions that can be answered with just a "yes" or "no"; they will stop the conversation—what else is there to say? To break this unproductive rhythm of interchanges, you might ask, "Tell me how you felt in that situation" rather than "Were you happy in that situation?"

Some kind of rejoinder by the interviewer is important to stimulate full responses. Lansing, Withey, and Wolfe (1971) found that typically, only 28% of interviewers gave enough feedback for an adequate response by the interviewee. Unfortunately, a similar percentage (24%) elicited an inadequate response. Still worse, 55% earned a refusal to answer. The 55% may consist largely of probes, but if we consider any interviewer response as positive reinforcement (which their study shows it nearly always is), this pattern reinforces the wrong response tendencies. Remembering to reinforce full and thorough responses is essential.

The emphasis needs to be on the respondent. Patton (1987) quotes Zeno of Citium in 300 BC, who advised, "The reason why we have two ears and only one mouth is that we may listen the more and talk the less" (p. 108). As Dick DeLuca, Ely's (1991) student, put it:

> The best advice anyone can give is to LISTEN, LISTEN—AND LISTEN SOME MORE. . . . Take care to observe . . . body language—tone, gestures, posture, eye movements. For example, if a question evokes a startled look, . . . ask, "From that look, I assume you didn't expect that question, could you tell me why?" (pp. 66–67)

Recall that Whyte (1957), when he asked an inappropriate question, was told to be quiet and listen. He did and found the answers to questions he didn't know enough to ask.

Particularly if you have an agenda for the interview, it is easy to slip out of the listening mode. This happened to Rosengarten (1981): "I played over the morning's tape. . . . I was astonished at how little of Ned's talk had reached my inner ear. The problem was, I had set out to question, not to listen. My mind was full of chatter and thoughts about my questions" (p. 124).

The solution reached by Rosengarten is worth noting:

> Let the machine record and you listen. Afterwards, listen to the recording with an adversarial ear. . . . [That is what I did.] I got into the pattern of listening deliberately to our tapes the evenings of the days we recorded. In these hours I planned questions, . . . listened for gaps in the stories, . . . for allusions to people or incidents I wanted to hear more about, . . . for extraordinary events [to follow up], . . . and for inconsistencies. (p. 124)

Using the time out of the interview situation to analyze and plan allowed him the best of both worlds, what he called "pure listening" and "deliberate listening." He found that "You need to listen both ways. . . . Whenever I was stymied, I found . . . going back to pure listening had the effect of sharpening my sense of Ned." Thus, he managed to put together Ned's autobiography "in a way that conformed to this sense—or essence—of him" (p. 124).

The interviewer telegraphs messages by body language, voice intonation, and other subtle clues. If the interviewer signals discomfort, the tension often spreads to the respondent. In a nonthreatening situation the reverse may occur, and a secure respondent may put the interviewer at ease. But because setting the mood mostly depends on the interviewer, it is very important to learn the art of building rapport.

Respondents realize they are being interviewed when an interview is requested and its purpose given (Patton, 1980). In an unstructured interview, however, respondents may not even realize they are being interviewed; indeed, if questioned, the interviewer may give a false reason. This tactic is subject to the same ethical and practical problems as covert participant observation.

Interview location can be important. Interviewing in the respondents' home or office allows them to relax in their own territory, but phone calls and other business may create complications. There also may be other distractions; for example, Skipper and McCaghy (1972, from Hammersley & Atkinson, 1995) interviewed a stripper in her dressing room. "It was clear to us that the nudity and perceived seductiveness of the stripper, and the general permissiveness of the setting had interfered with our role as researchers" (pp. 239–240). Thereafter, they conducted their interviews in a restaurant.

> ▶ Establish rapport to get full and truthful responses.
>
> ▶ Establish a comfortable rhythm of back-and-forth conversation.
>
> ▶ Use questions that require more response than a mere "yes" and "no."
>
> ▶ Be sure to respond positively to the kind of responses you want to encourage.
>
> ▶ Interview in a place where you both can be comfortable.
>
> ▶ Use body language to set the mood of the interview.
>
> ▶ Above all, *listen!*

The Nondirective Approach

This is an approach that every interviewer should master. It requires the interviewer to rephrase and reflect to the interviewee the underlying feelings and central significance of the previous response. For instance, in a study of voting literature, the initial question might be, "What do you think of the literature you received on voting?" Respondent: "I don't like people bringing literature to my home that implies I am not a good citizen if I didn't vote; I pay my taxes like anyone else." Interviewer: "I just want to be sure I'm getting this right; you were unhappy with the literature you received? It seemed too preachy?" When followed by the interviewer's look of anticipation, the respondent is encouraged to elaborate on the answer and, if necessary, correct the rephrasing. Note also, that the interviewer found the underlying feeling of unhappiness as the significant emotion to reflect. In nondirective interchanges, the interviewer is attentive, and the restatement implicitly conveys the personal worth and acceptance of a person whose answer was important enough to rephrase.

Nondirective interviewing doesn't mean that the interviewer cedes all direction to the respondent. Whyte (1953, as found in Hammersley & Atkinson, 1995) gives an example of "steering" in the responses given to a union official handling grievances in a steel plant:

> *Whyte:* I'm trying to catch up on things that have happened since I was last here to study this case. . . . I think probably the best thing to start [with] would be if you could give your own impressions. . . . Do you think things are getting better or worse, or staying about the same? . . .

> *Whyte:* That's interesting. You mean that it isn't that you don't have problems, but you take them up and talk them over before you write them up, is that it? . . .

> *Whyte:* That's very interesting. I wonder if you could give me an example of a problem that came up recently, or not so recently, that would illustrate how you handled it sort of informally without writing it down. . . .

> *Whyte:* That's a good example. I wonder if you could give me a little more detail about the beginning of it. Did Mr. Grosscup first tell you about it? How did you first find out? . . .

> *Whyte:* I see. He first explained it to you and you went to the people on the job to tell them about it, but then you saw that they didn't understand it?

Notice, that, in contrast to reflecting the underlying feelings, which is what is normally practiced in the nondirective approach, the interviewer is responding to the overt content in the responses. He then questions to get more depth and detail. He uses the restating and reflecting of the nondirective approach, which maintains rapport but keeps control of the direction of the discussion in the choice of what is restated.

Nondirective responses build rapport and are particularly valuable in getting respondents to talk about their answers. The implied *is-that-correct?* response has an unfinished quality that calls for further elaboration, yet it conveys the direction of what is significant to the interviewer. If incorrect or inadequate, the respondent can correct it: "I felt really mad." The result is that whereas, on average, structured questions result in more talk by the interviewer than the respondent, the nondirective approach reverses this ratio.

In many instances the best response is minimal—a simple "Uh huh" or "Yes" said with a rising inflection that signifies *tell me more*. "Yes, I see, I never thought of that, but . . ." Sometimes a wave of the hand, a questioning eyebrow, or a similar natural gesture implicitly says "and . . ." At other times more direct probes are needed: "Tell me about . . . ," "Could you tell me more about that," "If I understand you correctly, . . ." Note how Whyte's responses start with approving comments: "That's interesting . . . ," "That's a good example . . . ," "I see." Sometimes materials are used for prompts. For example, Lancy and Zupsic (1991), studying parent–child interaction in learning to read, used a list of activities with which the parent was familiar as the interview basis, asking questions like, "What do you think about item #8, 'Share family stories with your children'?" (p. 16).

> ▶ Nondirective interviewing involves rephrasing and reflecting to the interviewee the underlying feelings and central significance of the previous response. It is an important skill to learn.

ELECTRONIC INTERVIEWING

E-mail, instant messaging, and telephone interviewing (including low-cost voice-over-Internet protocol—e.g., VoIP, like Skype) have advantages and disadvantages over face-to-face interviewing, depending on what is wanted. For instance, all make it possible to interview individuals who would be difficult or costly to access for face-to-face sessions. Besides eliminating travel, these methods may make it possible to discuss sensitive topics, to engage shy individuals, and to access individuals in places that are difficult (e.g., hospitals) or dangerous (e.g., war zones) to enter. All require access to appropriate equipment; e-mail and instant messaging limit the choice of respondents to those with computer familiarity and access. All provide fewer social clues than face-to-face contact; clues successively decrease with telephone usage, instant messaging, and e-mail—with emoticons and without them (i.e., graphics that portray mood, such as ☺ or ☹). There is some evidence that emoticons don't make much difference. Similarly, the likelihood of a spontaneous response is greatest with face-to-face and telephone, and less with answer-when-convenient instant messaging and e-mail. E-mail and instant messaging are less intrusive and self-transcribing, thus eliminating a costly step.

"The best words . . . to separate . . . [face-to-face] from e-mail interviews are FLOW and DYNAMICS [spontaneous slowing down, getting louder, laughing together], both of which . . . contribute to greater depth and quality of information" (Hodkinson, 2000, emphasis in original, as found in Mann & Stewart, 2000, p. 127). Schaefer and Dillman (1998) compared conventional mail and e-mail questionnaire returns in an experimental study involving a computer literate sample (university faculty). They found comparable response rates, but faster returns from e-mail as well as more complete and longer responses, especially for open-ended questions. Web-based questionnaires, with some technical savvy, can appear just as a paper questionnaire would, but open-end questions require some keyboarding skill of respondents. (For more, see Bampton & Cowton, 2002 and Mann & Stewart, 2000; for telephone interviewing see chapter 24.)

SAMPLING INTERVIEWEES

Selecting interviewees is, of course, determined by what information is sought. Purposive interviewing or theoretical sampling (Glaser & Strauss, 1967) is the most common pattern—that of selecting individuals who meet some information need or provide special access. The article by Hoffmann-Riem in chapter 1 provides an excellent example of sampling decisions. Wanting a representative sample, she considered using the adoption agency records for a random or stratified sample. But she rejected the idea (see "sampling," p. 12) because doing so would have reminded parents of whatever experiences they might have had with the agency's administration. Instead, she chose a discussion group and compared its characteristics with those of a year's applicants to show typicality.

Access and openness to supplying information are important reasons for choosing interviewees but they are often overtaken by the requirements of *purposive sampling*, which is used:

• to fill in a missing piece of information;

• to check another person's statement;

• to cover a kind or type of person not yet included;

• to find those who can extend in depth what is already known;

• to take the interview into new areas; or

• to corroborate a hypothesis or theory by finding varied new cases where it ought also to apply, as well as those borderline and inapplicable cases that define its generality limits. (Refer to the sidebar on conceptual analysis on pp. 279–280.)

There may be times, however, when you are simply trying to characterize a group as a whole. Then, either stratified sampling (if you know certain characteristics that should properly be represented) or random sampling may be best. In an observation situation, constructing a sampling plan ahead of time using a random number table avoids unconsciously being drawn toward better dressed or otherwise attractive individuals (for example, plan to interview the fifth person you meet, then the third, and so forth).

Multiple Interviewers and Respondents

Anyone who has done interviewing knows there are times when help would have been extremely welcome. For example, an exasperated interviewer may need to repair rapport and regain composure. Having someone else record responses allows the interviewer to concentrate on the interaction. **Tandem interviewing** is one answer. It is more difficult to "pull the wool over the eyes" of two people. Kincaid and Bright (1957) used a male–female team to interview business elites. The help available for rephrasing increased the accuracy of questioning. Leading questions with suggested answers were caught; ambiguous replies were pressed to resolution. Rapport was greater because respondents always had at least one interviewer's full attention as well as a same-gender person to relate to. It also simplified recording and coding.

Interviewing multiple respondents in a group permits discrimination of unique from mainstream responses merely by asking for a show of hands in agreement. By demonstrating a situation's range of meanings to various individuals, such groups help us learn what to ask and how best to ask it. They can illuminate how people feel about an issue, political stand, or product and what is significant about it. Widely used in product development and advertising, they find the effectiveness of television commercials, the desired characteristics of projected products, and reactions to new ones.

Focus groups.   The focus group is an interview of a typically small (7- to 10-person), relatively homogeneous group representative of a target population—too much diversity causes some persons to withdraw. Circular seating facilitates spontaneous responses and interchange. Unless intended to obtain reactions to a specific item (e.g., a television commercial), focus-group interviews frequently start broadly. Wide inquiry provides the context in which to understand responses to more specific questions. One individual's comments may stimulate others. With time to collect their thoughts before speaking, responses are often more considered than in an individual interview but also more censored. At the same time, in contrast to a one-on-one interview, any person speaking out on a sensitive issue in a group often releases the inhibitions of others. However, individuals with views contrary to those of the group may be less likely to share them than in individual interviews. Although focus groups yield almost as much as individual interviews, and they are quicker and less expensive, individual interviewing is typically used to obtain depth and detail.

Morgan (2002) notes that most novices adopt a structured questioning approach:

> The ideal group would start with an opening question designed to capture the participants' interest, so that they themselves would explore nearly all of the issues that a moderator might have probed . . . a less structured approach to moderating can keep the discussion going with little more than a smile and a nod. (pp. 148–149)

Problems of focus groups include difficulties in scheduling and getting the right mix of people—educational homogeneity seems to be important. In contrast to the one-on-one interview, the group moderator doesn't have the same control over the discussion. Strong chairing may be required to prevent individuals from monopolizing the discussion or to shift its focus from interesting but largely irrelevant material. There may be a selection effect as to who can or is willing to attend and to speak. (See Krueger & Casey, 2000, for more on focus groups.)

Virtual focus groups can be convened by telephone, through instant messaging, or online as well as face-to-face. They permit geographically disparate individuals to participate, making it possible for persons unable otherwise to do so. Online groups can be synchronous (everyone online at the same time; conferencing software is available) or asynchronous (everyone contributes to the online discussion as they get around to it—like chat rooms).

After the initial online identifying contact is established, it may be difficult to be sure who is actually at the keyboard with virtual groups. Gaiser (1997, as found in Mann & Stewart, 2000) notes that unless asynchronous sessions develop a sense of self-discipline, they can wander badly or get into trouble. That means the role of the facilitator is even more important in virtual groups than in face-to-face focus groups. It may take awhile to establish a friendly atmosphere in which participants contribute freely. However, once established, there may be less inhibition than there would be in face-to-face sessions (Mann & Stewart, 2000)—a bit like opening up to a stranger whom one does not expect to see again. Nonverbal clues and verbal intonations are lacking, however, and computer access may be a limiting sampling factor. While synchronous groups' size must be limited to establish a group atmosphere, asynchronous online groups do not have this limiting factor.

> ▶ Multiple interviewers may facilitate both the conducting of the interview and the recording of the responses.
>
> ▶ Focus groups, well suited to certain problems, gather data economically. Virtual focus groups by telephone, instant messaging, e-mail, or online make it possible to assemble nonlocal groups.

How Interviewer Characteristics Affect Responses

The aim of the interview, like observation where the invisible observer is the ideal, is to minimize the impact of the interviewer on what the respondent says. This may be difficult when the interviewer is touched emotionally. For example, Ely's (1991) student Flora Keshishian "found that I was too busy trying to imagine how he felt when called 'fat' to follow him, let alone tease a question out of that conversation. . . . In fact it was Sam who reminded me to take notes" (p. 60).

When a respondent describes an emotion-laden experience, in an effort to build rapport, interviewers are often moved to share their own similar past. While this does build rapport, care must be taken. Ewa Iracka, Ely's (1991) student who interviewed immigrants, learned this: "Being a foreign born person myself, I wanted to tell them that I understood what they were feeling . . . . [But] expressing these thoughts . . . would have slanted the interview. . . . Detachment was and is a difficult state for me to maintain" (p. 60).

Numerous studies have investigated how interviewer characteristics such as race, gender, status, sex, and religion affect the interview. It was originally thought that it was best to match the race of the interviewer to the respondent. However, a number of studies have shown significantly different responses under matching and mismatching conditions.

For unknown reasons, as Ornstein and Phillips (1978) point out, some questions produce different results from white and African American interviewers but others do not (p. 233). They note, for example, that Schuman and Converse (1971) used both African American and white interviewers to question African Americans two weeks after the assassination of Martin Luther King, Jr. Although they discovered differences, they also found no differences where some might be expected. For example, the race of the interviewer made no difference on questions such as whether the assassination would likely drive African Americans and whites further apart or whether interviewees had ever taken part in nonviolent civil rights protests.

But Daves, Krosnick, Callegaro, and De Keulenaer (2006) found that in a mayoral race between an African American woman and a white male, there was an interaction effect between race and gender of the interviewer—the highest likelihood of voting for the African American woman was found with an African American woman interviewer. The race effect continues to be difficult to predict.

Status and race are often intertwined because whites are often perceived as high in status when interviewing low socioeconomic-status African Americans. Considering status alone, however, the results are still mixed. Some investigators have concluded that lack of rapport is a problem when levels of status are different; but when they are alike and rapport is high, it is possible that the interview "takes on the quality of a social visit . . . as both of the participants become overly concerned about maintaining the pleasant atmosphere." As a result, good reporting suffers (Ornstein & Phillips, 1978, p. 234).

Religion may seem an invisible characteristic, but it has also been found to bias responses even when no apparent identification of the interviewer's religion is given. Cosper (1972), for example, found results regarding consumption of alcoholic beverages related to the stereotype of drinking in the interviewer's religion. Protestant fundamentalists found few reports of heavy drinking; Catholics and liberal Protestants found more. Hyman (1954), querying about Jewish influence in the business world, found more negative responses addressed to non-Jewish interviewers. Perhaps an interviewer's values are conveyed either more consistently than are differences in race or status, or more subtly so that they work subliminally and thus they are harder for the interviewer to control.

Studies also show response differences with respect to same- and different-gender interviewers, but contemporary changes in attitudes toward women make past data questionably applicable.

Though most of these findings involve hired interviewers, when doing your own interviewing they should sensitize you to the potential influence of race, gender, religion, and other bias sources. Such sources should be written about in memos, considered in interpreting data, and those considerations conveyed to the audience. Further, if you suspect bias due to the match between interviewer and respondent characteristics, a pilot study of matches and mismatches may well be worth the effort.

> ▶ Interviewer–respondent interaction effects appear to be quite subtle but can influence interview responses. Where they are suspected, use pilot studies to determine the nature and seriousness of such effects and write about it in memos.

Tips on Interviewing and Hallmarks of an Interview

Heeding the following suggestions[2] will improve your interviewing technique and are hallmarks of good interview procedures.

- Identify yourself and set the respondent at ease; then prepare to listen. "Listen more, talk less" (Seidman, 1991, p. 56).

- The respondent's reaction often mirrors that of the interviewer. The respondent will know if you are uncertain and uneasy. Your pleasant, positive, well-informed approach will be reflected in the interviewee's readiness to respond.

- If you want longer and detailed responses, reinforce those kinds of answers—say, "Yes," "Okay," or "I see," or nod. Using similar reinforcers for nonresponsive answers gives the wrong signal; save them for responsive answers.

- Teach and motivate the respondent by using feedback expressions like these: "Thanks, this is the sort of information we're looking for in this research." "It's important to us to get this information." "These details are helpful." "It's useful to get your ideas (your opinion) on this." "I see; that's useful information." "Let me get that down" (Cannell, 1985b).

(continued)

- Master the **probe**: repeat the question; give an expectant pause (an expectant look or nod of the head); possibly repeat, summarize, or reflect the feeling tone of the reply. Say: "Anything else?" "How do you mean?" "Could you tell me more about it?" "I'm not sure I know what you mean by that (bewildered look)." "Could you tell me a little bit more?" However, don't overuse these kinds of questions, or the respondent will think you can't recognize a valid answer.

- When probing recall, use probes that give memory cues of items likely to be forgotten. For example, if probing hospitalization, say, "Well, people quite frequently forget; it is more difficult to remember just an overnight hospitalization, for instance. Was there any chance you had something like this?" (Cannell, 1985a).

- "The key to asking questions . . . is to let them follow, as much as possible, from what the participant is saying" (Seidman, 1991, p. 59).

- Explore discordant responses such as laughter after something that isn't funny in order to get in-depth responses (Seidman, 1991, pp. 67–68). Similarly, probing where body language—gestures, posture—is incongruent with what is said may open up new areas.

- Rather than interrupting, make a note when something incidental but of particular interest to you comes up; then bring it up later in the interview: "Awhile back you talked about . . ." (Seidman, 1991, pp. 60–61).

- Tolerate silence. Your discomfort with silence will be telegraphed to your respondent. "Thoughtfulness takes time; if interviewers can learn to tolerate . . . silence . . . they may hear things they would never have heard if they had leapt in with another question . . . ." (Seidman, 1991, p. 70).

- Maintain enough control of the interview to achieve your purpose. You may need to interrupt long-winded, unfocused responses with something like, "Let me stop you here . . . I want to make sure I understand something you said earlier" (and then ask an on-target question) or "I want to get to that later. First I want to ask . . ." (Patton, 1987, p. 132).

- When overtly interviewing, sit in a comfortable spot without distractions where you can record the responses verbatim, using abbreviations to get them down. Record abbreviations, probes, and interviewer comments in parentheses. Write as the respondent talks.

ADDITIONAL READING

For general discussions on interviewing: Whyte (1984), chapter 6; Ely (1991), pp. 57–69; Seidman (1991); Gubrium and Holstein (2002); and Weiss (1994). For an example of using structured, semi-structured, and unstructured interviews to study learning, see DeGroot (2002). For comparison of face-to-face with electronic interview forms, see Opdenakker (2006).

For an example of grounded theory interview questions, see Charmaz (2002, pp. 679–680); for focus groups, Morgan (2002) and Krueger (1994); for Internet interviewing, Bampton and Cowton (2002), Mann and Stewart (2002). See also chapter 24 of this book regarding the formulation of questions; questionnaire development is similar to preplanning interviews.

For free cross-platform transcription software visit the Express Scribe Web site at http://www.nch.com.au/scribe. For useful information on transcribing see http://www.audiotranskription.de/english/.

IMPORTANT TERMS AND CONCEPTS

focus group
focused interview
nondirective interviewing
probe

structured interview
tandem interviewing
unstructured interview

OPPORTUNITIES FOR ADDITIONAL LEARNING

1. David Apple is a researcher who is interested in establishing what barriers, if any, exist to children's use of personal computers at the elementary school level. He has received permission to carry out his study at selected elementary schools and has decided to supplement his participant observation by interviewing a sample of students from all grade levels (kindergarten to grade 6). What style of interview might he use?

2. Margy Darby is studying how the roles of secretaries have changed in her university as computerized word processing made faculty more responsible for their own correspondence. She knows she needs data on time spent on various kinds of activities, but she also wants to determine any other ramifications. What kind of interview should she use?

3. Suggest a nondirective interviewer response that would build rapport, yet elicit further details to the following comment by a respondent female:

> I tried working as a salesperson in the funeral business and thought I was quite good at it. But no matter how hard I tried, I couldn't win the respect of the men. It was a boys' network and I just couldn't break into it. Finally I just couldn't take it any longer.

How would your response differ, depending on whether you are a male or a female interviewer? Compose sample responses from interviewers of both sexes.

4. Comment on the interviewer's response in this interchange:

Female informant: I know I owe him a considerable amount of money, and it could affect our relationship of living together if I don't pay it back. Yet I don't seem to be able to set aside enough to make payments.

Male interviewer: You seem increasingly uncomfortable about owing money, but not guilty enough to change the situation. How do you think it will get changed?

Compare your answers with those following the Application Exercise.

APPLICATION EXERCISE

How might interview data facilitate your understanding of the phenomena you plan to study? Whom might you interview, and for what purpose? How would you select that sample? How would you record the data? How much structure of interviewer roles would be most helpful? Of respondent roles? What kinds of interviewer–respondent interactions, if any, would you expect to arise?

KEY TO ADDITIONAL LEARNING OPPORTUNITIES

1. Children represent a special and often difficult group with which to conduct interviews. Further, the responses David might obtain from the youngest will likely be quite different from those of the older children. Given that and the fact that his purpose here is exploratory, he will want to use either an unstructured or a partially structured style. These approaches will allow him to ask open-end questions and to follow up any leads or unusual answers. Use of a nondirective technique would allow him to establish better rapport with the children and to encourage freer responses. Conducting group interviews, particularly with the younger children, might help overcome their natural shyness toward strangers.

2. Margy's best choice would be a focused interview that begins with broad questions and then narrows to the specific "hard" data she needs regarding time allocations. The latter could even take the form of a questionnaire for respondents to complete.

3. A female interviewer might say, "You felt really shut out didn't you! Do you recall what made you first feel that way?" This suggested response, by stressing "really," shows the interviewer's sympathy for her respondent's situation. The female interviewer's probe asking the respondent to recall the onset of her feelings provides a clear field to probe wherever it seems profitable between the time of the incident and the present.

   A male interviewer might change the lead to "Those guys really made you feel shut out didn't they!" "Those guys" is intended to distance himself from the males in that situation and thus to make him appear responsive to her feelings.

4. Presumably, because the final question is aimed at next steps, that is the direction the interviewer wants the interview to take. However, prior to that probe, his response far exceeds in feeling tone what the informant has admitted. The interviewer may be quite correct that she feels guilty, but she has not said so. His response forces the issue out in the open and could well dispel what rapport exists. Even if it doesn't, it is more likely to become the focus of the following interchanges than taking steps to do something about the problem. The first part of his response is closer in style to nondirective and, phrased as a question, might be more appropriate: "You seem increasingly uncomfortable owing money but equally disturbed by your inability to begin paying it back?"

SUMMARY

The tips section summarizes important points to be aware of in interviewing. Structuring refers to preplanning the interviewer's role. Both the interviewer's and the respondent's roles may be relatively unstructured or quite structured. Unstructured interviews are more likely to be used with the qualitative approach, and structured interviews with quantitative research. In order of increasing amounts of structure, preplanning might include: general areas to cover, specific topics to include, suggested questions to ask, specific questions to ask, or specific questions to ask in a particular order. Similarly, the respondent's role may be unstructured with open-end responses, or quite structured with the response limited to a choice among options. Exploratory interviews follow whatever leads turn up. More often, however, interviews are structured because researchers know what information they are seeking, or areas they want to cover. Interviews often start with broad exploratory questions, successively focusing on the target of interest closer to the session's end.

The skill of the interviewer is critical to getting good information. Rapport builders, which create a good feeling between interviewer and respondent, help create an atmosphere conducive to full and honest responses. The nondirective response, which reflects not only the content but especially the feeling tone of the respondent's last response, is an important tool to learn. It encourages the respondent to answer more fully, conveys an attitude of respect and worth to the respondent, and assures that the interviewer is not misinterpreting the reply.

Purposive sampling is the dominant sampling mode in qualitative method. Cases to interview are chosen to densify examples of key concepts, to find the boundaries and general outline of applicable cases, and to determine how far a generalization will transfer.

The use of multiple interviewers and/or multiple respondents is frequently advantageous. For example, multiple interviewers permit one interviewer to pick up cues the other missed, or allow the other to take over when one has lost composure. One concentrates on questioning while the other focuses on making the record.

With multiple respondents (group interviews) the interviewer can separate representative responses from those peculiar to certain individuals. In a group, a shy respondent may talk when another adopts a frank manner. Focus groups, chosen to represent a particular population, are widely used by political and commercial researchers to fathom reactions to particular communications and products.

Although the characteristics of interviewers can bias responses, research has shown that it is difficult to predict its sometimes counterintuitive direction and nature. Because bias may be subtler than researchers might anticipate, pilot studies are mandatory whenever bias is a possibility.

A Look Ahead

Because the analysis step in the qualitative research process is so critical to a study's success, we will examine it in detail in the next chapter.

Notes

[1] Excerpts in this chapter from *Doing Qualitative Research: Circles in Circles* by Margot Ely et al. (Copyright © 1991) are reprinted by permission of the author and Taylor & Francis Books, U.K.

[2] Portions of this section are based on Institute for Social Research, *Interviewer's Manual* (rev. ed.) (1976). Ann Arbor: Survey Research Center, University of Michigan, 1976.

Links to previous research

Explanation, rationale, theory, or point of view

Questions, hypotheses, models

Preplanned and emergent designs

Design/procedure

Focus   Records   Time   Comparison and Contrast   Situation   Participants

Data

Statistical analysis and/or
Narrative analysis

Conclusion

Link to next study

Explanation or rationale
of next study, etc.

chapter
15

Qualitative Data Analysis

> Art is the elimination of the unnecessary.
>
> —Pablo Picasso
>
> You will need roughly two to five times as much time for processing and ordering data as the time needed to collect it.
>
> —M. Q. Patton, *Qualitative Evaluation Methods*

In this chapter we consider starting points for developing codes and coding, including the increasingly important role of qualitative-analysis computer software. If explanations of the data are to be accepted by the audience, equally plausible rival explanations must be eliminated—one of the five judgments involved in Internal Integrity. Knowing common rival explanations that have plagued past research helps avoid future problems so in this chapter, we discuss those rival explanations potentially affecting qualitative studies. (These and others appear again in sample surveys, chapter 24, and in experimentation, chapter 21.) A discussion of the process of drawing and verifying conclusions begins in this chapter and continues in chapter 16. Finally, we end with tips on analysis.

INTRODUCTION

Analysis is the process that facilitates making interpretations from fieldwork, observation, and interviewing. It was introduced in chapter 13, where it was integrated into fieldwork; this chapter features a more detailed examination. Fieldwork tends to be an all-consuming activity with energy single-mindedly devoted to building a substantial database of notes. Fieldnotes pile up rapidly and become extensive as observation proceeds. Lila Sussman's fieldnotes for one day of observation at an elementary school, for example, amounted to 34 typewritten pages (Ornstein & Phillips, 1978, p. 327). Some studies fill many file drawers of notes. **Data reduction** quickly becomes important.

313

You probably have never thought of art as the "elimination of the unnecessary" as suggested by Picasso, but this is what the sculptor does in revealing the form hidden within the stone. Likewise the painter selects the elements in a composition and arranges them creatively. Doing good research is also part art—and part of the art of qualitative research is cutting away those notes and details that are not of consequence in order to concentrate on what is. One does this by selecting and naming those items that seem important, analyzing them, and organizing them.

If you were manually indexing this book, you would create an index card for all the items the author deemed important and organize them, collecting those dealing with the same topics into headings with subentries. In qualitative research, **coding** is the process of selecting what is important from the rest (comparable to making index cards) and naming it. Whereas the author has done much of the work of naming and organizing for the indexer, the researcher must creatively do those tasks.

This chapter is written from the standpoint of an emergent study. Some studies have a clear focus from the outset; others are fuzzier, and some mainly choose the situation to study. For the latter type, an *emergent study*, the process of selecting what is important dominates the early and middle stages of analysis. At the initial data-gathering stage, we attend to everything that might be important as well as to that which commands our attention. For beginners it is especially hard to focus. "In the early stages of a study, most of . . . [the data] looks promising. If you don't know what matters more, everything matters" (Miles & Huberman, 1994, p. 55).

But we can't record everything! Sometimes, foci emerge almost unconsciously at the outset and selectively rise above irrelevant detail. Other times, it is hard work; it takes much rereading of fieldnotes and reflection on their content to select what is significant. Gradually we sense more clearly what is important, and we write interpretive memos about the meaning of significant events, selecting them for more attention.

Through coding we selectively attach meaningful tags to words, phrases, events, situations, and so forth, naming what is potentially important about them and distinguishing them from the rest of the data. This successive selectivity culminates in purposive sampling to find those individuals and situations needed to flesh out the study. Finally, by setting forth generalizations that grew out of the data and stand above its detail—the ultimate stripping away of the unnecessary—we contribute to social science knowledge.

TECHNIQUES TO IDENTIFY CODES

Ryan and Bernard's study (2003) of the ways to induce themes from qualitative data found four categories of helpful techniques: analysis of words, scrutiny of large text blocks, analysis of linguistic features, and physical manipulation of text.

The first of these, analysis of words, corresponds closely to the discussion of indexing. It involves finding the most frequently used words (computers easily compile word-frequency lists), searching for the context in which they are used, and, in particular, noting unusual words, often local slang, or familiar words used in unfamiliar ways.

Scrutiny of large text blocks involves

- comparing and contrasting text (How does this differ from that preceding it? What is common to both? How would meaning differ coming from someone different in age, gender, race, etc.?).
- using previous experience or social science knowledge to suggest things to look for (e.g., social conflict, power and control, using theoretical perspectives).
- searching for missing information (topics expected to arise but didn't, silences where comments might be anticipated—e.g., resistance to an official government policy).

Analyzing linguistic features includes looking for metaphors, transitions, and connectors. Metaphors are ways of representing thoughts, behaviors, and experiences. Deducing what underlies different metaphors for the same phenomenon often points to themes. Transitions, paragraphs, or section headings in written text, and pauses, changes in tone of voice, or certain phrases often indicate a change in content or new theme. Linguistic connectors signify relationships that form the basis for themes. Causal relationships may be indicated by words like "because," "since," and "as a result." For conditional relationships search for "if," "or," "rather than," and "instead of."

Physically manipulating text involves marking or moving the data into categories. Thus, marking up the text with colored highlighters, using one color per theme, catches the obvious categories. Additional multiple readings turn up less obtrusive and subtle ones.

CODING ON PAPER

For years, and still today, coding for simple projects has been done with physical manipulation of text (fieldnotes, interview transcripts, etc.) and file folders. Codes were applied to selected sections of the text, and these are cut out of their context and placed in folders with other material of the same code. Material in the folders is sometimes divided into subcodes; at other times it's consolidated with like material under a coding that includes both categories. Clearly this is a laborious and, for large data sets, a cumbersome process.

CODING ON COMPUTERS

Just as quantitative researchers have for years used software to avoid routine computation, qualitative researchers increasingly use qualitative-analysis software programs to ease their labor. Once the text is put in digital form by typing or scanning it into a computer or by using speech-recognition software, the above process can be handled with qualitative data-analysis software. Such programs do "not render one's assertions more valid than using the time-honored method of cutting up fieldnotes and putting sections in file folders" (Behrens & Smith, 1996, p. 984). But the software is a significant advance as it makes coding, recoding, and retrieving text, as well as ordering, structuring, and visualizing code structure of vast and cumbersome qualitative data files feasible, leading to more complete analyses. Most individuals who dismissed computers as merely high-priced page-turners have changed their minds. But, some researchers have resisted computer usage to stay closer to their data and avoid features that may make the process seem mechanical.

The next section describes fourteen steps in the coding and analysis process. *The comments in italics embedded in nearly every step describe the role of computer software in that step's accomplishment.* The advantages and concerns of using qualitative software are summarized in a following section.

STEPS IN CODING AND ANALYSIS

The most basic process of analysis is coding. Coding is interpreting. As my colleague Sari Biklen tells her classes, "It is making decisions about what things mean." What do you code, and where do these codes come from? What you code depends on what you consider relevant and important. In coding, you assign a descriptive word or phrase to each unit of notes (not necessarily everything—some clearly will be irrelevant). Use the informant's language in a brief code title if you can (although numbers are shorter, they are removed from the concept involved and difficult to remember).

If you entered the study with a purpose, that purpose will help you decide what to code and what will be a codable unit—a phrase, a sentence, a line, a paragraph, or any selected section of text. (*Newer qualitative software is flexible regarding codable unit length; some older software isn't.*)

As we might expect, considering the varied styles people use to organize material for their own writing, there is no standard order to coding for analysis. Some researchers do all analysis after they have collected their data. Most qualitative researchers, however, concomitantly engage in observing, creating and assigning codes, and code consolidation and interpretation, but with successively shifting emphases over the study's course from observing to interpretation.

Following are the steps that can profitably be covered in the analysis process, although not necessarily in this order. A section later in the chapter offers starting points for developing codes.

1. Finding What Is Significant

The first time you sit down to read through your data is the only time you come to it fresh. Search the data for common phrases as well as surprising, counterintuitive, and unexpected material. Underline significant parts and make marginal notes to avoid losing initial impressions. Intervening experience changes perceptions. Early impressions may be especially insightful—or wrong; you will know better later.

Video recording creates extensive records that must be reviewed for analysis. But some software tools facilitate assembling segments of video, just as one uses software to assemble coded notes (see Secrist, de Koeyer, Bell, & Fogel, 2002). Artifacts may be included as data by using descriptive titles as placeholders.

Once you find the characteristics, aspects, or wording that is significant, a computer is invaluable in very quickly finding other similar occurrences. Reading your notes into a microphone for computer transcription may call your attention to inflections, asides, or phrases that might have been missed with silent reading. It slows down your processing of the material, facilitating the search for significance.

2. Loading Your Mind

Study and restudy the raw data to develop detailed, intimate knowledge of it. Reading and rereading the data seems to facilitate seeing patterns. It chunks the material in your mind so that you get past the details to the larger picture.

Look for repetitions and relationships and note these; they help devise codes. To get started, use text analysis software (find it by searching "word frequency count software") and have it compile a listing of the most common words found in the data and their frequencies. Unexpected high word frequency may suggest overlooked aspects. *Some software allows you to look for words in conjunction with others (proximity searches—two words within a specified number of words of each other), permitting you to find the location of these patterns in the fieldnotes. You may also infer such multiple word search patterns from the frequency listing. But, if what you are seeking can be expressed many different ways, you will have to supply the search alternatives.*

Figure out what is important about these similarities. Qualitative method is particularly useful for examining systems and processes where there are interactive relations among variables. Reflect complex relations in your coding and analyses instead of confining yourself to single dependent and independent variables. Look for commonalties across individuals and conditions that identify types of persons or common situations that are important to what you are studying. "Unusual participant terms are always worth following up since they often mark theoretically important or interesting phenomena" (Hammersley & Atkinson, 1995, p. 211). Reflect participants' terms in your code names as much as possible to keep the "flavor" of the situation.

3. Letting Your Unconscious Process the Data

The process suggested for finding an organization for your problem creation notes (p. 94) applies equally well to qualitative data analysis: fill your conscious mind and let your unconscious sort it out while you do other things. Your mind will be processing and organizing even while you are away from coding and sorting. Be prepared to make a record when the ideas pop into your conscious mind so they won't get lost—a note or two helps. The process of making notes itself helps fix something in your mind, and the data helps you create the rest.

In emergent studies, one doesn't initially know where one is going, so writing tends to be disorganized and subject to revision. Using a computer's word processor, which makes it easy to change, reorganize, and produce clean text without crossed-out material, facilitates the thinking process.

4. Beginning with Initial Codes

Make a list of tentative categories and code the raw data using this initial set. For example, consider the following paragraph selected from fieldnotes:

> Before class started, it was obvious that Mr. Johnson had decided to video record the segment on statistics and place it in the Instructional Materials Center so students could review it at their convenience. But it was equally obvious that he had

never handled a video camera before and, even after class started, he was still fid-
dling with the equipment, apparently attempting to get it to work. He was heard
commenting to a student, "The Dean insists we provide after-class follow-up for
all class sessions."

In a study of what kind of instructional technology was being used, you might
code this note fragment *vid* for video recording or *cl vid* for in-class video. In a study
of the technology problems of new teachers the focus might be on the difficulty with
the video camera resulting from no training. You might code it *NT/cl vid* if you're
seeking understanding of teaching behavior, rather than letting teachers' comments
"speak for themselves." We might, in Lillian Rubin's words, "try to understand what
lies behind . . . without violating their spirit or intent; to bring to the surface the
latent meanings that may lie outside the immediate awareness of the person who
speaks them" (Rubin, 1981, p. 102). Thus, depending on the tone of voice used, we
might code the teacher's remark to a student for resentment of work rules (*rsmnt*).
Each of these codes emphasizes a different aspect of this note fragment. In a study
without a preplanned purpose (an emergent study), what code should you assign?
You might code for any of these or apply multiple codes, realizing that as you accu-
mulate coded data, what is significant will emerge.

Some qualitative researchers suggest *line-by-line coding*. This results in very intensive and dense coding and can result in what is referred to as the "coding trap"—
avidly assigning codes to everything and "losing sight of the forest for the trees."
*Researchers switching from paper to computer coding are particularly susceptible to this
because of the comparative ease of coding (Gilbert, 2002).* Take a break after an intense
period of coding to consider where the work is going; write memos. You are also more
likely to avoid the coding trap if you follow the sequence of steps being described.

*Some programs require you to decide on how to chunk your data at the time of
input, and you are then limited to coding those chunks. Other programs allow what
Weitzman and Miles (1995) call* free-form coding. *It allows you to select any portion of
a text for coding, whether paragraphed or not, even allowing for selection of overlapping
sections to receive different codes. For emergent studies, where the foci may change with
the analysis, ability to free-form code can be very important.*

*Computer programs enable you to recode, consolidate, change, or divide codes with
a few keystrokes. Most software can assign multiple codes to overlapping text without
recopying the overlapped material. Some programs infer rules from your coding and can
automatically suggest codes for sections of text, refining their rules if you reject their suggestions. Where a code is triggered by the presence of a key word or phrase, in some programs you can activate automatic assignment of that code thereby saving considerable
time and energy. However, the automatic appearance of suggested code may bias one's
decision making or may lead to too readily adopting what the software suggests. In
essence this lets the computer make the decision rather than allowing you to adequately
think it through. In most instances such practice should be subjected to human review.*

5. Checking the Consistency of Title with Coded Material

Examine the relation of each code title to the actual coded material for consistency both with the title and across the material. If you use the paper method, sort

the raw data into the code titles by putting the coded and cut-out scraps of paper in piles or folders. Consider using colored paper to designate different interviews, time periods, and so on; colored highlighters to code sections of text; pinking and ordinary shears to clip corners or otherwise shape cut-out segments to code for whatever you want to keep track of: variables; codes; data sources (observations, interviews, cases, persons, sites); types of data (fieldnotes, memos); and so forth (Radnofsky, 1995).

Here is where the computer shines; it makes it easy to bring together all the material for a code in one place. This facilitates "constant comparisons of all indicators of a given code or concept" (Legeiwe, 1998, p. 277). Because reading from a monitor is limiting, you may want to print them out to scan them quickly.

6. Adjusting Code Titles for Better Fit

As you do steps 4 and 5, evaluate how well the material fits the code title. As appropriate, change the title for a better fit as you proceed. You may also find that distinctions you initially thought important aren't; combine and retitle those codes. *Easy computer recoding with the find and replace command (so much easier than relabeling all the slips of paper) is a revelation to those who formerly considered keeping a barely adequate or poor code because of the labor required to change.*

Check also for adequacy of examples for each code. Use purposive sampling to select persons and situations for additional data to bolster weak spots, as well as to fish for material to flesh out the coding picture. *Computers link code titles with their underlying material, making it easy to find underdeveloped categories.*

7. Recoding at an Interpretive Level

After this initial coding you might recode this same material at an interpretive level. In the above example of a technology use study, you might infer the intended use of the technology: *rev* (content review), *sk* (skill learning), *sk p* (skill practice), and so on. At a still deeper level of analysis, later, you might code patterns of activities, themes, causal links, and other more complex aspects that relate to a theory you are building. For example, you might discover a repeated pattern—the instructor who decides abruptly with no training or forethought to introduce technology into the instruction—and code it as *imp instr* (impulsive instructor). *You can locate the instances of these events for coding using search or find commands. Some software can do proximity searches for a combination of words within a certain number of words of each other.*

8. Developing and Testing Working Hypotheses

Develop working hypotheses about repeating patterns, especially things that follow one another regularly. These will yield classifications and principles that permit you to sort the data and observe the consistency or inconsistency of that regularity. Test these patterns with other data to see whether the proposed explanation works well enough to be a satisfactory explanation for a significant segment of the data. Then similarly analyze the rest of the data, testing with provisional trials until you are satisfied with the emerging explanations. *Again, computer searches make it easy to find other instances in the data where the explanation can be tested.*

9. Developing and Testing Generalizations

In some studies, you may seek generalizations. For example, most teachers are enticed into using technology by its promise as a labor saver. Once they begin using it, however, they concentrate on instructional improvement instead of the labor-saving aspects. Developing such a generalization requires certain steps:

1. Determine to what expectations the generalization would lead and see if those expectations are supported by the data (e.g., new technology leading teachers to try to cover more content).

2. If the expectations are not supported, determine if you can revise the generalization so as to fit both the new implications and the original data from which it was derived. (E.g., teachers becoming disillusioned with technology by trying to add too much content. Technology aids instruction when help is given during its introduction.)

3. Repeat steps (1) and (2) to see if support can be found for the revised generalization.

4. Look for data providing counterexamples of this generalization.

5. Review the case that can be made for the generalization and assemble the data that bears on it, pro and con. (Remember conceptual analysis, pp. 279–280?)

Often the difficulty is to find a generalization to test; nothing seems to emerge. Strauss and Corbin (1998) note:

> What we have discovered is that researchers often carry their analytic problems around in their heads as they go about their daily activities. Then, perhaps while reading the newspaper . . . insights occur and the analysts are able to make sense out of the previously unexplainable data. (p. 48)

It is the same advice of working off center given in the section in chapter 5 on problem creating (p. 94).

10. Developing and Testing Descriptive Types

In some studies you may seek to construct descriptive types. Assemble the best examples and describe the common features that characterize the group. For example, there may be a group of teachers making considerable use of instructional technology who have these common characteristics: (1) they were either the first or one of the earliest in the building to use instructional technology, (2) they devised their own instructional technology materials, and (3) they are perceived as more oriented to things than to people. Presumably, these three characteristics identify a teacher type. Then:

(a) Look for persons who were not included in this initial set but who are characterized by the initial distinguishing characteristic. In the case of our example, this would be a search for other teachers who make considerable use of instructional technology.

(b) Determine if additions or modifications in the initial set of characteristics will permit inclusion of the new examples, making sure the set still fits the original group. For instance, do the new teacher examples have some of these characteristics but not others (such as being early adopters and more oriented to things than to people, but using commercially prepared materials)? Depending on the purpose of the study, the type might be better defined by only characteristics (1) and (3) above, if instructional material preparation was not relevant.

(c) If the statement cannot be modified to cover both new and original data, you have a new type. Determine if there is a set of distinctive features that characterize all or a part of the new group. For example, there may be a group of intensive users who (i) were late adopters, (ii) used commercially prepared material heavily, and (iii) were perceived as more oriented to people than to things.

(d) Continue with this process until there are no more groups with common characteristics of sufficient size to be of interest. Then review the set of types to determine whether there is redundancy across types or whether similar types can be clustered into families of types. For example, these two might constitute a family of types dealing with the time of adoption; there may be other families concerned with other aspects of technology use. *As with developing any generalizations, computer search capacities facilitate type development.* (Again note the relation to conceptual analysis.)

11. Developing Graphics to Examine Code Relationships

My colleague, Anne Shelley—because a picture is worth a thousand words—argues for laying out the codes in a graphic. Graphics help us see the relation of one variable to another and facilitate developing explanations and theory. Further, they highlight code categories where the relationships are obscure—these may call for more data. Consider whether some categories ought to be hierarchically related so that there are different levels of coding. For instance, there might be a family of different errors in the use of technology that are made by new teachers that would bear the coding both for "new teachers" (*nt*), and the "kind of error": interfering technologies (*nt no mix*), or inappropriate technology for goal (*nt inapp*), and so on.

Where major codes are differentiated into more specific subcodes, lay out the relationships in outline form or as you might a hierarchical genealogical chart of your relatives, with inclusive codes for parents and the specific codes for their children. Use dotted lines to show relationships between codes. If a hierarchical structure doesn't fit, use pattern noting (see p. 102).

As another example, Anfara, Brown, and Mangione (2002) present a coding tree that shows how detailed coding is consolidated into more comprehensive codes. For example, in a study of the characteristics of middle-school teachers, the more detailed codes of "Gender issues/equity?" "Nurturing ability?" "Male advisors?" and "Only women care?" were consolidated into "Caring is women's work." It is a gradually evolving process that develops out of greater understanding of the data.

Some software programs facilitate this process by displaying the codes in a tree-like graphic, or in network diagrams with the relation of one code to another shown by arrows or labeling on the lines relating them (e.g., "are examples of," "result in," "follows," "belongs to"). "By a few mouse clicks, even the most abstract concept can be easily connected with all its indicators within the data, thus testing its groundedness" (Legeiwe, 1998, p. 278, emphasis in original). *Glesne and Peshkin (1992) note that use of graphical displays forces organization and planning and encourages systematic work, all of which help provide an audit trail for those who wish to review the work later.*

12. Developing Explicit Definitions of Each Code

Write a definition of each code. Delineate what falls under the code title. The definition shows its generality but also helps to define the boundaries of what is included. Provide at least a couple of instances of verbatim narrative from the data for each of the codes. If you seek to view the situation as perceived by those in it, select material in the informant's own words.

Constructing definitions often helps you see other relationships among the codes as well as the necessity for further refinement and revision of the structure. Figure 15.1 shows the interconnectedness through which codes affect analysis and are affected by it as the study involves memoing, defining, coding, searching for new positive and negative instances, relating to other codes, and contributing to the report. Arrows are double headed to indicate the flow goes both ways. A memo or an idea added to the introductory and final chapter files may suggest a code or a change in a code. That in turn may cause the creation of a new code or a change in related codes that triggers changes in what text is coded. These may result in adjustments to the network of code relationships. In short, this process often has unanticipated conse-

Figure 15.1   The relation of a code to the parts of the analysis it affects and is affected by as analysis progresses (adapted from Gibbs, 2002, p. 59).

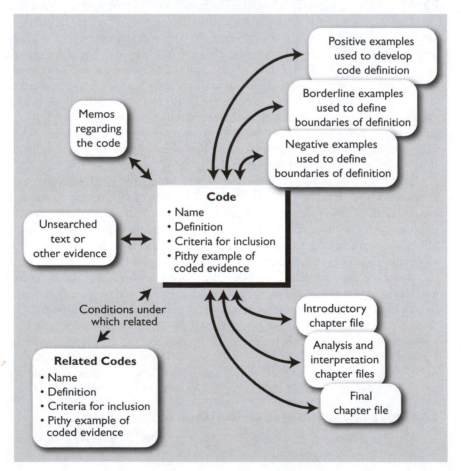

quences, but the coding structure that develops is usually stronger and better integrated as a result. *Computer hyperlinks ease the tracing of the ripple effect by showing what is linked to what else.*

Software programs facilitate this process by:

- *providing templates for each code with places for definitions and other attributes;*
- *easily searching for new examples;*
- *linking codes to memos;*
- *showing coded text in context;*
- *bringing together all the text for each code for a check on consistency and homogeneity, thereby expediting revisions and refinements; and*
- *joining codes in relationship with hyperlinks as you trace the ripple effect of changes.*

13. Relating Your Findings to Those of Other Researchers

If not done previously, but certainly before finalizing your coding and explanation, do a literature search to determine what others have learned about your topic. The search may give support to the directions in which you were already going and strengthen the case you will present when you write it up. Conversely, it may cause you to rethink or modify your coding and hypothesizing, or possibly even require you to start over in a new direction. In some instances, it will suggest rival explanations to the one you had found, thereby requiring additional field data that will test which explanation is best supported by the evidence. *See the example of a literature search* (pp. 320–327) *to see how the computer can facilitate the process.*

14. Developing the Report

Now (or better still, starting earlier), write statements describing what you believe you can best draw from the data: generalities, general perceptions or perspectives, types of individuals, actions, situations, central events, processes, strategies, interactions, and so forth. *Software programs provide hyperlinks to memos with links to related text, to other memos, and to parts of the data. This makes for easy retrieval of that material when writing the report, or acting on the suggestions in a memo.*

COMPUTER SOFTWARE FOR QUALITATIVE DATA ANALYSIS

Let's first summarize the pros and cons of using qualitative data-analysis software (the italicized material in the 14 steps above).

What Computer Software Can Do for You

Qualitative data-analysis software vary in their capabilities, but programs are available that will:

- provide for coding of text, multiple codes of material, coding of text overlapping previously coded material.
- allow annotation of text and codes.
- make video clips part of the viewable and analyzable base.

- show coded material in the context of the material that surrounds it.
- as text is coded, search for and show similar material and, if desired, link it for coding.
- automatically code where certain words or phrases appear.
- suggest codes based on previous codings.
- learn from your rejection of suggestions and appropriately modify future suggestions.
- tell what is linked to something else so you can search, find, and link to related material.
- link materials as hypertext, allowing you to immediately pull up and view the linked text.
- provide easy correction of coding as well as changes or consolidation of codes and reorganization of data.
- encourage theorizing with easy consultation across data, memos, fieldnotes, structural maps of data, interviews, and so on.
- provide graphic representations of relationships among codes and their relation to the researcher's conceptualizations of the situation.
- make complete searches of data for supporting and contradicting instances.
- connect to software that facilitates quantitative analysis of qualitative data.
- handle large sets of data.
- provide an audit trail.

Concerns about Using Software for Analysis

One possible disadvantage of computer analysis is that the learning time required to use the software makes some researchers hesitant to leave the scissors-and-paper approach. Computer users, however, argue that programs have become easier to use and that the increased ability to analyze the data leads to better studies. The cost of the programs, in terms of both money and training time, make manual processing more practical for small projects.

Unless one works from handwritten notes, the big task is typing the material into a word processor—a labor-intensive process. Although scanners can shortcut this step for already existing documents, output must be treated with a spelling program and proofread. As already noted (chapter 13, p. 288), voice translation software can practically eliminate the keyboarding step for dictation and notes read aloud. With analog-to-digital software (search "analog recordings to digital software"), recordings fed into the computer are converted into digital sound files that may be listened to and annotated (coded) for later search and retrieval. Thus, one can reduce transcription to those key stretches needed for reporting.

Perhaps the main objection to qualitative software is the concern that users will focus on the mechanical instead of on empathetic understanding, which can distance researchers from their data. The mechanical auto-code feature that seeks out and codes material similar to that already coded requires human review to add to understanding. As is often the case with technology, it is the way that it is likely to be used rather than the product of the technology itself that is often of concern.

Analysis with Word Processors Rather than Specialized Software

To avoid purchasing a costly software package, a word processor or spreadsheet program can be used for simple projects. For example, Nideröst (2002), using Microsoft Word, suggests using paragraph marks to section the data. Then use the "convert to table" function to place the paragraphs in a table, one to a row. Add a column, and number the paragraphs in the new column by using the "auto number" feature. Sorting on this column regains the original sequence at any later time. Add a column for codes. Use the sort command to bring together paragraphs with the same code. Search for causal relations by putting words in the "search" command like "because," "therefore," "of," and "why." Obtain counts of words or codes using "search and replace," entering the word to be counted and commanding it to replace itself, so that there is no actual change yet the number of changes is reported. Using "replace," one can recode and combine codes. Use a new column for subcodes of each main code, or add a numerical suffix to the main code name. This process is similar to that described for sorting notes for the literature review (see p. 126). An example of the table described above is included there as well. Carney, Joiner, and Tragou (1997) provide a similar example using WordPerfect.

Most computer-literate individuals undertaking a project of considerable size will benefit from using one of the qualitative-analysis software programs. Some programs encourage quantitative analysis of qualitative data by making it easy to tabulate and export data to qualitative-research software programs.

Choosing Qualitative-Analysis Software Programs

A very useful examination of qualitative-analysis software has been prepared by Ann Lewins and Christina Silver of the UK's CAQDAS (Computer Assisted Qualitative Data Analysis Software) Networking Project. Besides general advice they provide analyses (including screenshots) of the major qualitative-analysis software packages, a glossary of qualitative terms, and links to resources for qualitative data analysis. Note especially their final section under each package analysis under the heading "CAQDAS Networking Project Comments on . . ." Access this information at http://caqdas.soc.surrey.ac.uk/ChoosingLewins&SilverV5July06.pdf.

Harald Klein maintains a larger compilation of software descriptions. Access this information at http://textanalysis.info/.

Although Weitzman and Miles's (1995) analysis of computer programs is out-of-date, their advice regarding considerations in the choice of software programs is not. Nor is their conclusion that choice of the most appropriate software program varies with the expected nature of the study.

Choose software that has the capacities you need, but also consider other factors—for example, listservs for updates, help and discussion, and Web sites for demonstrations. Nearly all programs have free downloadable demonstration programs that you can try out for yourself. Thus, in addition to the above analyses, you can try out the program to see how easy you find it to learn.

Here are Web sites for a number of currently available software programs. The operating system is designated in parentheses:

- *ATLAS.ti*   http://www.atlasti.com/index.html (Windows)
- *The Ethnograph*   http://www.qualisresearch.com/ (Windows)
- *HyperResearch*   http://www.researchware.com/ (Macintosh and Windows)
- *Kwalitan*   http://www.kwalitan.nl/engels/index/html (Macintosh [click on "engels"])
- *MAXqda*   http://www.maxqda.com/ (Windows)
- *NVivo 7* and *XSigh*   http://www.qsrinternational.com/default.aspx (Windows) (Using data from a previous study, di Gregorio [2003] illustrates the use of NVivo for grounded theory analysis at http://latrobe.edu.au/aqr. Click on "journals" and then on "Special Issue 2003," pages 78–94.)
- *Qualrus*   http://www.ideaworks.com/qualrus/index.html (Windows)
- *SuperHperQual*   http://www.home.satx.rr.com/hyperqual/ (Macintosh)
- *TAMS*   http://www.tamsys.sf.net/osxtams/download.html (freeware Mac OS X)
- *Weft QDA*   http://www.pressure.to/qda/ (freeware for Windows and GNU/Linux)
- *QDA Miner*   http://www.provalisresearch.com/ (Windows)

QDA Miner is a qualitative-analysis program in three coordinated programs, one of which straddles the boundary between qualitative and quantitative analysis. It is supported by WordStat for text analysis and by SimStat for numeric analysis. Through word counts and the association of certain words with particular others, it can show the similarity of individuals in terms of codes and identify subgroups of people and problems. For examples of how these tools can be used see the following Web sites:

- http://www.provalisresearch.com/QDAMiner/QDAMinerShots.html
- http://www.provalisresearch.com/wordstat/WordStatstudies.php

Welsh (2002), in a comparison of manual and computer analyses, notes instances where manual actions are needed (such as in searches) to supplement those of computer software and concludes, "It is important that researchers recognize the value of both manual and electronic tools in qualitative data analysis and management and do not reify one over the other but instead remain open to, and make use of, the advantages of each."

> ▶ The mechanical aspects of handling data can be substantial. This task is increasingly being taken over by specialized computer programs.
>
> ▶ Computer processing eases data management, but its greatest contribution is to facilitate development of better coding structures.
>
> ▶ Ease of recoding means the researcher is likely to work longer at getting a good fit.
>
> ▶ By providing graphical portrayals of the code structure, some software gives a perspective that facilitates theory building.
>
> ▶ Some programs can incorporate video clips as data, as well as export and import tables and data for quantitative analysis.

SUGGESTED STARTING POINTS FOR CODING

We noted earlier that, especially with focused and preplanned studies (for example, the evaluation of a program against its stated goals), we could establish a set of tentative codes at the outset. For studies in which the problem is emergent, many qualitative researchers, including Strauss (1987), suggest reading the fieldnotes and inductively picking out the important aspects as provisional codes that can be revised later as necessary. Certainly, our initial ideas about what is significant will bear heavily on what we look for. How should you start? Some alternatives:

Strauss's Process

Strauss (1987) suggests, as a way of getting started, coding *conditions, interaction among actors, strategies and tactics,* and *consequences* (pp. 28–29). To find conditions, look for words like: "because," "since," "as," and "on account of" (easily done with the "find" command on the computer). To find consequences, look for: "as a result of," "because of," and similar expressions.

Next, Strauss (1987) suggests moving to *dimensions* (abstractions, concepts, constructs, generalizations) as quickly as possible, each of which will suggest comparative cases to be examined for these dimensions. Strauss calls this *axial coding,* because items are coded around the axis of a dimension. For example, in observing outbreaks of disruptive student behavior, Kounin (see p. 36 of this book) noticed the impact of connectedness of instruction. He termed this "momentum," a dimension along which the observations of teachers could be coded.

Lofland's Generic Codes

By way of providing more structure, especially for beginners, Miles and Huberman (1994, p. 61) suggest using Lofland's (1971) generic scheme to code:

- *Acts*—action in a situation that is temporarily brief, consuming only a few seconds, minutes, or hours.
- *Activities*—action in a setting of longer duration (days, weeks, months) constituting significant elements of people's involvement.
- *Meanings*—the verbal productions of participants that define and direct action.
- *Participation*—people's holistic involvement in, or adaptation to, a situation or setting under study.
- *Relationships*—interrelationships among several persons considered simultaneously.
- *Settings*—the entire setting under study conceived as the unit of analysis.

Bogdan and Biklen

A different scheme is provided by Bogdan and Biklen[1] (2007, pp. 174–179):

- *Setting/context codes*—general description of the setting that allows you to place the study into a larger context (e.g., descriptions of elementary schools).
- *Definition-of-the-situation codes*—how subjects understand, define, or perceive their setting or relevant study topics (e.g., feminist perspectives).

- *Perspectives held by subjects*—ways of thinking shared by subjects toward the setting or some aspect of it. Try to capture shared understandings (e.g., "be honest but not cruel" is a recognition of what is best in informing parents in a medical setting).

- *Subjects' ways of thinking about people and objects*—understandings of each other, of outsiders, and objects that make up their world (e.g., teachers differentiate students as "immature" or "ready for school").

- *Process codes*—sequences of events, transitions from one status to another, changes over time (e.g., turning points, benchmarks, stages, phases, and careers).

- *Activity codes*—regularly occurring kinds of behavior (e.g., the showing of films, morning exercises, and so on).

- *Event codes*—particular happenings that occur infrequently or once (e.g., a strike or a pageant).

- *Strategy codes*—ways people accomplish things using tactics, methods, techniques, or ploys (e.g., how students get out of hall duty).

- *Relationship and social structure codes*—cliques, friendships, romances, coalitions, enemies, and other regular behavior not defined on the organizational chart.

- *Narrative codes*—the structure of talk, the narrative, itself.

- *Methods*—problems, joys, dilemmas of the research process (usually consisting of observer comments).

Understanding the Data

While the starting points above may provide clues regarding what kinds of things to look for, Miller (Crabtree & Miller, 1999b) describes the process of gaining understanding of data as a series of readings of the data:

> The first time I just read . . . without any preconceptions, . . . and look at key themes, emotions and surprises. . . . I reflect back on moments where I was surprised . . . and where did I notice emotions in my self.
>
> In second readings, I specifically read for those themes [I noticed on first pass], the evidence that supports those themes, [and evidence that is] against [them]. . . . I am looking to better understand.
>
> In the third readings, I will go back again to see if there is anything else important that I missed.
>
> In the fourth reading, I force myself to come up with one, two or three alternative understandings . . . . Fourth readings force me to take on other personas— would I have a different perspective if I were another person.
>
> Fifth readings: If I come up with discrepancies [during the fourth reading], are there ways to link them together? (p. 186)

These many rereadings are likely to be time consuming, but they facilitate a thorough understanding of what is in the data as well as reducing the likelihood of bias by forcing the researcher to explore the data from different angles.

EXAMPLES OF CODING AND INFERENCE

One process of coding and inference is briefly but clearly described in the Hoffmann-Riem study in chapter 1. Reread the section on Data Interpretation (p. 13). Note how the author wrote up each couple's story, sectioning them into standard broad areas: motivation, adoption process, and relation development (a coarse coding to be further refined). Then she proceeds across the cases to find commonalities. Next, using certain common aspects within each of her broad initial three categories, she seeks their boundaries by determining case variety. Finally she constructs *polar*— that is, opposite—types to see how cases differed from one another and fills in the gaps between the extremes with other cases. Her process in perspective: establishing rough coding, seeking commonalities, developing finer coding, relating codes to dimensions representing major findings, and selecting cases to illustrate and give meaning to the ends and middle of each dimension. This is a common sequence.

How to find interrelationships and generalizations, however, seems to vary with the individual. Bosk (1979) kept a running analysis separate from his fieldnotes. Gans (1962) abstracted generalizations from his field diary onto more than 200 cards, which he sorted and classified. He then digested these into notes listing the major generalizations. He reread the diary and wrote the report. Strauss (1987) suggests finding families of categories and core categories that represent the higher-level abstractions making up the theoretical network. Notice that these methods all involve writing down ideas. Putting ideas on paper, as we noted earlier, does more than provide a record; it helps to organize our thoughts.

FACILITATING ANALYSIS WITH MATRICES

Miles and Huberman (1994) find that matrices and diagrams displaying the interrelationships among variables, persons, and situations are of considerable help in organizing the data, finding relationships, and eliminating alternative hypotheses. In qualitative analysis, a matrix is a table displaying information that describes the relation between two or more variables. An example is Table 15.1 (on the following page), which is part of a matrix summarizing the results of a school improvement program across sites. Sites were arranged from high (Masepa), to medium (Carson), to low program impact (Burton). Successive columns across the page describe program objectives, the direct positive and negative results, and the indirect effects and side effects for each site. Each effect is marked to indicate the sources of data: U for user (teacher), A for administrator, C for counselor, P for parent, E for evaluator, and S for student. Bold, italicized letters indicate a mention by at least two persons; x indicates the presence of a dissenting or conflicting opinion.

Use of such a symbol system, when combined with juxtaposition of the data in such a matrix, facilitates the interpretation of a tremendous amount and variety of information. For example, by comparing rows, you can see that at a high-impact school (Masepa) many effects were observed, both direct and indirect; whereas at a low-impact school (Burton) there were few effects and only direct ones. Some impor-

Table 15.1 Matrix Summarizing the Effects of a School Improvement Program across Different Schools

Sites	Objectives	Direct Effects		Indirect and Side Effects	
		Positive	Negative	Positive	Negative
Masepa (externally developed innovation)	Improvement in full range of language arts skills More on-task behavior Improved discipline	Improved skills: vocabulary U, A, P; spelling *U*, A; phonetics *Ux*; punctuation *U*; reading comprehension Ux, E; reading decoding U; grammar U; written expression U Low achievers more productive Ux	Retention levels not good *U* Too little diversity U Student fatigue U	Concentration, study skills U, A Fewer discipline problems *U*, A More attentive to errors *U* Better academic self-concept *U* More enjoyment, enthusiasm U, A	Some lagging, failing mastery tests *U* Boredom *U*
Carson (locally developed innovation)	Increased achievement Clearer career interests Friendliness Improved self-concept as a learner More internal locus of control	Career knowledge U, A, C		Achievement composite (use of resources) E Better classroom attitude U Attitude to school E, *U* Self-concept as a learner (high school) E Friendliness E Self-understanding U	Little effect on achievement U
Burton (externally developed innovation)	Knowledge & practical skills re political/ government/ legal processes (voter education, state government, individual rights)	Concept learning by being in different roles U Experienced active learning approach A	No effects discernible *U*		

Source: Adapted from M. B. Miles & A. M. Huberman, *Qualitative Data Analysis* (2nd ed.), p. 191. Copyright © 1994 Sage Publications.

tant effects were both observed by the teacher users and confirmed by an administrator or counselor (those labeled U, A, C). Few observations are labeled "x," indicating that dissenting opinions were rare, although one appears next to what would otherwise be a very important result at Masepa: "Low achievers more productive." Thus, from this matrix, in addition to comparing the impact of the program at different schools, you can assess evidence in terms of the source of the data and whether it was confirmed by more than one source or contradicted by a dissenting opinion.

In addition, matrices such as Table 15.1 enable us to see other things. Do administrators always show up only on the positive comment side? Apparently. Are locally developed innovations (Carson) more successful? Not according to these data. They make clear where we have data and where they are missing (Burton's "Indirect and Side Effects"). Like Mendeleyev's periodic table of the chemical elements, they permit prediction and search for missing entries, sometimes with useful and surprising results.

Miles and Huberman (1994) is a superb source of suggestions for such matrices, graphic displays, and network designs. Their book contains many examples as well as advice on their construction and use. Graphic displays and networks can show events in time sequence or their relationships.

Not everyone thinks visually and, to some researchers, such devices suggest too structured an approach to method. For example, Miles and Huberman (1994) advise that at the outset the researcher should roughly sketch matrices from the research questions and key variables, and then get colleagues and others to help examine the assumptions and to suggest alternatives. Provided the researcher can stay open to the unexpected, such an approach works well with structured and focused research questions; when research uses an emergent approach, such displays may be more appropriate later in the analysis process.

Audit Trails

In addition to facilitating understanding, matrices and memos provide an **audit trail** that others can follow to reconstruct how an analysis developed, to check how well coding terms are grounded in the data, and to determine the logical validity of conclusions. Researchers argue that leaving a clear audit trail helps critics to track the steps of qualitative method and is likely to provide for greater methodological rigor. Without in any way restricting the options available to the researcher, an audit trail allows others to check the reasoning; it makes the process explicit. Studying trails of past research can provide a perspective on the qualitative-analysis process that would help novice researchers decide how best to proceed with their studies.

FACTORS THAT POTENTIALLY BIAS ANALYSIS

In Sadler's (1981) analysis of the mind's cognitive limitations (see p. 268), we considered concerns possibly affecting observation. Others factors in Sadler's list may affect analysis. (Sadler cites research studies that support each of these points.) Knowing these limitations is the first step toward disciplining their effect.

Positive and negative instances. Evidence that supports tentative hypotheses is much more likely to be noticed. Research shows that people tended to ignore information that conflicted with already held hypotheses; "even intelligent individuals adhered to their own hypotheses with remarkable tenacity" (p. 28).

Correlation and co-occurrences. Co-occurrences are often seen as evidence of correlation when they may actually be chance occurrences. Having a reasonable explanation helps distinguish chance occurrences from correlated ones.

Novelty of information. One observer watching a teacher discipline a student describes it in routine terms; another reports it quite graphically as an aberration. Which report is more likely to affect the study? The novelty of aberration makes it stand out, and we tend to discount less extreme data. Positive and negative information do not typically cancel each other; the more extreme tends to win. This is more likely to occur where there is a paucity of information than when, with more information, the less novel behavior is shown to be closer to typical.

Base-rate proportion. The base rate is the natural frequency with which a behavior occurs (e.g., aggressive acts in daily life) independent of some intervention such as an experimental treatment (e.g., aggression when losing a chess game), or of some cause one is studying such as a particular influence or context (e.g., aggression among spectators at a boxing match). Judging base rates from small samples with their greater variability is very difficult—occurrence may appear large but may actually be small in a larger sample. Individuals tend to base their judgment on the sample's perceived representativeness rather than on the actual proportion of the population it constitutes. Insensitivity to base rate and a tendency to form impressions from small amounts of observational data seem to be common problems and may account for the above noted novelty problem.

Uneven reliability of information. There is a tendency to treat data from an unreliable source almost the same way as data from reliable sources. In one study, subjects arrived at a conclusion, and then each source was shown to be less credible than originally thought. As each source was discredited, the revisions of the original hypothesis became smaller. Even when all sources had been discredited, a residual of commitment to the hypothesis still remained.

Overconfidence in judgment. As noted, "once an assessment is made, people have been shown to have an almost unshakable confidence in the correctness of their decisions, even in the face of considerable, relevant, contrary evidence" (Sadler, 1981, p. 30). Training to remain open to new evidence is very important for the qualitative researcher.

Since the researcher is the data collection instrument, the last item (as well as others in the list above) indicates that temperamental characteristics affect qualitative research. Impulsiveness, for example, might cause individuals to jump to generalizations too early. A tendency toward holistic approaches in contrast to "missing the forest for the trees" seems a necessity to induction. Flexibility, openness, and willingness to entertain the "new" are important, though not to the point that the new automatically displaces the old. This ability to appropriately integrate new information into the whole may be one of the most critical, since the order of events is beyond the researcher's control and initial events form the base on which the rest is built.

Tips on Analysis

1. Underline or highlight notes for future ease of coding, scanning, and sorting. Code not only for what is present, but also for significant missing items (e.g., no feelings of regret or guilt in a teacher who has physically punished a student).

2. Look for themes. Frequently, people's language gives clues. Look for repeating events, routines, and concepts.

3. Develop types and classification schemes of how people categorize other people and things.

4. Ask professionals in your field who are unfamiliar with what you are studying to read the notes and point out what they see as themes, commonalties, and points of significance.

5. Consult the literature of others who have studied the same phenomenon and see what themes and explanations their work suggests. Include relevant fiction because, removed from the constraints of scientific precision, such authors' intuitive insights may be suggestive of useful ideas.

6. Give priority to memoing over everything else. Sort your memos from time to time, and link them conceptually.

7. Begin early to set the goal of your study by trying various one-sentence titles, and by establishing files for the introductory and the final chapters of the report. Also set up a sensitivity (reflexivity) file to remind you of your reactions, attitudes, and other concerns that might bias your interpretations.

8. There is a fine balance between sticking to a particular line of thinking and abandoning it to the lure of a seemingly more promising one. You don't want to get stuck in unproductive tracks, yet you need to follow them far enough to sense their potential. Strauss (1987) advises that you trust yourself, "your subliminal thought processes as well as your memory, [and the process of sorting to bring back your older ideas] when the time is ripe. They all integrate better that way" (p. 211).

9. Remember, there is no one right way to handle your data; there are lots of "roads to Rome." Pick one that makes sense to you and is comfortable.

10. Once you have determined your core coding categories, those central to the support of your explanation, relate other categories to them. Examine what is left to see whether the core needs modifying or whether there is something significant that has been missed. After this process, discard categories that are totally or relatively unrelated.

11. Test each major code for completeness, and whether it hangs together. This process can result in the need to recode old data or gather new. Beginning early reduces the extent of such work.

12. Consider portraying your coding structure graphically.

13. Examine the structure for ways of relating codes in a hierarchical or other structure; look for generalizations and types.

14. Writing the report is an excellent integrating mechanism. Strauss (1987, p. 213) suggests beginning it even before integration is complete.

ADDITIONAL READING

See Ryan and Bernard (2000) on matrices, graphics, causal analyses, networks, and graphical forms of analysis. See Strauss and Corbin (1998) on coding and analysis. See Charmaz (2006) regarding grounded theory and, for an example, Huehls (2005). For tutorials on NVivo 7, see Richards at http://sagepub.co.uk/richards/.

The following online portals will guide you to sources of qualitative-analysis information and software):

The Qualitative Research Web Ring is a ring of Web sites devoted to qualitative research; enter it at: http://ringsurf.com/ring/QualitativeResearch/

QualPage—extensive resources for qualitative research: http://qualitativeresearch.uga.edu/QualPage/

Resources for text analysis: http://www.textanalysis.info/

For a list of quality criteria, see Brantlinger, Jimenez, Klingman, Pugach, and Richardson (2005).

For analysis processes closer to quantitative method, see the qualitative comparative analysis of Ragin (1987 and 1993), a halfway house between quantitative and qualitative. He uses the presence or absence of target items and Boolean algebra to build a case for causation. Griffin and Ragin (1994) introduce a special issue of *Sociological Methods and Research* devoted to further discussion of this and other "in-between" methods.

IMPORTANT TERMS AND CONCEPTS

audit trail
coding

data reduction
reflexivity

OPPORTUNITIES FOR ADDITIONAL LEARNING

1. How might you code this segment from a study of the onset of Alzheimer's disease? Would you code it differently if the study were of caregivers' reactions to the disease? If so, how?

   Interviewer: Tell me when you first noticed your wife's memory problems.

   Dave: She was a very bright lady who had a much better memory than mine. Then suddenly, as we left on a long trip, for which she had exhausted herself in preparation, her memory was gone! I just couldn't believe it. She seemed not to be able to remember what had happened yesterday. I was shocked! But then after we arrived at our destination, her disability disappeared as suddenly as it had come. So I didn't really think about it again until years later when she began to have trouble handling numbers.

2. Frank Annanias has gathered data in a number of school libraries regarding its usage by the students. He has interviewed students in their classrooms and in the library itself. He has also recorded data about the make-up of the library, the way shelves are arranged, the training of the librarian, and many other factors. He is interested in the factors that make for increased library usage. How would you suggest that he analyze these data?

3. Wharton (1996)[2] interviewed 30 women from 17 real estate firms "to identify the factors that lead women to choose and keep this occupation" (p. 217). Following are excerpts from her interviews. If you were doing this study, how would you code these? Code each quotation in turn, adjusting your codes as you move through the set.

a. The flexible hours: thinking that I'd be able to play tennis and do some other things that I wanted to do during the day. In teaching I got really tired of being stuck in a classroom from 8:00 in the morning until 3:30.

b. I can schedule my home time and my time away from home. . . . Like in the summer, every Wednesday we [her family] go out on the boat. And I've had my weekend that I take off. I allow more time. I go to all the kids' games. I find that I can control my time better now: Once I learned that I had to say I had another appointment or commitment, then I could block off time.

c. Without a college education, I found myself limited in what I could do that would have income potential, let alone flexibility. Real estate did not require college, gave me unlimited potential depending on how hard I elected to work, allowed me to be my own boss while I could juggle my schedule around my family and basically take control of myself.

d. At that point in time, I thought the nicest thing about real estate would be that if I didn't like somebody, I just wouldn't have to work for them! I wouldn't have to worry about it!

e. Every transaction is a little bit different. I think the part that I like best is, that it is a dream and to see that face when that dream comes true, you know, when they get into the house. I just like real estate basically because I have that personality where I like helping people. I like to make money too [laughs], but I like helping people and it gives me gratification when you get into that house.

Compare your answers with those following the short Application Exercise below.

APPLICATION EXERCISE

Considering the questions you hope to investigate, the data that you plan to gather, and its likely key terms and important foci, can you begin to set up a possible set of codes that might help you get started on your data analysis? What problems of analysis do you expect at this point? Does one of the coding suggestions in this chapter seem to fit your problem better than another? Are there likely relationships that lend themselves to your developing tentative blank matrices that you will fill in later? Can you devise graphics depicting sequences or interrelationships of events that you anticipate encountering?

KEY TO ADDITIONAL LEARNING OPPORTUNITIES

1. What is coded depends on what you consider significant for your study. Researchers coding this passage with different studies in mind would code it quite differently. Studies of the development of the symptoms of Alzheimer's might give it one or more of several codes such as "short-term memory loss recovered," or "short-term memory loss from stress," or "numeric aphasia," or "slow symptom appearance." All of these are potentially important characteristics mentioned in this segment of the interview, and might be relevant to the analysis. Note: The actual codes would be some abbreviation of the code titles that were easy for the researcher to remember—for example, for the above codes: strec, ststress, numaph, or slosymp.

Were the researcher studying caregivers' responses, the codings might be "denial of seriousness of symptom"; "I was shocked" (using the informants' words for a code title); or "slowness in observing onset." It is quite possible that the first and third of these might be merged if other examples showed little distinction between them. They might then be more appropriately titled to fit the whole body of excerpts.

2. This problem is ideally suited to a matrix display. Frank should list the names of the schools, in order from most usage to least, down the left side of the page, one school to a row. Next he should draw as many columns as he has information items about the libraries, including those items on which he may have data for some but not all the schools. He should label the columns across the top with the items of information they are to contain and then proceed to fill in each row with the information he has on the school designated by that row.

Finally, he should scan down each column and look for consistent, gradual change. Some columns will be a jumble with no consistency, but those that change in a consistent direction from top to bottom are the factors associated with increased usage. Where there is only partial data in the column, he will want to go back to the schools with the missing data, fill it in, and see if it completes the pattern. Once he has one or more characteristics that show the pattern of change from top to bottom, he should add some new schools, especially ones for which the data might be expected to not support the generalizations developed from the initial set. He should then fill in the matrix for them on the same items as showed trends in the initial set and see if the generalizations hold, need to be modified, or are invalidated.

3. As in so many of these application questions, there is no single correct answer. The following answers show one coder's process as she "thinks aloud" on each successive quotation. Your answer may pick up some insight missed in them.

   a. "It is desirable to use the language of the informants for codes where possible; such language usually captures the feeling tone more accurately. Therefore, in this instance, the first code might be "flexible hours." I'll use multiple codes to capture other ideas in the statement; this one has at least a couple of ideas. Something reflecting freedom would capture the idea in the last sentence, perhaps "autonomy." That code term captures the idea but is far removed from the informants' language! Maybe other interview segments will provide a better name.

   b. Here we have the idea of autonomy again! But this statement suggests there are different aspects to autonomy that may need to be separated out. The first statement suggests "freedom from confinement." The statement adds "freedom to enjoy family," and "control of time." Perhaps "autonomy" is a good concept after all since it captures the different meanings, but it should be viewed as a major code with subcodes under it.

   c. Perceived job characteristics suggest two new codes: "low education requirement" and "earning potential." Apparently we can divide job characteristics into three groups, those characteristics set: (1) by the job requirements, like the education requirements, (2) jointly by the salesperson and the real estate organization, like earning potential; and (3) by the salesperson, like their freedom to enjoy family. These might be considered superordinate categories for which you might write a memo to yourself describing this idea, then set it aside to see whether it is still helpful as coding proceeds.

   In addition, this statement adds a new subcategory to autonomy: "own boss." Another subcategory, "autonomy–control of time," is a repeat of an earlier theme.

   d. Still another new aspect of autonomy: "control over those worked with." This seems to apply to bosses, colleagues, and clients.

   e. Even more new attractive facets of the job: "every transaction is different" and "gratification of helping people." The theme of earning potential repeats."

   Note how in the above, we devise new codes, preferably in the informants' language, as new aspects are encountered. However, we try to relate them to what has gone before, and to see whether a deeper concept, in this instance autonomy, captures the essence of many of them. We then revise our coding scheme to capture this, and go back and recode previously coded sections. Using computer software makes recoding easier—a major advantage. Note, too, the attempt to find all the themes in each statement, and to use multiple codes for the statement. Then, with computer software (or by sorting if they are on separate cards), gather all the statements with a common code to determine whether the name still fits or whether something better can be found. As you develop an encompassing explanation of what attracts and holds women as real estate salespersons, you will also further interrelate codes into a structure, often hierarchical with major codes and subcodes. You can see the beginnings of the hierarchical structure in the "autonomy" code above.

Incidentally, do you think these women really talked in nice, neat sentences as portrayed by Wharton (1996) in these quotations? Probably not, it seems likely Wharton cleaned them up while retaining the feel of the original statement. This common practice avoids embarrassing your informants when they see themselves in print.

SUMMARY

Observation and interviewing often result in amounts of data that are well beyond human memory capacity to retain and integrate.

Coding and analysis are the data-reduction processes that make the database manageable; the mound of data is winnowed to that which is directly relevant to the study's focus.

Coding is the process of tagging the significant parts of the data with names, thus indicating their importance to the study and describing their relation to its central focus.

In preplanned studies, codes can be deductively derived from the goals of the study.

In emergent studies, coding, an inductive reasoning process, involves extracting similarities in behavior or perceptions from the data and determining the important concepts and dimensions that underlie them.

Coding and memoing go hand in hand. Memos capture inferences about the concepts and dimensions underlying the codes.

Codes are concepts, and the coded data are the definitions of the concepts. In turn, codes are knit into an explanation, or theory, hence the term grounded theory; it is "grounded" in—that is, built from—the coded data.

Various generic coding systems are suggestive starting points for novices.

Once put in digital form by typing, scanning, or speech-recognition software, the above process can be handled with qualitative data-analysis software.

Qualitative data-analysis software markedly eases coding, recoding, and retrieving text, as well as ordering, structuring, and visualizing code structure. Vast and cumbersome qualitative data files become feasible. The software leads to more complete analyses.

A variety of information processing concerns potentially affect the researcher. These can constitute special problems for qualitative researchers since they are the data-recording instruments.

Graphics and matrices provide a perspective on data that facilitates spotting trends and relationships, missing data, and data that does not follow the pattern.

Providing an "audit trail" is important not only for others but also for the researchers themselves; it gives them some perspective on the process.

A Look Ahead

In the next chapter, we will discuss the final step in the qualitative study, developing the report. In addition, we will examine some of the quality indicators of such research and how to ensure that our research meets these standards.

Notes

[1] From Robert c. Bogdan and Sari Knopp Biklen, *Qualitative Research for Education: An Introduction to Theory and Methods* (2nd ed.). Copyright © 1992. Reprinted with permission of Pearson Education.

[2] From C. S. Wharton (1996), Making people feel good: Workers' constructions of meaning in interactive service jobs. *Qualitative Sociology, 19*, 217–233.

Links to previous research

Explanation, rationale, theory, or point of view

Questions, hypotheses, models

Preplanned and emergent designs

Design/procedure

Focus   Records   Time   Comparison and Contrast   Situation   Participants

Data

Statistical and narrative analyses

Conclusion

Link to next study

Explanation or rationale
of next study, etc.

16

Quality Considerations, Conclusions, and Reporting in Qualitative Research

> Of all the roles, the role of interpreter, and gatherer of interpretation is central.
> —R. E. Stake, *The Art of Case Study Research*
>
> How do I know what I think until I see it in writing?
> —M. B. Miles and A. M. Huberman, *Qualitative Data Analysis*

Trust is absolutely essential to accepting the findings of a study. Critical to building that trust is the quality of the research (optimizing audience credibility again). What characteristics of qualitative research indicate its quality? This chapter shows that Internal Integrity and External Generality apply to qualitative as well as quantitative studies. We will discuss how they, as well as other hallmarks of qualitative research, contribute to trust. Discussion of the criteria of quality, begun in the previous chapter to help guide analysis, is continued in this chapter as a check on what appropriately belongs in the study's report.

How must the researcher write the report of a qualitative study to develop trust and display the study's quality? Just as the analytic phase can follow many different paths, so can reports. Yet, regardless of the research method used in the study, there is certain basic information readers need in order to understand it, to determine whether to trust the evidence presented, to judge whether the evidence supports the findings, and to learn how the findings bear on whatever the study is addressing. In addition, readers of qualitative research have certain additional expectations, especially in terms of the researcher disclosing potentially biasing influences. Therefore we can indicate what a report of a qualitative study should contain.

But what about format and style? If the findings result in one or more generalizations, they are usually presented deductively as a chain of reasoning, although some links may not be in the usual order.

INTRODUCTION

The foundation of a quality study is high-quality data, so in the chapter on field methods (chapter 13) we described means of data checking such as triangulation across persons, situations, and methods. In addition, we specified the necessity of memoing regarding the researcher's background, prior experiences, and other sources of potential bias such as how what we read, hear, or observe is affecting us. What else indicates quality?

Considering the wide variability in qualitative methods, can there be standards against which to judge quality? Some researchers suggest that such standards are impossible:

> They hold the position that analysis is their . . . [unique] creation which can only be internally confirmed by them, and if they do a good job of communicating their reasoning, perhaps their results can be understood and even supported by others. (Ely, 1991, p. 164)

Others take the stand that "there is a reasonable view of 'what happened' . . . and . . . we who render accounts of it can do so well or poorly" (Miles & Huberman, 1994, p. 277). Because qualitative inquiry, like all research, has real-world consequences, qualitative researchers cannot escape quality judgments, whether or not they subscribe to standards. They can suggest reasonable bases for making such judgments. Many have sought to do so, often adapting and supplementing criteria common to quantitative to fit qualitative research (see, e.g., Anfara, Brown, & Mangione, 2002; Guba & Lincoln, 1989; Kvale, 2002; LeCompte & Preissle, 1994; Lincoln, 1995; Miles & Huberman, 1984, 1994).

In chapter 3 we noted that if the research is to be used, it is the consumers who must be satisfied—they are the arbiters of the study's validity. How do consumers judge? Criteria are described in chapters 7 through 9, but these criteria apply mainly to studies concerned with generalizations, with showing cause and effect or processes. Some qualitative studies do have this as their purpose; but others, like Whyte's *Street Corner Society*, or Liebow's *Talley's Corner*, are mainly descriptive. Many are in between, providing case or small sample data supporting what may be a generalization, but without enough evidence to make a very strong generality claim—for example, the Hoffmann-Riem study in chapter 1. What criteria should we apply to these other kinds of studies? There are two ways we could approach this problem: operationally and conceptually. If we look at it operationally—that is, in practical terms—we ask: What kinds of actions in a study result in quality research? If we approach it conceptually, we ask: What are the standards that distinguish quality research?

AN OPERATIONAL APPROACH TO DEFINING QUALITY

Let us begin with the operational or practical approach, spelling out a variety of data collection and analytic actions that one should look for in the report of a quality study. It would include items discussed in the previous chapters, such as:

- unobtrusive entry and participation in the field
- prolonged engagement with the field
- thick description
- reflections by the researchers on their reactions to data gathering, analysis, and possible biasing factors
- triangulation using different methods, along with samples of persons, times, and places
- detailing their research procedures, leaving an audit trail
- active search for discrepant data
- active search for rival explanations for the phenomenon
- use of participant quotations in the report
- member checking (described later in this chapter)

We might add that having others view the work, especially if they independently recode the data, provides a check on one's lack of bias and effectiveness. In addition, such **peer checking** audits the researcher's interpretation. Providing a backup recording for observations, such as an audio or video recording may be helpful in assuring that the fieldnotes accurately reflect what went on.

A CONCEPTUAL APPROACH TO DEFINING QUALITY

There might be general agreement on the above list as operationally defining quality, but it does little to advance the conceptual definition. Furthermore, in contrast to agreement at the operational level, there is little agreement at the conceptual level. This is not for lack of many thoughtful efforts (for example, Kvale, 2002; Polkinghorn, 1983; or the references in Lincoln, 2001 and Lather, 2001). In part the differences arise from the many orientations to qualitative research. In addition, some researchers differ on the issues of epistemology, the conception of the nature of knowledge. Is there one reality out there to be discovered, or multiple realities (e.g., Lincoln, 2001; Lincoln & Guba, 1995)? For others, the epistemological discussion is "unhelpful fiction" (Donmoyer, 2001).

Respect for the rights of those studied and concern over ethical issues add participatory, empowerment, and cooperative criteria (Lincoln, 1995). Racial and ethnic issues as well as other concerns with social change can add criteria as well. In addition, there are critical theorist and constructivist versions of validity.

Given the variety of qualitative orientations and their accompanying varied purposes, Donmoyer's (2001) proposal that the criteria of validity vary with the purpose of the study makes sense. He suggests a categorization of purposes:

- Academic knowledge—what relationships and theory explain the data (e.g., Hoffmann-Riem).

- Emic description—how people perceive their world (e.g., how the gang members and "corner boys" perceived their community in *Street Corner Society)*.

- Describing a process or change over time (e.g., how interns become surgeons in *Forgive and Remember*).

- Presenting a personal point of view (e.g., what unique and useful meaning the researcher can construct of the data).

- Achieving social change (e.g., how we can make advocacy for change part of our research design). (Donmoyer has other names for these study types, but these are more accurately descriptive.)

Examples of these and other validities can be found in Lincoln (2001) and Lather (2001).

Where does that leave us? Is there no generally acceptable formulation? For purely descriptive studies like *Street Corner Society* the applicable operational strategies listed above will have to do. For studies like Hoffmann-Riem or those providing evidence of a generality, perhaps the standards closest to being widely adopted are Guba and Lincoln's (1982) translations of four common quantitative criteria into terms more compatible with qualitative research. They are presented in Table 16.1 on the following page.

The third column of Table 16.1 displays Anfara, Brown, and Mangione's (2002) operational strategies (with additional strategies from the operational definition listing above) for achieving the standards of quality displayed in the first two columns. Guba and Lincoln (1982) sum the overall effect of the above criteria in the term **trustworthiness** and set it parallel to *scientific rigor* in quantitative terms. *Building credibility with the audience* was noted as a criterion to maximize in chapter 9, and trustworthiness is an apt synonym for it. So trustworthiness is a suitable overall goal for qualitative research. Let's examine in more detail the criteria of credibility/Internal Integrity and transferability/External Generality and in the process, include dependability/reliability and confirmability/objectivity.

CREDIBILITY/INTERNAL INTEGRITY IN QUALITATIVE RESEARCH

Guba and Lincoln prefer the term credibility to Internal Integrity, the latter defined earlier as a judgment of a study's ability to link variables in a cause-and-effect relationship (p. 138). Certainly, credibility results when a study has strong Internal Integrity. Internal Integrity is composed of five subjudgments: (1) explanation credibility, (2) translation validity, (3) demonstrated result, (4) rival explanations eliminated, and (5) credible result. While Guba and Lincoln may have had in mind a more global judgment of the credibility of a study than processing five subjudgments would imply, this conception of Internal Integrity is applicable to qualitative research. Here's how.

Table 16.1   Quantitative and Qualitative Criteria for Assessing Research Quality and Rigor

Quantitative Term*	Conceptual Qualitative Term*	Operational Strategy Employed
Internal Integrity (internal validity)**	credibility	prolonged engagement in the field triangulation member checking peer checking time sampling active search for discrepant data active search for rival explanations for the phenomenon
External Generality (external validity)**	transferability	provide thick description purposive sampling
reliability	dependability	create an audit trail code–recode strategy triangulation peer examination prolonged engagement
objectivity	confirmability	triangulation practice of self-reflection (reflexivity) use of participants' quotations audit trail

*The first two columns use the terms of Guba & Lincoln (1982).
**Guba and Lincoln used the terms internal validity and external validity; translated into this book's terms they become the more descriptive: Internal Integrity and External Generality.

Source: Adapted from Anfara, Brown, & Mangione, 2002.

1. Explanation Credibility

This criterion applies whenever an explanation is advanced, as, for instance, when Hoffmann-Riem explained the drive for adoption as normalization. No special interpretation of explanation credibility is needed for such qualitative research.

2. Translation Validity

This criterion applies equally obviously to qualitative and quantitative research. Translation validity requires judging the congruence of the construct as identified in the data with the characteristics of the construct as the term is used in the study— whether the construct is faithfully (with fidelity) represented in the way it is measured or in the case of qualitative, otherwise empirically portrayed. For instance, Hoffmann-Riem (see p. 15) relates the construct of *normalization* to data excerpts, like "It is your own child, and that's it." Translation validity is the judgment of whether this, together with her other descriptive quotations, exemplifies what we mean by "normalization." (As we'll see in chapter 18, this is comparable to evidence of construct validity with quantitative data.)

However, translation validity implies as well for both qualitative and quantitative that the basic data from which description, explanation, or theory are derived are of sufficient quality. This involves the other pairs of terms in Table 16.1, that the data are dependable/reliable and confirmable/objective, so, let's examine these as well.

Dependability/reliability.   To qualitative researchers the term dependability (which they link to consistency) is preferable to reliability (Lincoln & Guba, 1994). *Consistency* is a good synonym for reliability, as it is used in both quantitative and qualitative research. There are many kinds of consistency—for example, from one observation time to another (i.e., the behavior identified with a particular construct is stable between records of the same situation) or when a secretary's minutes of a meeting reinforce observation fieldnotes.

Triangulation (see p. 285) is basically about consistency and is a way of assuring it. As was noted in an earlier discussion, you can triangulate for consistency across social situations, time of observation, locations, observers, and methods of data collection. In addition, there is consistency of coding that can be verified by peer checking (i.e., would others using the same coding scheme classify data the same way and draw the same conclusions?).

Evidence of consistency over time results from prolonged engagement and deep familiarity with the phenomenon being studied. Some experienced qualitative researchers are unhappy with the short periods of fieldwork in many current qualitative studies; the observation period does not seem sufficiently long for depth and representativeness. But it is also true that repeated close contact over time changes our perceptions of and our relations with those being observed. Separating such changes from those unrelated to observation and interaction can be a serious problem.

Leaving a clear audit trail is also a way of helping to assure that you have attended to dependability and consistency concerns.

Exactly where the audience looks for assurance of consistency depends on the nature of the study. A study of creativity under stress would be concerned with consistency in identifying when the individual is stressed and with what constitutes creativity. Showing consistency across the various kinds of stressful situations relevant to the study indicates that the findings can be relied on (dependability) as characterizing the person or kind of behavior (etc.) rather than being a function of that social situation, particular time, or location (etc.). Clearly, we must consider data consistency in judging the translation validity of qualitative studies.

Confirmability/objectivity.   "The major technique for establishing confirmability is the . . . audit" (Lincoln & Guba, 1985, p. 328). Retracing the audit trail confirms that the procedures used conform to what would be expected of such a study. The auditor will especially wish to look at the researcher's self-reflection (reflexivity) journal and memos to determine whether concerns about bias have been taken into account in interpretation.

Another procedure is having gatekeepers and the study participants read the researcher's report to determine whether it has portrayed them accurately—a process referred to as **member checking**. It provides a useful review of both data and its interpretation. Whyte (1993), for instance, went over the various parts of his report with his informant, "Doc": "His criticisms were invaluable in my revision" (p. 341). This practice has its dangers, however. Grant (1979), in a study of competency-based education, found the case study of one university so objectionable to its administrators that he had to delete it from the final draft. Even when informants recognize the accuracy of the description, they may reject this view of themselves, claiming it is inaccurate. Bloor (1997) warns that member checking is "a social event, constrained . . . by the social dictates of polite conversation and shaped by the biographies and circumstances of the discussants" (p. 47). Overall, however, most researchers believe they benefit from this process.

Some qualitative researchers reject the quantitative definition of objectivity, defined as the consistency of two or more observers in describing the same phenomenon. These researchers argue that observers view situations from their own perspectives. For instance, one person may concentrate on details, the other on the big picture; one on the person at the center of attention, the other at those on the periphery; one on the interviewer, the other on the interviewee. Each brings a perspective that the other does not, enhancing the data and making the interpretation richer and more complex. From this viewpoint, the fact that the fieldnotes are not similar is not important. But where there is concern that a situation may be poorly portrayed, comparing fieldnotes with a second observer may be helpful.

Whether objectivity is an issue is, in part, a matter of the intent of the study. If it is about overt behavior, then it is reasonable to expect some kind of congruence of observers. But if it is about covert behavior, about inferring intent, about unobservable perceptions by others, then observers may reasonably differ. It might be found that one observer viewed a teacher's ignoring a girl's raised hand as bias—a preference for boys over girls—while another, recognizing that girls participate in discussion more, viewed it as simply giving all pupils a chance to participate. Note that in instances like this, however, differences may highlight observer attitudes that must be dealt with in memos and discounted in further analyses.

3. Demonstrated Result

In an experimental quantitative study, demonstrated result indicates the treatment had its expected effect thereby linking cause and effect—in a study of a process, that it proceeded as expected. What is qualitative's parallel? The fact that the explanation or theory arises from and is grounded in the data, links the data with the explanation, and serves much the same purpose. So does detailed, thick description, and a search for other positive instances without instances where it should have appeared but didn't. Also contributing evidence are instances where the relationship should not appear and didn't. The tighter the fit of the explanation or theory to such supporting evidence, the more convincing are the findings and the less likely this is a chance relationship. This can be a real strength of qualitative method, particularly if it satisfies the following criterion.

4. Rival Explanations Eliminated

Regardless of whether a research method is qualitative, quantitative, or a combination, once you have found an explanation for a relationship in data or a theory that explains it, you must determine that no rival explanation accounts for the data as well as the one being advanced. Campbell and Stanley (1963) coined the phrase *threats to validity* for such especially plausible rival explanations. In some cases researchers may not be aware of rivals; in others they may be aware but did not, or could not, protect against them. Zimbardo's study was chosen as an example in chapter 1 partly because it is so good at showing how one eliminates rival explanations. (See the list of strengths on pp. 9–11 that indicate how treating the groups in the same way except for the treatment eliminated rival explanations.)

All research is besieged by rivals: commonly encountered ones that we can name in advance, specific ones that plague certain research methods, unique ones that result from the configuration of a particular study (e.g., the use of hypnosis in Zimbardo's study). However, even one uneliminated rival that is apparent to the audience (e.g., for some readers, Zimbardo's use of college students) may be sufficient to destroy a consensus that the proposed explanation is a valid one. Thus, these are serious matters.

Some of the common rival explanations defined by Campbell and Stanley (1963) and Cook and Campbell (1979) have applicability to qualitative methods. You will find the discussion of rival explanations placed in the discussion of experimental methods in most research texts. It is important that the applicability of rival explanations be recognized as relevant to *any* (not just quantitative) work. Therefore, we begin describing them here and note them elsewhere as they are relevant, especially when we discuss them in detail in connection with experimentation in chapter 21.

Although their names are descriptive (mortality, instrument decay, selection), some initially bring the wrong picture to mind—for instance, mortality refers not to death but rather to the loss of individuals from a group, thereby changing what the group represents.

Mortality.   Is mortality a threat to validity in qualitative research? It often is, and most important, it sometimes occurs unnoticed. Concentrating on the persons active in a group may leave you blind to persons who have left but might have had an effect had they remained. For example, in trying to understand the impact of new playground equipment on children's play patterns, you concentrate on how children take turns, their ease in adapting to the equipment, and similar aspects. You might not notice that some former playground users, afraid of the new equipment, have avoided the playground altogether and played elsewhere. The mortality in the group suggests that had they stayed, one might have an equally plausible yet quite different picture of adaptability to the new equipment.

Instrument decay.   This refers to inconsistency in a measuring instrument or in observation. For instance, rules for using an observation checklist can fail to cover some situations; for these situations researchers make arbitrary judgments but may make different judgments in the next such encounter.

In qualitative research, the observer is the instrument. We have noted previously how relations between observer and those observed change over time and how these, in turn, change perception. Wax (1971), while studying Japanese Americans interned during World War II, found data gathering "made it impossible that I ever again approach or talk to them in the way that I had . . . three or four months before" (p.

31). Clearly, the observer must be alert to such changes, write memos that describe their impact on the study's findings, and take them into account in the study report.

The most serious change of this type is "going native," becoming one with the group being observed and losing perspective. Lang and Lang (1960) reported that during a 1957 Billy Graham crusade, an observer left her observation task and "somewhere in the course of the sermon she decided to step forward. . . . The next thing she knew was that she had risen and was hurrying to the main floor to declare herself [a believer]" (p. 424).

A variation of instrument decay is the tendency to overlook or ignore the negative aspects of a group with which the researcher has come to identify. Thus, Ornstein and Phillips (1978) criticize Liebow's (1967) "compelling description of street corner men" because he "presents no description of their involvement in crime or drugs or violence; he describes few instances of cruelty or times when they actually were impulsive or improvident, as we all are sometimes" (p. 350).

Other rival explanations.   Other rivals arise out of a particular study configuration, the sample, the methodology, and so forth. Researchers should think ahead while still in the field and gather data to eliminate them. With changing conditions, returning to the field may be too late or impossible. Qualitative or quantitative researchers who wish to build audience credibility must attend to these concerns and allay them in their research report.

5. Credible Result

Credible result calls for judging the credibility of the findings in the light of the previous four judgments and of prior research. The strength of the judgments of explanation credibility, translation validity, demonstrated result, and the elimination of rival explanations together with the congruence of the study to prior research, all make up the strength of Internal Integrity. As the previous discussion indicates, there is no reason why qualitative studies cannot have strong Internal Integrity.

> ▶ Internal Integrity and its five judgments apply to qualitative research studies concerned with providing evidence for a generalization.
>
> ▶ Explanation credibility requires that the generalization being advanced is plausible and credible.
>
> ▶ Translation validity requires that terms used for constructs or concepts match well the data excerpts intended to illustrate them. Problems can arise from a number of inconsistencies: of the behavior identified with a construct over time, in the way an observer takes fieldnotes, in the records of two recorders of the same phenomena, from inconsistency in the coding process by an individual coder over time, or the way different persons apply the codes (determined by peer checking). Member checking is a way of authenticating that the data agree with participants' own view of their situation.
>
> ▶ The elimination of rival explanations is a concern of all methods, including qualitative.
>
> ▶ Certain common rival explanations, or "threats to validity" as they have been called, are applicable to qualitative methods. Examples are mortality and instrument decay.

> ❱ Eliminating rival explanations may be difficult if evidence to eliminate them is not gathered while still in the field. Often unique to an individual study, they are the responsibility of the researcher to ferret out.
>
> ❱ The anticipation of rival explanations that will be of concern to the audience is essential if a consensus is to be formed around the proposed interpretation of the data.
>
> ❱ Data gathered in support of emergent explanations or theories provide evidence for a demonstrated result, particularly as it is bolstered by examples beyond those in which the theory was first developed as well as by reasonable instances where the result should not appear and did not.
>
> ❱ Credible results occur when the judgments of explanation credibility, translation validity, demonstrated result, and rival explanations eliminated are positive and findings are consistent with previous related work.

TRANSFERABILITY/EXTERNAL GENERALITY IN QUALITATIVE RESEARCH

Because of the small and purposive (instead of representative) samples used in qualitative research, evidence of transferability/External Generality is often problematic. Indeed, many studies make no claim to it, and some discussion of standards or criteria do not even mention it. Miles and Huberman (1994), Stake (1995), and Lincoln and Guba (1985), however, do—the last using the term *transferability* and the first adding *fittingness*. With the exception of studies that do cross-site sampling, the local nature of the data and the limited, purposive sampling of most studies provide little empirical evidence for it.

However, the rich, detailed illustrations in qualitative research allow readers to "try on the examples for size" to see whether they fit their experience and thus facilitate transfer to new situations. Some studies gain considerable generality; an example is Margaret Mead's (1928) *Coming of Age in Samoa*, one of the first widely read qualitative studies. In her Samoan data, she found insights with implications for raising children in America, which, although later challenged, had substantial impact at the time. Although not all researchers are explicit about the implications for generality, nearly all researchers hope their work will provide useful insights for other situations. If you took advantage of Additional Learning Opportunity #6 in chapter 8 (p. 183), you realize that this is certainly true for Hoffmann-Riem. Review the answer to that problem (p. 184) to refresh your memory of the judgments that enter into External Generality.

Generality always involves an inferential leap—a leap of faith. Although that leap is often not supported by empirical qualitative evidence, it is clear that many useful conceptualizations have been found in qualitative research. Often they have later been validated with additional qualitative or quantitative studies. Indeed, the synthesis of similar studies in literature reviews is a more likely source of evidence for External Generality for qualitative research than large, multi-site studies.

Increasingly, however, qualitative researchers are using multiple sites and multiple case studies to expand the generality of their findings. **Multisite studies**, especially in instances where the additional sites are used to confirm and validate generalizations derived from a prior site, may develop considerable External Generality—particularly if the additional sites are chosen randomly from an appropriate sampling frame. But, as Miles and Huberman (1984) point out, "If each site produces 200–300 pages of field notes and ancillary material, we are rapidly awash in waves of data" (p. 151). These data must be managed well or they will be poorly analyzed. Extending the methods of single-site analysis to those of cross-site analysis, Miles and Huberman note the necessity of standardizing the codes, reporting formats, and organizing data displays for each site. They then suggest a number of tools for managing and comparing the data across sites using matrix-type displays such as Table 15.1, where the data desired make up the vertical divisions and each row is a site (see also Ragin, 1987).

> ▶ External generality involves a conceptual leap from the evidence of one study to similar situations. Although this leap occurs in all research, the limited and selective nature of qualitative evidence may make it more speculative.
>
> ▶ Multiple-site and multiple-case studies employing standardization of data gathering and analysis can provide strong evidence of External Generality, especially when cases or sites are chosen by probability sampling methods. But such studies are rare because they are so labor intensive.
>
> ▶ Although the empirical evidence is typically lacking, most qualitative researchers hope their findings will have generality. The examples through which the explanation is usually presented facilitate readers' successful testing of it against their own experience to show its generality.

SOCIAL CONSEQUENCES—AN ADDITIONAL CRITERION?

Although there are implications for all methodologies, qualitative researchers—perhaps because of the relationship they establish with those studied—have been especially concerned with the **social consequences** of their research for their participants. Therefore, many would argue that attending to social consequences is an additional criterion to be met by qualitative research of quality.

Researchers often comment on how significantly their view of those they studied has changed. Lincoln (1995) notes that some researchers helped their needy informants long after the study ended and at least one shared royalties with them. She lists a whole series of social concerns: "Does it speak for those who do not have access to the corridors of knowledge or the venues of academic disciplines?" (p. 12). Does it empower them? Are they educated by it? "Have we 'come clean' about the advantages which accrue to us as knowledge 'producers'?" (p. 17). She argues that "the new research is a relational research—a research grounded in the recognition and valuing of 'connectedness' between researcher and researched, and between knowledge elites and the societies and communities in which they live and labor" (p. 19).

Many researchers are still content to do the research, publish it, and let it go at that, and undoubtedly there is much research for which this is quite appropriate. The question of social consequences, however, adds another criterion and highlights considerations that have not been taken into account by many researchers.

WRITING THE REPORT

Up to this point we have been writing analytic memos and other material, much of which will find itself, in one form or another, in the report. But writing the report raises questions, like "Am I sure of that?" "How consistently did this event actually follow that one?" and "Maybe I'd better look at the data again!" Yet there comes a time when, rather than satisfying our own curiosity, our emphasis must shift to assembling the material for presentation to others. The line distinguishing analysis from the preparation of the report of findings is a permeable one. As Glesne and Peshkin's (1992) student, Gordon, comments: "Another interesting discovery is that the writing process actually is an important part of the analysis. A lot of my insights . . . came through . . . writing. . . . Next time I will begin writing sooner" (p. 149). That is an important insight worth heeding! One works back and forth between the analysis and conclusions; the attempt to draw conclusions forces one to go back and check the analysis or perhaps add to it, which in turn leads to modified conclusions.

There is an art to doing analysis and drawing conclusions. It helps to work with someone who can model it for you. Stabb's (1999) advice from a student is: "Number one: Get organized. Number two: Allow for time, time, time. Third thing: The member checks and cross-validation are absolutely invaluable. And the fourth one: Set a stopping place and stick to it" (p. 97).

Report Format and Organization

Whether a qualitative or quantitative study, the researcher must convince the reader that the evidence warrants the conclusions. When presenting a case for a generality, most qualitative researchers use a deductive format like the chain of reasoning. In place of numbers and statistics for a "demonstrated result," they intermingle their interpretation with vignettes, quotations, and other examples to illustrate the points they are developing. The Hoffmann-Riem study reproduced in chapter 1 exemplifies such a study. Note that she starts by laying the groundwork for her method, and discusses her research questions (p. 12). These two steps lead to her description of the sample and methods of data collection (pp. 12–13). Her analysis of what she found includes a number of interview quotations illustrating the points she is making about normalization (pp. 13–14). Her final section deals with her generalizations, tying together the material in the previous analytic section (p. 17). Thus, she develops a chain of reasoning: question statement, followed by a section on research design, a large section on analysis and data presentation, and conclusions. Hoffmann-Riem lacks the literature review and the search for rival explanations that are typical of quantitative studies, but she grounds the analysis and conclusions in well-chosen interview excerpts. Hers is not a great variation from the chain-of-reasoning format, and many qualitative studies include the links that she omitted.

Although many qualitative reports follow this pattern, especially those advancing a generalization, there really is no standard reporting format. The 1974 observation by Lofland that "qualitative researchers lack a public, shared and codified conception of how what they do is done and how what they report should be reformulated" (p. 101) is still true thirty-plus years later. For instance, instead of a chain of reasoning the researcher may prefer that the report reflect the inductive nature of the qualitative process. For example, the data's description gives rise to the generalization at the end rather than being anticipated in the problem statement. "A write-up can be organized any way that contributes to the reader's understanding of the case" (Stake, 1995, p. 122).

The standard report format of quantitative research has the advantage that the reader knows where to expect certain parts of the study and so may move directly to a part of special interest. Readers of qualitative studies, however, must encounter the study as presented since, not knowing where to expect what, it is difficult to intelligently skip around. And qualitative researchers do show considerable creativity in organizing and presenting their material. "The challenge is to combine theoretical elegance and credibility appropriately, . . . to combine propositional thinking of most conventional studies and more figurative thinking [of qualitative research]" (Miles & Huberman, 1994, p. 299).

Often, qualitative research is written as a *case study*. Case studies have their origins in the medical and legal profession where, vividly and precisely conveying the characteristics of a single individual, situation, or problem, they are used to illuminate a generic problem. Case studies are bounded by a particular individual, situation, program, institution, time period, or set of events. Within those boundaries, whatever is the focus of attention is described within the perspective of the context surrounding it. Case studies are ideal for illustrating the complexity of causation. The case study is sometimes a step in a larger study where cases are combined in support of an overall explanation or theory that arises out of cross-site analysis. In many instances, the time-bound nature of the material results in a timeline type of narration that organizes the presentation of a qualitative study.

We can make an informed choice if we consider different organization arrangements and their analytic implications. Hammersley and Atkinson (1983) suggest five for consideration:

- *Natural history*—tells the story of the investigation, how understanding unfolded, the history of progressive discovery.

- *Chronology*—focuses on the evolution over time, the development and unfolding of a character, or the situation.

- *Narrowing or expanding the focus*—starts small and gradually increases in generality, like those hollow Russian doll sets with increasingly larger dolls enclosing one another; or the reverse—starting large and successively narrowing the focus.

- *Separation of narration and analysis*—provides a section for the narration and follows it with analysis. Note, however, that the narrative implicitly, by what it includes and what it excludes, is itself analytic.

- *Thematic organization*—(a) presents the culture or social structure in terms of sociological components such as kinship and marriage, political institutions, economic institutions, and so on; or (b) presents the insider's view in terms of how those studied organize and view themselves.

The researcher can embed organization in the explanation. For this method, Strauss (1987) argues for clearly specifying all the theoretical elements and their connections and then adding such illustrative material as is needed to convey reality, enhance comprehension, and build trust.

Content to Include

While the reporting format may differ from study to study, there is certain information the reader needs to know in order to determine whether to trust the findings. Generally we look for certain descriptive aspects that are integrated into the body of the study report, as they are in the Hoffmann-Riem study. This is especially true of studies presenting a generalization. Other times, especially when it is a descriptive case study and such details would get in the way of the narration, they are put in a methodological appendix, as they are, for instance, in Whyte's (1955) classic *Street Corner Society*. The report should include:

- What the study is about—the area of investigation, questions, hypotheses, theories, or models around which the study is framed.
- What was done, by whom, when, where, and how key concepts emerged; problems in the field and in data collection (if any); and problems of bias or tendencies to "go native."
- The development of a rationale, explanation, or theory.
- An indication of how this study stands on the shoulders of others and goes beyond any previous work in the area.
- A complete meshing of facts and theory. Choice of facts must demonstrate intelligence and internal consistency. Honesty must shine through the description to show how well facts support theory. Include efforts to test the theory by disconfirming it as well as to find evidence to support it.
- A talented selection of vignettes, stories, and quotations that illustrate and interpenetrate the rationale, explanation, or theory, making the extent of the match clear.
- Possible rival explanations and, where able to do so, evidence of their elimination.
- Description of the researcher's background and how it affects data collection, analysis, and interpretation. More often thought of as negative and potentially biasing, such disclosure can be quite positive, as when an individual has special knowledge and experience in an area.
- The likely questions of the intended audience are answered with respect to both content and method. If concerns are not allayed, reasons are given.

Where and how each of these items is covered is the province of the writer, but all should be included.

Writers differ in how much of the interpretation they do for the reader. Stake[1] (1995), noted for presenting large amounts of data for the readers to self-analyze, suggests seven sections:

1. Open the report with a selected vignette—"I want my readers immediately to start developing a vicarious experience, to get the feel of the place, time."

2. Describe the issues "that will help them understand the case," as well as who the researcher is and how the study developed.

3. Present a body of data "not unlike that they would make themselves if they had been there."

4. Develop a few key issues, "not for the purpose of generalizing . . . but for understanding the complexity."

5. Probe the issues with considerable experiential data and indications of how points were confirmed and attempts made to disconfirm them.

6. Summarize understandings about the case and how the generalizations have "changed conceptually or in level of confidence."

7. Use a closing vignette—"I like to close on an experiential note, reminding the reader this is just one person's encounter with a complex case" (p. 123).

"For a while we worry about having enough to say; before we know it, we have too much. . . . It is an effective author who tells what is needed and leaves the rest to the reader" (p. 121). Stake's own work exemplifies his recipe except that he tends to underweight the even-numbered points and to overweight the odd-numbered ones, especially number 3; he presents large chunks of data. The outline, however, is a good one when presentation and interpretation are balanced.

Try to find a study like yours in the literature and note what is included, how it is organized, how the parts go together, and how transitions are made from one section to the next.

▶ Many qualitative investigations are written up as case studies, which are ideal for describing complex causal systems "in living color."

▶ Inclusion of many illustrations from the data is a characteristic of these reports; it makes them highly readable. Empathy permits readers to "try on" the explanation to test its validity and estimate its generality.

Style

Whereas academic writing is generally formal and uses the third person, qualitative research is often informal and frequently uses the first person. For instance, Hoffmann-Riem's section describing her study is full of "I examined . . ." "I sought . . ." and so on. Hammersley and Atkinson (1983) note that the use of "I" may be appropriate when these instances are personal choices, personal interpretations, or the result of personal characteristics or biases. Reporting the procedure section in the first-person active voice shows your pride in having made these design choices.

We face a number of perplexing problems in preparing materials to communicate with others. For example, what can we do about the grammatically flawed material we would like to quote from the data? Use quotes just as they are? How many of us talk in complete sentences, especially when under stress or in a hurry? These problems may well convey the reality of the person or situation but can embarrass informants. By now, they seem more like friends than persons "out there to be studied." It is a matter of judgment, but many researchers prefer to clean up the quotes as much as possible while still making them sound as if recorded. Incomplete sentences can include a description of a nonverbal gesture to show that it was finished.

How many examples are enough? The inclusion of "real" illustrative material is a strength of the qualitative path, which consists of "the concrete particulars of events," as Erickson (1986, p. 150) puts it. The narrative "persuades the reader that things were in the setting as the author claims . . . because the sense of immediate presence captures the reader's attention" (p. 150). Strauss (1987), however, warns not to over-load because the material is "colorful and interesting—at least to the author"; "data should function . . . in the service of . . . theory" (p. 220). It is a judgment call, but there is a strong tendency to include too many examples because they are particularly well phrased, clever, or "right on target." They become decorations instead of serving to connect evidence with claims. Marshall (2002) gives good advice:

> Give me a short juicy quote that tells me . . . the essence of the category/code/theme. . . . Then give me a sense of its importance. . . . Next I like to know about the complexity—what variations occurred? What do you make of them? . . . [Here] I would expect to see some analytical comments . . . comparisons between participants, links between themes . . . little comments about how the analysis was done. . . . You move between illustrating . . . and telling me in what way I should read the data.

Unfortunately, if illustrative material leads to a person's identification, the authenticity so well achieved by such material can also cause loss of privacy and embarrassment to informants. Unless there is reason to identify them, they should be protected not only by pseudonyms but also by the deletion of material that would uniquely identify them or their situation. Usually you can do this easily without losing the feel of reality. As extra protection, it sometimes is useful to have your colleagues try to identify locations and individuals and, if they are successful, query them for the clues they used to see whether your audience would know such clues.

Can you mix numbers and words? Why not? Some qualitative researchers believe that numbers have no place in their work. But the problem faced by the researcher is how best to convey the sense of the data. If that is best done with words alone, so be it. But if you are trying to convey relative sizes, frequencies, averages, and similar concepts, then numbers and statistics are as appropriate for qualitative research as for quantitative.

Another dilemma is how to convey trustworthiness and be taken seriously yet write in such a way that one's audiences feel what one is describing "at the gut level." One of the appeals of qualitative methods is that they get behind the intellectual side of problems to the affective, the emotional. Some researchers suggest that poetry in reports may help convey this side of the data (see Cahnmann, 2003). Qualitative researchers often deal with problems they want the audience not just to "under-stand" but also to "feel," to have empathy and concern. Rothman (1986) expresses the problem exceptionally well. She studied women who had undergone amniocente-sis to learn whether they carried defective fetuses and whether to consider abortion. Worth reading in the original, here are some excerpts:

> The heart of the book is the women who got the bad news. I used their experience of grief and anguish for what it tells about motherhood, about pregnancy, and about a society that develops this kind of technology—and expects gratitude for it. . . . The challenge was to write it in such a way that others . . . would feel the emotion. . . .

> Yet I know that when we do that . . . we open ourselves to charges of being not scientific, of being journalistic, . . . sensational journalism. . . . It is a real bind. If I stick to the neat hypotheses . . . I don't get to . . . the core of the experience women face when they use amniocentesis. But when I share the horror at the core I risk being dismissed as not only not scholarly . . . but just plain hysterical, overemotional.
>
> When I wrote the chapter on their grief, I let it go . . . wrote like a person possessed. I cried—you cry. . . . At every level, from their most intimate relationships to the medical institutions, these women suffered. I wanted the whole society to know it, to know what we are doing. (pp. 52–53)

Such research deeply involves the researcher in the data-gathering process, but then she must distance herself from it long enough to get it into perspective to write it up. The researcher "who fails to achieve distance will easily fall into the trap of recounting 'what happened' without imposing a coherent thematic or analytic framework" (Hammersley & Atkinson, 1983, p. 213). Having "made the strange familiar," she must now stand back to "make the familiar strange." Yet, to have the intended affective impact, she must keep that emotional edge. The title of Rothman's article says it well: "Reflection: On Hard Work." No question, it was—and is.

▶ Qualitative reports can be organized in any way that contributes to the reader's understanding.

▶ They are often written in an informal style using the first person.

▶ Quotations are often "cleaned up" enough to avoid embarrassing the informant but still retain a sense of authenticity.

▶ Informants are protected from identification by using pseudonyms and removing or changing identifying context.

▶ Inclusion of examples and direct quotations contribute to the success of qualitative methods but can be overdone.

▶ Numbers and words can be mixed; numbers should be used wherever they can be helpful.

▶ In some studies, writers must balance the tone of their writing to achieve the emotional impact they seek without destroying the trust usually attributed to a scientific study.

Hallmarks of Qualitative Research

A list of hallmarks is included for each of the research methods described in this book. A hallmark was the mark a guild used in the Middle Ages to signal a work of quality. These listings similarly indicate quality characteristics. This one includes *considerations that are universal to research*, regardless of method; these are marked with an asterisk and will not be repeated in later lists. (Some have been adapted from Stake [1995] or Miles and Huberman [1994].)

(continued)

*1. The author has special competence in the research method used as evidenced by previous work in the area, or by the details given about method in the body of the report or its methodological appendix. Methodological detail is especially important if the author lacks a prior reputation for competence.

*2. Unless it is strictly a descriptive report, the study includes a conceptual structure (verbal description of the phenomenon relating it to previous knowledge) that guides questions, explanations, rationales, or theories.

*3. Research questions are clear and the features of the design are congruent with them.

*4. Data were collected across the ranges of situations, settings, persons, and times that are implied by the research questions and by such generality claims as are made in the study.

*5. If multiple fieldworkers and/or sites were involved, consistency was observed across researchers and sites in both data gathering and analysis.

*6. There is no reason to believe that the researchers have special biases that would distort their view of the phenomena; or, if they have such biases, they have been described so that they can be taken into account in judging the findings.

*7. The study was not sponsored in such a way as to create expectations regarding its outcomes. If it was, explanations are given as to why one should discount this concern.

*8. Observations appear to have been made in such a way that the process of observation did not change the behavior observed. If it was, changes were documented and allowances made in interpretation.

*9. From the excerpts given in the report, recording of observations appears to reflect accurately what was observed. There was not an inappropriate overemphasis on the exotic or unusual.

10. The research examines a phenomenon in context rather than excluding aspects that might give a different perspective.

11. Observations and interpretations appear to have been triangulated and/or otherwise checked. Triangulation was done across persons, situations, and methods as needed to substantiate findings. The role and point of view of the researcher are apparent.

12. Findings are tested by checking for possible disconfirming as well as confirming evidence.

13. Where appropriate, observations seem to reflect how those that were studied understand or view a phenomenon.

*14. The time required to complete the study was long enough to provide deep familiarity with the phenomenon and provide a representative sample of the phenomenon being studied. But it was not so long that investigators have "gone native"— that is, to so overidentify with those being studied as to lose research perspective and their sense of naive curiosity.

*15. A thorough search for rival explanations has been made, and they have either been eliminated or the remaining ones are discussed.

16. The consistency of coding across coders, time, and data samples was checked.

17. When shown to the informants (member checking), the analyses are confirmed, the rejection can be reasonably explained, or members' comments are incorporated into the report.

*18. Findings are consistent with the data that are presented—conclusions are neither over- nor underinterpreted, and areas of uncertainty are identified.

*19. Findings are connected to prior theory, and their congruence or lack of it is discussed.

20. The report appropriately illustrates the complexity of the phenomenon with rich detail. It includes enough appropriate quotations and examples so that the match between observations and generalizations can be judged. Data summaries are displayed where appropriate. The study appropriately takes into account the influences of personalities, politics, and time on the phenomenon.

*21. The characteristics of the sample of persons, settings, processes, and so forth are sufficiently fully described to permit adequate comparisons with other samples, and any limiting aspects are discussed. Where feasible, the generality of findings is tested in other circumstances.

*22. Any ethical concerns raised by the research have been allayed.

*23. Enough methodological detail is presented as to provide an audit trail; another researcher can replicate the study by making reasonable inferences about procedures where there are gaps in the account.

ADDITIONAL READING

The many general works cited in Additional Reading for chapter 12 have something to say on writing the report. In addition, some researchers like Firestone (1993), for example, have examined the kinds of generality possible with qualitative research. Two useful books on writing up research reports are Wolcott (2001) and Becker (2007). See Fischer (1999) on preparing reports for publication. On qualitative research quality standards, see Freeman, deMarrais, Preissle, Roulston, and St. Pierre (2007).

IMPORTANT TERMS AND CONCEPTS

confirmability/objectivity
credibility/Internal Integrity
dependability/reliability
instrument decay
member checking
mortality

multisite studies
peer checking
social consequences
transferability/External Generality
trustworthiness

OPPORTUNITIES FOR ADDITIONAL LEARNING

1. In her study, Margaret Johnson concluded from her interviews that in contrast with men, women talked about the difficulty of handling their work, both on the job and in the home, as though it were their responsibility to handle both. Using the first person throughout, she

wrote the research report as a narrative, describing how she came to interview these particular people, the nature of the interviews, and so forth. The report concluded with the generalization that women have not yet internalized men's conception of the workplace.
Comment on the nature of her report.

2. Describe how well you think the Hoffmann-Riem study in chapter 1 meets the quality standards of this chapter.

3. Genevieve Le Conte is studying the effect of the availability of day care on families. Will
day care allow the mother to become a wage earner, or will she use the time for less economically helpful purposes? She starts interviewing every mother with an odd-number
address in a low-income housing unit where a free day-care program has been established
and plans to reinterview them every month. About this time, a new and better housing unit
opens across town. Some of her informants move to these new units. Since the new unit
does not yet have day care, Genevieve decides to continue her study with the cases at the
unit where day care is already established. Comment on this decision.

4. How could Hoffmann-Riem (chapter 1) have increased the External Generality of her study?

5. What do you suppose was the point of providing both operational (practical) and conceptual criteria of quality in qualitative research?

APPLICATION EXERCISE

In writing up your proposed study, what format seems to be most appropriate? A sequential narration of what occurred? A chain of reasoning? Another format? What data-quality
problems do you anticipate, and what can you do about them? Try to find a study like yours in
the literature and note what is included, how it is organized, how the parts fit together, and
how transitions are made from one section to the next.

KEY TO ADDITIONAL LEARNING OPPORTUNITIES

1. In one sense, she can write the report anyway she wants to, because there is no standard
format. In another sense, if she wishes to focus on acceptance of the conclusion of her
study, she would do well to write it as a chain of reasoning and reserve the use of the first
person for those instances where she is expressing her opinion or describing the decisions
she made in methodology.

2. Christa Hoffmann-Riem's presentation of the research is very professional and inspires
confidence in her findings; trustworthiness as well as credibility with the audience are not
problems. She provides sufficient description of the way she did the study so that the reader
can follow the general outline and another researcher could probably replicate it. But this
assumes that such a researcher has the interviewing skills of Hoffmann-Riem who, without
a set of preinterview-developed questions, appears to have been able to draw the information she wanted from the parents.

The Internal Integrity and External Generality of the study were already analyzed in,
respectively, Additional Learning Opportunity #6 in chapter 7 (p. 150) and Additional
Learning Opportunity #6 in chapter 8 (p. 183). If you did not yet complete those problems,
do them now. Next read the answers to the problems and then the paragraphs below.

Two of the additional characteristics we would expect to find in a solid qualitative study are
evidence of data checking and of self-disclosure. With regard to checking the data for validity, we have no indication of any kind of triangulation—person, situation, or method. There

is no evidence that she used other than interviews as data; for instance, she did not observe the parents and children in their homes. She is the sole data gatherer. Although this is not atypical, having another person observe or interview can provide a basis for determining whether there may be a bias affecting the inductive reasoning.

Do we need triangulation in this instance? Is there any reason to doubt the validity of the parent interviews? Should we be concerned that what is actually happening is different from what the parents say it is? Would the parents have anything to gain by their statements? Respondents generally try to be cooperative and give the interviewer what is being sought; they want the interviewers to think well of them and want to please them. Did Hoffmann-Riem cue the parents to the answers she sought? Probably not, if we believe her interview procedure, because it starts broadly. If all the normalization statements came at the end when she was narrowing in on what interested her, this might be true, but we are given the impression that they just tumbled out in the interview.

If we sensed that her findings were counterintuitive, we might press such concerns further. Where findings confirm what seems to make good sense, however, it seems petty to raise such considerations. This is part of what makes up explanation credibility—and her explanation is highly credible.

One can question whether "raising the bar" and pressing such concerns is appropriate. Sometimes, it is precisely because someone questioned what nobody previously had that a significant finding comes about. Since far fewer counterintuitive findings turn out to be true than intuitively true ones, this can be a very expensive way to spend your energy. You need either to be sharp enough or lucky enough to question the right findings.

With respect to self-disclosure, we would look for some background to indicate possible biases. Since she is the main data-collecting instrument, were there any personal reactions during the study that might have affected her interpretation of events? She gives no such indication. Further, she does not comment on why this particular problem intrigued her, so we don't know if there are any prior dispositions that might have influenced her. Some comments on this point would have allayed such concerns.

In summary, the report does not offer any clues that suggest that bias is a problem, or that others might have used an alternative strategy for the interviews or analyzed or interpreted the data differently. Again this kind of question might be pursued further if the findings did not make such good sense.

3. This is an example of what is called mortality: Individuals have left the initial sample whose absence could well account for, or at least affect, the study's outcome. It is quite possible that the more ambitious individuals who took advantage of the day-care center to find employment are the same ones who would be most likely to try to improve their lot by applying for new and better housing. Thus, those leaving the sample might be a selective group. If the center were not found effective in creating wage earners, mortality is a rival explanation since those most likely to use it for its intended purpose moved away.

4. Here are several ways: comparing her findings with similar studies, using a probability sample, or replicating the study with a new sample. The generality of qualitative studies often arises from synthesis with similar studies. Had Hoffmann-Riem cited other studies of adoption that found similar results with different kinds of participants, this would have markedly strengthened External Generality.

Hers was a convenience sample. Since "birds of a feather flock together," one doesn't know whether the kinds of persons who participated in the discussion groups differed from the adopting population. The fact that they were from one discussion group raises questions. She mentions considering using the records of the adoption agency to obtain a probability sample, but she discarded the idea because it would associate her with the agency and its problems. Here is one of the many trade-offs a researcher must make. Does she emphasize possible greater External Generality by using their records over possibly more valid responses to her queries by disassociating herself from the agency and using the convenience sample? She chose the latter. Note, however, that as a substitute for a probability sampling, she showed the similarity in demographic statistics of the members of these discussion groups to "the universe of applicants for one year."

Finally, replicating her study with a new sample of a different nature and obtaining the same findings would have strengthened External Generality by making it much less likely that the findings applied only to her original group,

This answer adds to the thinking behind the answer to Additional Learning Opportunity #6 in chapter 8 (p. 184).

5. There is no way for me to know what you suppose, but you might be helped in examining your answer by the following. In the absence of current, and, likely, future differences in what constitutes appropriate criteria, Donmoyer's suggestion (p. 343) that one adjust the criteria to the purpose of the study is probably good advice. Including both approaches provides a basis for doing so. The operational and conceptual approaches compliment each other in "covering the waterfront."

Further, both are important, but in different ways. As indicated in the chapter, standards can't be avoided in work that is to be accepted by others. Conceptual criteria are needed by those not familiar with qualitative work to help them judge it; they are unlikely to be satisfied with a laundry list of things to attend to. But it is also important to qualitative researchers to provide a basis for discussion about the priorities for those doing qualitative studies.

The operational definition, the list, is important for qualitative researchers because conceptual criteria often do not translate immediately into operational terms.

SUMMARY

We can try to characterize the indicators of quality in qualitative research operationally, by describing the kinds of methodological steps to look for in a study, or try to characterize them conceptually. We did the former by assembling a list of methodological strategies from the previous chapters. The latter is more difficult because of the variety of conceptions of qualitative standards. For descriptive studies without claim to generality, the operational criteria will have to suffice. For those claiming generality, or studies like Hoffmann-Riem that obviously hope for it, an examination of the judgments of Internal Integrity of chapter 7 as named and discussed by Guba and Lincoln (1982) showed that Internal Integrity criteria are applicable. Also, the criteria for External Generality from chapter 8 are applicable where generality is claimed. The listing of hallmarks together with the operational criteria listed on page 343 summarize things to look for in qualitative reports.

Descriptive qualitative studies are frequently written as case studies of an individual, group of persons, situation, event, or phenomenon. These, in particular, can be written in any format that adequately presents the case. Studies advancing a generalization, however, usually follow the chain-of-reasoning pattern; if not in exact order, at least the pieces are present. A key to a good qualitative report is combining the explanation with sufficient (but not too many) informant quotations to give the feel of the individuals, the climate of the situation, and the atmosphere of events.

Qualitative reports create pictures in the minds of the readers that are fleshed out with feelings as well as factual details—not only the "concrete particulars of events" but also the immediate presence of the individuals who are involved. This ability is one of the unique advantages of the qualitative method. The writing can be appropriately informal to achieve factual trueness to the original situation. Although words may carry the main message, where numbers would convey the meaning more appropriately there is every reason to combine verbal description with numbers, charts, and graphs. Although format is not specified, we can clearly indicate what the report should include as indicated by the listing on page 354.

A Look Ahead

In the next section we jump to the quantitative end of the continuum before coming back to the middle for research using sample surveys and doing evaluation. They fall in the middle of the continuum by using both qualitative and quantitative methods. The quantitative section opens with chapter 17 on the use of numbers to describe the characteristics of data with statistics.

Note

[1] From R. E. Stake, *Art of case study research: Perspectives on practice*. Copyright © 1995. Reprinted with permission of Sage Publications.

The Continuum of Research Methods
Quantitative Side

This section explores quantitative methods, beginning with the tools of the method—descriptive statistics, measurement, and inferential statistics—and then describes experimentation and meta-analysis, which use these tools. These are the tools most commonly used to establish causation and to eliminate rival explanations. Able to handle large data quantities, they can provide evidence for generality.

- Chapter 17 deals with the numerical description of data. We routinely describe our world in verbal terms, but we must also understand the ideas involved in describing phenomena with numbers. This chapter shows how to display data and summarize them into statistics descriptive of central tendency, variation, and relationship.

- Chapter 18 explores measurement, testing, and structured observation. Some things can be counted (number of words produced in a minute) or measured (time between each response) and described by numbers. Other things, such as concepts and constructs, must have their definitions translated into the observable behaviors that constitute a testing, measurement, or observation scheme. This chapter uses the descriptive statistics of the previous chapter as it examines the criteria of good measurement and the means for determining how well the criteria have been met.

- Chapter 19 also builds on the descriptive statistics chapter to describe the logic of inferential statistics. They show whether it is likely a real effect exists and disconfirms or adds confirmatory evidence for a hypothesis. They eliminate the rival explanation of sampling error.

- Chapter 20 describes and gives application examples of some of the most commonly used inferential statistics—t test, chi-square, and analysis of variance.

- Chapter 21 describes how experimental design can eliminate a host of other common alternative explanations that plague studies. From simple to more complex designs, the logic of controlling to eliminate rival explanations is explored and rules for constructing new designs are discussed.

- Chapter 22 describes meta-analysis, both (1) as a method of combining quantitative findings across studies to determine the average size of an effect or relationship, and (2) as a method of research in its own right to tease out likely causative factors embedded in those studies. Meta-analysis was expected to replace verbal literature summaries, but researchers have realized that the two can be complementary.

Links to previous research

Explanation, rationale, theory, or point of view

Questions, hypotheses, models

Preplanned and emergent designs

Design/procedure

Focus   Records   Time   Comparison and Contrast   Situation   Participants

Data

Statistical analysis and/or narrative analysis

Conclusion

Link to next study

Explanation or rationale of next study, etc.

17

The Numeric Description of Data
Descriptive Statistics

> For in relation to economics, to politics and to all the arts, no single branch of educational science possesses so great an influence as the study of numbers.
>
> —Plato
>
> All models are wrong, some are useful.
>
> —George Box

As we saw in the Zimbardo study in chapter 1, researchers collecting data that is quantified are often faced with a large amount of raw data that must be organized and summarized because there are too many pieces of information to understand at face value. Only as we summarize them in some way can we see patterns and draw conclusions from them. Descriptive statistics such as Zimbardo's do this very well. But what we see presented in the Zimbardo report is only a small sample of methods that researchers use to understand what their data can tell them.

This chapter first briefly shows how to portray a set of data in different graphic formats and then concentrates on common descriptive statistics such as mean, median, mode, measures of variation, and correlation and its relation to causation. Descriptive statistics facilitate analyzing and summarizing data and thus undergird the final links of the chain of reasoning.

Correctly interpreting data is essential to its use. This requires using the proper statistic. For example, shall we use the mean, median, or mode, two of these, or all three? Each of these statistics is a summary that emphasizes some aspects of the data and overlooks others. They all provide information we need to get a full picture of the world we are trying to understand.

INTRODUCTION

The process of describing something requires that we abstract its important parts: in painting a scene, we select the important features to sketch in. Similarly, in describing phenomena in words, we almost automatically select what is important to us. Doing so is second nature—indeed, so much so that Travers (1961) used it as a predictor of teaching ability. To find what was important to teachers, he asked them to draw a classroom. Did they include pupils? Where did they put the teacher? The more successful teachers not only included pupils but also drew the teacher in the classroom working with children rather than behind a desk.

Similarly, we often point out the significant aspects of our world with numbers: the gross national product, the population of a community, the size of a table lamp, or the Scholastic Aptitude Test (SAT) score of a college freshman. Nouns name these objects or characteristics: product, population, heat, verbal learning ability. We select each of these names from a range of possible nouns to fit the phenomena we wish to convey. To further convey them, when describing in words, we use adjectives to modify those nouns: enormous gross national product, small town population, hot oven, bright college freshman. When describing numerically, numbers take the place of adjectives: $4 billion gross national product, a population of 267 persons, a 12-inch table lamp, a freshman with an SAT verbal score of 800. We speak of a batting average of .325, or an average income of $20,000. As used in the social sciences, numbers specify some condition in a category (such as how many) or a point on some scale.

Numbers can modify their nouns by giving us a count of units (267 persons), by indicating a rank (the twelfth-smallest town in the state), or by placing the characteristics on some scale (12 inches, SAT score of 800 with a mean of 500). They refer to only a single dimension, or characteristic, at a time, just as an adjective does—32 inches tall, a mean of $20,000. Numbers have the considerable advantage that we can differentiate far more precisely with numbers than we can with words. For example, students with SAT scores of 800 and 735 are both very bright, but their scores differentiate them. Even using a less-than-perfect measuring instrument, with a scale running over a large range we can differentiate many more levels of learning ability than we have adjectives to describe them.

All the advanced fields of science that can predict and control use numbers to describe phenomena. In fact, using numbers has come to be such a hallmark of science that some people look down on fields that do not use them. It is true that the use of numbers has proven effective and efficient in describing phenomena. Some experts, however, believe that because certain characteristics have not yet been measured adequately, words still do a better job. At the current level of development of the social sciences, there is room for both points of view—and both have merit.

> ▶ As used in the social and behavioral sciences, numbers specify a condition in a category or on some scale. Scientific fields that have made advances in prediction or control have used numbers to describe their phenomena. Social scientists' measurements are still sufficiently limited such that describing in words is required in many instances.

CATEGORIES OF NUMERIC INFORMATION

We have noted three operations for numbers: naming and counting, ranking, and placing on a scale. These correspond to different levels of measurement, each containing more information than the previous and requiring a greater degree of precision. Thus, if we discriminate no more finely than to put people into categories (Caucasian, African American, Hispanic, Asian, Native American), all we can do is to name the categories and count their contents. Such use is designated as the **nominal level of measurement**. Names apply to persons or things with common characteristics that we place into the same category. The UPC bar code on merchandise that is read at the cash register by a laser scanner is a nominal use of numbers; it names the product. We can also use numbers to modify that name by telling how many of a thing there are, that is, by counting them.

If we can differentiate among the individuals within a group, we can move to the next higher level of measurement: ranking (ordering of objects), or the **ordinal level of measurement**. We can rank several teachers in terms of their apparent skill but perhaps would not want to say that the differences in skill between the first and second and between second and third are equal. So we are not placing them on an equal-unit scale, but we do know that one is more skillful than another. The Mohs' hardness scale is an example of a very useful ordinal scale. It is formed by determining which mineral will scratch the other when the two are rubbed together; diamonds, scratching everything else, rate the hardest. We have no way of expressing diamond's hardness other than this ranking.

Finally, at the next two levels of measurement, we place numbers on scales: one with an arbitrary zero point like the Fahrenheit temperature scale—an **interval scale**—and one with a real zero point like the scale of inches—a **ratio scale**.[1] The advantage of the latter is that we can say that a distance of 12 inches is twice as long as one of 6 inches. Conversely, we cannot say that a day on which the temperature reaches 80 degrees is twice as warm as one on which it reaches 40 degrees. Similarly, a student with an SAT verbal score of 400 does not have half the verbal learning ability of the student with the top score of 800. Most psychological and educational measures are of the arbitrary-zero type. These are called interval scales because the units from one score point to the next (400 to 401, 401 to 402) are presumed equal, but the zero point is arbitrary.

Just where ordinal scales cease to be useful and interval scale statistics become permissible has been much discussed (for an excellent discussion, see Knapp, 1990). A response scale such as "never," "sometimes," "frequently," and "always" is clearly ordinal. We often assign the values 1, 2, 3, 4 to these responses and compute averages; that is, we treat them as though the attribute were being measured on an interval scale. We have no evidence that the distance from "never" to "sometimes" equals that from "sometimes" to "frequently." However, if the data yield useful generalizations when interpreted—it works—we use it!

Where the zero point is not arbitrary, it is a ratio scale because we can legitimately interpret ratios such as twice as much or half as much. Time and most physical measures have this property. It makes sense that one can do something in half the time or that one person is half as tall as another. What does a zero SAT score mean? There is no such thing.

Some statistics are designed to deal with categorical data or nominal measurement, some with ranked data, and most with interval or ratio scale measurement where it is assumed we have a scale that measures in equal units.

Four uses of numbers are:

▶ Nominal—numbers name the members of a category or indicate the number in the category.

▶ Ordinal—successive numbers order data in terms of some common characteristic (size, hardness, ability, etc.). No assumption is made that the differences between the numbers are equal.

▶ Interval—successive numbers on a scale mark off equal units, but the scale's zero point is arbitrarily chosen.

▶ Ratio—not only do numbers mark off equal units, but also zero indicates an absence of whatever the scale measures.

REPRESENTATIONS OF GROUPS OF NUMBERS (DATA SETS)

A *data set* is the list of data describing one or more characteristics of a group. How would one best describe each of these data sets: The gross national product of a variety of countries? The populations of the communities of a state? The heights of a shipment of table lamps? The SAT scores of a freshman class? A common way is to use *descriptive statistics*, summarizing one feature of the data at a time—the average, the spread, the bias toward high or low, and so forth.

We tend to rush to use statistics or graphs, forgetting that clever use of words can also bring life to a disembodied set of numbers. Consider this from Wurman (1989, p. 176):

> Statistics about the distribution of income may not mean much, but imagine if people's height reflected their income. An hour-long parade of 30 million British income earners would start with several minutes of people with no height at all (people who, although working, are losing money), to more than a half-hour's worth of very short people (mostly women, pensioners and teenagers). Only after forty minutes would people of average height appear, followed by a few people who would be ridiculously tall, towering 20 miles over the heads of the people who started the parade.

This dramatic quotation also lends itself to a pictorial representation, the use of a graph or chart. Graphs and charts can depict all of this at once, holistically, and in easily understood pictorial form, letting us instantly grasp what is significant about it. Although the rest of this chapter is devoted to descriptive statistics, before using statistics you must first consider whether they are the best means of communicating what you wish to convey. Graphical representation has been underused, perhaps because of the extra preparation required and printing costs. Today, however, they are so easily generated by a variety of computer programs that their use should be increasing. And, as Wurman's verbal illustration nicely shows, creativity and imagination help enormously.

We saw in our sections on qualitative research that a primary function of the researcher was to extract the gist or themes from a set of data. As with qualitative, so it is also with quantitative data: the analyst's job is to bring out the salient points and communicate as much about the data as possible and to do so in a succinct and revealing way.

Consider the following data from a subset of states in the United States:

22, 28, 33, 32, 27, 31, 20, 32, 18, 33, 26, 26, 26, 27, 35, 29

These are percentage scores, indicating the percentage of fourth-grade students in 16 states who are estimated to score proficient or higher as measured on the National Assessment of Educational Progress. Before we begin thrashing around in the data, it is important to make sure we know something about where the numbers have come from. Are they based on samples? How are the scores derived: teacher observation, multiple-choice tests, computer-based tests? How are the participants determined: random sampling, convenience sampling? Why are only these states presented? Are data for all states available?

Let's answer these questions first. The goal of the National Assessment of Educational Progress (http://www.nces.ed.gov) is to estimate state-level achievement, not the achievement of individual students. The test is multiple choice and administered to everyone in a classroom. Schools and classrooms are picked at random, with the sampling stratified to ensure there are sufficient numbers of schools from within each state. We have only presented states that are listed as being in the South according to the regional definitions given by the U.S. Census Bureau (http://www.census.gov). The original data included results from the District of Columbia. However, we wanted to present a state-level picture. Because the District of Columbia is a city, and because all the states are combinations of city and noncity influences, we decided to set it aside.

Some researchers will forget to stop and reflect on what is known and not known about the data in advance. This is a very important step that will help you anticipate and identify problems in the data and the analysis. Do not bypass this step.

BRINGING ORDER TO THE DATA

Returning to the data, it is often helpful to reorder the data from lowest to highest, to develop a sense of the **frequency distribution**. The frequency distribution refers to how the numbers are distributed along a scale in terms of frequency (how many 1s, how many 2s, etc.). In this case, the scale is percentages, so we know already that it has a minimum of zero and a maximum of 100. The reordered data for the states are presented in Table 17.1.

The table helps us see some things that might have been hard to see before. There are 16 values and only one state with a percentage below 20; all but three are between 25 and 35. Let's go further and make a frequency table showing which states had each percentage (Table 17.2).

Table 17.1 States in the Southern Census Region Listed by Percent Proficient in Reading at Fourth-Grade Level

Mississippi	18	Arkansas	28
Louisiana	20	West Virginia	29
Alabama	22	Kentucky	31
Oklahoma	26	Florida	32
South Carolina	26	Maryland	32
Tennessee	26	Delaware	33
Georgia	27	North Carolina	33
Texas	27	Virginia	35

Source: National Assessment of Educational Progress (nces.ed.gov/)

Table 17.2 Data from Table 17.1, Tabulated by Frequency of States at Each Percentage

Value	Frequency	States	Value	Frequency	States
18	1	MS	27	2	GA, TX
19			28	1	AR
20	1	LA	29	1	WV
21			30		
22	1	AL	31	1	KY
23			32	2	FL, MD
24			33	2	DE, NC
25			34		
26	3	OK, SC, TN	35	1	VA

The frequency table shows the basic shape of the distribution of scores. It also shows that the Gulf Coast states have the lowest values, and there is a cluster of states around the District of Columbia that do quite well. In one picture, a frequency distribution conveys multiple layers of information: the spread of scores, the location of the middle scores, whether the scores cluster around one or more points, and whether the distribution is symmetrical, among other things. To paraphrase Cohen (1990), without a frequency distribution: "You won't know that there are no cases between scores of 23 and 25, or that the scores 22 and below are somewhere in left field, or that there is a pileup of scores of 26. These . . . become immediately evident with simple graphic representation" (p. 1305).

The frequency table can be represented by a variety of graphics to communicate a visual sense of the data. For example, in Figure 17.1, the same data are presented three ways, each bringing out some important aspect of the data, while making other aspects less salient. For example, the *bar chart* (panel A in Figure 17.1) provides bars of length equal to the frequency of each row in the frequency table, thereby identifying peaks and valleys in the data. Bar charts are most commonly used as counts of data in nominal categories.

Panel B consists of a *stem-and-leaf plot*. In this text-based graphic the left column indicates the 10s place of each number (the stem), and the remaining portion of each number is represented in the right hand side (the leaf). Here again, bins are used, and when multiple numbers occur in the same bin, multiple leaves are lined up to give a graphical sense of the distribution. In this way, the graphic communicates both the overall sense of the distribution, while allowing the viewer to see the individual values in the leaves. This graph uses bins of size 2. (The hinges—H—are quartiles. The M stands for median.)

Panel C is a *box-and-whisker plot*. The ends of the box are drawn at the location of the first and third quartiles. The **quartiles** are the values at or below which one, two, or three quarters of the data fall. For example, in Figure 17.6 (p. 385), on the percentiles scale the 25th percentile is Q1, the 50th percentile is Q2 (median), and the 75th percentile is Q3.

The difference between the first and third quartiles, and hence the length of the box, is called the *interquartile range*—the location of the middle 50% of the data. The second quartile, which marks the point above and below which half the values fall, is called the median. The line inside the box is drawn at the location of the median. The lines above and below the box extend out to the minimum and maximum, indicating the full range of data. As the reader can see, the box plot provides a quick visual summary that effectively communicates the bunching of data at the low end of the box.

The variety of charts and graphs in Figure 17.1 only scratches the sur-

Figure 17.1   Different graphic representations of the data in Table 17.2: (A) bar chart, (B) stem-and-leaf plot, (C) box-and-whisker plot.

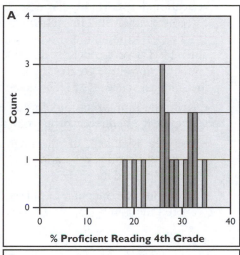

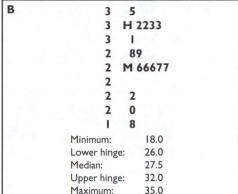

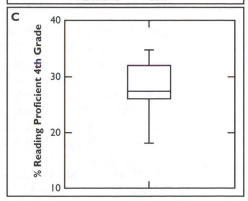

face; the number of forms they can take are limited only by the scope of human ingenuity. For example, quality of life can be portrayed by superimposing faces on the states of a U.S. map. Each feature of the face can represent a quality-of-life characteristic (e.g., eyebrows = crime; mouth = education, etc.) and can be given a positive or negative look to reflect that aspect. A high crime rate has arched eyebrows; lots of educational opportunity has a smiling mouth, little a frowning one; and so on. We can convey an overall impression of a state yet allow specification of a characteristic.

Proper formulation of charts and graphs is essential to avoid misconceptions. Tufte (1983) very concisely describes the goal: "Graphical excellence is that which gives the viewer the greatest number of ideas in the shortest time with the least ink in the smallest space" (p. 51). To achieve this, he suggests:

- Keep the representation of numbers, as physically measured on the surface of the graphic itself, directly proportional to the numerical quantities represented.

- Use clear, detailed, and thorough labeling to defeat graphical distortion and ambiguity. Write out explanations of the data on the graphic itself. Label important events in the data.

- Don't let the number of information-carrying (variables) dimensions depicted exceed the number of dimensions in the data (p. 77).

> ▶ Charts and graphs have the advantage of showing the data while highlighting certain aspects of them. Unlike a descriptive statistic, such as an average, they can show more than one aspect at a time. Some, such as the frequency distribution, bar chart, and stem-and-leaf diagram, show all the individual data points while displaying the shape of the distribution.
>
> ▶ As you consider using descriptive statistics, determine whether the goal of your communication can be as well or better conveyed by a graphic. If it can, remember to heed Tufte's maxim to convey "the greatest number of ideas in the shortest time with the least ink in the smallest space."

SHAPES OF DISTRIBUTIONS

In general, distributions vary by where on the scale the bulk of the data occur (low, medium, or high), and how spread out the data are (bunched up or spread out). Data related to human populations often have a lot of small values. For example, there are many small towns in most countries, and a few large cities. Graphically, this leads to a tall peak of bars far on the left side of the bar chart, with a long line of small bars as one moves to the right. Figure 17.2 shows this common pattern in a plot of the enrollment of students in each school in a state in the southwestern United States. Notice that the pattern reflects the fact that most schools are small (that is, less than 750), but that some are in the 2500 range.

Distributions are often described as having peaks and tails; the tails are the sides of the distribution that "tail off." When a frequency distribution has a single peak and symmetric sides it is referred to as "bell shaped." Some such distributions are called **normal frequency distributions**. Asymmetry is referred to in terms of **skewness**: if positively skewed, the long tail is pointing to the large-values end of the scale; if negatively skewed, it points to the small-values end. The distributions portrayed in Figure 17.1 have some mild negative skew. The distribution in Figure 17.2 has moderate positive skew.

A negatively skewed distribution may result when we have a test with a "ceiling" effect: The test is too easy for high-achieving students, nearly all of whom get very high scores, yet it discriminates well (provides a spread of scores) among low-achieving ones.

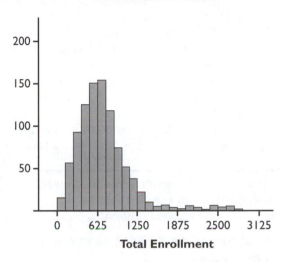

Figure 17.2   School sizes in a southwestern state.

Similarly, a test that is too difficult for low-achieving students will bunch up the very low scores and therefore have a "floor" effect, but it will spread out the high-achieving students.

DESCRIPTIVE STATISTICS

The graphics we have seen so far perform an important function. They take numeric values and represent them in ways that are easy memorable, and they promote the recognition of usual or unusual patterns. Efforts at describing sets of data are usually focused on two things: where the bulk of the data lie, and how spread out the data are. Statistics describing the location of the bulk of the data are commonly called *measures of central tendency*. Statistics that describe the degree to which data are spread out or bunched up are called *measures of variability*. Alternately, these measures are sometimes called *level* and *spread*. The role of descriptive statistics is to summarize batches of data, preferably using as few summary values as possible.

Measures of Central Tendency

The common indicators of central tendency are the mode, median, and mean. The **mode** is simply the score, measure, or category that occurs the most often. Categorical (nominal-level measurement) data have a mode; it is the category with the most persons or things in it. In the case of the frequency distribution of Figure 17.1 (panel A), 26 is the mode—the score with the highest frequency.

We have already met the median in the box-and-whisker plot. The **median** is the point below which half the scores lie and assumes only ordinal-level measurement. In a sample with an odd number of observations, it is the middle observation, or score: In the sequence 10, 14, 15, 17, 20, the median is 15. With an even number, it is the score halfway between the two middle ones: In the sequence 10, 14, 16, 17, the median is 15, half the interval between the middle scores. No median can be formed for nominal data because they have no order, but we can find one for ordinal or higher-level data.

By far the most commonly used indicator of central tendency is the arithmetic **mean**, more often called just the mean, or average. This is simply the sum of the observations divided by the number of them. It assumes that the data are at least at the interval level of measurement. If the scores are displayed as a frequency distribution (Figure 17.1, panel A), it is the point on the baseline around which the distribution would balance if it were cut out of cardboard and put on a knife-edge.

Like a seesaw on a child's playground, cases that are on the extremes have a major effect on the mean. Picture two children in balance on the seesaw but sitting in toward the center. Now move one child to the far end of the board. Because the fulcrum has to be moved toward the distant child to restore the balance, an extreme score pulls the mean significantly toward it.

Figure 17.3   Symmetrical and skewed distributions and their effect on measures of central tendency.

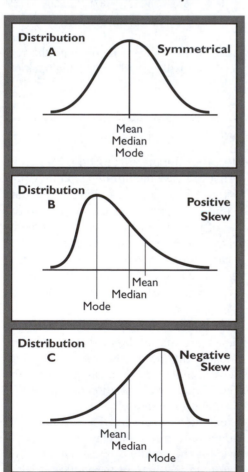

A skewed distribution can be detected by the order of mean, median, and mode. When the mean is largest, the median next, and the mode smallest, as in frequency distribution B of Figure 17.3, the skew is positive; when the size order of these measures is the opposite, the skew is negative (distribution C). When they are all very close, the distribution A is likely to be symmetrical. (Note that we say *likely* to be symmetrical but not *certain*. Large clumps of scores close to the mean on one side can be offset by small clusters on the other side distanced further from the mean. This distribution will be asymmetrical even though the mean, median, and mode are all lined up in the middle.)

With a skewed distribution, we are more likely to use the median or the mode rather than the mean to represent the data's central tendency. For example, the distribution of pay in large corporations is usually skewed with the mean moved higher by the salaries of top executives. The pay of a typical employee is better represented by the median or mode.

Not all distributions are bell-shaped.[2] Those that deal with social conformity, for instance, are likely to be J-shaped. In Figure 17.4, graph A shows such a distribution

Figure 17.4 Frequency distributions for a social conformity variable and a bimodal variable.

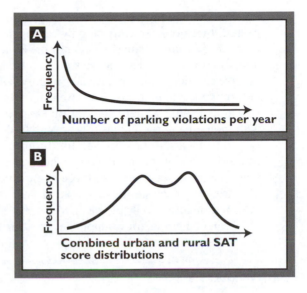

for the number of parking tickets acquired by individuals in a year. Most had none, one, or two, and the drop-off is severe from there. Some curves have more than one peak and are multimodal. An example is the bimodal graph B in Figure 17.4, which is a frequency distribution of SAT scores for a high school within a combined rural and urban attendance area. The score distribution of the urban feeder elementary school is represented by the higher peak, and that for the rural feeder school by the lower one. When the students are merged in the high school, the combined distribution still shows these two peaks.

> ▶ Three statistics describe the central tendency of a data set:
>
>   1. The mode is the most numerous category, measure, or score.
>
>   2. The median is the point below which half of the scores, or measures, lie.
>
>   3. The mean is the arithmetic average, the sum of the scores divided by their number: the balance point of the score distribution.
>
> ▶ In a symmetrical frequency distribution, the mean, median, and mode are nearly equal.
>
> ▶ In a negatively skewed distribution (tail to left), the mean is smallest, the median is in between, and the mode is largest.
>
> ▶ Conversely, in a positively skewed distribution (tail to the right), the mean is largest and the mode is smallest.
>
> ▶ Negative skewness can result from a "ceiling" effect (measure is too easy for high-scoring students).
>
> ▶ Positive skewness can result from a "floor" effect (measure is too hard for low-scoring students) or simply the fact that many things exist in small quantities.

We began this chapter with a discussion of four different levels of measurement: nominal, ordinal, interval, and ratio. Each level contains more information about the phenomenon being described than the previous level. Nominal measures group people, ordinal measures rank them, interval measures use scales with an arbitrary zero point to show distance between ranks, and ratio measures use scales with a true zero.

Statistics require a certain level of information in order to be correctly interpreted; therefore, we can use only certain statistics on the lower levels of measurement. For example, since we cannot order nominal measures, they have no median and, of course, no mean. Since we can tell which category contains the largest number, we can determine the modal category. Where we have ordinal measures, we can determine the middle case; thus we can find a median. If there are ties in rank, there is a modal rank; without ties, all ranks have one case, so there is no peak. Finally, with interval and ratio measures, we can find all three—mean, median, and mode.

In using a statistic designed for lower-level data on higher-level data, we discard the additional information of the higher scale. Thus, the mode alone includes no information from cases other than those in the modal category. The median finds the middle case, but the clustering or spread of cases on both sides of it does not affect it; such information affects only the mean. As we have discussed earlier, this differential sensitivity can be helpful, for example, in detecting the presence and direction of skewness.

VARIABILITY

Sometimes we are concerned with the variability in the data or the phenomenon, whether the scores are spread out or bunched up. A measure of spread or variability tells us about how dissimilar or inconsistent the scores are. For example, when we choose a doctor, we would consider not only her overall quality but also her consistency or variability. We certainly wouldn't want a doctor who says, "How well I perform the operation really depends on the day you catch me—on average I'm good, but some days I'm great and other days I'm terrible!" Likewise, we would not be happy with people who are "on-time on average" but are either an hour early or an hour late.

Range

One method for describing variability is how far apart the most extreme scores are. It is the distance from the highest to the lowest observations. The **range** for the frequency distribution in Figure 17.1 as shown by the maximum and minimum in panel B is $35 - 18 = 17$. Because the range is totally dependent on the two extreme scores, it is likely to vary considerably from sample to sample and to be easily affected by an extreme score. Be careful not to assume that there is data throughout that range.

Semi-Interquartile Range

Another way to represent dispersion is to exchange the extreme scores of the range for the spread of middle scores—how far points in the middle of the distribution are apart. We introduced the interquartile range above with box plots—the difference between the third and first quartile determines the size of the box (Figure 17.1, panel C). We more commonly use half the interquartile range, called the **semi-interquartile range,** for descriptive purposes to make it comparable to the standard deviation (discussed below). The semi-interquartile range has the disadvantage of not using information from each piece of data—long tails and bunching up between quartiles are not represented. Further, it has no use in inferential statistics, but the standard deviation does.

Using Multiple Statistics

Because summaries affected by a single rare value may mislead us from a true sense of the distribution, it is always important to consider multiple summary statistics. Table 17.3 shows summary values for all the U.S. census regions for the same test and grade used previously. As you can see, the South clearly has the largest spread of scores. This is reflected in the extremely large range (34), but this is due in large part to the extremely low value of one state. When we compare the range difference between the South and the West (34 vs. 22) the difference is considerable; however, when we look at the variation in the bulk of the data as reflected in the semi-interquartile range, we see they are much closer at 4.75 versus 4.38. Clearly, the Midwestern states have the smallest variability or spread combined with a high central tendency or location.

Table 17.3   Mean, Median, Range, and Interquartile Range for Census Regions Using the Percent Proficient in Reading at the Fourth-Grade Level

Group	Count	Mean	Median	Standard Deviation	Min	Max	Range	Semi-Interquartile Range	25th Percentile (Q1)	75th Percentile (Q3)
Midwest	12	35.25	34.5	3.36087	30	42	12	1	34	36
Northeast	9	37.4444	39	5.0277	28	43	15	3.75	33.75	41.25
South	17	26.1765	26	8.0408	7	41	34	4.75	21.75	31.25
West	13	29.0769	31	6.13	17	39	22	4.38	24.5	33.25

Source: National Assessment of Educational Progress (nces.ed.gov/)

Variance and Standard Deviation

To create a measure that tells us something about how spread out or bunched up scores are, a common method is to pick a point, such as the mean, in the middle of the distribution, and measure how far each value is from that point. If data are spread out, then the distance from each data-point to the center will be large. If data are bunched up, then the distance from each data-point to the center will be smaller. Table 17.1 is reproduced in the first two columns of Table 17.4. The mean of the second column was calculated and placed in the third column to expedite finding its distance from the entries in column two. That difference, the deviations from the mean, is in the fourth column.

If we look at deviations on average, we would like to think we could get a sense of variability on average. As you can see, however, the sum and average of the deviations from the mean are zero. This is because we describe the mean as the balancing point, as we mentioned earlier, which is equivalent to saying it is the spot where the deviations sum to zero. To get around this problem, statisticians and scientists have

Table 17.4   The Mean of This Group of States, the Distance of Each State from That Mean, and Its Squared Distance (added to Table 7.1 data)

State	Percent Proficient	Group Mean	Distance from Mean	Squared Distance
Mississippi	18	27.8	−9.8	96
Louisiana	20	27.8	−7.8	60.8
Alabama	22	27.8	−5.8	33.6
Oklahoma	26	27.8	−1.8	3.2
South Carolina	26	27.8	−1.8	3.2
Tennessee	26	27.8	−1.8	3.2
Georgia	27	27.8	−.8	.6
Texas	27	27.8	−.8	.6
Arkansas	28	27.8	.2	.04
West Virginia	29	27.8	1.2	1.4
Kentucky	31	27.8	3.2	10.2
Florida	32	27.8	4.2	17.6
Maryland	32	27.8	4.2	17.6
Delaware	33	27.8	5.2	27
North Carolina	33	27.8	5.2	27
Virginia	35	27.8	7.2	51.8
Sum	445	445	0	354
Average	27.8	27.8	0	22.2

squared the deviations to keep the information about size, while putting them in a form for which we can get a sum and thereby an average. You can see in the fifth column that squared deviations accentuate the difference between values and show the variability more sharply.

By summing them, we can have a measure of variability based on the sum of squared deviations or, as they are also called, the sums of squares. Of course, as we noted before, sums have problems of interpretation so more commonly we average the squared distance. This is called the **variance**. In practice, the problem with the variance is that it is far outside the scale of the data. To address this, we use the **standard deviation** (SD), which is the positive square root of the variance. Engineers call this the *root mean square deviation*, which states the computational operations in reverse order. The standard deviation thus has all the information of the variance, with the additional advantage of providing a number in the original scale.

The formula for the standard deviation of a set of scores is:

$$\sqrt{\frac{\Sigma(X-M)^2}{N}}$$

where Σ indicates summation, X stands for each score, M for the mean, and N for the total number of scores.

This formula is used when describing the variation in sets of data. When we are trying to use an observed set of data to infer the variance or standard deviation of a larger unobserved group, we use $N - 1$ rather than N in the denominator in order to estimate the population standard deviation. This correction is necessary in order to adjust for a bias in estimation, which is of greater concern with small samples—the effect of subtracting 1 from a large N is negligible.

The standard deviation is affected by extreme values even more strongly than the mean (on which it is based). The distance of a score from the mean is squared, and the squares of numbers rise much faster than the numbers themselves. For example, let's consider scores of 5, 6, 7, and 8, which are but one unit apart. Their squares (25, 36, 49, 64), however, are 11, 13, and 15 units apart, respectively, and the distance between numbers continues to increase as the numbers get larger. Thus, the more extreme the case, the more leverage it will have.

Figure 17.5 shows the two measures of dispersion on a *bell-shaped frequency distribution*, also sometimes referred to as the normal curve. It corresponds closely enough to the score distributions of many behavioral measures to be useful. Note that the interquartile range, by definition, includes the middle half of the cases—the semi-interquartile range is half that distance. The standard deviation usually includes about the middle two-thirds of the cases. Therefore, the middle band including ±1 SD on each side of the mean is broader than the interquartile range. The range is not shown, because the highest score for a normal distribution is infinity, and the lowest is minus infinity.

Numerous test score distributions resemble the bell-shaped curve or normal curve, as do many physiological functions such as height. We will see many more uses for it as we look at making inferences to unobserved populations. Examine Figure 17.5, which

---

Figure 17.5   Two measures of dispersion, standard deviation, and semi-interquartile range, shown for a normal frequency distribution (normal curve).

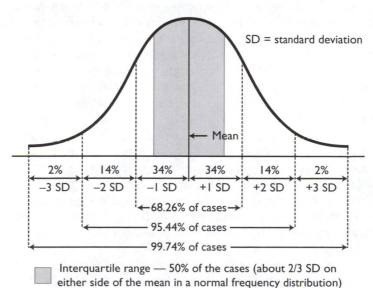

SD = standard deviation

| 2% | 14% | 34% | 34% | 14% | 2% |
| −3 SD | −2 SD | −1 SD | +1 SD | +2 SD | +3 SD |

←68.26% of cases→

95.44% of cases

99.74% of cases

☐ Interquartile range — 50% of the cases (about 2/3 SD on either side of the mean in a normal frequency distribution)

is an approximation of a normal curve. The curve is really a frequency distribution, just like the charts in Figure 17.1. The normal curve joins the tops of an infinite number of columns running from the highest to the lowest score. When we mark off successive standard deviation distances on the baseline, starting at the mean, we will find that ±1 SD falls just at the points where the curve changes from convex to concave.

One of the advantages of the normal curve is that we know what proportion of the cases fall between any two scores. The percentages between successive standard deviation demarcations in Figure 17.5 indicate what proportion of the scores falls into each area. Adding the figures for the two areas adjacent to the mean gives 68%; thus, slightly more than two-thirds of the cases lie between ±1 standard deviation. When we extend the range to ±2 SD, we cover 95% of the observations, with about .26% of the cases in the tails beyond ± 3 SD.

Three measures of dispersion are:

▶ The range is the distance from the lowest to the highest score.

▶ The semi-interquartile range is half the distance from the point below which a quarter of the observations lie (Q1, first quartile) to the point below, which three-fourths of them lie (Q3, third quartile).

▶ The standard deviation is the root mean square of the deviations from the mean. The square of the standard deviation is the variance. The standard deviation is the dispersion measure most used; it is strongly affected by cases far from the mean.

Standard and Derived Scores

Just as the inch and the meter serve as standard units of length, so standard deviations provide a constant scale across measures. Using it, we can compare scores to show relative standing on very different tests. A raw score typically conveys little information—some tests are easy, others difficult; some are extremely long and some very short. But whereas the inch and meter have a true zero point, test scores as interval scales do not. However, describing a score in standard deviation units, especially if the score distribution is roughly a symmetrical bell-shaped curve, tells us whether that score is high, low, or in the middle of the score distribution.

Standard scores (or *z-scores*) are simply the raw (original) score translated into its distance from the mean in standard deviation units. For example, in a distribution with a mean of 100 and a standard deviation of 25, a raw score of 75—a score that is one standard deviation below the mean—will have a standard score of –1.00. Standard scores, as such, are not much used because negative numbers for scores below the mean are troublesome to handle and carry a negative connotation. Instead, a close relative, **derived scores** (also called *scaled scores)* are commonly used.

With the addition of a constant like 50, 100, or 500 to the standard scores so that the mean becomes 50, 100, or 500 instead of zero, derived scores translate standard scores to a scale where all scores are positive. Figure 17.6 shows a variety of score scales that set some arbitrary serviceable number as the mean, similarly set the standard deviation conveniently, and then translate the scores to that scale. Standard scores are used most often to compare scores on different tests—the relative standing of a student on a verbal ability test with his standing on an English test. We would expect comparable standard scores on each if students were living up to their potential.

Many intelligence test results are reported in deviation IQ scores with a mean set at 100 and the standard deviation at 16 (for example, the Stanford-Binet; the Wechsler tests use 15). From our knowledge of the normal distribution, we can then interpret an intelligence test score of 148 as very high, for it is three standard deviations from the mean. Since less than 1% of the cases exceed ±3 standard deviations, and

Figure 17.6   A variety of score scales shown in relation to the normal curve.

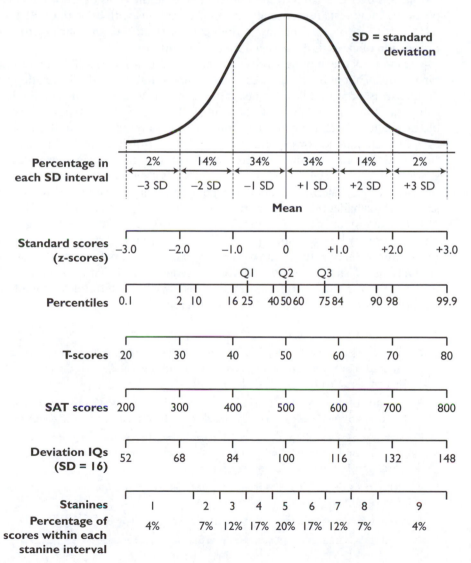

that includes the observations in both tails, still less might be expected in the upper tail alone. Similarly, a score of 84 is one standard deviation below the mean. With half of the cases above the mean and about 34% between the mean and one standard deviation below it, we know that 34 + 50 = 84% of the cases are above the score of 84 and only 16% below it. Whether such inferences are accurate depends on how closely the shape of the sample's frequency distribution approximates that of a normal curve.

The percentage below a given score is called the **percentile** score. Figure 17.6 shows where some percentile values fall in terms of standard deviations. Knowing the proportion of cases at points along the normal distribution, we can easily translate raw, standard, and derived scores into percentiles. Many tests have tables showing the translation.

To ensure the accuracy of inferences made on the basis of a normal curve's proportions, some tests use normalized T scores, usually with a mean of 50 and a standard deviation of 10. The raw score scale is stretched and shrunk to make the proportion of cases fit those of a normal distribution.

Some tests use **stanine scores**. The name is a contraction of "standard nine" for nine scores. Except the end scores, each stanine is half a standard deviation wide; the middle score of 5 straddles the mean. Because so few cases normally fall into the end categories they are open ended, extending to the highest and the lowest scores possible on the test. Like normalized T scores, stanines are normalized; thus, the percentages in each stanine correspond to those of the normal curve. Using half-deviation steps to define each stanine, however, results in different percentages in each stanine score (4, 7, 12, 17, 20, 17, 12, 7, 4, respectively). It is easier to remember that a fifth of the cases (20%) fall in the middle category and that the categories to each side are successively smaller by 3, 5, 5, 3 percentage points (see the bottom line of Figure 17.6).

If we consider the lack of precision of most tests, this cruder categorization of nine scores may be more appropriate. Two- and three-digit derived scores invite spurious interpretations. In a scale with a possible range of 600 points like the SAT, the comparison of small score differences (e.g., a score of 704 and one of 720) may reflect only one more correct question. This trivial real difference is made to seem important by the 16-point derived score difference.

▶ Using the standard deviation as the unit of measure and the mean as a base point, standard scores replace the raw score mean with zero and adjust the raw score standard deviation to 1.

▶ A variety of derived or scaled scores are available to translate raw scores into scales with easy-to-use means and standard deviations that facilitate usage and interpretation.

▶ With these new scales, or "rulers," we can translate any score to show where it will fall on a standard or derived score scale—we can then compare relative standings of scores across tests for individuals.

▶ Such scores typically use the frequency distribution of the normal curve as a basis for interpretation.

▶ Percentile scores indicate the percentage of scores falling below a given raw score.

MEASURES OF RELATIONSHIPS

So far we have dealt with the description of a single variable, but more often we deal with at least two variables and wish to describe the extent of the relationship between them. Suppose we have grade point averages (GPAs) for a group of students in both their high school and college freshman years. Thus, we have a pair of GPAs, one high school and one college, for each individual. We can then plot each pair as a point on a graph, as in Figure 17.7, where each x represents a pair. We can see that, in general, individuals who did well in high school also did well in college, because the two variables vary together—they co-vary or are *correlated*. Such a plot is called by several names: **scatterplot**, scatter diagram, and scattergram. The oval line surrounding the points is added to show the area within which the pairs of scores fall. Not a part of the computation of a correlation, the oval line will be used in other figures to represent the scatter diagram.

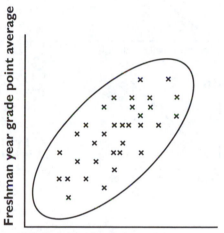

Figure 17.7   Correlation of high school and college grade point averages.

Pearson Product–Moment Correlation

The **Pearson product-moment correlation**, more commonly referred to just as "the correlation," is represented by the symbol r and indicates the extent of relationship by a number between $+1.00$ and -1.00; thus it is usually reported as a two-digit decimal—for example, .85. Each individual has a pair of scores, one on each of the two variables on which the correlation is being computed; the correlation is computed from these pairs of scores. A correlation of $+1.00$ indicates a perfect relationship such that if we know that the individual has the highest score on one variable, we also know she has the highest score on the other and all the pairs of scores are similarly predictable.

With a negative correlation, they track one another inversely; with a correlation of -1.00, the highest score on one variable is paired with the lowest score on the other. A correlation of less than one, either positive or negative, indicates that each member of a pair of scores tracks the other less than perfectly so that the highest score on one variable in a positive correlation might be accompanied by a medium high score on the other variable. The lower the correlation, the more poorly one tracks the other until, with a zero correlation, there is no regular relationship between the two scores. From one of the pair, we cannot predict the other.

Correlation scatterplots.   Just as we learned to interpret the standard deviation, so we also learn the meanings of different sizes of correlation. Coat or sweater size

**Figure 17.8
Representations of
the scatterplots for
correlations of
various sizes.**

High positive correlation

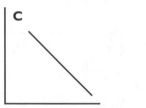

Perfect positive correlation

Perfect negative correlation

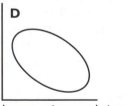

Low negative correlation

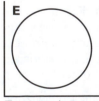

Zero correlation

bears a close-to-perfect positive relationship to the distance around a man's chest. High school academic achievement bears a zero relationship to shoe size or social security number, a negative but less-than-perfect relationship to the amount of conflict in the family or hours of television watching, and a positive but less-than-perfect relationship to the level of education of one's parents or to achievements in elementary school.

Correlations are often portrayed by encircling the majority of the points with an oval. Anyone using correlations is well advised to create a scatterplot of the observations. Figure 17.8 shows representations of scatterplots for correlations of various sizes. As the oval narrows from a high correlation such as plot A (r = about .80 to .90), it becomes a straight line for a perfect correlation, as in scatterplot B (r = +1.00). Plot C (r = −1.00) is also a perfect correlation, but a negative one. When the correlation decreases, from a low correlation such as plot D (r = −.20 to −.30), the oval gets fatter until, at the zero point, it becomes a circle, as in plot E (r = .00). An exact size is not given for each scatterplot because the correlation depends on the distribution of the scores as well as the shape of the oval. Thus, these are approximations.

Importance of scatterplots.   We noted earlier the importance of examining the scatterplot of a correlation. This is underscored by data from Anscombe's quartet (Anscombe, 1973, as given in Tufte, 1983, pp. 13–14). These are four sets of data of 11 cases, each of which produces exactly the same correlation of .82; they all even have the same means for both variables.

However, the sets produce the four scatterplots shown in Figure 17.9. Note how different they are from one another. A is a typical correlation scatterplot; B is a curvilinear plot; C is an almost perfect positive correlation except for one point (X = 12, Y = 13). In D, all the Y scores but one (X = 12, Y = 19) are the same. Were we to try to infer the nature of the relationship between the variables from just the number .82, the size of the correlation alone, we would make a grave mistake. Yes, the figures were adjusted to make a point, and they do make it—examining the scatterplots as well as the statistics is very important! Computerized software can easily provide scatterplots.

Effect of outliers on the correlation.   As you can sense from the example above, the size of a correlation is particularly strongly affected by one or more extreme scores. Called *outliers*, these are observations that lie outside the ellipse that

Figure 17.9   Scatterplots of four very different sets of scores for 11 subjects.

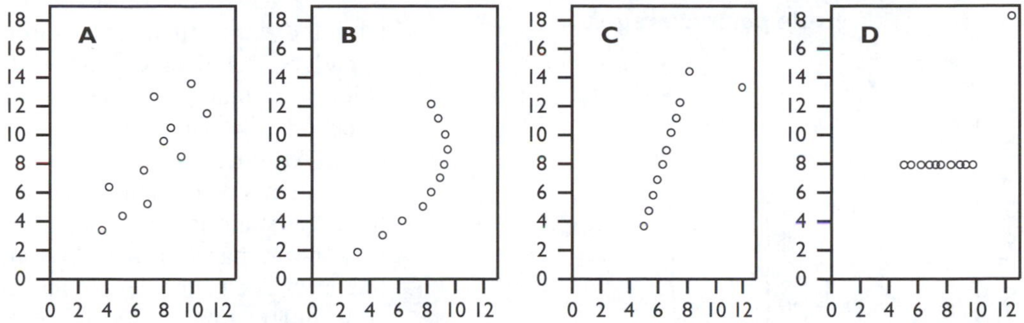

Source: After Anscombe (1973), as found in Tufte (1983)

would normally encompass them. An example is the observation $(X = 12, Y = 13)$ at the far right in scatterplot C of Figure 17.9. It is considerably off the line formed by the others, and notably lowers what would otherwise be a perfect correlation. In opposite fashion, in scatterplot D, there is no relationship between the y-axis scores (which are all 8s), and the x-axis scores (which vary over the score range) except for the outlier far up in the right-hand corner, which changes the correlation to .82. Without the outlier there is no variability; without variability there can be no correlation. Without variability the standard deviation in the denominator of the equation is zero. Recall from your study of algebra that dividing by zero makes no sense; thus, there is no meaningful correlation coefficient. As these examples indicate, the effect of outliers on correlations can make interpretation difficult.

Treatment of outliers.   So, outliers strongly affect certain statistics such as means, standard deviations, and correlations. Should you, then, discard them? Or do they tell us something special about the topic? You must judge each situation on its own. Interview persons with extreme scores to find an explanation. An outlier may be the result of illness, trauma, or English as a second language and you might appropriately discard it. Be careful, however. For example, an art test outlier's score that is due to color blindness raises questions about what is really being measured. Whether you decide to keep outliers or discard them, tell what you know and explain your action in the report. Calculate statistics both with and without the outliers so that readers can see their effect and judge for themselves.

Effect of range on the correlation.   Because the correlation is sensitive to extreme cases, the score range of the variables making up a correlation should be typical of the relationship of interest. An atypical **restriction of range** leads to an underestimate of the size of the typical relationship, just as an atypical extension of range leads to an overestimate.

Figure 17.10 on the following page shows how we might underestimate the effectiveness of selection into college because of restriction of range. The data in the entire figure are what we would like to have—an unselected sample—to evaluate the effectiveness of using the high school grade point average (GPA) to estimate success

Figure 17.10   Selection of students for college on the basis of their high school grade point average.

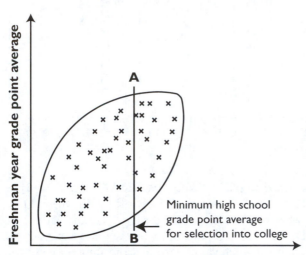

in college. The typical situation, however, is that a test, or variable, is used to select those to be admitted, and then only those already selected cases are available to estimate the success of selection—the cases to the right of the AB line. It is readily apparent that a correlation based on those cases alone would be markedly lower than that based on all the data. The former would markedly underestimate the selection value of high school GPA, yet it is frequently the only data available.

Thorndike (1947, as found in Guilford & Fruchter, 1978) describes one of the rare selection evaluations using unselected groups, thereby training individuals who would otherwise have been excluded—a costly study. The task was to evaluate the effectiveness of tests in predicting success in training pilots during World War II. The correlation between scores on a test of complex coordination and training success was .40 for the 1,036 unselected group, but only –.03 in the top 13% of the pilots that would have otherwise been selected. Evaluating the test on that 13%, which is all that would typically have been available, would have caused the test to appear useless.

In parallel fashion, if the range is extended to cover cases not typically included, the correlation will be an overestimate. Suppose you are considering the use of a read-

Figure 17.11   Effect of extended range on correlation.

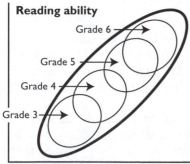

ing test as a measure of how well a student is likely to achieve. Figure 17.11 shows the relationship of a reading test to overall achievement for each of grades 3 through 6. Note that the correlation within any one of these grades is not very high. The scatterplot for each grade is almost the circle that you obtain for a modest or low correlation. But the children do learn as they progress from grade to grade, which stretches the overall range of scores. When combined into a single scatterplot, the total range of scores increases markedly. Although the correlation was moderate to low in each of the grades taken individually, it is high (the heavily outlined ellipse) over the course of four grades. If you wish to use the reading test to examine children's likely progress in their own grade, the more modest correlation is the one you should heed.

Effect of nonlinearity on the correlation.   From the fact that a perfect correlation is a straight line, you might guess that the Pearson product-moment correlation assumes that the relationship we are examining is a **linear relationship** (also called a *straight-line relationship*). As one variable changes, the other also changes in a proportionate amount. Relationships are not always linear, however. Correlations of many ability scores with age are often nonlinear, with growth spurts and plateaus.

Figure 17.12 shows a scatterplot for a class, some members of which have too much anxiety about the test, some too little, and some just enough to be well motivated. Such relationships yield an inverted U-shaped, or curvilinear, scatterplot. These would be markedly underestimated by the Pearson product-moment correlation so a special statistic, the *correlation ratio,* is usually used.

Figure 17.12   Curvilinear relationship between level of test anxiety and an achievement test score.

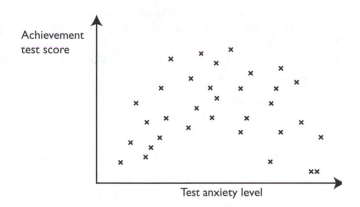

Correlation as proportion of variance.   The extent of relationship is indicated more accurately by the square of the correlation coefficient than by the coefficient itself. Thus, the amount of relationship displayed by a correlation of .40 is more accurately represented by .16, which is considerably lower. Further, an increase of .05 in correlation from .90 to .95 when these are squared is a change from .81 to .90, a change of .09. This is the same as the difference between a correlation of .10 and one of .32 $[(.32)^2 - (.10)^2 = .10 - .01 = .09]$, but it is a difference of .22 in terms of the unsquared coefficients. Because the connection between the amount of relationship and the size of the correlation coefficient is not constant from .00 to 1.00, a large change is needed at the low end of the correlation scale to achieve the same amount of increase in relationship as a small change attains at the top end of the scale.

The square of the correlation indicates the proportion of the variance that is accounted for by the relationship. For example, with a correlation of 1.00, 100% of the variance of the variables is common or accounted for by the relationship. With a correlation of .80, the proportion of variance that is common is .64, or 64%.

Computing the correlation.   Although the computation is currently rarely done by hand, understanding the formula aids interpretation. The formula for the Pearson product-moment correlation is simple in standard score form; it is the average of the products of the standard scores (z-scores). Therefore, we multiply the pair of z-scores for each individual $(Z_x Z_y)$, sum those products, and divide by the number of scores: $\Sigma(Z_x Z_y)/N$. The formula using raw scores (X and Y) is:

$$r_{xy} = \frac{N \sum XY - (\sum X)(\sum Y)}{\sqrt{\left(N \sum X^2 - (\sum X)^2\right)\left(N \sum Y^2 - (\sum Y)^2\right)}}$$

Other Correlations for Special Conditions

Although designed for use with interval data, Pearson product-moment correlations are often computed on categorical (nominal) or ordinal data to show relationships with variables of interest. One can use ranks or assign arbitrary numbers to categories such as 0 to elementary-level education, 1 to high school, 2 to college, and 3 to beyond college to provide data for a Pearson product-moment correlation. But a better solution is to use one of the correlations designed to handle data from special situations.

A variety of correlation statistics have been devised for special situations:

• *Spearman's rank correlation* (two ranked variables),

• *Biserial correlation* (interval or ratio scale variables, one of which has been arbitrarily dichotomized),

• *Point biserial correlation* (same as biserial but the dichotomy is real, such as gender),

• *Tetrachoric correlation* (two normally distributed arbitrarily dichotomized variables),

• *Contingency coefficient* (two categorical variables, e.g., male–female, living–dead), and

• *Correlation ratio* (one interval variable with one ordinal or interval level variable— used primarily with **nonlinear relationships**).

Some of these correlations have the same properties as the Pearson product-moment correlation coefficient; many of them do not.

Many predictions of a dependent variable (e.g., success in college) from an independent variable (e.g., success in high school) can be done with an offshoot of correlation, *regression*. Often this involves more than one independent variable (e.g., a motivation measure, a mental health measure, etc.). In such cases, multiple correlation and multiple regression are used to optimally weight the measures for the best prediction.

▶ The Pearson product-moment correlation shows the extent of a linear relationship between two variables on a scale from −1.00 to +1.00. It is usually reported as a two-digit decimal, for example, $r = .76$.

▶ A correlation is computed from pairs of scores, a pair from each individual in the sample. For a correlation between variables A and B, the pair consists of an individual's scores on A and on B.

▶ A correlation of .00 indicates no linear relationship.

▶ A positive correlation shows that the members of the pair vary together; when one is high the other is also.

▶ A negative correlation indicates that the variables vary inversely; low scores on one variable are associated with high scores on the other.

> ▶ The extent of a relationship is portrayed more accurately by the square of the coefficient than by the coefficient itself.
>
> ▶ Size of the correlation is affected by outliers, nonlinearity, and inappropriate range (restriction in range or too broad a range to estimate the relationship in typical situations).
>
> ▶ The Pearson product-moment correlation assumes interval-level continuous variables; there are a variety of correlations based on data fitting different assumptions.

CORRELATION AND CAUSATION

The fact that a relationship exists as shown by a correlation does not allow us to infer that the relationship is causal. Often the relationship is the result of a third variable or a combination of other variables. The statistician Helen Walker was fond of noting that comparing footprints in the sand of older women next to footprints of younger women might lead to the conclusion that women tended increasingly to walk with their toes pointing outward as they grew older. Actually, there is no causal relationship here; rather it was considered a sign of femininity to walk with toes pointed out when these older women were young. Because the link often occurs earlier in the causal chain, we must be careful in inferring causation from a correlation.

Regardless of whether a relationship is causal, a correlation allows prediction; thus, such relationships are extremely useful. An extensive body of literature describes predictors of various kinds: to enhance learning conditions, to increase the effectiveness of teaching, to predict the stock market, to forecast college success. The higher the correlation, the more accurate the prediction. Unless the correlation is perfect, however, the predicted value is always less extreme—that is, closer to its mean—than the value from which it was predicted. This is referred to as *regression to the mean;* and the smaller the correlation, the greater the regression. Regression toward the mean reaches its maximum with a zero correlation; then the best prediction we can make from any score (such as high school GPA) is the mean of the other variable (mean college GPA). The prediction of one variable from another is discussed in statistics books under the topic of regression.

APPROPRIATE INTERPRETATION OF STATISTICS

Assuming that statistics were properly applied, basic to proper interpretation is (1) examining the sample for representativeness, and (2) examining what underlies the data from the standpoint of those from whom it was collected. If we expect to attain a consensus around the interpretation of data, we must anticipate any problems our audience may have in these areas.

Representativeness of Sample

We are rarely interested in the sample itself, but rather in what it tells us about some larger group or population of which it is representative. If our sample comes from a laboratory school, our readers will suspect that, compared to students in typical public schools, these students are well above average in ability and the ability range is smaller. If our research is to apply beyond the laboratory school, we should indicate the effect that range curtailment had on the data, what might be expected under more typical conditions, and how all these atypicalities affect the interpretation and generality of the results.

Understanding What Underlies Data

We are always tempted to take data at face value, but qualitative researchers in particular remind us that data are always the result of a social construction and may not mean what we think they do. As Bogdan and Biklen (1992) point out, the very act of gathering data often changes it. When Congress mandated that 10% of a remedial program should consist of handicapped children, the programs magically produced the required number of such children. Were there really that many previously unrecognized handicapped children? Was the local definition of handicapped changed? "Statistical data on minority, or handicapped children . . . the number of athletic injuries, acts of violence, or incidence of drug use in schools does more than numerically portray phenomena; it changes how we experience them" (p. 149).

Depending on the reward or penalty for reporting them, data collection itself may increase or decrease the visibility of violence, injuries, or drug use; result in recruiting of minority groups; strengthen countermeasures toward undesirable behavior; and so forth. Changes in rates must be particularly scrutinized for such influences as well as the effects of newly visible efforts to collect the data, changes in definitions, new ways of data gathering (such as a more sensitive test), and inconsistency in data-collection procedure. Counts can be strongly influenced where the funding level depends on a quantitative indicator. Remember, accuracy depends on the data produced, and "some commonly heard terms among data collectors include fudge factor, numbers game, massaging the data, and padding" (Bogdan & Biklen, p. 151). Understanding what underlies the data is critical to its proper interpretation.

EXPLORING WITH STATISTICS

We usually don't think of statistics as useful in an exploratory mode, because their use in the research literature is almost always to provide evidence for or to disconfirm some hypothesis, structure, or model. However, statistics have long been used to check data for unexpected relationships, although that activity is not usually mentioned in the reports. Scatterplots are universally used in this way. Researchers love the exhilaration of finding in them something unexpected that sometimes results in restructuring the whole direction of a study.

Having once experienced that "high," experienced researchers use descriptive statistics for the titillating exploration of data. They love looking for the next curiosity that could be just around the corner. Novice researchers should try exploration with simple statistics; it is a major joy of research. If you are interested in reading more about exploratory statistics, see Tukey (1977) or Leinhardt and Leinhardt (1980).

Exploration has been discouraged by the dictum that it is cheating to look at the data to see what they show, then develop a hypothesis, and finally proclaim to all that the data confirm it. When you know the hypothesis will be confirmed from the start—that is not research. Most statistics books warn against exploration as "data dredging" or "bottom fishing." As the derogatory names imply, such practices are deemed undesirable since chance relationships that are not generalizable may be interpreted as real.

Even if you rationalize after the fact, however, "Ah, now I see why," results that make reasonable sense may be worth further exploration. If you can, show that the explanation holds in a new sample; if it is confirmed, it probably is not happenstance. If you don't have time, leave testing for later or point it out for someone else to follow up. With clear indications that the results were found during exploration and explained after the fact, you may include exploratory results in your report separately from the original hypotheses. Considering the time and effort invested in data collection, it is only sensible to seek all it can tell you. Wherever feasible, researchers ought to probe for additional findings that appear to make sense and then follow them up with further research.

ADDITIONAL READING

In addition to Tufte (1983), recommended earlier, see Henry (1997) for examples and discussion of graphical presentations. Guilford and Fruchter (1978) is a conventional but understandable statistics text; Jaeger (1990) is unconventional and an easy read. For exploratory data analysis, Tukey (1977) is the classic presentation; also see Leinhardt and Leinhardt (1980). Huff (1954) remains an excellent survey of statistics misuse.

IMPORTANT TERMS AND CONCEPTS

derived scores
frequency distribution
interval scale
linear relationship
mean
median
mode
nominal level of measurement
nonlinear relationship
normal frequency distribution
ordinal level of measurement
Pearson product-moment correlation
percentile

quartile
range
ratio scale
restriction of range
scaled score
scatterplot
semi-interquartile range
skewness
standard deviation
standard score
stanine score
variance

OPPORTUNITIES FOR ADDITIONAL LEARNING

1. A Department of Guidance and Counseling faculty member wished to determine how the graduates of its master's program rated the effectiveness of instruction they had received. She asked graduate students to rate each course on a scale of 1 to 5 (in which 1 = inferior and 5 = superior). She then calculated the mean rating for each course. The department's statistics course was given a mean rating of 1.56; the course in theories of counseling and the one in techniques of counseling had mean ratings of 3.05 and 3.21, respectively. Sup-

pose she had concluded, on the basis of the mean ratings, that these graduates considered the instruction in the latter two courses twice as effective as that in statistics. Would she be correct in her assumption?

2. Following is a frequency distribution of an eighth grade science test in a large high school:

Score	No. students getting that score
67	3
66	5
65	15
64	25
63	35
62	55
61	40
60	8

No. of students = 186

a. Calculate the median score.

b. If the sum of all the scores was 11,461, what was the mean score?

c. Which is the better representation of central tendency of this distribution, the median or the mean?

3. A newly hired chemistry professor at Beltline University is put in charge of the first-year undergraduate chemistry course, which has an enrollment of over 200 students. He decides to teach the class in sections. He will assess students by a midterm and a final examination, each worth 50% of their grade. He wants a way of making it possible for students to compare their standing on successive examinations, even though the difficulty of the examinations varies. What do you advise him to do? How should he go about it?

4. Drawing on Bandura's (1978) self-efficacy theory of motivation, Salomon (1981) suggested that the relationship between attitude toward media and learning can be conceptualized as an inverted U. He hypothesized that students invest effort on the basis of two factors: the perceived difficulty of the task and the students' assessment of their skills in relation to the task requirements. Thus, students who perceive a medium such as television as easy will invest little effort in television instruction. The more difficult students perceive the medium to be, the more their effort increases until they begin to consider it too difficult. At that point, effort begins to decrease. Dr. Gladys Southwind conducted an experiment to test this relationship, examining subjects' ratings of the difficulty of various media and their effort on a task using the medium. A Pearson product-moment correlation coefficient determined that the strength of the relationship was only .35. Dr. Southwind concluded that there was not a strong relationship. Do you agree or disagree with her? Why?

Compare your answers with those following the Application Exercise.

APPLICATION EXERCISE

Consider the data that you are likely to collect for your study. How can you best summarize them? Why did you choose that way? What kinds of symbols or graphs will best convey what you want understood? Would translation into some form of standard scores be helpful? How else could they be presented? Would you use correlations to display the strength of relationships among your variables?

Some students lay out "dummy tables" so that they can anticipate what data analysis they plan to do and can then fill in the tables when they get the data. Although this method avoids surprises, it can also lead them to believe they can anticipate all they are going to find. However, half the fun of research is playing with the data to explore what is there. Don't limit yourself—plan to explore as well.

KEY TO ADDITIONAL LEARNING OPPORTUNITIES

1. No! Scales such as this have no real zero point; therefore, they are not ratio scales. The scales are at least ordinal, but we treat the data as though they were interval. We do so because, while we don't know for sure they are equal unit scales, we have found that when interpreted as interval scales they usefully predict real-world phenomena. Although it is convenient and useful to calculate mean ratings by way of comparison between groups, it is not correct to interpret them in terms of ratios.

2. (a) To get the middle case, divide the number of cases by 2; $186 \div 2 = 93$, which is in the third category from the bottom, or 62. (b) Mean score $= 11,461 \div 186 = 61.6$. The median would be a better representation than the mean because the frequency distribution is positively skewed; the long tail points to the higher scores. The position of the mean is sensitive to the higher scores.

3. Advise him to change the raw scores to a derived score with some easy-to-remember mean and standard deviation, such as a mean of 50 and a standard deviation of 10. To do this, he would subtract the test's mean from each raw score on that test, divide that difference by the raw score standard deviation, multiply that standard score by 10, and add 50. Then all the tests would have a mean of 50 and a standard deviation of 10, regardless of how easy or hard they happened to be.

4. From the description of Salomon's theory, Dr. Southwind probably should have expected a curvilinear relationship: little effort for easy media, increased effort as a medium was perceived as more difficult, and effort falling off again as the medium was seen as very difficult. Nonlinear relationships are underestimated by the Pearson product-moment correlation. Statistics like the correlation ratio would provide a more accurate estimate of the relationship. A scatterplot would be very useful in showing whether the relationship really is U-shaped.

SUMMARY

The problem of describing a set of data is parallel to that of describing a situation in words. In both cases we select the features that are important to convey, name them, and then modify them with words and/or numbers to portray the situation more accurately. Graphs and charts convey more than one feature of a data set and therefore can communicate the sense of the data very effectively, but they are underused. Statistics convey single features such as central tendency, dispersion or variation, and relationship, but they can be combined to portray more complex phenomena. With descriptive statistics, we select the features that are important (such as central tendency) and then describe them with numbers that convey more exactly the location or amount of those features.

The statistics that convey central tendency are the mean, median, and mode; those that convey variation are the range, interquartile range, and standard deviation. The order of the mean, median, and mode relative to one another can be used to sense skewness. The mean and standard deviation are the most commonly used descriptive statistics and form the basis for standard scores. They can be used to translate raw scores into a variety of convenient score scales that are, in combination with the normal frequency distribution, more easily interpreted. Translating raw scores into a common derived score scale facilitates comparison of an individual's results on different tests.

The Pearson product-moment is the correlation most often used to convey the strength of relationships. Relationships can be portrayed by means of a scatterplot, the shape of which indicates the general size and nature of the relationship. The Pearson product-moment correlation assumes that the relationship is linear—a change in one of the two variables is accompanied by a proportional change in the other. A perfect correlation is described by a straight line, successively less-than-perfect correlations by progressively rounder ovals, until at zero correlation it is roughly a circle. Outliers and nonlinearity strongly affect correlations. A correlation between two variables does not necessarily imply causation; both may be influenced by other variables. Regression permits the prediction of one variable from the other; the accuracy of prediction increases as the correlation increases. A variety of special correlation statistics have been developed for special situations.

A Look Ahead

In the next chapter on measurement, testing, and observation we will use many of this chapter's statistics to determine quality of measurement. Chapter 19 on statistical inference, inferring the size of a population value from a sample's statistics, also will build on this chapter's statistics.

Notes

[1] This discussion of nominal, ordinal, interval, and ratio measures perpetuates a legacy of S. S. Stevens (1946, 1951), which, some statisticians argue, is best left forgotten. Certainly, Stevens' scale types are incomplete, as Duncan (1984) observantly notes. Further, this textbook includes counting (which Stevens ignored) in the nominal category. It deserves a place, for when combined with good theory, counting can be as important as measurement and is certainly less controversial than measurement. Discussion of these measurement levels is needed because the interpretation of statistics is determined by the level of data from which they were computed. We can calculate arithmetic averages on ordinal data, but a comparison of such averages is meaningless unless we assume that the data come from scales or measures whose units we can assume are approximately equal.

[2] But many are, and even Plato noticed this. In *Phaedo*, Plato remarks to Socrates, "There are not many very good or very bad people, but the great majority are something between the two. . . . Have you never realized that extreme instances are few and rare, while intermediate ones are many and plentiful?" (Duncan, 1984).

Links to previous research

Explanation, rationale, theory, or point of view

Questions, hypotheses, models

Preplanned and emergent designs

Design/procedure

Focus   **Records**   Time   Comparison
and Contrast   Situation   Participants

Data

Statistical analysis and/or
narrative analysis

Conclusion

Link to next study

Explanation or rationale
of next study, etc.

Measurement, Testing, and Observation

> It is the faith of all science that an unlimited number of phenomena can be comprehended in terms of a limited number of concepts [constructs]. . . . The constructs are . . . man-made inventions . . . not a part of nature. It is only a way of comprehending nature.
>
> —L. L. Thurstone, *Vectors of the Mind*
>
> There is no descriptive language that does not consist of general words, that is, of concepts. The gift of humanity is precisely that, unlike animals, we form concepts.
> —Jacob Bronowski, *The Identity of Man*

In chapter 17, we noted that numbers are adjectives indicating "how many" or "how much." In this chapter, we look at the nouns the adjectives modify, the items or observations that are counted or measured. The problems of measurement are few when the scale can be physically sensed—for example, length (how far an individual moved) or time (latency or duration of response). The measurement of concepts and constructs that cannot be directly sensed is more problematic.

How do we know, if we cannot sense them, that we are measuring those constructs? What evidence can we find that an instrument has, in measurement terminology, **validity**? There is considerable evidence, but we must learn which to use and when to use it. Consistency is also a problem. Scores may vary from one measurement to another or from one measurement form to a parallel one; the testee may be less motivated or more tired. Evidence of consistency of measurement—of **reliability**, as it is called—is also important. This chapter examines the characteristics of good measurement.

Constructing good measures is time-consuming and costly. What aids exist for finding already developed measures? (There are many!) What are the strengths and weaknesses of various data-gathering methods? We will explore these questions in this chapter. Whenever the word *test* is used throughout the chapter, the material applies equally well to any kind of measure—for instance, rating scales, structured observation instruments, and so forth.

INTRODUCTION

Measures record or "freeze in time" a sample of behavior for later evaluation—for example, the ability to visualize the rotation of figures in space. Observation scales provide a means for recording perceptions of a sample of behavior (who talks in the classroom, who listens), judgments of persons' behavior (actively discussing, inattentive), internal state (happy, bored), and characterizations of the environment (accepting, everyone feels free to contribute). When properly summarized and interpreted, these evaluations, judgments, and perceptions convey information about variables of interest (spatial ability, classroom climate). They provide a symbolic representation of the perception of behavior and allow inferences about the state of constructs affecting it.

We tend to think of units and measures, especially physical ones, as obvious or "givens." Indeed, some dimensions of phenomena stand out, whereas others, such as "good character," are more difficult to discern even when we are clear about them conceptually—and often we are not. It is worth noting, however, that dimensions and measures, even of physical characteristics, are social constructions. As Duncan (1984) observes, what we now think of as the result of multiplying width by length (area),

> was measured by cultivators in southeast [sic] Asia by the number of baskets of rice seed required to sow a field. . . . The Chinese even defined a standard vessel for measuring grain and wine in terms of the musical pitch produced when it was struck, so that a pitch pipe, its length measured by millet grains, was . . . [the] measure of capacity. (p. 15)

Thus, cultures choose aspects from phenomena, name dimensions, and select ways to describe them—in our culture, usually in units and numbers. Measurement is also part of a theme begun in the early chapters, which shows knowledge as the result of a social process.

> ▶ Measures select from our world concepts of interest to us and operationalize them in ways determined by our culture.
>
> ▶ Measures record information for later use and provide a representation of one or more dimensions. Measures of constructs symbolize their state.

MEASUREMENT—A SAMPLING PROCESS

Measures and observation scales represent phenomena by sampling:

- The content of a course to find how well a student has learned on the assumption that the questions represent the material in the course (*content* or *domain sampling*).

- A student's behavior with respect to that content on the assumption that the sample represents that student's typical behavior with that content (*behavior sampling*).

- A candidate's ability to solve typical problems involved in a position he or she is seeking on the assumption that today's demonstrated ability is representative of tomorrows' ability on the job (*time sampling and content—job description—sampling*).

- The interaction of a group, coding at specified intervals the nature of the focus of the group and its interaction, on the assumption that this record of the group's behavior (e.g., a video recording) is representative of a complete record (*time and behavior sampling*).

- A pool of questions regarding ways of handling various interpersonal situations on the assumption that certain answers represent the construct—for example, an individual's assertiveness (*domain sampling*).

All sampling principles apply to measurement. In order to measure with the same degree of precision—all things being equal—the more heterogeneous the target area or skill we are sampling, the larger our sample will need to be. For instance, one needs a longer instrument (a bigger sample of behavior) or period of observation (a longer test) to cover the heterogeneous complexities of American history in comparison with the relative homogeneity of the short test that is adequate for evaluating the multiplication of single-digit numbers.

Similarly, the more precise we wish our measurement to be, the larger our sample will need to be (e.g., a longer test is required if we want to have confidence that an individual's true score is within 2 rather than 5 points of his observed score as expressed by odds of 1 to 20).

Stratified sampling and sequential sampling are also used in measurement.

> ▶ Measuring is taking a sample of behavior at a sample time (which is a sample of possible times) on a sample of items taken from a domain that is a sample of a larger universe. The principles of sampling apply to measurement; some measures use stratified or sequential sampling methods.

Pros and Cons of Measurement and Observation Records

Knowledge growth seems to follow the ability to record, analyze, and measure the phenomena of a field. Measures extend our senses, gathering more data than we can otherwise comfortably digest and summarizing them in a single number or a profile of numbers. They allow us to differentiate individuals, groups, or classes as having more or less of whatever we are measuring. An alternative is to observe or interview individuals to obtain certain desired information, judge it, and then verbally summarize it in ways that differentiate hundreds of individuals. This comparison makes apparent the efficiency of instruments like the Scholastic Aptitude Test (SAT), which, with all its faults, still gathers a great deal of information—simultaneously, in a single day's time, from tens of thousands of potential college students—and puts it into usable form.

Measurement often corrects faulty impressions. We may believe that dissatisfaction is widespread but be shown by a survey instrument that the problem is confined to a very vocal few. Or, when a student does poorly in high school but attains high scores on the SAT, we learn that the individual is not stupid, as we might infer from the grades, but is perhaps bored or otherwise not academically motivated.

Observation scales are used to make records of targeted persons (for instance, the group leader), to describe kinds of interaction (praise or reinforcing statements), and to indicate who interacts with whom and how. An example is Flanders's (1970) interaction analysis in which an observer classifies student and teacher talk in a set of categories. It is only a partial record, colored by the viewpoints of the scale and observer; but since categorizing and coding occur simultaneously with observation, the record is less voluminous than a video recording and is immediately ready for analysis and interpretation. It is targeted so as to select, out of all that is there, the information we are seeking. Use of observation scales with video recordings allow more detailed analysis—like the instant replay used in telecasting professional sports—than is possible when observations are done in the field.

Many observation scales require observers to record the frequency of certain behaviors, rate certain dimensions, or record their observations in similarly structured ways. Simon and Boyer (1974) is a collection of such observation scales for the classroom. Although not mentioned in the remainder of this chapter, nearly everything in the chapter is applicable to such instruments; just consider a rating on a dimension, or the frequencies of a particular action as a test item.

On the negative side, however, many feel that especially multidimensional behavior such as affective responses are too complex to capture by measures which do best reflecting one dimension at a time. This is a frequent concern of measures of intellectual ability, so-called intelligence tests, which measure only part of what we generally mean by "intelligence." Another limitation is that when certain behaviors (e.g., social behaviors) are brought to a person's attention by the act of measurement, the individual—now having become self-conscious—often changes the behavior.

▶ Some evidence shows that a field of research develops more rapidly as the precision of its measures increases.

▶ Measures allow us to differentiate individuals more precisely and accurately than we can with words.

▶ Measures permit us to collect enormous amounts of information efficiently and quickly.

▶ Observation scales abstract from behavior the characteristics of interest. We can use them either in the field or with film, audio, or video records of field experiences.

▶ Some multidimensional behaviors do not lend themselves well to measurement.

▶ The measurement process itself changes some behaviors.

Measures as Operational Definitions

We refer to the measure of a construct as its **operational definition** because the operations performed in measuring the construct determine what our data really represent. The ability to answer the problems on a spatial ability instrument becomes what we mean by "spatial ability"; responses to questions about how we feel about financial assistance for destitute people become what we mean by "attitude toward welfare programs."

The operational definition of a construct may specify:

- operations that bring the construct about.

- situations and circumstances that may evoke the construct.

- descriptions of behaviors that occur when the construct is present and so may be used as indicators of it.

We often use the first form of definition to bring about conditions we are interested in studying. For instance, to examine the effect of the constructs *hunger* and *thirst* on ability to concentrate, we would use deprivation of food and water as the operations to bring them about.

The second form describes most of our measures; test items are situations developed to evoke a behavior, and the testing situation is the circumstance in which those situations are presented. For example, we set a problem in a test situation intended to elicit the correct behavior: "Predict the increase in temperature of hydrogen gas when the pressure on a 20°C 10-gram sample is doubled from 15 ppi." If the student knows Boyle's law, this problem should evoke a correct response.

The third form is reflected in observation rating scales: for example, tally the number of times each individual was an asserter, where assertiveness is defined as interrupting another person or not giving another a chance to talk. (Other specific behaviors could be listed, perhaps as a checklist with space for tallies of occurrences.)

All three forms are useful ways of defining constructs.

> ▶ The operations followed in measuring a construct are its operational definition. Operational definitions may specify the operations that bring it about, the situation that evokes it, or the behaviors that, being regular concomitants of it, can be used as indicators of it.

EVIDENCE OF VALIDITY

"Validity refers to the degree to which evidence and theory support the interpretation of test scores entailed by proposed uses of tests" (Joint Committee on Standards for Educational and Psychological Testing [U.S.], 1999, p. 9).[1] The closeness with which the study's intended meaning of constructs matches their operationalization is the translation validity, one of the important aspects of Internal Integrity. It assures that the construct intended is indeed being measured—the operational definition faithfully reflects what was intended. To show score interpretations are valid, we provide an evaluative summary of the evidence for them. Basically, the evidence sought is that the instrument behaves as would be expected if it were a valid measure.

Note that since an instrument can be used in different ways, *validity applies to the intended score's interpretation and use rather than being a property of the instrument*. The evidence usually combines theoretical and empirical sources: theoretical in the sense that our knowledge of the construct allows us to predict what to expect under certain conditions, and empirical in that we gather data to confirm the prediction. We look for certain kinds of data in assembling the evaluative summary of evidence:

- We seek evidence based on *content* when we want to assure that the score represents mastery of the content in a particular domain, such as achievement in a particular subject matter, or mastery of certain job aspects.

- We seek evidence based on *response processes* when we want to assure that the instrument is not only assessing the proper content but also that intended mental processes, skills, and abilities are being displayed in response to the measure.

- We seek evidence based on the measure's *internal structure* when we want to assure that the structure of the instrument conforms to our understanding of the nature of the construct. For example, if the construct (anxiety, for example) has two dimensions (current conceptions of anxiety suggest it has state and trait dimensions), then an analysis of a measure of the construct should display that structure—a context-dependent dimension (*state*) and a person-dependent one (*trait*).

- We seek evidence based on relations to other variables when we want to further assure the instrument is tapping the proper construct in relation to other possibilities. That is, we seek convergent and discriminant evidence—*convergent evidence* that other measures of the construct with which we would expect the instrument to relate, do indeed correlate with it as expected, and *discriminant evidence* "indicating a distinctness from measures of other constructs" (Messick, 1995, p. 746) such that low, zero, or negative correlations with them are found.

- We seek evidence of the *consequences of measurement* to assure that the positive value of using the instrument outweighs any possible harm.

We will examine these different kinds of evidence in detail below.

Standards for Educational and Psychological Testing

Because of the widespread use of tests in important educational, personnel, and policy decisions, interested professional associations (the American Educational Research Association, American Psychological Association, and National Council on Measurement in Education) jointly appointed a committee to develop standards that provide guidance for the development of tests as well as for their proper use. The resultant *Standards for Educational and Psychological Testing* (Joint Committee on Standards for Educational and Psychological Testing [U.S.], 1999) have been revised periodically, as additional uses for and new understandings about tests have developed. A new joint committee is currently working on further revision.

While the standards have no legal standing, they have become quite influential and are often cited in discussions of test use, court cases, and policy statements. Their importance is attested to by the organization of this chapter as well as by frequent references to them.

Face Validity

First, however, note that there is a kind of validity evidence not recognized in the Test Standards. When laypersons must accept the results of important decisions obtained from measurement, it is imperative the instrument appears valid to these unsophisticated users. This becomes especially important if there is considerable discrepancy between what the instrument appears to measure and what it is claimed to measure. For example, studies have long shown that ability to write well is predicted almost as well by a multiple-choice test of English usage as by a carefully scored written composition (Breland, 1987). Nevertheless, the College Entrance Examination Board still includes actual composition samples. A single multiple-choice test would be less expensive, less time-consuming, and faster and easier to score. But the reality is that the appearance of validity—the **face validity**—of the multiple-choice test is such that many clients refuse to accept it in place of an actual writing sample.

> ▶ That an instrument looks as though it would be valid (face validity) is often as important as data-based validity for test-based important decisions and/or where laypersons are involved.

Evidence Based on Content

Evidence of **content validity** (also called *curricular validity*) is important for instruments that are used to measure academic achievement, or competency. Once we know the content of the subject matter that the instrument is intended to sample, we can analyze the instrument to show that it does, indeed, representatively sample it. Examples are minimal competency examinations required for high school graduation or for obtaining a teaching certificate. The term *content*, usually thought of as a curriculum area, is used broadly to include, for example, assembling a rifle or using specific software. In some instances a job analysis provides specifications of the skills and content with which an instrument can be compared, just as a curriculum does for a course in school. Measures provide evidence of content validity if they adequately represent the content of the curriculum, task, job analysis, or construct. Validity is a judgment supported by both empirical evidence and theoretical rationales.

Evidence of content validity is a representation problem and therefore involves sampling. We show how well the various parts of the measure represent the content by comparing it with a table of specifications.

Table 18.1 shows such a table for an examination dealing with the main topics of this chapter: validity, reliability, and objectivity. The whole table represents the domain to be sampled, and it is constructed from behavioral objectives or goals of instruction. Such objectives show the behavior (described by the column designation) that individuals should be able to show upon completion of instruction with particular content (described by the row designation). Each cell is considered a subdomain combining the column's behavior with the row's content and containing a pool of items of varying levels of difficulty to be sampled.

Table 18.1   Table of Specifications for an Instrument Measuring Achievement of the Concepts Validity, Reliability, and Objectivity

| | Skills | | | | | |
Subject Matter	Knowledge of Major Terms and Concepts	Can Use Terms Correctly and Intelligently	Can Apply the Concepts to a Situation	Can Construct a Table of Specifications	Can Evaluate Study's Use of Terms	Row Weight in %
Validity	9	9	18	10	18	64
Construct	(4)	(4)	(8)		(8)	
Predictive	(2)	(2)	(4)		(4)	
Content	(2)	(2)	(4)	(10)	(4)	
Face	(1)	(1)	(2)		(2)	
Reliability	5	5	10		10	30
Internal consistency	(2)	(2)	(4)		(4)	
Stability	(1)	(1)	(2)		(2)	
Equivalence	(1)	(1)	(2)		(2)	
Stability and equivalence	(1)	(1)	(2)		(2)	
Objectivity	1	1	2		2	6
Column weight in %	15	15	30	10	30	100

Because some behaviors and certain content may be more important than others, we weight the columns and rows to indicate the proportion of the whole instrument that should come from each. These are shown as percentages at the bottom of each column and at the far right of each row. Each cell entry shows the percentage of the whole instrument that is to come from that cell. By comparing the instrument's actual sampling of items with those in the table of specifications, we provide evidence of content validity.

If programs rather than individuals are being evaluated, each student may be given a different sample of only a few items from the table so that testing time for an individual is minimized but coverage of the program is obtained. This process, called *matrix sampling*, is used by the National Assessment of Educational Progress.

Evidence Based on Response Processes

In addition to assuring that the expected content is appropriately sampled by the measure, we must also be concerned that the expected response processes are being sampled as well and that the persons actually use these processes in responding to the instrument. For example, a student taking a multiple-choice arithmetic test may be solving the problem not by doing the arithmetic as intended, but by eliminating the most unreasonable answers and guessing among the rest. Having the students talk aloud about their thought processes as they take the test often provides evidence of the actual response process, which can then be compared with those expected.

Response times and/or eye movement records may provide evidence as well. So might stimulated recall (see p. 271). Similarly, keeping a record of the development of writing skill by comparing successive drafts would provide evidence of process.

Studying the response processes of different groups of examinees may turn up differences in meaning or in the interpretation of certain items as a result of previous experiences or capabilities that should be reflected in the proper interpretation of their scores.

Evidence Based on Internal Structure

"Analysis of the internal structure . . . can indicate the degree to which the relationships among items and test components conform to the construct on which the proposed score interpretations are based" (Joint Committee on Standards for Educational and Psychological Testing [U.S.], 1999, p. 15). The internal structure of the construct is often known or hypothesized from its nature. For instance, some have argued that intelligence is a multidimensional construct with many, at least partially independent, aspects. If that were the case, then that is the structure we would expect to find when analyzing the intelligence test by factor analysis.

Factor analysis is a statistical procedure that, by examining interrelationships among items, helps to identify the dimensions underlying a measure and hence what it is measuring. Suppose we correlate the scores of each item in an instrument with the scores of every other item in that instrument across a sample of individuals. A factor analysis identifies clusters of items that correlate highly with each other and thus are measuring the same things—factors. One determines the number of factors making up the test and infers from the common characteristics of its items what each factor measures. Factors that correspond to what the instrument was intended to measure provide evidence of **construct validity**. The items of a homogeneous instrument will all belong to a single factor.

Evidence Based on Relations with Other Variables

By factor analyzing a battery of test scores that include new measures along with instruments already accepted as valid, we can also gain evidence of the validity of the new instruments. For example, we might anticipate that verbal fluency and flexibility will be two of the factors underlying a new measure of verbal creativity. A factor analysis of the intercorrelations of a battery of test scores that includes already accepted measures of verbal fluency and flexibility will show how the new instrument relates to these factors—evidence of validity.

We make predictions about how we expect the properties of the construct to manifest themselves under particular conditions, or with certain kinds of people, and then we provide evidence that they do. For example, given a new measure of creativity, we can develop a set of propositions about how individuals who are creative will behave in certain artistic situations. We might expect that creative people will be flexible, but not that all flexible people are creative. Therefore, flexibility is a **contingent** (necessary but not sufficient) **condition** for artistic creativity. Thus, there might be people with both high and low creativity in their art who are flexible, but no inflexible people will be highly creative. We can inspect a scatterplot of the creativity measure against a flexibility measure to see whether it is triangular—people with high flexibility scores and both high and low creativity scores but no persons with high creativity scores combined with low flexibility scores. This would provide evidence of validity.

Similarly, we can correlate daydreaming with creativity. Again, however, we expect a low correlation in that daydreaming might facilitate creativity—but as a contributing condition, not a necessary condition for it. A low positive correlation under these circumstances would be further evidence of validity.

Convergent and discriminant evidence.   If we examine the network of measures of which our instrument is a part and find that other measures correlate with it as we would expect—while others that shouldn't correlate don't—we have convergent and discriminant evidence of validity. Convergent evidence comes from the fact that already accepted measures of the construct correlate highly with it and that measures expected to be only weakly related to it show only low correlations or, if inversely related, have negative correlations. Discriminant evidence comes from the zero or nearly-so correlations with those distinct from it and not related to it.

Suppose we have a new measure of children's reading ability; we expect it to show a high correlation with widely accepted reading tests like the reading part of the Iowa Test of Basic Skills. We might expect a moderate-to-small correlation between mathematical achievement and reading achievement and a low or zero correlation with a test of spatial visualization. Showing expected relations to other measures provides evidence of validity.

Does this procedure sound familiar? It should! Recall that when describing the constant comparative method and delineating a coding category (construct) in our study of qualitative method, we were to find (a) key instances of it, (b) borderline instances, and (c) instances that were beyond the border (see p. 279). We noted that this was a general procedure called conceptual analysis. We use that same logic here to examine whether the instrument we are validating appropriately correlates highly (key instances), correlates weakly (borderline instances), or does not correlate at all—or negatively with inverse measures (those beyond the border).

Recall also the concept of triangulation, wherein we used data from different sources (across persons, situations, and methods) to ensure that our data were not overly influenced by one point of view. So too with construct validity, we are seeking data from different methods of validating measures: relating it to other measures, showing that the instrument relates to how the construct would display itself, and showing that the instrument samples its domain or context appropriately. *The logic we apply to both quantitative and qualitative methods is basically the same, but we adapt it to the specific kind of data.*

A combination of convergent and discriminant evidence with multiple methods of measuring (e.g., free response, multiple choice, observation) provides very persuasive validity evidence—method triangulation (see pp. 285–286). It is known as *multitrait, multimethod evidence.* For example, to assure his audience that the construct paranoia was being measured, the Zimbardo et al. study in chapter 1 provided three measures in two modalities: a clinically derived paranoia scale (self-report), the Minnesota Multiphasic Personality Inventory (self-report), and judges (observation). They would be expected to show congruent results, and they did.

Evidence based on test-criterion relationship.   Evidence showing that the instrument might usefully predict certain criteria also contributes evidence of validity. A **criterion** is a measure generally accepted as valid. We show that an instrument (e.g., SAT) can predict a criterion measure (e.g., college grade point average) to select individuals for college.

We usually divide **criterion-related validity** into **concurrent validity** (criterion and test score obtained at same time) and **predictive validity** (criterion obtained after test score—e.g., SAT in high school, GPA in college).

The correlation of SAT with freshman GPA provides evidence of predictive validity, but since some unsuccessful students drop out of college during the first year, the test must discriminate among the students that survive. This restriction in range results in a lowered correlation similar to that in Figure 17.10 on page 390.

Evidence based on the consequences of measuring.   Measuring may have consequences beyond those that were intended. For instance, an individual's poor showing on a measure may become a self-fulfilling prophecy—individuals fail because they believe they couldn't do the work, when perhaps they could. Is this occurrence sufficiently rare and the diagnostic value of measures sufficiently great that their use is justified?

"[I]t is important to distinguish between evidence that is directly relevant to validity and evidence that may inform decision about social policy but falls outside the realm of validity" (Joint Committee on Standards for Educational and Psychological Testing [U.S.], 1999, p. 16). This distinction is particularly important in cases such as those involving effects on certain groups, selection and promotion, special education placement, and changing school curriculum. "Although information about the consequence of testing may influence decisions about test use, such consequences do not in and of themselves detract from the validity of intended test interpretations" (ibid., p. 16).

The societal consequences of testing can affect how validity is viewed and can change with time. The National Teacher Examination (NTE) was originally hailed as valid when legislation in some states allowed African American teachers to use a high enough score to attain the same pay scale as Caucasians. Later, when racial discrimination in pay was largely erased, the NTE came to be viewed as invalidly discriminating against the minorities it had originally helped.

There is no debate that the consequences of testing are important and should be considered, but some believe they should not be included in the definition of validity. This is another of the increasing instances in the social sciences where exploration of the interlocking of values and science makes still more apparent the socially constructed nature of science.

The Specificity of Validity

Evidence of validity is always gathered in a particular context, and typically, one of our concerns is the generality of that context. An instrument that is useful for selecting individuals for entrance to one college may be too selective for another. Until recently local validation studies were always required. (The case of *Griggs v. Duke Power Co.*, 401 U.S. 424 [1971] was interpreted as mandating it.)

However, the Test Standards have provided some leeway since analysis showed that once corrections were made for some statistical artifacts, "the remaining variance in validity coefficients is relatively small" (Joint Committee on Standards for Educational and Psychological Testing [U.S.], 1999, p. 19).

> ▶ "Validity refers to the degree to which evidence and theory support the interpretation of test scores entailed by proposed uses of tests" (Joint Committee on Standards for Educational and Psychological Testing [U.S.], 1999, p. 9).
>
> ▶ Evidence of validity may come from a comparison of the instrument's content with what it was intended to measure.
>
> ▶ Evidence of validity may come from a comparison of the response processes the instrument actually elicits with those it is intended to elicit.
>
> ▶ Evidence of validity may come from a comparison of the internal structure of the instrument with its theoretically expected structure.
>
> ▶ Evidence of validity may come from a comparison of its relations with other variables with the expectations held for such relations.
>
> ▶ Evidence of validity may come from instrument-criterion relationships where there is a criterion measure.
>
> ▶ Evidence of validity may come from the pattern of convergent evidence that supports its expected positive relationship with other measures, and from discriminant evidence that supports its expected distinctiveness and lack of relationship with other measures.
>
> ▶ The societal consequences of testing may affect how validity evidence is viewed.

RELIABILITY OF MEASURES

If the evidence for validity is adequate for our intended purpose, then in providing such evidence we will have also shown that the instrument has adequate reliability. There are three different ways of assessing reliability: classical test theory (which has been the most common way), generalizability theory, and item response theory.

Classical Test Theory

In classical test theory, reliability refers to the consistency with which an instrument measures whatever it measures. Think of a measure's reliability as comparable to firing a gun at a target where the bull's-eye represents a person's construct to be measured and each shot represents an attempt to measure it—a score. Validity involves repeatedly hitting the heart of the target, as in the middle target of Figure 18.1, which shows a measure with both validity and reliability. When the measure is reliable, it tightly clusters the shots wherever it is aimed, as in the middle and right-hand targets. The right-hand target represents a reliable but invalid measure; the shots are clustered but, not hitting the bull's-eye, are measuring something else. An unreliable measure, as in the left-hand target, spreads shots (scores) all over; it will not accurately measure the attribute in any given instance. We might, however, get an estimate of the attribute

Figure 18.1   Reliability and validity portrayed as an analogy to firing consistent and inconsistent guns at a target.

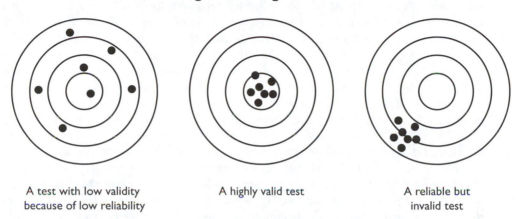

A test with low validity
because of low reliability

A highly valid test

A reliable but
invalid test

by averaging the shots—in essence, lots of measurings—or by taking a very long measure. Indeed, lengthening the measure is one strategy we use to increase reliability.

Without evidence of validity, an instrument may be reliably consistent in measuring the wrong thing. Thus, reliability is a necessary condition for validity, but it is not a sufficient condition, not a guarantee that the measure is valid.

Operationally, reliability is the consistency with which persons evidencing the same amount of whatever is being measured are assigned the same score. Because various factors may prevent this consistency, there are different measures of reliability:

- The measure may consist of items from different, unrelated domains (e.g., spatial visualization and creativity) so that a score may represent excellence in only one (spatial visualization) or the other (creativity) or middling levels in both. As a result, we would not know how to interpret the score—the measure lacks **internal consistency reliability**.

- Different samples of items assign a different score to the same level of competence or ability. Form A of an instrument yields scores different from those of form B— the scores from the different forms lack **equivalence reliability**.

- Individuals' responses vary over time, either because their perceptions of items change or because the level of the construct changes. Today the world looks rosy and I respond accordingly; yesterday I felt depressed by the rain and darkness and it affected my answers—the scores lack **stability reliability**.

Coefficients of reliability of commercial instruments usually are in the .80s and .90s.

▶ Reliability refers to the consistency of results produced by a measure.

▶ Reliability is a necessary but not sufficient condition for high validity. An instrument that is valid for a given purpose is reliable, but a reliable instrument may or may not be valid.

▶ As with validity, we seek evidence of reliability to fit the kind of consistency desired.

Internal Consistency Reliability

Internal consistency refers to the consistency with which all items measure the same thing. An instrument affected only by a single construct will have high internal consistency reliability (i.e., it is homogeneous). Homogeneity is lowered by items evoking different responses, depending on how they are perceived. For example, double-barreled questions such as "Do you approve lowering taxes for the poor and veterans?" might elicit answers that reflect attitudes toward the poor, or veterans, or both. Similarly, items can measure different unrelated or only partially related skills (e.g., algebra items in a mathematics test that require recall of both algebraic and geometric knowledge). Random errors can occur under distracting testing conditions. When low reliability results from some combination of these factors, what does the score represent? Score interpretability requires internal consistency reliability.

For achievement tests and other learned responses, the homogeneity of the measure is not solely a function of the measure itself but is also affected by the way the content was experienced or learned. Homogeneity indices can be high for tests of students shown how events of the twentieth century had their roots in the nineteenth, but low for those who do not see them as interrelated because they learned about the two centuries independently. Some subject areas tend to be homogeneous. Mathematics is such a subject, since those who do better at puzzling out one geometric proof or solving one equation can usually do other, similar problems. The more differently individuals experience the material, the more they will diverge in terms of what is easy and what is hard, and this will lower the internal consistency or homogeneity.

Measuring internal consistency reliability.   There are several ways of estimating the internal consistency of a measure. One is to split the measure into two halves, randomly assigning the items to halves and correlating the scores on the halves. Considering the fact that half the test is a smaller sample of behavior than the whole test, the half-test correlation will underrepresent the reliability. Fortunately, there is a way of estimating whole-test reliability: the *Spearman-Brown formula* (see the addendum to this chapter). Such reliabilities are often referred to as *Spearman-Brown reliabilities*.

Where similar items are grouped (e.g., a math section, a social studies section), we assign odd-numbered items to one half and even-numbered to the other—*parallel split-half reliability*. Because this method stratifies the halves so that each correctly represents the groups, these reliabilities will be higher than random splits.

Because there are many possible random splits, each slightly different, we need an estimate of the average reliability for all random ones. **Kuder-Richardson reliability** formula 21 (KR21) for tests where answers are scored either right or wrong, and *Cronbach's alpha coefficient* (or *Hoyt's analysis of variance reliability*) for any kind of scoring, provide estimates. (See the addendum to this chapter for the formulas.) Because KR21 requires only the mean, the variance, and the number of items, it is widely used. Because it assumes that all items are equally difficult, it yields a lower estimate of reliability than the parallel split-halves procedure. Maydeu-Olivares, Coffman, and Hartmann (2007) suggest the use of a *confidence interval* (see p. 428) approach to Cronbach's alpha that gives a truer estimate of internal consistency reliability.

Too-short time limits that result in many unattempted items yield artificially inflated internal consistency reliability estimates because all such items are scored as wrong.

Equivalence Reliability

This form of reliability is like parallel split-half reliability except that it uses different forms of an instrument. Because familiarity with one form may allow scores to increase with the second, with *equivalence reliability* we counterbalance testings—a general technique for eliminating serial order effect. We divide the sample equally into as many groups as there are possible orderings. With two test forms, we divide the group in half, one receiving form A first and the other form B. With three forms we divide into six: ABC, ACB, BAC, BCA, CAB, and CBA. The combined data from these groups is used to correlate the scores on one form with those on the other for equivalence reliability.

Stability Reliability

When we ask, "How consistent are the scores over time?" we are measuring stability reliability. It is the correlation of two score sets—a test and then a retest of the same individuals—obtained at different times. How much elapsed time? Whatever period over which you wish to estimate stability. If you are comparing achievement test scores at the semester's beginning with those at its end, ideally you will use testings a semester apart. However, since over such a long period some learning is likely, in practice such periods are shorter. The trade-off between using the proper interval and avoiding irrelevant influences is a matter of researcher judgment.

What if we plan to use one form of an instrument at the opening of a semester and the other at the end? Then we need a combination of stability and equivalence reliability—we correlate scores from different test forms we have administered with a suitable intervening period. The two sources of inconsistency typically yield a reliability lower than either alone.

Standard Error of Measurement

Where we interpret measurements for individuals, we are generally more concerned with the standard error of measurement. It makes practical use of the reliability estimate, using it to provide a band that, with a given probability (e.g., odds of 19 to 1), includes the person's score. Considerably more on this standard error is included in the addendum to this chapter.

Generalizability Theory

Cronbach developed *generalizability theory* by extending the approach he originally employed in developing his internal consistency reliability formula (which yields an **alpha coefficient**), to estimate a variety of other sources of unreliability (Brennan, 2001; Cronbach et al., 1972; Shavelson, Webb, & Rowley, 1989). Generalizability theory allows us to examine whether, for instance, the reliability of a measure is best increased by making it longer, by using more raters to evaluate each response, by improving the conditions under which measurement was made, or by some combination of these processes.

Generalizability theory considers a score to be a sample from a universe of possible scores and reliability to be the accuracy with which it estimates the universe's value of these scores (the "true" score). It requires a partitioning of the variability of scores (analysis of variance, see p. 466) to determine, as does Cronbach's alpha coefficient, the variability due to the items (item homogeneity). Beyond that, it also determines the contribution of such attributes as different samples of persons being measured, different samples of items making up the measure (such as different forms), different conditions of measurement, and lack of consistency in scoring from rater to rater. From such an analysis, we can estimate the expected variance of the scores in the universe and the expected variance of the scores in the sample; their ratio yields a generalizability coefficient. This figure indicates how well the measure embodies the variability of the universe it is intended to represent.

Generalizability theory has many useful aspects, especially for indicating the sources of unreliability in order to construct a cost-efficient measurement. Researchers are increasingly using it. However, Jones and Appelbaum (1990) suggest that, "given the complex assumption base, both conceptual and mathematical, and the basic difficulties in the definition of a domain [universe in generalizability terms], a cautious approach to the use of generalizability theory still appears warranted" (p. 31).

> ▶ Generalizability theory extends the internal consistency approach from merely estimating the impact of a lack of item homogeneity to assessing the variability of additional definable sources of inconsistency. It is particularly useful as a diagnostic procedure to determine how best to improve measurement by showing the contribution of these various sources to measurement and to error.

Item Response Theory

Reliability indices yielded by classical test theory are estimates of the average precision of measurement across the range of the trait. But **item response theory** (IRT) shows that scores generally include more error at the highest and lowest score ranges than in the middle of the score distribution. In place of reliability, IRT uses a test information function that summarizes how well the test discriminates among individuals at different levels of whatever the test is measuring. The item characteristic curve for a given item plots the proportion giving the desired response at successive levels of the trait measured.

Figure 18.2 on the following page shows two sample item characteristic curves. One, for a difficult test item, is j-shaped; and the other, which is more typical, is s-shaped. These provide a measure of the information contributed by the item at each trait level. The plot of the sum of the information over all the items at each trait level tells us how efficient the test is at that level. A test information function is derived from summing the contribution of each item over the trait levels. Its reciprocal is comparable to the standard error of measurement in classical test theory.

NORM–REFERENCED AND CRITERION–REFERENCED TESTS

Tests that provide a range of scores achieved by a norm group and show the standing of an individual in that group are called **norm-referenced tests**. The group

Figure 18.2   Two item characteristic curves, one for a difficult test item and one for a more typical test item.

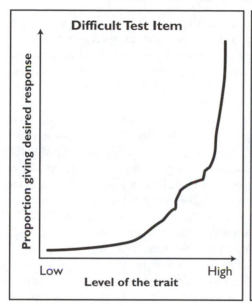 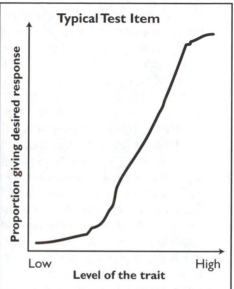

may be the current class, or a group representative of a particular grade, or other prior experience (e.g., graduates from a particular program). For instance, an achievement test's grade norms indicate how far a student is working above or below others at that grade level.

Criterion-referenced tests determine whether an individual has achieved a given criterion level with respect to particular content or skill and ability. The criterion is a level accepted as satisfactory—for instance, by a teacher, a standard-setting group, a research-determined mastery level for advanced training, or for certification. High school graduation tests sampling the content and skills individuals should have mastered are an example.

Since many criterion-referenced tests are built so that most students obtain a nearly perfect or passing score, conventional reliability estimates are not appropriate. Alternative measures have been devised by Berk (1986) and Subkoviak (1988).

> ▶ Norm-referenced tests spread the scores along a scale so that the researcher can determine how well individuals did relative to a norm group.
>
> ▶ Criterion-referenced measures determine whether certain content has been mastered or a certain level of mastery has been reached. Special measures are needed to assess their reliability.

Improving Validity and/or Reliability through Item Analysis

Measures designed for norm-referenced testing are designed differently from those for criterion-referenced testing. We can use **item analysis** to improve the efficacy of both types. With norm-referenced measures, we seek to increase validity, reliability, or both. Usually, we first examine whether some items are too easy or too hard for most examinees. The percentage passing an item is its **item difficulty index**; Items with too high or too low a difficulty index—too easy or too hard for most students—contribute less to overall validity and reliability than do items in the middle range. We then either rewrite items to adjust their level of difficulty, or we substitute new ones.

Next, if using the test to predict, we usually consider item discrimination, the contribution of the item to predictive validity. Suppose that on a test predicting writing ability, we ask the question "Do you outline before writing?" We can correlate a valid criterion measure, such as grades in English composition, with responses to this question (1 for yes and 0 for no, using special correlation methods, p. 392). The correlation, called the **item discrimination index**, shows whether persons with high composition grades answered the question differently from those with low grades. If they did, the item was a good predictor of success, and perhaps we might add similar questions. While we might expect a "yes" answer to predict writing ability, we aren't interested in the direction of correlation—positive or negative—since a "no" answer predictive of success is also useful (see empirical keying in the next section). But if successful and unsuccessful writers answer the same way, we can drop this question from the test, try to repair it, or substitute a functioning item.

If we have no valid criterion with which to check validity, we can at least improve internal consistency reliability using the test score itself as the criterion. The item discrimination index shows how well each item contributes to the total score. Items measuring something different from most other items will have a low correlation with the total score. Eliminating them usually increases reliability, even as it shortens the test. Patterning new items after the remaining ones augments reliability.

Criterion-referenced tests are typically built so that individuals with adequate levels of whatever is measured (knowledge, skill, trait) give the expected answer. This is often 100% in the case of basic learning. Instruments used to select persons over a certain criterion level should have items clustered around the 50% difficulty level for the population of individuals among which it is intended to select. See the discussion of cut scores in the section on the standard error of measurement in the addendum to this chapter.

Item response theory (IRT) not only examines the contribution of the correct response through correlational statistics but also plots the relationship of each possible response in a multiple-choice item to the criterion. The Rasch model, a part of item response theory, is increasingly used to place items on a scale of difficulty independent of the sample of testees (see Bond & Fox, 2007).

Empirical Keying

Empirical keying goes a step further than item analysis in assembling responses that significantly correlate with the criterion into a scoring key of "right" answers.

Each response that is negatively correlated is either subtracted from "right" answers or tallied as a separate score with its own interpretation. For example, the U.S. Army wished to retain the best of its officers at World War II's end. While units were still intact, they obtained peer ratings by fellow officers as a criterion measure on a large sample. These officers also took a large questionnaire about background and attitudes. Items discriminating the best from poorest officers were keyed as the best officers answered them. So scored, the test successfully predicted the criterion. The key showed that the best came from small towns, were from large families, and were the firstborn.

Could the Army have anticipated this? Probably not. Can we rationalize **empirical keying** after the fact? Yes, but there are also counterarguments. Because of their weak face validity, such findings are usually subjected to repeated studies (called *cross-validation*). Empirical keyings require large numbers of representative cases to get keys that are stable from sample to sample. But these tests often succeed where others have failed, as is shown by two of the most widely used measures, the *Strong-Campbell Interest Inventory* and the *Minnesota Multiphasic Personality Inventory* (the latter was used in the Zimbardo study in chapter 1).

> ▶ In item analysis we identify too-easy or too-difficult items. Modifying or replacing them improves the test.
>
> ▶ To improve predictive validity, we correlate the items with the criterion we want to predict. Items that correlate poorly with the criterion are modified or replaced.
>
> ▶ To improve internal consistency reliability, we correlate items with the total test score. Items that correlate poorly with that total are modified or replaced.
>
> ▶ To best predict a criterion (empirical keying), we use item analysis to determine those responses that are answered differently by persons with high criterion scores than they are by low scorers and assemble them into a key. Responses that correlate positively are scored "right," and responses that correlate negatively are subtracted from the total as "wrong" (or interpreted separately). Counterintuitive "right" responses may require new studies to back up original findings.

OBJECTIVITY OF MEASURES

The consistency of two or more independent records of the same phenomenon is referred to as **objectivity**—as for example, when two or more judges agree on the score of a given performance, or when they make similar records of or categorizations of their observations of the same behavior. Judgment of responses is easy with low-inference measures, more difficult with high-inference ones. A judgment of the chosen response must be made in either case. If done beforehand, as in low-inference, multiple-choice format, consistency of scoring is ensured. But the responses a testee can make are limited, unlike with high-inference, free-response items where we defer judgment of responses until the test is given.

High- and Low-Inference Measures

The very definition of creativity excludes multiple-choice format as a way of measuring it. So, for it and for other similar skills, we obtain constructed responses. Since various students may answer essay test questions quite differently, the task of judging the answers is often difficult. Therefore we must work with judges to ensure their consistent—that is to say, as objective as possible—scoring. Judging is a high-inference task because the judge must infer what the student meant and compare it with the desired response. Raters are more likely to be in agreement if they carefully work out in advance their scoring basis for at least the most common answers.

Multiple-choice tests are low-inference, more objective measures because the desired answer is decided before the test is given. This need not be the barrier it is generally considered to be, however. There are many more forms of multiple-choice items than are typically used (Bloom, 1956; Gerberich, 1956; Gulliksen, 1986; Haladyna, 2004). Computer programs allow objective measurement of a student's knowledge structure. Students develop graphics that describe their structure (*cognitive maps*) or arrange *knowledge trees* that are derivatives of it (see Lane, 1991). The similarity of student and instructor's structures indicates instructional effectiveness (see the example in chapter 5's addendum). These methods and others (see Frederiksen et al., 1980 and especially Marshall, 1990) not only extend the range of skills and abilities that can be tapped by such instruments, but better integrate instruction and assessment as well.

Observation scales of social interaction vary greatly in the objectivity of the inferences to be made. High-inference scales require the observer to rate dimensions or statements such as, "Group members reinforce each other's actions ___ always, ___ most of the time, ___ about half of the time, ___ occasionally, ___ almost never." Such scales require training to ensure that observers have a common framework for deciding what is "most of the time" or "occasionally."

In contrast, low-inference and, therefore, more objective scales specify the target behaviors sufficiently so that they need only be seen to be recognized. For example, Flanders's (1970) interaction analysis for school classrooms consists of ten easily learned, clearly specified categories. The observer categorizes the behavior in the classroom every five seconds, recording a sequence of category numbers. This record permits analysis of questions such as "What happens when a child finishes talking?" Does the teacher try to clarify the child's ideas, ignore them, go off in another direction? Many such rating scales for instruction exist. Simon and Boyer (1974) is a compilation of them.

Although low-inference scales have the advantage of objectivity, because of their highly targeted nature they may miss the larger picture. This can be captured by high-inference measures, which provide a summary judgment on a range of group characteristics. Which is better? The researcher is facing a trade-off.

Objectivity is also a problem for projective measures—for example, the Rorschach Test, the Thematic Apperception Test (TAT), and the House–Tree–Person Test, which are closer to qualitative than to quantitative measures. Rorschach testees report what they see in black or multicolored inkblots that look much like symmetrical clouds. Testees read meaning into the TAT's illustrations depicting people in ambiguous situations by constructing a story about each one. Skill and training are required to interpret these free responses. Bellak (1993), Exner (2003), and Aronow, Reznikoff, and Moreland (1994) make the scoring of these tests more objective. However, many believe that although something may be gained in objectivity and in comparability of one person's test with another, much clinical evidence is missed by structured scoring formats.

Assessing Agreement among Judges

Determining the degree of correspondence between ratings by different judges is a common problem when scoring free-response material. The temptation is to use percent of agreement, but it does not take into account chance agreements. Correlating judgments takes account of the pattern of agreements, but not the level. If one is a harder grader than another, and their pattern is the same, the difference in grades will not decrease in the correlation. It will, however, show with an intraclass correlation, which is a better measure. Also better are *Krippendorff's alpha* (http://www.asc.upenn.edu/usr/krippendorff/webreliability2.pdf), *Cohen's Kappa* (http://www.niwascience.co.nz/services/free/statistical/kappa), and *Kendall's coefficient of concordance* for three or more judges. Use one of these better measures.

> ▶ A measure has objectivity when different individuals judging the same evidence arrive at the same score or rating.
>
> ▶ Multiple-choice tests are considered objective because two persons can score them identically except for clerical errors.
>
> ▶ Essay tests and projective tests require greater effort to achieve objectivity.
>
> ▶ Measures calling for low inference have greater objectivity; those requiring high inference, less of it.
>
> ▶ There are better ways of assessing agreement among judges than percent of agreement.

TAILORED AND ADAPTIVE TESTING

Computers have made it possible to shorten conventional testing times using **tailored tests**, also called *adaptive tests*. The software starts everyone in the middle of the trait range and then branches to easier or harder items, depending on whether the preceding item was answered incorrectly or correctly. Such tests make maximum use of testing time, because the items are so chosen as to accurately place the individual on the scale with a minimum number of items. They require high internal consistency reliability to achieve the same accuracy of classification in less testing time. In structure, these tests are analogous to the sequential sampling plans described on page 173 in chapter 8. A set of guidelines for computer-adaptive tests have been developed (American Council on Education, 1995).

> ▶ Adaptive (tailored) tests in homogeneous domains require the testee to take fewer test items, which reduces testing time. Computer software analyzes each individual's previously passed or failed items to determine the most appropriate next item in order to extract maximum information.

LOCATING EXISTING MEASURES

Because the construction of new measures is such an expensive and lengthy process, retrieval materials have been developed to help find already developed tests. Commercially available tests are listed in *Tests in Print VII* (Murphy, Spies, & Plake, 2006), which "serves as a comprehensive bibliography to all known commercially available tests that are currently in print in the English language." Such tests are reviewed in the *Mental Measurement Yearbooks* (Geisinger, Spies, Carlson, & Plake, 2007, new volumes every two years) and Pro-Ed's *Test Critiques, Vol. 11* (Keyser & Sweetland, 2004). *Tests in Print* and the *Yearbooks* are produced by the Buros Institute at the University of Nebraska at Lincoln (http://www.unl.edu/buros/). *Yearbook* test reviews are also available for a small fee.

Test Link (http://ets.org) provides access to the Educational Testing Service Test Collection of over 25,000 tests collected since the early 1900s, and claims to be the largest collection in the world. Scroll to the bottom of their home page, click on Site Map, scroll to Tests, and click on Test Link.

In addition, there are some useful sources of information in print:

Backer, T. E. (1977). *A directory of information on tests*. ERIC TM Report 62–1977. Princeton, NJ: ERIC Clearinghouse on Tests, Measurement and Evaluation, Educational Testing Service.

Fabiano, E., & O'Brien, N. (1987). *Testing information sources for educators*. TME Report 94. Princeton, NJ: ERIC Center on Tests and Measurements, Educational Testing Service. Fabiano and O'Brien bring Backer's 1977 publication up to 1987 but is not as comprehensive.

Goldman, B. A., Mitchell, D. F., & Egelson, P. (1974–2007). *Directory of unpublished experimental mental measures*. Vols. 1–9. Washington, DC: American Psychological Association.

Krug, S. E. (1993). *Psychware sourcebook*. Champaign, IL: MetriTech. A directory of 500+ computer-based assessment tools: tests, scoring, and interpretation systems.

Rubin, R. B., Palmgreen, P., & Sypher, H. E. (1994). *Communication research measures: A sourcebook*. New York: Guilford Press. Covers four communication contexts: interpersonal, mass, organizational, and instructional.

With many sources of information, in most instances, researchers can devote energies to adapting and improving measures rather than starting anew.

MEASUREMENT TRADE-OFFS

There are a number of trade-offs in measurement. Here are some:

- using professional time either beforehand in constructing hard-to-measure complex skills or afterward in grading them.

- measuring broadly but shallowly versus measuring narrowly but deeply. Measuring broadly yields little information about weaknesses and strengths, too small a sample of items for reliable diagnostic scoring.

- attaining audience credibility by using an established but only partially relevant test with trusted results, versus a not-yet-accepted instrument that is right on target but will require convincing evidence of its validity.

- obvious evidence gathering versus unobtrusive measurement. Obtrusively seeking target information or behavior resulting in possibly suppressing or changing it versus only obliquely, and possibly inaccurately, getting at what is wanted. (See Webb et al., 1981, for a more complete discussion.)

ADDITIONAL READING

The American Psychological Association Testing Information Clearinghouse contains information and links on test use and locating tests: http://www.apa.org/science/testclearinghs.html. For a collection of instruments see: http://oerl.sri.com/instruments/instruments.html. For links to articles on a variety of testing topics: http://www.ericae.net/nav-ar.htm. For general treatments, see Anastasi and Urbina (1997). Brennan (2006) is a handbook on measurement. For classical test theory: Allen and Yen (2002), Weiss and Davison (1981), and Linn (1989). For item response theory (IRT): Bond and Fox (2007) and Baker (2001). For multiple-choice test item development and validation: Downing and Haladyna (2006). For free useful software: http://www.unt.edu/benchmarks/archives/2002/november02/rss.htm (scroll to software).

IMPORTANT TERMS AND CONCEPTS

alpha coefficient	item analysis
concurrent validity	item difficulty index
construct validity	item discrimination index
content validity	item response theory
contingent condition	Kuder-Richardson reliability
criterion	norm-referenced tests
criterion-referenced tests	objectivity
criterion-related validity	operational definition
empirical keying	predictive validity
equivalence reliability	reliability
face validity	stability reliability
factor analysis	tailored (adaptive) tests
internal consistency reliability	validity

confidence interval   Spearman-Brown formula
correction for attenuation   standard error of measurement

OPPORTUNITIES FOR ADDITIONAL LEARNING

1. Refer to the description of Jonassen's study in the Additional Learning Opportunities for chapter 4 (p. 76). The purpose of the study was to "validate" the use of pattern notes as a measure of cognitive structure. With what source of validity evidence was Jonassen concerned, and why?

2. The dean of Watertown University was concerned about the number of freshmen who were failing and dropping out. She decided to try a prestigious testing firm's new University Entrance Competency Test (UECT) and carefully examined the data indicating the test's validity. (a) What kind of validity evidence should she look for? (b) How might she improve the test's validity?

3. Dr. Keith devised a typology that assigns an individual to one of four personality styles: spontaneous external, spontaneous internal, systematic external, and systematic internal. Coscarelli and Stonewater (1979) proposed that consultants use this model to help understand client decision-making behavior and thus to allow themselves to respond to the client in a supportive manner. In what sort of validity evidence would these researchers be interested if they were to develop a scale to measure these constructs?

4. Elizabeth Cleghorn developed a computer-based course for teaching introductory calculus that should result in increased achievement. To verify this hypothesis, she compared a randomly selected group of 30 first-year college students with a "control" group who were taught by the "regular" (lecture) method. Each group was given a calculus achievement test at the beginning of the semester and a parallel form at the end. With what kinds of validity and reliability evidence would this investigator have been concerned?

5. Recall the investigator who thought that there might be a relationship between a teacher's effectiveness and the teacher's enthusiasm. She had to measure both effectiveness and enthusiasm. To measure the latter, she decided to use two techniques: ratings by independent observers and a diary kept by the teachers. The observers were trained and filled out a five-point rating scale for a series of indicators of enthusiasm such as facial expression, body movements, and varied vocal delivery. The diary was open-ended. Assess the strengths and weaknesses of each measure.

Compare your answers with those following the Application Exercise.

APPLICATION EXERCISE

Can you find measures for the study you are thinking about? If you are dealing with variables that are standard, look up possible measures in *Tests in Print*, or search Buros' *Mental Measurement Yearbooks* on the Internet (http://buros.unl.edu/buros/jsp/search.jsp). Given the kind of study you plan, what kinds of validity and reliability will you look for? Do the tests that are candidates for your study appear to have useful levels of validity for your purposes? What about reliability? As you can tell from the foregoing material, creating your own measures is likely to be difficult and time-consuming—a study in and of itself. Try to find measures in experimental form that you can build on if nothing seems to fit exactly.

Key to Additional Learning Opportunities

1. Jonassen's study sought evidence that the technique of pattern notes measured cognitive structure—the latter being a construct that is not directly measurable. To demonstrate the technique's validity, Jonassen provided evidence based on relations with other variables. He showed that it related to the free word-association technique, a cognitive structure measure already accepted as valid.

2. (a) She would have been interested in instrument-criterion validity evidence, a predictor of a student's first-year grade point average. Presumably she is into the academic year when she notices freshmen dropping out because of failing grades. She could ask the remaining freshmen to take the UECT and correlate its scores with the end-of-year grade point averages. This would be concurrent validity evidence, which would underestimate predictive validity because students who have already dropped out are not included in the testing. To obtain predictive validity evidence, the UECT should be given to next year's freshmen at the beginning of the academic year and be correlated with their GPA at the end of the year or at the time the students dropped out.

   (b) To improve predictive validity, she might item-analyze the test to determine which items did not predict failing dropouts, replacing them with new items similar to those that did predict them. To do this, she would compare the way dropouts answered each item with the way those who did not drop out answered it. Items that showed a large difference would be predictive of dropping out.

3. They would first be interested in knowing whether the scale truly did measure the existence of the four personality styles theorized by Keith's model. For this, they might gather convergent evidence of validity. For example, they might ask individuals to nominate people who know them well. The latter persons would then be asked to rate the individuals on each of the four personality types, and these ratings would be correlated with the test scores. High correlations would be evidence of validity.

   Second, after developing a scale that would indicate to which of these four types a participant belonged, consultants would administer the scale to the participants prior to working with them. The participant's scale classifications would then be compared with the consultants' judgments of their decision-making styles after the consultants had worked with them long enough to determine it. Since the judgment data was gathered later than the scale data, a comparison of them would provide predictive validity evidence.

4. She should check the content validity of the test against the course. The table of specifications for the examination should match the content and skills taught in the course in both coverage and emphasis. In terms of reliability, she would be concerned with a combination of stability and equivalence reliability. Since she will be measuring the effect of semester-long instruction, she will be comparing the results from two tests given several months apart. She would want to know that without instruction, the control-group students' scores would stay approximately the same over that period of time. She will also be comparing the students on two parallel forms of the test and would be concerned that the two forms consistently measure the same concepts—that is, that they are truly equivalent.

5. The data collected by the observers were a direct measure of the teachers' behavior and perhaps the most objective measure available to the investigator. Since a checklist was used, analysis of the data would have been straightforward. However, the presence of the observers likely had an effect on both the teachers and the students. Moreover, the observers were restricted to predetermined indicators of enthusiasm, which may or may not have been valid measures. Thus, enthusiastic behavior not reflected by the checklist may have been

overlooked. These observations would have been time-consuming, and, if the investigator had to pay the observers, possibly costly.

The diaries were a form of data produced by the teachers themselves. Their flexible form could have provided comprehensive insight into the teachers' behavior, particularly into private thoughts and feelings. They were inexpensive. The major weakness of this form of measure is that it depends on self-perception and may not accurately reflect how others (in this case, the students) would have perceived the teachers' level of enthusiasm. In addition, filling out a diary requires recall of past events, albeit recent ones, which may have been modified by a teacher's memory. Finally, the diary data would have been time-consuming, and possibly difficult to analyze and summarize.

SUMMARY

Measurement, an important characteristic of any field, increases the distinctions that we can make among phenomena and improves our ability to describe them. Measurement is basically a sampling problem: We are sampling an individual's behavior at a single time or a series of times with respect to a sample of content or of situations.

Validity is the most important characteristic of measuring; "it is the degree to which all the accumulated evidence supports the intended interpretation of test scores for the intended purpose" (Joint Committee on Standards for Educational and Psychological Testing [U.S.], 1999, p. 11). Evidence of validity forms the basis for intended score interpretation. To show validity is to provide an evaluative summary of the evidence for intended score interpretation.

Evidence of validity may come from a variety of sources. For instance, it might come from showing that a measure is a representative sample of the content domain it was intended to measure. We gather evidence from response processes to show that the individuals are using the intended mental processes, skills, and abilities when being measured. We gather evidence of the measure's internal structure to assure that it conforms to our understanding of the nature of the construct. To assure that it is a measure of the intended construct we examine its relations to other variables. For example, we show that the measure correlates strongly with other measures of the construct and less strongly with associated constructs (convergent validity evidence) and does not correlate with unrelated constructs (discriminant validity evidence). We show that the test predicts a criterion measure—either when the criterion measure is gathered long enough after testing to determine how well the individual did (e.g., succeeded on a job or in school—predictive validity evidence), or when both test and criterion measures are gathered at the same time (concurrent validity evidence). We gather evidence to assure that the positive value of measuring outweighs its consequences, even unintended ones. Face validity—that the test appears intuitively valid—is an important factor for tests used in critical decision making, since the tests must undergo scrutiny by laypersons who may not be impressed by statistical evidence they do not understand.

Reliability is a necessary but not sufficient condition for validity. Reliability indicates consistency—whether the measure's sample of behavior is sufficiently representative so that there is consistency across different samples of test items (internal consistency reliability), of tests (equivalence reliability), and over test samples obtained at different times (stability reliability). When one form of a test is used at the beginning of a program and a comparable form at the end, we require both stability and equivalence reliability.

Norm-referenced measures show where an individual's score stands relative to some norm group—for example, whether at, above, or below the achievement of a representative sample of students at their school grade level. Criterion-referenced measures show whether an individual can achieve at a required level—for example, a high school proficiency test. Since such mastery measures result in a large proportion of high or perfect scores, reliability measures for criterion-referenced measures are different from norm-referenced ones.

Item analysis is used to improve the validity and/or reliability of an instrument. To improve validity, responses to each item are correlated with a criterion that is a valid measure. To improve the internal consistency reliability, the total score is used as the criterion. Items that do not correlate with the criterion are either discarded to shorten the measure or changed to improve the correlation.

The Spearman-Brown formula, the correction for attenuation, and the standard error of measurement are covered in the addendum to this chapter. We can estimate the effect on reliability of changing the length of any test by any amount with the *Spearman-Brown formula*. With the *correction for attenuation*, the correlation between two tests that are less than perfectly reliable can be estimated as if they were perfectly reliable. Given the reliability of the test, the *standard error of measurement* is useful for indicating, with an expressed confidence, the range within which the true score lies.

A Look Ahead

Just as this chapter showed how one gathers evidence into an argument for the validity of a measure, the next shows the logic used to marshal evidence in support of a proposition.

Note

[1] Conceptions of test validity have gradually changed over the years as experts in measurement have revised the Test Standards. The discussion of test validity and reliability are based on the 1999 version of the Test Standards, which was heavily influenced by, and follows closely, Messick (1995).

CHAPTER ADDENDUM:
THE STANDARD ERROR OF MEASUREMENT

The standard error of measurement (SEM) not only is critical for score interpretation, understanding it will also pave the way for understanding the concepts covered in the next chapter.

Consider the test score as composed of two parts: a true score—the score if the measure were perfectly accurate—and an error component—the influence of all the factors that might cause inconsistency in measurement. (This is a classical test theory formulation; a more modern test theory, like item response theory, deals with the latent variables underlying a test. The classical formulation is simpler and serves our purposes here.) The true score will not vary with re-measures (unless the underlying construct does—so assume stability). The error component will vary at random— sometimes positive, sometimes negative, usually small, rarely large—the bell-shaped normal probability curve of chapter 17. With no reliability, the standard deviation of this error distribution, called the **standard error of measurement** (SEM), is as big as the standard deviation of the scores themselves but approaches zero as reliability improves. Its formula is $\text{SEM} = \text{SD}\sqrt{1-r}$, where SD is the standard deviation of the measure and r is the reliability. (Comparable item response theory formulations are slightly different, producing larger score ranges for extreme scores.)

We often accompany a person's score with an interval erected around it using the standard error of measurement. Called a **confidence interval** (a topic developed further in chapter 19), its size depends on how confident we wish to be that the interval includes the true score. Our confidence is expressed as odds, as in a wager.

Let's suppose we had a test with a reliability of .91 and a standard deviation of 10. The SEM is 3. Since we have some unreliability error, the scores for persons with a true score of 63 scatter around 63, as shown by Figure 18.3. Approximately two-thirds of the observed scores will lie between ±1 SEM (or 60 and 66), 95% between ±2 SEM (or 57 and 69), and 99.9% between ±3 SEM (or 54 and 72).

Figure 18.3 Distribution of observed scores for persons with a true score of 63.

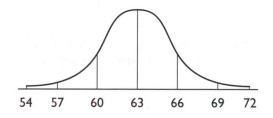

| 54 | 57 | 60 | 63 | 66 | 69 | 72 |

Given Rebecca scores 59 on a test, suppose we wish to locate Rebecca's true score with a certainty expressed by odds of 2 to 1. Graph A in Figure 18.4 shows an interval from 56 to 62, one SEM on each side of her observed score of 59. This is the confidence interval within which the true score lies with odds of 2 to 1. Setting those odds assumes our willingness to be wrong the one time out of three when Rebecca's true score lies outside the confidence interval.

Put another way, the confidence interval in graph A locates the set of true score distributions to which her score of 59 can belong: 56, 57, 58, 59, 60, 61, and 62. We don't know which it is, but graph B shows that since 59 falls within their central ±1 SEM bands, it can be any. With confidence expressed by odds of 2 to 1, therefore, her true score is between 56 and 62. We do not know whether we are right or wrong, just the odds—2 to 1, we will be wrong a third of the time.

We would have been wrong if Rebecca's true score were 63. But at odds of 19 to 1 (a band ±2 or four SEM wide, from 53 to 65, as shown in graph C), our confidence interval includes her true score in its 12-point span. Precision of location is traded off for certainty; we must decide the optimum balance.

Knowing the SEM is important for scores that make decisions about an individual. Let's suppose scores of 60 or below fail the nurses' licensing examination; we can say with a confidence expressed by the odds of 1 in 6 that Mary Jane, with a score of 57, has a passing score! Why 1 in 6? With a standard error of measurement of 3, at odds of 2 in 3, Mary Jane's score lies in the area labeled B in Figure 18.5. Therefore, at odds of 1 in 3, it lies in the remaining areas, A and C, with equal probability of being in either. However, we are interested only in the odds of its being in C, the area above the passing score; therefore, the odds are half the 1 in 3, or 1 in 6.

Because candidates who fail a certification examination can legitimately use this argument, actual cut scores are often placed one or more SEM below the desired cut score. Some who should fail will pass, but, considering the personal devastation caused by an error, this may be the lesser evil. However, in licensing nuclear engineers or airline pilots with the safety of large numbers at stake, we may switch errors. Setting the cut score above the minimum level of competency increases the chances that those certified have a passing true score. Some will fail who deserve to pass, but consider the consequences of an error at a nuclear power plant or 35,000 feet in the air! Adjusting cut scores involves trade-offs for the "greatest" good.

Figure 18.4   An observed score of 59 surrounded by a confidence interval one SEM wide and the one-SEM-wide bands of true scores that overlap that confidence interval.

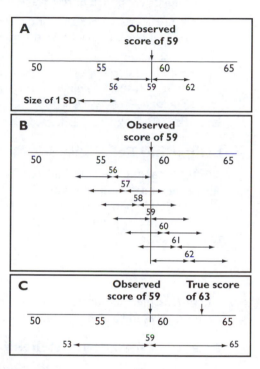

Figure 18.5   A score one SEM below a cut score on a certification examination and the chances of being failed in error.

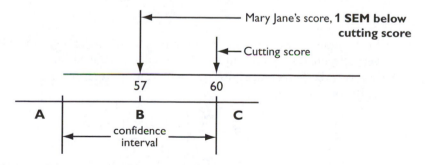

▶ The standard error of measurement permits us to establish a confidence interval within which we can say that a person's true score will lie, with a confidence expressed by specified odds.

▶ The size of the confidence interval reflects the amount and kind of unreliability used in the determination of reliability—stability, equivalence, and so on.

▶ Requiring greater certainty increases the size of the confidence interval, thereby reducing precision in locating the true score.

▶ The standard error of measurement is often used in establishing a cut score for licensing and certifying examinations. The direction in which potential error is allowed depends on whether the individual's or society's protection is the prime consideration—a trade-off.

Estimating Reliability for Measures of Different Length

In discussing the split-half reliability we noted that, to avoid an underestimate, the **Spearman-Brown formula** adjusts the reliability for a measure to full length from the correlation between split-half tests. We can use the following formula to estimate reliability for any amount of change in the length of the measure (halving it, tripling it, and so on):

$$\frac{Kr}{1+(K-1)r}$$

where K is the ratio of items in the new measure to those in the original form (for example, it would be 2 to double the length) and r is the reliability of the original form.

Internal Consistency Reliability Formulas

The earlier discussion of the Kuder-Richardson formulas indicated that one of them, KR21, assumes that all items are equally difficult. This formula is simple to compute and therefore widely used. Its formula is:

$$r - \frac{k}{k-1}\left(1 - \frac{M(k-M)}{k(\text{SD})^2}\right)$$

where k is the number of items in the measure (and the maximum possible score), M is the average score on the test, and SD is the standard deviation of the measure.

KR21 uses the percentage passing each item and therefore is a more accurate estimate. Its formula is:

$$r = \frac{k}{k-1}\left(1 - \frac{\Sigma pq}{(\text{SD})^2}\right)$$

where p is the proportion of students passing an item and q is the proportion of students not passing it. The Σ indicates that these pq values are summed over all the items on the measure.

Coefficient alpha is a more generalized form of KR21 in which the sum of the variances of the parts of the measure replaces Σpq in the numerator of KR21. For example, in an instance where items are scored on a 10-point scale, each item is considered a part of the measure, and the variances of the items are summed.

Estimates of Relationships under Conditions of Perfect Reliability

Predictive validity is reduced by unreliability of either the predicting measure or the criterion. The **correction for attenuation** is a handy way to estimate the improvement in correlation if both criterion and measure were perfectly reliable. Its formula is:

$$\frac{r_{xy}}{\sqrt{r_{xx}r_{yy}}}$$

where r_{xy} is the correlation to be corrected and r_{xx} and r_{yy} are the reliabilities of the measures involved in that correlation (see Guilford & Fruchter, 1978). Used to correct any correlation between two imperfectly measured variables, the formula determines the size of the relationship between them with perfectly reliable measurement. We use it to eliminate measurement error when we build theory or to determine whether improving a measure's reliability is worthwhile. The sources of inconsistency (equivalence? stability?) in the reliability coefficients should reflect the sources of error we wish to eliminate.

> ▶ The correction for attenuation estimates the size of a correlation if both the measures involved were perfectly reliable. It is useful as predictive validity evidence showing that a measure is "on target" and merely needs to have its reliability improved. Its estimate of the size of the relationship between constructs without measurement error is useful in theory building.

Links to previous research

Explanation, rationale, theory, or point of view

Questions, hypotheses, models

Preplanned and emergent designs

Design/procedure

Focus   Records   Time   Comparison and Contrast   Situation   Participants

Data

Statistical analysis and/or narrative analysis

Conclusion

Link to next study

Explanation or rationale of next study, etc.

The Logic of Inferential Statistics

> Like many things, statistics, though opaque in bulk, is transparent in thin slices.
> —Anonymous

Chapter 17 explained how we use numbers for description—descriptive statistics. This chapter shows how inferential statistics build on them to provide supportive or disconfirming evidence for a hypothesis—a validating role. Further, just as descriptive statistics can be used in an exploratory role to check out hunches, so too can inferential statistics. Often they guide us to new insights or provide leads to next research. Both roles are important. Because the exploration prior to problem finding is rarely included in research reports, the exploratory role gets little visibility.

INTRODUCTION

Inferential statistics do two jobs:

1. They are so named because they permit us to infer the characteristics of a population from a representative sample. Applying inferential statistics to data from a random sample, we can estimate the size of a population characteristic of interest, such as the mean of a population. By using the data of the sample and setting the level of certainty (for instance, odds of 95 to 5), we construct an interval that tells the range within which the population value lies.

2. With a certainty expressed by the odds that we set, we can determine whether an effect other than that of sampling and chance error exists in a study. We do this by determining whether an interval such as that described above includes zero, which would be the size if there were no effect (the **null hypothesis**). If it does not, with a certainty expressed by odds we set, we can rule out sampling and chance variability as causative factors. However, whether the effect is due to the cause we hypothesized depends on ruling out all other plausible explanations—a matter of study design instead of inferential statistics.

Thus, inferential statistics contribute to two of the five key judgments of Internal Integrity: rival explanations eliminated (namely, sampling and chance error) and demonstrated result (the effect showed as we hypothesized it would).

Because the logic of estimation and hypothesis testing is the same regardless of the inferential statistic used (e.g., *t* test, analysis of variance, chi-square), this chapter concentrates on the logic. Once we understand the logic, it is easier for us to understand how a given statistic works and when and how it is appropriate to use it. Related to this logic are the concepts of statistical power (sensitivity), Type I and Type II error, and the difference between statistical and practical significance.

THE LOGIC OF INFERENCE

Inferential statistics seem to be made up of complex operations foreign to any of us but the initiated. Nevertheless, they are omnipresent. Although we do not use statistical terms, we are continually making inferences in our daily lives. Indeed, a large chunk of the workforce earns its living because it is good at making inferences! Further, the logic structure we daily use resembles inferential statistics in important ways. Consider this example.

When you drive someone else's car or rent one, one of the first things you do is learn the normal noises that the car makes, especially older models with lots of rattles. Having learned what is typical, you can detect subtle but atypical noises, such as a dragging brake pad or a wheel bearing starting to break up. You then take the car to a garage. A flat tire is easy to sense—the effect is so great that you can recognize it immediately without knowing the normal background noise. In the same way, we don't need inferential statistics to determine that penicillin is effective because the before-and-after contrast is so great. When the effect is small, however, inferential statistics become important.

Continuing with our car example, garage service managers make a good living determining what is atypical in car noises, and why. How do they learn this? Probably from listening to lots of cars. A few normal cars are very quiet, a few are very noisy even though they are OK, but most are just slightly noisy—that bell-shaped curve we keep encountering. Service managers know what is typical. The manager takes your car for a test ride—but only a five-minute ride because other customers are waiting. It is a small sample to use for a decision, but it is a typical one; we usually have less information to make decisions than we wish. From this small sample the manager must judge the kind and range of noise that currently characterizes this car. He practices estimation, inferring the population value from a sample—the car's typical noise over a long normal drive.

The next inference is whether the noise belongs to a population of noises made by "healthy" cars or to a population made by cars with defective wheel bearings—a serious problem. If ignored, they become more expensive to repair and, on a highway, can even get hot enough to seize up, freeze the wheel, and cause an accident. Is the sound atypical enough that something may be wrong? The manager can tell for sure only by pulling off the wheel. This will deprive the owner of the use of the car and cost something for the labor. Figure 19.1 illustrates the dilemma.

Figure 19.1   Type I and Type II errors of inference (puns are intended as mnemonics)

		DECISION BASED ON SAMPLE DATA	
		Manager says car is okay; noise is typical.	Manager says car is not okay; you should leave it for check and repair.
TRUE STATE OF AFFAIRS	**Car is okay; noise is typical**	Manager is correct. Customer has no further problems and has increased trust in manager's judgment.	Type I error in judgment (*alpha* error). Customer says "If you're wrong, do I *alpha* pay da bill?"
	Car is not okay; noise is atypical. Bearing is starting to break up, could cause accident if not corrected!	Type II error in judgment or *beta* error. Customer has accident on road and says, "I *beta* never go there for service again!"	Manager is correct; repair is made. Potential accident is averted; customer builds trust in manager's judgment.

These are the risks we run in making inferences. We can determine what is to be judged atypical at whatever level we wish. That will determine our **Type I**, or **alpha error**—saying the bearing is failing when it is OK. If it is cheap to pull a wheel, we might not mind making such errors because it will avoid a possible accident and a **Type II**, or **beta error**—saying the car was OK when the bearing was failing. But if the level of what is judged atypical is set too conservatively, thereby increasing Type I error so that many noises are said to be atypical when they are really typical, we will anger many unhappy customers who will have paid to pull the wheel when nothing was wrong.

Thus, we can decrease Type II (beta) errors, all other things being equal, by increasing Type I (alpha) errors (i.e., being conservative in saying there is a problem when there may not be). Alternatively, we can increase the accuracy of our diagnostic judgments by taking a bigger sample on which to base the judgment—a longer test drive—or otherwise increase sensitivity to the atypical—use a stethoscope or an electronic amplifier to increase the loudness for sound location.

The problem faced by the mechanic is also faced by the surgeon deciding whether surgery is warranted (every human being is built a little differently), the physician prescribing a drug (each of us metabolizes chemicals at different rates), the teacher determining whether a student needs special placement, the librarian trying to decide how open the shelves can be without unacceptable rates of book loss, the social worker trying to decide how much aid can be given to a family without its becoming dependent on it, the economist trying to determine the interest rate that will stimulate the economy yet not cause inflation.

Thus, the consequences of Type II (beta) errors may be quite a bit more far-reaching than our wheel-bearing example. For example, researchers may judge a medication to be ineffective when it is efficacious and thus miss the use of a valuable drug. Each situation has its own set of consequences and its own possibilities for increasing the sensitivity of the study to make a better diagnosis.

The logic of inference is obviously not foreign to any of us, nor is its use in statistical inference.

ESTIMATION

Perhaps the easiest way to understand estimation is also by way of an example. As head of the Governor's Department of Education, you need to know the average hours of in-service education and teacher conferencing of the teachers of the state for a report on in-service training for the legislature. One of your assistants queries 100 teachers and finds an average of 10.3 days with a standard deviation of 2.5. How useful is that information? Not very, unless you can relate it in some way to the in-service hours of the rest of the state's teacher population. It is a sample statistic, whereas the population value is what you want. Without further information you would have to say that the mean of the sample, 10.3, is your best estimate of the population mean. (This is called *point estimation*. More often, however, we use *interval estimation*; we turn to it next.)

Each random sample is different, however, and this one might have more teachers from rural areas where in-service training is less expected, or more from larger districts where in-service education is regularly scheduled. In either case, the sample's mean might not be exactly the population average. In any event, you can't be sure the sample's mean is the same as the population mean, even though most random sample means will be closer to the population mean than not. Their variability depends on the variability in in-service days from teacher to teacher.

Because the variability of samples reflects that of the population, there ought to be a way to estimate the **standard error of the mean** from the sample's variability. Statisticians have found a way: Divide the standard deviation of the sample by the square root of the sample size. For the sample data, this means you divide 2.5 by the square root of the sample size of 100, which is 10, yielding a standard error of .25. How does this help us?

Confidence Intervals

Descriptive statistics are often reported along with an interval that expresses our confidence that the interval includes the population value. This is common in opinion polling, where the percent in favor of a candidate might be given as "42% ±2.1% at odds of 2 to 1" (the phrase "at odds of 2 to 1" is often assumed and therefore omitted in reports). (The media often say, "the chances are 2 to 1 that the real vote proportion is between 67 and 73%." The chances [odds] actually reflect our confidence in where the population value lies with respect to this observed value—a subtle distinction but one to keep in mind.) The ±2.1% indicates the upper and lower boundaries of a one-standard error interval erected around the statistic to which it is attached. In the polling example, we add and subtract 2.1 from 42% and the interval would run from 39.9% to 44.1%. Called a **confidence interval**, it represents the range of values that includes the population value with a given confidence expressed by a percentage (for example, a 95% confidence interval) or odds (19 to 1) as in a wager. The ends of such intervals are the **confidence limits** (for example, the 95% confidence limit). We adjust its size depending on how confident we wish to be that the interval includes the population value.

In practice, we never know the population's mean for sure unless we actually gather the population's data; we have to work from the sample's data. So let's suppose that we would be satisfied to estimate the population mean with a certainty expressed by odds of 2 to 1. Figure 19.2 shows an interval labeled A from 10.05 to 10.55 (one standard error on either side of our sample's mean of 10.3), and one labeled B that is two standard errors on either side and goes from 9.8 to 10.8.

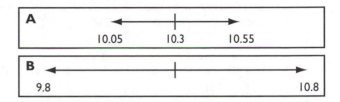

Figure 19.2   Two confidence intervals extending one standard error on either side of the sample mean in A and two standard errors in B.

Confidence interval A is the interval within which we state that the population mean lies with odds of 2 to 1. Setting those odds, we do not know whether we are right or wrong, nor for that matter where in that interval it lies if we are right—just that the odds at 2 to 1 express our certainty that it lies in the interval as well as our willingness to be wrong a third of the time. Two-thirds of such intervals constructed on random samples from the population will contain the population value. The downside of this, however, is that a third of them will not. When you are reporting to the state legislature, that big a chance of being wrong seems pretty risky. But being 95% confident it is bracketed, as in interval B, gives a band a full day wide.

Multiplied by all the teachers in the state, that's a lot of in-service training. Were you this department head, given the opportunity, you should get additional data to refine the estimates! One way of reducing the size of the standard error of mean is to increase the size of the sample. This reduces the standard error of the mean by reducing the variability of the sample means. (Imagine two separate samples—one of five women and the other of 10,000 women. Count the money in their purses. The average value for samples of 10,000 will likely vary from one another at less than the penny level, and samples of five at the dollar level.)

But given that the report is already overdue, which **confidence level** do you use? That depends on many factors, such as how much of a problem an error in estimation causes, how quickly it can be corrected, and how tolerant you might expect the legislature to be of error. The purpose for which the data are to be used is the most important factor in determining the confidence level. If you already plan to replicate the study and will be able to remedy any error, the odds of being wrong, on average 1 time out of 2, seem quite acceptable. However, we will never know in any given instance whether our study is that wrong one!

Public opinion pollsters tend to use the ±1 standard error (SE) level, but most social and behavioral science researchers use 95% and 99% levels. If a great deal is at stake, as in a life-or-death matter or when the decision involves considerable expense, then we may wish to be wrong only once in 10,000 or 100,000 instances. Then we would extend the size of the confidence interval accordingly. Although we tend to use intervals of 1, 2, or 3 standard errors (68%, 95%, 99% confidence levels), we can set any confidence level we wish, making a choice based on all the factors involved.

Where do we find levels other than those already noted? Tables that statisticians provide show what proportion of the cases lies in the tails of a probability distribution. Table 19.1 presents selected entries from a table of the normal probability distribution to give an idea of what it looks like and how the percentages change as we go further from the center of the distribution. Most of the statistics social scientists commonly use are distributed as one of five theoretical sampling distributions (the normal, binomial, *t*, *F*, and chi-square distributions). Tables (such as Table 19.1) for all the distributions are available in most statistics texts, but they typically show values for more and smaller intervals than appear here.

Table 19.1 Selected Entries from the Normal Probability Distributions

Distance from the Mean of the Distribution	Percent of the Sampling Distribution in Both Tails	Percent of the Sampling Distribution in One Tail
0.00	100.0	50.0
0.44	66.0	33.0
0.50	62.0	31.0
1.00	32.0	16.0
1.65	10.0	5.0
1.96	5.0	2.5
2.00	4.6	2.3
2.58	2.0	1.0
3.00	0.3	0.1

▶ If we calculate a descriptive statistic (for example, a mean) on repeated random samples from a population, the frequency distribution of the resulting values is called the sampling distribution of that statistic (for example, the sampling distribution of the mean). The standard deviation of that distribution is called its standard error (for example, the standard error of the mean).

▶ A multiple of the estimated standard error, determined by the confidence level we have chosen, marks off the boundaries of the confidence interval (the confidence limits) around the sample value.

▶ The confidence level expresses our certainty that the population statistic falls within the confidence interval. Conventionally used levels are 68, 95, and 99%. A confidence expressed by odds of 2 to 1 accompanies a 68% confidence interval, which is ±1 SE wide; odds of 19 to 1 accompany a 95% confidence interval, which is ±1.96 SE wide; and odds of 99 to 1 accompany a 99% confidence interval, which is ±2.58 SE wide. Although these choices have become standard, we can set any level appropriate to the data's use.

▶ We determine the width of the confidence interval by how confident we wish to be that it contains the population value. The wider we make it, the more certain we can be that it contains the population value. Since a broader interval locates the population value less exactly, however, we trade off exactness for certainty.

▶ We must set the confidence level in relation to the kind of decision that flows from the data.

THE LOGIC OF HYPOTHESIS TESTING

We can extend the logic of estimation to hypothesis testing. In **estimation**, we are seeking a range of values that probably contains the population value. Therefore, we focus on the values inside the confidence interval. In **hypothesis testing**, by contrast, we are looking at differences. These might be differences between the mean of a sample and some population value. Therefore, our question is whether our sample differs from the population value (e.g., "Are our students like a normal hearing group?"). We would usually hypothesize that they are not (they are partially deaf or have extra-sensitive hearing), that they lie outside the "normal." Our focus, then, is on those values that fall outside the confidence interval, values that occur with a low frequency.

As another example, we often have two means (for example, in the chapter 1 Zimbardo study, one mean from a sample of subjects had been hypnotized and told they would be hard of hearing and not realize it, and one from a similarly treated group were told they would realize they had a hearing deficit). We examine the difference between them in relation to a sampling distribution of differences between means. Our question is whether the difference is atypical, larger than the researchers would expect as a result of sampling variation and random error built into a study. The logic involved in "Is this difference between means typical?" is simply a twist in the focus of the same logic we used in: "Does this value belong to this population?" to "Is this mean atypical?" Returning to the Zimbardo example, these researchers set as atypical any result that would be expected on average to occur as rarely as five times or less out of a hundred as shown by use of the word "significant" to describe these results. Indeed, some results far exceed this standard, occurring as low as once out of a hundred or once in a thousand or less. See Zimbardo's Table 1.1 (p. 8) and its interpretation.

Determination of the Atypicality of a Mean (or "Does This Mean Belong to This Population?")

The logic of hypothesis testing builds on estimation by adding some steps. Suppose we are concerned that adolescents who are repeatedly exposed to loud music from headphones, dances, and concerts are ruining their hearing. We test a randomly selected sample of 26 teenagers attending a recent concert who say they regularly listen to loud music. We find that on the Syracuse Hearing Tests, their mean score is only 69, whereas normal-hearing samples have a mean of 80. We are about to go public with our results when one of our colleagues says that she is not at all sure that these students are hearing deficient. This sample could be no different from the normal hearing population except for random sampling variation and the error built into the study, such as the error of measurement of the Syracuse Hearing Tests. This seems to pass the explanation credibility test, the first judgment in Internal Integrity.

Our question is whether we can reasonably account for the difference between the sample mean of 69 and the mean of a normal-hearing population of 80 by sampling and chance variation. Inferential statistics permit us to determine whether this explanation is reasonable or unreasonable. Figure 19.3 is helpful in illustrating the logic.

Figure 19.3   The logic in hypothesis testing: Statement of the problem.

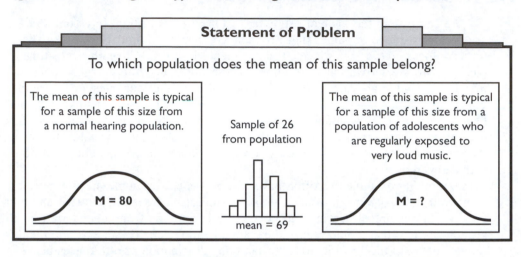

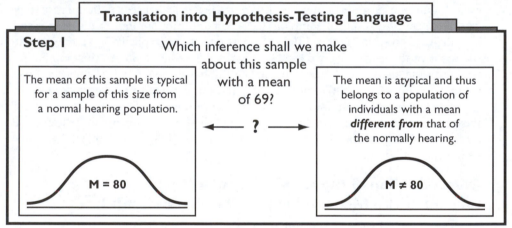

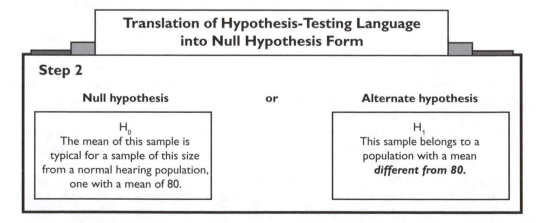

The problem is stated in the first frame of Figure 19.3. The upper right bell-shaped curve is the frequency distribution of hearing scores for a population of adolescents who are regularly exposed to loud music, from which we have taken our sample of 26 that is shown in the middle. The mean of this population is unknown, as is indicated by the question mark. We are trying to establish whether that mean, whatever it is, differs from that of a normally hearing group, the frequency distribution on the left.

This problem is illustrated in step 1, the figure's middle frame. From what population was our sample taken? Is its mean from a population with a hearing-test mean of 80—that is, a mean typical of a sample of this size from a normally hearing population? We define "typical" as the range within which most means (for example, 95%) of random samples will fall. Or is it atypical (for example, 5% or less) and therefore more likely from a population with a mean different from 80? Notice that it is the population value about which we make inferences. This is the beginning of *translation validity*, the second judgment in Internal Integrity, and the translation continues in the next paragraph.

Step 2 in the figure's bottom frame translates the hypotheses of our problem into proper logical form for this statistical test. This step involves establishing two hypotheses: the null hypothesis and an alternate hypothesis. The null hypothesis (H_0) is that when we take into account the sampling and random error of the study, the sample value is typical for a sample of this size from a normal-hearing population. Put another way, it is suggesting that in reality there is no (null) difference between the mean of the sampling distribution from which this sample came and that of a normal-hearing population. Put still another way, the strategy is to nullify, or reject, this hypothesis (Cohen, 1990). The alternative hypothesis (H_1), which we must consider if the first hypothesis proves false, is that the sample came from a population with a mean different from 80. That is, the question is whether or not we can reject the null hypothesis.

In Figure 19.4 on the following page, we find a way to choose between the two inferences. Step 3 shows the calculation of the standard error of the mean, which for this example is 6.2. Just as we did in discussing estimation earlier, in step 4 we have extended a confidence interval around the mean of 80 at an appropriate confidence level, in this instance a 95% confidence level. Therefore it is ±1.96 standard errors wide. The confidence interval is the region within which we will find samples that differ only by sampling and chance error from the true mean of 80. Thus, it is the region within which we will accept the null hypothesis (there is no real difference)—a region of acceptance.

In hypothesis testing, however, we concentrate on whether the value is atypical, that it falls within the shaded tails (which are regions of rejection of the null hypothesis). We are concerned with **significance levels**, the complement (for example, $1 - .95 = .05$) of the confidence level. This is the error we are willing to tolerate in saying that the value is atypical when it really is not—that is, when the null hypothesis is true. It is usually indicated by $p = .05$ ("p" for probability) or by the lower-case Greek letter alpha (α), $\alpha = .05$. We say, "The **alpha level** is .05" or "The significance level is .05." In statistical tables, this is often indicated with asterisks, a single asterisk for the .05 level and two asterisks for the .01 level. In our examples we have used the 5% significance level.

Figure 19.4   The logic of hypothesis testing: The solution.

Calculating the Standard Error of the Mean

Step 3

Sample of 26
from population

M = 69
SD = 31

Estimation from the sample SD of the
standard error of a population of
means of samples of size 26:

$$SE = \frac{SD}{\sqrt{n-1}} = \frac{31}{\sqrt{25}} = 6.2$$

Locating the Sample Mean in the Normal Hearing Population and Locating Acceptance and Rejection Regions for the Null Hypothesis

Step 4

Locate the sample mean of 69 in the
sampling distribution of means of
samples of size 26 taken from the
population of the normal hearing.

X

80

67.8   92.2

69

Sampling distribution of means of samples,
n = 26, taken from the
normal hearing population.
Mean = 80, standard error = 6.2.

Region of acceptance extends
± (1.96 × 6.2), which is 67.8 and 92.2.

Sample mean of 69
falls in the region between the arrows
which mark the ends of the region of
acceptance of the null hypothesis.

Region of rejection: Shaded areas mark the ranges
within which means defined as atypical will fall.

Interpreting the Data of Step 4 for the Original Hypothesis

Step 5

Since 69 falls within the region of acceptance, it is a typical value,
one likely to have been a random sample from a population with a mean of 80.

Thus, we have failed to reject the null hypothesis, H_0.

We cannot, therefore, accept the alternative hypothesis that it is a sample
from a population with a mean different from 80. We would have been wrong
had we concluded that this group was hearing impaired simply because its mean
hearing level was lower than that of the normal group.

In making such judgments we have confidence we will be right 95% of the time
but will be wrong 5% of the time.

We are trying to determine whether 69 falls inside or outside the range of values within which we will typically expect to find the population mean. If it falls inside, there is no reason to say that the sample mean of 69 comes from a population with a mean different from 80. Although it is numerically different from 80, it differs by an amount that we can easily account for by sampling and measurement error. Therefore, in step 4, the arrowed line under distribution X is the region of acceptance of the null hypothesis if we assume the null hypothesis to be true. It shows the range of values around the mean of 80 within which we will find the population value in 95% of samples of size 26. This interval extends across the center of the distribution from 67.8 to 92.2. It encloses all but the most extreme 2.5% of the means in either tail, which are the shaded parts at opposite ends of the distribution. It includes our sample mean of 69. As sample means falling inside the region of acceptance are typical, we accept the null hypothesis as true. Means falling inside the shaded areas are considered atypical, and not from a normal-hearing population with a mean of 80. These are the regions for rejection of the null hypothesis as false.

Since the mean of 69 does not fall within the shaded regions—it falls inside the region of acceptance—the data support H_0. Acceptance of the null hypothesis simply means that within the **statistical sensitivity** of this study we cannot reject it. We say that the size of the difference between this mean and the mean of 80 is not **statistically significant**. This means it can be accounted for by the rival hypothesis of random sampling variation and chance error as well as by a loss of hearing. If we cannot reject the null hypothesis, we cannot accept the alternative hypothesis H_1, which is usually what we wish to do. Thus, we would have been in error had we concluded that this group was hearing impaired simply because its mean hearing level was lower than that of the normal group.

Accepting the null hypothesis, however, does not mean we assume that the mean of the population of which it is a sample is really 80. But, if it isn't 80, what is it? Using the technique of estimation covered earlier in this chapter, we can construct a confidence interval around the sample mean, with whatever confidence level we desire, to show the range within which the true mean will likely fall.

> ▶ A difference between an observed and an expected value that falls within a region of acceptance is considered to be typical; the difference can be accounted for by sampling and chance error.
>
> ▶ A difference that falls outside that region is considered to be atypical, more extreme than would be accounted for by sampling and chance error. It is considered a statistically significant difference.

One-Tailed and Two-Tailed Tests of Statistical Significance

Notice that in our example we defined atypical values as being in both extremes of the distribution. Our alternative to the null hypothesis in step 2 was that the sample belonged to a population with a mean not equal to ($\neq$) 80. We were saying that a mean that was atypical in either direction was of interest. But defining the upper tail as atypical is tantamount to saying that our expectations include the possibility that the hearing of this group might be more acute than normal as a result of being exposed to loud sounds (that is, the mean of the sample is statistically significantly higher than that of the normal-hearing group). This hypothesis seems highly unlikely. We are expecting hearing to be diminished. Therefore, we should confine our search for atypical values to the lower extreme. The alternative to the null hypothesis then becomes that the mean from which our sample came is less than (<) 80. (In the addendum to chapter 18, this reasoning was demonstrated in the case of Mary Jane [p. 429]. There, however, we were looking at the upper extreme rather than the lower.)

We originally made what is called a **two-tailed test** for statistical significance where the alternative is nondirectional. This is appropriate when we do not know what to expect—for example, whether hearing might be made more sensitive or diminished. In our example, however, our hypothesis tells us to look in the lower tail. The alternative hypothesis is $H_1 < 80$; a one-tailed test is more appropriate.

Figure 19.5 indicates in boldface italic type the changes that we must make in Figure 19.3 to accommodate a **one-tailed test** of the hypothesis. Notice that the definition of the population with abnormal hearing has changed to be not merely different from normal but lower than normal (< 80). This has also changed the alternate hypothesis, which we will accept if we change the null hypothesis from "different from 80" to "less than 80."

In parallel fashion, Figure 19.6 (on p. 446) shows in boldface italic type the changes that we must make in Figure 19.4 to accommodate a directional hypothesis and its accompanying one-tailed test. Note that the shaded area is all in the lower tail of distribution X in step 4 of Figure 19.6 rather than split between the two tails as in Figure 19.4. When split between both tails, half the 5% was in the lower tail, and a mean had to exceed –1.96 SE to be defined as atypical. To include 5% of the cases in one tail we need only go out as far as –1.65 SE, however. (Where does the 1.65 come from? See Table 19.1, p. 438.) Since $80 – (1.65 \times 6.2) = 69.8$ with a one-tailed test, 69 is just a bit smaller than this confidence limit and would be atypical. With a two-tailed test, it was not. Thus, with a one-tailed test, we reject the null hypothesis that the sample belongs to the population with a mean of 80 and accept the alternative hypothesis that it belongs to one with a mean lower than 80. Compared with the normal-hearing population, this group hears less well on average.

With the one-tailed test, we have increased the *statistical sensitivity* of the study. That is, the sample mean did not have to be so extreme to be judged statistically significant. If the logic of the study permits us to make a sound directional prediction so that differences in only one direction are of interest, using a one-tailed test is one of the easiest ways of increasing statistical sensitivity. It requires no changes in design, nor does it incur the cost of gathering additional data or increasing the size of the sample (the latter is the most common way of increasing statistical sensitivity). As we shall shortly see, there are other ways of increasing the statistical sensitivity.

Directional hypotheses and therefore one-tailed tests are appropriate whenever we are studying a treatment with an expected effect, and we can ignore a finding of the opposite effect (for example, an alleged sleeping pill causes agitation rather than sleep) and consider it as not resulting in new information (it can cause some agitation, but we thought it would be overcome by sleep). In improving reading scores, keeping students from dropping out, or reducing an individual's anxiety, we are inter-

Figure 19.5   A one-tailed test (problem statement and steps 1 and 2).

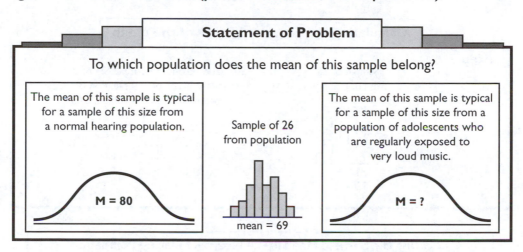

Statement of Problem

To which population does the mean of this sample belong?

The mean of this sample is typical for a sample of this size from a normal hearing population.

M = 80

Sample of 26 from population

mean = 69

The mean of this sample is typical for a sample of this size from a population of adolescents who are regularly exposed to very loud music.

M = ?

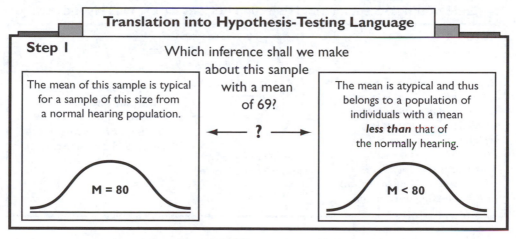

Translation into Hypothesis-Testing Language

Step 1

Which inference shall we make about this sample with a mean of 69?

The mean of this sample is typical for a sample of this size from a normal hearing population.

M = 80

← ? →

The mean is atypical and thus belongs to a population of individuals with a mean **less than** that of the normally hearing.

M < 80

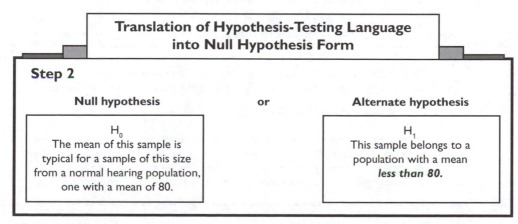

Translation of Hypothesis-Testing Language into Null Hypothesis Form

Step 2

Null hypothesis   or   **Alternate hypothesis**

H_0
The mean of this sample is typical for a sample of this size from a normal hearing population, one with a mean of 80.

H_1
This sample belongs to a population with a mean **less than 80.**

Figure 19.6 A one-tailed test (steps 3 through 5).

Calculating the Standard Error of the Mean

Step 3

Sample of 26
from population

M = 69
SD = 31

Estimation from the sample SD of the
standard error of a population of
means of samples of size 26:

$$SE = \frac{SD}{\sqrt{n-1}} = \frac{31}{\sqrt{25}} = 6.2$$

Locating the Sample Mean in the Normal Hearing Population and Locating Acceptance and Rejection Regions for the Null Hypothesis

Step 4

*Region of rejection: Since we are
interested only in the lower tail,
the shaded area begins at
−1.65 SE below the mean,
which is the score of
80 − (1.65 × 6.2) = 69.8.
This marks the boundary
of the lowest 5% of the means
in the sampling distribution.*

Distribution of
means of samples
of size $n = 26$.

80
69.8
69

*Sample mean of 69
falls in shaded region.*

*Region of acceptance
with the lower boundary
specified as 80 − 1.65 × 6.2 = 69.8
(no upper boundary in this
one-tailed directional test).*

Interpreting the Data of Step 4 for the Original Hypothesis

Step 5

Since 69 falls **outside** the region of acceptance, it is an **atypical** value,
one **unlikely** to have been a random sample from a population with a mean of 80.

Thus we **reject** the null hypothesis, H_0.

We **accept** the alternative hypothesis that it is a sample from a population with a
mean **lower than** 80. *If we can think of no reasonable alternative explanation
for the sample having less-than-normal hearing, we would accept the
hypothesis that exposure to loud music was a reasonable explanation.*

ested in positive treatment effects. We do not expect negative effects or, if they occur, we presume them to be the result of chance or some factor other than the treatment. Of course, should we find the opposite of the expected, we will have the basis for another study to see why it happened and whether it is an artifact of the way the study was done. If we can replicate it and it is a real effect, then clearly our understanding of what is going on is in error and we must remedy it.

> ▶ One-tailed tests of statistical significance increase the statistical sensitivity of a statistical test. We can use them whenever we have a directional hypothesis, one that tells us in which direction to look for results that will be statistically significant. In that context, we would consider a result in the opposite direction an aberration rather than a reliable result.

Returning to our example, since 69 is statistically significant, we have a *demonstrated effect*, the third judgment in Internal Integrity. There is a cause at work. What cause? We would like to say that it is exposure to loud music. If (1) the previous three judgments in Internal Integrity are positive; (2) we can find no other reasonable rival explanation (we have *eliminated rival explanations*, the fourth judgment of Internal Integrity); and (3) there is no other reason for us to assume that we do not have a *credible result* (the fifth judgment), then the study has Internal Integrity, and we would say that the loss in hearing is due to the teenagers' being exposed to loud sounds.

> Summary of the Logic:
>
> ▶ In abstract form, the logic of inference to determine whether an observed value belongs to a particular population is as follows:
>
> 1. We translate the study's hypothesis into two statistical hypotheses: the one we test, the null hypothesis (H_0); and the alternative (H_1), which we wish to accept if H_0 is rejected:
>
>   • H_0: The observed value is typical of means for a sample of this size from the sampling distribution of means created by random sampling and chance error.
>
>   • H_1: The observed value is atypical, not one that belongs to the population sampling distribution created by random sampling and chance error. It belongs to a population with a mean that differs from the mean of the chance distribution (or, for a directional hypothesis with one-tailed tests, a population with a mean that is higher—or lower—than the mean of the chance distribution).
>
> 2. We set a significance level that expresses the risk we are willing to run of being wrong in this particular instance. Whether the observed value is atypical depends on whether it falls outside the region of acceptance of the null hypothesis constructed around the expected value.
>
> ▶ If it does not fall outside, we have failed to reject H_0 and cannot accept H_1.
>
> ▶ If it does fall outside, we reject H_0 and accept H_1 with a "maybe so."

Determination of the Atypicality
of a Difference between Two Means

Suppose we believe that studying from the general to the specific is more conducive to learning than studying from the specific to the general. For instance, learning the logic of inferential statistics before studying specific statistical tests should result in superior achievement to studying specific statistical tests first. A pool of 40 volunteer students is randomly assigned: 20 undergo the general-to-specific treatment and 20 the specific-to-general. A post-test is given to both groups. The general-to-specific group's mean on the test was 46.5, and that of the specific-to-general was 38.0.

Do these means come from populations with the same mean so that the difference results from sampling variation and chance error? Or are they from populations with different means and the treatments presumably made a difference? Translated into generic form, a group received some experimental treatment, and a control group received either a neutral treatment or, as in this case, a less favorable alternative treatment. We want to know whether the difference between them is statistically significant—that is, reliably different from zero. This is among the most common questions asked of inferential statistics.

Here we appear to compare two means whereas before we located one in the distribution of its expected value. How do we proceed now? We reduce the problem to the same formulation. Instead of dealing with the two means, we deal with the difference between them and test it against the sampling distribution of differences between means. We follow the same logic as before: Is the observed difference atypical in a distribution of differences between means?

Let's assume that these two means are from sampling distributions with the same mean and same standard error. We have one observed difference between two random samples from these distributions. Presumably we could take many samples, find their means and, subtracting the first from the second, construct a distribution composed of differences between means. On the average, the two means would be about equal; only occasionally would a large positive or negative difference occur. Therefore, the mean of this distribution would be zero, and it would have the shape of a normal distribution as the number of differences grew larger. Obviously, we don't go through this process in practice, but this is conceptually what we mean when we talk about the sampling distribution of the differences between means.

The variability in differences between means will be a function of the variability in each of the sampling distributions from which the means came. Therefore, we use the standard errors of both distributions in estimating the standard error of the sampling distribution of the differences between means. The standard error of the differences between means is the square root of the sum of the squared standard errors of the two individual distributions:

$$\sqrt{SE_1^2 + SE_2^2} \text{ or } \sqrt{\left(\frac{SD_1}{\sqrt{n_1 - 1}}\right)^2 + \left(\frac{SD_2}{\sqrt{n_2 - 1}}\right)^2}$$

This formula holds for independent means. If the means come from samples where individuals are matched or paired, the product $2r_{12}(SE_1)(SE_2)$ is subtracted from the amount under the square root sign (r_{12} is the correlation between the scores for the paired subjects).

The logic is similar to that we used before, but here we want to know whether the difference between the two groups belongs to a sampling distribution of differences between means with a mean of zero or to one with a mean greater than zero. Figure 19.7 on the following page shows the logic in the same kind of diagram as we used for previous examples. The top box states our study question and reduces the problem of dealing with two means by translating the problem into an examination of the difference between means. Step 1 shows how this translates into hypothesis-testing language (the box in the center) and in turn, step 2 shows the null hypothesis logic applied to step 1.

Since our hypothesis is directional—we expect the general-to-specific treatment, M_1, to be superior—we use a one-tailed test. Since we expect the difference, M_1 – M_2, to be positive, all the atypical values will be in the right tail. Therefore, we build a region of acceptance around the expected value, which includes the left tail and extends to the right to a point determined by the error we are willing to tolerate, for instance, 5%. We consult Table 19.1 earlier in the chapter and find 5% is in one tail at 1.65 SD so the region of acceptance runs all the way from the left tail to +1.65 SD. We then determine in which region the difference falls. If it falls within the area where values are typical, we cannot reject the null hypothesis and thus cannot accept the alternative. There is no statistically significant difference between the two methods of study. If the difference falls outside the region of acceptance, inside the region of rejection, we reject the null and say "maybe so" to the alternative—that in this instance it pays to learn the general logic of inference first.

▶ Hypothesis testing of a difference between two observed values involves a null hypothesis: The difference between the two means is typical of differences in a sampling distribution of differences between means from samples of these sizes, where the mean is the same in both populations from which the samples came. A simpler way of saying this is that the mean of the sampling distribution of differences is zero. We wish to nullify the null hypothesis.

▶ The nondirectional alternative hypothesis is that the difference between means belongs to a population of differences with a mean other than zero. With a directional hypothesis, the alternative states whether the difference is greater or less than zero.

▶ Working with the difference between means rather than the two means individually allows us to reduce the problem to the logic we used previously for whether a value was typical or atypical of those in its distribution.

STATISTICAL SENSITIVITY AND STATISTICAL POWER

Statistical sensitivity and statistical power are names for the same thing, the ability of a statistical test to sense a difference of a size of interest to us. Studies should be designed with appropriate statistical sensitivity if they are to be successful. If the

Figure 19.7   The logic of inference applied to a difference between two sample means with a one-tailed test of significance.

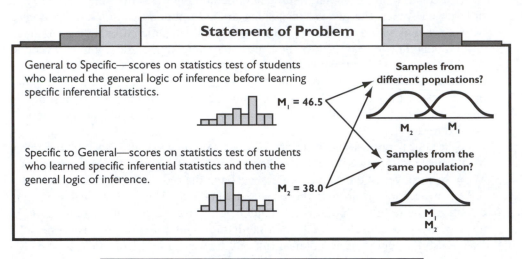

Statement of Problem

General to Specific—scores on statistics test of students who learned the general logic of inference before learning specific inferential statistics.

$M_1 = 46.5$

Samples from different populations?

M_2 M_1

Specific to General—scores on statistics test of students who learned specific inferential statistics and then the general logic of inference.

$M_2 = 38.0$

Samples from the same population?

M_1
M_2

Translation into Hypothesis-Testing Language

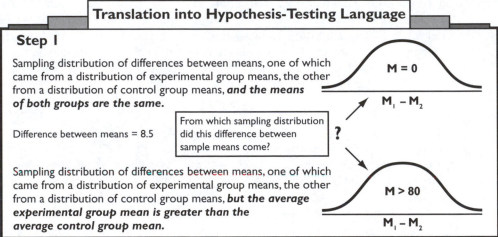

Step 1

Sampling distribution of differences between means, one of which came from a distribution of experimental group means, the other from a distribution of control group means, *and the means of both groups are the same.*

$M = 0$

$M_1 - M_2$

Difference between means = 8.5

From which sampling distribution did this difference between sample means come?

?

Sampling distribution of differences between means, one of which came from a distribution of experimental group means, the other from a distribution of control group means, *but the average experimental group mean is greater than the average control group mean.*

$M > 80$

$M_1 - M_2$

Translation into Null Hypothesis Form

Step 2

Null hypothesis   or   **Alternate hypothesis**

H_0
This difference is typical of those in a sampling distribution of differences between means for samples of these sizes where the mean is the same in both distributions from which the samples came.

H_1
This difference between means is atypically large in the sampling distribution of differences; therefore, the sample means must have come from populations where M_1 is greater than M_2.

study is not sensitive enough, the researcher risks missing the result that is sought. Since most ways of increasing statistical sensitivity require resources, an overly sensitive study uses resources that could have been put into further studies. An exception is a study that must be large enough to be intuitively convincing to laypersons or others relatively unsophisticated in research methods.

Errors of Inference

As we have already noted, when we set a confidence or significance level, we are accepting a certain level of error. With one type of error we reject the null hypothesis, which claims we have a real difference when in actuality the difference is not real but is due to sampling and chance variation—that is, saying the treatment was effective when it was not. As noted earlier in this chapter, this kind of error has been labeled a Type I (alpha, α) error. Type I error is always under our direct control as a result of setting significance levels, say, at 5%. On the average, when H_0 is true, with a 5% significance level we will be wrong 5 times in 100 when we say that there is a real difference.

Such error can be serious when we are relying on a finding as representing the true facts. We want to be sure, for instance, that a treatment is making a difference. For important decisions, like building special equipment into a classroom building or adopting an expensive way of teaching reading, we ought to rely on accumulated evidence rather than on a single study. If we must depend on a single study, however, we reduce Type I error by using a confidence level of 99, or 99.9, or even 99.99%.

If that is the case, why not always use such stringent confidence levels? Because, for a given set of data, decreasing Type I error causes its opposite, Type II (beta, β) error, to increase. The latter occurs when we miss a real difference and call it chance error; we fail to reject the null hypothesis when we should have.

As much as we pay special attention to Type I error in validating a finding, we want to attend to Type II error when exploring. When screening cancer cures, we do not want to discard an option by judging the improvement no greater than chance when the treatment was effective. If the effect is too small to be sensed, we run the danger of lumping it with chance errors. In exploring, we want a study that is sensitive enough to show any effect of possible interest as statistically significant. Figure 19.8 summarizes these two types of errors.

Does Figure 19.8 look familiar? It should! It reflects exactly the same logic as that illustrated by Figure 19.1. In fact, the section in which the first figure appears introduced this very same logic and pointed out its every-

Figure 19.8   Type I and Type II errors and the null hypothesis.

		DECISION BASED ON SAMPLE DATA	
		Do not reject null hypothesis	Reject null hypothesis
TRUE STATE OF AFFAIRS	H_0 is true	Correct decision $1 - \alpha *$	Type I error $\alpha *$
	H_0 is false	Type II error $\beta *$	Correct decision $1 - \beta *$

* These are the probabilities of that event occurring.

day use. Correct decisions build trust in a service manager's judgment, and incorrect ones lead to distrust. Similarly, correct decisions lead to trust of science by laypersons and incorrect ones to distrust. In comparison with laypersons, however, when an inference is wrong, scientists continue to trust science because they understand the probabilities and realize that errors will occur. This shows how important it is to educate everyone about how science works and the role of inference in it!

Figure 19.8 also indicates the probability of occurrence of each of the events. Thus, defining the Type I error as α (say, 5%) makes the probability of a correct decision when H_0 is true, $1 - \alpha$ (95%). Unless we do some estimation ahead of time, we do not usually know the size of β, the Type II error. Whatever it is, however, we know that $1 - \beta$ is the probability of a correct decision where we should reject the null hypothesis. Indeed, because we want correct decisions, $1 - \beta$ indicates their likelihood and therefore the sensitivity of a statistical test in a given instance. Hence, we define $1 - \beta$ as the **power or sensitivity of a statistical test**.

Conventions, like 5% for Type I error, are not well established for Type II error. If the study is but a small step in the search for knowledge, a Type II error of 10%, 20%, or even larger may be acceptable. A large Type II error seems better tolerated than a large Type I. This bias reflects the preference of most scientists to miss a possible real effect rather than to be publicly embarrassed by a false knowledge claim that cannot be replicated. Missing a finding is regrettable, but since negative-result studies are rarely published it is a private matter, and nobody is the wiser. Further, if it is not published, it won't foreclose the work of someone else who might study it with sufficient statistical sensitivity to obtain a statistically significant finding.

▶ Type I (alpha, α) errors occur when we decide that an observed value is atypical and not the result of sampling and chance error when it really is. Type I errors are particularly serious when we are attempting to validate a hypothesis that supports an important decision.

▶ Type II (beta, β) errors occur when we decide that an observed value is not atypical and therefore not statistically significant when in fact it results from a real effect. Type II errors occur when a study's statistical sensitivity is insufficient so that a real effect does not cross the threshold and show statistical significance. They are especially serious in screening for possible treatments when a beneficial effect may not only be missed but therefore also possibly be excluded from further research.

Ways to Increase Statistical Power

How can a researcher increase statistical power? We have already noted one way, using a one-tailed instead of a two-tailed test when it is appropriate to do so. Usually, increasing sample size comes to our mind as well.

Statistical power and sample size.   When we see a poll that indicates a candidate is winning, we want to know "What was the sample size?" Intuitively, a poll based on 50 cases is not nearly as trustworthy as one based on 500 or 5,000 cases. This makes good sense because the larger sample is more likely to be representative of the population (unless there is a sampling bias, as in selecting all the cases from only one social class). However, there is a statistical reason as well: The standard error decreases with larger sample size, as shown in Figure 19.9.

Attend especially to the size of the standard errors. Although it is clear that the curves become more peaked and narrow, it is a bit difficult to judge the standard error change from the shape. If we start with a standard deviation of 10, with samples of size 1 the standard error is still 10. Doubling sample size reduces it only to 7.07. To cut it in half, we must quadruple the sample size. Similarly, to cut this in half, we must go to 16 cases. Reductions occur as a function of the square of the change in sample size. To cut the standard error by a third, we must have 9 times the cases; by a fifth, 25 times the cases; and so on. With each halving in the chart, the drop in the size of the standard error is smaller and the number of cases needed to bring it about is substantially larger.

Figure 19.9   Reduction in the standard error of the mean with increases in sample size.

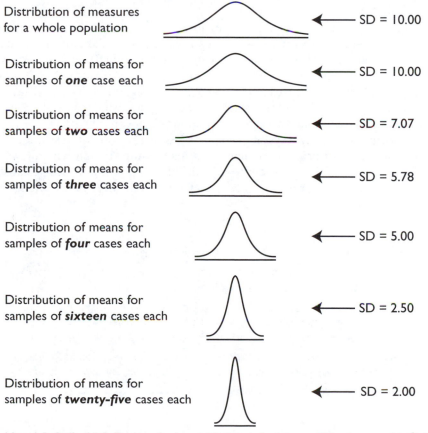

Distribution of measures for a whole population — SD = 10.00

Distribution of means for samples of **one** case each — SD = 10.00

Distribution of means for samples of **two** cases each — SD = 7.07

Distribution of means for samples of **three** cases each — SD = 5.78

Distribution of means for samples of **four** cases each — SD = 5.00

Distribution of means for samples of **sixteen** cases each — SD = 2.50

Distribution of means for samples of **twenty-five** cases each — SD = 2.00

Adapted from J. P. Guilford & B. Fruchter, *Fundamental Statistics in Psychology and Education*, copyright © 1978. Reprinted by permission of the authors.

Other ways to increase the power of a statistical test.   We want the result of dividing the difference between the means by its standard error to be large enough to reach statistical significance. We can make it larger by increasing the difference or by decreasing the standard error. We can increase the difference between the means by: increasing the strength of the treatment, choosing for both control and experimental groups individuals who are especially susceptible to the treatment, increasing the motivation of the subjects, administering the treatment over a longer period of time so that the cumulative effect is greater, and other similar efforts.

Besides increasing sample size, we can decrease the standard error by reducing the variances of the samples. We can do that by: choosing homogeneous samples, eliminating all extraneous distractions by moving the study into the laboratory, masking distracting noises, and other similar efforts. There are also statistics, such as analysis of covariance and partial correlation, that would reduce variability by removing the effect of contaminating variables. Using highly reliable measures also reduces variability, and using unreliable ones increases it.

We have already noted that a directional hypothesis with its one-tailed test increases statistical power, but we can also change the level of significance. Moving the significance level from 1% in the direction of 5% increases statistical sensitivity as well.

Finally, some statistical tests are more powerful than others under certain conditions. In general, tests based on interval or ratio scale data are more sensitive than those based on ranked (ordinal) or categorical (nominal) data. However, there are special conditions, such as those in sampling from non-normal distributions, when using ranked data—for example, the Wilcoxon signed-ranks test (May, Masson, & Hunter, 1990, pp. 491–494)—is more powerful than using the *t* test (Blair & Higgins, 1980, 1985). Exploring such special conditions is beyond the scope of this book.

With these many ways of changing statistical sensitivity, researchers clearly will want to do a statistical power analysis during the study design. This allows determination of a sample size sufficient to provide adequate power. Search "statistical power analysis" on the Internet for software. *This is the one-and-only answer to the question, "When is the sample big enough?".*

▶ The power of a statistical test $(1 - \beta)$ is its ability to avoid Type II error.

▶ Increasing the statistical power (sensitivity) of the test makes a statistically significant result more likely if a non-chance effect is present.

▶ We can increase statistical power by increasing sample size, the size of the effect (a stronger treatment), reducing variability (moving from field into laboratory or using more reliable measures), or other ways of reducing the standard error.

▶ A power analysis shows the sample size needed for adequate statistical sensitivity and is the only way to determine what constitutes a "big enough" sample.

THE LEVEL OF SIGNIFICANCE TO REPORT

Look at the table in the Culler and Holahan study on page 464. They reported statistical significance at the .002 level, which is .2%—considerably less than the conventional 1 or 5%. Authors use significance levels like this to indicate that the finding was not borderline. Indeed, it is common journal practice not just to indicate whether a result is or is not statistically significant but also to tell how rare it is. We find exact probabilities like 6%, 10%, .003%, or even .00004%.

Interpreting such probabilities is difficult, however, since the level of significance depends on a study's statistical sensitivity—and studies vary greatly. How does one compare the highly significant .01% result of a study of 10 cases with different findings from a 100-case study that barely made the 5% level? Repeated borderline results are probably due to more than chance, however, and deserve to be so interpreted. Reporting exact probabilities facilitates meta-analysis, the process we use to combine data across comparable studies (see chapter 22).

Although there are accepted conventions, all research and statistical practices are not cut and dried. Indeed, mathematical statisticians recognize two points of view regarding inference: (1) Fisher's and (2) Neyman and Pearson's. Fisher's (1959) concentrates on rejecting the null hypothesis and uses predetermined levels of significance (often 5%) and confidence intervals. Decisions are presumably based on a body of studies, and the goal is understanding. Neyman and Pearson (1933) give the alternate hypothesis equal importance with the null hypothesis and are concerned with Type II errors as well as Type I. Their goal is decision making between the null and the alternative hypothesis. This distinction may seem minor, as May, Masson, and Hunter (1990) note. In practice, however, the two views often merge—studies follow the logic of a 5% significance level but then report whatever level is achieved. Indeed, this chapter is Fisherian in the discussion of the logic of inference, and Neyman-Pearsonian in its discussion of power analyses. For more, see May, Masson, and Hunter (1990, chapter 7). Incidentally, if one considers the study as ultimately mainly fodder for a *meta-analysis*, the distinction is moot.

STATISTICAL AND PRACTICAL SIGNIFICANCE

Very large samples can make the tiniest values to be statistically significant. We can increase statistical sensitivity so that any real difference can be statistically significant. Not all statistically significant findings, however, have practical significance. Let's consider an experimental group receiving a $10,000-per-pupil reading treatment to get only a one-point gain in achievement. This difference might be statistically significant and, from the point of view of a researcher, might lead to further useful research.

From a school's standpoint, however, such an expenditure for so little gain completely lacks practical significance. Thus, **practical significance** is a function of the purpose for which the results are to be used. What is practically significant is a judgment of the value of the results in a particular context; for example, the school might be willing to add $300 to per-pupil costs for a 10-point gain.

> ▶ It is possible to increase the statistical sensitivity of a study to the point where, if there is any effect at all—no matter how infinitesimal—it can be made statistically significant. However, whether it is practically significant is another matter entirely, a judgment based on the value of the result in particular contexts.

PROOF OF A PROPOSITION VERSUS ITS ESCAPING DISCONFIRMATION

Suppose a study shows a statistically significant effect in the expected direction. Have we proved the proposition? Don't we wish it! In Section I of this book we noted that all knowledge is not permanently true but must be held as tentatively true until new knowledge modifies or replaces it. Beyond this limitation, however, the logic of statistical inference is such that we are never sure a given finding is not the result of error and chance variation. Positive results simply increase the odds of saying that the results are real; that is, they increase our confidence in our assertion. In any given instance, we can merely say that a proposition has escaped disconfirmation.

Popper (1959) and others have argued that the job of the researcher is to subject each proposition to tests of disconfirmation—to try actively to disconfirm it! Then each escape from disconfirmation creates added confidence about its validity. Unfortunately, in the social and behavioral sciences we are not as prone to attempt disconfirmation as we are confirmations in new circumstances. If the data support the proposition in a new context or an extension of the old one, we feel increasingly confident about its validity. Eventually, it crosses the threshold of what we are willing to accept as knowledge—still tentative but firm enough to act on. However, if we design a sufficiently sensitive study and the result does not appear or a different result appears and we cannot otherwise justify it, we must go back to the now disconfirmed study to seek an explanation.

A meta-analysis that integrates the body of studies bearing on a finding significantly increases our confidence in it.

> ▶ A statistically significant result proves not that the hypothesis is true but that it has escaped disconfirmation in this instance. Each such instance contributes to confidence that the proposition is valid. With enough such evidence, a proposition becomes accepted as knowledge that, though tentatively held as true, is considered firm enough to act on.
>
> ▶ Combining the results of studies, as in meta-analysis, increases our confidence in the findings.

ADDITIONAL READING

For useful statistics texts: Freedman, Pisani and Purves (1997), Guilford and Fruchter (1978), Hays (1994), and May, Masson, and Hunter (1990). For statistics books minimizing formulas and mathematics: Abelson (1995) and Dichter and Roznowski (2005). For exploratory statistical techniques: Tukey (1977). For nonparametric statistics: Siegel and Castellan (1988). For sage statistical advice: Cohen (1990). For comparison of multiple means: Hancock and Klockars (1996). For analysis of pre- to post-change: Collins and Horn (1991) and Collins and Sayer (2001). For a primer on multiple regression analysis, path analysis, multidimensional scaling, logistic regression, analysis of variance, and multiple analysis of variance: Grim and Yarnold (1995). For links to a wealth of statistics material online: http://statpages.org/javastat.html.

IMPORTANT TERMS AND CONCEPTS

alpha error	one-tailed test
alpha level	power or sensitivity of a statistical test
beta error	practical significance
confidence interval	significance level
confidence level	standard error of the mean
confidence limits	statistical sensitivity
estimation	statistical significance
hypothesis testing	two-tailed test
inferential statistics	Type I error
null hypothesis	Type II error

OPPORTUNITIES FOR ADDITIONAL LEARNING

1. Some researchers were interested in comparing the performance of learners working independently on a computer-assisted instruction program with that of learners working on the computers cooperatively in pairs. They were able to conduct the experiment with 60 eighth-grade students (31 male and 29 female) drawn from several health education classes and randomly assigned to either the individual learning group or the cooperative learning group. The students were given a parallel series of 16 lessons on the topic of sex education. Despite the sensitivity of the subject matter, the investigators predicted that the cooperative method would yield superior performances on a written posttest. How might the investigators proceed to show the superiority of the cooperative method?

2. A medical researcher was interested in the long-term effects of marijuana on users. She administered a test of automobile braking-reaction time to a sample of 49 long-term users. She compared the results with the adult population average for her city (previously computed in a series of studies conducted by the local traffic safety board for use in licensing tests). The users sample had a mean reaction time of 0.98 seconds, whereas the population average was 0.90. The standard error for the sample was calculated to be 0.043 seconds, with the confidence interval for 95% ranging from 0.896 to 1.064 seconds using a two-tailed test and 0.909 seconds for a one-tailed test looking in just the lower tail. Given these results, should the researcher accept or reject the null hypothesis that there is no difference between this sample's mean and that of the adult population?

3. Sandra Fayette showed that college students who generated their own questions to a passage of text would demonstrate higher comprehension rates than those who were presented with relevant questions. She decided to replicate her study with high school students to see if this effect would also be found with younger students. Her results came very close to showing a statistically significant difference between the two approaches in favor of the generative question hypothesis. When she examined her data, she noticed that the compre-

hension score for one particular student, who was part of the generative strategy group, was considerably lower than the average scores for that group. She also realized that if she were to discard his score, she would have a statistically significant result. What is her dilemma regarding Type I and Type II error? Is it possible for her to demonstrate statistical significance using her current data without discarding the score?

4. Comment on this statement: "As we change from validation to a discovery orientation, we typically change the level of significance from 10% toward .1%."

5. Comment on this statement: "If we reject the null hypothesis, we can say that the observed result proves that the proposition we are testing is true."

6. Teresa Wright is the superintendent of a suburban school system. Her director of research tells her that the new curriculum is superior at a statistically significant level to the old curriculum. What questions should she ask the director?

7. Dr. Gerrard Goetz is up for tenure. He wants to be sure that his study shows a significant result so that he can get it published. He is comparing the effectiveness of beginning-of-chapter advanced organizers on learning scientific laws with end-of-chapter traditionally written summaries. What might he do in designing and conducting the study to make it more likely he will get a publishable result?

8. Sally Stoltz has to use a convenience sample of teachers in New York State for her questionnaire, but she would like to show that this group of teachers is typical of those of the state. She has 25 returns. She runs a statistical test on their ages, years of experience, and grade level and finds that the means of all three are not statistically different at the 5% level from those for the state, as published by the state education department. She concludes that she can generalize her sample to the teachers of the state. Is she justified? Why or why not?

9. The following statements appear in Schmidt (1996, p. 126):

    a. If my findings are not significant, then I know that they probably just occurred by chance and the true difference is probably zero.

    b. If the result is significant, then I know I have a reliable finding.

    c. The level-of-statistical-significance test tells me whether the relationships in my data are large enough to be important or not.

    Which of these statements is true and which false? If false, why?

    Compare your answers with those following the Application Exercise.

APPLICATION EXERCISE

Consider how you might set up your study with an experimental and a control group (which you will learn more about in the next chapter). How might you apply the logic of inference? What would be the null hypothesis? The alternative hypothesis? Would a one- or two-tailed test of significance be most appropriate? What would be an appropriate significance level? Why? Are you concerned with statistical or practical significance?

KEY TO ADDITIONAL LEARNING OPPORTUNITIES

1. The investigators would be interested in examining the difference between the means of the two groups. Expecting a greater effect for the cooperative learning group, they would adopt the null hypothesis that the difference between the means of the two groups belongs to a population of differences with a mean of zero. According to this logic, any observed differ-

ence is due to chance and sampling error, and the two samples actually belong to the same population. They would use a directional test involving the positive tail of the distribution of differences between means. If they were able to reject the null hypothesis, they would likely accept the alternative hypothesis that the difference between the means belongs to a population of differences with a mean greater than zero. Failing to find a plausible alternative cause, they would state that there was a significant difference between the instructional treatments in favor of the cooperative treatment.

2. The answer depends on the researcher's prior expectations—the alternative hypothesis that would be accepted if the null hypothesis can be rejected. And that determines whether the researcher chooses the one-tailed or the two-tailed test. The latter includes the population mean within the 95% confidence interval; the former does not. Thus the one-tailed test is more sensitive and indicates statistical significance. But is the researcher justified in using it here? It depends on whether there was an expectation that the drug would slow or quicken an individual's reaction time—leading to a directional hypothesis—or simply expecting an effect, but not knowing which direction it might be. The choice of the one-tailed test is justified if the researcher had a directional hypothesis, two-tailed if nondirectional.

   If she hypothesized that reaction time slowed (one-tailed test) but found that marijuana actually speeded up reaction time, she would have to consider that an aberration rather than a finding. If she could find nothing wrong with the study, she might then switch her hypothesis and replicate the study with a new sample.

3. Sandra's dilemma is that she does not want to reject the null hypothesis and claim an effect that really does not exist—that is, commit a Type I (α) error. But it seems as though that one extra low case may cause her to commit a Type II (β) error (i.e., say the generative treatment may not be more effective when it really is).

   Can she show statistical significance without discarding the score? The problem doesn't state whether she used a one-tailed or two-tailed test when she just missed statistical significance, but given this was a replication, she already knew which should be the better treatment. If she ran a two-tailed test in error, she might reach statistical significance with a one-tailed test. If her sample were small, it might be possible to gather data on an additional group and combine them for a larger sample. Finally, if she is able to return to her original sample, she could increase the treatment time (perhaps test the subjects with more text passages) to strengthen its effect.

   Alternatively, provided that she can demonstrate a valid reason for doing so (e.g., perhaps the student was ill that day, or English was a second language and not yet mastered), she could consider discarding data for the one subject. If she does this she should explain it in the study's report and, usually, the data is presented both with and without that case so readers can judge for themselves.

4. With a discovery orientation, such as in screening remedial reading programs for one that works, we don't want to miss a potentially good one. We are willing to tolerate what we call false positives, programs that show up as statistically significant but are Type I—chance—errors. Thus, we change the confidence level in the opposite direction from that stated in the problem, from 0.1% toward 10%. Portions of the 10% that show statistically significant effects do so by chance, but they will be caught by studying that group further.

5. If that were the case, it would make research much easier! No, all we can say is that the null hypothesis escaped disconfirmation this time. We ought to be putting our propositions to the most rigorous tests we can find. Each time we test a proposition and the data shows what we expected, we say that it escaped disconfirmation. After it has escaped enough times, we are confident about our results and eventually act as though it were a true proposition. But

science is the only method of knowing wherein every proposition is held as tentatively true until disconfirmed. Thus, even well-established propositions could, in theory at least, be disconfirmed at any time. Of course, this might markedly upset our ideas about the way the world works, but consider that it's just what Einstein did with the theory of relativity!

6. Here we run into the problem of statistical significance versus practical significance. Wright needs to know not only that the effect was statistically significant but also whether it was large enough to be practically significant. Thus, she wants to know how big it is in terms of the gains that children normally show at that grade. She may also want to know how many additional resources were required to achieve that gain.

7. Dr. Goetz should conduct a pilot study to find estimates of the standard deviations of his variables, as well as an estimated difference between treatments. When he has these, he can do a power analysis to help him design a sufficiently sensitive study so that if that size of effect appears again, it will be statistically significant.

   Alternatively (or at the same time), he can devise a design that is as sensitive as possible. To do this, he can change the confidence level from 1% toward 5%, use a directional hypothesis and a one-tailed test of significance, increase the size of the difference between treatments by writing the advance organizers for maximum effect, comparing the two treatments over many samples of material, giving the two treatments to a bright group that might be more susceptible to the effect of advance organizers, and so on. In addition, he could use the largest sample possible or decrease its variability. The latter can be done by using more reliable tests or measures, by moving into the laboratory to decrease random noise that would decrease attention, by uniformly motivating the students but ensuring that different trials used the same directions for testing, and similar things.

8. Apparently, the difference between the means for these characteristics in Stoltz's sample and those of the population give sufficient reason to attribute them to sampling error for samples of 25. But that assumes that the sensitivity of the statistical test that she ran was powerful enough to pick up a difference that was practically significant so far as she was concerned. Sally must determine what magnitude of difference between means is a practically significant difference between her sample and the population. If this turns out to be within the statistical sensitivity of her study as already designed, all is well. If not, then getting a larger sample is probably the easiest way to fix the study.

9. They are all false! Here are the reasons:

   a. The true difference is not necessarily zero; you only know that it was too small to sense with the statistical power of that study.

   b. It may be a chance finding rather than a reliable finding. On average, 5% of them will be such if that was the level of significance used.

   c. The level of statistical significance does not indicate the importance of the finding; that is a value judgment made by a human. It could be a real difference that is too small to be considered practically important.

SUMMARY

Understanding the logic of inference unlocks the mystery of many inferential statistics; the context of its application differs, but the basic logic doesn't. Estimation with interval or ratio data involves finding ways of determining what would be typical values for a statistic due to random sampling variability and the chance error built into the variables used in the study. When applying the logic to questions about the mean, imagine computing the mean from an infinite number of samples from the population of interest. Form the frequency distribution of these means; the standard deviation of this distribution is the standard error of the mean. From this distribution and standard error, given a specified level of confidence, we can form a confidence interval that includes means that are typical of this distribution. By typical we mean that the interval includes a given proportion of the population means. The confidence interval is expressed as a range, and a percentage or odds indicates the level of our confidence that the interval contains the given percentage. These confidence levels are usually 95% (odds of 19 to 1) or 99% (99 to 1) but can be set wherever is appropriate for the decision involved.

We can test a sample mean to see whether it differs from the typical values in a given distribution (for example, normal hearing). We define "typical" as the level of confidence we set for the confidence interval, such as 95% confidence or odds of 19 to 1. Thus odds of 19 to 1 express our confidence that a 95% confidence interval includes 95% of the means in the frequency distribution. An atypical mean is defined as falling outside this confidence interval. This is the alpha (α) level (1 – confidence level), the level we set as being wrong when due to error we say that a mean is atypical when it is typical.

With hypothesis testing, the logic assumes that a given sample statistic—for example, a difference between means—is typical of such differences from samples of those sizes taken from the same population (the null hypothesis). The alternative hypothesis is that the differences come from different populations in which one population's mean is larger than the other. We then compare the observed difference between means, with the typical range for differences between samples from the same population, to determine whether the difference falls within that range. Values lying outside the typical range are likely to have been influenced by something other than sampling and error variability (the alternative hypothesis). Atypical values permit our rejection of the null hypothesis and acceptance of the alternative—that is, that the means of the populations from which the sample means come differ. If we fail to reject the null hypothesis, we cannot accept the alternate hypothesis. If our hypothesis was directional, it will indicate which one is the larger, and we should have used a one-tailed rather than a two-tailed test of significance.

Sometimes we fail to reject the null hypothesis when we should have. In this instance, we make a Type II (β) error. The statistical sensitivity of a study is determined by the extent to which such errors are avoided (1 – β). Studies should be designed to appropriate levels of sensitivity by conducting a statistical power analysis in the planning stages. Sensitivity can be made greater by increasing the size of the sample, increasing treatment effect, or decreasing the variability of the measures (as by increasing their reliability).

A Look Ahead

Now that we have the necessary tools—descriptive statistics and an understanding of the logic of inference—we will examine some common statistics that make use of this logic in the next chapter.

Links to previous research

Explanation, rationale, theory, or point of view

Questions, hypotheses, models

Preplanned and emergent designs

Design/procedure

Focus   Records   Time   Comparison and Contrast   Situation   Participants

Data

Statistical analysis and/or narrative analysis

Conclusion

Link to next study

Explanation or rationale of next study, etc.

20

Common Inferential Statistics and Examples

> Mathematics does not develop the scientist's powers but puts its powers at his disposal; [with] its creation, something of the genius of the mathematician . . . is made available to every schoolboy.
>
> —A. Kaplan, *The Conduct of Inquiry*

In this chapter we'll take up a few commonly used statistics: the *t* test, chi-square, and analysis of variance and discuss two topics you'll likely encounter: showing two statistics are the same, and the assumptions of statistical tests and their violation. Computation by computers, which has markedly eased that task, has had implications.

INTRODUCTION

Now that you understand the logic of inference, you may wonder what specific statistics use it in research. The range of such statistics is beyond the scope of this book and more suited to a statistics course, but we can introduce you to some common statistics that you are likely to encounter in your reading. With the rich resources of the Internet, the additional reading references in the previous chapter, and this chapter, you can explore further on your own.

SEEKING NON-CHANCE DIFFERENCES AMONG MEANS

Many studies examine a difference between two means with the *t* test, especially in relatively simple designs involving either a comparison of two experimental treatments or a comparison of a control with an experimental group. Many more use analysis of variance in studies comparing more than two means. These are probably the two most commonly used inferential statistics in the behavioral sciences.

The *t* Test

This test uses the same logic that we examined in the previous chapter but adds a couple of refinements. First, instead of using the normal probability distribution, it uses a sampling distribution called the *t* distribution. Although this distribution becomes normally distributed with large samples, it differs for small samples. Whereas the 5% level of the normal distribution requires 1.96 standard error (SE) for statistical significance, for 6 cases the *t* **test** requires the higher value of 2.5 SE but drops back to 1.98 SE for 100 cases. To use the *t* table, we use *degrees of freedom* (usually abbreviated as *df*). For most *t* tests of differences between means, this is simply 2 less than the sum of the sample sizes ($n_1 + n_2 - 2$).

Second, the formula we usually use assumes a common variance for the populations from which the samples came and pools the samples' variability for a better estimate of the population value. This formula also gives greater weight to samples of larger size:

$$\text{SE}_{\text{M}_1-\text{M}_2} \sqrt{\frac{(n_1-1)\text{SD}_1{}^2 + (n_2-1)\text{SD}_2{}^2}{n_1+n_2-2} \cdot \frac{n_1+n_2}{n_1 n_2}}$$

Then:

$$t = \frac{\text{M}_1 - \text{M}_2}{\text{SE}_{\text{M}_1-\text{M}_2}}$$

The *t* test also assumes that the groups are independent samples of a population. This is not the case where individuals are matched and then assigned to groups. As we noted before, where matching occurs we should use a special formula. If we do not, we may make a Type II error and attribute a possible real difference to sampling and chance error (see May, Masson, & Hunter, 1990, pp. 272–276).

A *t* Test Example

Culler and Holahan (1980) used the *t* test to examine the differences in study-related behaviors between two groups of college freshmen, one with low test anxiety ($n = 31$) as measured by Sarason, Pederson, and Nyman's Test Anxiety Scale, and the other with high test anxiety ($n = 65$). It is one of a large number of studies examining this problem among students. Test anxiety is "thought to produce task-irrelevant responses (concern for passing, thoughts of leaving, etc.) in the testing situation that interfere with the task-relevant responses necessary for good test performance" (p. 16). A rival explanation is that the well-documented poorer grade performance of those with high test anxiety is "at least partially a function of differential study-related behaviors between high and low test-anxious individuals" (p. 16). Both groups of students completed the Study Habits scale of the Brown-Holtzman Survey of Study Habits and Attitudes and responded to a questionnaire. The results are summarized in Table 20.1.

The data were consistent with the hypothesis that the study habits of those students with high test anxiety were statistically significantly poorer (at the 0.2% level, using a two-tailed test) than those of students with low test anxiety. Also statistically

Table 20.1   Relationship of High and Low Test Anxiety to Various Study Patterns

Variable	High Test Anxiety		Low Test Anxiety		
	M	**SD**	**M**	**SD**	**t**
Study habits	37.2	14.8	53.4	14.2	5.42*
Total study hours	21.7	12.7	14.1	7.0	–3.11*
Cramming	4.5	1.4	4.7	1.4	0.57
Missing classes	10.5	7.7	10.7	11.1	0.08
Late exams	0.6	1.1	0.3	0.6	–1.52

*p < .002.

Source: R. E. Culler & C. J. Holahan, Test Anxiety and Academic Performance, *Journal of Educational Psychology*, 27, p. 18. Copyright © 1980 by The American Psychological Association. Used by permission.

significant were the total study hours, but the difference was in the opposite direction—a good reason for using a two-tailed test! The authors were surprised by this finding and suggested that perhaps the high test-anxious students attempted to compensate for their lower study competence by studying longer. The other comparisons, degree of cramming for tests, number of classes missed, and number of exams missed and made up at a later date, were all statistically nonsignificant.

The Mann–Whitney *U* Test

A rank test comparable to the *t* test and easy to use on small samples is the **Mann-Whitney *U* Test**. It involves combining both sets of scores into a single distribution and then assigning ranks to the scores, giving the rank of 1 to the lowest, 2 to the next, and so on. We next sort out the ranks belonging to each group and sum them. If the experimental treatment is effective, the sum of its ranks should be higher than that of the control group's. Use the simple formula:

$$U = n_L n_S + \frac{n_L (n_L + 1)}{2} - T_L$$

In the formula, n_L is the size of the sample with the larger sum of ranks and n_S that of the smaller, and T_L is the larger sum of ranks (see Hays, 1994; Shavelson, 1996; or Siegel & Castellan, 1988). We consult the table of the *U* distribution to determine whether the product of the formula is significant.

We can use this Mann-Whitney test in place of the *t* test in cases where we suspect the populations deviate significantly from normal or the variances are unequal. However, if the variances are nearly equal we can use the *t* test, and fairly large departures from normality can be tolerated (Hays, 1994).

> ▶ A *t* test, which allows us to test the difference between two means for statistical significance, is a commonly used statistical test. It substitutes the *t* table for the normal probability distribution for more accurate probabilities with small samples, and it uses a formula that provides a more accurate estimate of the standard error.
>
> ▶ The Mann-Whitney *U* Test may be used in place of the *t* test for nonnormal distributions and when the variances are unequal.

SHOWING THAT TWO STATISTICS ARE THE SAME

There are instances where we wish to show that two statistics or distributions are the same rather than different. For instance, a rival explanation of some polling results is that our sample is older than the town's average age, but we thought the sample was not deviant. We test the difference between the mean of the sample and the average age given by the latest census data and find that it is not statistically significant. We never accept the null hypothesis as meaning the difference is really zero; we merely fail to reject it—that is, it could be zero or too close to it to be sensed as atypical.

How close it must be to be judged typical depends on the sensitivity of our statistical test. This is another instance in which we cannot escape making a judgment. We must decide what age difference between the sample and the population is big enough to say our sample is atypical. Then, with a statistical power analysis, we can determine whether the existing study is sensitive enough to detect such a difference if it exists, or we can design one that is. Only then can we say that the particular sample does not differ significantly from the population of which it is presumed representative. Failure to follow this logic is a common error. Cohen (1990, p. 1309), however, notes that in most instances, especially when we are required to sense a very small difference, a power analysis will demonstrate that an impractically large sample size is necessary and that showing similarity with considerable precision may be difficult.

THE INFLATION OF PROBABILITIES PROBLEM

Note that there were five *t* tests in the above Culler and Holahan study. The more significance tests we run, the more likely we are to encounter a significant one by chance. At the 5% level, on average, we can expect one in twenty to be significant due to chance factors alone—the **inflation of probabilities** problem. The true likelihood of a Type I error with a 5% level of significance becomes greater than 5% as the number of tests of significance required by a study increases. One answer to this problem is to require a more unusual event to call it significant—instead of the 5% level, use 1% or .1%. Another is to use analysis of variance in place of multiple *t* tests.

Analysis of Variance: Testing Differences among Several Means

In complex experimental designs in which more than two groups, or multiple conditions, are being compared, **analysis of variance** (ANOVA) is widely used. For example, we can use ANOVA to study the effect of directive and nondirective counseling or no treatment (three treatment conditions) under conditions where the counselors are of the same or opposite gender (two conditions). These treatments might apply to teenagers, adults, and the elderly (three categories) and for male and female participants (two categories). This is a $2 \times 3 \times 3 \times 2$ design resulting in 48 cells (combinations of the variables) and lends itself to ANOVA. Think of all the t tests (comparisons of two conditions like directive counseling and no treatment) that would have to be done—8 just to test for effects of the major variables, resulting in a 40% likelihood of a chance finding at the 5% level.

Analysis of variance allows us to partition the variance of the study to find the part that is attributable to each of the variables. We can test the statistical significance of the contribution to effective counseling of gender of subject, age of subject, counseling treatment (directive, nondirective, or none), and matching counselor gender. In addition, we can test the combined effect of variables (gender of subject combined with counseling treatment, age of subject with matching counselor gender, age of subject with gender of subject with counseling treatment, and so forth). After accounting for these variables and their combinations, the residual variance is a purer measure of sampling and chance error, thus providing for more precise tests of statistical significance.

With so many groups and categories, there are many pairs of means to examine with a t test. ANOVA avoids the inflation-of-probabilities problem and keeps the Type I error at 5% by, in essence, making a single simultaneous test of all means. This tells us whether the means are equivalent except for differences traceable to chance variation. If they are not, we can find which variables' data are statistically significant.

The logic used by analysis of variance involves deriving two estimates of the population variance: first, an estimate that includes the effect of the one or more variables (e.g., the effect of treatment and of other independent variables), and second, an estimate which is free of it. If there is no effect, on average, the two variance estimates are equal and the expected value of dividing the first by the second, called an F *ratio*, is one. However, given a possible effect and, in any event, sampling and chance error, the first of these estimates will typically be the larger, so the ratio will usually be greater than one. We consult an F table to determine how much above one to allow for sampling and chance error.

An Analysis of Variance Example

Darley and Batson (1973) examined the reactions of seminary students to a person apparently ill and in need of help. The "ill" person, an accomplice, was stationed on a path that subjects were directed to follow. Seminarians were randomly assigned to one of two conditions: They were given instructions to hurry to an appointment (hurry condition) or sent to speak on the parable of the Good Samaritan (message condition). The question was whether these conditions individually or together would influence the seminarians' willingness to stop and help an individual apparently in trouble. Table 20.2 on the following page shows the results in terms of ratings of helpfulness.

ANOVA data are usually presented in a standard format such as that from the Darley-Batson (1973) study shown in Table 20.3 on the following page. Data in the first two rows show the effect of message and hurry respectively, and the third row shows the effect of their interaction (speech but no hurry, speech and hurry, no speech but hurry, no speech and no hurry).

Table 20.2   Helpfulness Means for Combinations of the Three Levels of Hurry Condition and Two of the Message Condition

	Hurry			Summary over Hurry Conditions
Message	Low	Medium	High	
Helping relevant (go to preach)	3.8	2.0	1.0	2.3
Task relevant (go to appointment)	1.7	1.7	0.5	1.3
Summary over message conditions	3.0	1.8	0.7	

Source: Adapted with permission from J. M. Darley & C. D. Batson, From Jerusalem to Jericho: A study of situational and dispositional variables in helping behavior, in *Journal of Personality and Social Psychology,* 27. Copyright 1973 by the American Psychological Association.

Table 20.3   A Typical ANOVA Data Table

	Sum of Squares	df	Mean Square	F	p
Whether or not the subject was being sent to speak on the parable (message)	7.766	1	7.766	2.65	NS
How much of a hurry the subject was in (hurry)	20.844	2	10.422	3.56	<. 05
Hurry by message interaction	5.237	2	2.619	.89	NS
Error	99.633	34	2.930		

Source: Adapted with permission from J. M. Darley & C. D. Batson, From Jerusalem to Jericho: A study of situational and dispositional variables in helping behavior, in *Journal of Personality and Social Psychology,* 27. Copyright 1973 by the American Psychological Association.

The row labeled *error* is the measure of sampling and chance error. Entries in the *sum of squares* column are divided by the degrees of freedom (the column labeled *df*) to yield an estimate of the population variance, labeled *mean square*. The ratio of the mean square to error yields the F ratios shown in the next column. Those *F* ratios can then be compared with the tabled value for 1 and 34 degrees of freedom for hurry, and for 2 and 34 *df* for both message and interaction. These provide the probability values shown in the right-hand column.

Only the probability for the hurry condition is statistically significant at less than the 5% level (NS means "not statistically significant"). The interaction condition asks whether some combination of hurry with message (such as low hurry with thinking about the parable) is more effective than hurry or message alone. In this instance, since *F* is less than 1 and since only ratios larger than 1 can be statistically significant, this one is not. We might have expected such an interaction, but it apparently did not occur. We should note that the data for the message condition are in the hypothesized direction but are not significant. A more powerful design might have avoided what appears now to be a possible Type II error.

> ▶ Analysis of variance (ANOVA) allows for more precise inference by estimating and removing the variance due to factors built into the design. The variance remaining provides a more accurate estimate of the error variance and a more powerful design.
>
> ▶ It allows the testing of the statistical significance of each variable in the design as well as the combined effect of these variables.
>
> ▶ It avoids the inflation-of-probabilities problem that would result when more than two means are compared. Otherwise, the probability of getting a statistically significant difference by chance increases as more tests are run, and the true Type I error level becomes inflated over the stated level.

SEEKING NON-CHANCE DIFFERENCES BETWEEN FREQUENCIES

Chi-Square

Another commonly used statistic is **chi-square**, which handles only categorical data, frequencies, or figures based on them like percentages or probabilities. Besides eliminating the alternate explanation of sampling and chance error, chi-square can:

- Test a hypothesis about whether one variable is related to another;
- Examine patterns of frequency counts for deviations from chance or test whether the data fit a particular model or distribution (for example, were the data normally distributed?); and
- Combine probabilities derived from independent samples in a single study or across studies into a single probability (another way of doing meta-analysis).

The formula for chi-square (χ^2) is simple. It involves finding the difference between the observed frequency and the frequency that would be expected by chance, squaring it, dividing it by the expected frequency, and summing these over all the observed data.

$$\chi^2 = \sum \frac{(f_o - f_e)^2}{f_e}$$

where f_o is the observed frequency found in the data, f_e is the expected frequency, and Σ indicates that the fractions are to be summed. (If one or more expected frequency is less than 10 for a 2 × 2 table, we must use Yates's correction for continuity. We subtract 0.5 from observed frequencies greater than expected and add 0.5 to those lower than expected.)

A Chi-Square Example

Let's consider, for example, whether political party affiliation is related to gender. Answers to the question "Are you registered to vote as a Democrat or a Republican?" were tabulated for males and females and Table 20.4 was created. The data appear to be a significant deviation from a chance distribution. But are they? Chi-square will tell us.

Table 20.4   Responses to the Question "Are you registered to vote as a Democrat or Republican?" Tabulated by Gender

Gender	Actual Frequencies		Expected Frequencies		Row totals
	Democrat	Republican	Democrat	Republican	
Females	42	21	29.96	33.04	63
Males	36	65	48.04	52.96	101
Column totals	78	86	78	86	164

In Table 20.4, numbers at the left are the actual frequencies; those at the right show us how the frequencies would have been distributed if chance were at work. There are 42 + 21 = 63 females. If this were a chance distribution, since the ratio of Democrats to Republicans for the whole sample is 78 to 86 out of 164 cases, then 78 out of 164 or 47.56% of the 63 females would be Democrats and 86 out of 164 (or 52.44%) would be Republicans. These data give us the figures 29.96 and 33.04 in the top row of the expected frequency table. We similarly derive the next row. We insert these figures for each cell in the chi-square formula and sum across them:

$$\chi^2 = \frac{(42-29.96)^2}{29.96} + \frac{(33.04-21)^2}{33.04} + \frac{(48.04-36)^2}{48.04} + \frac{(65-52.96)^2}{52.96} = 14.99$$

We need the number of degrees of freedom to find our probabilities in the chi-square table. The concept of **degrees of freedom** refers to the freedom of the cell data in successive samples to vary once the column and row totals are fixed. In 2 × 2 tables, once we determine one cell entry, we can determine the other three. Thus, such tables have only one degree of freedom. (Try this yourself: Put a new frequency, 63 or lower, in the top left cell and you can find the other three entries using the column and row totals.)

In general, they have $(r-1)(c-1)$ degrees of freedom, where r is the number of rows and c the number of columns. Looking in any chi-square table (such as May, Masson, & Hunter, 1990, p. 556) under the 5% significance level and one degree of freedom, we find that anything larger than 3.84 is atypical. Since the chi-square of 14.99 is clearly atypical, with a confidence expressed by odds of 19 to 1, we can say that we cannot account for this distribution of males and females into political parties by sampling and chance error. Females are more likely Democrats, and males are more likely Republicans.

▶ For categorical and frequency data (and percentages and probabilities based on them), chi-square can test the fit of a model or of expectations against chance, can show whether there is a regularity to the frequencies or whether it is a chance arrangement, and can combine the probabilities from studies into a single one, as in meta-analysis.

ASSUMPTIONS OF PARAMETRIC AND NONPARAMETRIC TESTS

All statistical tests begin with certain assumptions that, together with the laws of probability, enable statisticians to develop the tables we use to determine statistical significance such as the normal distribution, t, chi-square, and F. Use of random sampling is a common underlying assumption of many statistical tests. Many further assume that such sampling is from normally distributed populations and that where two or more samples are involved, their variances differ by no more than would be "typical." Such statistical tests, called **parametric tests**, are the focus of most texts and computer programs and are the most widely used and understood.

Nonparametric statistics are based on ranked or categorical data (e.g., this chapter's Mann-Whitney U and chi-square tests). They ask whether the patterning of the data is typically random or atypically regular. For example, order the merged scores from an experimental and a control group by size and, if nothing is at work, we expect a random alternation between experimental and control (the Mann-Whitney). But if the experimental group's scores are the highest ranks and the control group's are the lowest, something is at work. Such departures trigger statistical significance in nonparametric tests. Whereas random sampling provides the chance element with parametric statistics that statisticians assume to estimate probabilities (as in t tables), random ordering or patterning does so for nonparametric statistics. For both parametric and nonparametric statistics, random sampling supports generalizability of findings by, on average, providing samples representative of the population.

With nonparametric tests, as with parametric ones, however, what appears to be atypical may not be. On average, even ten pennies will come up all heads about once in 1,000 times. Thus, the same inferential logic applies to both kinds of tests, and Types I and II errors must be considered. Other commonly used nonparametric tests are the sign test, rank test, run test, and Wilcoxon signed-rank test for matched samples.

Violation of Assumptions

Though parametric statistics are the norm, few studies use random samples. What is the justification for violating this assumption? May, Masson, and Hunter (1990) state that in most situations, since parametric statistics approximate the nonparametric results, they result in meaningful and useful interpretations without random sampling. They also suggest, however, that nonparametric statistics assumptions are more appropriate for most behavioral science studies. When we are concerned with building a consensus around the interpretation of data and developing credibility with a statistically unsophisticated audience, however, using unfamiliar nonparametric statistics may fail to be convincing. In situations where parametric assumptions are seriously violated, nonparametric statistics clearly are more appropriate. As long as useful interpretations result, however, familiar parametric statistics will continue to be the major tools.

An important assumption of tests of differences between means (t tests, analysis of variance) is that although the means may be affected by a treatment, the variability of the distribution is not. That is, the treatment is assumed to add or subtract a constant from all scores. Affecting them differentially would increase the variance (e.g., a nutritional supplement increases IQs more for high scorers than low ones, increasing the treatment group's variance). We say that a statistic is **robust** if we can interpret it meaningfully even when one of its assumptions has been violated. Fortunately, many parametric statistics have proven surprisingly robust in the face of sampling from skewed distributions or unequal variances.

For the *t* test and analysis of variance one can correct for these violations by using a 1% instead of the 5% significance level (Hays, 1994). In a situation where assumptions have been violated and no evidence on the robustness of the statistic is available, it may be desirable to use a nonparametric test.

▶ Assumptions allow statisticians to use probability theory to develop the tables we use to determine statistical significance.

▶ Parametric statistics such as those discussed in this chapter assume random sampling. Sometimes they also assume sampling from normally distributed populations with equal variances before treatment.

▶ Nonparametric statistics using the same inference logic assume that random ordering is at work and examine rankings and categorizations for regularity that is atypical and nonrandom.

▶ Even without random sampling, parametric statistics lead to useful results—perhaps because their results parallel nonparametric statistics, which do not assume random sampling.

▶ A robust statistical test is one that permits accurate interpretation of the data even when an assumption on which the test is based has been violated. Most parametric tests are fairly robust in the face of minor violations and even with major violations can often be used with adjustments, usually in the probability level (for example, with a 1% instead of the 5% level).

COMPUTERIZED STATISTICAL PROGRAMS

Computerized statistical programs make available a wide range of possibilities that statistics users would not have otherwise considered. The ease of computation makes possible studies so complex that researchers are like laboratory workers who manipulate mechanical hands by remote control from a room outside a sealed data container. With no sense of the data there is little basis for suspecting an absurd result, and one is at the mercy of the computer printout. Pictures are worth a thousand numbers. We are sensitive to patterns in plots, graphs, and other displays of the kind provided by these same computer programs. Request them. Make certain that the numbers are congruent with what you see in the data plots, and look for other patterns not caught by your planned analyses.

It nearly always pays to play with a sample of the data using either exploratory data analysis techniques like those described in Tukey (1977) or easily computed nonparametric tests. In addition, such exploration is fun! It gives us an idea of what to expect so that, if the computer analysis differs, we become aware of a possible error. The popular computer programs have ks for support and interchange of ideas and some trial programs; they can be very helpful.

TRENDS IN INFERENTIAL STATISTICS

Some researchers (e.g., Cohen, 1990) suggest that, in contrast to just determining whether or not an effect exists, we should determine the effect size as well as a confidence interval, showing the range within which the effect lies. Similarly, in place of analysis of variance that yields primarily only statistical significance, we should use statistics that yield the sizes of relationships. All this ties into meta-analysis (the topic of chapter 22), which combines the effect sizes of multiple studies for a single overall effect size. Further, instead of just using the 5% or 1% significance levels, published articles increasingly give the exact probabilities that facilitate their use in meta-analyses.

ADDITIONAL READING

The statistics texts recommended in the previous chapter have sections on the statistics described in this chapter as well as other methods of handling these situations.

IMPORTANT TERMS AND CONCEPTS

analysis of variance

chi-square

degrees of freedom

inflation of probabilities

Mann-Whitney *U* Test

nonparametric statistics

parametric statistics

robust

t test

OPPORTUNITIES FOR ADDITIONAL LEARNING

Because of the extreme difficulty of anticipating the expected depth of mastery of this chapter's content, application problems (if any are needed) are at the instructor's discretion. With major emphasis on the prior chapter, this chapter might be assigned as additional reading. Others may devote considerable time to this chapter's topics, using supplementary material.

APPLICATION EXERCISE

Are any of the statistics applicable to the problem you have chosen? If so, how would they be employed? Do you have an inflation-of-probabilities problem? What will you do about it?

SUMMARY

Especially for small samples, the *t* test of differences between means is widely regarded as accurate and sensitive. It assumes interval or ratio scale data. In addition, sometimes one wants to show two estimates are the same (as when, because its mean does not deviate significantly from the population value, one claims a sample is representative of a population). However, statistical significance depends on the sensitivity of the test, which can be very sensitive with large samples. Therefore, to claim similarity, the size difference signifying dissimilarity must be specified. Then, a power analysis can determine the sample size needed to sense the existence of such a difference as well as its size. For ordinal data, the Mann-Whitney U Test substitutes for the t test.

Complex studies often require comparisons of many means. This encounters an inflation-of-probabilities problem. The more tests of statistical significance a study requires, the greater the true rate of a Type I error above the established significance level. Switching from less stringent levels (5%) to more stringent (1% or rarer) is one solution. Analysis of variance is another. It avoids the inflation-of-probabilities problem where multiple t tests must be performed. It is particularly useful for complex designs.

Chi-square is widely used for nominal or categorical data. It can show whether a regularity exists, whether data fits a model or expectations, or combine probabilities across studies to summarize their combined probability.

A Look Ahead

Analysis of variance, discussed in this chapter, is sometimes used to determine the effect of possible rival explanations and determine whether there is an effect with their influence removed. In the next chapter we examine experimentation, which is the most common way of removing such competing explanations.

Links to previous research

Explanation, rationale, theory, or point of view

Questions, hypotheses, models

Preplanned and emergent designs

Design/procedure

Focus   Records   Time   Comparison and Contrast   Situation   Participants

Data

Statistical analysis and/or narrative analysis

Conclusion

Link to next study

Explanation or rationale of next study, etc.

Experimentation and Experimental Design

INTRODUCTION

Because good experimental conditions rarely occur naturally, many social scientists argue that the strongest chains of reasoning can be built by creating proper conditions through experimental design. Of course, history, as well as much of economics, astronomy, and jurisprudence—fields where doing experiments are impossible—also build strong causal chains. And like these fields, experimentation too depends on careful reasoning. It often requires creative thinking to create the desired conditions—partly an art. But being able to experiment has certain advantages. Its effectiveness, however, depends on

1. a treatment to provide clear identification of the presumed active ingredient

2. application of treatment as intended (or its accurate recognition in natural experiments)

3. comparison with the same situation without the active treatment ingredient

4. manipulation of treatment for contrast between treatment presence and absence (or ability to clearly identify in a natural experiment)

5. a design to

   a. tightly link cause to effect

   b. identify best methods to control for rival explanations

   c. identify common rival explanations so we will know what to look for to obtain

      • Internal Integrity

      • External Generality

The use of common designs that protect against common rival explanations makes it more likely that readers will trust the results, because they know their strengths and weaknesses.

477

The outline above illustrates the general plan of the chapter, which ends by summarizing the hallmarks of good design and looking backward and forward at the maturation of design.

THE ART OF EXPERIMENTAL DESIGN

Because experimentation is one of the most structured of research methods, we might think of it as a cut-and-dried procedure. But, while it is part deductive reasoning, it is also part art. From the analysis we made of Zimbardo et al. in chapter 1, the many design decisions required are apparent, and yet the published report did not cover prior exploration, pilot studies, and decisions regarding resource planning and allocation. Researchers balance many things and choose among multiple alternatives. Creatively combining these decisions is an art in itself, to which one must add the creative touches: Zimbardo's use of hypnosis, employing three instead of just two comparison groups, training confederates, and using audiotapes and slides for instructions.

There is considerable need for good judgment, originality in adapting standard designs, and benefiting from pilot studies and provisional tries to create new ones. Except with very simple problems, these are all part of normal procedure, but because they are rarely part of the published report, we are unaware of them.

Typically experiments involve the method of differences we described in chapter 11 (p. 224). One or more experimental individuals or groups receive(s) a treatment (or possess[es] the independent variable), and control individuals or groups receive either no treatment—a situation just like the treatment but without the "active ingredient"—or a competing treatment (the individual or group does not have the independent variable). Alternatively, for treatments that leave no residual effect, individuals are tested or observed pre- and posttreatment. The method of differences requires that two or more situations be exactly alike except for one thing—the presence of a treatment or whatever independent variable we are studying. Although it is true that no two individuals or groups can be exactly alike—even the same individual or group is different at a later time—the intent is to use **functionally equivalent groups**. That is, they must function as if they were exactly equivalent for the purposes of this study. Making the groups functionally equivalent is the purpose of some control procedures.

Reifman sums this up with 5 Es: "Everything Equal Except Essential Element!" (http://courses.ttu.edu/hdfs3390-reifman/causal.htm).

> ▶ Design is part science and part art—multiple choices can be creatively combined in many ways to tightly link cause to effect, explain the relationship, and protect against rival explanations that otherwise would be as plausible as the intended one.

THE TREATMENT

Defining the Experimental Treatment

Essential to defining a treatment is the determination of the "active ingredient" that distinguishes the treatment. Since control and experimental treatments must be alike except for that one aspect, it must be accurately described (conceptualized) and translated into those operations used to apply it (operationalized). Explaining the theory or rationale underlying the active ingredient aids *explanation credibility* (p. 139). It also facilitates defining what to look for in **treatment fidelity** for optimal effect (p. 177).

As an example, let's consider Tinto's (1987) hypothesis: "The greater students' active participation in the social and academic campus life, the less likely they will become college dropouts." We can operationalize the treatment, "active participation in social and academic life," in many ways. We find that Tinto drew a parallel to Durkheim's analysis of suicide cases as persons too isolated from their society to benefit from its support. He argued that potential college dropouts likely also have isolated themselves from social and academic support. Therefore, we define activity levels of "participation in social and academic life" in terms of their capacity to involve and support students and prevent feelings of isolation and disconnectedness.

> ▶ Conceptually defining the treatment involves delineating the parts of the treatment that are the "active ingredient." Relating treatment to its conceptual base in an underlying theory or rationale helps both to conceptualize the treatment and to find optimal operationalizations of it.

Defining the Placebo or Control Treatment

The *"Swahili syndrome,"*[1] involving a comparison of something with nothing, sounds simple on the face of it: One teaches Swahili to the experimental group and not to the control and, lo and behold, the experimental group learns more Swahili. Before you consider this example ridiculous, recall that the treatment always has something the control doesn't. It is in the reasonableness of the comparison of the "active ingredient" with the lack of it that the definition of the control treatment avoids the Swahili syndrome and the placebo treatment gains definition. A placebo has all the characteristics of the experimental treatment except for the "active ingredient," or cause.

Suppose, instead of learning to solve the variety of mathematical problems usually taught, a researcher has found they can be combined into five problem types. These, once learned, allow access to the usual variety. Learning and using the problem types are the "active ingredient." Additional conditions of treatment are: The teacher can devote as much time as she wishes, teach however she pleases, and involve the students in any way and as much or little as she desires, as long as the students learn the problem types above a specified minimum ability to use them. These experimental conditions help to define the placebo treatment, which should devote an equal amount of time to content, follow the same teaching style (including involvement of students), and in all other ways be like the teaching in the experimental section. There is only one difference—it should not include the five problem types as such or the test of their use. The teacher might teach solutions to similar problems, but she would teach them as solutions to specific problems rather than as types. By making the placebo a completely parallel treatment, the researcher also eliminates many potential rival causes: length of instruction, kinds of instruction, involvement of students in active learning, and so on.

> ▶ The placebo treatment should be exactly like the experimental treatment or as much like it as possible, except for the characteristic that delineates the treatment—the "active ingredient."

It has long been recognized that placebos can have an effect, but it was only recently realized that the effect is, in many respects, a genuine organismic response. Medical placebos, for example, develop antibodies and in other ways muster the body's therapeutic defenses. In many situations, the **placebo effect**, the expectation of efficacy of treatment, is an intended part of treatment. For example, counseling and psychological therapy can be effective only if the client wants to participate in it and has some hope, however small, of benefiting from it.

But in many instances we wish to disentangle placebo from treatment effect and its interaction with treatment. We can do this by experimental design. For example, consider an experiment to determine whether personal adaptation of instruction to the individual is effective or the placebo effect makes it appear so—the students expect improved learning because the adjusted instruction fits them personally. A new, very flexible set of materials on the history of the U.S. Constitution can be adapted to fit three text-learning styles: aural, visual-graphic, and visual. You assign students randomly to four groups and randomly assign treatments to groups:

Condition 1, treatment plus placebo expectancy—You very conspicuously promote this wonderful new approach, which should ensure raising student grades when material is fitted to their learning style. You make changes in the material very obtrusively, posting the unit assignments for each student on a large wall chart for all to see. You make assignments according to your diagnosis of learning style in such a way as to maximize learning.

Condition 2, placebo expectancy treatment—Like condition 1, but assignment type is random.

Condition 3, treatment, no placebo expectancy—Nothing special is said about the course material; it is just another assignment. But you make your individual learning style assignments unobtrusively according to your diagnosis of learning style as you walk around the room interacting with students as you normally would.

Condition 4, no treatment or expectancy—Like condition 3 but the student assignment type is random.

Comparison of conditions 2 and 4 tells whether obtrusively changing the course material increases learning—that is, whether there is a placebo effect. Comparison of 3 with 4 shows whether intentional individual assignment results in greater learning than random assignment—that is, whether the treatment is effective. Comparison of conditions 1 and 3 indicates whether the placebo effect strengthens the treatment effect—that is, whether it improves the effectiveness of the individual assignments.

> ▶ If the treatment can be given without the participants' being aware they are receiving it (silent administration), the placebo effect can be determined by varying the obtrusiveness of placebo and treatment.
>
> ▶ The placebo effect is often consciously made a part of treatment to increase the treatment's effectiveness.

Ensuring Treatment Fidelity

Treatment fidelity ensures that "treatment administered was treatment intended." This includes three aspects: (1) congruence of operational with conceptual definition (already noted but needing further discussion), (2) assurance that the administered treatment was the intended treatment, and (3) representativeness of the generality intended by the operational definition.

Congruence of operational and conceptual definitions of treatment. Regardless of what was intended, operationalization defines the treatment. What can be involved in such judgments is often surprising. Consider the questions arising in a study of teaching a unit on any topic:

How much time must be devoted to this topic for treatment to be authentic? Must all the content be covered? If not, how much? Must it be spread over a certain period, or can it be concentrated? If the latter, how much? Can other material be included in the teaching of these concepts, or must these be the only things taught in this block? What constitutes teaching? Lecture? Material that is organized and delivered in a certain way? Discussion? What kinds of questions are asked by the teacher? Are questions drawn from text, class, or both? What accuracy level must the answers reach before continuing to the next lesson? What proportion of discussion is involved in problem solving? What level of absenteeism constitutes the threshold for noncompletion of treatment?

Substitute your treatment's terms for "teaching," "topic," and similar specific items and you will find that most of these questions have general applicability—yet the list is clearly far from exhaustive. That, of course, is the point; we must decide which are the "active ingredients" to ensure treatment fidelity (see also Walker & Schaffarzick, 1974).

Availability can snare us into less-than-optimal operationalization: "Full-time students who become members of university-recognized clubs are less likely to become dropouts than those who never join." The university has a definition for "full-time student" and "dropouts," and campus clubs list members—easy hypothesis translation? Not so! The treatment's original context included feeling supported by being involved; being listed as a member is no guarantee of participation, much less of feeling supported.

Operational definitions need to be appropriate for each situation yet true to their original conceptualization, a likely problem with multisite studies. "Active involvement" for commuting students at a junior college may differ from that at a residential college.

> ▶ Treatment fidelity involves translation of the concepts in which treatment is expressed into operational terms.
>
> ▶ The operational definition is the treatment.

Treatment administration.   Was the treatment really given as intended? The latitude exercised in giving the treatment may be so great that variations in administration may blur treatment definition or constitute an experimental variable in its own right. How do we ensure fidelity of treatment implementation? Usually, with detailed structure, instructions, and/or training and low-inference observation with, for example, an observation checklist of "active ingredients."

Although the need for monitoring the experimental treatment is clear, we often must also monitor control and placebo treatments to ensure maintenance of the expected contrast. Experimental treatment often diffuses to them through informal contact.

> ▶ Detailed description of the active ingredients and training helps ensure treatment fidelity. Monitoring treatment administration, both experimental and placebo, ensures fidelity as well as maintaining appropriate contrast of treatments.

Representativeness of treatment.   Are we interested in this local use of the treatment—these teachers' use of a specific curriculum? Or in what it represents—that a specific curriculum is representative of curricula in general that are built from the same rationale?[2] For example, in a study of the effectiveness of prewriting outlining in English composition, the treatment should be typical either of the way outlining is usually taught, or, if it can be taught in many ways, of the breadth of those methods.

> ▶ Where generality is desired, treatments selected for study may be typical examples, or, where we seek the boundaries of generality, representative of that range.
>
> ▶ For maximum generality, conditions of treatment administration should be realistically like those under which the treatment is intended to be used.

Laboratory vs. Field: Emphasis on Internal Integrity or External Generality?

Laboratory experimentation clearly can build strong Internal Integrity—linking cause to effect. But what about External Generality? Typically it is weakened—a trade-off! The number of laboratory experiments with little apparent practical application reinforces the stereotype of lack of generality for laboratory findings. In their defense, some researchers (e.g., Berkowitz & Donnerstein, 1982 and Henshel, 1980a, 1980b, among others) note that the purpose of such studies is simply understanding the phenomenon. Once we can explain how something works in the laboratory, we often can build to eventual practical applicability. Analyzing studies of basic research—research done just for understanding—Mosteller (1981) found a long lead time (often 20 to 30 years) between publication of results and their incorporation into major developments. A substantial portion of research contributing to a given development had no relation to application when the research was done—for example, between 1945 and 1975, this was true of 41% of the advances in cardiopulmonary medicine and surgery. Further, Henshel (1980b) argues that learning in an artificial situation may enable us to see how we can make the real situation resemble the artificial one. We learn about phenomena "that are capable of existing," permitting "the creation of entirely new social structures and institutions heretofore unknown" (p. 194).

Experimentation is not confined to artificial settings, however; and it has been used in large-scale trials of social reforms. One of the largest, the income maintenance experiment (guaranteed annual income), was even replicated in different cities. It showed an important policy flaw: not that individuals would become lazy (the expected problem) but rather that families would break up—an unanticipated side effect (Rossi & Lyall, 1976).

There are also "natural experiments" wherein we study the effect of a "treatment" applied by nature. For example, early studies of how societies cope with disaster (Baker & Chapman, 1962) led to studies with new understandings following other catastrophes—earthquakes, volcano eruptions, and so on (Kreps, 1989; Raphael, 1986). The Disaster Research Center at the University of Delaware collects such research.

Part of the art of experimental design is choosing study situations that achieve the appropriate balance between Internal Integrity and External Generality.

> ❱ Experimental control has its greatest potential in the laboratory study, where strong Internal Integrity is usually gained at the expense of External Generality.
>
> ❱ Natural experiments, which wait for a treatment to occur spontaneously, or experiments in which a treatment is applied under field conditions, gain greater External Generality, usually at the expense of Internal Integrity.
>
> ❱ The researcher's task is to achieve a balance of the two characteristics that is appropriate to the goal of the study.
>
> ❱ Basic research, which aims at understanding phenomena, or at inventing conditions that do not yet exist but might, is often considered a first step toward application.

TIGHTLY LINKING TREATMENT TO EFFECT

How do we maximize the effect of the treatment, so that if there is an effect it is easily sensed and its possible strength estimated? There are many ways:

- Making the effect more obvious—increase the strength of the treatment by higher doses, applying it longer, applying it at repeated intervals, and so on.
- Selecting susceptible persons (Zimbardo's study in chapter 1 used the most hypnotizable).

- Using a controllable situation such as a laboratory (Zimbardo used a laboratory situation with trained persons for interaction, and tapes and slides to communicate instructions).

- Using the most valid and reliable way of getting records and measures (Zimbardo assured validity with three measures of paranoia).

- Maximizing the contrast between treated and control groups (e.g., varying the strength of the treatment both positively and negatively over time or with different treatment groups, and a placebo treated control group).

- Using a theory or a rationale to predict the appearance of the effect. Do so in as much detail as possible, indicating when it will appear, how strongly, how long it will last, and so on. Show the agreement of prediction and results.

- Using the best method of control, as explained in the next section.

CONTROL METHODS TO ELIMINATE PLAUSIBLE RIVAL EXPLANATIONS

Methods of control protect a study from the effect of a *confounding variable*—an unwanted variable present at the time of treatment that could affect the study's outcome. We control by one of four methods: (1) *removing* the variable and/or excluding it, (2) *measuring and adjusting* for it, (3) *spreading its effect* across all the groups being compared so that they are equally affected, or (4) *random selection* of participants and *random assignment* to groups and of treatment to groups (*randomization*). Of these, removing and excluding is the most desirable when loss of generality is not a problem. Measuring and adjusting is difficult to do properly with available methods. Spreading across comparison groups adds variability that reduces the sensitivity of a statistical test to an effect, and we usually need all the sensitivity we can get. Nonetheless, spreading the effect is the most common method. Randomization is really a subcategory of spreading across groups since in randomly selecting participants, on average, we equate the groups for all characteristics.

Removing and Excluding

Use of the laboratory, or an area where we can control what goes on, is the usually preferred method. However, other more practical techniques with less reduction of generalizability often have the same effect and can sometimes be substituted. **Camouflage**, for instance, was used by Kounin (1970), who placed a box on a pedestal in classrooms. Because students and teachers never knew whether the box was empty or held a camera, they soon came to ignore it. Similarly, the participant observer, by participating, seeks to lose the stigma of an outsider and to take on the role of group member.

Masking of one variable with another is sometimes effective. "Landscaped" offices illustrate the principle. Five-foot partitions substitute for walls, and "white noise" is introduced to mask sounds coming over the partitions. In a study of autokinesis as a personality variable, Thurstone (1947) used complete darkness as a mask. After moving a penlight in a designated pattern he placed it in a holder. Participants were to record their perception of the light's movement. Because the holder was masked by the dark, perceived movement long after the pen was stationary—the autokinetic effect—could be measured.

Compensatory action often reduces parents' demands that their children also receive the experimental treatment—for example, as when administrators promise that the control group will be treated next or they build a waiting list that they use as a control group.

Restricting the range of a variable to be controlled reduces or eliminates its power. For example, using a very bright group in which IQs vary little eliminates its variability so that differences in IQ are less of a factor in the effect.

Measuring and Adjusting

Partial correlation and analysis of covariance are the two methods most commonly used for reducing the effect of unwanted variables. When measurement is accurate and valid, the methods work well (as in controlling for length of practice time, which can be measured precisely). But just as in trimming fat from a piece of meat—neither too much nor too little—these methods entail problems in making the proper adjustment in most social science uses.

A very large-scale comparison of public with private school achievement (Coleman, Hoffer, & Kilgore, 1982) used analysis of covariance to correct for the socioeconomic bias. The considerable controversy that erupted over the adequacy of the correction was indicative of the distrust of such methods even by other sophisticated researchers (e.g., Goldberger & Cain, 1982). Alternatively, we can sometimes build the unwanted variation into the study as an independent variable, as in the factorial designs described later in this chapter.

Spreading the Effect to All Comparison Groups

Assuring that the groups are alike in all respects except the treatment is the goal of spreading the effect of variables that are rival explanations. If a pretest can boost posttest scores, we must also pretest the control group so its scores are equally boosted. If the recipients of the experimental treatment feel special because the treatment was *obtrusive*, we must give the control group a placebo treatment devoid of the treatment's "active ingredient" to make them feel special, too. Because individuals react differently to the same situation, using a pretest or an obtrusive treatment will add to the variance of the study. This added variability would decrease the statistical sensitivity to an effect, but that is the trade-off for control of these variables.

Randomization

When the variable to be controlled is a characteristic of the participants, randomization is a form of spreading the effect of the confounding variable to the groups being compared. It involves randomly selecting individuals from a population by a random number table or a computer's random number generator, random assignment of individuals to groups by a flip of a coin or throw of dice, and then randomly assigning groups to treatment(s) and control. It is the statistician's preferred way of ensuring that groups are comparable and of avoiding bias in assigning treatments.

Most important, on average, random assignment of individuals makes groups comparable in all variables—even eyelash length. On average, it equates not only variables we anticipate might present problems, but also unanticipated ones that we didn't. Randomization buys a lot for little!

Campbell and Stanley (1963) thought random assignment so important that they applied the term *true* to experimental designs using random assignment, naming other designs *quasi-experimental*. Unfortunately, this terminology sounds as though "true experimental designs" protect against all rival hypotheses—which, of course, they do not. For example, obtrusive random assignment alerts participants to their participation in an experiment and may result in "onstage" behavior.

Researchers intuitively tend to resist random assignment, both because failure of chance to equate a key variable may ruin the study and because it is difficult to do unobtrusively (random assignment is rare under normal conditions). But when it is not known which treatment is most effective, random assignment gives participants an equal chance of being in a treatment or control group. Boruch, McSweeney, and Soderstrom (1978) compiled a list of 300 field tests where random assignment was used, including delicate situations. Further, to show how random assignment can be used to study important policy matters, Boruch and Wothke (1985, Appendix 1) added ten additional such studies and described eight social experiments. They make a strong case for our considering random assignment even where we might think it impossible. Appendix 2 in Boruch and Wothke (1985) lists six objections to random assignment with counterarguments, and the book's final chapter describes strategies for increasing the chances of making randomization feasible through advance planning.

It is cold comfort when, by chance, random assignment fails to equate a very plausible rival cause. Random assignment within blocks (*strata* become *blocks* in experimental design terms), like random sampling within strata in stratified sampling, ensures representativeness of the **blocking** (stratifying) variable. For example, to control for socioeconomic status, we would sort individuals into high, middle, and low-socioeconomic-class blocks and randomly assign individuals within each class block to experimental and control groups. Especially with small groups where outliers in only one group could be devastating, stratification can be important. Matching individuals and randomly assigning to groups is the extreme of blocking: every pair constitutes a block. Blocking provides cheap insurance and, as with stratification, we lose only the labor we have spent if no gain results.

▶ Random selection of individuals, and random assignment of individuals to groups and of groups to treatment, protects from selection bias as well as on-average equating for the effects of variables not previously considered as potential rival explanations but might be.

▶ Random assignment of individuals to groups from within blocks (strata) provides additional assurance of equating important variables through stratification.

▶ So-called "true" experimental designs are those in which the groups are equated by random assignment. Despite the name's connotation, these designs are not immune from all rival explanations. Designs without such random assignment have been labeled as "quasi-experimental."

COMMON RIVAL EXPLANATIONS AFFECTING INTERNAL INTEGRITY AND/OR EXTERNAL GENERALITY

The terms *rival explanation*, *rival hypothesis*, *alternative explanation*, and *threat to validity* all refer to the same thing: a condition that is confounded with the effect being studied. **Confounding** occurs when two conditions (e.g., the treatment and a condition that could be a rival explanation) are present at the same time. Then we cannot tell which might have been the cause of whatever effect occurred—or whether both contributed.

Triangulation can sometimes help us identify a confounding variable. We first met triangulation in chapter 7 (p. 141) and again in chapter 13 (p. 285). The multimeasure-multimethod procedure in looking at the same phenomenon or attribute with different measures and methods shows whether one of these is affecting the results. Often it is the result of one of the common rival explanations examined below; once identified, one can then take appropriate steps.

Unless we can rule out alternatives by the design of the study, they present rival explanations to the intended one. Depending on their nature, they can threaten the Internal Integrity or the External Generality of the study. The first of these common rival explanations, sampling and chance error, is universal to all studies.

Sampling and Chance Error

Quantitative studies estimate the likelihood that sampling and chance error is a plausible rival by the use of inferential statistics. It is in the rejection of the null hypothesis that the rival hypothesis of sampling and chance error is eliminated. Qualitative studies do so by showing that the phenomenon replicates.

Let's take a simple case. Ms. Kimball, a first-grade teacher in the inner city, is concerned about her children's progress. She has heard that the University of Chicago's School Mathematics Curriculum has been highly successful. She gives it a four-month trial and then tests the children on the Stanford Achievement Test. In comparison with the test's norms, she reports, "It appears that my group's score, though still below what I expected, is better than the norm average." We wonder, "Really, was there any effect?" (the null hypothesis). After all, with different samples of participants (sampling error) and measurement error, the mean would bounce around. An upward bounce instead of treatment effect is a reasonable rival explanation. By using inferential statistics (see chapter 19), we can determine whether the gap between achievement and norms is statistically significant, or whether it is due to chance error. We must also judge whether it has practical significance.

> ◗ The likelihood that sampling and chance error is a rival explanation can be estimated by inferential statistics. However, the study must have adequate statistical power to show statistical significance and its practical significance must also be judged.

Campbell and Stanley (1963), Cook and Campbell (1979), Shadish, Cook, and Campbell (2002), and Reichardt (2006) named and described a variety of common rival explanations. Although some studies may have other unique rival explanations, these authors have provided very useful lists. In alphabetical order, we discuss many of them and the means of their control.

Their original names have been kept because they are so referred to in the literature, but don't take their names literally. For instance, *maturation* includes individual changes due to growth but also includes other changes over time, such as becoming more tired, less motivated, or more test-wise.

Base Rate Problems

Method of Control	How to Control
Measure and adjust	Dividing the frequency of the effect by the frequency of the cause changes a frequency to a percentage and eliminates the effect of base rate.

Here is an example: Contrary to conventional wisdom, when Baron and Ransberger (1978) examined 102 major riots in the United States between 1967 and 1971, they found a curvilinear relationship between the number of riots and the day's average temperature. Riots increased when the temperature varied between 81 and 85 degrees; with higher temperatures they were less frequent. Carlsmith, Merrill, and Anderson (1979) believed that **base rate** explained this finding—the hotter the days, the fewer such days, and hence fewer riots. Adjusting for temperature base rate by dividing frequency of riots at each temperature level by the frequency of such days, riots increased linearly with hotter weather.

Instrument Decay

Method of Control	How to Control	Consequences
Eliminate	Use low-inference measures, train for use of instruments, use calibration checks, use double-blind conditions, resolve use and interpretation problems through regular meetings.	A pilot study is needed to tell how much training is sufficient; training is expensive; determining the success of training requires checks on reliability.

As also described in the discussion of qualitative research (p. 348), instrument decay refers to changes in the measurement or observation process in ways that might account for the observed effect—as in reinterpreting the meaning of categories of an observation instrument, moderating the strictness of grading on an essay test from earliest to latest, or differing instrument usage over time or by different observers.

When the observer is the instrument, as the setting grows more familiar the observer has more realistic expectations and becomes more sympathetic; unusual behavior is perceived as a rational response. Similarly, teachers' expectations are highest and marks lowest for the first essay examination papers they read, and marks become more realistic for later ones.

Instrument decay is especially likely with relatively unstructured and high-inference measures and understandably rare with multiple-choice tests and observation devices in which coding is clear and unambiguous. Even with the latter, however, observers may become more skilled in using it, create different rules for new situations, or change rules to make observation easier. Interviewers may become more comfortable with an interview schedule or more skilled in eliciting responses. Any of these and similar instances can account for an instrument-decay effect.

Another source involves changing the scale between pre- and posttest due to ceiling or floor effects. A measure that spreads the group across the scale at pretest, because of growth, may be too easy on posttest. Limited by the top score, the mean is lower than it should be—a *ceiling effect*. Too difficult a measure creates a pileup at the opposite end—a *floor effect*. Graphing or charting the scores reveals both. Using instruments that differentiate across the entire range avoids this rival explanation.

Local History

Method of Control	How to Control	Consequences
Eliminate	Discard affected cases, such as those tests interrupted by a fire drill.	Discarding cases decreases statistical power by reducing sample size. Researcher may not know all persons exposed. Exposure may have been selective. Trades more Internal Integrity for less External Generality. Replicating study expensive and may be impossible.
Equalize across groups	Assure that the control group is as likely to be exposed to the same events as the experimental; keep groups in close proximity.	Proximity may result in increased chance of rivalry, other reactivity, and diffusion.

Ms. Kimball's Stanford Achievement Test scores may be higher because many of her students were watching a television program that, to illustrate the power of mathematics to the layperson, happened to give practice on the kinds of problems the test emphasized. Alternative events that could have caused the target effect are called **local history**, or just history. A comparable control group protects against local history; they were as likely to have also watched the television program. Local history is one of the most difficult to control; it is impossible to predict what to expect, when, or how serious it will be. Keeping close to the groups and being alert to the possibility of something untoward occurring are the main lines of defense.

Maturation

Method of Control	How to Control	Consequences
Measure and adjust	Use norms to determine growth of comparable groups or measure trend prior to treatment and extrapolate to posttreatment expectation.	Norms on comparable group may not be available. Nonlinear growth is hard to extrapolate; growth could be linear prior to treatment and nonlinear after.
Equalize across groups	Use randomly assigned and blocked, or matched, groups, at least one serving as control group.	If stratifying variable is related to phenomenon variables, blocking and matching decrease variability and thus increase the sensitivity of the study.

Maturation includes "all those biological and psychological processes which systematically vary with the passage of time, independent of specific external events" (Campbell & Stanley, 1963, pp. 177–178). Thus, between observations students might have grown older, more tired, bored, capable of more mature reasoning, or more serious about getting an education, as well as more biologically and socially advanced. If Ms. Kimball's treatment lasted only four months, biological growth is an unlikely factor. Nor would such factors as growing bored or tired have persisted over four months. Thus, maturation seems an unlikely alternative in our particular example. However, in a longitudinal study lasting several years or a two-hour study in which pre-kindergarten children were expected to sit quietly, maturation might well be an issue. Once again, a control group would presumably be affected by maturation in the same way as the experimental group and so would protect against it.

Mortality

Method of Control	How to Control	Consequences
Eliminate	Provide incentive for completion of study.	Incentives are likely to be obtrusive; reward becomes part of the treatment. Trades more Internal Integrity for less External Generality.
Measure and adjust	Discern the kinds of individuals who dropped out and remove equivalent individuals from the other groups.	Loss of cases reduces the statistical power and generality of the study. Trades more Internal Integrity for less External Generality.
Equalize across groups	Assign to groups randomly and make placebo treatment of the control group as similar to the experimental treatment as possible.	Mortality by treatment interaction may occur if the "effective ingredient" is too unpleasant or difficult. Then it trades more Internal Integrity for less External Generality.

Mortality was introduced in the discussion of qualitative research (p. 348). It is a rival explanation whenever individuals leave an experimental group prior to completion of the study. The danger is that the composition of the group is changed by the loss—for instance, the absence of Ms. Kimball's lowest-achieving students during the posttest, which is not unlikely since such students often have the poorest attendance records. Such selective dropout would have raised the test's average, and mortality is a rival explanation. A comparable control group would also be affected by absenteeism and protect against mortality. However, if those remaining in the control and experimental groups after dropout differ in relevant characteristics from the target to which we hope to generalize, External Generality may be diminished.

Regression

Method of Control	How to Control	Consequences
Reduce	Use the most reliable measures possible; double-test individuals.	Reliable measures and double testing do not correct for the type of regression that occurs when corrective measures are instigated at the peak of a problem that would subside without remediation.
Equalize across groups	Use randomly assigned experimental and control groups.	Control group measures gain due to regression.

Whenever you find a high or low group that was selected on the basis of some test and has then been retested with the same or a similar test, suspect one of the two types of regression, one of the subtlest rival hypotheses. For instance, suppose Ms. Kimball used the Stanford Achievement Test as a pretest to select the lowest quarter of her students for treatment with a remedial curriculum. This group, labeled R for remedial, is the group to the left of the cut score in Figure 21.1.

When she retests them, even if her treatment is totally ineffective, she will observe an improvement in scores due to the regression effect—a frequent claim of remedial groups unless there was a control group to measure against. Regression causes the *means* of split-off groups to "regress" on retest, that is, to be closer to the mean of the parent group. Therefore, as shown in the

Figure 21.1   Groups R and A are subject to the regression effect as a result of having been separated from a parent group by means of a selection test later used to measure treatment effect.

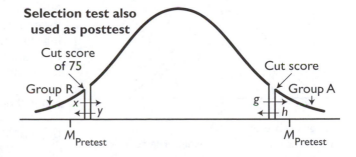

Figure 21.2   Regression effect in the selected groups at retest.

Pretest (Selection Test)

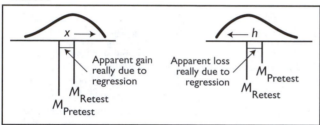

Retest

lower part of Figure 21.2, the mean of remedial group R is higher, showing an apparent gain. If there is any treatment effect, it looks better than it should because regression effect is added to it.

In similar fashion, an especially capable group, labeled A for accelerated, able, or enriched in Figure 21.1, was selected for faster instruction. In such a group, as a result of regression alone the posttest mean would be lower, as shown in Figure 21.2. Since regression and treatment effect typically work in opposite directions, the apparent treatment effect will be less than the actual effect and, when re-gression exceeds a weak or zero treatment effect, the posttest will be lower than the pretest—participants will appear to have lost!

In pretest–posttest designs, regression results from the unreliability of the test. Consider participant Xavier's score: It is one of those in the remedial group in Figure 21.1 and is represented by the *x* adjacent to the cut score for Group R in both Figure 21.1 and the top-left part of Figure 21.2. Suppose you hypnotize him, test him an infinite number of times with the same test, and each time give him the posthypnotic suggestion to forget taking it previously. Due to various sources of testing error—for example, day-to-day variation in motivation—his scores will vary from their true score and form a normal, bell-shaped curve. The mean of those scores is our best estimate of his true score of 80, which is above the cut score of 75. Figure 21.3 shows the score distribution created by the multiple retesting.

Figure 21.3   Distribution of Xavier's scores with multiple testings with the X representing his score in the example's testing.

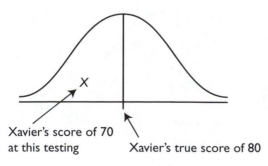

Xavier's score of 70 at this testing

Xavier's true score of 80

The mean of the distribution is the best estimate of Xavier's true score. Note that Xavier's score, the *x*, is in the lower part of the distribution on this testing. On retest, it could be anywhere in the distribution, one can't tell where, but it is clear that the odds are that, because most of the scores are to the right of his *x*, it will be higher.

But, as it turns out, Xavier's true score of 80 is above the remedial group's cut score of 75—he doesn't really belong in that group. He should be over with Yolanda, represented by the *y* in Figure 21.1; her score of 79 is above the cut score. Yolanda would have a distribution of her own, similar in shape to Xavier's. But, if we test her multiple times as we did Xavier, we find her true score of 73 is below the cut score. Her score in this particular testing, like Xavier's, misclassifies her also, because with a true score of 73 most of the scores in her distribution would be to the left (that is, lower than 79).

If the whole class were kept together instead of being divided by cut scores, Xavier's score on retest would likely be closer to his true score since most of the scores in his distribution are higher then his. Similarly, since most scores in Yolanda's distribution are lower, her retest score would be lower. So, moving in opposite directions, the shape of the whole group would not change.

But consider what happens when the remedial group is removed from the class and retested, as shown in the lower half of Figure 21.2. Yolanda and persons like her are no longer present to offset changes in the remedial group. Now, only Xavier and persons like him affect the mean. There is no longer a clean drop at the cut score, but a tail of scores to the right whose true scores were above the cut score. So even with zero treatment effect, the retest mean is higher. And if the treatment is effective, it adds to regression effect so it appears to be more effective than it really is.

In like manner, in accelerated group A, George (represented by the *g*) takes the role of Xavier and Harry (represented by the *h*) the role of Yolanda. But now when Harry alone is left in the accelerated group, his retested scores are closer to his lower-than-the-cut true score. Thus, he and others like him counteract whatever treatment effect there is, and they appear to lose if the regression effect overpowers the treatment as shown in the lower half of Figure 21.2.

Since retested control groups are also affected by regression, any difference in posttest means between the treated and control groups indicates true treatment effect. Control groups provide protection against regression effect. As an alternative control for regression, retest the selected group *before* treatment and average the two for a pretest score. Retesting provides a larger and thus more reliable sample of the participant's behavior—scores of individuals that were too high will drop on retest, and those that were too low will rise.

Another instance of regression results from instigating a remedial treatment when an effect is at a peak that would subside toward its mean without intervention. For example, critiquing a study comparing the arrest records before and after treatment of 365 delinquents, McCleary, Gordon, McDowall, Maltz, and colleagues (1979) noted "in each case the time of intervention . . . [was] selected apparently, as a reaction to a particularly high rate of arrest" (p. 633). Put another way, the arrest rate for these delinquents was at a peak in comparison with both their own personal record of arrests and the pool in general. This example illustrates the difficulty of assessing a remedial program's effectiveness without a control group or pre-intervention trend measure. Remediation is unlikely to begin before the problem is sufficiently serious for ameliorating societal mechanisms to come into play.

> ▶ Regression is a rival explanation wherever an extremely high or low group is selected for treatment (remediation, enrichment, or special treatment) when researchers use a pretest-posttest design with no control group.
>
> ▶ Regression may also be found where a remedial treatment is employed at the height of a problem that in time would subside without treatment.
>
> ▶ Since a control group will also be affected by regression, comparison of its mean with that of the experimental group controls for this problem.

Selection

Method of Control	How to Control	Consequences
Eliminate	Use random assignment with matching and blocking on all relevant variables.	Procedures for random assignment may result in obtrusiveness and its effects and thus trade more Internal Integrity for less External Generality.
Measure and adjust	Use analysis of covariance, partial correlation, or build in a variable used in selection as an independent variable.	Elimination may be incomplete, depending on the validity and reliability of the measuring instrument.

Selection occurs when a factor that determines group membership also affects the outcome of treatment. Unrecognized, it can lead to wrong conclusions. For example, judging from bottles washed up on a beach we conclude that all bottles are discarded in the ocean with their caps on. Of course, we see only the survivors; the others sank. Similarly, some of the groups we study—seniors in high school and college, and graduate students—are survivors.

Commonly, we use groups formed by a regularly occurring process such as participants' availability in a certain time block, participants' typical choice, or an institutional scheduling procedure. But unrecognized selection factors are often at work—especially when student choice is involved. A student's interest in a subject, a group of friends, or an easy-grading teacher may be the selective factor and thus a rival explanation for an effect. The use of preformed instead of randomly sampled and assigned groups is always open to suspicion.

A common example of selection is the use of volunteers to constitute the experimental group, and nonvolunteers the control group. From Rosenthal and Rosnow's (1975) review of the literature, we know that, in contrast to nonvolunteers, volunteers had many positive characteristics. They were found to be more intelligent, better educated, higher in social status, more sociable, higher in need for social approval, more likely to be female (except for physically demanding or stressful situations, where males are more likely to volunteer), more likely to be interested in arousal-seeking situations, and more likely to be somewhat unconventional. Volunteers tended to be less authoritarian and even more likely to be Jewish than Protestant, and more likely Protestant than Catholic. (This listing includes only findings that Rosenthal and Rosnow [1975] believed were supported by enough research to merit considerable confidence. They list other differences with less evidence that could be important under particular circumstances.) Though cultures change, similar findings were later validated in Wilson and Musick's (1997) theory of volunteering.

Establishment of a control group similarly affected by selection strengthens Internal Integrity, but External Generality is impaired since we can only generalize to those similarly selected.

> ▶ Selection is a rival explanation when choice of participants includes a selective factor that affects the measure of treatment effect. A common example is the use of volunteers for the experimental group but nonvolunteers for the control. Volunteers typically differ from nonvolunteers on a wide variety of characteristics.
>
> ▶ Random assignment to groups, including a control group, usually avoids the selection effect.

Testing

Method of Control	How to Control	Consequences
Eliminate	Use posttest only.	Posttest only eliminates testing-treatment interaction, reduces testing cost, and necessitates only one test form. But without pretest researchers may not be sure the groups were initially equivalent.
Reduce testing effect	Use different forms of test or different tests at pretest and posttest.	The more alike the forms are, the greater the comparability of pretest and posttest but the greater the likelihood of a residual testing effect. The latter is reduced with the use of different tests, but so is the comparability of pretest and posttest, a trade-off.
	Use a different group for each testing; use the Solomon four-group design (see p. 503 in this chapter).	Use of extra groups as in the Solomon four-group design requires a much larger sample, and groups may not be comparable unless randomly assigned. It increases the cost of testing but controls for testing-treatment interaction.
Equalize across groups	Use the same pattern of observation or testing with experimental and control groups.	Testing by treatment interaction is not eliminated, so it trades more Internal Integrity for less External Generality.

Crane and Heim (1950) showed that students gained 3 to 5 IQ points solely as a result of retaking the test. **Testing** shows in retests of personality measures as an apparent increase in "adjustment" (Windle, 1954); sensitized participants have increased awareness of socially approved answers.

> ▶ Testing, as a rival hypothesis, occurs whenever two or more measurements occur with the same or closely related instruments, because the experience of having been tested earlier may affect later testings.

Interactions Affecting Internal Integrity

Interaction effects result when the treatment effect is inappropriately strengthened or weakened by another treatment, the situation, or the individuals in it. Some examples:

Instrument decay by treatment interaction. An observer studying democratic and authoritarian-led groups is pleased by the democratic group's collaboration and focuses on its positive attributes. Conversely, reacting to the stifling authoritarian milieu, he is especially sensitive to negative aspects. These biases make democracy look better, authoritarianism worse, and their difference greater than appropriate. A structured instrument combined with training might be the best antidote.

Selection-maturation interaction. A selection factor creates groups with widely differing maturation levels. Suppose, because of a scheduling conflict, an unusually high proportion of senior students enrolled in an experimental physical education section, a situation that naturally depleted such students from the section used as the control. Seniors might differ sufficiently in skills and motivation from freshmen to create a between-groups difference that could inappropriately be interpreted as due solely to the experimental curriculum. Random assignment to groups can control for this.

Selection by treatment interaction. People attracted to or with a special need for treatment (especially therapeutic treatment) seek entrance, and are accepted into the experimental group. Conversely, individuals may avoid an aversive treatment. Neither case estimates true treatment effect, which can be estimated with random assignment.

In another scenario, that of seeking institutions for a study, all but a few turn you down because of treatment characteristics—it disrupts the schedule, is not compatible with their goals, and so on. Are those that welcome you representative? Not likely. Creating both treatment and control groups from volunteers, the usual remedy, strengthens Internal Integrity but weakens External Generality.

RIVAL EXPLANATIONS AFFECTING GENERALITY

Rival explanations affecting generality are better thought of as restrictions on generality. A number of the consequences boxes above contain the phrase "Trades more Internal Integrity for less External Generality." Actions taken to eliminate these rival explanations restrict generality to situations and conditions similar to those of the study. The following sections describe other common ones.

Reactivity to Obtrusiveness

Method of Control	How to Control	Consequences
Eliminate	Use low obtrusiveness conditions for treatment and measurement or observation. Isolate groups from one another.	Groups and situations may not be comparable; local history may cause variation in effects.
Equalize across groups	Apply placebo treatment with equal obtrusiveness to a control group.	Obtrusiveness may interact with treatment, potentiating or weakening it over normal use. Trades more Internal Integrity for less External Generality.

The term **reactivity** covers effects resulting when procedures are sufficiently obtrusive that individuals realize they are the participants in a study. **Obtrusiveness** can increase or decrease treatment effect, depending on study conditions. Here's how:

Increasing Treatment Effect (or, Lacking Any, Creating It)

- "I'm special!"—the **Hawthorne effect,** so named after an experiment at Western Electric Company's Hawthorne plant by Roethlisberger and Dickson (1939), intended to show that the improvement of a department's working conditions resulted in increased production, the study also found that production increased following negative changes such as reduced lighting. They concluded that the real cause was the effect of giving special attention.

  Adair, Sharpe, and Huynh (1989) examined the 86 studies they believe are the body of Hawthorne effect studies involving use of control groups. They classified control treatments as alternate activity, special attention, or awareness of being studied. Attention had the largest effect but was not statistically significant. Since 86 studies did not find it, they concluded that Hawthorne effect, as currently operationally defined, is too small to be of significance. On the other hand, Hawthorne effect is not so dissimilar from placebo effect, which has been confirmed as real even to the point of being able to show physiological changes (see p. 480). The difference may be that the nature of expected effect is usually clear with placebo but often less so with Hawthorne.

- "What does she expect from me? I'd like to please her!"—**Hypothesis guessing** by participants is common and correct guesses enhance treatment effect. Especially where there is a status difference, participants show eager-to-please behavior—for example, when instructors use their advisees as participants. (See also a study's demand characteristics later in this chapter.)

- "That's new and interesting: I like it!"—the novelty effect. Extra work required by a new curriculum is met with enthusiasm the first time and maybe even the second, but the gusto wears off.

- "I'm especially pleased he's studying me."—In one-on-one situations, a close emotional bond may develop between the participant and investigator. If the treatment is always so administered, reactivity is part of treatment. But findings clearly may not generalize to larger group situations.

Decreasing or Negating Treatment Effect

- "I don't want to be a guinea pig!"—The treatment is perceived to be aversive or dangerous or the research site is too frequently used (for example, laboratory schools). May reduce or sabotage treatment effect.

- "I don't want my group disadvantaged because a coin flip made it the control group!"—compensatory rivalry. It decreases apparent treatment effect. Conscientious teachers try to offset any experimental benefits. Also called the "John Henry effect," after the legendary railroad worker who tried to outdo a steam railroad spike driver (for example, see Zdep & Irvine, 1970).

- "We can't compete with special help! Why try? Let's quit."—Demoralization and feelings of dismay may lower the effect measure in the comparison group; the treatment looks better than it should.

- One experimental group participant to a control-group participant: "Have you heard about the easy new way we are learning long division?"—**Diffusion,** where a treatment is communicated (for example, during recess), may occur without reactivity but is more likely under nonroutine conditions. It decreases the apparent treatment effect.

- "I want my child to get that special treatment!"—Yielding to parental pressure, administrators provide compensatory treatment to the control, decreasing the apparent treatment effectiveness.

Controlling Obtrusiveness

Obviously, the best way to reduce reactivity is through **unobtrusiveness.** Unless the treatment itself is too novel, have the regular staff (e.g., the teacher) simply routinely work measures and treatment into the day's ordinary activities. Present novel treatments simply as program improvements. Concealed observations (or unconcealed after accommodation) reduce or eliminate obtrusiveness. Two-way mirrors fool few participants but are usually forgotten, especially with the realization they are not always in use. Webb and colleagues (1981) provide a very useful discussion of unobtrusive measurement and offer suggestions. If other steps fail, similarly obtrusive treatment of control groups spreads its effect to both groups.

> ▶ Reactivity is the reaction to the unusual circumstances of being observed or participating in a research study. Obtrusive procedures increase it, whereas unobtrusive methods of treatment, observation, or measurement reduce it. Spread the effect to the control groups by obtrusively treating them as well.

Researcher Expectancy Effects

Method of Control	How to Control	Consequences
Eliminate	Use double-blind procedures—treatment, test administrators, observers, and participants have no idea which group is experimental and which is control.	When special knowledge is required of those giving the treatment, only judges must be blind; the rest need not be.

"Did the mouse find the target? Since he stuck his nose in the box, I'll count it." Especially if what counts as "success" is open to interpretation, researchers are more likely to perceive events in the desired direction. Also called the *Pygmalion effect*, after George Bernard Shaw's play, Rosenthal (1969, 1976) named it the **researcher expectancy effect.** Researchers may inadvertently tip the scales in a variety of ways—verbally (for example, with encouragement and clues) and nonverbally (smiling for right answers or frowning for wrong ones).

Rosenthal and Rubin (1980) examined 345 interpersonal expectancy effects studies—for example, experimenters were told that their subjects were "especially able" mice, or teachers with "unusually capable" children. Even though randomly chosen, mice and children showed expectancy effects. Only 2 of 9 reaction-time studies showed these effects, but 11 of 15 animal studies did so. Unintended expectancy effects may be as large as intended ones.

Double-blind procedures control expectancy effects when no one involved with treatment administration (administrators or recipients) nor anyone observing effects can tell which is the control group and which the experimental group. Participants or groups are coded so that an uninvolved party can tell them apart. Double-blind procedures cannot be used when:

- Expectancy of benefit is part of the treatment itself.
- Treatment can be identified by merely observing, being exposed to it, or from side effects.
- Withholding a more favorable treatment would have ethical consequences.
- Treatment effectiveness is reduced by the elimination of clues to its identity.

To eliminate expectancy effect, use independent judges called in only to assess results and kept "blind" to group identity (Guy, Gross, & Dennis, 1967). But, even after every effort, were treatment administrators and evaluators really blind? With multiple judges, investigate this by asking them to identify the experimental groups and compare their guesses with chance. If you find a statistically significant result and therefore possible expectancy effect, interpret the data conservatively (Kazdin, 1980).

▶ Researcher expectancy effects may appear when persons can identify those treated prior to assessment (especially those presumably kept "blind" who are responsible for giving the treatment or assessing its effects). Keeping observers, measurers, treatment administrators, and participants blind to which groups are experimental and the nature of the treatment (or in lieu of that, having independent evaluators who are) may eliminate these effects.

▶ Whether such efforts are successful is an empirical question that should be checked where feasible.

▶ Unintended expectancy effects can be as large or larger than some intended experimental effects.

Demand Characteristics of a Study

Method of Control	How to Control	Consequences
Measure and adjust or redesign study	Use stimulated recall (p. 248), think-aloud procedures, or interviews to obtain representative participants' perceptions of the study as it proceeds.	Obtaining participants' perceptions determines whether the design worked as intended. But think-aloud procedures may change the way participants approach what is asked. Recall may not be accurate or may be modified to please the researcher.

The researcher expectancy effect and many of the obtrusiveness problems described above are all part of a study's **demand characteristics** or conditions. What participants perceive the study wants of them may not be what the researcher intended. Determining these perceptions can be important to interpreting findings accurately.

Demand conditions explained a surprising finding in Payne, Krathwohl, and Gordon's (1967) study of the importance of sequence in programmed instruction. Three sequences of questions and their answers were developed: tightly sequenced, moderately sequenced (according to judges), and random. Surprisingly, performance on the randomly scrambled questions was not markedly degraded.

Why? Interviews showed that the study's demand conditions were such that students saw the scrambled material as a challenging puzzle. Forced to be active learners, students mentally rehearsed questions and answers to keep them available as they were organized into proper sequence—thus facilitating learning. Once discovered, the researchers felt they should have anticipated it. Hindsight is 20/20; research design never is!

Postexperiment debriefings, stimulated recall techniques, and think-aloud procedures can help determine the actual versus the intended demand conditions.

> ▶ The demand characteristics of a study are determined by how the participants perceive the study. This perception may or may not be what the researcher intended, but it can seriously affect results.

Interactions Affecting Generality

Multiple-treatment interaction. The effect of prior treatment(s) on later ones makes it difficult to generalize to a treatment administered alone. For instance, having found the University of Chicago program only moderately successful, Ms. Kimball switches to a new curriculum by the Southwest Educational Laboratory. She finds it more effective, but because of possible multiple-treatment interaction, these findings are limited to situations where Southwest follows prior use of the Chicago curriculum—a restrictive condition on generality. She encounters this limitation when, beginning with Southwest alone the next fall, it is no more effective than the

Chicago program. Prior learning from the Chicago program increased the effectiveness of the Southwest curriculum.

To estimate sequence effect, establish as many groups as there are treatments, and rotate each treatment into the first position. You can find any sequencing effect on the treatment's singular effectiveness by comparison with the sample in which it was given first. These are called **counterbalanced designs.**

Testing-treatment interaction. This demand characteristic occurs when similarities to a pretest sensitize individuals to comparable parts of the treatment. By perhaps motivating them to better learn these parts, pretests likely increase treatment effectiveness. (Hovland, Lumsdaine, and Sheffield [1949] found interaction, but it was negative; their movies were less effective changers of attitude when used with a pretest. So beware—pretests don't always make treatment more effective.) Research findings apply only to treatment accompanied by a pretest, a restrictive condition on generality. Testing-treatment interaction may be present in any pretest-posttest design but is eliminated by the posttest-only design and the **Solomon four-group design**. The latter provides an estimate of its size.

Mortality by treatment interaction. This would have taken place in Ms. Kimball's class if children had high absenteeism because they disliked the curriculum— the interaction between treatment and the absent participants. This may artificially raise the average score. Though difficult, obtaining data from the full initial group membership provides evidence with more generality.

> ▶ Multiple-treatment interaction occurs when the residual effects of one treatment influences a later one such that its apparent effect is different from the one without the residual influence. Putting each treatment into first position provides an estimate of its effectiveness alone.
>
> ▶ Testing-treatment interaction occurs when the treatment effect is strengthened or weakened as a result of pretesting.
>
> ▶ Mortality by treatment interaction occurs when individuals selectively drop out of the treated group in reaction to the treatment.

UNIQUE RIVAL EXPLANATIONS

Besides the standard rival explanations, alternatives may exist that are unique to a particular study, its setting, or its procedure. For example, Zeigarnik (1927; see also Denmark, 1984) argued that unreleased tension has an effect on memory. She proceeded to illustrate this hypothesis by giving participants a series of common tasks (such as winding thread), a randomly selected half of which were interrupted when the participants were thoroughly engaged. The other tasks were completed without interruption. Zeigarnik then asked participants to recall all the tasks. She found that the interrupted tasks were better remembered.

Critics argued, however, that the impact of being interrupted was what caused the increased memory. To answer this rival explanation, she then arranged that all the tasks were interrupted with a new set of participants; half of them were then allowed to complete their tasks. Again, the uncompleted tasks were better remembered.

But maybe these tasks were better remembered because they were to be completed later? Thus, Zeigarnik did two more studies with instructions indicating that either the task would be completed later or it would not be worked on anymore. Again, interrupted tasks were better remembered. This cascade of studies to answer new objections not only nicely illustrates the process of science at work but also how alternatives unique to a study arise.

Should the researcher have anticipated these alternatives and designed protections into the original study? The better such predictions, the shorter the route to building a consensus around the interpretation of the data and acceptance as a contribution to knowledge.

SAMPLE SIMPLE EXPERIMENTAL DESIGNS

There is a wide variety of designs and this text can examine only a small sample of them. To provide a basis for understanding how designs protect against rival explanations, let's look at six simple single-treatment designs. Each successive design has an advantage over the previous and thus illustrates both some desirable design characteristics and the way designs evolve. A standard notation for such depiction, developed by Campbell and Stanley (1963), uses X to indicate a treatment and O to indicate an observation or measurement. Events are sequenced in time from left to right, and each group occupies a separate line.

Ms. Kimball's trial of a new curriculum and her evaluation of her students' success is a case study. We diagram it as X O, where X is the new curriculum and O is her evaluation of it. The sequence indicates that the curriculum was applied (X) and then the students were measured with the Stanford Achievement Test (O). If her students are like those on which the Stanford was normed, she can compare her students with them. But they might have started as high as they ended.

A stronger design would have tested both before and after the treatment—**one-group pretest-posttest design** (O X O). Students are being used as their own control group—compared with themselves. The mention of a control group suggests that the teacher might have used one in her study. She might use another teacher's class, a preformed group formed for other than experimental purposes. We do not know the two groups' comparability, which is indicated by a line between the rows in the **nonequivalent control group design**. The C indicates a control treatment:

$$\frac{O\ X\ O}{O\ C\ O}$$

Establishing groups specifically for the study can ensure, on average, that the groups will be comparable. By the flip of a coin, individuals from a pool of participants are randomly assigned to either the control or the treatment group. Then, by a coin flip, one of the two teachers is assigned to administer the treatment. Random assignment of participants and treatment to groups is designated by the R in a square. The pretest in this **pretest-posttest control group design** ensures that randomization did equate the groups:

$$\boxed{R}\ \begin{matrix} O\ X\ O \\ O\ C\ O \end{matrix}$$

Trusting randomization to make groups really comparable eliminates the need for pretest. A **posttest-only control group design** simply compares them at the posttest:

$$\boxed{R}\ \begin{matrix} X\ O \\ C\ O \end{matrix}$$

To make sure randomization worked; let's combine the last two into a single design, the Solomon four-group design:

$$\boxed{R}\ \begin{matrix} O\ X\ O \\ O\ C\ O \\ X\ O \\ C\ O \end{matrix}$$

The combination of random assignment with a control group in the last three designs confers a great deal of protection. In general, the combination protects against the rival explanations of: history, instrument decay, maturation, mortality, regression, selection, and the interaction of selection with maturation. The posttest only and Solomon four-group designs also protect against testing and testing with treatment interaction; they are very strong designs.

Because of its prevalence, and the fact that we must often use already formed groups, the nonequivalent control group design (O X O/O C O) deserves further attention. Much has been written about it, especially by Cook and Campbell (1979), who discuss a number of variations. Bracht and Glass (1968) noted that this design is most interpretable when the experimental group begins below the control and their positions are reversed at posttest (Figure 21.4). An initially lower treatment group might draw even with the control because of a ceiling effect but would not draw ahead. The initially lower-scoring group might be expected to regress upward toward the group mean but would not overtake it.

Typically one assigns the lower group at pretest to the experimental treatment and hopes it overtakes the control. But as Cook and Campbell (1979) warn, as possibly indicated by its lower start, its growth rate may be lower than that of the control's. If it is, the lines may not cross or, even if they do, they will underestimate the effect, possibly showing no statistically significant difference. We cannot tell whether there was no treatment effect, or an unsensed change due to slow growth rate.

Figure 21.4   Outcome of the nonequivalent control group design when the treatment group overtakes the control group.

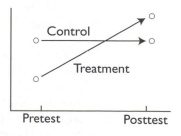

Pretest   Posttest

> ▶ The nonequivalent control group design is in common use because researchers must often work with preformed groups. The design is interpretable if the experimental group begins below the control group and then overtakes it. Deliberately designing a study in this way, however, may underestimate the effect.

DESIGNS WITH MORE COMPLEXITY

Time-Series Designs

These designs (O O O X O O O) are especially useful for studies of single participants, but they can be employed with groups as well. Longitudinal studies are time-series designs, some with a manipulated treatment and others merely allowing nature to take its course. An individual is initially observed until a **baseline** is established (O O O), then a treatment or new variable is introduced (X) and finally a new baseline is found (O O O). In time-series notation they are often designated as **ABA designs** where A indicates measurement and/or observation and B a treatment or introduction of a new variable.

Local history would not be measured without a control group, though single participants might be questioned if it is suspected. Maturation is automatically built into repeated observations. Testing effect wears off with repeated measurements, as does regression. Testing-treatment interaction and researcher expectancy effect can be a problem. If "blind" conditions can be established for either participants or researcher, researcher expectancy can be reduced or, under double-blind conditions, eliminated. Protection from instrument decay requires continued calibration of instruments or observers. Depending on the participants' needs and the procedure's obtrusiveness, there might or might not be selection by treatment interaction (a person who sought treatment) and reactivity. From the foregoing, we can see how the circumstances of a particular study modify protection.

Multiple measurements to establish a baseline also sense any trends, whether linear or curvilinear. Extrapolating it provides a prediction of post baseline without treatment, deviations from which we assume to have resulted from treatment. This variation of the time-series design, called a *regression discontinuity design*, is discussed extensively in Cook and Campbell (1979) and Shadish, Cook, and Campbell (2002).

A stronger design repeats the treatment as in O O O X O O O X O O O, or with multiple replications. Replication in the form of a pattern of treatments, each of which is successively different from the previous, possibly one or more being control or placebo treatments (e.g., O O X_1 O O C O O X_2 O O X_3 O O O), is a very strong design. Only a recurring local history event would be a problem, and its timing would have to match that of the treatment's. Unless treatment was repeated unobtrusively, reactivity might be present. If the real treatment is distinguishable from the control treatment, researcher or participant expectancy may be a problem. Depending on the persistence of the effect of treatment, there may be multiple-treatment interaction. Given a nonpersistent effect and unobtrusive and double-blind treatments, adding a control group would provide very strong evidence of causation.

> ▶ Time-series designs provide good control for a number of the common rival explanations and gain especially strong Internal Integrity with a patterning of the treatment that is reflected in the effect.

Patched-Up Designs

Patched-up designs solve particular problems of control with peculiar patterns of groups or of testing. As Campbell and Stanley (1963) note, this approach should be typical of the spirit in which designs are developed. For example, when observation of a group is easier to arrange than its treatment, the simulated before-and-after design (Jahoda, Deutsch, & Cook, 1951) shown below overcomes the common field limitation of using intact groups (school classes, churches, and so forth). It involves pairs of two separate experimental and control groups. The $\boxed{R}$ indicates that the groups are randomly assigned to experimental conditions within the first pair and last pair; thus, the two sets of pairs may not be equivalent. The (X) stands for any treatment that is administered with obtrusiveness comparable to that of X, the treatment of interest.

Since both of the first pair receive treatments and neither of the second does,

$$\boxed{R} \begin{array}{l} O\,(X) \\ X\,O \end{array}$$
$$\boxed{R} \begin{array}{l} O \\ \quad O \end{array}$$

reactivity is controlled within each pair. The second pair controls for history, maturation, and mortality. It is possible there is a selection difference between the two sets of pairs (for example, one pair of classes is older and less likely to grow tired than the others). Selection might interact with time (interaction of selection and maturation). The lack of a pretest in the experimental group controls for testing and for testing-treatment interaction.

> ▶ Many designs are "patched-up" designs that use peculiar patterns of groups and measures to fit particular situations. They are so designed as to provide the kind of protection that is important for a given study.

Factorial Designs

Over the years, studies have increasingly involved more than one variable comparing two or more treatments or examining the effects of such characteristics as demographic, situational, personality, or ability variables. **Factorial designs** facilitate estimation not only of the effects of these variables singly, but also of their **interactions** in all possible combinations. Factor is simply another term for a variable that is present in two or more levels: gender has two, male and female; a strong, medium, and weak treatment has three. (Don't confuse factorial design with factor analysis, which helps determine the underlying factors—constructs—that account for a set of relationships among variables.)

Let's consider a study of ways to control speeding on the New York State Thruway involving three factors: (1) two kinds of police cars—marked and unmarked; (2) five ways of handling a violation: (a) require immediate court appearance, (b) issue a ticket for later court appearance, (c) issue a ticket that can be handled by mail, (d) give a stern warning, (e) do whatever police normally would (control group); (3) two kinds of driver—commuter and noncommuter (commuters will have passes that can be detected by a sensor in the road).

Factorial designs collect data for each combination of factors that, in this $2 \times 5 \times 2$ design, is 20 sites as diagrammed in Figure 21.5. Each "x" of "site x" would designate one of 20 randomly assigned five-mile stretches of highway over which we would find the average speed of randomly sampled cars for the treatment assigned that site with each of the four combinations of car marking and commuting.

Figure 21.5   A 2 × 5 × 2 factorial design for a study of speeding violator treatment.

	Treatment of Violators									
	Control		Immediate court appearance		Delayed court appearance		Mail		Warning	
	Commuter	Noncommuter	Commuter	Noncommuter	Commuter	Noncommuter	Commuter	Noncommuter	Commuter	Noncommuter
Marked car	Site X	Site X	Site X	Site X	Site X	Site X	Site X	Site X	Site X	Site X
Unmarked car	Site X	Site X	Site X	Site X	Site X	Site X	Site X	Site X	Site X	Site X

By analysis of variance (see p. 466), we can determine (1) whether marking a police car makes a difference, (2) whether average speed is reduced by violator treatment in general and by certain treatments in particular, and (3) whether commuters react differently to the treatments from noncommuters. In addition, we can determine whether each variable interacts with others to form a more potent or weaker effect than alone. For example, was the mail-in ticket treatment more effective with commuter or noncommuter traffic? With marked or unmarked cars? We can examine whether the three characteristics formed a pattern that together raised or lowered the average speed. Thus, we can check the effect of each major factor by itself and in all possible combinations. This makes it possible to determine how treatments are affected by context variables.

Nested Designs

Nested designs reduce the number of groups to those combinations in which we are particularly interested. Let's suppose we are convinced that marked cars are more effective in reducing the number of speeding commuters, so we need no further data on that issue and can collapse this distinction. In the language of experimental design, we allow these two variables to be confounded.

We assign marked cars to attend to stopping commuting speeders, the most effective speed reducing combination, leaving unmarked cars to monitor noncom-

Figure 21.6   A nested factorial design for a study of speeding violator treatment.

	Treatment of Violators									
	Control		Immediate court appearance		Delayed court appearance		Mail		Warning	
	Commuter	Noncommuter	Commuter	Noncommuter	Commuter	Noncommuter	Commuter	Noncommuter	Commuter	Noncommuter
Marked car	Site X		Site X		Site X		Site X		Site X	
Unmarked car		Site X		Site X		Site X		Site X		Site X

muting speeders. Thus, in each column designating a violator treatment (warning, mail, etc.) there will be two cells: the upper-left commuter-marked car cell and the lower-right noncommuter-unmarked car cell. This still gives us information on the marked versus unmarked cars in relation to the different treatments of violators as well as commuters versus noncommuters in relation to these violator treatments. However, this nested design has only 10 cells and thus needs only 10 sites.

> ▶ Factorial designs are popular because they permit estimation of the effect of the treatment and other independent variables singly and in all possible combinations.
>
> ▶ Building variables we wish to control into such designs as independent variables (for example, commuting) allows us to determine their effect. This design shows us the effect of context variables.
>
> ▶ When we are not interested in all possible combinations of variables, use of nested designs reduces the demand for cases and possibly sites as well.

After-the-Fact Designs (Causal Comparison, Ex Post Facto Studies, and After-the-Fact Natural Experiments)

The world is such that we can't manipulate many of the phenomena that interest us most. What is the effect of low socioeconomic class on school achievement? Or low spatial visualization on creativity? Manipulating these variables as a treatment is impossible. We must examine them and their consequences as they exist in the world—that is, we must create after-the-fact designs. Causal comparison, ex post facto studies, and after-the-fact natural experiments are all names for **after-the-fact designs**. Kerlinger (1986) used the too-inclusive name *nonexperimental studies* in his 1986 edition. Babbie (1992) refers to them as the *elaboration model*. None of these names seems entirely satisfactory.

Causal comparative method usually refers to studies where data are gathered from preformed groups and the independent variable is not manipulated as in an experiment. They are also called *ex post facto* studies (after-the-fact) because in most instances data are gathered retrospectively. They all have the common characteristic that they deal with situations in which the variables are not manipulated but occur naturally. In most of the studies of this type the events occurred in the past, and the study uses available data sets or assembles such sets for the purposes of the study.

We will refer to them all as after-the-fact designs, but "after-the-fact natural experiments" is also nicely descriptive since, like experiments, they contrast two or more groups, and since they use data created under natural circumstances. These experiments are formed "after-the-fact," because the cause, the effect, or both are already present—sometimes in preformed groups, sometimes in groups specially constructed to certain characteristics. They are "natural experiments" in that the "treatment" or the effect of some variable occurs naturally and is observed either after the fact or as it occurs. For example, Hollowood, Salisbury, and Rainforth (1995) contrasted six students with severe disabilities with twelve nondisabled students in the use of time in the classroom. Arguing for inclusion of the handicapped in normal classrooms, they found that groups had comparable levels of engaged time and that the disabled did not cause loss of instructional time for the nondisabled.

Such studies can test a hunch, extend previous research, or search for causative variables. For example, we have a hunch that highly creative individuals have higher verbal fluency than less creative ones. Since no known treatment changes verbal fluency, we must find (or create) groups with high and low verbal fluency and determine their difference in creativity, or find (or create) groups with high and low creativity and see if they differ in verbal fluency.

Problems of After-the-Fact Designs

Finding comparable groups.   Often, particularly in the health field, the effect of interest has already occurred (for example, individuals with emphysema). We accept such individuals, selected from the natural environment, just as they are. Creating a functionally equivalent control group (for example, nonemphysema victims), however, can be a problem. We must provide a functional equivalence on all relevant variables. But what variables are relevant? We don't always know! Further, variables like gender, socioeconomic status, and personality tend not to act independently; they come in "bundles" or "constellations"—a complicating factor. Consider that smokers' self-selected lifestyle may be almost impossible to duplicate in the control group—otherwise, they might also become smokers. It is possible that nonsmokers, health-conscious and self-controlled enough to avoid smoking, have attitudes and personality characteristics that, independent of smoking, relate to low lung cancer incidence. Such constellations make it hard to analyze variables separately to build a strong case. Because there are rarely "before" data on both groups, the causal relationship is usually analogous to a posttest-only control group design (X O/O). The actual equivalence of the groups is always a nagging question in such studies.

Relying on available data. In retrospective studies, we must make do with what data are available. Such data may not have been gathered with the same thoroughness as we would employ if we knew its future use. It may have missing cases at critical points or outliers for which there may have been a reasonable explanation that is no longer known. Further, data based on peoples' recall, which is the nature of a good deal of such data, always creates nagging doubts regarding accuracy.

Difficulty of retrospectively establishing precedence of cause.   Without data on prior conditions, order of precedence may be hard to determine. If lung cancer patients both smoke more and are nervous, is the prior cause nervousness, which caused smoking, or vice versa?

Lack of control over the independent variable or treatment.   We cannot vary the cause in a particular pattern to show the effect follows it; if natural variation happens to do so, we are very fortunate.

Concentrating on late links when early links may be the cause.   After-the-fact designs may concentrate on late links in the causal chain of events (see p. 135) instead of the critical earlier ones. For example, perhaps the underlying cause was stress, which led to nervousness, which triggered smoking, which caused lung cancer.

Despite these problems and the barrages of rival explanations by groups desiring to undercut confidence in the findings (e.g., the long battle regarding the effects of smoking), the evidence for many policy decisions rests on after-the-fact designs. Despite concerns about their adequacy, findings from such studies are often widely embraced when they suggest inexpensive problem solutions (for example, large doses of red grape seed extract) that could possibly reduce the risk of a costly effect (e.g., heart attacks).

> ▶ After-the-fact natural experiments provide us with a comparison of a target group of interest possessing a cause, an effect, or both, with a group so constructed as to be comparable in all important ways except for the presence of the presumed cause. The intent is to show a causal relation.
>
> ▶ In studies intended to validate a relationship, we check the comparable comparison group for an absence of the effect. Alternatively, we start with persons having the effect and show they were exposed to the cause, whereas similar persons without the effect were not.
>
> ▶ For exploration studies, we look for differences between groups with and without the effect but otherwise comparable, seeking potential causes for which we can construct reasonable rationales. We then use these findings to construct validation studies.
>
> ▶ Although they often provide evidence when experimentation is difficult or impossible, after-the-fact designs have many weaknesses: the difficulty of constructing comparable groups that exclude all reasonable rival explanations is especially serious; the accuracy of data gathered retrospectively is often suspect; precedence of cause may be difficult to establish from existing records; relevant data may be missing or not be as reliable as if they were gathered for research purposes; and because the treatment or independent variable cannot be manipulated, unless it occurs naturally, we cannot obtain strong patterns of evidence such as the reflection of an on-off-on-off pattern of cause in the effect.
>
> ▶ Despite these weaknesses, in the absence of stronger evidence we often effectively employ after-the-fact designs to gather evidence for policy decisions when experimentation is impossible.

Hallmarks of Experimental Design and Tips on Constructing Them

All of the following are hallmarks of good experimental design. The tips are aimed primarily at the developmental process. The others—hallmarks—are characteristics of the published report that can help you judge the product. Remember also that all the asterisked items in the similar list for qualitative methods (14 of the 19 listed on pp. 357–359) are equally applicable to quantitative methods. Be sure to reread them, because they should be considered part of this list as well.

1. Start with a translation of the hypothesis; then add features to protect against rival explanations likely to be important in the eyes of your intended audience.

2. Experimental designs are often developed through a series of iterations and result in a patched-up design (see p. 505).[3] Make a provisional try at developing the design. Then, when you see a flaw, fix it. This repair may make apparent either a new rival explanation or one not previously noticed. It, too, will require changes, and so it goes. Continue until you are satisfied, but remember that nearly all designs are compromises because of the trade-offs involved.

3. Control undesired variables by eliminating them if their elimination does not unduly affect whatever External Generality is required (for example, laboratory versus field). If possible, control others by building them into the design as independent variables. As a last resort, spread their effect equally among the groups.

4. Describe in your write-up any rival explanations not protected against but of possible concern to your audience; indicate that they were left that way by conscious choice, usually as a result of a trade-off compromise, not ignorance. Explain why this design was the best choice.

5. Don't decide on a final design until you have done a pilot study, including the gathering of qualitative data (see point 17 below). Use the pilot's results for a power analysis to ensure that the study is statistically sensitive enough to detect a finding of interest.

6. Random assignment of treatment to groups and of individuals to experimental groups and a well-constructed placebo control group ensure more protection than any other design feature. Block (stratify) on important variables not otherwise controlled. You lose only your labor if the variable turns out not to be important, but you make the study more sensitive if it is. Using such procedures obtrusively, however, may reduce External Generality.

7. Use double-blind methods to control for expectancy effects. (Follow up with point 17 below—the participants may not have been as blind as you thought!)

8. In learning studies, tests of later retention are often more sensitive to differences in treatment than immediate posttests. This is an easy way to increase the power (sensitivity) of your study.

9. In studies of treatments that do not have residual effects, for maximally convincing results, vary the treatment in an on-off-on-off pattern, possibly at random intervals or in randomly constructed patterns.

10. Besides an on-off pattern, use different levels of treatment or reverse the treatment—use its opposite where feasible and ethical. For example, in studying the

effect of praise on achievement, vary the frequency of praise or even scold instead of praise. But be sure they are really opposites; for example, extreme praise and extreme punishment may not have opposite effects (see Cook & Campbell, 1979).

11. Where preexisting growth or change might be a plausible rival explanation, multiple observations—at least three for a curvilinear one—will reveal a trend. Use a regression discontinuity type design to sense changes in trend resulting from treatment. An effective treatment will show that the trend has been displaced upward and may also angle upward more sharply (see Cook & Campbell, 1979; Shadish, Cook, & Campbell, 2002).

12. Carefully delineate the "active ingredients" in the treatment by a supporting rationale or theory. Build these ingredients into the experimental treatment, putting all the treatment's other characteristics in the control (placebo) treatment.

13. Assign a group to each separate combination of independent variables. For ease of analysis, vary them systematically from group to group (for example, use a factorial design).

14. Counterbalance the order of measures or multiple treatments when you expect their order to have an effect.

15. Use unobtrusive measures and administer treatments as unobtrusively as possible for increased External Generality.

16. Remember that replication is the ultimate validation. Repeating a study with different measures and designs yet finding the same or similar results is very strong evidence.

17. Every experimental study should include an element of qualitative research to help understand the point of view of the participant, the treatment administrator, and the observer or measurer. Interviewing the participants after the study often reveals that the treatment was perceived quite differently from what was intended (the demand characteristics of the study) and leads to new and important rival explanations. It also provides anecdotes that help to verify the phenomenon being studied and make the statistics more meaningful.

18. When the effect of repeated testing is expected to be significant, establish multiple comparable groups (possibly by splitting experimental and control groups), one for each testing.

19. Evaluate carefully all of the design changes you plan to make after the pilot study. Let them gestate for 24 hours before acting on them.

20. Conduct data gathering in the least amount of time that is appropriate. Reducing study length decreases the likelihood of local history events; the possibility of selection, mortality, and maturation effects; and personnel costs (usually the largest budgeted item). Remember: Even if your time is not budgeted, you still incur what economists call "opportunity costs," the potential value of using that time in other ways.

21. Although experimental studies usually test hypotheses, afterward explore! Gathering data is too expensive not to extract all you can out of it. Talk to participants and coworkers about their experiences. Explore conceptually some "what ifs" and gather a bit of information about some of the more promising leads. Explore your data with scatterplots and distributions; try different cross-breaks and look for patterns. It's exciting, fun, and often fruitful! Keep your horizons wide. Your most precious finding may be something other than what you were looking for.

THE FUTURE OF DESIGN

So many experimental studies are designed to contrast one form or level of treatment with another, asking, "Does this variable make a significant difference?" This is a relatively primitive inquiry. The next higher level of question is, "How strongly and in what way is this variable related to the effect?" Though such designs are more complex, with the information they yield we are in a much better position to utilize the phenomena constructively and to construct theory.

The future of the social and behavioral sciences lies in going beyond which variables make a difference toward determining effect sizes (see next chapter) and the strength and nature of relationships between variables. This direction requires that we refocus research questions so that the strength or nature of the treatment and effect can be measured, otherwise quantified, or is present at several distinguishable levels. Then we can use statistics to show the strength of the relationship, or graphics to portray its nature.

This next level is already present. As noted at the outset, history, much of economics, astronomy, and jurisprudence also build causal chains—astronomy and economics with quantitative models. This pattern is appearing in funded psychology research with linear models and **structural equation modeling**. Such models depend on having an understanding of the complexities of a phenomenon and translating these into measures that predict their effect. This is then matched with the actual data to determine the effectiveness of the model. As a base of knowledge develops to build from, we can expect research to move in these directions—not yet replacing analysis of variance-type models but increasingly using correlational, regression, and equation-type models.

ADDITIONAL READING

Campbell and Stanley (1963), Cook and Campbell (1979), and Shadish, Cook, and Campbell (2002) are excellent materials to read for the detailed analysis of a great many designs. In addition, all contain a variety of examples that make the principles come alive. The latter also has an excellent section on analysis of causation. Ellsworth (1977) suggests guidelines for choosing natural research settings for experimentation. For program treatment fidelity see O'Donnell (2008), and Cronbach (1982) has useful discussions of treatment, especially chapter 8. Seligman (1995) uses many of this chapter's design suggestions to evaluate psychotherapy effectiveness. Reichardt's (2006) discussion of the logic of design and of rival explanations is unique in its approach and very useful. See also Schneider, Carnoy, Kilpatrick, Schmidt, and Shavelson (2007). For time-series designs, see Brandt and Williams (2007). For single-subject designs, see Barlow, Nock, and Hersen (2008).

IMPORTANT TERMS AND CONCEPTS

ABA design	blocking
after-the-fact designs	camouflage
base rate	confounding
baseline	counterbalanced design

demand characteristics
diffusion
double-blind procedures
factorial design
functionally equivalent groups
Hawthorne effect
hypothesis guessing
instrument decay by treatment interaction
interactions
local history
masking
maturation
mortality by treatment interaction
multiple-treatment interaction
nested designs
nonequivalent control group design
obtrusiveness
one-group pretest-posttest design

placebo effect
posttest-only control group design
pretest-posttest control group design
random assignment
reactivity
regression
researcher expectancy effect
restriction of range
selection
selection by treatment interaction
selection-maturation interaction
Solomon four-group design
structural equation modeling
testing
testing-treatment interaction
time-series designs
treatment fidelity
unobtrusiveness

OPPORTUNITIES FOR ADDITIONAL LEARNING

1. As a researcher in science education, you are interested in the role of diagrams in instruction. These are usually combinations of text and arrows to indicate what phenomenon leads to another. Examples are the oxygen and water cycles. You wish to investigate whether using small pictures in place of text within the diagrams will facilitate comprehension of the principles and concepts that are taught. To do so, you have developed eighth-grade biology units on the water and oxygen cycles that incorporate the liberal use of diagrams. How would you design your study?

2. A state government curriculum team wished to demonstrate the superiority of its new approach to the social studies program at the junior high-school level. Team members selected a sample of teachers from around the state to carry out a one-year pilot study of the new program. All the teachers were volunteers.

    a. Assume that students who were taught using the new approach scored significantly higher on a test of comprehension of key concepts than did comparable students in the regular program. What rival explanations can you advance to the claim that the new approach was better? How can these be avoided?

    b. Assume that the control (regular curriculum) group scored significantly higher. What could explain this result?

3. A university mathematics instructor has developed and incorporated an extensive computer-assisted instructional (CAI) program into his own course on introductory calculus. Wanting to assess the effectiveness of his approach, he decides he will randomly assign students to his and the other instructor's section of the course and compare the mean scores on the final exam at the end of the semester (the posttest-only control group design). He hypothesizes a significant difference between the means in favor of his approach. What rival explanations represent a threat to his design? How can he avoid them?

4. A group of researchers were investigating the interaction between the age of viewers of an instructional film and the gender of the narrator. Participants in the second and fifth grades were randomly assigned to one of two groups. One group watched a film narrated by an

adult female, and the other group viewed the same film narrated by an adult male. During the film, the investigators measured the children's visual attention to the program. They also tested recall of the story ideas using a multiple-choice test. What research design would these investigators probably have used, and why?

5. A nursing graduate student investigated the neurological problem of unilateral neglect (in which a patient is unaware of one side of the body). She decided to compare unilateral neglect patients who also suffered from another related problem, anosognosia (the inability to recognize that anything is wrong with them), with those who did not. She believed the patients with both unilateral neglect and anosognosia would experience more difficulties with self-care activities. Assuming she had located a reliable measure of self-care, how would she design a study to compare the two groups? Note that these disorders are relatively rare. Take into account, as well, that such medical conditions tend to be unstable—that is, the severity of the symptoms varies with such factors as patient fatigue and stress. In addition, such patients do tend to improve, albeit slowly.

6. A 1986 study by DeBack and Mentkowski (1986)attempted to answer the question of whether or not nurses with baccalaureate degree preparation were more competent than those graduating from a hospital-based or two-year diploma program. They hypothesized that baccalaureate graduate nurses would have more nursing competencies than other graduates, as would nurses with more experience regardless of training. They broadly defined these competencies as a set of "generic" abilities that represent the underlying characteristics of nursing performance. The investigators described these in behavioral terms inferred from descriptions of effective and ineffective behaviors on the part of professional nurses.

To do so, they selected three Midwestern health-care settings with excellent reputations: an acute-care setting, a long-term care environment, and a community agency. Nursing staff members were asked to cite "outstanding" and "good" nurses; 90% of them returned the questionnaire. A group of 45 "outstanding" nurses and 38 "good" nurses equally weighted for education were selected for interview. They were asked to describe three critical incidents in which they believed they were effective and three in which they were ineffective. They also completed a biographical questionnaire. There was no significant relationship between the nominations and either education or experience.

A codebook model of nine generic nursing competencies (conceptualizing, emotional stamina, ego strength, positive expectations, independence, reflective thinking, helping, influencing, and coaching) was developed from the interviews and used to evaluate the 502 critical incidents gathered. A 2×2 analysis of variance (education $\times$ experience) yielded statistically significant results in favor of baccalaureate preparation for six of the nine competencies: independence, ego strength, coaching, helping, conceptualizing, and reflective thinking. Three statistically significant effects favoring the two-year program were also shown (influencing, conceptualizing, and helping). There were no significant interaction effects (between education and experience), but level of education was significantly correlated with setting (the community agency had almost all baccalaureate-prepared nurses) and, in the acute-care setting, with supervisory position.

DeBack and Mentkowski concluded from this analysis that nurses with baccalaureate preparation exhibited more competencies than those with associate degrees or diplomas and that such education had long-term benefits. Was this an after-the-fact natural experiment? Are the researchers' conclusions warranted?

Compare your answers with those following the Application Exercise.

In order to explore the possibilities of using experimentation with your problem, you need some kind of hypothesis and treatment. If these are not normally part of your problem, find an aspect about which enough is known that setting forth a hypothesis is reasonable. What kind of experiment does a translation of the hypothesis lead to? What terms in the hypothesis translate into design features?

How would you define the treatment? Should you check to be sure it is being administered faithfully to what is intended? How would you do so? Are you interested in the treatment per se? Or do you intend it to be representative? If so, of what? What are the implications of this?

How might you administer the treatment so as to have the most convincing evidence of cause and effect? What kind of design does that suggest? Do you need an alternative or a placebo treatment? Of what will it consist? What essential characteristics of treatment must you exclude from it, and what other characteristics must you include because they go with the treatment but are not really part of it?

What rival explanations are likely to be a threat to the Internal Integrity of the study? How will you protect against them? Can you protect against the worst threats? If you can't, what would you do? Are there alternative designs among which you could choose? What trade-offs would be involved in selecting one design over another?

Will you be concerned with generality? If so, what restrictive conditions should you be aware of that might limit External Generality? What design considerations might be involved?

Can you examine your problem with an after-the-fact design? What might be the problems of constructing an adequate comparison group? To what rival explanations might such a group be open? Is there any way of reducing their plausibility or eliminating them?

KEY TO ADDITIONAL LEARNING OPPORTUNITIES

1. You will be designing a single-variable study and have many options depending on the availability of participants and your control over the situation. If you are able to bring the students to a laboratory or otherwise rearrange their natural classroom groupings for the purposes of the study, you may be able to assign your participants randomly to each treatment. It is unlikely that you could successfully assign different treatments (with or without the pictures within the diagrams) on a random basis within each classroom, as the students would soon realize the differences and compare materials (the rival explanation of diffusion). If you were able to assign participants randomly (rearrange the classes), the best choice would be the randomized posttest-only control group design, in which the no-pictures group is the control. This would allow you to avoid any testing effect caused by a pretest.

   Most likely, however, you will have to give each treatment to existing, presumably comparable classes. The time required to cover both units might stretch the cooperation of the school authorities, so your design choice would probably be the nonequivalent control group design with two sets of control and experimental groups. For analysis, either combine the oxygen and water data to compare the experimental and control groups or, using analysis of variance, examine differences between both units and treatments. Since this design includes a pretest, you could assign the class with the lower mean to the treatment. But remember, only if the experimental group catches up and outscores the control on the posttest will you have an interpretable result.

2. (a) If the treatment group did score significantly higher, we could point to several rival explanations:

   • selection, since all the pilot study teachers were volunteers;

- reactivity, since the students would likely have been aware of belonging to an experimental group;

- novelty effect, if the approach was substantially different from standard classroom procedure; and

- researcher expectancy effect, if members of the curriculum team or its supporters were involved in the evaluation of the effect.

(b) A significant result in favor of the control group might have resulted from compensatory rivalry, or the John Henry effect. This is more likely if the teachers using the regular program were opposed to the introduction of the new approach. They may well have made an extra effort to demonstrate that the old approach was equally effective or even more effective.

3. We could argue for several rival explanations: a researcher expectancy effect, reactivity (or novelty effect), and, if the other section were superior, the John Henry effect (compensatory rivalry). The instructor could not very well keep the other section leader blind to the treatment, given its obvious inclusion in the course. One way that he could avoid the expectancy and John Henry threats is by gaining the other section instructor's support and involving her in the experiment. This might reduce, though not entirely eliminate, researcher expectancy, since she may not have the same vested interest in the outcome. Gaining her agreement to allow use of the CAI material would also remove the possibility of her trying to improve the standard approach to compete with the CAI.

Eliminating reactivity (or novelty effect) might be more difficult because of the obvious and unusual nature of the treatment, communication between students, and other factors. One possibility is using a placebo (perhaps a CAI program containing topics not examined) so that all students are exposed to CAI in the course and are kept blind to the actual treatment. Lastly, the researcher could use the nonequivalent control group design by using the CAI with all the introductory calculus students one semester and comparing results with past exam results or with those of a future group not exposed to the treatment.

4. The investigators would probably have used a $2 \times 2 \times 2$ factorial design because they tested children of two different age groups (second and fifth grades) on two variables (recall and attending) to determine the effects of two treatments (a film with a male narrator and the same film with a female narrator). Use of analysis of variance would have allowed them to determine the effect of each factor in turn and also the various possible combinations. In actual fact, Klein and colleagues (1987) did report a combination effect: second graders showed a significant difference on attending in favor of the male narrator.

5. She is restricted in her choice of design for several reasons. The most obvious is that her study is actually observational and not truly experimental. That is, it is a "natural experiment" in which she intends to study the "treatment" applied by nature. In effect, the treatment is the disorder of anosognosia acting in concert with unilateral neglect. So rather than apply a treatment, she would need to locate, in sufficient numbers, two groups of neurological patients: one whose members exhibit unilateral neglect only and another whose members have that disorder and anosognosia. If she considers the disorders to be a form of treatment, she could consider one of the experimental designs, the nonequivalent control group design. She could not, of course, apply a pretest, because she cannot identify ahead of time who will develop the disorders. The randomized posttest-only control group design would be the strongest choice, but she could not randomly assign the participants to each group, as they have to suffer from each particular disease. In actuality, she would have to conduct a series of case studies.

Consequently, her study would be subject to a variety of threats to Internal Integrity, the most serious of which are selection, local history, and maturation. The first is important because it might be argued that the participants who volunteered (or whose families agreed to the study) might well differ from those who did not. The second, local history, is a serious threat because the severity of these syndromes varies with such factors as patient stress and fatigue. The third, maturation, is perhaps the biggest threat, as patients do tend to get better. Since the numbers of such patients are small, she may be compelled to assess various participants in different stages of the progress of disease.

She might be able to control for the threats of local history and maturation by using a variation on the time-series design and conducting several assessments of each of the participants throughout their convalescence. The problem of selection, however, may be difficult to avoid, since the numbers of such patients are small, and the researcher may have to accept the patients to whom she can gain access.

6. It was an after-the-fact natural experiment. The investigators were unable to control the variable of interest, which was the possession of baccalaureate nursing training. They were, however, able to select a stratified random sample, which provided them with comparable groups in most respects. They could not, however, control for self-selection. This, since they are arguing for baccalaureate preparation for nurses, is an important rival explanation. Perhaps nurses who complete the higher degree have greater ability (for example, intelligence) or are more strongly motivated. It may be that these characteristics are responsible for the difference in these competencies and would display their effect regardless of education.

Also, to agree with their conclusion, one would have to accept DeBack and Mentkowski's definition of nursing competencies. Does their rationale make sense? Does it support their hypotheses? Though not presented in this summary, the investigators did indeed develop their hypotheses from a theoretical basis and from past research evidence. The operationalization of the hypotheses also appears to be sound since the codebook was developed from the participants' descriptions of effective and ineffective nursing behavior.

SUMMARY

Experimentation produces one of the strongest chains of reasoning for testing a cause-and-effect hypothesis. Design is at the heart of experimentation—development of a plan for data collection and analysis providing the strongest possible chain of reasoning. Random or intentionally complex manipulation of the treatment, which is reproduced in the effect, provides especially strong cause-and-effect linkage. Control is also a hallmark of a strong design. Through control, we provide protection against rival explanations (rival hypotheses, threats to validity) and potential weakeners of Internal Integrity, as well as against restrictive explanations or conditions that reduce generality. Control by removing the effect of unwanted variables increases statistical sensitivity more than control by spreading their effect to both control and experimental groups. The latter is often more feasible, however.

Although each study may have unique rival explanations or restrictive conditions, Campbell and Stanley (1963) and others have formulated a useful set of prevalent ones. Though developed in the context of experimentation, many apply equally well to other research methods. A number of common design configurations have been analyzed for their strengths and weaknesses in protecting against rival hypotheses. When these are not feasible or inadequate, you can use either other designs (described in the additional readings) or create a patched-up design. When the best choice of design does not eliminate possibly important rival explanations, make clear that your choice was intentional and show why it is the best one.

Experimentation runs the range from laboratory to so-called natural experiments where society or nature are the treatment administrators. In between are treatments applied under field conditions. The laboratory approach offers considerable control over problem variables and hence provides evidence with strong Internal Integrity. Field studies and natural experiments seek greater External Generality, possibly at the expense of Internal Integrity.

After-the-fact designs involve the comparison of previously gathered, retrospective, or new data gathered from a target group with groups intentionally formed to be comparable in relevant ways. The intent is to show a relationship, ideally a causal one, between variables present in different amounts in the two groups. Many policy studies regarding the effects of drugs, lifestyles, and educational practices are of this nature. Such studies are subject to a variety of problems, however, because of the limitations of using prior data and the difficulty of eliminating rival explanations.

A Look Ahead

The next chapter shows how the results of multiple quantitative studies—meta-analysis—can be combined to yield a more stable and more definitive finding regarding the phenomena in question.

Notes

[1] I am indebted to Gavriel Solomon for this stark rendition of the problem.

[2] Readers familiar with models of analysis of variance will recognize being "interested in this treatment itself" as parallel to the fixed model. "What it represents" (The Chicago Curriculum) is representative of curricula built from the same rationale as parallel to the random model.

[3] In contrast, Abelson (1997) argues, when starting out in a new area, "avoid messing with flimsy phenomena. . . . [Pursue those] with characteristically large effect sizes (further enhanced by 'sledge-hammer' manipulations). . . . Once . . . confident that large effect sizes can be reliably observed, . . . strip the experimental manipulations to their essentials and repeat. If the phenomenon is robust enough, . . . supportive results will still emerge" (p. 14).

22

Syntheses of Findings—
Meta-Analysis

> Like the artisans who construct a building . . . , scientists contribute to a common edifice called knowledge. Theorists provide the blueprints and researchers collect the data that are the bricks. . . . researchers are the bricklayers and hodcarriers. . . . It is their job to stack the bricks according to plan and apply the mortar that holds the structure together.
>
> —H. Cooper & L. V. Hedges, *Research Synthesis as a Scientific Enterprise*
>
> Meta-analysis has . . . revealed how little information there typically is in any single study. . . . Any individual study must be considered a data point to be contributed to a future meta-analysis.
>
> —F. L. Schmidt,
> *Statistical Significance Testing and Cumulative Knowledge in Psychology*

INTRODUCTION

An implicit assumption of all literature reviews is that rarely is a single study sufficient to provide a definitive and generalizable answer to a question. The pooling of similar research in a literature review is generally perceived as the best way to determine the real state of affairs and its generality. But, since studies are rarely exact replications of previous ones, how can we combine these apples and oranges? Does putting them together make fruit salad? Or garbage?

NARRATIVE LITERATURE SUMMARIES

For years, *narrative literature reviews* have sought to evaluate and integrate the body of research relevant to a question or proposition. Typically, this is strictly a conceptual process resulting in a traditional summary of selected studies from respected journals. A reviewer estimates the contribution of a given study to the synthesis being constructed by weighting such characteristics as centrality to the target phenomenon, sample representativeness and size, tightness of design, control of important moderating conditions such as socioeconomic class, time on task, and validity of instrumentation. Next the reviewer assesses the combined nature and direction of the studies, bearing in mind the appropriate weighting for the above characteristics. Since the human mind can juggle only seven to nine things at a time, this large set of characteristics immediately suggests a very difficult task, further complicated when there are conflicting results. Reviews differ because the reviewers may have found different pools of studies, used various research methods, or were interpreted differently by reviewers who used varied criteria for inclusion and/or analysis. Particularly with conflicting results, this has resulted in a call for more research because there is insufficient evidence for a conclusion—when by meta-analysis, there may have been enough.

META-ANALYSIS

Meta-analysis gained attention when Glass (1976) showed how to average results after conversion to a standard metric called effect size and coined the term **meta-analysis.** Attention was particularly brought to it when Smith and Glass's (1977) meta-analysis decisively showed positive results for psychotherapy, a conclusion that researchers had unconvincingly sought since clinical psychology began—what is the effectiveness of "just talking about a problem" with a trained therapist?

And where narrative reviews so often showed inconclusive results, Lipsey and Wilson (1993), on examining meta-analyses of psychological, educational, and behavioral interventions, found the results overwhelmingly positive. Only 6 of 302 meta-analytic studies showed negative results! Furthermore, 85% found treatment strengths such that 55% of the treated group would exceed their untreated or placebo-treated controls.

> The aim of meta-analysis . . . [has been] to discipline research synthesis by the same methodological standards that apply to primary research. . . . Reviews should be just as replicable as any other piece of scientific work. . . . Disagreements among the experts should become more a matter of method than opinion. (Wanner, 1995, p. vii)

The latter expectation has not been realized, however. Just as researchers may differ about how a study is best done, especially what various trade-offs should be made and how resources are best employed, so meta-analyses require considerable judgment—what studies to include, how best to organize them, how best to weight them, and so on.

The Methods of Meta-Analysis

All methods of meta-analysis start with an exact enough definition of the phenomenon to be studied so that the body of literature pertaining to it can be located. With the methods described in chapter 6, a search is conducted that is as complete as is feasible, including unpublished federal research reports, convention papers, and dissertations, as well as published sources. We often find that the phenomenon of interest is confounded with other variables, and we must broaden our search to include these. Next we must decide whether to use all the studies or some select group of them. (Glass [1976], for example, discarded those without control groups.) Then we must decide how we will synthesize results. Whatever the method, we must translate the results into a common "currency." Votes, effect sizes, and correlations are the most common. With the latter two, just as we would with any data set, we must make a distribution and see if it fits our expectations. *Outliers*, or deviations from the normal bell-shaped curve, usually suggest the influence of one or more variables additional to the study's focus. It is worth examining the aberrations to see what they are and how they relate to what we are studying.

Glass (1976) proposed that effects measured by different operational definitions of the same construct could be compared if results were translated into a standard-score-like form. These are called **effect sizes**. Basically, effect sizes are measures of treatment effects in a common measure. Routinely used to compare different test results, standard scores remove the contexts of raw scores—the number correct on measure A, or the number of statements chosen as self-descriptive on measure B—by dividing them by each measure's standard deviation. Standard scores, and therefore also effect sizes, can be expressed in standard deviation units. Correlations from various studies may also be translated to a linear metric, averaged, and translated back to a correlation as the combined effect size. With certain assumptions, effect sizes can be translated from standard deviation form to correlations and vice versa.

With results from an experiment, it is the score difference between two means, usually the means of the experimental and control groups, that is divided by a standard deviation—but what standard deviation? Glass suggested using either the standard deviation of the control group or an estimate of the population's standard deviation derived from the pooled standard deviations of the samples. The latter are presumed to be uncontaminated by treatment. Given that the effect sizes collected in a study are random samples of a population of effect sizes, their mean estimates the true size of treatment effect.

For example, Smith, Glass, and Miller (1980)—seeking the mean effect size of psychotherapy—found that more than 1,000 studies had been done to convince skeptics. They selected for intensive analysis the 375 studies that had both an untreated and a treated group, even though some were weak designs. These yielded 833 effect sizes from more than 25,000 subjects. Eighty-eight percent of the effect sizes were positive. Although only 12% were negative, fully half would have been negative had there been no effect!

An average effect size of 1 would indicate that the average treated person's score exceeded that of an untreated person by one standard deviation. The average effect size over all measures of psychotherapy improvement was .67. What is considered a strong or a weak effect seems relative to the field. Effects of 1 are considered strong in the behavioral sciences; effects of .3 or below, weak. By assuming the sample effect sizes are normally distributed we can translate a gain into percentiles. For example, the average client in the psychotherapy treated group was about two-thirds of a standard deviation better off than the average person in the untreated control—that is, better off than the person at the 75th percentile in that group. Expressing gains in percentiles puts synthesized results into more understandable terms. Effect sizes are also frequently expressed as correlations or Cohen's *d* (small .2–.3, large .8–1.0).

Meta-analysis gives a different perspective on a mixture of negative, not statistically significant, and positive results. From that perspective one realizes that, by chance, half the results will fall above and half below the mean, which is the true population effect size. If that mean is not far from zero, the effect size distribution will include negative and no-effect findings as a matter of course. Therefore, such a mixture of results simply indicates a weak relationship rather than none. Negative effect sizes seem devastating to narrative reviewers; the subjective feeling is: "any is too many." The latter is what a narrative reviewer who did not give consideration to this meta-analytic expectation might be inclined to conclude.

We can determine the dependence of the effect on various factors by categorizing studies in terms of study conditions. For instance, Smith and Glass (1977), coding the studies on overall quality, found no difference in effect size between stronger or weaker studies. This has not always proven true, however; stronger designs often yield larger effects.

Rosenthal (1994) asked whether our expectations are too high in the social sciences. He cites a study of the effects of aspirin in reducing heart attacks that was prematurely ended because "it had become so clear that aspirin prevented heart attacks . . . that it would be unethical to continue to give half the . . . subjects a placebo" (p. 242). What was the magnitude of this dramatic finding, he asks? Was it correlations in the .60s, .70s, or .80s? No, the correlation was .034 and would be considered insignificant in a social science study! However, Rosenthal notes even that low a correlation reflected a 4% decrease in heart attacks. Granted, because life-and-death issues are involved, the stakes are higher. Still, it makes one reconsider whether we are presenting our findings in an appropriately compelling way.

▶ Each study yields one or more estimates of a population effect size.

▶ Just as standard scores translate the scores for an individual from different measures into a common scale, so translation of findings on measures of a construct into effect sizes converts them into a standard scale so they may be meaningfully combined into an average effect size.

▶ We find an effect size by dividing the difference between experimental and control group means by the population standard deviation estimated from the pooled sample standard deviations, or by the standard deviation of the control group. We can also average correlation coefficients to obtain an effect size. Effect sizes in standard deviation form can be translated into correlations and vice versa.

▶ Meta-analyses average effect sizes across studies to get a better population estimate. To more easily understand the effect of treatment, we can assume the effect sizes are normally distributed and translate them into percentiles of the untreated group.

▶ A mixture of weak negative, no-effect, and positive effect sizes for a phenomenon indicates a weak relationship rather than no relationship.

▶ Meta-analysis has evolved as a new research method. As subsets of data provide estimates of effect sizes under contrasting conditions, we are able to determine whether a phenomenon is strengthened or weakened by certain conditions. With enough data, we can map the nature of that relationship.

The Difference in Sensitivity between Narrative Literature Reviews and Meta-Analyses

Research findings can be summarized either narratively or quantitatively, as in meta-analyses. Early on, Cooper and Rosenthal (1980) demonstrated a major advantage of quantitative literature summaries by showing they are more likely than narrative ones to yield a clear-cut answer. They gave seven studies supporting the same hypothesis to 41 judges who were randomly assigned to prepare either meta-analytic or narrative analyses. Judges were asked to determine whether the studies upheld the proposition. More than twice as many of the narrative reviewers (73%) as meta-analytic reviewers (32%) found "probably or definitely" no support for the proposition. In commenting on the study, Glass, McGaw, and Smith (1981) note: "The entire set of studies occupied . . . fewer than 56 journal pages. One can imagine how much more pronounced would be the difference between these two approaches with bodies of literature typical of the size that are increasingly being addressed with meta-analytic techniques" (p. 17).

> ▶ Reviewers using meta-analytic procedures are more likely than narrative literature reviewers to give clear-cut answers regarding the existence of a relationship.

The conceptual difficulty of balancing so many factors in narrative syntheses may be part of the reason for the difference in conclusivity of results, but there are others:

The tendency to vote-count.   This means tabulating study results as positive if statistically significant, and negative if not. Hedges and Olkin (1985) showed that vote-counting procedures, especially with small samples, are very likely to miss small effect sizes.

Near misses don't count.   A study's result may align with the hypothesis but, because of insufficient statistical power, may not be statistically significant. Although several such near-misses may seem more than happenstance, by widely accepted statistical logic near-misses do not count. However, combining such studies in a meta-analysis yields statistical power greater than any one study and may show statistical significance whereas the individual studies did not.

Hard to judge the effect of moderating variables.   From a single study, it is hard to judge the effect of moderating variables such as personal attributes, characteristics of the context, and the way the study was done. Combining results of studies can help us to target the effect of moderating variables and find the specific set of circumstances under which an intervention can be most effective.

Advantages of Meta-Analytic Reviews

In addition to the advantages implicit in the preceding material, meta-analytic reviews can yield information unlikely to be found in narrative reviews such as:

Showing the shape of the relationship.   For instance, Glass and Smith (1979) and Glass, McGaw, and Smith (1981) plotted class size against achievement. They found that achievement increases only very slightly from huge classes sizes to those in the low teens, and then accelerates rapidly for class sizes below ten to a maximum with size one—tutoring. By plotting the effect sizes against class size, they provided a much clearer idea of the nature of the relationship than could be derived from a narrative review that does not turn results into effect sizes.

Plotting the variables coded in doing the literature review often turns up interesting findings. For instance, coding for quality in the above-noted class size and achievement study showed that small sample studies with stronger designs yielded larger effect sizes than did comparably sized studies with weaker designs.

Extracting construct effect through the multimethod multimeasures technique. As Hall, Rosenthal, Tickle-Degnen, and Mosteller (1994) point out, combining multiple operationalizations of variables extracts the essence of a construct, giving the effect size greater construct validity than does any single study: "For example, to learn about the construct 'anxiety,' we may use a self-report anxiety scale, a coding of observed anxiety behavior, or electrodermal skin response. Through aggregation, meta-analysis extracts the essential anxiety effect, while sloughing off residuals due to instrumentation factors" (p. 20).

Extracting generality. Meta-analytic techniques are "ideal . . . for confidently answering a question about the generality of an effect . . . [since they provide] empirical assessment . . . to an extent rarely available to a single primary study" (ibid., p. 20). The reviewer must still judgmentally assess whether the populations of subjects, situations, and procedures involved in the combined result are adequately representative for the intended generality. But the effect size indicates the generality over whatever groups were studied.

Identifying the critical features in implementation. Light (1984) notes research syntheses can explain which features of a treatment are critical. For example, Raudenbusch (1984), examining 18 studies of expectancy effect, found only a small effect overall (.11). However, by comparing studies having a strong expectancy effect with those having a weak one, he discovered an important finding: Teachers who met their children after they were given information creating the expectancy showed a strong effect. Those who met the children first showed almost none. Unless a researcher entered a study with this hypothesis, it is unlikely that it would have been determined from a single study. In the same way, by using syntheses researchers can demonstrate the robustness of treatment across sites and sometimes explain conflicting results.

Suggesting a research strategy. Designing a series of studies to explore and understand a phenomenon is a strategy. Glass saw a strength of meta-analysis as the synthesis of studies using different methods in which the strengths of one made up for the weaknesses of another—like a combination of fishnets where the rips and tears of one are covered by another (Guba & Lincoln, 1985). Extending this, Shadish (1993) suggests that we should use *critical multiplism*, different research patterns to design a series of studies so as to achieve this mutually reinforcing result. Certainly, after completing a meta-analysis, a researcher is in an excellent position to suggest a strategy for future studies such as Shadish recommends.

For all these reasons and more, meta-analyses now appear in a wide range of disciplines: business, meteorology, all the social sciences, and especially in medicine.

> ▶ Meta-analysis may be able to extract positive findings from statistically underpowered studies and studies with weak designs.
>
> ▶ From meta-analysis data researchers can determine the shape and nature of a relationship.
>
> ▶ Similarly, researchers can find the critical features in implementation.
>
> ▶ Researchers can also find the best strategy for designing future studies of a phenomenon.

EVIDENCE-BASED PRACTICE MOVEMENTS

The capacity of meta-analysis to digest a series of studies of treatments and determine not only whether they were effective, but also which had the largest effect sizes, attracted attention in professional fields of practice, especially health care. This has had four results:

1. The establishment of organizations—the Cochrane and Campbell Collaborations—devoted to the application of the finest of meta-analytic practices to their fields to find the best evidence-based practices.

2. The development of libraries consisting of meta-analyses that have been reviewed by peers and an editorial team before acceptance into the library.

3. The continued development of meta-analytic methods and the rapid integration of new developments into a semistandard method (semistandard because there is still much room for good judgment in doing a review).

4. The development of a body of professionals familiar with meta-analysis.

The Cochrane Collaboration

The Cochrane Collaboration, founded in 1993, is an international nonprofit independent organization. Its meta-analytic reviews of health-care practices are prepared by "mostly health-care professionals who volunteer to work in one of the many Cochrane Review Groups, with editorial teams overseeing the preparation and maintenance of the reviews, as well as application of the rigorous quality standards" (ibid). The result has been the establishment of evidence-based practices that have been adopted as standards for their fields. To guide their reviewers, their self-instructional *Cochrane Handbook for Systematic Reviews of Interventions* is continually revised with new developments in meta-analytic methods. This valuable resource is openly available online at http://www.cochrane.org/resources/handbook/index.htm.

The Campbell Collaboration

Founded in 1999, the Campbell Collaboration was set up on the model of the Cochrane Collaboration to provide a library of reviews in the social, behavioral, and education areas, giving priority to education, social welfare, and crime and justice. Equally valuable are its reviewer's guidelines, available online (http:// www.campbellcollaboration.org/systematic_reviews/index.php). The site lists the steps in conducting a Campbell review.

JUDGMENTS REQUIRED BY META-ANALYSES

As has been noted throughout this chapter, although there once was hope that judgment could be eliminated from meta-analysis, this is clearly impossible. Good judgment is required at nearly every step in the meta-analytic process. Recounted below are some of the common problems reviewers face and how they are operationally resolved.

Determining the Pool of Studies

Determining the pool of studies on which a meta-analysis is based is a critical judgment in the process. As indicated in the description of the method at this chapter's beginning, a thorough search of the literature using chapter 6's suggestions is a first step. Different selection criteria will likely lead to different results. Confining the search to published materials probably inflates effect size, since published studies have more positive and larger effects than unpublished—what Rosenthal (1979) called the "file-drawer effect." (Rosenthal assumes that researchers have file drawers bulging with studies showing null results that, therefore deemed unpublishable, were never submitted.) Including unpublished research reports or dissertations corrects this. Rosenthal (1979) provides a way of estimating a "fail-safe n"—how many "file-drawer studies" would be required to nullify the effect found. An implausibly large number suggests that publication bias is not serious. Hedges and Vevea (1996a) developed a correction for such bias that is included in some software (e.g., SPSS).

Broadening the inclusion rules may be important if the target to which we plan to generalize is not well represented by the studies we initially chose. For example, selecting only sites where the treatment was well implemented may be closer to a purposive than a representative sample, as Crain (1984), for example, showed. He found that studies selected by the National Institute of Education to evaluate the effectiveness of school desegregation differed in important ways from typical practice.

Often the search finds that the phenomenon of interest is confounded with other variables and we must broaden our search to include these. For example, in a meta-analysis of whole versus part learning of psychomotor skills, LaMura (1987) had to develop a system for classifying the studies in terms of what pattern of whole and part learning was used. Using W for practicing the whole skill, P1 to designate the first part practiced, P2 for the second and so forth, she could describe the variety of possible patterns and classify the studies. One pattern might begin with practicing the whole, concentrating on a part, returning to the whole, and similarly proceeding through all the parts (WP1W, WP2W...). Alternatively one might add successive parts: (P1), (P1 + P2), (P1 + P2 + P3) until W is reached.

However, examination of the literature showed that these variations of treatment were administered under conditions of massed practice (all at one learning session), or distributed practice (distributed over several sessions), or both. Thus, a second variable was introduced, and studies had to be sorted into all the possible combinations of whole-versus-part learning variations with massed versus distributed practice. Developing such an organizational structure from a review of the literature is one of the most important tasks of the meta-analyst. The structure facilitates understanding the field, points to the existence and effect of moderating variables, and also shows where research has and has not been done and hence where new research is most needed.

Still another factor to consider in evaluating the adequacy of the pool of studies is whether the methods being used to study the phenomena of interest are beyond those that meta-analysts can handle. As Kennedy (2007) points out, the technical capacity of meta-analysis lags behind that of researchers. Studies using structural equation modeling and other complex statistics and designs may have to be excluded from the meta-analysis pool, thus introducing a methods bias (but they may be interpreted separately as part of a literature synthesis as did Cooper, Robinson, and Patall, in their 2006 meta-analysis of homework and achievement).

Depending on the intent and audience of the study, one must decide whether to use all the studies, or some select group of them. Smith, Glass, and Miller's (1980) meta-analysis of psychotherapy, for example, selected from over a thousand studies only those with a treated and untreated group, because those would likely present the most convincing argument.

Correcting for Sample Size

In general, we would expect larger samples to yield estimates closer to the population value than small studies. Therefore, when a small sample effect is given equal weight in an average with the results from large samples, another question arises. Weighting the samples by the inverse of their variance gives more weight to large samples and is done by some software (e.g., SPSS). Hedges and Olkin (1985) provide a correction for the bias of small samples. Hunter and Schmidt's meta-analysis (2004) weights studies in relation to sample size, more being given to larger samples, and excludes outlier studies. Be sure to report the latter.

Correcting for the Unreliability of Measures

It seems reasonable that reliable measures would give better estimates of a relationship than unreliable ones. In their psychometric meta-analysis, Hunter and Schmidt (2004) use the correction for attenuation (see p. 431) to correct for the unreliability of both the cause and effect measures.

Correcting for Multiple Effect Sizes in the Same Study

Many studies use more than one measure of the constructs of interest; each is translated into an effect size. When these estimates are combined with others to estimate the population average, because those studies' errors are multiply represented, the estimate is not composed of independent appraisals. For example, were the Zimbardo study in chapter 1 used in a meta-analysis, it would yield three effect sizes since there were three measures of paranoia. Flaws in the Zimbardo design would therefore be represented three times in a meta-analysis.

Four common ways of handling this are:

1. Choose one of the effect measures to represent the study. For example, a curriculum had three positive effects: achievement, attitudinal, and study skills. We could choose one of these, probably achievement, to represent the study. This throws away useful information. Alternatively, we could show the effect of multiple measures by displaying the results with and without them.

2. Average all its effect sizes to get a single estimate for that study. This can conceal the nature of the measures making up the average.

3. Weight each measure inversely by the number of measures in the study ($1/n$, where n is the number of measures in a study). Each of the three measures in the Zimbardo study would be weighted .333. This gives the study the same weight as the previous method but reveals the nature of the variables in the study.

4. Group studies by those measuring the same kind of effect and analyze such groups separately—for example, achievement, attitude, study skills. This reveals which aspect is contributing most to the overall result.

The last example is the most common way of solving the apples-and-oranges problem. Suppose, using measures of changes in attitude with changes in skills, we find that the effect of psychotherapy is moderated by the kind of effect we are measuring. Should we report each separately or give a combined effect size? Is there a single best measure of psychotherapy—or any other intervention? These are all judgmental issues that the researcher must decide and then inform the audience of the rationale for the decision.

Correcting for Study Quality

It seems reasonable that high-quality studies are more likely to provide a better estimate than those of low quality, when quality includes such things as treatment implementation as well as a design that eliminates rival explanations. Coding the studies for quality on a 3- or 5-point scale is fairly common. Correlating the codes with effect size indicates the extent to which study quality is contributing to a better estimate, and we can weight the studies accordingly.

Cordray (1993), however, notes that in selecting quality studies, one often confounds quality of treatment implementation with quality of the research. He constructs a fourfold table of the intersections of well and poorly implemented interventions with strong and weak studies, noting that only well-implemented interventions in strong studies are usually selected for meta-analysis. However, this method limits generality and discards important information. Contrasting strong studies of well-implemented interventions with strong studies having poorly implemented interventions, he notes, "might reveal why program implementation is weak, and corrective actions could be proposed" (p. 83). It may also provide information about the dose-response relationship and the added value of increasing the strength of the intervention. Most important is how "*out-puts*, or *benefits*, or *effect sizes* vary from one set of circumstances to another . . . [since the meta-analyst] rarely works on a collection of data that can sensibly be described as a probability sample from anything" (Glass, 1995, p. 738, emphasis in the original).

Determining Whether the Phenomenon Has the Same Effect over All the Studies

If the phenomenon being studied has the same effect over all the studies, we would anticipate that the effect sizes of the studies would be distributed approximately as a normal curve with a variance no greater than would be expected due to random sampling. Hedges (1982) and Rosenthal and Rubin (1982) worked out statistical tests for the homogeneity of effect sizes so as to determine whether the data are estimating a single value—one population measure. If one plots the 95% confidence interval of the effect sizes, the intervals nearly all overlap a common value. Such a plot, referred to as a *forest plot*, is shown in Figure 22.1. Each row is one of 7 studies labeled A–G. On each row, the line running between the vertical crossties depicts the 95% confidence interval of that study's effect size as shown on the scale at the bottom. The effect size is at the center of the box. The size of the box is proportional to the study's weighted contribution to the overall effect size. The vertical line running through the studies indicates the weighted average of the effect sizes, which is .38. Since all of the confidence intervals are intersected by the weighted average, the estimates are homogeneous and differ no more than would be expected by random sampling variation. Presumably they are samples from a single homogeneous population of measures of the phenomenon being meta-analyzed.

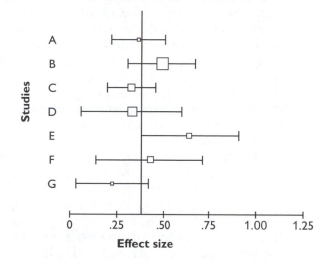

Figure 22.1   A forest plot in which each row represents a study.

Outliers, or deviations from the normal bell-shaped curve, usually suggest the influence of one or more variables additional to the study's focus. Since outliers can dramatically affect averages, deciding how to handle them is important. It is worth examining the aberrations to see what they are, how they relate to what we are studying, and what reasonable basis there is for excluding or including them from the pool.

Extracting the Phenomenon When It Doesn't Have the Same Effect over All the Studies: Fixed vs. Random Effect Analysis

Ideally, if studies were replications of one another, instead of using the study as the unit, we could pool individual subjects into one giant definitive study with a huge number of cases. The source of variability would be the individual differences of the participants. However, studies are not replications, application of treatments differ, treatment dose varies, and so on. The variability in the results is often so great that the results are clearly the consequence not only of the treatment variable but also of variations in method, instruments, and other factors. Therefore, we can only approximate data pooling. To researchers with a background in analysis of variance (ANOVA), this broad variability suggested the parallel to fixed and random-effects analysis of variance—using fixed-effects ANOVA for pools with homogeneity of effect sizes, and random-effects ANOVA for heterogeneous ones (Hedges & Vevea, 1996b).

For heterogeneous pools, after determining the effects of the various sources of variance, one could subtract each of them from the total variance so that what remains is more clearly the effect of the independent variable of interest. This involves partitioning the variance into subgroups on some reasonable basis (by type of outcome measure, by treatment variation, by research quality, etc.) and subtracting it until one could show that what remains is homogeneous.

Hunter and Schmidt (2004) argue that the purpose of meta-analysis is not just to summarize the relation between variables in the available studies, but also to estimate "the construct-level relationships in the population . . . because these are the relationships of scientific interest" (p. 512). Therefore, in their psychometric meta-analysis they correct for all the artifacts potentially related to the phenomenon under study—for instance, coding the studies for a variety of characteristics (by type of outcome measure, by treatment variation, gender, etc.) and noting any study artifacts that might systematically affect the pool of results (e.g., artificial dichotomization of continuous variables or restriction in range). A partition may be suggested by an outlier study; what caused it to be an outlier may mediate the effect in less extreme ways in other studies as well.

Hunter and Schmidt suggest ways of correcting for these artifacts and for unreliability in the measures in both the cause and effect variables. They then correlate each of the study-characteristic codings with the reliability-corrected effect sizes. The correlations show whether there are relationships between these coded variables and a measure of the effects. Further, the square of each correlation indicates relatively how much each coded variable explains the effect measure's variance. They highlight the presumed causal relationships between these study characteristics and effect. Although many assumptions are involved, this method is an attempt to find potential inaccuracies in the estimates and to make allowances for them. For the method to be explanatory, however, substantive theory has to guide both the selection and grouping of the variables to be coded and the manner in which they are employed in the analysis. Otherwise, exploration may lead to treating chance relationships as real ones.

Most meta-analyses analyze the data as both fixed and random effects and present both results (which are the same if the data are homogenous). Software is available for translating study data into effect sizes (e.g., Borenstein & Rothstein, 1999) and for doing fixed and random-effect analyses (e.g., as a macro for SPSS, Lipsey & Wilson, 2001). Hunter, Oh, and Hayes's study (2007) suggests that the confidence intervals for most fixed-effects analyses overstate the study's precision. Indeed, Schmidt (2008) agrees, further arguing that fixed-effects meta-analyses are rarely justified; random-effects models give more accurate estimates.

BEST–EVIDENCE SYNTHESIS

Despite the fact that meta-analyses require many judgments, as do narrative reviews, meta-analytic techniques are here to stay. Combining them with traditional judgmental qualifications about the strengths and weaknesses of the studies, and their influence on the composite results, is probably the most reasonable course to follow. Slavin (1986, 1987) has argued for **best-evidence synthesis**, a combination of judgmental and meta-analytic methods. In the same vein, Light and Pillemer (1984) is still an excellent analysis of problems in both narrative and quantitative reviews. Of interest along these lines is the Iterative Best Evidence Synthesis of the Ministry of Education of New Zealand. It considers all kinds of evidence "rather than just

Hallmarks of Meta-Analytic Studies and Tips for Doing Them

A good meta-analytic study should meet the following guidelines:

1. Describe the search pattern used to find studies as well as the criteria for selecting from these.

2. Either enter each study in the meta-analysis only once or, alternatively, show the effect size with and without multiple measures from the same sample.

3. Develop a reasonable framework for organizing the studies into homogeneous groups around the variables likely to moderate phenomena in that domain.

4. Indicate the basis of organization of the studies and how they were selected and coded.

5. Where multiple judges are used in categorizing or classifying studies or their characteristics, indicate the extent of their agreement.

6. Estimate average effect size from the best studies as well as from the total composite.

7. Compare the composite effect sizes of published studies with unpublished ones such as dissertations and convention papers.

8. Examine the distribution of effect sizes: look for outliers or deviations from the expected bell-shaped curve, and seek their explanation by examining the apparently aberrant studies.

9. Check for homogeneity of effect sizes. If not homogeneous, do a random analysis of variance of the data, subtracting the effect of coded characteristics to get a better measure of the phenomenon and of error. Consider doing both fixed and random analysis of variance.

10. Discuss any interesting results or side effects discerned in borderline studies that just missed being included in the set analyzed because of the definition of the variables.

11. Evaluate judgmentally the adequacy of the kinds of studies included. This is especially important if all research in the area is weak, or if weak studies predominate.

12. Indicate where there are inadequate studies for the analysis and where more research is needed.

13. In an appendix, list the studies, their sample sizes, and the effect sizes they contribute (if not published it should be available on request).

bringing in an elite group to make decisions and push them downward. They are actively getting input from all sorts of stakeholders and seeking to negotiate as broad a consensus as possible" (Jere Brophy in New Zealand Ministry of Education, 2004).

ADDITIONAL READING

Glass, McGaw, and Smith (1981) is one of the earliest treatments; it gets across the basic ideas without the complexities of later discussions. For a recounting of the development of meta-analysis by one of its inventors as well as a look into a future of data synthesis, see Glass (2000). Hedges and Olkin (1985) requires statistical knowledge to appreciate what they accomplished. Hunter and Schmidt (2004) is one of the most readable accounts. See Lipsey and Wilson (2001) besides the material made available by the Cochrane and Campbell Collaborations referred to in the chapter. Regarding meta-analysis as a research method in its own right, see Shadish (1996). For a well-done example that combines meta-analysis and narrative, see Cooper, Nye, Charlton, Lindsay, and Greathouse (1996). Meta-analyses of research on a topic are typically published in journals covering that topic; those of general interest may be found in the *Review of Educational Research* and *Psychological Bulletin.*

IMPORTANT TERMS AND CONCEPTS

best-evidence synthesis   effect size   meta-analysis

OPPORTUNITY FOR ADDITIONAL LEARNING

Dave Cummings decides to repeat the meta-analysis of Cooper, Robinson, and Patall (2006) regarding the effect of homework on academic achievement—see Cooper (2006). Without having read that study, what things would you advise Mr. Cummings to scrutinize in the study before beginning his?

Compare your answer with that following the Application Exercise.

APPLICATION EXERCISE

Have enough studies been done on some aspect of your study to mount a meta-analysis? If so, how might the results from such an analysis help in the reformulation of your problem? For what moderating variables would it be desirable to code the studies? Quality? Which form might such a meta-analysis take? Vote count? Average all the effect sizes found in the studies? Average in subgroups?

KEY TO ADDITIONAL LEARNING OPPORTUNITY

With this little information about the Cooper study, one can only imagine places where individuals might differ in doing a meta-analysis, see which choice was made, and whether it makes sense in the context of the study. Here is a beginning list:

1. Some of the biggest differences in how researchers would tackle this problem might lie in the pool of studies chosen in answer to two key questions:

   • What was the definition of homework? What was assigned? What was the measure of compliance? Amount of time reported by students, parents? Kind of homework assigned?

- What was the definition of academic achievement? Teachers' grades? Tests? How did they get a standard measure across schools?

2. If academic achievement was measured by tests, were correlations corrected for their unreliability (correction for attenuation—see addendum to chapter 18)?

3. How was the size of study taken into account?

4. For what moderating variables were the studies coded? Amount of homework? Kind of homework—memorization versus problem solving? Quality?

5. Were tests for homogeneity made? Should random ANOVA have been used? Or both fixed and random?

SUMMARY

Meta-analysis combines the quantitative results of studies of a relationship to produce an overall estimate of its size. It provides a perspective on mixtures of positive, zero, and negative effect sizes. The latter two are difficult for narrative reviewers to handle. However, they must be expected in pools of studies involving weak treatments, since they are simply the low end in a distribution of effect sizes. Providing a logical framework within which the studies can be analyzed throws light on the important variables and their interrelationships; it is conducive to theory and model building. Meta-analysis can show the moderating effect of variables, of research methods, and of measures, in addition to estimating the overall treatment effect and its shape in relation to treatment strength (dose-response). It is one of the most important advances in integrating findings and unifying a fragmented field of research results. It may be most effective when combined with qualitative research reviews in a best-evidence synthesis.

A Look Ahead

Having explored research methods that deal with the quantitative approach, we turn to areas where a mixture of methods borrows from both qualitative and quantitative approaches and adds to them as appropriate to devise the best study possible. We turn first to evaluation and action research as an example of such research.

section VI

The Continuum of Research Methods
The Qualitative/ Quantitative Middle

The differentiation between qualitatively oriented and quantitatively oriented research tools is easily exaggerated. In fact they are often used complementarily. Indeed, where applicable, the strongest studies borrow the most appropriate aspects of all methods to present their case, as is described in chapter 26 of this section. The other chapters describe areas of research that use whatever is the best fit—one, the other, or both.

- Chapter 23 describes evaluation and action research. In the latter, the researcher is both the doer and the prime audience. Both formative and summative evaluation are discussed, and particularly the conditions under which evaluations are likely to be applied, including stakeholder participation.

- Chapter 24 discusses sample surveys and questionnaires—from the building of instruments, through the gathering of data by face-to-face interviews, telephone interviews, mail surveys, and Internet and e-mail surveys to the coding, analysis, and reporting of the results.

- Chapter 25 describes historical research and how Internal Integrity and External Generality relate to it.

- Chapter 26 examines the advantages of using multiple and mixed-method approaches to a problem. This chapter reinforces their complementarities and notes the ever-present trade-offs in both method and design choices.

535

23

Evaluation Studies and Action Research

> Conceptualizing an evaluation depends on understanding self-interest: yours and theirs. Useful evaluations put theirs first.
> —M. Q. Patton, *Qualitative Evaluation Methods*
>
> Evaluative investigation is an art. The design must be chosen afresh in each new undertaking and the choices to be made are almost innumerable. Each feature . . . offers particular advantages and entails particular sacrifices.
> —L. J. Cronbach, *Designing Evaluations of Educational and Social Programs*

INTRODUCTION[1]

Evaluations provide evidence of the worth of something for decision making, such as how to improve something, how to maintain quality control, which is the best alternative, or which policy to pursue (i.e., discontinue, continue, add resources, or disseminate). In contrast with research, evaluations are said to be *decision-driven*, meaning that each successive step of the evaluation process is aimed at providing the best possible decision-relevant information. Because policy choices are nearly always made on the basis of incomplete information, an evaluation's information-rich decision-making environment is helpful in reducing that uncertainty.

Evaluators use all the methods of the social sciences—quantitative, qualitative, survey, whatever is most appropriate given the requirements of the task at hand. However, some evaluators, because of their special skills or epistemological beliefs (see chapter 12), give preference to certain methods.

Utilization of the evaluation's findings in decision making is the mark of success. Because utilization requires trust in the results, if the evaluation's audience is to have faith in the product of the evaluation, they must have faith in the process that produced it. The knowledge anyone trusts most is that which grows out of their own experiences (see p. 46). The greater involvement one has in the evaluation, the greater one's personal identification with the evaluation findings and the more likely one is to accept and use them. As a result, considerable attention has been given to involvement of persons with a stake in the evaluation's outcome. The process of conducting the evaluation becomes as important as its product. Action researchers solve this problem, since those who will use the findings—themselves—conduct the evaluation entirely or in large part. (As used in sociology, the term **action research** usually refers to research undertaken to bring about social change.)

EXAMPLES OF EVALUATION

Just as the examples of meta-analyses considered in the previous chapter come from the full range of social, educational, psychological, and economic problems, so do evaluations. In fact many meta-analyses intended to find best practices—for example, those in the fields of health and education—are syntheses of evaluations. See for instance, the library of reviews of the Campbell Collaboration (http://www.campbellcollaboration.org/campbell_library/index.php). Some program evaluations have had an important impact on policy, such as the evaluation of the Perry Preschool Program, which showed the effectiveness of preschool programs such as Head Start when they were carefully developed. Its evaluation extended longitudinally, following the students to age 19 (Berrueta-Clement, Barnett, & Weikart, 1985).

> ▶ Evaluation studies are used to improve a product, policy, or program and/or determine its value or worth.

THREE BASIC QUESTIONS

There has been much discussion on the evaluation scene as to who and what is properly the primary focus of evaluation. Much like the blind men who each characterized the whole elephant by the part they happened to touch, so individuals have characterized evaluation by emphasizing particular aspects. For example, there is goal-directed evaluation (Madaus & Stufflebeam, 1989; Tyler & Waples, 1930); goal-free evaluation (Scriven, 1972); connoisseurial evaluation (Eisner, 1976, 1981); adversarial evaluation (Wolf, 1975, 1979); management-oriented evaluation (Stufflebeam & Shinkfield, 1985); consumer-oriented evaluation (Scriven, 1967, 2007); objectives-oriented evaluation (Tyler et al., 1976); and responsive-naturalistic evaluation (Stake, 1975). They each have a point, their arguments are worth considering, and this chapter could be structured to good advantage around a discussion of these different points of view. Indeed, this chapter in the first and second editions of this book was so structured. But viewed in retrospect, it seems better to take a step back and ask what are the basic questions that underlie every evaluation and, for that matter, lie behind the points of view undertaken by these experienced evaluators. It turns out that there are three basic questions (see Figure 23.1).

Figure 23.1   The basic questions that underlie evaluation.

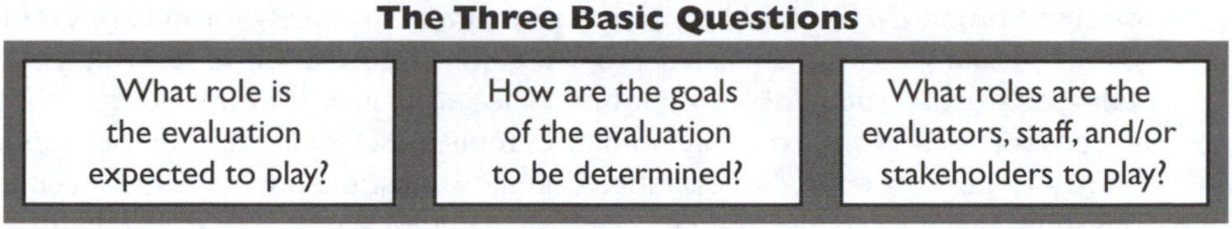

The Three Basic Questions

What role is the evaluation expected to play?	How are the goals of the evaluation to be determined?	What roles are the evaluators, staff, and/or stakeholders to play?

Each of these, in turn, spawns a series of subquestions. For some of us who are visually minded, it may help to visualize the subquestions that arise for each of the three in its own two-dimensional space. The choice made in each of these spaces guides respectively what evidence is to be gathered, for what purpose, and who does it. But in gathering data, evaluators may choose among many different research methods—quantitative, qualitative, experiment, survey, and so on. These in turn determine what analyses are appropriate, and what can be reported and disseminated. The perceptions of the situation of those involved and their preferences are important factors in determining which alternatives are chosen. A variety of "right" answers is possible. And of course, new ones may replace the original choices when unseen factors are encountered as the evaluation proceeds.

What questions arise in each of these three arenas? In order to make them clear, each arena is next discussed in detail, and a series of examples further helps to show how the answers to these three questions can be used to plan an evaluation.

THE ROLE OF THE EVALUATION

Two decisions are considered in this arena: how the evaluation findings are intended to be used, and who has access to the results. Figure 23.2 details the role-of-the-evaluation decisions and the choices available in terms of the intended use of the evaluation's results and access to the evaluation's findings. The circled number 1 indicates the location in the figure of the text's illustrative evaluation.

Figure 23.2   The role the evaluation is to play.

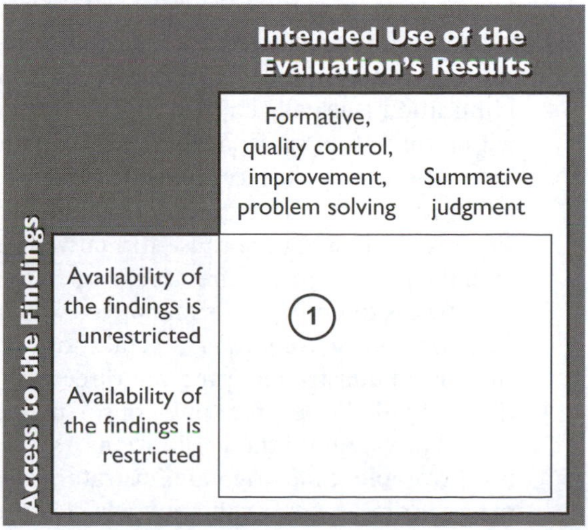

	Intended Use of the Evaluation's Results	
	Formative, quality control, improvement, problem solving	Summative judgment
Availability of the findings is unrestricted	①	
Availability of the findings is restricted		

Access to the Findings

Intended Use of the Results

Some evaluations, especially those done early in the developmental process, are oriented primarily toward improving a program or product—**formative evaluation**. Others, usually of an established project, gather information to help determine its value or worth—**summative evaluation**. The latter may be for resource allocation purposes (discontinue, continue, enhance, replicate elsewhere, etc.). Scriven (1991) quotes Robert Stake on the formative/summative distinction: "When the cook tastes the soup, that's formative evaluation; when the guest tastes it, that's summative evaluation" (p. 19). In practice the distinction is often moot, since thoughtful consideration of formative findings may lead to project termination, just as careful analyses of summative findings often result in redirecting a continuing project. But knowing where the initial emphasis lies helps in guiding what kind of evidence will be most relevant to the originally intended decision.

The criteria of Internal Integrity usually take priority in formative evaluations, and those of External Generality in summary evaluations—especially in programs intended for wider dissemination or to influence policy.

Personnel external to the project are often chosen at least to supervise and more often to conduct a summative evaluation because of the obvious conflict of interest staff members have in the outcome.

Access to the Findings

Determining access is important because those with access come into possession of information about whatever is being evaluated that others either don't know or, if they suspect, don't have the evidence to confirm their suspicions. Such information represents the power to suggest, make, and/or even require changes. Whoever is in charge of the evaluation process or does the evaluation possesses the results. Therefore, they can selectively disseminate them or not and/or can potentially make use of them; these are issues of potential concern—and possibly contention.

Although access to findings also has implications, both for the goals of the evaluation and for who does what parts of the evaluation (decisions considered in the next sections), it is considered here because access decisions are often explicitly or implicitly affected by choice of formative or summative roles. If formative is chosen the implication is usually implicit that the process and its results will be open so that all with information can contribute and can use the results to benefit the program's clients. There may be exceptions, however, as when a program is under fire and the administrator wants to quickly evaluate and turn the program around without outside distractions. But because formative evaluations are primarily for those involved with the project, results are usually open to anyone who wants to learn from them.

Access to findings of summative evaluations can become an issue when program continuation and/or jobs are at stake, or when clients desire changes in fundamentals such as administration, program direction, goals, funding, or staffing. If the evaluation is funded, the program sponsor may claim to be the sole client and keep the results private until the implications are clear, perhaps planning to suppress them if not favorable. Similarly, administrators who are unsure the results will be positive may restrict access. Evaluators who lean toward using evaluation to empower the powerless (usually the clients) may especially be concerned in such cases and may have little choice other than to refuse to do the evaluation.

The term *sponsor* in this chapter is used as a shorthand for three kinds of persons: (1) those funding a requested, or contracted for, evaluation (e.g., government agencies, foundations, school boards); (2) those from whom you obtain permission to do the evaluation if it is unsolicited (superintendents, principals, school boards); and (3) those from whom you must get day-to-day cooperation, even though they work for the person who solicited the evaluation or gave permission to do it (teachers, clerical workers). Sometimes one or more, or perhaps all three groups, are involved; the context usually makes clear which ones.

In most evaluations it is in everyone's interest to provide open access to results and, to some degree, involve those that will be affected by the results in evaluation planning and/or execution. This includes those directly affected by the program: administrators, staff with jobs on the line, and other **stakeholders**—persons whose lives and perhaps livelihood may be affected. It also suggests at least informing and listening for responses from those indirectly affected such as taxpayers or other supporters. Involving the program's administration and stakeholders is likely to bring useful viewpoints to bear on the decisions and has the added benefit, as Patton (2003–2004) puts it, of getting them to think evaluatively. That is, it makes them more aware of goals and the relation of goals to methods of achieving them; it makes them more cognizant of the need to look for evidence of results.

An Example

Consider, as an example, action research in which evaluation results are to be used formatively to help devise changes in the curriculum toward greater effectiveness. Dissemination of the results is to be unrestricted; they are mainly of use to the teachers who are also the evaluators. The circled "one" in Figure 23.2 indicates the location of this illustrative example at the junction of the column "Formative, quality control . . ." and the row "Availability of the findings is unrestricted." However, were they to find problems in the curriculum, to prevent such knowledge from opening them to criticism by the school administration they might temporarily restrict knowledge of the results until the problems have been diagnosed and remedies proposed.

HOW THE GOALS OF THE EVALUATION ARE DETERMINED

Within the formative or summative role is the determination of what goals are to be evaluated. For instance, is the target of evaluation the original goals for which resources were allocated? Is it the goals as they evolved? Is it what those affected hoped would be the goals? And who decides? As shown in Figure 23.3 on the following page, there are two subquestions to be considered here: (1) the possible goals of the evaluation, and (2) who is involved in setting the goals. The columns of the figure indicate the possible goals of the evaluation, and the rows show who is involved in determining them.

Figure 23.3   The determination of the goals of the evaluation.

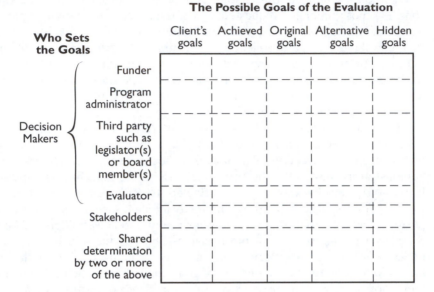

Who Sets the Evaluation's Goals?

This is among the evaluator's first tasks. The categories arrayed vertically in Figure 23.3 describe who determines the goals of the evaluation: the decision makers alone, the stakeholders alone, or both are involved (the more common alternative).

Decision makers.   The decision makers are those with power who were involved in starting and running a program, and most likely are those evaluating it. These may be persons allocating funds for the program (a funding agency). A decision maker may be a third party such as an institution or a policy-shaping center—often pluralistic in interests (e.g., a legislature, a consortium of lobbying or interest groups, or a professional association). The decision maker might be the program administrator, who, given a broad mandate, must now determine the specific goals, alone or with others. This is not unusual when the program results from a political compromise and the originators can only agree on a broad, general description, leaving the tough work of the specifics to administrators and staff. Or the decision makers may be some combination of the above.

If the program's real results are to be assessed, regardless of whether they were the intended ones, the evaluator becomes the determiner through inferring the goals actually achieved from the evaluation's data. This is referred to as a *goal-free evaluation* (Scriven, 1972, 1991; discussed later in this chapter). In contrast, if the client's goals are to guide the evaluation, it may be preceded by a needs evaluation to determine what the client's needs really are rather than presupposing what they are. Needs analyses often turn up problems, such as child care, that can prevent the success of an otherwise good program but are often overlooked by program developers.

Stakeholders.   At a different power level are those affected by these decisions, the stakeholders, who are often unorganized and disparate. But when organized and aroused and with focused goals they can have a powerful impact on decision making, even though they have no direct decision-making power. However, some evaluators view evaluation as a means of empowerment of those affected by programs (e.g., Cronbach, 1982; Fetterman, Kaftarian, & Wandersman, 1996; House, 1976, 1980). Sometimes stakeholders believe that they have the right to determine the goals against which the project should to be evaluated. For example, what are the really important goals of the Head Start Program: preparation for grade school entry, medical and nutritional diagnosis and remediation, reduction of the disadvantage of lower-class children, socialization into school behavioral norms, or any or all of these? They face a bewildering array. *Another of the first and most important initial tasks of an evaluator is to clarify the evaluation's goals.*

Shared determination.   If we return to the prime assumption that a successful evaluation is one with findings that are used, then clearly one of the most effective ways of getting the evidence used is for both decision makers and stakeholders to be involved. Many evaluators believe in involving the stakeholders in as much of the evaluation process as possible (Rippey [1973] gave it an apt name, transactional evaluation). Not only do the stakeholders gain ownership in the process and therefore more reason to trust it, but the process also concurrently educates them about the evaluation's problems. It makes them aware of the fallibility and inevitably incomplete nature of the evidence as well as making them more properly cautious about drawing inferences from it.

Evaluation Goals

Categories of goals for the evaluation are (1) a needs evaluation to determine what the goals should be; (2) a goal-free evaluation to determine what goals are actually being achieved by a program already underway; (3) accepting the originating goals of a program, process, or product; (4) establishing alternative goals or additions to the original ones; and (5) hidden goals. Let's explore these categories.

Needs.   Needs evaluation, also called a *needs analysis* or assessment, is basically a first step to determine what client needs exist that might be addressed by a program, product, or process, usually with the intent of establishing a program to alleviate or fulfill those needs. It may involve consulting individuals to determine expressed needs, or evaluating the status quo against a standard (as in using a diagnostic test to determine achievement weaknesses and strengths) to guide remediation efforts. While it may be the first step in the inauguration of a program to determine its future directions, it may also be undertaken in an established program to assure that the most important needs are being addressed—which may not be those most easily perceived.

Achieved goals.   Goal-free evaluations, as indicated earlier, involve already established programs. Starting free of preconceptions requires an evaluator without knowledge of the prior goals of the project or, barring that, someone as unfamiliar with it as feasible. The evaluator has minimal contact with the program manager and staff until the achieved outcomes have been inferred. Such evaluations should be sensitive to side effects that often lay outside typical data collection, which is usually focused on the originating goals. For example, the key goal of a toy-lending library program, intended to give poor children certain advantages of the middle-class home, was to make available otherwise unaffordable toys. Mothers typically asked for recommendations from the "librarian" who, seizing on this opportunity to teach parenting skills, thereby produced the project's most important outcome. Formative evaluators following the original goals, and focusing on the children and the toys they were playing with, might have missed the most important aspect of the project—the parent education. A goal-based evaluation pursued by an internal evaluator—a staff person—and a goal-free evaluation simultaneously conducted by an external evaluator can complement each other.

Original goals. Accepting the originating goals of a program, process, or product to determine how effectively they are being achieved is the most commonly chosen of these alternatives. A goal-based evaluation usually requires that the goals or objectives of an intervention be stated in terms of **behavioral objectives**—the behaviors the intervention is to bring about. Such specification requires most interveners to think about their program's outcomes in concrete ways and in detail they have not previously considered. It assumes, however, that we can translate all goals into observable behaviors without losing a wholeness or essence that may be a prime characteristic. For example, it is difficult to specify and observe the affective thrill of seeing a painting, a result that may be considered a key goal of art appreciation instruction.

Covert behaviors, such as "The student should be able to appreciate a painting," are translated into overt behaviors that can be recognized, such as "On studying a painting, the student should be able to describe how the artist used perspective to achieve her purposes." Any relevant evidence should be used, not just paper and pencil. Evidence of appreciation of painting might include library records indicating that the student checked out prints from the library's collection of reproductions. Records of art gallery attendance might be checked for number of visits.

The investigator has an important role in teasing out the implications of a policy or the dimensions of a program (Cronbach, 1982). For example, an evaluation of most written policies on mainstreaming will show they apply equally well to keeping gifted children as well as the handicapped in the mainstream. That implication may not be acceptable and may call for rethinking what mainstreaming means. Often, the evaluator must assume the additional role of educator.

Rossi and Wright (1986) find goal-based evaluation too restrictive.

> Social programs tend to develop their goals as they proceed; thus to saddle them with evaluations that stress a priori goals does an injustice to the evolving nature of most programs. . . . Many potentially innovative social projects are funded with vague goals supposed to be achieved using unspecified procedures. An experimental approach that demands fixed procedures and unchanging goals simply does not work in the "real world" where both goals and procedures are continually being changed in an effort to find something that appears to work. (p. 60)

Though this is often the case because, for instance, meeting state-established standards of educational achievement is often mandatory, evaluation of original goals is common.

Alternative goals. An example of an alternative goal is that of empowering consumers and stakeholders. This is often a goal of *product evaluation* (e.g., Consumers Union) and various efforts such as establishing standards and providing feedback forums. A close relative is so-called *responsive evaluation* (Stake, 1991), which provides ample data for the consumers to judge for themselves. Delaying the design of the evaluation until the program is understood, the evaluator is responsive to the evolving needs of the program and its stakeholders. Stake (1975) provides details of this approach as applied to the arts.

A wide range of goals can be added to the originals. Many of these have been discussed in the evaluation literature. An example is comparing the effectiveness, efficiency, or both of alternative programs. Another is educating a program's variety of clients. One way of achieving both these goals for complex issues is *adversarial evaluation*. It aims at creating an understanding of the pros and cons of a program through a court-like proceeding. The object is not so much to win the litigation as to provide an insightful examination that educates the audience to the complexity of the issues. Wolf (1975, 1979) proposed a *judicial evaluation model* that included a statement of charges, opposing presenters of the cases who could call witnesses (including experts), a judge or hearings officer, and a jury or panel to render a verdict. The National Institute of Education's trial of minimum competency testing is an example. It was televised and the two opposing evaluators, Popham (1981) and Madaus (1981), reproduced their arguments in print.

Education is often an additional goal of *connoisseurial* or *expert-judgment evaluation* (Eisner, 1976, 1981, 1991) which seeks to help consumers understand and appreciate "the subtle, often unnoticed yet significant aspects of a situation" (Eisner, 1991, p. 175). It is most widely used when measurement is impossible because of the many "right" answers. For example, a pilot can fly from Chicago to New York many different ways under a variety of flight conditions. Evaluation by a flight observer is not only considered the fairest method of assessing such a performance, but it also provides an opportunity to highlight the subtleties involved.

Cost-benefit analysis (Rossi, Lipsey, & Freeman, 2003), which weighs the costs of the program against its benefits, usually in monetary terms, may also be an evaluation goal. Such information is often sought when programs compete for the same resources. Related is **cost-effectiveness analysis**, which determines the cost of achieving certain benefits, often against alternatives to achieving them.

Hidden goals. Often added to the stated goals of the evaluation are additional unstated intentions. For example, stakeholders may wish to show the program was poorly administered; funders, to assess staff morale or adequacy of staffing; administrators, to show the need for more resources; innovators, to show off the superiority of their innovation; or stakeholders, to show that a side-effect of the program should be given more prominence (e.g., greater provision for parents to learn how to teach their children in a kindergarten program). As these examples suggest, calling the goals "additional" is often an understatement; to those holding them, they often are a main reason for evaluating.

An Illustrative Example

In its very earliest years (1954–1959), the Ford Foundation funded an evaluation to determine whether their teacher-training model would produce better teachers than the usual conventional bachelor's program. It involved moving teacher training to the master's degree level, making a four-year liberal arts degree a prerequisite, consolidating all teacher-training programs in the state at the University of Arkansas, and moving much of the training from the university into the schools in the form of apprenticeships. The circled number 2s in Figure 23.4 portray the kind of goals involved in the evaluation and who was involved in the decision.

Figure 23.4   The determination of the goals of an evaluation.

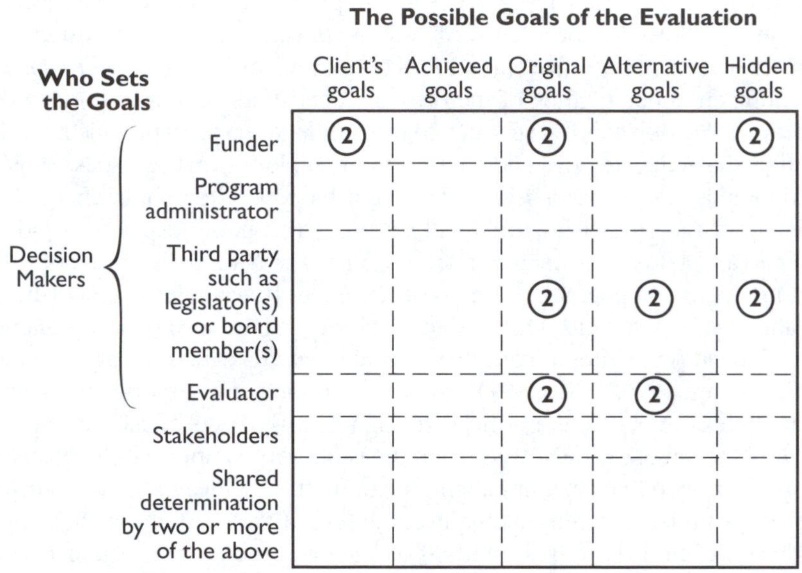

The Possible Goals of the Evaluation

Who Sets the Goals		Client's goals	Achieved goals	Original goals	Alternative goals	Hidden goals
Decision Makers	Funder	②		②		②
	Program administrator					
	Third party such as legislator(s) or board member(s)			②	②	②
	Evaluator		②	②		
Stakeholders						
Shared determination by two or more of the above						

Three decision-making centers were involved—the funder, the board, and the evaluator.

1. The funder of the evaluation—the foundation—of course wanted its original goals to be the main evaluation focus; the circled numeral 2 in the top row of the diagram under original goals indicates this. The other circled 2 in the top row shows that the foundation also had a hidden agenda—this prototype's success was to show the nation how to improve teacher education.

2. A board made up of the presidents of all the higher education institutions in Arkansas oversaw the program. They needed the money promised by the program and so were willing to set up an experimental program at the University of Arkansas, provided some went to their institutions as well. But they were not happy about giving up their teacher education programs, which, for the teacher's colleges, were their most important programs. So their hidden agenda was to get foundation funds for their institution and allow the fund an experimental program that would not be better than those of their own. They found a way to achieve the goals when the foundation agreed to fund the strengthening of their liberal arts programs—thereby adding alternative goals. And, although funds would have

allowed hiring the best persons in the country to develop the University of Arkansas program, they did not conduct such a search. Thus, there are circled 2s in the third-party row under original, alternative, and hidden goals.

3. The evaluators found that evaluation funds had to be spread to include changes in the liberal arts programs (alternative goals) as well as the original goals, hence the circled numerals in that row (Spalding & Krathwohl, 1959).

THE ROLE OF THE EVALUATOR

The person doing the evaluation may be an outside evaluator (a person with no formal connection with the program) or an inside evaluator (such as an administrator or staff person). Sometimes stakeholders too are involved, as in the first example, where the teachers themselves evaluated the program. Figure 23.5 displays the roles of evaluator, staff, and/or stakeholder(s) in the evaluation process. Two subquestions are considered here: (1) who does the evaluating, and (2) in which steps in the evaluation process they do it.

The shading in Figure 23.5 is coded to indicate who is involved, and the filled proportion of the bar indicates the extent of their responsibility for that step. In addition, if one wishes, the relative height of each horizontal bar may show the proportion of the resources allocated to it or its relative importance. The figure was drawn to match the example in which the teachers were stakeholders.

Figure 23.5   **The roles of evaluator, staff, and stakeholders in each step of the evaluation process.**

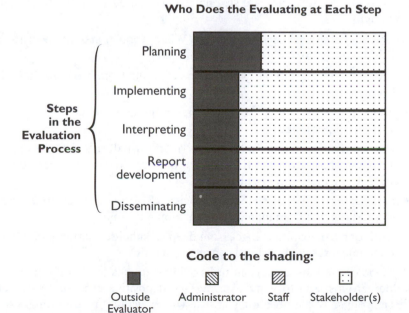

The degree to which an outside evaluator is involved can vary considerably—from helping to initiate, to consulting as needed, to doing the evaluation in its entirety. In many instances, even where the evaluator bears the major responsibility, he or she may use inside staff for data gathering. In the first illustrative example, we noted that teachers were evaluating their curriculum and its effectiveness, so they are the real stakeholders. As described by the coding of the steps in Figure 23.5, they had an outside evaluator help in planning the evaluation, but in the remaining steps that person's role was reduced to an "as-needed" basis. Clearly the teachers—as stakeholders—did the bulk of the work.

An outside evaluator is especially likely to be brought in as a neutral third party when two or more of the parties (funders, administrators, or various stakeholders) do not agree or trust one another. It is expected that an outside evaluator will bring an open mind, no prior preferences or prejudices, and especially their expertise and experience.

The evaluator's role is usually set at the same time that decisions are made about the role and goals of the evaluation, although it may change as findings emerge. Who hires an evaluator and how that evaluator is then perceived by all the stakeholders can be critical in determining cooperation in data gathering and thus what data are available, and how its analysis and resulting conclusions are perceived.

Similarly, how much the stakeholders participate can vary from instances where they basically do the evaluation, to as-needed consultation, to serving advisory roles, to merely reacting to the findings. Weaver and Cousins (2004) analyzed collaborative involvement and proposed three aims of stakeholder participation: pragmatic (which gets the job done more easily and effectively), political (which promotes fairness and provides a voice for the socially oppressed and for social justice), and epistemological (which increases the likelihood that the results of the evaluation will be more meaningful to others than with the evaluator alone). As adapted from Weaver and Cousins (2004), following are six dimensions that describe the forms that collaboration might take:

- control of technical decision making (What proportion of the decision making rests with the evaluator? With the stakeholders?)
- extent of diversity among stakeholders (ranging from broad to limited inclusion of diverse interests)
- power relations among stakeholders (ranging from conflicting, to aligned, to actively cooperating)
- power weighting among stakeholders (if any, usually it's in terms of ability to effect change in accord with the findings, but political goals may supersede—ranges from equal to unequal to very unequal)
- manageability of the evaluation (logistical—time and resource constraints may impede: ranging from manageable to unmanageable)
- depth of participation (ranges from deep stakeholder participation in full spectrum of technical research tasks to consultation only)

One of the most important tasks of evaluators is to identify their relevant stakeholder groups, and to work to bring about positive evaluator role perceptions by these groups. This is absolutely critical where evaluators are brought in as a neutral third party. Note that almost regardless of what the evaluators believe to be the reality, it is the stakeholders' perception of the evaluator's role that is usually a major determining factor in accepting and using the evaluation findings. Evaluators must address these perceptions in addition to their other responsibilities.

TWO MORE EVALUATION EXAMPLES

A Goal-Free Evaluation

Consider an evaluation in which a policy maker such as an administrator in a funding agency needs information to decide whether to continue to support a project. The funder would like to know not only whether it is effective in achieving its intended goal, but also what is actually being achieved, whether intended or not. She decides on a **goal-free evaluation** and employs an outside evaluator who purposely avoids initial awareness of the intended goals of the project until he can infer the achieved outcomes. He compares these with intended ones. Figure 23.6 is a goal-free, summative evaluation conducted by an evaluator. Dissemination of the results is restricted. The figure shows the location of such an evaluation as a circled 3 in the middle diagram under *achieved goals*, since he is searching for such goals as are being achieved, be they new or the original goals of the project.

As indicated by the location of the circled 3 in the left diagram, the evaluation is considered summative in the sense that the results are summed toward a judgment for a policy decision. Dissemination is restricted because a funder might prefer to restrict dissemination of the results if the original goals were not achieved or were supplanted by a side effect. This would be especially true if the results make the original funding decision appear foolish.

In the right-hand diagram, the solid dark coding of all phases of the evaluation indicates that the evaluator did it all from beginning to end.

Figure 23.6   A goal-free summative evaluation with restricted results conducted entirely by an evaluator.

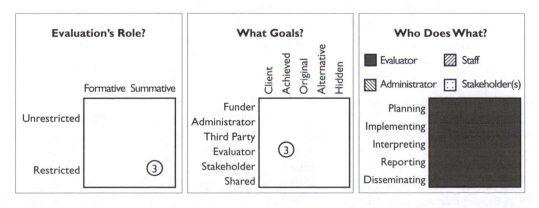

A Comparison of the Effectiveness of Two Alternative Programs

Consider the following: An administrator, who is the science-teaching coordinator for a large school system, decides to compare two programs for teaching science, each intending to achieve the same goals. He is undertaking the comparison because of pressure from a group of parents. They are enamored of school material developed by a foundation that is propagating a curriculum with an unusual view of evolution. He has obtained a grant from that foundation to support the installation of their curriculum and to evaluate it in comparison with the school's current curriculum. The foundation claims students will meet the state's eighth-grade science standards with their curriculum just as well as the school's curriculum, and it is against those goals that both are to be evaluated.

Figure 23.7 is a formative comparison of competing programs largely planned by an outside evaluator, implemented with administrator and staff, and involving stakeholders with a hidden agenda in all phases. The middle diagram shows the locations of such an evaluation as three circled numeral 4s to indicate that there are original, alternative, and hidden goals. The original goal is to meet the state's standards for a course and grade level, a goal shared by all involved. The alternative goal results from the fact that the administrator has added the goal of determining the most effective elements to possibly enable combining the best of both curricula. Parents (stakeholders) have the not-so-hidden goal of seeking to replace the current curriculum with the foundation's, which they favor. All of these goals have important implications for the evaluation. To meet the original goals, the examination based on state standards must be used as one of the evaluating instruments. To meet the administrator's goal, reliable subscores for significant segments of the curriculum must be established, probably by augmenting the state's test. To meet the credibility requirements of parents, who are likely to be distrustful of results that do not favor their point of view, they must be made to feel that the comparison gave their preferred course a fair trial.

The left-hand diagram indicates that the evaluation is formative in that it aims to find the best parts of the curriculums. Dissemination of the results is restricted, at

Figure 23.7   A comparison of two programs.

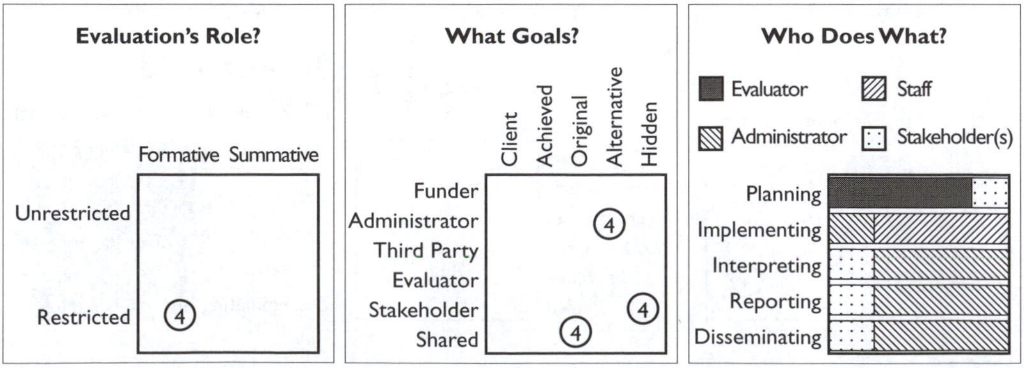

least initially. That way, if the foundation's program turns out to be inferior, as a courtesy the administrator can make the results first available only to the funding agency and parents to give them time to get comfortable with the results before disseminating them to the public.

The right-hand diagram shows that an outside evaluator basically lays out the plan of the evaluation. He was brought in by the administrator with the approval of the parents to assure them that a fair evaluation was being performed. Parents, being involved in all the stages except data collection, should be able to better understand and trust the results. Implementing data collection is largely the staff's responsibility. The administrator, with some overview from parents, takes major responsibility for interpreting the data, developing the report, and disseminating the findings.

The three evaluation questions and the decisions that flow from them can provide a useful framework for planning and analyzing evaluations, reminding one of various aspects that should be given adequate consideration.

▶ Formative evaluation is used in the development stage to guide an evolutionary process.

▶ Summative evaluation determines the worth of a mature program or process. In a sense, however, even this is formative since it usually leads to appropriate program modification.

▶ Some evaluations use needs surveys to determine what the goals should be.

▶ Goal-free evaluations are begun without the evaluators knowing the goals of what is being evaluated. They infer goals from what has occurred and then compare these inferences with what was intended.

▶ Most evaluations begin with specified goals, both for the evaluation and for the project, process, or product being evaluated. These may be given by the funder, administration, stakeholders, or some combination.

▶ Two of the evaluators' most important tasks are (1) clearly identifying who their client(s) are (negotiating an understanding satisfactory to the parties involved as to who the clients are) and (2) clearly identifying the goals: client's, achieved, original, alternate, and hidden.

▶ Using a model in planning an evaluation (such as that developed above) can help assure that all important aspects have been considered. It can also help critique an evaluation by pointing to characteristics that need to be judged.

OTHER CHARACTERISTICS OF EVALUATIONS

As evaluation is typically practiced, there are some characteristics worth noting. Among these are that evaluations are

• political, when they empower one group over another;

• threatening, especially if results are likely to be negative;

• conservative, when findings reinforce the status quo;

• afterthoughts, when getting the project up and running overpowers planning ahead for the evaluation;

- difficult to time so that findings arrive during complex policy discussions when they can be most effective; and
- most useful when tailored to the clientele.

Let's examine each of these points.

Evaluations as Almost Inevitably Political

> Evaluators take a political stand . . . when they undertake . . . a study. The message is . . . : (1) the program is problematic enough to need evaluating, and (2) the program is a serious enough effort to be worth the time and effort to evaluate. . . . Programs with powerless clientele . . . lack the coalition of support that shields more mainstream groups [from evaluation]. (Weiss, 1991, pp. 221–222)

Indeed, the political nature of evaluation manifests itself whenever stakeholders have concerns but no voice in the evaluation process. As noted earlier, some evaluators argue that evaluation should empower the powerless by seeking recognition and inclusion of all stakeholders. If use of evaluation results is considered a prime criterion of success, and if stakeholders are important in their implementation, then both sponsor and evaluator, recognizing this reality, must take stakeholder's goals and priorities into account. The evaluator as the active agent in the situation becomes the negotiator searching for a design and procedure mutually satisfactory for all parties—the "art of the possible," a phrase often used to define politics!

Whether formative or summative, internal or external, evaluations are subject to political pressures. Internal formative evaluations appear less threatening and therefore less likely to stir political winds. However, negative or inconclusive findings often embolden "I told you so" advocates of alternative solutions to press their point of view.

Because careers may be at stake, an internal evaluator may find it harder to convey a summative evaluation's negative findings than an external evaluator may. But external summative evaluations often create the strongest political turmoil. "Programs come into being through political processes, through the rough and tumble of political support, opposition, and bargaining" (Weiss, 1991, p. 214). To gain broad political support, program goals are often unrealistic and fuzzy, designed mainly to placate all or many concerned parties. Their translation into operational goals, either to direct the evaluation or to compare with program achievements, makes transparent what the fuzzy goals concealed; this pleases some competing factions and displeases others. It is difficult for an evaluator to be perceived as neutral. Evaluations of new programs seem less likely to be contentious than those with established clientele who have strong political connections.

Evaluations as Threats

Pressures for a favorable evaluation.   The life-or-death stakes for programs undergoing evaluation can lead to pressures for a favorable report. "The view some managers hold about their programs is *nil nisi bonum*, speak nothing but good; it is a phrase usually reserved for the dead" (Weiss, 1991, p. 215). For example, Brickell (1978), evaluating the impact of teacher aides, was warned early. Although Brickell was employed by the board of education, the district superintendents employed the teacher aides and one offered this advice:

"Okay you evaluators. Let's get one thing straight . . . these paraprofessionals . . . not only . . . help kids learn but . . . link us to the community [not a criterion the evaluator was employed to consider]. We're not looking for a report . . . that will cause any trouble . . . downtown. They've got their reasons . . . we've got ours. . . . We're going to keep our paraprofessionals. Don't make it difficult." Alerted thus, we made our study. And we were lucky that time. We found that the presence of paraprofessionals did in fact improve pupil achievement. (p. 95)

Sponsors may ask to see the report before it is released; they may demand the right to edit the final report. Even if a report is not censored, it can be made unavailable. Coleman (1972) reports that the federal bureau sponsoring his widely discussed *Equality of Educational Opportunity* perceived it as damaging the case for programs aiding minorities. Despite wide publicity and interest in the findings, the full report remained largely unavailable during its first year. The right to edit, censor, and limit the availability of the report are some of many conditions that should be agreed on at the outset of an evaluation.

Countering by withholding cooperation.   Administrators and staff can make access and data gathering very difficult if they perceive the evaluation as threatening. To overtly deny access is too obvious, but they can defer it well beyond the evaluator's frustration threshold—by holding up scheduling interviews, requiring approval of all instruments by boards or committees, subtly undermining their own requests to teachers or parents to cooperate by the way they are phrased or delivered, informally marshaling the "insiders" to resist the "outsiders," and so on—repeatedly and indefinitely. Similarly, those being evaluated, if antagonistic to the evaluation, can delay returning questionnaires, leave items blank, change or remove code numbers, give vague responses, and limit observations to favorable times and places. Data givers who have a stake in the outcome control the whole process.

Bogdan and Biklen (1998) argue, "You can only afford to do evaluation if you can afford not to do it" (p. 217). Bogdan is not implying that evaluations can never be done where there are hostile staff or participants, but the difficulties increase the importance of making stakeholders participants in the evaluation process in these situations.

Evaluations as Inherently Conservative

Berk and Rossi (1976) argue that evaluations are inherently conservative because they are usually limited to the politically feasible. The income maintenance experiment mentioned in chapter 21 (guaranteed annual income) was restricted to the narrow range of incentives that Congress might consider instead of a much wider range that would have contributed to understanding the phenomenon. Additionally, evaluations converge on the politically dominant view of social problems (e.g., the income maintenance centered on the concern that persons, satisfied with being on public assistance, would withdraw from the workforce. The outcomes of improved health and enriched lives were neglected or downplayed).

Evaluation findings of "close-to-zero effects" and "no significant difference" conservatively reinforce the status quo and discourage change. "When 'no significant difference' is interpreted as a program failure, the burden of proof is placed on the innovation" (Cronbach, 1982, p. 33). However, insufficient statistical power resulting from too small a sample to sense the effect may be the real problem.

It may also lie in program execution (no pun intended), that is, the considerable slippage between conceptualization and implementation. The challenge for program designers is to develop programs that are effective over a variety of implementation strategies or have "natural" paths to correct implementation. Alternatively, with trial implementation runs, they can see how and why modifications took place and can determine whether they can be controlled (Fairweather & Tornatzky, 1977; Hamilton, 1979).

Control of the study by a sponsor or manager seems obviously to exert a conservative force. "Evaluators help political figures remain in power if they supply them with information that other participants in the political process do not possess" (Cronbach, 1982, p. 35). The many voices arguing for the evaluator to negotiate for powerless publics is a reaction to this concern. Evaluators give evidence of their personal values by the evaluation opportunities they accept.

Evaluations as Afterthoughts

Evaluations are often afterthoughts: "First let's get the program up and running! What then? Oh, yes, we ought to evaluate it!" This is often after the intervention has occurred; too late for pre- and post-measurement. Clearly, we can develop a more satisfactory evaluation plan if it is included from the outset.

Difficulty in Timing the Findings of Complex Policy Evaluations

Evaluation's contribution to policy is considered further in pages 647–649, especially the problem of appropriate timing. It is almost impossible to conform study completion to political deadlines. But studies that gather data about real contexts are helpful to policy makers who accept them as indicative of results if the policy were adopted. Examples are the large-scale evaluations of the 1960s and 1970s, which were essentially "true-to-life" field experiments.[2] The income maintenance studies took place over six years. They demonstrated that such randomized experimentation was logistically and politically feasible, but also very difficult. It was hard to keep the experimental groups uncontaminated over a sufficiently long period for the effects of intervention to develop naturally. Interventions involving provision of services often evolve in response to conditions and clientele, making it almost impossible to track effects to a cause. Interventions that do not change over the course of the study, like payments to recently released inmates to reduce recidivism, seem more likely candidates for policy studies.

By contrast some evaluators, such as House (2001), are pessimistic about the value of large-scale experiments, viewing them as typically producing equivocal results. He cites the Follow-Through Study as an example; it evaluated the fruits of Head Start, the early school-years program. Follow-Through evaluation had to be reduced in size when it initially produced twelve tons of data. He argues that, as it was in Follow-Through, social causation is so complex that the variance in achievement measures across programs is as great as that within programs, thus yielding no clear-cut results.

House (2001) suggests that qualitative studies are more successful by reducing the complexity to one of a local context, with certain kinds of personnel producing particular results. Meta-analytic studies (see chapter 22) are similarly successful by summarizing results over variations in circumstances, thus making generalization more possible.

Evaluations Tailored to Clientele

Evaluators should consider the preferences of the client and stakeholder for certain kinds of research methods and evidence in planning their evaluations and reports. For example, administrators who favor businesslike approaches to management likely prefer analytic reports and so respond favorably to quantitative evidence. Whereas an administrator may find a statistical report interpretable and useful, however, others less accustomed to such data (e.g., an elementary school teacher, librarian, or social worker) may find a case-study approach describing the impact on specific individuals more meaningful. Evaluators unable or unwilling to adjust their personal preferences for methods and reporting styles to reflect client preferences and capabilities risk failing to have the desired impact.

▶ Evaluations almost inevitably stir up political forces, especially when they are perceived as threatening or when studying a program with political origins. Involvement of stakeholders in evaluation planning and implementation can raise questions of power and program control. If utilization is a prime criterion, negotiations to find "the art of the possible" often limit evaluations to the politically feasible.

▶ Individuals who perceive an evaluation as threatening can appear to be cooperating in data collection while subtly sabotaging it; they control the process. There may be pressures for a favorable report from individuals jeopardized by unfavorable results.

▶ Evaluations are a conservative force when they reinforce the dominant views in a society and stay within the bounds of the politically feasible. New programs often show effects too close to zero to overcome status-quo momentum. Sponsor control of evaluations tends to reinforce this conservative bent. Some evaluators argue that evaluation should seek to empower the powerless.

▶ Evaluations initiated as afterthoughts are likely to be weaker than those integrated into program implementation plans from the outset.

▶ Timing the availability of policy findings is critical to their use, but add in the complexity of policy evaluations and it is difficult to coordinate the evaluation process with political moods and deadlines.

▶ Evaluations can usefully explore social policy effectiveness and side effects. The large government studies of the 1960s and 1970s demonstrated the feasibility of large-scale experiments that employed randomization.

▶ Evaluators need to take into account the audience's preferences for certain kinds of research methods and evidence in planning and implementing an evaluation.

EVALUATION STANDARDS: PROTECTION FOR EVALUATORS AND CLIENTS

To ameliorate many of the earlier noted problems, evaluators representing interested professional associations developed standards that describe appropriate conduct for both evaluator and client. Like the test standards in chapter 18, they were a joint project of the interested professional associations (Joint Committee on Standards for Educational Evaluation, 1994). Thirty standards are grouped under the four main evaluation concerns: utility, feasibility, propriety, and accuracy. Each standard includes (1) an overview of intent, (2) guidelines for application, (3) common pitfalls, (4) caveats (trade-offs where more than one standard applies), and (5) an illustration of the standard's application. A summary of the standards is available at http://www.eval.org/EvaluationDocuments/progeval.html.

Although aimed at education projects, the standards have much wider applicability. The standards are particularly useful in the development of a contract between sponsor and evaluator. They indicate potential points of conflict that might evolve from their relationship as the project progresses. The standards can also be helpful in what has been termed *meta-evaluation*, the assessment of how well an evaluation study was done.

In addition, there are guidelines for evaluators at http://www.eval.org/Publications/GuidingPrinciplesPrintable.asp. A product of the American Evaluation Association, they "are intended to guide the professional practice of evaluators, and inform evaluation clients and the general public about the principles they can expect to be upheld by professional evaluators."

ACTION RESEARCH

Action research—research by practitioners to improve practice—carries participant-oriented evaluation to its ultimate conclusion: Participants do the research. *Practitioners* refers not only to frontline fieldworkers—teachers, social workers, librarians, journalists, and so forth—but also to their supervisors and administrators, who often are equally frustrated by the gap between academic and practitioner knowledge. Practitioners want "knowledge that is concrete, timely, prudent, and particular to their own circumstances" (Atkin, 1994, p. 105). Contrast this goal with the typical goals of academic researchers: broadly applicable, abstract propositions loosely related to specific situations. Like most enthusiasms, action research activity seems to capture the center of attention sporadically. When does it come to the fore? Examples are when practitioners find following academic research findings to be difficult, and/or they think they can do better; when reform movements threaten professional practice (they are omnipresent but pressure sometimes peaks); and when a group of proactive professionals find the time to improve practice.

An important appeal of action research is its empowerment of practitioners who, even though they are the prime stakeholders of many evaluations, have so often been made to feel inadequate by academics. The tension between academe and field is endemic; academics, with the responsibility, time, and resources to continually work at improving practice, believe they should always be ahead of the field. To the practitioner, however, their ideas are often impractical, unrealistic, and overly complex; worst of all, despite their confident demeanor, experts are not always right. Action research, controlled and done by practitioners, redistributes the balance of power. If and when practitioners need professional evaluation expertise, they call for it as colleagues.

Many academics have welcomed and encouraged some form of action research as the most effective tool for institutional reform (e.g., Altrichter, Posch, & Somekh, 1993; Gallego, Hollingsworth, & Whitenack, 2001; Hargreaves, 1996). It follows the dictum, "Feed them a fish and you satisfy today's hunger; teach them to fish, and you satisfy a lifetime's."

Action research is "day-to-day reflection made more systematic and intensive" (Altrichter, Posch, & Somekh, 1993, p. 154). It targets successive cycles of reflection, planning, action, and evaluation on a given problem or, more often, on a cascade of evolving problems. Characterized by simple research methods, usually qualitative, it is tailored to what can be achieved without disrupting practice. Sometimes the process is written up as a narrative to share with others facing similar problems.

An Instructive Example

The above characteristics are illustrated in this account of action research by an elementary school principal who became concerned about extensive fifth-grade discipline problems (Soffer, 1995).[3] Parallel examples can be found in any profession. This principal kept a journal of her thoughts and actions that could be used to reflect on where she had been, where she was, and where she was going. Many action researchers find such journals invaluable as a way of "keeping on the beam." It also facilitates sharing experiences with others.

Starting with a reconnaissance of how others perceived her handling of discipline problems, she found "such things as 'a need for more strictness with upper grades,' 'more evenness with application of rules,' 'need for more follow-through with discipline,' and 'need for more consistency'" (p. 117). Agreeing with these comments, she planned to focus on consistency and persistence—beginning with the development and consistent use of a standard form for her disciplinary records and a spreadsheet categorizing incidents so that she could spot trends and patterns.

Although she had to force herself to use these records, "given my distaste for repetitive . . . paperwork" (p. 119), by the end of the first week she realized that patterns were emerging: A small group of boys accounted for many of the incidents that involved disrespect for persons, and her records indicated "she had warned Bob . . ." or "told Ann . . ." "I did not feel they were learning . . . simply being punished" (ibid.).

How could she make the disciplinary conferences learning experiences? This goal led to a second cycle where, in consulting books on the subject, she found a "responsibility model." She would ask students about their responsibility for the incident, and what they might do to avoid future problems. Her evaluation both on the forms and in her journal noted a marked change: Students got involved and "became more responsive and active in solving their own problems" (p. 120).

In her third cycle, reflecting on her journal notes she noticed that the majority of incidents involved playground aides rather than teachers. Would her occasional presence with the aides enduringly affect student behavior? Her presence three days a week during recreation depressed incident frequency, but it rebounded without her attendance. This discovery made her wonder what she could "do to invest the aides with more authority in the eyes of the students" (p. 121).

In her fourth cycle she noted that even these changes in practice had not affected three fifth-grade boys on whom she had "used almost every approach I knew" (p. 122). After consultation with teachers and parents, she decided to move the two who were followers to separate classrooms, isolating the leader. Then, instead of viewing them "as a triumvirate with the same problems, I was able to see them as individuals with different problems" (p. 122). The two continued to misbehave, running to meet the "'powerful' boy" to brag about their exploits, though—without his friends—he had ceased to be a problem.

In her fifth cycle, reflecting on her failure with the two boys, she decided to draw up behavioral contracts with specified consequences of both rewards and punishments. This step reduced the negative behavior! That consequence reminded her of an approach she had read about that varied the disciplinary approach to fit the student. She sought to learn more about it.

During the following school year she continued her research, now keeping several cycles going simultaneously. She found that 54% of the school's referrals were to 6% of the students, thus narrowing the focus. Further, referrals rose two weeks before a major vacation, information she shared with staff in order to plan appropriate interventions. She took actions at the beginning of the school year designed to reinforce the authority of the aides.

Reflecting on the whole process, however, she realized that changing her role was of limited value; she needed to shift the whole environment, getting teachers to use the responsibility model. However, believing that this course would be manipulating them to her own ends, she decided to discuss the situation openly, to face the tension raised by her role as principal. She also recognized that her journal was "the vehicle that made it possible for my research to be reflective and flexible. [It] . . . captured . . . fleeting but important ideas not reflected in more formal data collection" (p. 123). She resolved to make her journal notes more extensive in the future.

This example captures many of the important characteristics of action research.

▶ Action research provides professionals with a concrete, timely, targeted, pragmatic orientation toward improvement of practice.

▶ It involves systematic and intensive reflection and is characterized by reflection-planning-acting-evaluation cycles.

▶ Each cycle provides a better understanding of an evolving cascade of problems.

▶ Keeping a journal of ongoing reflections and actions helps researchers see where they have been and where they should best go next.

▶ The simplest data collection methods adequate to the task minimize interruptions of practice.

▶ Researchers can call for specialized outside expertise as needed.

▶ Translating the journal into a written narrative helps others.

Hallmarks and Tips for Evaluators

The following tips for evaluators also indicate the hallmarks of a good evaluation.

1. Try to anticipate potential problems and work through the gray areas with the sponsor(s) regarding problem definition and scope, stakeholders' rights in the evaluation, report editing and documentation, the public's right to know, the time schedule, and fiscal details. Be sure they meet your personal and professional standards. Put the agreement in writing.

2. Have a means of modifying the agreement in case sponsor/evaluator cooperation fails; provide for flexibility and accommodation.

3. Check the provisions of the agreement with the Standards for Educational Evaluation (http://www.eval.org/EvaluationDocuments/progeval.html).

4. An advisory group of have-a-right-to-know audiences may be helpful in identifying potential "minefields." Depending on your philosophy and that of your sponsor, probe for additional audiences not apparent earlier, and work through their acceptance.

5. Using the advisory group and the sponsor, decide whether a goal-free or targeted evaluation is appropriate, possibly the former preceding the latter. Use such a group for a targeted evaluation to explore what questions are of concern (called the *divergent phase* by Cronbach, 1982). Find those questions important to all, those negotiated as important to enough groups to include, and those with no agreement (Cronbach's *convergent phase*). Allocate resources to the first type of questions and to the second as resources allow. Consider questions of the third type in terms of their intrinsic merit, the powerlessness of the group to get them attended to, resources available, and so on.

6. Act as an institutional resource by bringing appropriate outside research findings to bear, and organize them into a conceptual scheme related to the decisions to be made.

7. Choose methods of investigation appropriate to the questions and to the preferences for types of evidence of relevant stakeholders. Facilitate the development of trust by remembering the importance of perception in the evaluation process: "It is . . . of fundamental importance that justice be done, but it should manifestly and undoubtedly be seen to be done".[4]

8. Educate the advisory committee and sponsor regarding trade-offs in the study; have them help make the trade-off decisions.

9. Do not take for granted that a program was implemented as either planned or conceptualized. Reasons for any discrepancy may bear on the feasibility of implementation in a wider sphere.

10. Expect political pressures to increase in the later stages as the study's potential impact gets closer.

11. Use a format (written or oral report, graphics), style (informal, formal), and wording (technical, nontechnical) that will best communicate with your audience. "Don't expect decision makers to change their style of receiving information just for your evaluation" (Hendricks & Papagiannis, 1990, p. 124).

(continued)

12. Pace reporting so that it is absorbed. Leak results early in small interim reports dealing with easily understood segments. Recipients can accommodate negative evidence more comfortably this way. A big report's summary may restore perspective, but the report itself may be mainly archived.

13. Reinforce the limits and constraints of the study to the audience.

14. Separate recommendations and advocacy from interpretation of findings; make clear the judgmental aspects and possible biases. Clarify goal and policy implications.

15. In reporting, remember that audiences reading it will want to know the special competencies of the authors, who sponsored the study and why, what their responsibility was, how well these results match those of comparable studies, and, if the evaluation is controversial, where the response of opposing parties can be found (Hoaglin et al., 1982).

Tips for Doing Action Research

1. Work with one or more colleagues. Not only does this procedure provide motivation over the low spots, but discussion among colleagues also enhances the reflection critical to all phases of the process.

2. Careful observation and reflection are often the key. Remember that others may see things to which you are oblivious.

3. Consider a range of solutions. Don't worry about feasibility initially—it is the new perspective that can be most helpful.

4. Making a flow diagram of an action strategy is often helpful in seeing how it can be improved.

5. Improved practice resulting from particular actions is very reinforcing. Once you have found something that works, test it under the normal variety of contexts. Increase improvement through successive experiments with changes.

6. Actions in social situations often have unforeseen side effects. Look for them and, where negative, consider the trade-offs.

7. Complex problems may require complex solutions; they were not created nor are they likely to be solved overnight. Since they typically require more than single actions, you must successively adapt strategies over a period of time.

8. Keeping a journal, log, or other record not only will force you to reflect on your observations, but reviewing it from time to time will also reinforce your perception of how far you have come and provide a rudder to guide future progress. If you decide to share your experiences with others, it gives them a head start.

ADDITIONAL READING

Perhaps one of the most valuable sources of help in doing evaluations is the National Science Foundation's Online Evaluation Resource Library (OERL). Its sections on plans, instruments, and reports cover a wide range of evaluation types and problems (http://www.oerl.sri.com).

Logic models are a way to plan the evaluation of a program or project. Most models specify some variation of goals, inputs, activities, outputs, short-range impact, and long-range impact. Some of the many sources are listed below.

The Kellogg Foundation's Evaluation Handbook is online at http://www.wkkf.org/pubs/tools/evaluation/pub770.pdf.

A tutorial is available at http://www.usablellc.net/html/links_we_like.html#logic_models.

A rather complete model with checklists is at http://ec.europa.eu/europeaid/evaluation/methodology/foreword_en.htm.

Free software is at http://www.easyoutcomes.org/.

Visit http://www.outcomesmodels.org/ for a site where evaluators place their logic models for general use, each aimed at a particular kind of problem (e.g., in psychotherapy, school, community, etc.).

For useful evaluation discussions, see Cronbach (1982); House (1980, 1990, 2001); Rossi, Lipsey, and Freeman (2003); and Boruch (1997).

For Internet links see the American Evaluation Association's site at http://www.eval.org (click on "resources" at the page's top)—it links to university academic departments and centers where recent preprints are often posted.

There are also links to comparable sites at http://www.eval.org/Resources/Collections.asp. For an Encyclopedia of Evaluation, see Mathison (2005). A Wikipedia evaluation is being undertaken at http://www.evaluationwiki.org/wiki/index.php?Main_page.

For particular evaluation approaches: Eisner (1991), Guba and Lincoln (1986), Patton (2002, 2003/2004), and Stake (1991). See exemplars from various fields in Reason and Bradbury (2006). For an overview of approaches, see Worthen, Sanders, and Kirkpatrick (2004) and Stufflebeam and Shinkfield (2007).

For action research, see Altrichter, Posch, and Somekh (1993), Friedman and Rothman (1999), and Hollingsworth and Sockett (1994). For a handbook, see Reason and Bradbury (2006). For Internet links, see Martin Ryders' site at http://carbon.cudenver.edu/~mryder/itc/act_res.html.

IMPORTANT TERMS AND CONCEPTS

action research

behavioral objectives

cost-benefit analysis

cost-effectiveness analysis

evaluation

formative evaluation

goal-free evaluation

stakeholders

summative evaluation

OPPORTUNITIES FOR ADDITIONAL LEARNING

1. The success of the Children's Television Workshop (CTW), especially its best-known program, *Sesame Street*, has been attributed to CTW's unique three-stage program development model, summarized as follows:

   a. There is a long preproduction stage (up to one year).

      (1) Instructional designers conduct needs analysis and hammer out detailed behavioral objectives linked to the founder's definition of the educational problem to be solved.

      (2) The executive producer and designers agree on the behavioral objectives.

      (3) Educational researchers and production staff develop program philosophy and format.

  b. There is a pilot show.

      (1) Internal, laboratory-style research is done on comprehensibility, on appeals to the viewer population, and on consequent modification of program segments. Small groups of preschool children are brought to the studios.

      (2) A pilot show is produced and used to estimate achievement, audience appeal, and comprehensibility (as measured by interview, questionnaire, and assessment of eye movement) and to select the best program and features.

      (3) Findings are discussed through informal, supportive teamwork.

  c. Full production takes place with continuing feedback from researchers and subject content experts.

Consider the activities described in stages b and c. Are they research or evaluation? Explain your answer.

2. Two doctoral candidates at Upstate University were asked to evaluate the Developmental Economic Educational Program (DEEP) run by a local community college. The Joint Council for Economic Education, a private, nonprofit organization, primarily funded this program, and additional funds came from the state education department. A director and four faculty advisors administered the local DEEP Center. It had contracts with 35 school districts, each of which had a resident DEEP coordinator. It ran in-service workshops designed to familiarize the primary and secondary teachers in the districts with the DEEP curriculum (now mandated by the state) and to aid them in developing and implementing their own individual curricula. The director wished to determine if the teachers were really using the DEEP curriculum and if so, to what extent. He wanted to know whether the workshop was successful in helping them to do so and if it met their expectations. What approach might the evaluators have taken? How would you diagram the evaluation in the three decision spaces?

3. The superintendent of curriculum of the Fayetteville school board was given the task of developing a teacher evaluation process after the state education department disbanded its inspection system and turned control over to the school boards. How would you advise her to proceed?

4. The directors of a large charity organization in Sandstone City are concerned about the program at their halfway house for teenage girls. The halfway house serves local girls who have no alternative home life and are referred by child-care agencies. Most are in legal trouble. At any one time, the home might have between half-dozen and a dozen residents. The program attempts to teach the girls life skills such as self-care, personal hygiene, home care, and shopping skills. The basis of the program is a behavior modification system in which they earn points to move up level by level and obtain increased privileges. Some of the directors are concerned about the persistent reports that the program is being used to maintain control over the residents and that the point system is merely a means of punishment. They are also alarmed at the high rate of turnover of both staff and residents. They have hired you to evaluate the program. How would you proceed?

    Compare your answers with those following the Application Exercise.

APPLICATION EXERCISE

Are there aspects of your problem that could benefit from evaluation? If so, who are the stakeholders that ought to be involved? How? What problems might this create? Which of the evaluation standards might cause the greatest problems? Are there evaluation hallmarks that might also do so? How might you find your way around them?

KEY TO ADDITIONAL LEARNING OPPORTUNITIES

1. Although there are elements of research involved here, this is formative evaluation. It is decision-driven, designed to render judgments about what to include in the programs (pedagogical decisions) and whether particular program segments appeal to and are understood by the intended audience (programming decisions). The emphasis is on in-house teamwork in which a consensus is sought at each stage of development. The purpose is to make production decisions rather than to test hypotheses about the effectiveness of programs as instructional treatments.

2. The intent of this formative evaluation was to provide information that would improve the administration of the particular intervention, the DEEP program. Their client was the local director, who was interested in assessment of classroom impact, coverage of all the affected teachers in the districts, and the delivery of service. However, since there were many stakeholders, including the program's sponsors (the state education department and the joint council) and the clients of the program (the school districts' administrators and the teachers), whose input might have been important, the evaluator should try to convince the client that the inclusion of stakeholders in the process might provide evidence responsive to her concerns as well as be politically expedient.

    In terms of diagramming the evaluation's three basic questions, the role of the evaluation is formative and results are available unrestricted. The client of the evaluation, the program administrator, has specified the original goals of the program as achieved through the workshops as the goal. But you, as evaluator, should try to get recognition of the state education department and joint council as well as the school districts' administrators and teachers as also having a role in guiding the direction of the evaluation. This applies as well to the determination of roles in doing the evaluation where those groups might well have an advisory role in planning the evaluation. They may be particularly helpful in gathering and interpreting the data. And their information needs and preferences as well as those of the client should be considered in formulating the report.

3. The evaluation of teaching competency, looked at from the administrator's point of view, requires current knowledge of both teaching practice and curriculum. But since utilization is a prime criterion for an evaluation, and since these evaluations will clearly affect stakeholders such as the teachers evaluated, they are of concern to more than the sponsor. Further, they may well be affected by local circumstances of which teachers would be aware (teaching practice certainly being different in a large city from that in a rural setting). Therefore, some kind of evaluation that involves the stakeholders in the development of the evaluation process would be important: teachers, parents, school board, administrators, and experts in the evaluation of teaching would need to be included (though members of the stakeholder group guiding the evaluation might study the literature to become their own experts).

    A common strategy is to develop a standard teacher evaluation procedure with an appeal process. The evaluation should be structured, making clear who will make the judgment, when, and on the basis of what criteria. These criteria should be jointly developed by the stakeholders and be made publicly available in written form. Such evaluations should be conducted by more than one person—for example, by two different school administrators or peers. A written report of the evaluation should be given to the teacher with the opportunity to respond and, if possible (or desired), have the evaluation judged by a review group selected to be fair (again, possibly including peers).

4. Since you want to understand what is truly happening at the home, you would need to collect information that is responsive to the staff and residents as well as the directors. This is, in effect, a case study. In this situation, a naturalistic or qualitative approach (in which you conduct unstructured interviews or engage in participant observation) would be most informative. Entering with few preconceptions, you may get a better grasp of the differing perceptions of the people involved, understand the pluralistic nature of the situation, and come up with alternative recommendations. Perhaps only by involving the staff and the residents in every stage of the evaluation will you be able to overcome suspicions and resentment and make a viable recommendation.

SUMMARY

In contrast to research that may be considered hypothesis-driven, evaluations are typically decision-driven and the success of an evaluation is in the use of the results for decisions. The decisions may result from formative evaluations that are intended to help a program improve or from summative evaluations designed to determine whether and, if so, how to continue a program, or which of several programs is best.

Important decisions with respect to planning an evaluation involve three basic arenas: (1) the role the evaluation is to play, (2) the determination of the goals of the evaluation, and (3) the role of the evaluator, staff, and/or stakeholders in the process. The decisions involved in these questions can be graphically represented as three decision spaces.

With respect to the first basic question ("What is the role the evaluation is to play?") we locate the role of the evaluation between formative or summative and between allowing restricted or unrestricted access to the findings.

The second question ("What are the goals of the evaluation and who determines them?") locates the evaluation among the possible goals:

- the client's goals,
- those achieved by the program being evaluated,
- the original goals the program was intended to achieve,
- alternative goals (e.g., goals growing out of experience with the program), or
- hidden goals (e.g., to gain attention for the program and, hence, new resources).

The goals can be determined by decision makers: those funding the program and/or evaluation, the originator or program administrator, the evaluator, or a third party such as a legislature or school board. The stakeholders may have a say in determining the goals. More likely, the decision will be made by some combination of certain decision makers and stakeholders.

The third question ("Who does what?") involves determining the responsibility of the evaluator, the administration, the staff, and the stakeholders for each step in the process—planning, implementing, interpreting, reporting, and disseminating.

If the results are to be utilized, stakeholders must trust the process that produced them, and this usually means giving them some responsibility in one or more stages of the process. The process by which the evaluation is carried out is often as important as the product.

Once these decisions are made, they guide the choice of research methods used to collect data, analyze and interpret it, and develop the report. The panorama of such methods—from qualitative to quantitative, including various combinations—is available to and selected from evaluators.

Goal-free evaluation determines what has actually been achieved by a program. The side effects of a program are often as much of consequence as the intended goals. Without knowledge of the original goals, the evaluator determines what changes the program has achieved and then compares them with those originally intended.

Certain characteristics are inherent in the nature of evaluations. Because having knowledge is power, and evaluations produce knowledge, evaluations are almost unavoidably political. Evaluations are often threatening, especially if negative results are likely to be found. Because they are usually limited to the politically feasible, evaluations tend to be conservative, to reinforce the status quo. Because so much planning and energy is required to get a new program up and running, evaluations are often afterthoughts. Higher-quality evaluation likely results if planned for from the program's outset. The complexity of policy evaluation makes timing the production of results when most needed for policy making very difficult. Providing evaluation results in the same style as the audience typically expects them enhances their usefulness. Evaluation standards have been developed to guide both sponsors and evaluators.

A Look Ahead

In the next chapter we examine survey research methods, which can use either qualitative, quantitative, or both approaches. Survey use of questionnaires with pre-set choices yields quantitative data for analysis, whereas interviewing produces responses to questions that require qualitative skills for analysis. As we might expect of a research method that falls at a midpoint on the quantitative–qualitative continuum, much of the chapter has relevance for both approaches.

Notes

[1] The author gratefully thanks Kristen Evans Flint, Syracuse University, for suggested changes.

[2] Such studies include five negative income tax/income maintenance experiments (Berk & Rossi, 1976; Moffitt, 1979; Robins et al., 1980; Rossi & Lyall, 1976; Watts & Rees, 1976; important negative side effect: family breakup); transitional aid to prisoners that provided unemployment compensation to prisoners during time of transition and helped to reduce recidivism (Berk, Lenihan, & Rossi, 1980; it reduced theft but not other crimes). Other examples concerned a housing allowance that paid subsidies to poor families to permit them to purchase better housing (Bradbury & Downs, 1981; Friedman & Weinberg, 1983; Struyk & Bendick, 1981). Other studies concerned the effects of alternative police patrols on crime rates (Kelling et al., 1974); and subsidized medical insurance on consumption of health care (Newhouse et al., 1980).

[3] This example is from E. Soffer, "The Principal as Action Researcher: A Study of Disciplinary Practice," in Susan E. Noffke and Robert B. Stevenson, *Educational Action Research: Becoming Practically Critical*. New York: Teachers College Press, © 1995 by Teachers College, Columbia University. All rights reserved. Reprinted by permission of the publisher.

[4] This old statement by Lord Heward in *Rex v. Sussex Justices* [1924] 1 KB 256 [1923] All ER 233 has been repeated hundreds of times in case law.

Survey Research
and Questionnaires

> The validity of survey data depends on persuading a scientifically selected group of people to provide accurate and detailed information about themselves, their opinions and expectations, their sense of well-being, their activities, their family finances and educational background—all to a complete stranger.
>
> —C. F. Cannell,
> *Overview: Response Bias and Interview Variability in Surveys*

The chapter begins with the steps typically involved in developing a survey and then examines the decisions that shape its nature. This is followed by discussions of each of the major data sources: questionnaires (including what and how to ask); face-to-face interviews (including focus groups); telephone interviewing (including computer-assisted telephone interviewing, CATI); and mail, e-mail, and Internet surveys. The analysis of the data follows, along with how to avoid and cure survey problems. Sources of help are described.

INTRODUCTION

The practical effect of surveys on your daily life is amazing. They influence what television programs you watch (and therefore what is scheduled), what foods show up on the grocer's shelves and how they will be packaged, and even which potential jurors a lawyer should accept or reject. Surveys guide politics—what election campaign strategy a candidate will use and how she will counter her opponent's tactics. Preelection polls help voters identify front runners, and potential financial supporters rush to jump on rising candidates' bandwagons.

Survey researchers gather data from a carefully selected sample of a population, all of whom are considered informants. They choose among all the modes of communication for appropriate ways to contact their sample and gather their data: face-to-

face interviews, group interviews or focus groups, telephone interviews (usually computer assisted), mail surveys, fax, e-mail, and the Internet.

While highly sophisticated interviewing and/or instrumentation is often involved,
surveys basically involve getting reactions to questions or other stimuli from a representative sample of a target population, to which the researcher expects to generalize. The researcher is usually interested in the commonality of their responses, how
and how much their responses differ—their variability, how closely some responses
are related to others—and how responses vary with certain demographic variables or
with measures of social, political, or psychological variables. The response record
may be in the form of an interviewer's account of an interview, self-report answers by
the respondent to multiple-choice or open-end questions, an audio or video recording of an interview, an immediate coding as the response is given on an interviewer
form (called an *interview schedule*), or some combination of these.

As in qualitative research, some research intends mainly to describe rather than
to show relationships—surveys that seek to determine the nature of persons, their
perceptions, actions, intentions, and so on. Internal Integrity's criteria of translation
validity and rival explanations eliminated, as well as credible result's check of other
relevant research, are all particularly important in such studies, especially with surveys involving constructs. Because nearly all surveys are intended to generalize from a
sample to a population, the parallel criteria of External Generality—*translation generality, restrictive conditions eliminated, and replicable result*—are nearly always relevant.

Researchers face trade-offs in order to stay within resource limits as they decide
on appropriate sample size, adequate breadth, needed depth, and the most valid data
gathering and analysis. With the same amount of resources, we can collect considerably more information about a target population with surveys than we could afford to
collect from the entire population—and more efficiently than a census could.

THE STEPS IN THE SURVEY PROCESS

Though survey researchers use qualitative and quantitative methods, qualitative
surveys are typically more targeted than such qualitative research as begins with only
a hunch about what is significant. Surveys range, however, from only slightly more
targeted (interviewing school social workers to learn how they perceive their responsibilities) to highly targeted (asking how often during each day a social worker meets
with parents). Because surveys are targeted, they usually require some preplanning.
Plans include the sample, the instrument, the method of gathering data, and initial
plans for analysis.

A Survey Plan Guide

The sequence of steps in this typical **sample survey** plan can be used as a guide.

- Determine the purpose of the survey; try to state it in about 25 words. Check it
  with colleagues and your survey sponsor, if any. For some problem areas it is
  worth checking with typical informants from the target population for potential
  hidden problems.

- Given available resources, decide on the basic design trade-offs (e.g., the relative emphasis to be given Internal Integrity vs. External Generality). Such decisions in turn bear on sample size, breadth, depth, and validity of data gathering and analysis. Limited resources can preclude large samples, long questionnaires, and face-to-face interviewing with open-end questions. Gathering data broadly and/or deeply is something only the resource rich can afford.

- Develop a sampling plan appropriate for the survey's purpose. Determine its feasibility and the availability of required information (e.g., entries for the sampling frame, completeness of stratifying information for all individuals, cost of acquiring, and so forth).

- Form a representative group from the target population. Describe the purpose of the survey and get their help in formulating relevant questions. Try out questions of your own and get the group's reactions; move from broad to more specific questions. Refine questions with them until there is only one interpretation—the one you intend. (See discussion of focus groups, p. 304.)

- Develop your instrument, interview, questionnaire, or Web site. Get feedback from colleagues and your survey sponsor, if any. Do a pilot test with a small sample of the target group, using a feedback technique to determine if they interpreted questions as intended, had appropriate knowledge, and, as far as possible, answered honestly.

- Develop a preliminary coding scheme and analysis plan and make sure that they are congruent with each other and with your survey's purpose. As these steps require, reformulate the instrument and repilot. For quantitative studies, determine the needed sample size from the pilot data (this may result in the readjustment of the basic trade-offs initially made to stay within available resources, or a search for additional ones).

- For Internet surveys, consider using one of the Web sites established to host, receive, and compile responses and, sometimes, help interpret the results. Their software may markedly simplify the process.

- When using questionnaires, prenotify participants. When mailing, use first-class service with stamped return envelopes (which generally get a higher rate of return than business reply envelopes). When e-mailing, you may want to provide a way for the respondent to certify the authenticity of the request, such as a notice about the study on an established site—a university's, association's, or other reputable organization's. Send reminder postcards one week later so they will arrive while questionnaires are still on the respondents' desks. For interviews, prenotify and then phone to confirm the appointment. Follow up nonrespondents with second questionnaire mailings, postcards, e-mails, and callbacks as appropriate. Do callbacks in the early evenings or on Saturday mornings to reach weekday workers. Aware that their answers may differ from a normal response, contact questionnaire nonrespondents by phone to ask the most important questions.

- Record times of questionnaire returns. Analyze responses in order of receipt to determine if there is a pattern, since late mailers may be like nonrespondents. A trend may indicate the nature of a nonresponse bias.

- Consider interviews with key informants in the target group to determine reactions to both the query and the querying process that should be taken into account in interpretation.
- Compile, analyze, and interpret responses with computer software tools.

MAJOR DECISIONS THAT SHAPE THE SURVEY

Mode of Data Gathering

Survey research's rich combinations of modes of communication, question selection and ordering, and open-end and closed-end questions are illustrated in Figure 24.1. In it, a project is assumed to be sufficiently targeted so that a standard set of questions would gather the desired data, the most common case. For example, one may gather data in person, by telephone, directly on a computer, through the Internet, or by mail, e-mail, or fax. Within each of these methods, everyone can be asked to respond to the same set of questions, usually in a standard order, or the order and choice of questions may be made interactively so the selection of questions and their order changes, depending on the response—prior questions determine what questions follow.

Questionnaires given interactively rarely leave the follow-up of a response to the discretion of the interviewer; generally, the branch to the next question is specified.

Figure 24.1   Alternative survey research modes.

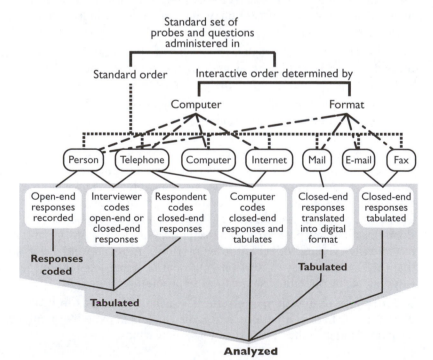

With nonnative-speaking interviewees, however, interviewers may probe to assure the question is understood and then use suggested or impromptu explanations to reach understanding before proceeding. As indicated in the figure, the next question may be indicated by instrument "yes"/"no" formatting ("yes" responders skip to question 71, "no" to question 84) or by the computer. In addition to paper formats, questionnaires may be presented through audio or video recordings or such recordings may present supplementary materials.

Whether the questions are open-end (respondent formulates response) or closed-end (response is chosen from a set of predetermined alternatives) is usually also a factor in choice of mode. All modes can be composed entirely of either open- or closed-end questions or can be a mixture. Figure 24.1, however, indicates the likely preference of open- or closed-end questions for each of the survey modes. The advantages and disadvantages of each type of question are discussed in greater detail later in this chapter.

While the mode of questioning limits the mode of response, the way those responses are processed for analysis has time, human resources, and fiscal implications. Responses to open-end questions posed by an interviewer may be electronically recorded, or described in writing by the interviewer as notes—usually as close to verbatim as possible—for later analysis. This adds a time consuming and costly step. Alternatively, the interviewer may immediately classify the response as corresponding to one of a predetermined alternative response list, leaving only the translation into digital format and tabulation before analysis. With CATI or computer-administered self-interviews (the respondent takes the instrument on a computer), the latter step is eliminated as responses are immediately tabulated for analysis.

Closed-end questions may be administered by an automated process using a telephone with responses made by the responder using the telephone touch pad; this format is usually introduced by an interviewer who then switches to the automated process. Responses so made to questionnaires on the Internet, and sometimes responses by e-mail or fax, are already in digital form and ready for tabulation and analysis. Responses on paper are usually translated into proper digital form for tabulation and analysis. Sometimes, particularly if typed, written responses can be scanned and digitized with optical character recognition (OCR) software.

Clearly, with these various alternatives there are a number of factors to take into consideration in any given survey. Table 24.1 on the following page, adapted from Turner and Martin (1984), is suggestive of when to choose interview over questionnaire. We discuss each mode in more detail later in the chapter.

Sampling a Population

A distinguishing characteristic of survey research is the care used in selecting the sample of respondents from the population. Cluster and quota sampling, discussed in chapter 8, are an outgrowth of survey methodology.

Sampling plans.   The first step in choosing a sample is determining precisely who is included in the population of interest. In trying to predict a town council election, it would seem evident that the population is all persons eligible to vote. Not so! It is those who actually will vote! Persons who have never voted in these elections,

Table 24.1   Appropriate Use of Interviews versus Questionnaires

Use an interview:	Use a questionnaire:	Use telephone interviewing:
• For immediacy of response, where speed is of the essence	• To economically get responses	• For sensitive topics
• Because CATI can reduce the questions asked as quotas for individual questions are filled	• To get a large number of responses or where the responses of a particular population are of interest	• To accurately measure latency in judging saliency
• To judge latency (time between question and response)	• When one knows or can accurately guess the likely range of responses of interest	• For gaining access to residences in poor neighborhoods where interviewers might be at risk and would stand out, and in wealthy areas where doormen would bar access
• To get at saliency (how readily item comes to mind)	• When a limited body of material is to be explored	
• To develop rapport and get a higher response rate	• When a sensitive topic is being explored that might get more honest answers from anonymity	• To reduce interviewer travel, particularly with a spread-out sample, and increase number of interviews per hour
• To determine the kind and range of responses that ought to be used in a questionnaire	• When responses might be affected by the gender, ethnicity, race, religion, or other characteristics of the interviewer	• For speed in getting results, especially with CATI where cumulative compiled results are immediately available
• When a large body of material is to be explored	• To get past screening of secretaries and doormen	
• When the range of individual responses is of more interest than the central tendency of the responses		
• When depth is wanted and responses can be probed (people will say more than they will write)		

who can't get to the polls, or who are too disaffected to vote will not help the researcher to predict the outcome. Precise definition of the population is critical to sample choice.

The stereotype of a sample survey is that it typically picks a random sample of the population. The sample is actually taken from the sampling frame, which is an enumeration of the population or that part of it that we are sampling. Where the frame is incomplete—for example, the telephone directory omits unlisted numbers, individuals who cannot afford a phone, and cell-phone-only residences—this will be reflected in the sample.

Surveying changes over time.   Because results can be available while the question is still of interest and because they are less expensive, most studies that examine change over time are **cross-sectional studies** (see the upper left corner in Figure 24.2). These, for instance, compare older respondents with younger ones in a cross-sectional sample of the target population. Inferences from such samples are subject to important alternative interpretations, however. Older individuals are a product of the events and context they have experienced. Therefore, differences between age

Figure 24.2   Graphic representation of cross-sectional, trend, cohort, and panel sampling.

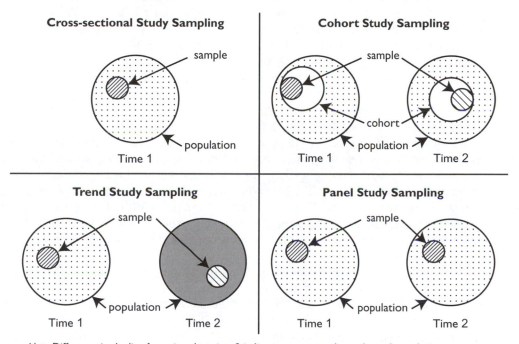

Note: Difference in shading from time 1 to time 2 indicates a new sample or changed population.

groups are often better traced to the age group's developmental history—for example, a flu epidemic or economic depression. Equally important, selection may change the composition of the older group—for example, college satisfaction is overestimated by comparing seniors with freshmen; it omits the pre-senior dissatisfied dropouts. Thus, we must view conclusions from cross-sectional studies with caution.

Longitudinal studies, which take samples over time, solve some of these problems but, depending on the particular sampling process, may incur others. Several kinds of longitudinal patterns—trend, cohort, and panel—are graphically depicted in Figure 24.2.

A **trend study** follows the changes in a particular population (lower left in the figure). In following the change in attitude of college students toward being involving in the institution's educational policy, we might sample students at three-year intervals. Not only may the population itself change over this time, but because we will be taking new samples, observed changes may also be due to the sampling variability involved in taking new samples or to persons leaving or entering the population.

A **cohort study** keeps the population constant but takes new samples from it. The cohort serves as the sampling frame but is usually a preformed sample of a population, as is shown by the white circles in the figure at upper right. For example, the cohort might be the class of 2006, which we follow through college, taking new samples of that class to determine their attitude toward being involved in policy making.

A rival explanation of observed changes in mortality (see p. 348) is the selective drop-out of cohort members.

A **panel sample** is a cohort study in which the sample is retained throughout the study and is queried two or more times (lower right in the figure). It gives a stable basis for comparison provided the panel stays relatively intact during the study. If the likelihood of member loss is great, we could compensate by starting with a larger panel or find satisfactory replacements. Because "movers" and "stayers" tend to differ on certain characteristics, if these are related to what we are studying, then exact replacement may prove difficult. Again, mortality may provide a rival explanation for observed changes. Because of the problem of retaining an intact group over time, panel studies tend to be of short duration.

Retesting or reobservation in panel studies, however, can have effects. Having experienced the instrument or interview once, individuals have time to consider their answers for the next data collection. Known as **testing**, we first encountered it in experimentation (p. 495). Further, knowing that they are panel members may create expectations. For example, Terman's study of talent identified a panel of child geniuses. The identification itself probably created expectations that may have been self-fulfilling and changed the nature of the results (Burks, Jensen, & Terman, 1930; Cox, 1926; Terman et al., 1926; Terman & Oden, 1947, 1959).

A panel study shows individual as well as group changes and shows who is changing and how. We can then track back to the events, the characteristics of the individuals, and the situations that might have contributed to the change. Further, since the same individuals are remeasured, it is more sensitive to small changes than comparably sized random samples. Thus, there are advantages and disadvantages to each kind of study.

Sample size.   The most common sampling question is, "How big a sample must I have?" The precise answer to this question is given on pp. 452–454. In brief, additional cases increase accuracy considerably for small samples, but much bigger increases in sample size are required for proportionally comparable increases in accuracy in large samples. A useful rule is that halving the error requires a quadrupling of cases. For instance, suppose there is a question to which the population responds 50% "yes" and 50% "no." If 100 cases will give a 10% error, an additional 300 cases (total 400) cuts it to a 5% error. But an additional 1,200 cases (1,600 total) are required to cut it in half again! Keep in mind that unless the population is small and the sample is a substantial part of it (10% or more), the *population size is not an important variable*. For example, we can estimate the salinity of a body of water from a representative thimble full of water, whether the body of water is a small pond, or it is the ocean. The size of population (the pond or the ocean) doesn't require a different size sample provided the water is well mixed so it is homogenous. The latter is an assumption that one makes in sampling.

You might argue that if you took a quart of water instead of a thimble full, you would get a more accurate estimate. That is true, the variability of the estimates will be smaller, but that decrease occurs whether you are estimating for a pond or for the ocean.

> Studies tracking changes over time may use cross-sectional, trend, cohort, or panel sampling.

> Cross-sectional studies estimate such things as the effect of growth, experience, or the passage of time by comparing younger with older persons at a given point in time in a cross-section of the population. They are the least expensive and quickest to do because the researcher does not have to wait to collect the data.

> Trend studies collect data from different samples of a population over time; the population is allowed to change as it naturally would.

> Cohort studies collect data from different samples of an identified group of individuals over time; that is, the sampling frame is kept constant.

> Panel studies collect data from the same selected sample of individuals over time.

> Larger samples are needed to increase the accuracy of estimates of population characteristics.

Sampling the Behavior of Respondents

Sampling enters survey research at two levels. At the population level you are interested in learning something in particular about a defined group of people; the sample is so designed as to represent that population. This was the focus of the previous section. But sampling also enters at the individual level—sampling the behavior in the particular area of interest from each reached member of the chosen population. The sample is assumed to be representative of that person's behavior in that area but is restricted to the breadth, depth, and quality of information that can be obtained in such a limited contact.

Though not often thought of in the sampling context, as a behavioral sample it is subject to the rules of sampling in chapter 8. Other things being equal, the greater the level of accuracy desired, the larger the sample required; with a more homogeneous sample, a greater level of accuracy of information can be obtained in the same size sample; the more heterogeneous the sample, the larger the sample required to obtain the same level of accuracy of information. These are reflected in the mode of data gathering used, the length of the interview or questionnaire, the nature of the questions and the proportion of the instrument devoted to each area to be covered. This results in trade-offs, noted in the discussion of data-gathering modes below.

THE SURVEY INSTRUMENT

The term *survey instrument* is used in its broadest sense to include, for example, interviewer's survey guide, and CATI program questions. So this material applies to *all* modes: face-to-face interviews as well as the standard questionnaire used in mail, e-mail, fax, and Internet surveys.

Important considerations in instrument construction are what to ask, how to ask it, how to order the questions, how to format the instrument, and how to improve it. These topics form the basis of the following discussion, much of which applies equally well to interviewing, especially as it relates to question development.

What to Ask

Although some instruments are simply probes to explore an area, most are targeted. An early step in planning what to ask is to lay out a "blueprint" to guide question construction. Called a **table of specifications**, such a table is shown in Table 24.2 for a study of the impact of various election events on the voter. We encountered these tables earlier in chapter 18 in the discussion of test construction. Subjects of the query are listed down the left; queries are listed across the top. The cells where queries meet content specify the nature of the question (for example, in the cell designated by where the first row meets the first column, the item elicits the respondent's initial reaction to the first positive television advertisement of a candidate). The numbers in the cells indicate the number of questions on that topic. Clearly, the largest proportion of questions in this 15-item instrument will emphasize the impact of television on voting. Some researchers work backward—from what the report should contain to the needed questions to minimize the "get-that-now-in-case-I-can't-later" tendency.

Table 24.2   Table of Specifications to Guide Question Construction for a Study of the Impact of Various Election Events on Voting Behavior

Study of Impact of Various Election Events on Voting Behavior	Initial Reaction	Considered Reaction	Expected Effect on Vote	Actual Effect on Vote
Television advertisement for candidate				
First positive ad	I	I		I
Second positive ad		I	I	I
Negative ad		I		I
Newspaper ad for candidate				I
Newspaper endorsement of candidate	I			I
Candidate's performance during televised debate			I	I
Literature delivered to home	I			I

How to Ask It

Careful wording is essential to portray accurately what is to be asked, to avoid biased or leading questions, and to ensure that the response is to the full question without confusion over which part was answered or what else caused the response.

The variety of question types is limited only by your imagination. Almost immediately this brings up the question of whether to use open- or closed-end questions. Each has its advantages and disadvantages, which are summarized in Table 24.3.

In addition to open-end questions, common types include short answer, checklists, rankings, response on a verbal scale ("very difficult, somewhat difficult, not difficult"; "very poor, poor, good, very good"; "Use the following scale to judge the expressions of opinion: strongly agree, agree, undecided, disagree, strongly disagree"), response on a graphical scale ("Check on the bar to show how clearly this

Table 24.3   A Summary of the Advantages and Disadvantages of Open-End and Closed-End Questions (after Peterson, 2000; and Turner & Martin, 1984)

Open-End Questions	Closed-End Questions
Less likely to influence responses.	The nature of alternative responses and their order may influence response.
Explores the range of possible responses and creativity of responses (including projective techniques).	Limits the range of responses to those suggested by the instrument.
Can probe response, determine understanding of question.	Unable to probe response.
Can give a measure of salience.	No measure of salience.
Possibility of bias in fieldnotes or in categorization of response.	Fieldnotes are rare; answer key does the categorization.
Requires more time per question; fewer questions in given contact time.	Less time per question; more questions in given contact time.
Usually sample size is limited by resources.	Sample size is less likely to be limited by resources.
Less likely to get an accurate response to sensitive questions, but can be used with devices to conceal response.	More likely to get accurate responses to sensitive topics; format easily lends itself to devices used to conceal response.
Possibly less expensive to develop; more expensive to administer in interviews and then to code, tabulate, and analyze.	Probably more expensive to develop; less expensive to administer, response is ready to tabulate and analyze.

instruction is written: very clearly __ __ __ __ __ not clearly at all"), weighing alternatives ("Indicate the relative importance of these statements by distributing 10 points among them"), and a variety of other multiple-choice formats. Measurement books with sample test items may suggest formats. Bradburn, Sudman, and Wansink (2006), among others, give excellent advice and suggest item formats. Past surveys are often helpful in suggesting the wording of questions. Gale Research Company (1983–present) lists databases of past surveys from 1983 on.

Projective techniques.   Private attitudes that control our behavior are often different from those publicly expressed. Therefore, direct measurement through scales asking the extent of agreement with certain stated positions may fail. Hence indirect measures are often used (see Webb et al., 1981). **Projective techniques** are one form of indirect measurement. Three commonly used projective approaches are association, fantasy and ambiguous stimuli, and categorizing (Oppenheim, 1966).

In word-association measures, we ask for the first thing that comes into the respondent's mind in response to a stimulus. The stimulus may be a word, a picture, or a graphic. This technique tends to work better in an interview because the respondent does not have time to think and censor responses. Even with a questionnaire, especially if there are a large number of items, over time the responses tend to become less guarded and more revealing of underlying attitudes.

Respondents can be asked to construct a story suggested by fantasy ("Tell me a story about a class clown") or respond to a specific stimulus (e.g., while viewing a picture of an African American child and a Caucasian child playing together, the interviewer asks, "What are they saying to each other?"). Such responses are revealing of the person's "building blocks" of experience and attitudes. Using ambiguous stimuli, such as cloud or inkblot pictures ("Tell me what you see in these pictures") requires respondents to assign meaning and reveal their personal outlook.

Categorizing and labeling reveal how individuals see the world and thus their attitudes. Asking them to cluster photographs of faces "in whatever way you think they belong together" and then requesting that they "please explain the groupings" may tell how respondents categorize people and what characteristics of individuals are dominant in their minds. These reveal underlying thinking and suggest the attitude structure.

Ordering the Questions

The order of the questions is important. The opening of the instrument sets the tone for the respondents regarding both motivation and purpose. Grabbing their attention and "pulling them in" is good practice, and titles often help. Erdos (1970) suggests instrument titles that appeal to the ego ("A Survey of Industry Leaders"), emphasize the topic and its relevance ("Taking Inventory of Your Personal Health"), underline its importance ("A Nationwide Survey of . . ."), or emphasize the respondent-researcher tie ("For Alumni Only—A Confidential Survey").

The first few items are important in setting the tone, reducing defensiveness, and allaying anxiety. Begin by asking easy-to-answer questions that personally involve the respondent: "What do you like about the location of your home?" Questions that arouse the interest or curiosity of the respondent are a good beginning, even if you don't tabulate them later. Early questions also set the frame of reference for later ones. The **funnel-sequenced questionnaire** parallels the focus interview in design; it starts broadly and then narrows to the topic of specific interest. As with the focus interview, the intent is to prevent the early responses from biasing later ones. Broad questions obtain the respondent's general frame of reference. When asking about a new topic about which an informed opinion is desired, invert the funnel and cover the aspects of the question in detail. Then, at the end, you ask, "Now, taking all these things into consideration . . ."

FACE-TO-FACE INTERVIEWS

Much of the "nuts and bolts" of interviews is covered in chapter 14, which is devoted to the topic. Survey researchers usually use structured interviews as described in the second column of Table 14.1 on page 298.

There is extensive literature on the techniques of interviewing, some of which borrows from counseling and clinical techniques. Various approaches to interviewing have been proposed, each with its own advantages. Chapter 14 notes different

Hallmarks of Survey Instruments and Tips on Question Construction

Each of the construction tips below is a hallmark of an effective instrument when followed and is therefore useful in critiquing one.

- Keep both the instrument and individual items short and simple. Short, simple questions are better than long, complex ones for maintaining interest and imparting a feeling of movement. They are also more likely to be understood.

- Avoid qualifying phrases and clauses. Be specific and concrete.

- Use phrasing and language that will be understood and will appeal to all segments of the intended population. This is sometimes difficult because education and experience may vary widely, so that what is simple enough and clear for one person may seem condescending to another. Be sure to pretest with varied groups.

- Be careful of colloquial terms and jargon ("winnow" may be known to farmers but not city dwellers). Slang becomes outdated quickly and may vary in interpretation from place to place.

- Choice of words may result in bias. Anglos react differently to the term "wetbacks" than they do to the term "Mexican Americans." Asking about "big business" gets a response different from that for just "business." Every modifier can make a difference!

- Be sure respondents interpret the question as intended; pretesting is essential for this. ("What kind of headache remedy do you use?" may refer to the brand, type of medicine, or therapy—pills, liquids, or lying down in a dark room for an hour.)

- Be aware of the importance of the **framing of questions.** Slovic, Fischhoff, and Lichtenstein (1982) found mandatory seat belts favored by only 54% of respondents when the likelihood of being injured was expressed as once in 100,000 trips. However, when the question was phrased in terms of a lifetime of driving—which changes this to a chance of one person in three—fully 78% favored it. When Harris (1973) asked, "How long was the movie?" the average estimate was 130 minutes; when he asked, "How short was the movie?" the average estimate was 100 minutes.

  Tversky and Kahneman (1981) give a number of examples showing how "seemingly inconsequential changes in the formulation of choice problems caused significant shifts of preference" (p. 457). They reinforce the importance of trying out all formulations on small groups ahead of time to be sure they communicate as intended.

- Make sure the context in which a question is asked is appropriate. In an instrument about the reasons for buying a new car, a series of questions about conservation of energy preceded the main issue. Not surprisingly, "fuel economy" turned out to be the most frequent response. For a more accurate answer, the question regarding purchase of a car should have been asked before the questions on conservation of energy.

- Avoid the **double-barreled question,** which poses two issues at once, obscuring the one being responded to. ("Have Russia's improved housing and industrialization raised the standard of living?" What if the respondent believes that housing has but industrialization hasn't?)

(continued)

- Avoid the equally subtle one-and-a-half-barreled question, where the second issue is introduced into the alternatives, for example:

  The United States is now negotiating a strategic arms agreement with the Soviet Union in what is known as SALT II. Which one of the following statements is closest to your opinion on these negotiations?

  — I strongly support SALT II.

  — SALT II is somewhat disappointing, but on balance I have to support it.

  — I would like to see more protection for the United States before I would be ready to support SALT II.

  — I strongly oppose the SALT II arms agreement with the Soviets.

  — I don't know enough about SALT II to have an opinion yet (Sudman & Bradburn, 1982, p. 136).

  The third response introduced adequacy of defense as a new issue and swayed responses negatively, whereas other surveys reported stronger support for the treaty.

- Avoid biasing the response by the question—an obvious point, but often both sides of the issue are not included in the lead. Payne (1951) notes that when questioned on whether companies could arrange things to avoid layoffs, 63% of respondents said they could and 22% said they could not. But adding the other side of the question—"or do you think layoffs are unavoidable?"—dropped the 63% to 43% and almost doubled the 22% to 43%.

- Allow respondents to protect their egos while responding. Otherwise, they may make up answers to avoid embarrassment. For example, lead with a question undercutting the expectation of a response. Instead of starting with, "What books does your child read?" first inquire, "Are you able to keep track of your child's reading?" Rephrase questions such as "Did you graduate from college?" to "What is the highest grade in school you completed?"

- Assuage the guilt of responding negatively by first asking for the positive: "What do you like about General Bullmoose?" "What do you dislike about him?"

- Use an impersonal lead, because it often gets responses when direct questions cannot: "Do persons like yourself generally believe . . . ?" "Are you like them?"

- Avoid negative questions, if possible: "We should not admit tiny nations to the United Nations." Respondents may miss the not. If the affective tone would be lost by positive phrasing, emphasize the *not* with underlining or italics.

- With multiple-choice questions, be sure that the list of alternatives is complete or an "other than the above" alternative is provided. Trying out the questions in an open-ended form with a sample of the target group helps determine the range of likely responses and whether a "none of the above" or "other, please specify" is necessary. Supplying the respondent with an incomplete list reflects negatively on instrument preparation, which, in turn, may be reflected in the care taken with responses.

- Comparison with results from an earlier poll is often helpful in determining whether new results are trustworthy. Such analyses help spot context and wording effects not otherwise noticeable. Because such effects are so pervasive and important, for very important issues some pollsters suggest being very wary of a question from one poll.

- Cluster similar questions to minimize the respondent's "mental set" changes.
- Order logically for flow and movement across topic coverage—such orderings as specific to general, past to present, or familiar to unfamiliar.
- Leave demographic questions to the end unless you are trying to determine whether the respondent should be questioned at all. It is well to explain why the demographics are important: "To determine how people of different backgrounds respond to these questions, we'd like a few facts about you."
- Leave sensitive questions to the end; usually, respondents feel they have invested enough time in the instrument to answer them rather than discard the whole effort.
- Save respondent time and reading with "Skip to question X" where questions in between are irrelevant. Arrows leading to the next pertinent question or other clever devices can help ensure that directions are followed.
- Check the effect of question order with a preliminary trial by using different orderings that seem to have merit. Often ordering affects the nature, length, and spontaneity of responses.

styles of interviewing and some of the factors affecting them. The nondirective approach is especially important for interviewers to master. Interviews are particularly useful in tracing causes, especially when they lie in the personal meanings of a common experience—what was significant to the respondent. For example, if literature was used to stimulate voting in an experiment, interviews might be used to find the significant aspects of the literature, the most effective aspects, and with what groups they were effective.

Interviewers typically gain more access with "I'd like to come in and talk with you about . . ." than with "May I come in . . ." It is important to collect the data uniformly, asking questions exactly as worded, and, where used, carefully following the interview form. If not recorded, get responses close to verbatim; abbreviations help. Keep probes and interviewer comments separate with parentheses. Figure 24.3 on the following page shows part of a sample interview form; note how the interviewer handled a less than cooperative interviewee.

Focus Groups and Group Interviews

Group interviews that are usually aimed at getting a samples' reaction to a particular question, product, or situation are called **focus groups**. Many consider them to be as good an information source as individual interviews, and they are conducted in less time with less labor. Focus groups and telephone interviewing are usually the methods of choice when getting information quickly is of major importance. Virtual focus groups can be held by telephone or online as well as face-to-face. They permit geographically disparate individuals to participate. Online groups can be synchronous (everyone online at the same time in conference mode) or asynchronous (everyone contributes to the online discussion as they get around to it—like chat rooms). A more complete discussion of focus groups appeared earlier, page 304.

Figure 24.3   A completed page from an interview form.

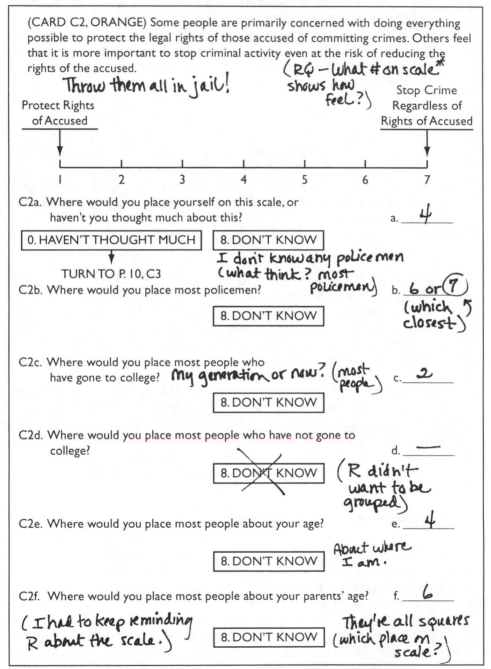

(CARD C2, ORANGE) Some people are primarily concerned with doing everything possible to protect the legal rights of those accused of committing crimes. Others feel that it is more important to stop criminal activity even at the risk of reducing the rights of the accused.

Throw them all in jail!   *(RQ — What # on scale* shows how feel?)*

Protect Rights of Accused   Stop Crime Regardless of Rights of Accused

1   2   3   4   5   6   7

C2a. Where would you place yourself on this scale, or haven't you thought much about this?   a. _____4_____

| 0. HAVEN'T THOUGHT MUCH | 8. DON'T KNOW |

TURN TO P. 10, C3

I don't know any policemen (what think? most policemen)

C2b. Where would you place most policemen?   b. _6 or ⑦_
(which closest)

| 8. DON'T KNOW |

C2c. Where would you place most people who have gone to college? *My generation or now? (most people)*   c. _____2_____

| 8. DON'T KNOW |

C2d. Where would you place most people who have not gone to college?   d. _____—_____

| 8. ~~DON'T KNOW~~ | *(R didn't want to be grouped)*

C2e. Where would you place most people about your age?   e. _____4_____

About where I am.

| 8. DON'T KNOW |

C2f. Where would you place most people about your parents' age?   f. _____6_____

(I had to keep reminding R about the scale.)

They're all squares (which place on scale?)

| 8. DON'T KNOW |

*RQ = repeats question (in parentheses because this was the respondent's question)

Source: Survey Research Center. *The Interviewer's Manual,* Revised Edition. Copyright © 1976 by the Institute for Social Research, University of Michigan, Ann Arbor, MI. Reprinted with permission.

Tips on Face-to-Face Interviewing[1]

Following are tips on survey interviewing that supplement chapter 14's tips on interviewing (p. 307).

- Don't ask, "May I come in?" Simply assume that the interview will take place: "I would like to come in and talk with you about . . ."

- Answer questions about the survey as if the person were interested and friendly. Comment in a nonspecific way that does not bias the interview: "We are interested in how people feel about . . ."

- Have literature or copies of clippings that show the value of past studies as an example of the worth of the interview.

- Collect the data uniformly. Ask questions exactly as they are worded. If there is an interview form, follow the specified order. Read slowly and repeat questions that are misunderstood.

- Record the responses verbatim, using abbreviations to get them down. Record probes and interviewer comments in parentheses. Write on the form as the respondent talks. Figure 24.3 shows a sample interview form.

COMPUTER–ASSISTED INTERVIEWING

Two types of computer-assisted interviewing are commonly used: computer-assisted telephone interviewing (CATI), and computer-assisted personal interviewing (CAPI). Both are discussed in the following sections.

Computer–Assisted Telephone Interviewing (CATI)

With CATI software as many aspects of interviewing are automated as possible. Once area codes and local telephone-number prefixes of the sample have been selected, random-digit dialing generates and dials the last four digits. The computer tracks whether the number responds. If not, the computer files it for callback at the most appropriate time to reach individuals in that community as determined by analyzing the accumulated information. Because random-digit dialing reaches many businesses and fax lines, usually the calling list is restricted to active household lines without blocks of numbers that are largely businesses or institutions. Once a potential respondent is reached, the call is switched to an interviewer who, reading the computer screen as in a conversation, is led through the interview by the computer.

Interviews usually begin with questions to determine whether the respondent is part of the target sample or to ask for the person in the household who qualifies. As the interviewer enters responses into the computer, it determines whether to break off the interview because the demographics do not fit quotas needed to fill the sampling plan or whether to continue. To personalize the interview, the computer can be programmed to insert the respondent's name or other demographic information at appropriate points in the script. It can recall previous answers and point out inconsistencies so that the interviewer can probe for reasons. The computer indicates when the interviewer has made a clerical error, for example, in case the coding doesn't fit any of the acceptable codes for a given item.

An important time saver is the computer's capacity to branch the interview to relevant questions, skipping whole blocks judged inappropriate on the basis of previous responses. Light pens or touch screens can eliminate the need for keyboard skills to enter data. Close control of the interviewing process (and useful research) is possible because all the interviewers are typically in the same location, and the supervisor can easily monitor and correct errors. Lavrakas (1993) argues that these quality control measures recommend CATI "as the preferred [survey] . . . mode" (p. 5) if the required data can be so gathered.

Telephone interviews tend to elicit shorter responses than face-to-face encounters, but total length does not seem to be shorter. With shorter responses and no transportation time between interviews, the number of interviews per worker-hour is much higher than with face-to-face interviews. Of course, nonverbal cues that add meaning are lost, and maintaining rapport may require additional interviewer responsiveness. In exchange, the impersonal aspect also permits a kind of anonymity that allows sensitive issues to be handled with less embarrassment. CATI does not have as high a return as face-to-face interviewing, but it is higher than with mail or Web questionnaires. Face-to-face has the highest rate of success in persuading the individual to cooperate.

Completely automated surveys have also been developed with recorded lead-ins and questions. Respondents answer by pressing telephone buttons: "Press 1, 2, 3, 4, and up to 5 to indicate how strongly you agree with this statement." The computer responds to such responses as if an interviewer had keyed them in, but the respondent has actually done so. This method does away with the trained interviewer, one of the most costly parts of the process. However, it introduces other selective factors, such as who is sufficiently motivated by the topic to be willing to respond to prerecorded queries.

Increasingly sophisticated software and decreasing equipment costs make CATI attractive to researchers, although there is resistance on the part of potential interviewees. Some experts argue that if the topic is of interest, individuals still enjoy the opportunity to express their opinions. This puts a premium on sample selection procedures.

The effect of cell-phone usage on CATI has yet to be assessed. As this is written, there is no centralized cell-phone directory, and the difficulty of obtaining numbers to include in a sampling frame precludes their inclusion in most surveys. Research in Finland suggests that the cell-phone-only households are largely young persons in unstable situations. Omitting such a group from a sampling frame could clearly bias results (Kuusela & Simpanen, 2002). Although this phone option appears to be growing, the majority still have both cell and land lines (ibid.). Clearly, this is a situation that will have to be monitored as cell-phone usage in the United States continues to grow.

CATI software, into which questions can be inserted, is available for personal computers. It is relatively inexpensive and is increasingly flexible. Search the Internet for "CATI or CAPI software."

Computer-Assisted Personal Interviewing (CAPI)

Notebook/laptop computers make **computer-assisted personal interviewing (CAPI)** feasible, so that responses can be entered into a computer instead of hand-written on a form. Completed interviews are downloaded into the main databank, providing quick data return and allowing interviewers to remain in the field. CAPI requires a skilled touch typist who can maintain eye contact with the respondent while recording answers. Unlike CATI, nonverbal responses may be noted. Further, many of the advantages of CATI, such as branching and catching inconsistent responses, are possibilities. However, be sure to encrypt data that has been promised privacy; this will protect it if the laptop is lost or stolen or if downloading is interrupted.

> ▶ Computer-assisted telephone interviewing retains many of the advantages of face-to-face interviews but has other pros and cons.
>
> • It can obtain results quickly,
> • It eliminates travel,
> • It tends to elicit shorter responses,
> • It can warn of respondents in already filled quotas, and
> • It can make automatic callbacks.
>
> ▶ If the computer leads the interviewer through the questions, it can use less skilled personnel and can automatically check the consistency of answers.
>
> ▶ Its main disadvantage is that it cannot pick up nonverbal cues.
>
> ▶ There may be a selective factor as to who responds to face-to-face but does not respond to telephone interviews, and vice versa.

MAIL SURVEYS

A mail survey gathers large amounts of data from many respondents very inexpensively. If the topic is of interest to the respondents and there are few questions, they may respond to open-ended queries, just as in an interview. The information will have less depth and richness, because people will always say more than they will write. Further, respondents have more opportunity to censor their replies. But mail questionnaires may get past the screening of doormen and secretaries who keep interviewers at bay. Also, you can ensure the confidentiality of responses if the questionnaire is returned anonymously.

The Letter of Transmittal[2]

Motivating the respondent is central to getting a reply with good data. The **letter of transmittal**, which, together with a return envelope, accompanies the questionnaire, is a major means of motivation. Respondents will answer many, many items and even open-end questions if they are inspired to do so. Erdos (1970) provides some excellent advice for composing a well-written letter of transmittal:

- Personalize the communication.
- Ask a favor.
- Indicate the importance of the research project and its purpose.
- Indicate the importance of the recipient—"You were chosen as part of a national survey of . . ."
- Stress the importance of replies in general—"Your answers will enable us to . . ."
- Note the importance of replies even from readers who consider themselves not qualified to respond.
- Indicate how the recipient or others may benefit from the research.
- Note that completing the questionnaire will take only a short time.
- Point out that the questionnaire can be answered easily.
- Include a stamped return envelope.
- Describe how the recipient was selected, making that person one of a special group.
- Indicate that answers are anonymous and confidential.
- Offer a report of the results.

Tips on Questionnaire Format

- Returns are highest on mail questionnaires that are short, easily responded to, attractive, and of personal interest.
- Keep the length within an uncrowded two to four pages—one or two pages is better; feature plenty of white space. Avoid a slick advertising look—otherwise recipients may confuse it with junk mail. A personal rather than commercial look makes it clear that the person's response is important to you.
- Make the first page especially appealing and easy to read.
- Don't number consecutively if there are many questions. Number within sections to provide a feeling of progress. Use sectioning with interesting headings ("About You and Your Department"). Break lists every five lines or so.
- Put write-in lines or boxes for responses in a uniform place, usually at the right, so that the question is visible as subjects respond (unless you are dealing with a left-handed sample).
- Use an easy-to-read typeface and be sure the printing is of high quality. Print both sides, so that the questionnaire appears shorter. Use good but lightweight paper.
- Arrange the questions on the page so that the respondent easily understands the flow through the questionnaire; this not only saves respondent time but also gives a feeling of progress.
- Use software that markedly simplifies questionnaire production. It provides templates from which answers can easily be scanned into computers to produce reports with spreadsheets, graphs, and charts. Do an Internet search on "survey host" or free survey software."

- Include a note of urgency in the request for response.
- Express the sender's appreciation for the response.
- Indicate the sender's importance to the respondent. Special populations respond to appeals from their own organizations.
- Make the letter look professional.
- If an incentive is included, describe it and indicate its purpose. Include tokens of appreciation instead of promising them for a return.
- Avoid anything in the letter that might bias responses.
- Keep the letter brief.
- If your IRB requires you to do so, list someone to contact if there are questions. This may be a good idea anyway, to gain feedback indicating problems that were not anticipated.

Note the number of items concerned with motivating the respondent through conveying the importance of the project, the respondent, and the reply—they make up almost half the list! Be sure that comments about the importance of the respondent sound sincere; obvious flattery may backfire. Limited sample size emphasizes the importance of replies ("You are one of few individuals who have moved into this area in the last 12 months; therefore . . ."). To avoid follow-ups ask for replies, even from those not qualified ("Send your return even if you are not a homeowner; otherwise, we'll never know").

Computer-personalized letters are so common these days that they may have lost some of their original appeal, but probably not all of it. If the topic is sensitive and confidentiality is important, it is better to make the letter impersonal and routine. If you are offering a report, supply a separate request form. A stamped envelope produces a higher response rate than a business reply envelope.

E-MAIL AND INTERNET SURVEYS

We conventionally think of questionnaires as being mailed, but survey researchers use all the two-way communication media. E-mail and Internet questionnaires have the advantage of low cost of distribution and rapid response. Costs of distribution and return are the least of any of the modes, 5 to 20% of paper surveys (Khosrow-Pour, 2002; Sheehan & Hoy, 1999), and the percentage decreases as sample size increases (Watt, 1999). Return percentages are comparable to those of mail, but Sheehan and McMillan (1999) found the average time for e-mail returns to be less (7.6 days) than for mail returns (11.8 days). Internet questionnaires can use graphics and motion where it would be helpful, but the look may differ with old browser versions and different platforms. Requiring a password limits responses to those invited. There can be unexpected hazards: Eliot (2006) offered an incentive and discovered that "a link to our study had been placed on a site that catered to folks looking for online contests."

Other things to consider:

- Samples are limited to those with e-mail addresses and Internet access. Avoidance of junk mail has made obtaining addresses difficult.

- The labor of scrolling to assure consistency with earlier responses may make for more spontaneous answers, but restriction to a screenful at a time may limit what can be asked and how it can be queried.

- Self-administration means that self-censorship of responses may occur.

- Inclusion of the sender's address in the response limits anonymity.

- The sender's name, subject, and possibly message size, all of which typically appear on an e-mail "in" box, can be critical in getting past a junk-mail filter.

- Like mail surveys, there is no guarantee that the actual respondent is the one who was targeted, nor that responding was done in a single, uninterrupted session.

- Using techniques to intrinsically motivate your respondents is as least as important as with mail questionnaires, maybe more so.

- Standards for the ethical use of the Internet have been approved by the Association of Internet Researchers and have been published (Ess & AoIR, 2002, online at http://www.Aoir.org/reports/ethics.pdf).

PILOT TESTING

Subject all interview schedules, questionnaires, and letters of transmittal to pilot testing before using! Use test respondents who closely resemble those you intend to query. Then have a sufficient sample of the pilot group think aloud as they move through the letter of transmittal and, item by item, the questionnaire. Review what they reacted to, what they meant by their answers, and why they answered as they did. Pilot test until you are saturated—not getting additional useful information. This will confirm that you have conveyed what you intended and that responses reflect what you were asking. The time and effort spent in pilot testing will be more than repaid by the elimination of questionnaire problems for both respondents and interviewers.

Interrupting an interview to ask about particular responses disrupts the flow. One remedy is to audio or video record the session for **stimulated recall**. This involves playing the recording for the respondent and stopping it where you wish to query responses. Given the stimulation of video or audio replays, respondents seem able to report both events and inner feelings with an apparent authenticity that suggests they were reliving those moments (Bloom, 1954; Kagan, Krathwohl & Farquhar, 1965).

When the questionnaire is intended to measure a construct, the procedures of item analysis used with tests (discussed on pp. 418–419) are applicable to questionnaires, as are estimates of test reliability and validity (discussed in chapter 18). Discovery of nonfunctional items may allow shortening the questionnaire.

CODING AND ANALYSIS OF SURVEY DATA

Coding and analysis of interview data is the same as analysis of qualitative data described in chapter 15. Because surveys are typically targeted to obtain particular information, you can establish the code system before you gather your data.

Coding of Interview and Questionnaire Responses

Try coding on your first interviews to assure that it is adequate and is not missing important unanticipated material. Reproducing the response codes on the form adds to the clutter and is usually unnecessary unless the interview is long and/or the coding system complex. Interviewers quickly become familiar with the codes and usually can code the responses as they are given. Keeping responses on the same edge of the paper speeds tabulation. If the equipment is available to you, machine-readable response forms and equipment save the time and labor involved in keying the codes into a computer, with its data-entry errors. If there are multiple coders, checking the consistency of coding across them is important; see inter-rater reliability (p. 421).

Following is some practical advice:

- At the outset, assign separate codes to distinctions and items of information that might be important. You can always merge codes later; for instance, categorize within "Other, please specify" responses to avoid recoding if one may later wish to distinguish among them.

- Make codes exhaustive of the response range but mutually exclusive so that a given response will always carry the same code.

- Be consistent (e.g., consistently use 1 for yes and 0 for no).

- If missing data may be a significant factor, distinguish the different causes: doesn't know, skipped question, refused to respond, indecipherable, inappropriate response, and so on.

- Assign codes to the most common patterns of multiple responses.

- Check consistency of coding across coders and over time.

- Provide each coder with a coding manual, and keep all manuals up-to-date as resolutions of coding problems are agreed upon.

Analysis of Interview and Questionnaire Data

Most survey data are tabulated, compiled, and analyzed with statistical computer programs. Many of the statistics commonly used were discussed in chapters 17–20. In general, using the simplest applicable analysis will require fewer assumptions and be understood by the widest audience. Simple percentages or averages often suffice. For instance, to determine the influence of education on voting behavior, construct **cross-tabulation** tables like the one in Table 24.4 on the following page. It contains data from two questions: "Did you vote in the last presidential election?" and "What is your highest level of education?" The raw data are given under the heading "Number of Cases."

Turning these first two columns into percentages of the whole group, as in the middle two columns, shows that they split roughly 60–40 with more nonvoters than voters. About half (29 + 19%) have only a high school education. From the last two columns it seems that the nonvoters have a lower level of education than the voters. There it is apparent that about twice as many nonvoters have only an elementary education (27% vs. 12%) and about half as many a college education or beyond (17 + 7 or 24% vs. 27 + 15 or 42%). For many purposes, such simple percentage analysis is enough.

Table 24.4   Cross-tabulation of Voting Behavior and Level of Education

Level of Education	Number of Cases N = 423		Percentage of Cases		Percentage by Education Level	
	Nonvoters	Voters	Nonvoters	Voters	Nonvoters	Voters
Elementary	68	21	16	5	27	12
High School	123	80	29	19	49	46
College	42	47	10	11	17	27
Beyond College	17	25	4	6	7	15
Total	250	173	59	41	100	100

▶ Coding must be done carefully to maintain data validity.

▶ Quality control can be provided by training coders, using code books that are kept up-to-date as questions are resolved, and sampling coded questionnaires for coding accuracy and consistency.

▶ Development and analysis of cross-tabulated tables provide information on the variation of responses with various demographic and other independent variables. These throw considerable light on the respondents' underlying characteristics, value structures, and thinking processes.

PROBLEMS AFFECTING SURVEY RESULTS

Inquiry into Sensitive Topics

Getting honest responses to questions regarding sensitive topics is a special problem. Wentland (1993) meta-analyzed studies where the accuracy of response could be checked. As might be expected, it showed accuracy negatively correlated with the sensitivity of the topic as well as the social desirability factor—with questionnaires less affected than interviews. However, for accuracy, respondents must believe their responses will be kept anonymous. Sins of shady researchers affect later honest efforts. If you promise anonymity, budget for follow-ups of everyone.

Various forms of the randomized response technique originated by Warner (1965) are useful in providing the respondent with greater security (Himmelfarb & Edgell, 1980; Schuman & Kalton, 1985). The respondent is confronted with two or more questions, one or more of which is not at all sensitive. A random device determines which question the respondent is to answer. For instance: "Please flip a coin, but do not show it to me. If the coin comes up heads, when I ask you to, please answer this question: 'Have you ever used marijuana, cocaine, or heroin or some form thereof?' If the coin comes up tails, please answer this one: 'Is your birthday in December?' Now tell me your answer, please." Assuming that the respondent understands the process, it removes most of the embarrassment surrounding the questioning.

How the Random Birthday Technique Works

With a random coin flip, half the sample will answer each question. Since birthdays are spread about equally across the year, about one-twelfth, or 8.33%, will answer "yes" to the second question and 91.67% will answer "no." Since they constitute half the cases, subtracting half the 8.33%, or 4.17%, from the yes responses and, similarly, 91.67/2, or 45.83%, from the no responses will yield the percentages of affirmative and negative responses for the other half of the group. Doubling the other half's percentages will yield an estimate of the percentages had all persons been asked the sensitive question, yet no one will know who answered which question. However, Umesh and Peterson (1991) found inconsistent results from the random response method; direct questioning often produced equally high results.

Miller (1984) suggests dividing a sample randomly in half, each getting a different list. One list contains only innocuous behaviors; the other includes the sensitive behavior as well. Subjects are asked to report only the number of activities engaged in on the list. The difference between the two lists provides an estimate of the frequency of the sensitive behavior. This method is simpler; there is nothing to be explained to the respondent, and it may appear less intrusive.

Neither technique links sensitive responses to other measures. Use the CDRGP (for "context-determined, rule-generated pseudonym") technique to link data gathered anonymously across different instruments or from the same one over a period of time. Everyone follows a common rule to generate pseudonyms for identification using the same pseudonym on each testing (Carifio & Biron, 1982). Using information well known to the respondent but not to the researcher eliminates error in pseudonym recall, since the same rule is used for all instrument administration in a given study. For example, respondents might be asked to record in successive boxes "the first letter of your birth month," "the first letter of your street's name," "the first letter of your mother's first name," and so on. For school research, you can base the questions on information that, by law, schools cannot disclose without the consent of those involved.

Response Sets

Interview and questionnaire responses can be affected by **response sets**, stances predisposing individuals to respond in certain ways (for example, toward social desirability, acquiescing, "nay-saying"). Particularly with attitude, personality, and interest scales, respondents may give false answers slanted toward their sense of what is desirable, possibly to gain social approval from the interviewer, to preserve their self-image or to avoid feelings of discomfort. For instance, when they were asked whether they had contributed to the Community Chest, a check of responses against records revealed that 44% of respondents gave false answers (Cahalan, 1968–1969).

Yea-sayers tend to answer "agree" to agree–disagree, "true" to true–false, and "yes" to yes–no response modes. Alternatively, one can make the desired response negative. However, although there are considerably fewer of them, there are some nay-sayer individuals who respond negatively to the same kinds of questions.

Another way is to include both negative and positive wordings in the same questionnaire and eliminate the responses of people who contradict themselves. However, dropping these individuals reduces sample size and also may affect generality—yea- and nay-sayers probably respond differently from others in a variety of areas. The best way of avoiding the problem of response sets is using item formats that do not incur them.

The Nonrespondent

Nonrespondents can be a serious problem for questionnaire interpretation; this is another example of mortality (see p. 348). Note that there are two potential sources of mortality: loss of members of a cohort or panel sample, and lack of response from one's sample. Refusals are rarest with personal interviews and rarer with telephone surveys. The number of callbacks to make contact has been increasing over the past few years, no doubt due in part to answering machines and caller ID used as "electronic peepholes" to screen calls. Professional survey organizations leave a message on answering machines designed to interest respondents sufficiently to return the call on a toll-free number.

What is a good return, and when should we be concerned about nonresponse? The answer lies in (a) the representativeness of the target population in the sample reached and (b) the difference in answers between respondents and nonrespondents. If those reached are representative and nonrespondents answer like respondents, a low response rate can be acceptable.

The problem is that respondents are essentially volunteers and therefore likely to conform to Rosenthal and Rosnow's (1975) list of volunteer characteristics—see page 494. These characteristics are relevant if they relate to what you are studying. A questionnaire study of welfare mothers would yield highly spurious results if only the better educated of them volunteered to reply.

The best defense against the nonrespondent problem is motivating respondents in the first place. In addition to an effective letter of transmittal, the presence of an incentive such as a coin or trinket may improve returns, but it probably does little to enhance quality of response. Include such incentives with the initial questionnaire; those offered on receipt of a return are not effective. (Cook, Heath, & Thompson, 2002). The best motivator is the internal one of wanting to respond to the questionnaire for its own sake rather than the external one of being bribed.

One of the most effective tools seems to be the "foot-in-the-door" technique—obtaining prior commitment from a potential respondent (Hansen & Robinson, 1980; Snyder & Cunningham, 1975). For example, send a postcard to be returned, indicating a willingness to complete the questionnaire. Telephone interviews are helped by solicitation of willingness to respond to a callback at a convenient time (Groves & Magilavy, 1981). Follow-ups do increase returns, although each successive one is less effective. A well-written postcard on first follow-up may do as much as a more expensive complete second mailing, but the latter is also often effective. Multiple follow-ups increase the legitimacy of the survey (Fox, Crask, & Kim, 1988). An effective sequence seems to be prenotification (obtaining consent if feasible), the questionnaire and letter of enclosure, a postcard reminder to reply, and multiple follow-ups. Results using alternative delivery methods (e.g., FedEx) are varied. Allow sufficient slack for follow-ups in the time schedule; the bulk of questionnaires are returned about two weeks after receipt but may dribble in for months. Set a cut-off date. Follow-ups can also use phoned reminders or e-mails, if contact information is available.

A way to estimate nonresponse effect is to assume that questionnaire nonrespondents are merely very late respondents. Then tabulating receipts by three- to five-day periods, or comparing those received before and after each follow-up, should reveal progressive response pattern changes. Extrapolating such patterns suggests the most extreme nonrespondents' responses so we can judge how seriously they diverge.

One can also phone nonrespondents for answers to essential questions. Especially for sensitive topics, however, these replies may differ from those of respondents. But it is difficult to estimate the nature of the difference because, no longer anonymous, their spontaneous response may or may not be censored by the socially acceptable one.

▶ Methods exist for maintaining respondent anonymity while querying sensitive topics and for anonymously linking data from several instruments.

▶ Researchers need to be alert to response sets, particularly the tendency to acquiesce to socially desirable responses; these can create data validity problems.

▶ Assuming nonrespondents are really very late responders, one can estimate their likely response by extrapolating trends from responses tabulated in successive three- to five-day periods. A phone follow-up with essential questions gathers some data on nonrespondents, but because they are clearly identified there may be a social desirability bias. The best nonresponse remedy, however, is motivating response in the first place (e.g., getting advance commitment).

SOURCES OF HELP

Survey Archives

Data archives contain a wealth of ideas for questions that may be useful as you develop your own instrument. Further, reused questions can show changes in attitude, opinion, and practices. Repositories of the major polling services, with access to archives and other information as well, can be found by accessing the links in the two Google directories listed at the end of this paragraph. In addition, data archives are listed by Gale Research Company (1983–present).

For surveys:
http://google.com/alpha/Top/Science/Social_Sciences/Methodology/Survey/

For polling:
http://google.com/alpha/Top/Society/Politics/Consultants/Polling

Online Survey Services

A surprising number of online services will provide templates for your survey, host it, and receive and tabulate the responses for a fee. Some sites are free or will let you try their services for smaller surveys at no charge. To locate them put "Web survey services" or "Web-hosting services" in a search engine. To use your computer as host, search "Web survey software."

Optical Mark Readers

Optical mark readers (OMRs) markedly ease the processing of paper-based questionnaires. Use a standard form for marking answers, or print the questions on the form. The machine reads these marks and compiles the scores. Queries with search engines for "optical mark readers" or "optical mark scanners" will find equipment, and similar searches for "optical mark forms" will turn up services that sell forms and will print to your specifications.

Additional Hallmarks of Survey Research

We have already noted hallmarks of interviews, questionnaires, and letters of transmittal. Following are additional survey hallmarks:

1. The intent of the survey is clearly defined.

2. The target population definition is consistent with the study's intent, and inferences to the target are made consistent with the quality of the sampling process.

3. The sampling technique is clearly specified. If possible and appropriate, probability samples are used and the sample is stratified on key variables. The likelihood of systematic bias is described and, if possible, shown not to have occurred by demographic data from the sample.

4. Interview questions, questionnaires, and letters of transmittal are pilot-tested to determine whether they elicit the intended response. As appropriate, "think aloud" or stimulated recall procedures are used to make sure that the respondent's interpretation corresponds to the intended one. As needed, revisions are also tested to ensure that corrections worked.

5. Interviewers are selected on appropriate bases—usually being matched to interviewees' background (there are instances in which matching does not work as intended and pilot tests are required). Data gatherers are adequately trained so that variations in their technique do not constitute an unintended contaminating variable.

6. If sensitive data are gathered, assurances of anonymity and procedures shown to be guaranteeing it are implemented. Data are so reported that individuals or institutions cannot be identified without their consent.

7. Appropriate data-gathering methods are employed (i.e., structured, partially structured, or unstructured interviews in person, by telephone, by chat sessions); questionnaires are administered in person, by mail, e-mail, chat, fax, or Web.

8. Procedures, including follow-up of nonrespondents, indicate that a representative sample was reached. Checks ensure that respondents represent nonrespondents as well. Comparison of late with early respondents or a similar practice gives clues about possible nonrespondent bias.

9. Sample size is adequate to ensure sufficient statistical sensitivity to differences between groups of interest (see pp. 452–454).

ADDITIONAL READING

For surveys in general, see Bradburn, Sudman, and Wansink (2006)—a revision of a classic—as well as Groves, Fowler, Couper, Lepkowski, Singer, and Tourangeau (2004); Peterson (2000); Foddy (1993); Schwartz and Sudman (1996); and Survey Research Center (1976). For telephone surveys, see Gwartney (2007).

Also see the Web Survey Methodology site at http://www.websm.org.

For detailed, concrete help and suggestions on question construction and layout design, see Dillman (2007). For online research see Mann and Stewart (2000), as well as Schonlau, Fricker, and Elliott (2002). See Norman (n.d.) on design. For computer-assisted telephone interviewing see Chen (2005), Frey and Oishi (1995), Groves (1990), and Lavrakas (1993). For a good self-instructional workbook for both telephone and personal interviews, see Guenzel, Berckmans, and Cannell (1983). For focus groups, see Morgan (1997a, 1997b) and Krueger and Casey (2000). For sensitive topics, see Lee (1993). To see examples of research done over the Internet, consult the American Psychological Society list of Psychological Research: http://psych.hanover.edu/Research/exponnet.html.

For a list of survey software, see the University Web Developers site: http://www.usask.ca/web_project/uwebd/links/web_applications/surveys/index.html

IMPORTANT TERMS AND CONCEPTS

cohort study
computer-assisted personal
   interviewing (CAPI)
computer-assisted telephone
   interviewing (CATI)
cross-sectional studies
cross-tabulations
double-barreled questions
focus group
framing of questions
funnel-sequenced questionnaire
letter of transmittal

longitudinal studies
nonrespondent
panel sample
pilot testing
projective techniques
response sets
sample survey
stimulated recall
table of specifications
testing
trend studies

OPPORTUNITIES FOR ADDITIONAL LEARNING

1. Christopher Easter, Dean of Student Services at Upstate University, wishes to determine how well his unit's services are contributing to the academic life of the university. It was his perception that there was a lack of awareness among faculty of the unit's contributions. He decided to conduct a survey to determine what information faculty had about the unit's program, how this information was received and utilized, and at what level the faculty was currently involved. How might he carry out this survey?

2. Ruth Anne Blanchard, dean of a privately run community college located in a city of 500,000, wished to gather information to help plan the courses the college would offer over the next five years. In order to develop projections, she decided to survey a sample of the city's residents to determine their perceived needs. How should she proceed?

3. Kristin Phillips, a member of a large national professional association, wished to know whether fellow members shared her view on the need for a local chapter and the activities and services it might offer. She mailed all members a questionnaire soliciting their opin-

ions. Assuming that she had constructed an appealing, well-designed instrument and an accompanying letter of transmittal, what further problems should she be alert to, and what should she do about them?

4. David Apple is a researcher interested in investigating what barriers, if any, exist to children's use of personal computers at the elementary-school level. He has received permission to carry out his study at selected elementary schools and has decided to supplement his participant observation by interviewing a sample of students from all grade levels (kindergarten to grade 6). What style of interview might he use?

5. Kathy Mentor, the family life and sex education teacher at a large urban school, offers a program on human sexuality beginning at grade 9 and continuing until the end of grade 12. She wishes to determine whether the approach she uses and the information she imparts are having an effect on the sexual behavior of the students. How might she do so using a questionnaire?

Compare your answers with those following the Application Exercise.

APPLICATION EXERCISE

Consider how you might explore your problem with a sample survey. Does it have aspects that might differ over time and be of interest? If so, what kind of design might you use to study them? Cross-sectional? Longitudinal? Which longitudinal design? Would interviewing gather useful data? What interview approach would you take? Nondirective? Structured? Funnel? Could you use a questionnaire? Who would be in your sample, and how would you choose these people? How would you learn what questions to ask? What kinds of questions might you use? Why? How might you pretest your questionnaire and, if a mail questionnaire, the letter of transmittal? What motivational appeal would you use? Would an e-mail or Internet questionnaire be feasible and easier?

KEY TO ADDITIONAL LEARNING OPPORTUNITIES

1. Dean Easter can use either a mailed, e-mailed, or Internet questionnaire or some form of interview, depending on whether or not he wishes to reach the entire faculty or a sample thereof and in how much depth. The choice may also depend, in part, on the urgency of getting the information. The questionnaire represents a method of reaching a majority of faculty easily, but unless the faculty views it as a priority they may be slow in responding. With support of the academic administration, however, a higher return rate might be expected. In light of a possible unwillingness to be critical of a colleague's operation, the anonymity of the questionnaire might provide more open and honest responses. On the other hand, structured questions might restrict the answers, possibly allowing important information to be missed.

Dean Easter could also consider two forms of interview: individual or telephone. Both offer the flexibility of probing answers and ensuring that questions are answered clearly, and examining in some depth any unusual and unexpected answers. Individual interviews offer the opportunity to establish rapport but are time consuming and would therefore likely restrict the survey to a small sample of the faculty. If the faculty could be convinced of the confidentiality of the responses, telephone interviews might permit more thorough coverage while retaining most of the advantages of both the individual interviews and the questionnaire and providing the most useful in-depth information.

2. Dean Blanchard is faced with two problems: finding the perceived educational needs and determining the size of the clientele for each educational program designed to answer a

need. These problems call for different survey techniques. An exploratory technique (such as some kind of in-depth open-end interviewing, either with individuals or groups, to find the unfilled perceived needs) is required for the initial phase. Perceived needs might come from the employers and also from employees. Although one might expect considerable overlap, they are not necessarily identical and call for research with both groups. Focus groups might be particularly useful, not only in more economically reaching a larger sample than individual interviews but also in providing information on how broadly the voiced needs were reinforced by others as they were raised.

Focus groups might initially be made up of selected graduates as well as employers whose needs had previously been served. Such persons may also be in the best position to identify groups who, similar in situation to themselves, might be usefully involved in successive focus groups.

Once perceived needs have been determined, the sampling plan for the second phase would depend on the kinds of programs proposed. If there is uncertainty about who might be interested in the programs, a random sample might be best. A mail questionnaire or telephone survey would permit estimation of demand. The questionnaire would be cheaper and easier, but individuals might say they would sign up just to preserve their options. A telephone interview might be able to probe just how serious they are about entering a program and so might provide better data.

3. After mailing her questionnaire, Kristin Phillips's major problem is one of response. She needs a good return rate, but she also needs to ensure that the people who do reply represent the membership. It may be, for instance, that those who responded are the members most supportive of establishing a chapter or most interested in specific services. To overcome this problem, Phillips would have begun by writing a good letter of transmittal to motivate as many respondents as possible to answer the first questionnaire. Next, she could have attempted to increase the return rate with a mailed follow-up, such as a reminder postcard. Then she might mail a replacement questionnaire with a letter appealing for a reply if there was no response to the first one.

   To determine whether the responses she is receiving represent the membership, she will want to see whether late-arriving responses are like early returns. If they are, the responses can probably be extrapolated to the population, even if the response rate is low. If late responses are not like early ones, it is quite possible that nonrespondents are different; a comparison of responses received in successive weeks might indicate the trend. Remembering that phone follow-ups may differ from written responses, Phillips may phone a sample of nonrespondents to approximate their written answers. Using the trends established from the comparison of early with late respondents and the answers of phone-contacted nonrespondents, she may extrapolate results for the total membership.

4. Children represent a special and often difficult group with which to conduct interviews. Further, the responses Apple might obtain from the youngest will likely be quite different from those of the older children. Given that, and the fact that his purpose here is exploratory, he will want to use either an unstructured or a partially structured style. These approaches will allow him to go with the give-and-take flow, using open-end questions. Yet he'll be able to obtain information on the desired queries, and to follow up leads or unusual answers. Use of a nondirective technique would allow him to establish better rapport with the children and to encourage freer responses. Conducting group interviews, particularly with the younger children, might help them overcome their natural shyness toward strangers.

5. Faced with the problem of querying a sensitive topic, Kathy Mentor will probably want to use a survey that provides anonymity, such as a questionnaire rather than interviews. She will want to clear the questionnaire with all parties: representative parents, school adminis-

trators and teachers, and the school board. Obviously, there should be no secret coding that would identify the responder. The simplest method would involve dividing her sample in two, choosing individuals randomly within grade strata.

Students would receive a questionnaire consisting of groups of seven activities to which they would respond by indicating how many of each group they had engaged in during the past two months (or a suitable period). A random half of the groups in questionnaire A would include some of the sensitive behaviors, the other half would consist entirely of non-sensitive activities. Questionnaire B would present exactly the same groups of activities, but would consist of all innocuous activities, omitting the sensitive ones. The difference in average number of activities engaged between lists, with and without sensitive activities, would indicate the frequency of the latter without revealing who engaged in what activity.

SUMMARY

There are a number of modes of data gathering available for surveys: face-to-face-interviews, computer-aided face-to-face interviews, computer-aided telephone interviews (CATI), automated telephone interviews, mail questionnaires, faxed questionnaires, e-mailed questionnaires, and Internet questionnaires.

- The mode of data gathering chosen is responsive to the nature of the information sought, the population to be sampled, and the timeliness of that need.

- Information is sought on a sample representative of a population. From each person reached in the population sample, a sample of behavior is taken as representative of that person's behavior in the target information area.

- The resource limits available to the survey and the limited time each respondent is willing to give to the survey both result in trade-offs among the various decisions affecting the nature of the survey.

- Each of the modes of data gathering has advantages and disadvantages.

- Surveys can be unstructured, as when one is exploring an area to see what is there, but are usually structured to obtain particular information about a specific area.

- Although structured, surveys can be composed of open- or closed-end questions or both. Each has its advantages.

- The term *questionnaire* in this chapter refers to that of a mail, fax, e-mail, or Internet questionnaire, but also to the interview guide and the computerized aide to interviewing.

- Questionnaires must be carefully developed, pilot tested, and revised.

- Proper framing and ordering of questions are important for obtaining valid data.

- Poor response rate is the single biggest problem for mail, e-mail, and Internet questionnaires. This is of concern when the answers of nonrespondents might have differed from those of respondents in ways related to whatever is being studied.

- The defenses against nonresponse involve motivating individuals to respond and correcting results for the extent and effect of nonresponse. There are multiple techniques for the former; the latter is more difficult.

- Prenotification and the letter of transmittal can be important in setting the frame for responding and in obtaining a high response rate; therefore, they warrant careful development and pilot testing.

- Research shows that prior commitment works, as may some kind of reward, but the best motivation is intrinsic interest by the respondents in having their responses count toward the results.

- An effective mail sequence involves prenotification (with reply commitment if feasible), the questionnaire and transmittal letter, a postcard reminder, and multiple follow-ups. Follow-ups increase returns. Although each wave brings decreasing results, multiple follow-ups increase the legitimacy of the survey.

- If respondents' and nonrespondents' answers differ, later responses may trend over time toward those of nonrespondents.

Table 24.5 on pp. 600–603 summarizes much that appears in the chapter, but it also provides some additional information, examining the relative advantages and disadvantages of five ways of gathering data.

Jaeger's (1984) questions below apply equally to interview and questionnaire data. Reminding yourself of the considerations involved in answering each of the following questions will help fix the major points of this chapter in your mind.[3]

- Was the sample representative of the target population?

- Was it large enough?

- Did the respondents understand the questions?

- Did the respondents interpret the questions as intended? Were they willing to respond?

- Did they have the knowledge or information needed to respond?

- Would responses change with equally appropriate rephrasing? With question order changes?

- Were respondents honest in their responses?

- Were responses recorded accurately?

- Were responses transcribed and aggregated accurately?

- Were responses interpreted accurately?

A Look Ahead

In the next chapter we explore another area that uses both qualitative and quantitative methods, that of historical research. While most historians would consider themselves most like qualitative researchers, some emphasize quantitative methods (usually in the context of mixed methods).

Notes

[1] Portions of this discussion are based on *Interviewer's Manual* (Rev. Ed.). Ann Arbor, MI: Survey Research Center, Institute for Social Research, 1976.

[2] Adapted from Erdos (1970), p. 102.

[3] From R. M. Jaeger, *Statistics: A Spectator Sport.* Copyright © 1990 by Sage Publications. Reprinted with permission.

Table 24.5   A Comparison of Five Survey Data Collection Modes

	Individual Interview	Group Interview	Computer-Assisted Telephone Interview	Mailed Questionnaire	Web- or Internet-Based Questionnaire
Sample	Restricted geographically and numerically by cost. Field interviewer determines those chosen. Possible bias toward those most accessible and pleasant if sampling plan is not carefully followed. With good interviewer, nature of sample can be better controlled than with other methods. Good sampling unavailable for some populations (e.g., working mothers). Highest response rate, as interviewers are able to cajole people to participate. Actual representativeness of the sample depends on persons reached.	If face to face, group is geographically restricted and number of groups is restrained by cost. Selectivity among invitees who actually attend may reduce representativeness. Not all ages, sexes, etc., available at same time. Right mix of people necessary for good response. Good sampling unavailable for some populations (e.g., working mothers). If telephone or online, some may not be attending group interviews.	No geographic restrictions. Geographically dispersed sample can be contacted quickly. Sequential sampling is easily implemented. Can control sample representativeness by screening respondents for match to unfilled quotas. Reaches unlisted numbers with random-digit dialing but, alas, also reaches businesses and fax lines. Good sampling unavailable for some populations (e.g., working mothers). Although poorest may be phoneless, reaches about 95% of households. Advantage over face-to-face where urban doors are closed to strangers.	No geographic restrictions. May get past secretaries that interviewers couldn't. Some segments will not respond (e.g., illiterates, disorganized people). Low cost allows mass mailings to find targets without sampling frame.	No geographic restrictions. Geographically dispersed sample can be contacted quickly. Sample limited to those who type and have Internet connections. Lengthy or complex sites require broadband. Selectivity in nonresponse (e.g., disorganized people, dial-up connections, out-of-date browsers). Password protection avoids answers from anyone finding the site. Flagging fends off search-engine indexers that might otherwise call attention to the site.
Length	Very long interviews of a day or more have been held successfully. Respondent motivation determines length limits.	Hard to keep a group together for long periods.	Generally shorter than face-to-face interviews.		

	Individual Interview	Group Interview	Computer-Assisted Telephone Interview	Mailed Questionnaire	Web- or Internet-Based Questionnaire
Nonresponse	Few people refuse; but callbacks are expensive.	Selectivity in those who respond to invitations.	Few people refuse, but more so than with face-to-face interviews. Callbacks are inexpensive.	Selectivity in those who respond to invitations. Low response rate can be somewhat reduced by follow-ups, by activating respondent motivation techniques, and by incentives.	Selectivity in those who respond to invitations. Low response rate can be somewhat reduced by follow-ups, by activating respondent motivation techniques, and by incentives.
Interviewer Bias or Coding Errors	Reduced through good training and regular supervisor checks for standardization, bias, or cheating.		Supervision is especially easy. The computer identifies interviewers with atypical rates (e.g., refusals). The computer shows inconsistencies in respondents' answers, which can be probed for cause or correction.	With proper forms and equipment, scanning is highly consistent. Training and supervision required for hand coding, the same as for interviewers.	The computer can be programmed to prevent inconsistencies in respondents' answers.
Anonymity	Respondent is known, but interviewer can reassure most persons.	Some anonymity in group responses, as when interviewer asks, "All those agreeing, say 'yes.'"	The impersonality of telephone is better for sensitive issues.	Respondent not known if return envelope *not* coded and respondent trusts the researcher's assurances.	Can provide genuine anonymity. Respondent known by e-mail address unless returned through anonymizer.

(continued)

	Individual Interview	Group Interview	Computer-Assisted Telephone Interview	Mailed Questionnaire	Web- or Internet-Based Questionnaire
Sensitive Issues	Characteristics of interviewer and respondent(s), as well as ability to observe race, socioeconomic status, dress, and other nonverbal clues, may affect both interviewers' questioning and respondents' answers.		Impersonality of phone encourages responses that would be limited to the socially desirable or inhibited in face-to-face interviews.	Anonymity encourages fuller responses than in face-to-face interviews.	
	Random response methods and pseudonyms provide anonymity.	Respondents who open up encourage others to do so.	Random response methods and pseudonyms can provide anonymity.		
Visuals	Can be used		No	Can be used; color printing adds to the cost.	Can be used; color is no more costly than black and white.
Speed	Slow	Relatively fast	Fastest; 10 interviewers @ 4 hrs. per day = 4 to 500 20-question interviews in 3 days (Lavrakas, 1993).	Slowest if a high return rate is required.	Relatively fast
Probing?	Yes. Can clarify questions, assure understanding and determine the underlying rationale for responses.	Yes. In addition, the generality of responses can be elicited by asking how many in the group agree or would answer similarly.	Yes, but somewhat limited if rapport is to be maintained. Can easily change the interview schedule to pursue leads.	No. Omissions are common but difficult to interpret. Probing by follow-up contact destroys anonymity.	No
Spontaneous Reactions, Unguarded Responses?	Yes—spontaneous, but more likely to get socially desirable responses. Can control that other persons present are not suggesting responses.	Yes—gets both initial, spontaneous, and (later) considered responses. Fear of contradiction by others minimizes information distortion.	Yes—spontaneous, but also shortest responses; likely to get socially desirable responses.	No—a person can mull over and change an answer. Respondent checking of previous answers can inflate consistency.	No—a person can mull over and change an answer. Unless programmed to prevent "return to previous page," respondent checking of previous answers can inflate consistency.

	Individual Interview	Group Interview	Computer-Assisted Telephone Interview	Mailed Questionnaire	Web- or Internet-Based Questionnaire
Adaptation of Language to Level of Respondent?	Yes		Yes, if the interviewer catches on soon enough.	No—must be preset as best one can to accommodate the sample.	
Inclusion of Persons Who Work?	Only with the increased cost of evening and weekend interviews.			Yes	
Pluses and Minuses Not Covered Elsewhere	Context for question interpretation is limited to respondent's memory of immediately preceding material; this makes the order of questions and responses within a question important. Provides flexibility to follow significant leads.			Less order dependence, since all questions are available.	
	Can establish rapport and control over interview environment; assures that others are not suggesting the answers.	Can establish rapport and control over interview environment but could have trouble with some in the group, which could affect other members.	Limited length; tiresome after 20–30 minutes. Most important advantage: control over data quality from sampling through interview supervision to data entry (Lavrakas, 1993).	No control over who actually formulates questionnaire responses.	
Cost	The most expensive and time consuming.	With large groups, can be the least costly of interviews on per-person basis. Some researchers believe the data is as good or better than that obtained in individual interviews.	Substitutes much lower phone costs for expensive travel; but adds equipment overhead costs.	Large samples contacted at very little cost, but extensive follow-ups of nonrespondents adds expense.	Large samples and extensive follow-ups of nonrespondents contacted at very little cost.

Source: Adapted from R. Ferber and P. J. Verdoorn (1962), *Research Methods in Economics and Business.* New York: Macmillan.

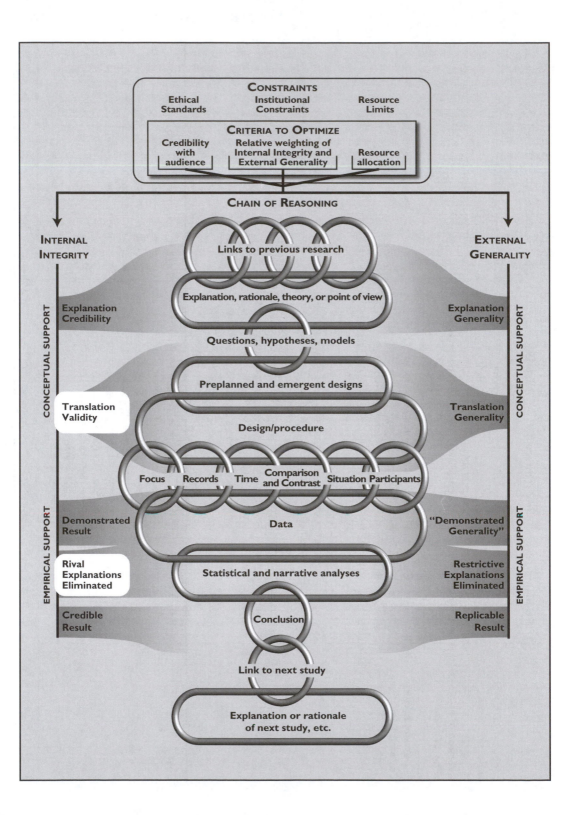

Historical Research

> Sometimes historians search for a single fact as when Mosteller and Wallace . . . sought to determine whether Madison or Hamilton wrote the Federalist papers. In other instances, they try to understand the meaning of the past to the living as when the black historian John Hope Franklin tutored the Supreme Court lawyers in the 1954 case that overturned the "separate but equal" doctrine. He demonstrated convincingly "in the view of the framers, the Amendment meant equality . . . and that if they were around today they wouldn't support segregation and discrimination."
>
> —J. Starr, "Above All, a Scholar"

Through an understanding of the past many historians seek to contribute to our current knowledge of the human condition. In this role they follow the same rules as do other behavioral scientists. For their finding of patterns in the past, historians are to be especially treasured. True, hindsight is on their side, but setting our own stage for data collection is difficult enough; making sense of the leavings of a culture is a tough job.

History consists of the discovery, selection, organization, and interpretation of evidence to describe a situation or to answer a question about past events. Free to choose and interpret their data, historians are judged by the intelligence and honesty they bring to the task as they seek to interpret data from a new standpoint. The chapter is titled *historical research* instead of *historical method* because history is distinguished mainly by content rather than method. Its methods include careful and sometimes clever application of logic, and it employs the basic social science research techniques we have already covered.

INTRODUCTION

Every research method has its special demands. Clearly, the ability to combine strong storytelling with an organizing rationale is critical to historical study. Nevins

(Billington, 1975) tells a story of Lincoln Steffens, who, on seeing a man bearing a glittering fragment of truth, warned Satan, "'That man has hold of some truth. He could kill you if he tried. . . .' 'No danger,' Satan replied. 'He will take that fragment home, chisel it, rub it, dull it until it has no power whatsoever.'" Not so, says Nevins: "Truth, like the South African diamond, is a dull cloudy pebble when first discovered. Long labor and the nicest art have to be applied to cut it into those well-polished facets that give it scintillating power" (pp. 41–42). That is the work of the historian.

INTERNAL INTEGRITY AND THE INFERENCE OF CAUSATION

Much of history is concerned with causation, often with a view to prediction— "Whoso desireth to know what will be hereafter, let him think of what is past, for the world hath ever been in a circular revolution" (Sir Walter Rowley, 1751). Where one is concerned with causation, Internal Integrity and those parts of it—*translation validity* and rival explanations eliminated—are especially important. Authenticity of evidence is also always a concern.

Historians have certain advantages. They can choose selectively among the wide scope of past events to prove their point. Not caught up with and blinded by the passions of the time, they have the advantage of hindsight, of knowing what happened, and they can trace backwards for causes. But, because of faulty and partial records, differing perspectives, and other problems, people who think deeply about causation generally believe only "highly plausible connections" can be demonstrated.

Historians, however, want to write forcefully and often dramatically when presenting a strong case. As though the cause were clear, they use words like inevitable, unavoidable, and inescapable. Carr (1962), in discussing causation, suggests that we should do without such terms: "Life will be drabber. But let us leave them to the poets and metaphysicians." (But he is nevertheless partial to vivid writing; on the next page, he asks to be excused for not getting rid of *inevitable* in his own work [p. 126].) Barzun and Graff (1992, p. 177) propose using the term *conditions* and talk of the *probability of events*. These are the exceptions. Just like all other behavioral scientists, historians make the strongest case the evidence permits for each of the Internal Integrity judgments.

Satisfying the Conditions for Inferring Causation

The rationale or explanation plays the same role in historical studies as in other subject areas. We show the fit of the rationale to the data and the extent to which changes in causes resulted in appropriate changes in effect. If we argue that emigration is a function of economic conditions, then the more tightly the rate of emigration follows the gyrations of the economic indicators, the stronger is the presumption of a causative relationship.

One of the most convincing conditions, the production of an effect at will, is denied the historian, who can only pick and choose to illustrate past events but cannot create them. In one important sense, however, there are predictive possibilities: predicting the as yet unknown or undiscovered on the basis of the known. The historian who supplies missing pieces that are later confirmed by new discoveries is in much the same position as the astronomer who predicts the existence of an unseen planet or moon that is later shown to be present. Such evidence is very convincing. Sometimes such predictions can be made by carrying over a method of analysis from one period to a second period when the data for the second period had not yet been analyzed in that way. This serves exactly the same purpose as a cross-validation sample or replication in quantitative research.

The presumption of causation is strengthened by showing repeated examples in varying circumstances—Mill's method of agreement applied to historical data. Toynbee (1948), for example, tracing his thesis about the rise and fall of civilizations over a range of cultures, shows that his argument holds under a variety of circumstances. It also shows External Generality.

Demonstrating that cause precedes effect is difficult. Fischer (1970), for instance, disagrees with Potter's (1954) *People of Plenty*, which argues that much of Americanism resulted from affluence. Only recently have people thought of themselves as affluent, says Fischer; "Portraits of our ancestors have a lean and hungry look. . . . They became American and then became affluent" (p. 172). Which came first? Were Americanism and affluence interactive? Have we found an amplifying loop? Precedence as a condition may not be possible to show, nor would it be likely to make much sense in this or other historical situations. The large number of historical phenomena that are really relatively self-contained, interactive systems makes precedence useful only for analyzing isolated sections of the chain of events.

Multiple Causes, Multiple Interpretations

Can historians ever claim to have found the single necessary and sufficient cause of an event? It is true that there are events in history that appear to be the key to what follows? For example, Fischer (1970, p. 173) notes that enemy possession of Confederate General Robert E. Lee's General Order 191 allowed Union General George B. McClellan to anticipate where Lee would mass his troops. It may have been fatal to the loss of Antietam, a defeat that may have cost the South the possibility of European intervention and hence the Civil War. Others, in return, may build competing chains of events. Which is correct? Perhaps all are! Perhaps the possession of the Confederate order is but one of multiple **contributing conditions**, which together produced the eventual outcome.

Like all behavioral scientists, historians abstract and simplify. In this pursuit they are confronted with complex people in biographies, with institutional histories, and with a range of people and institutions in important events and over periods of time. Therefore, historians are much less prone to the highly simplified single-variable descriptions; patterns of **multiple causation** are the norm instead of the exception. With the acceptance of multiple causation, complex social phenomena can be looked at from different points of view, each making good sense.

David Tyack (1976) demonstrates this very nicely in an essay explaining the rise of compulsory schooling as driven by five different intents or causes: (1) as a means of binding students to the nation-state, (2) as a means of satisfying the ethnocentric demands of religious and ethnic groups, (3) as an outgrowth of the developing school bureaucracy, (4) as an investment in human capital, and (5) as a way of reproducing the class structure of American society (a Marxian interpretation). Each explanation is shown to fit the facts, some better at certain periods than others, but all apparently having some validity.

Tyack's example not only demonstrates how a single event can be open to multiple understandings, it also indicates the creativity that historians bring to the reinterpretation of events. Often they reconstruct the past from a new angle, bringing a different insight to past explanations.

▶ Historians face the same problems of showing causality as other social scientists do. Those who have thought about it have serious doubts that tight cases are possible. Yet historians, like other social scientists, continually attempt to build convincing cases for causality.

▶ Historians cannot vary causes and show that effects follow, but they can selectively seek instances where that has occurred naturally.

▶ Precedence of cause may be difficult or impossible to prove.

▶ With complex phenomena, explanations involving multiple causes are the most common and usually make the most sense. While opening phenomena to multiple useful interpretations, they pave the way for reinterpretations, or revisionist history.

KEY CRITERIA OF INTERNAL INTEGRITY FOR HISTORICAL STUDIES

Two key criteria of Internal Integrity for historical studies are translation validity and rival explanations eliminated. We discuss them in the following sections.

Translation Validity

One of the criteria of Internal Integrity highlighted in the chapter's opening diagram is *translation validity*. In historical studies setting forth a generalization, we are concerned with three aspects: (1) the authenticity of the data, (2) the stability in the meaning of terms over the period studied, and (3) the match of construct to evidence.

Authenticity of the data. How can the researcher be sure that evidence is what it purports to be? Historical records may be drafts, an autobiography, or a biography. We typically look for consistencies in content, physical condition, and context. We examine the dates of material found with a record and subject ink and paper to chemical analysis, radioactive-carbon, or other dating techniques; examine watermarks and word usage for typicality at the time of presumed production; and look for facts and allusions appropriate for the time. To decide disputed authorship, we often use the resemblance of the document in question to the base rates of unusual word usages and constructions of the contending authors in other documents. For example, Mosteller and Wallace (1984) so analyzed the Federalist Papers and strengthened the prevailing opinion favoring Madison over Hamilton as author. (Authentication of artifacts has been called *external criticism*, and the problem of establishing their accuracy or worth, *internal criticism*. For a variety of reasons these terms seem less used these days; they are noted here in case you come across them.)

Like the lawyer who distrusts hearsay evidence, historians most value firsthand accounts by participants instead of secondary reports of persons who have heard about, read about, or perhaps talked to participants. They seek evidence in official records and reports, minutes of meetings, photographs, recordings, bulletins, catalogs, licenses, certificates, and other documents likely to be generated in the activities they are studying. The originating author's relation to the event is important. Was it an immediate or a retrospective account? If the latter, how much time elapsed between event and report? Was the event viewed directly, or is the account based on what other people saw?

Historians cannot manipulate treatment, create new data, or take new measures. Because they are confined to the objects, artifacts, and records left to them by the past, often they must resort to indirect evidence. A classic example is the problem of showing the growth of the British bureaucracy in the days before organizational charts. Records of the growth of government procurements of sealing wax very nicely documented the expansion. A good bit of ingenuity goes into divining evidence that might have been kept, as well as undertaking the detective work of finding it; a good bit of luck helps, too. Webb et al. (1981) and Lee (2000) may be sources of suggestions.

Stability in the meaning of terms over the period studied.   The relation of constructs to their operationalization, a problem for any researcher, contains a special twist for the historian. Is the meaning of the construct consistent from one time period to another, or does it change in ways that might suggest rival explanations? For example, does household size mean the same thing from census to census? Did a "family" include adult sisters and brothers, in addition to husband, wife, and children living together? Yes, at one time. Did it include boarders who ate and lived with the family? The latter, in particular, would not only significantly affect reported household size but would also constitute a different concept of a household.

Matching construct to evidence.   Whereas we usually think of operationalization as moving from construct to evidence, the reverse process is equally important for the historian when the intended purpose of an artifact in a culture is not clear. Consider the many spoofs of how today's toilets might be interpreted by historians of the future as places of religious ritual and sacrifice to unknown gods. The difficulty of inferring the meaning of things in another time and place is readily apparent.

Rival Explanations Eliminated

The prevalence of rival explanations in history is indicated by the fact that so much of historical writing is reinterpretation from a new angle to suggest another reasonable view of the evidence. Such reinterpretation is particularly dominant theme in so-called postmodern history. Rewriting history from the standpoint of African Americans or feminists, for example, yields new emphases, highlights different data, and provides new insights.

Most of the rival explanations listed in chapter 21 on experimentation apply to historical events as well. Especially prevalent is selection, since we nearly always use intact groups. No mystical figure from the past was out there, arranging randomly assigned groups for tomorrow's researchers! Groups form for a reason, so there is almost always some selection pressure, often related to the topic being studied. We are not even free of the problem of volunteers, since many groups are self-selected. For example, were people who immigrated to the United States those who were the most unhappy in their homeland, the most aggressive and proactive in seeking solutions to problems, the misfits and maladjusted, the uneducated? All of these are possible selection factors that might have contributed to the nature of their lives. Differential mortality among immigrants is also a factor in that those who returned disgruntled to their homeland were not a random sample of the original group. Although there was a draft, selection was a factor in the representativeness of the army during the U.S. Civil War. It was both legal and common practice for wealthy men to hire individuals to take their place.

Just as selection may occur with respect to the individuals involved, it may also occur with respect to the records. Laslett (1980), for example, noted the belief that extended families were the dominant form in preindustrial societies. She wondered whether this belief was a reflection less of commonality than of the fact that wealthier families tended to live in larger and more complex households. Since such families were more likely to create diaries, letters, and other artifacts as well as to preserve these records, the impression may have been more a function of the selective availability of records than of reality.

Society and culture determine what is important to record. The kinds of persons who make and retain records are different from those who don't. Only certain kinds of events are typically recorded. There are, for example, plenty of probate records in precolonial Maryland but no regular methods of recording births and marriages. Exactly the reverse is true of Massachusetts; both reflect what was important in the religion and life of that time. Clearly, knowledge of the culture is essential to correct interpretation.

Many rival explanations can be eliminated if there is a control group. Establishing such groups requires creativity and ingenuity. Briggs (1978), for example, wanted to show how children of Italian immigrants in the United States compared with their non-Italian classmates in achievement. He compared each child with an Italian surname in three Rochester public schools over the years 1910–1924 to the child nearest on the class roll with a non-Italian surname. With this group he could compare age in grade, attendance, and promotion to the next grade. Children of Italian immigrants tended to be older but had better attendance and had very slightly less chance of repeating a grade.

Historians face special problems of analysis:

▶ It is necessary to understand the meaning of constructs in the culture and at the time studied.

▶ There is a possibility that constructs have changed in meaning over time.

▶ It is difficult to infer the meaning of artifacts except as we understand their meaning in the culture at that time.

▶ The fact that society and culture determine what is important to record requires that the likely selectivity of records be considered.

▶ Much ingenuity is required to establish control or contrasting groups in past data.

▶ Historical studies are subject to the same rival explanations as other studies, but selection and mortality may be especially common.

Hallmarks of Historical Studies

In seeking to build a strong case, the historian will attempt to:

- Conduct a reasonably complete search for sources of evidence.
- Indicate the sources of information.
- Use primary sources, but where secondary sources were used, this is made clear.
- Lay out the approach to the evidence in an evenhanded and open fashion.
- Present a credible rationale or explanation. If it builds on previously available evidence, it extends, clarifies, and revises prior interpretations.
- Ensure that the evidence presented is appropriate to the constructs employed.
- Give sufficient instances of evidence so that the reader is able to judge its adequacy.
- Weigh carefully and present important rival explanations as appropriate, or explain why they were rejected.
- Show a close correspondence between the rationale and the evidence.
- Cite evidence from more than one instance where generality is claimed (preferably considerably more, depending on the generality sought).
- Team up with someone having the appropriate expertise if venturing into an unfamiliar field or time period.
- Make clear any biases that might have affected judgments.

ADDITIONAL READING

Aydelotte, Bogue, and Fogel (1972) present nine examples of historical studies demonstrating different quantitative approaches. Barzun and Graff (2003) is readable and practical, with much useful detail. Fischer (1970) is a fantastic laundry list of errors of historians, full of lively examples. See also Gottschalk (1956); Nevins (1975).

IMPORTANT TERMS AND CONCEPTS

contributing conditions   multiple causation

OPPORTUNITIES FOR ADDITIONAL LEARNING

1. Burton (1988) traced the evolution of school discipline in the United States from the mid-nineteenth century until the present. At the heart of her study was the analysis of 475 journal articles from 1940 to 1980 with a specific focus on elementary public schooling. This was supported by a general review of the history of school discipline and an analysis of the social, political, and economic changes in American society based on such social analysts as Galbraith, Henry, and Potter.

   Burton delineated three historical periods, indicating what she thought to be the overriding societal philosophy pertaining to school discipline for each, and compared them to the modern era. From the mid- to late-nineteenth century there was a search for a theory of discipline that would "provide self-disciplined citizens and workers for a rapidly growing, industrializing young nation"—a production-oriented society. During the first quarter of the twentieth century, the philosophy of John Dewey, the spirit of social cooperation, and community life dominated—interest was the key to discipline. During the mid-twentieth century, discipline was based on self-control and the recognition of each individual's "responsibilities to the group consonant with good citizenship in a democratic society." In the last half of the twentieth century, two major social changes affected both the purpose and the methods of school discipline. One was recognition of social diversity and individual rights. The second was a shift from a producer to a consumer society—increased consumption became the cornerstone of democratic and economic security.

On the basis of this analysis, Burton argued that American educators now face unrecognized and therefore unaddressed conflicting social purposes. They are disciplining for the needs of a consumer-oriented society, the purpose of which is instant gratification. This runs counter to traditional American beliefs and standards—"the production-oriented goals of thrift, sobriety, diligence, responsibility, hard work, and delayed gratification are not conducive to, [or] supportive of, a consumer society." The response of educators has been to concentrate on workable methods of immediate control in the classroom without regard to general, long-term, social purpose.

How does Burton demonstrate Internal Integrity in this study?

2. Laslett (1978) described past and present family structure in American society, how and why it has changed, and its importance in contemporary society. She begins her study with a brief discussion of two contradictory sociological views of family. The first is that the institution is in trouble—that it is "alive but not well," a view predicting its demise and borne out by a steady increase in divorce rates and in family violence. The second view is that the family is "here to stay," contending that society depends on it for the development of personal identity and the satisfaction of personal needs.

Laslett argues the second viewpoint, stating that "changes in household composition, in the demography of kinship, and in the relationship between family and other institutions have contributed to the greater emotional significance of the family through their impact on the socialization process" (p. 477) and have increased its significance for personal identity and emotional gratification. The problems of divorce and violence are the negative result of the intense feelings generated by this increased intimacy.

To make her argument, Laslett attempts to trace the changes over time and compare family in the past to that in the present. Thus, household composition of preindustrial society is held to have included others unrelated to the conjugal family unit, such as boarders, lodgers, and employees; today's family rarely does. Further, in the past, adolescence tended to be spent outside the family home (job hunting, apprenticeships, etc.). Today, adolescents tend to remain at home with increased identification of self, based on the particular family. Increased life span and improved means of communication have led to the modern availability of ascendant kin—grandparents, aunts, and uncles—who may elaborate the meaning of kinship.

Finally, the ideology of family living has changed from the Puritan view of family as guardian of the public good to that of the private family and the home as a personal sanctuary where a sense of personal control and intimacy can be found. This has been further accentuated by the separation of home and work and of home and schooling. These historical changes have resulted in an increased weight of meaning attached to the personal relations of the family.

What has Laslett attempted to do in this study? Is her argument convincing?

Compare your answers with those following the Application Exercise.

APPLICATION EXERCISE

How might your problem be examined in historical perspective? What might this add to your understanding of it? How might it give a clearer picture of the causal chain of events? What, if any, might be the problem of obtaining data and records? Of authenticating them?

KEY TO ADDITIONAL LEARNING OPPORTUNITIES

1. Remember that an important contribution of the historian is interpretation, the extent of which varies with the author, the author's purpose, and the reader's own perceptions. She has shown this in her credible characterization of school discipline in each of three periods (*explanation credibility*). She no doubt demonstrated *translation validity* by showing the correspondence between her characterizations of the period with descriptions of discipline from each period. Internal Integrity is demonstrated by effectively showing a correspondence between the explanation (how the construct, school discipline, changed) and the evidence (the data)—*demonstrated result*. There is evidence that she considered other writers covering these periods, which no doubt included explanations other than her own characterizations (*rival explanations eliminated*), but this is not made explicit. The fact that she took into account the analyses of others reinforces her characterizations (*credible result*). Her argument makes sense based on her selective interpretation of the evidence.

2. Laslett has tried to show causality. She has presented a thesis: that the role of the family has changed from preindustrial to modern times and that society is now dependent on it for the development of personal identity and the satisfaction of personal needs. To support her argument she has tried to demonstrate a pattern of multiple causes all acting together to produce the current situation. To be convincing she needed to satisfy the conditions for inferring causation. Does her rationale fit the data? Does it make sense? Insufficient information is presented in this summary to permit judgment, but she has at least put forward a convincing hypothesis.

SUMMARY

The historian, in advancing a rationale or explanation of an event (or set of them), provides the reasoning that persuades us that the interpretation of the evidence is a reasonable one. The better the match of rationale to events, the more convincing the case. The art and skill of the historian is in the selection and organization of the facts and data to show congruence without distorting either data or theory. Historians range widely, looking for strong and convincing explanations to encompass a set of events. From all the behavioral sciences they borrow the propositions, viewpoints, and research methods that can be applied to retrospective data. Authentication of data is a much greater problem than in other research fields.

A Look Ahead

In the next section we take the time to step back and seek perspective on the research process. Having studied a variety of approaches to research problems, the next chapter emphasizes using the best combination of approaches appropriate for a given study. It notes again the importance to effective research of handling the ever-present trade-offs.

Optimizing Research Effectiveness by Using Mixed Methods

> The issue is how we can use the contrast [between quantitative and qualitative methods] to highlight the taken-for-granted practices and perspectives of each approach and how, taken together, they can provide a more textured and productive view of the social phenomena we seek to understand.
> —P. Moss, *Enlarging the Dialogues in Educational Measurement*
>
> All quantities are measures of qualities.
> —J. T. Behrens & M. L. Smith, *Data and Data Analysis*

INTRODUCTION

Having reached this chapter in the book, you are well aware that all research methods have both strengths and weaknesses. No single method is research's be-all and end-all. Good research properly defines a problem so as to encompass all the necessary aspects to understand it as completely as possible, regardless of method (Phillips, 1992). Used for an appropriate purpose on the right problem in suitable contexts with adequate resources, a single method can often present a sufficiently convincing case to achieve the consensus that begins the journey to acceptance as knowledge. But some problems require more than any one method can deliver. For example, understanding a particular problem and/or its solution may require showing how it qualitatively affects individuals to supplement the quantitative data, and some problems first require exploration for understanding before validation of a solution. A mixed-method approach is often the solution.

In a book devoted to advancing multiple-method approaches, Brewer and Hunter (1989) argue: "Our individual methods may be flawed, but fortunately the flaws are not identical. A diversity of imperfection allows us to combine methods not only to gain their individual strengths but also to compensate for their particular faults and limitations" (pp. 16–17). Eisner (1981) notes, "The issue is not qualitative as contrasted with . . . quantitative. . . . With both we can achieve binocular vision. Looking through one eye never did provide much depth of field" (p. 9). Indeed, there is a long history of calls for mixed-method approaches as well as many examples in the literature. Since qualitative and quantitative methods both offer views of the same world, when they turn up the same findings they usefully reinforce one another. This is but one instance of the many purposes for which the methods can be usefully combined.

WAYS IN WHICH MIXED METHODS ENHANCE RESEARCH

Researchers have yoked multiple methods for a variety of purposes. Among the most common are:

- *Enhance, illustrate, and explain*—most often using qualitative data to flesh out the meaning of quantitative data.

- *Describe both process and product*—qualitative data is usually employed to describe a process. The results of the process are often best conveyed quantitatively.

- *Compensate or complement one another*—as noted in the Brewer and Hunter quotation above, the methods can reinforce one another; one catches what the other misses.

- *Explore for understanding*—using techniques that provide qualitative data, or a very broad questionnaire, one can develop leads that can then be explored by another method.

- *Check for unexpected effects*—with qualitative data or a very broad questionnaire, we can monitor a process for unexpected side effects.

- *Develop the basis for an instrument*—develop an understanding of a phenomenon with qualitative techniques that show how an instrument might be developed.

- *Show the extent of generality*—quantitative techniques involving larger samples than would be involved in qualitative study extend findings beyond the original group.

- *Validate, triangulate*—show that a proposition is not dependent on the method of investigation but holds with a different method.

- *Protect against a rival hypothesis*—show that an effect was not present that would otherwise provide a rival explanation.

- *Fulfill social or political purposes*—Greene and Caracelli (1997) and Mertens (2003) add another goal to the use of mixed-methods designs, that of the *transformation–emancipation agenda*. By this they refer to the use of mixed-method studies for some social or political purpose—for example, concerns growing out of feminist, ethnic, disability, and gay and lesbian scholarship.

While Creswell and Plano Clark (2007) combine these purposes into four designs (triangulation, embedded, explanatory, or exploratory), it would seem that for most instances the following two would do it, along with a third rare one:

- To add information to that extracted by a single method (usually complementary or supplemental, sometimes contradictory).

- To explore with one method to provide leads for a second (more often qualitative than quantitative, but as Tukey [1977] and Behrens and Yu [2003] showed, sometimes in reverse order).

- To show that a phenomenon was not a result (artifact) of the research method itself; it appears with a different method as well.

For such choices one must also decide whether (1) the methods are used simultaneously, in sequence, or some kind of phasing; and (2) which is given primary weight or whether they have equal emphasis.

THE USE OF MIXED-METHOD DESIGNS

Following are examples showing how qualitative and quantitative methods are used for one or more of the above purposes.

Enhance and Illustrate

This is, perhaps, the most frequent use of mixed-method designs. Qualitative stories can make quantitative analyses come alive, as in Clausen's (1993) longitudinal study of the developmental effects of the Depression on children of the 1920s. Though begun when research was technologically primitive—few psychological tests, and no tape recorders or computers—interview, observation, mailed questionnaire, and physical examination data were compiled into abstract numerical analyses that were made real with life-story accounts. A book reviewer commented: "In a display of methodological virtuosity, Clausen manages to combine longitudinal variable analysis with life histories and the analysis of these histories as narrative. . . . The combination is impressive" (Gerstel, 1993, p. 1157).

Smith, Gabriel, Schott, and Padia's (1976) combination of qualitative and quantitative methods in the evaluation of Outward Bound is another good example. Outward Bound is a voluntary program intended to increase participants' self-confidence and awareness of their dependence on others. Participants train for a wilderness experience that tests their physical, mental, and emotional capacities. Smith provided a qualitative account that conveyed the thoughts and feelings of a participant as she experienced it. This was accompanied by quantitative evidence of the program's success in achieving its goals.

Validating Findings of One Method with Another

A very nice example of the sequential use of qualitative and quantitative methods is found in the study of marriage by Gottman, Murray, Swanson, Tyson, and Swanson (2002, as found in Sandelowski, 2003). Marriage seems like an unlikely topic to tackle with mathematics, but qualitative psychology researcher Gottman, mathematical biologist Murray, and others (2002) teamed up to apply mathematical modeling to predict marriage stability. Quantitative research requires first knowing the variables involved; but what variables lead to stabilizing or destabilizing a marriage? The answer comes from Gottman's qualitative research, the observation of marriage partners in interaction—coding observations, and then synthesizing them into variables. Since the variables are grounded in observations, there are many ways one can turn them into measures—using frequency counts, making ratings on scales, assigning weights to certain behaviors to provide a score, and so on. As trends are established with these measures, the research moves from the qualitative into the quantitative realm.

Using Gottman's prior research, which was now built into measures, Swanson built a predictive model. The model's ultimate test was provided when a relationship was trending toward destabilization. Gottman, basing clinical actions on data from the model, showed he was able to move the interaction to a region of stability. Interestingly, although generally "nice" is better than "nasty," there were instances where reduction of too many positive forces produced a stable state.

In this study, as is often the case, qualitative data analysis provides an explanation through identifying the significant variables and their interrelationships. Quantitative methods confirm the explanation and can sometimes show the way to make adjustments leading to better theory and prediction.

Protect against Rival Explanations

As part of an effort to validate a proposition, mixed methods can protect against a rival explanation. Duffy and Roehler (1990) studied the effect of explicit instruction in mental processing on reading; volunteer teachers were randomly assigned to experimental and control treatments. Both sets of teachers were taught ways to improve student engagement on academic tasks. In addition, the experimental teachers were taught to provide instruction in mental processing. Both groups were observed seven times during the year to determine the explicitness of the teachers' instruction (qualitative data on treatment). The researchers also gathered qualitative data through interviews with students in both groups to determine the extent of their awareness of their mental processing (qualitative data to eliminate rival explanations for score changes). A standardized reading achievement test determined the effect of treatment (quantitative data on product). They were able to use this combination of quantitative and qualitative data to show the success of explicit instruction for students with poor reading skills. They used qualitative methods to assure that mental processing, not rote memory, was occurring.

As indicated in the comments in parentheses in the previous paragraph, different research methods are involved in different aspects of phenomena; qualitative methods are often used to describe process in studies where quantitative methods evaluate products. This also occurred in the Clausen study of Depression children and the Smith, Gabriel, Schott, and Padia (1976) evaluation of Outward Bound.

Enhancing, Illustrating, Finding Side Effects, Exploring, Explaining, Determining Generality

Multiple methods used sequentially may help decide a project's next steps. For example, qualitative methods can be used to explore and find effects and then quantitative methods can be used to determine their generality. Rossi and Lyall's (1976) income maintenance study combined a field experiment, intensive case studies, and survey methods. Together, these provided the picture that kept a seemingly promising plan for helping low-income families escape poverty from becoming policy. Qualitative case studies caught the family breakup that unexpectedly resulted and also helped the researchers understand why it occurred. Using survey methods, the researchers then determined the size and seriousness of this side effect as well as the intended desirable consequences of income maintenance that they had expected. The combination of three research methods provided evidence of side and main effects, and of relationships, as well as explanatory rationales.

The Rossi and Lyall example reinforces the mixed-method suggestion in chapter 21—that every experimental study should have, formally or informally, an element of the qualitative case study in it. Good researchers stay close to their treatment administration and data collection to learn whether things went according to plan, how participants viewed the study, what the participants were expecting, and how they reacted. Unanticipated events, side effects, or misperceptions can completely alter a study. Demand conditions (see p. 500) may convey unplanned perceptions to the participants. Researchers unaware of such events will completely misinterpret the data. Although assistants may gather some of the data, there is no substitute for the principal investigator also gathering some firsthand.

The Transformation—Emancipation Agenda

Mertens (2003) notes examples of mixed-methods designs used, for example, to try to transform college admissions (Bowen & Bok, 1998), to shed light on power relationships (Brown, 2000), and to best construct instruments for particular populations (Chelimsky, 1998).

Transforming college admissions: Bowen and Bok (1998) studied how race-sensitive admissions policies work and their effects on students of different races, abilities, and genders attending elite and nonelite colleges. They used both quantitative data from the College and Beyond Study database and interviews with a subsample. On the basis of these data they speculated as to the effects of terminating the race-sensitive policies, aiming their results at the "institutions that have the power to influence national policy on this issue" (Mertens, 2003, p. 146).

Shedding light on power relationships: Brown (2000) studied transcripts of focus groups, noting the contributions of men and women in both quantitative and qualitative terms. When structured by the moderator, men and women contributed equally. When less structured, she found disparity in the amount and quality of contributions, as well as in ways of obtaining the floor and introducing topics. She noted how important it is for the moderator to be aware of these differences if the voices of all are to be heard.

Constructing instruments to fit particular populations: Chelimsky (1998) surveyed disabled people before evaluating the effectiveness of the Americans With Disability Act. She used the responses in both the design and instruments, and from probing questions learned about "not just observable barriers, but also invisible ones" (p. 152).

▶ Instead of pursuing additional mixed-method uses and examples, let's simply note that they can enhance a study in ways limited only by the researcher's creativity.

▶ The emphasis, however, should always be on finding the most appropriate methods for a given study.

▶ In many cases, only mixed methods can provide the optimal combination required for the powerful development of evidence and an explanation that will gain a consensus around the interpretation of the data.

▶ Among the many roles played by mixed-method designs:

1. Triangulation and corroboration—"seeking convergence, corroboration, and correspondence of results across the different methods" (Greene, 2001, p. 252).

2. Complementing—"different methods . . . measur[ing] overlapping but distinct facets of the phenomena" (ibid., p. 253).

3. Development—"different methods sequentially . . . use the results of one method to help develop the other method or inform its implementation" (ibid.).

4. Expansion—"different methods for different inquiry components . . . extend[ing] the breadth and range of the inquiry" (ibid.).

5. Initiation—"designs are used to intentionally seek the discovery of . . . new perspectives or frameworks via the recasting of questions or results from one method with questions or results from the other method" (ibid.).

6. Transformative—designs used for political or social purposes; often to communicate across varied audiences or highlight injustices (Greene & Caracelli, 1997).

THE PHILOSOPHICAL PROBLEMS OF MIXED-METHOD APPROACHES

Some qualitative researchers argue that quantitative methods are incompatible with qualitative methods because of their underlying philosophical assumptions. Quantitative-method researchers assume that there is a reality out there to be discovered. Their important task is uncovering its nature, and the interrelationships among its parts.

Symbolic-interaction qualitative researchers emphasize that we know our world only through our perception of it. They argue that we react to things in terms of the meanings they come to have through our social interaction. Reality, therefore, is subjective and socially constructed. Further, since each individual perceives the world in terms of his or her own experiences, multiple realities can exist. Symbolic-interaction qualitative researchers' goals are to understand the social world from the viewpoint of its actors, and to see the world as they perceive it.

For these qualitative researchers to use a mixed-method design that includes quantitative techniques, they would have to accept quantitative's assumption of one external reality. Given a man's reaction to environmental changes, they would seek to learn how, if at all, he perceived the change, what meaning it had to him, and how this affected the way he reacted to it. In contrast, they might expect quantitative researchers to measure the environmental changes and his reactions to it and correlate these measures to show cause and effect.

This contrast shows the fundamental difference in how the problem is framed, what is being studied, and what information is sought and deemed useful. Thus, these qualitative researchers would not likely engage in mixed-methods research. This difference is often described as the methods having different paradigms.

In the last decade, several authors have suggested *pragmatism* as the philosophical basis for mixing methods. But, Maxcy (2003) shows it has a long prior history, tracing it primarily to Charles Sanders Pierce (1839–1914), William James, John Dewey, George Herbert Mead, and Arthur F. Bentley. From this viewpoint, "Only results count!" (ibid., p. 85). If there is a gain in using the techniques or point of view of other methods, use them! Greene and Caracelli (2003) agree, "inquirers choose from the full repertoire of methodological options . . . signaling both creativity and a view that paradigm characteristics are not intrinsically bound to particular methods or techniques" (p. 107). But, they argue, "each [paradigmatic tradition] has something valuable to offer to our understanding of our complex social world. If such differences are not attended to in practice, then the full potential of mixed methods inquiry will remain unfulfilled" (ibid.). So if point of view helps, use it.

ADDITIONAL READING

For mixed-research methods generally, Tashakkori and Teddlie (2003) has chapters on a wide variety of aspects and examples in a number of fields. See also Creswell and Plano Clark (2007), Brewer and Hunter (2005), and Fielding and Fielding (1985). For a discussion of the philosophical bases, see Maxcy (2003), Greene and Caracelli (2003), and Miller (2003). Shadish (1993) discusses mixed-method studies in the context of a research strategy. See also Brannen (2005) for good general discussion. Moss (1996) searches for the common ground in interpretivist and "naturalistic" (read "quantitative") traditions for a "more textured and productive view of . . . social phenomena" (p. 22). In the context of evaluation, see Mertens (2003), Greene and Caracelli (1997), Mark and Shotland (1987, an issue devoted to mixed-method evaluation), and Frechtling and Sharp (1997). Sieber (1973) shows how qualitative and survey research complement each other. Behrens and Smith (1996) is an excellent discussion of both quantitative and qualitative data analysis with emphasis on exploratory data analysis and multiple-method research. Patrick and Middleton (2002) provide an example of multiple-method research investigating self-regulated learning.

IMPORTANT TERM/CONCEPT

multiple and mixed-research methods

OPPORTUNITIES FOR ADDITIONAL LEARNING

1. A medical researcher wished to investigate the sensitive topic of incest in American society. Her problem was to find out what incest is and to understand the behavior of the participants. To conduct the study, she had to establish strong rapport with a sample of affected families. Further, to identify a sufficient number of cases, the investigator had to work with

an educational treatment agency. "Obtrusive" procedures such as surveys, questionnaires, and psychological tests were actively discouraged by the agency. However, the agency worked with about 500 families. What research method(s) might she have used?

2. McKim and Cowen (1987) published a study of young children's school adjustment, which they characterized as multiperspective. The main purpose of the study was "to assess the relationships among five perspectives of young school children's adjustment: teacher, peer, parent, and self-ratings and behavior observations." According to the authors, each of these "five measurement perspectives has its own substantial literature." Secondary purposes were to assess relationships between adjustment and achievement, to compare the adjustment of suburban and urban children, and to compare those children referred for mental health services to those not referred. The investigators studied 462 second- and third-grade children from four urban and two suburban schools. The measures, which were all quantitative, consisted of a series of rating scales completed by teachers, standardized achievement tests, and a classroom observation protocol. The scores obtained on the 27 dependent measures were compared using Pearson product-moment correlation coefficients. Analysis of variance was used to test for differences between location and gender.

Is this a mixed-method study in the spirit of what is suggested in this chapter?

Compare your answers with those following the Application Exercise.

APPLICATION EXERCISE

Consider how you might use multiple or mixed methods to bolster the study of your problem. Are you doing basic or applied research? If the former, are any of the four kinds of evidence contributing to Internal Integrity not covered by the method you were planning to use? Could another method cover them? As you considered your problem from the standpoint of different methods, were there some you considered useful? Would a combination of these strengthen your study? If you are doing applied research, what aspects of External Generality need strengthening, and how might other methods facilitate this?

Consider the different enhancements for any tentatively chosen design you may have developed. Examine the trade-offs for those enhancements that might make your design stronger. What are the positive and negative aspects of the enhancements? On balance, do the positives outweigh the negatives? If not, which enhancements would you drop to strengthen the overall picture? Which additional ones might you use?

KEY TO ADDITIONAL LEARNING OPPORTUNITIES

1. Strong Internal Integrity is the key criterion in this basic research study in which the investigator is interested in understanding and describing the phenomenon of incest. This very study was carried out by Patricia Phelan (1987) in San Francisco. She was able to mix qualitative and quantitative methodology in an innovative way to develop an explanation of the phenomenon. To gain entry, she became involved as an intern counselor in the treatment program and began with an ethnographic study using participant observation. This allowed her to understand the treatment community, including clients and staff, and the treatment model used.

Once accepted, she was able to conduct intensive interviews to reveal the family dynamics involved. Since surveys and other quantitative methods were not permitted and interviews with the large number of families were not feasible, Phelan conducted structured interviews with the counselors to gather detailed descriptions of incestuous relationships. From this information she was able to carry out a numeric analysis and test for statistical significance. Combining the two types of data, numeric and narrative, provided her with a comprehensive picture of the phenomenon.

2. Puzzled about how to respond? Good, you were expected to be! On the one hand, the data is all quantitative, but on the other, clearly it is tapping different perspectives on the individuals' behavior, just as a mixed-method study would be expected to do. It used achievement measures, classroom observations (apparently with a structured, low-inference device), and rating scales completed by teachers—three different points of view and three independent snapshots of behavior.

Is it mixed-method in the sense of using both quantitative and qualitative methods? No! It did not use qualitative methods at all. Might they have added something to the mix? Possibly; it depends on the intent and the audience.

But, more importantly, is it consistent with the intent and spirit of the chapter? Absolutely! The whole point of the chapter is that we should use such methods for gathering, analyzing, and interpreting such data as are adequate to encompass our problem and intent (e.g., convincing policy makers). Combinations of methods, more often than not, will build the strongest study. But what if the study were best implemented solely as a quantitative or qualitative study? Fine—whatever best fits the reality of the situation and the problem posed.

SUMMARY

Good research properly defines a problem so as to encompass all the necessary aspects for us to understand it as completely as possible, regardless of method. For some problems one method may be adequate. However, since the various research methods provide different kinds of evidence about phenomena, by combining methods not only can we compensate for the flaws of one method with the strengths of another, but we can obtain different perspectives, "depth of field," and detail. Using more than one method can provide complementary evidence that can reinforce our confidence in the results. It can bracket a phenomenon to reveal its dimensions. Replication of results with a variety of methods under a variety of circumstances is the strongest and ultimate validation of a generalization.

A Look Ahead

The next chapter is an unusual one in a research methods book. It asks that, as a researcher, you reflect upon your work. Step back from the routine analysis of a process, interview or observation coding, software application, statistical interpretation, or whatever aspect of the research you are deeply involved in. Stop to get some perspective, and ask yourself some questions you might not ordinarily consider.

The Larger Context of Research

Having studied the tools and methods of research, the two chapters in this section take a longer view, and they place the previous material into perspective. Much of what is discussed here has been foreshadowed.

Chapter 27 suggests that taking the time to get some perspective on one's research by reflecting on it will be of value to the researcher and may result in better research.

Chapter 28 examines the roles of social science research and what is involved in ensuring that it works properly at the individual level, the peer level, and the societal level. It is intended to raise questions for further thought rather than provide answers.

chapter 27

The Reflective Researcher

INTRODUCTION

In this chapter we weave together two quite different strands of thought. Taken together, they suggest that the results of research may be enhanced if, as a regular part of doing research, researchers stop from time to time—certainly before completing the write-up of the results—to reflect upon what they are about to do and/or what they have done. This may be "carrying water to the river" for some researchers, particularly some qualitative researchers who make this a regular part of their process. But, in addition to re-emphasizing the point for them, it is important to get researchers using quantitative and mixed methods into the practice as well. Furthermore, particularly for quantitative researchers, it is suggested that the reflection be broader in scope than a search for the usual suspects, the list of typical rival explanations—threats to validity.

INTUITIVE KNOWING IN ACTION

The first strand of thought grows out of Donald Schon's book, *The Reflective Practitioner: How Professionals Think in Action* (1983), which was accorded considerable attention when it was published. A summarization of his argument is online in his 1978 presentation to the American Educational Research Association (http://educ.queensu.ca/~ar/schon87.htm). (Schon describes what he calls "reflection in action" as the off-the-cuff reaction of professionals to new situations—their artistry in handling them. It is their spontaneous response that exhibits the intuitive "more" that we know by "what we do by the way in which we do it." He says this "is what I mean by knowing-in-action" [ibid.].) The term *intuitive knowing in action* better portrays what he is describing than *reflection in action*, because the term *reflection* implies a process of thinking and verbalization. To demonstrate, he asks the audience, "When riding a bicycle and it is leaning to the left, do you turn the wheel left? Right? Don't know? Quick!" He points out that, though many will say "right," if you put them on a bicycle, their intuitive actions contradict their words—"intuitive knowing in action."

But it *is* reflection in the usual sense that is his main concern, as Schon points out: Intuitive knowing in action *"IS an intellectual business, and it DOES require verbalization and symbolization"* (ibid., emphasis in the original). And he sees *this* kind of reflection, reflection on the whys and wherefores of the decisions of a professional process, as important. It produces useful knowledge that heals the split between research and practice—indeed, he believes it makes a "revolutionary difference" (ibid.).

PERCEPTIONS SHAPE HOW WE THINK ABOUT THINGS

The second strand of thought grows out of philosophy, the rejection of positivism and its replacement by post-positivism or postmodernism. Ridiculing the assumption of positivism that scientists could objectively stand outside their study completely unaffected by culture, race, gender, and other influences has consumed many journal pages. This literature delves into the relation between our perceptions of the world and the physical objects that give rise to those perceptions. These relationships have been extensively explored with points of view such as phenomenalism, representationalism, and direct realism, offering solutions with mixed success (see, e.g., BonJour, 2001). But the important point that grows out of these discussions is that perceptions do shape how we think about and verbalize things and that the perceptions are affected by the myriad things that positivism assumed we could be immune to.

JOINING THE STRANDS OF THOUGHT

It is here that we join the strands because Schon would have us reflect upon those perceptions, especially those of *knowing in action* and those on the constructed nature of explanation and interpretation. He gives as an example:

> I want to take an example from "The Teacher Project," which was a project initiated in 1978 by Jean Bamberger, who is here, and Eleanor Duckworth. And it was a project of in-service teacher education. The teachers were chosen from elementary schools in Cambridge; they attended seminars once a week. The vignette I want to pick is one in which these seven teachers are sitting watching a videotape. And on the videotape they're seeing two boys playing with pattern blocks—you know what pattern blocks are? And there's an opaque wall between them. One boy has a pattern in front of him; the other boy has a bunch of blocks. And the first boy, looking at his pattern, is trying to give the second boy directions for completing the pattern. And the teachers are watching this videotape. And the first boy gives a series of directions, and pretty soon it's clear that the second boy begins to go horribly awry, and his pattern gets more and more divergent from the ones that the teachers can see in front of the first boy. And the teachers begin to talk about what's going on. And they say the second boy is clearly a slow learner, and he doesn't know how to follow directions. And he seems to lack basic skills. And in the midst of that, Maggie Cauley who was assisting Jean and Eleanor, and who was watching, said, "Wait a second: I think the first boy gave an impossible instruction." And they went back and played the tape again, and they saw that

indeed the first boy had said, "Put down a green square," and there were no green squares, there were only orange squares, and the only green things were triangles. And then the teachers began to see the whole tape in a completely different way. And they perceived that the second boy was, in fact, a virtuoso at following instructions, a virtuoso at improvising instructions. And they said, "You know what we did was we gave the kid reason." (Schon, 1987)

This kind of reflection, showing how it changed the constructed explanation of the student's behavior, resulted from seeing the problem from the student's point of view. This particular point of view is typical of the kind that Schon and many qualitative researchers argue is important. We agree that it is, and we are suggesting here that in addition, it is important in many cases to go beyond that to reflection upon the whole research process prior to completing a final research report.

EXAMPLES OF QUESTIONS TO REFLECT ON

It is true that when doing the kind of research described in this book, particularly in quantitative and mixed-method research, many of the decisions are thoughtfully arrived at. But there are so very many ways of doing even the simplest research that some of the decisions often display that "artistry" of the researcher that results in spontaneous and perhaps surprising choices—intuitive knowing in action. This will be particularly true of fieldwork where the unexpected happens. Add to this the researcher's immersion in what is being studied, and the constructed nature of explanation and interpretation—whether qualitative or quantitative—and this indicates that there are times when a reflective stance may suggest alternative interpretations.

Researchers ought, at one or more points, to reflect on their research. Here is a basic set of questions to consider:

- Considering my interests, my capabilities, and my circumstances at this time, is this the best research to take on?
- What other ways are there of attacking this problem? How did I justify this one?
- Viewing the decisions made in the study so far, which of these might be considered intuitive knowing in action?
- Reflecting on these, were they the best of the alternatives?
- How else might the resources to be put into this study be used?
- How would the participants in this study view it?
- What if the participants were of a different gender, race, class, cultural, or socio-economic background? Would results be different? How would they view the study—what was asked of them—differently?
- How would I likely view the study if I looked at it through the lens of another gender, race, class, or cultural predisposition and affiliation?
- What if my institutional affiliation were different?
- Experience, training, and/or skill in method often makes it more likely that we will ignore certain choices or formulations of a problem because they do not lend themselves to our capabilities. Did that limit the study that should have been done?

(Fear of statistics may give the nod to qualitative method. Ability to easily produce statistics at little effort may favor that direction.)

Obviously this is just a start. Questions specific to the study, as well as more general ones, need to be added, but perhaps these will trigger others. As a researcher deep into the study, it may be that your reflections might benefit from some outside help, from colleagues without such an investment as yours. Discussions with them about these matters may be helpful.

With careful consideration the data may look different, as did data on the boy who received the impossible instruction in Schon's example above. While it seems such reflection may make little difference in some studies, it might make a great deal in others.

EXAMPLES FROM CHAPTER 1

As an example, let's do some reflection on the two studies with which we began the book. Consider the Hoffmann-Riem study of adoption in chapter 1. Would a male investigator have elicited the same data and arrived at the same conclusion? Might the data have been more likely to include statements on the part of husbands that "having a family represents a step into manliness, into an expected male role, into self-fulfillment as a virile man"? Would that have been part of the definition of "normalization"? Was the explanation advanced more likely to come to mind because the interviewer, the researcher, was female?

If we consider the finding from the standpoint of persons from cultures with different family structures, it seems the "normalization" drive might be stronger among those with extended close structures, strongest among those with traditional rural values, and weakest among those with cosmopolitan values—all raising questions for extending this research.

Consider the Zimbardo study as well. Here is a carefully controlled experimental study that seems an unlikely candidate for the kind of reflection suggested. Still, if we do reflect on the way it was done, the following thoughts occur:

The effect was shown with 18 male college undergraduates in a laboratory with good experimental procedure. One of the reasons to use a laboratory-like setting is that you are able to control so many things, and you tend to control everything that you can. This may limit the generalizability, but it also gives the effect the greatest chance to show itself, if it exists. In this instance Zimbardo, among other things, controlled for gender. If women reacted differently than men to the situation, this would increase the variance of the effect. That would, in turn, make it a less sensitive study (see p. 454).

Consider, however, that there is some evidence that females are more socially sensitive than males. Therefore, might female subjects have been more affected by what was presumably said about them when they couldn't understand because of their hypnotized deaf state? Might a study using all females have a larger effect?

Given when the study was done, it seems likely that all the subjects were Caucasian males. How would persons of other races have reacted? Having been exposed to Caucasian persons making presumed negative comments, might they have reacted more strongly, or would they be more able to brush such attacks off with less reaction? Given some noncaucasian persons who reacted more strongly and some who "brushed it off," might they have cancelled each other? That would leave the overall effect undifferentiated from an all-Caucasian group, but the variability would be larger, thus raising the likelihood of a less sensitive study.

These are college students at an age of considerable physical ability. They would have little expectation that anything is physically wrong with them, such as sudden deafness. But given the elderly condition in which bodily parts are failing regularly either on themselves or their colleagues, and given that deafness is a common condition of the elderly, might a failure of hearing be a more salient explanation for them than for college students? Would using college students actually have overestimated the effect in the elderly?

After-the-fact reflection seems to have suggested things that did not occur to us when we initially read these studies.

REFLECTION FOR ALL STUDIES?

Clearly, such reflection may not make a difference in every study. Are there kinds of studies where such concerns are relevant and others where they are not? If so, it doesn't seem that the dividing line is between qualitative and quantitative. There are both qualitative and quantitative studies where, for example, particularly at the interpretation of data level, persons of different gender, race, class, and cultural predisposition and affiliation might see the patterns differently. Is it causal studies that are exempt? It doesn't seem so; both Hoffmann-Riem and Zimbardo are causal. Because it isn't clear where the line is—if one exists—it is recommended that the process at least be attempted for all studies.

APPLICATION EXERCISE

Reflect on the questions above with respect to the study you have been using in these application exercises.

A Look Ahead

In the final chapter, we examine whether the research system works at the individual, peer, and societal levels, raising questions about the process at each level and examining possible answers.

The Macrosystem of Educational and Social Science Research

> Few of us realize how short the career of what we know as "science" has been. Three hundred and fifty years ago hardly any one believed in the Copernican planetary theory. . . . The circulation of the blood, the weight of air, the conduction of heat, the laws of motion were unknown; the common pump was inexplicable.
> —R. Reynolds & Sons, *Some Problems of Philosophy* (1911)

> After close to two centuries of passionate struggles, neither science nor faith has succeeded in discrediting its adversary. On the contrary, it becomes obvious that neither can develop normally without the other. And the reason is simple: The same life animates both. Neither in its impetus nor its achievements can science go to its limits without becoming tinged with mysticism and charged with faith.
> —P. T. de Chardin, *The Phenomenon of Man* (1961)

A heuristic aids in discovery and encourages inquiry. This chapter is a heuristic that raises questions to which there are not yet satisfactory answers. Indeed, perhaps there never will be, since many involve values about which persons differ. The goal is to suggest topics deserving of thought, to raise some questions you might otherwise take for granted. Then, because of your greater awareness, perhaps you will attend to them when encountered in future reading or even pursue deeper analysis of them. Here, however, we give them only such examination as we can.

We'll examine the building of a social science, starting at the individual researcher level and working successively through the peer to the societal level. Each depends on the workings of the previous one. Examining problems at each level, we ask whether and how well it works. Questioning how well the system works is important because, as Begley (1977) stated:

> Society is driven by science. The conclusions of researchers answer questions as important to ordinary people as the heritability of alcoholism and the merits of using IQ scores to assign 5-year-olds to "gifted" school programs. Science, in short, matters. (p. 56)

Lastly, we look at whether, as we have presumed throughout the book, a social science is possible.

INTRODUCTION

The natural sciences are largely supported as a matter of faith; the lay community seldom understands much of what natural scientists do but does see occasional important applications. In contrast,

> the social sciences seldom get full credit . . . because the discoveries, once labeled, are quickly absorbed into conventional wisdom. This is easily demonstrated: note the number of social science concepts common to our vocabulary: human capital, gross national product, identity crisis, span of control, the unconscious, price elasticity, acculturation, political party identification, reference group. (Prewitt, 1981, p. 659)

Furthermore, the stuff of everyday life in which all of us are our own "experts" is the content of social and behavioral science. (Really expert? Not necessarily—remember the research of Wong described on p. 45.) Everyone feels competent to judge such research. This "transparency" makes it even more important that the social science research process should work as well as possible, since, as problems are perceived, they tinge the source with suspicion in the minds of the public.

DOES SOCIAL SCIENCE FUNCTION AS INTENDED AT THE INDIVIDUAL LEVEL?

The "Packaging" of Findings

Consider the model of how findings become knowledge, described in chapter 3. It is a process whereby findings pass a series of hurdles and are finally accepted by a wide enough audience that they are generally acknowledged as true. It seems likely that someone in our present society must immediately ask, "Isn't it true that advertising also is concerned with getting a product accepted through a series of hurdles?" Ouch! Of course it is! And doesn't that raise the question, "Do the techniques of advertising also apply to the science process?" The answer is both yes and no. Yes, in the sense that knowledge products that fill a need and that are well "packaged" move quickly into acceptance, just as they do with an advertised product. What is meant by *well packaged*? For one thing, Slovic, Fischhoff, and Lichtenstein (1982) note that the way an issue is framed has a lot to do with its acceptance. The political bureaucracy has taken this to heart, leading the environmentalists to protest the "Clean Air Act" and the "Clear Forest Act"—in which using "clean" and "clear" is a perversion of their meaning.

But we would also have to say no to advertising in science, in the sense that researchers don't generally give much attention to the "packaging" of knowledge, nor would their colleagues like it if they did. Colleagues would perceive that the products might not stand on their own merits and that the researchers may be trying to "put one over on readers."

Let's look at a case where "packaging" played a role, though it was because the researcher published appropriately, not as the result of a conscious advertising role. It is the spread of meta-analysis, a technique described in chapter 22.

There are scattered examples of meta-analyses prior to its being labeled and defined (e.g., Bloom, 1976). But it blossomed when Glass (1976) coined the term *meta-analysis*, showing how to average results of previous studies, convert them to a standard metric called effect size, and use it to decisively show positive results for psychotherapy. This was a conclusion researchers had unconvincingly sought since the dawn of clinical psychology—what is the effectiveness of "just talking about a problem?" (Smith & Glass, 1977). Meta-analysis eventually grew an *evidence-based movement* in many fields, especially prominently in medicine and education (e.g., the Cochrane and Campbell collaborations—see p. 525).

There are several things at work here:

1. The need for this technique was clearly present in the search for the most effective practices in professional areas.

2. It was shown to be effective in an important situation.

3. The technique was given a label that was descriptive.

4. The procedure was well documented, clear, and doable.

5. Meta-analysts could make more definitive statements than those doing syntheses in words—especially those for whom negative findings were perceived as negating a relationship instead of perceiving such findings as a normal product of a weak relationship (see p. 522). (It no doubt helped that the effect size was linear in contrast to the nonlinearity of the correlation scale—a correlation of .40 is not just twice as "strong" as .20, but it accounts for four times the variance.)

Does all this suggest that researchers ought to give more thought to "packaging" their ideas?[1] Probably, because they call attention to some aspects to attend to, but mainly in the sense that there is a certain minimum the researcher should do. First in importance is reporting the study so it is easily understood (point 4 above). For those studies to which it is applicable, the model of the chain of reasoning in chapter 4 provides a framework that assures the logic has all its parts, and, if the links are followed in sequence, can ease understanding in many presentations. And if a finding or idea can be shown to fill a need (point 1 above) and advances the field (point 5) it is more likely to gain acceptance. If appropriate, it helps that the finding or idea can be named descriptively, as was the term meta-analysis. To do so gives it a reality that elevates it out of the background and gives a handle to the phenomenon that facilitates its use (point 3 above). All of the points above, with the exception of this last one, might appear obvious; but that last one is important. Consider that many of us had known about prior quantitative syntheses using chi-square. However, not until Glass pulled the procedure together and named it appropriately did it get the impetus it needed to gain acceptance as part of the body of knowledge.

Fraud in Science

We place an amazing amount of trust in the integrity of individual investigators. We think of their reports as containing enough information to judge the study, and in most respects this appraisal is accurate. But space limitations demand that research reports omit much detail. If you don't think so, consider replicating the Zimbardo study in chapter 1. It seems to be reported in sufficient detail, but think about all the aspects you would have to supply to replicate it—the method of hypnotism, many of the instruments, and—most surprisingly of all—a timetable. How long would you guess the sessions took? Thirty minutes? An hour? A day? Several days? They actually took only about half an hour to an hour. That information was contained in a newspaper article about the study (Hunt, 1982), not in the study itself.

Largely because of problems in the biomedical field, trust in the individual investigator is increasingly questioned. Tracing major cases of fraud, mostly in the natural sciences, Judson (2004) recently cites some in the social and behavioral sciences as well. For instance, he describes how critics at the time deemed Freud's theories, based on his cases, as without scientific merit, but "What's new is the finding that Sigmund Freud's cases were bogus from start to finish" (p. 86). He notes, "Sulloway [1979] showed that every one of Freud's case histories is rendered worthless by gross fabrications and falsifications" (p. 89). He also describes the famous case of Sir Cyril Burt, whose data on the heredity of the IQ "are simply not worthy of our current scientific attention" (Kamin, 1976, as quoted in Judson, 2004, p. 94). Mackintosh (1995) not only claimed that Burt fabricated data but also determined that two assistants credited as data gatherers never existed.

It is unknown, of course, how widespread fraud in science really is. A survey of 2,000 faculty members and 2,000 doctoral candidates (Swazey, 2004) had unusually high returns (79% of faculty, 59% of student samples). This survey found that half the faculty and 43% of the students reported direct knowledge of some kind of misconduct. While it is possible that those with such knowledge were more likely to reply, and it is possible that multiple individuals reported the same case, even with such discounts this is uncomfortably high.

De Vries, Anderson, and Martinson (2006) were more concerned with what they called *normal misbehavior*. Using focus groups of experienced researchers from major universities they found that while researchers were aware of the rare but highly publicized cases of falsification, plagiarism, and data falsification, "in their eyes misconduct generally is associated with more mundane, everyday problems in the work environment" (p. 43). They embodied such problems in a questionnaire sent to a national sample. In contrast to the Swazey study, where because they were reporting about their own milieu, the same event may have been reported by many different colleagues, they asked for self-reports. They found falsification, fabrication, and plagiarism "to be a minor problem (as indicated by self-report of these behaviors): just 0.3% of our respondents admitted to falsifying data, and 1.4% admitted to plagiarism" (p. 47).

For them, it was the problems in doing research that fall in "gray areas." Many examples were from hard sciences, but social scientists can relate to that of

> finding the line between "cleaning" data and "cooking" data. One scientist said: "I was defending my master's thesis . . . and the external examiner look[ed] at some of my graphs. And he said, 'You know, well I'd be much more convinced by your data if you'd chopped off the last two data points . . .' I was like, well, I wasn't sure that you could do that . . . those two data points may be more interesting than something that has happened before." (De Vries et al., p. 45)

Other examples involved changing design or method to please funders, withholding details of methodology or results, and not obtaining permission or giving credit for another's ideas. While the low percentages of outright fraud are reassuring, the amount of "misbehavior" is considerably less so.

The unexpectedness of any fraud at all, combined with the inability to determine how frequently it occurs, raises questions about the whole research enterprise. Each time an instance is uncovered, everyone is tainted with the stain.

Why does it occur? Pressure to publish, to win research grants, to succeed, and to be first with a significant finding no doubt all contribute. Various studies (among them Katz, 1973 and Tuckman, 1976) have shown that publications in all fields of research contribute significantly to salary increases. Centra (1977) showed that the most important information for tenure, salary, and promotions was the number of articles in quality journals and the excellence of the research as judged by peers. Clearly, these are pressures that every academic researcher feels. No doubt, although specific pressures differ, the situation is similar outside academia. The rush to publish is endemic to the scientist's world. As Price (1975) points out:

> At the root of the matter is the basic difference between creative effort in the sciences and . . . the arts. If Michelangelo or Beethoven had not existed, their works would have been replaced by different contributions. If Copernicus or Fermi had never existed, essentially the same contribution would have had to come from other people. There is, in fact, only one world to discover. (p. 69)

The first person to publish is recognized as the discoverer and gets the credit.[2]

It is difficult to convey adequately the excitement of the race to discover. Unfortunately, there are few reports of research competition. One is the story of the unraveling of DNA by Watson and Crick as told by one of those Nobel Prize-winning researchers (Watson, 1968). The intensity of that race is conveyed especially effectively when Watson tells of the laboratory visit of the son of Linus Pauling, who headed a rival team. Watson and Crick's efforts to covertly assess where the two teams stood with respect to the problem's solution and their elation at believing they were ahead make fascinating reading.

Another account is that of the marathon between Nobelists Guillemin and Schally to discover the interaction between the brain and the pituitary gland (Wade, 1978). Wade analyzes the way in which the rivalry shaped their approaches, trying to assess whether the competition helped or hindered. Although it certainly interfered with cooperation between the teams, it also "'stimulated both men to do their very best and check each other's work. They learned from each other'" (Wade quoting Meites, a historian of the field, p. 513). Although neither example is from the social sciences, its interpersonal relations and team experiences are likely to be similar.

Given these innate features of research, there is no easy solution to the problem of avoiding fraud. As with other ethical problems, we cannot have laboratory police. The responsibility rests with the individual researcher. In the long run, fraud may be uncovered by efforts to build on top of what proves to be false work. Meanwhile, however, there is the short-run damage of wasted efforts.

If you are involved in research, you—personally—are the bulwark against fraud! You must be vigilant to the possibility of fraud and, instead of letting possible incidents pass, must challenge your peers to guarantee that it is not present. Although we are inclined to think there is very little fraud in the social sciences, *any* fraud exacts too great a price, for trust once destroyed is very difficult to reestablish.

Can We Trust What We See?

Considerably more prevalent than fraud are the mechanisms likely to bias the interpretation of data. An example of this is the *expectancy effect* that Rosenthal and Rubin (1980) showed to be so pervasive—in which, regardless of the facts, results confirm the researcher's expectations (see p. 499).

Remember, "there is a lot more to seeing than meets the eyeball" (Hanson, 1958, p. 7); perception organizes what we see into learned patterns. Phillips (1987) cites research in which playing cards were flashed momentarily—trick cards, such as a black six of hearts, were mixed in. Regular cards could be routinely identified; trick cards were either misread or seen as a blur. Moreland and Zajonc (1977) flashed abstract designs on a screen at a speed so fast that the designs were not perceived as having been seen. Later these designs were mixed with other abstract designs, and the subjects were to indicate how well they liked each design. The designs with which they were familiar as a result of prior subliminal exposure were better liked! Ferris (1981) notes:

> The eye . . . delivers not television pictures to be observed . . . but processed information, much of it . . . hypotheses. . . . And in the dialogue between the eye and the rest of the brain, what we see can become what we expect to see. A field mouse is transformed into a snake to the hiker who fears snakes. (p. 61)

How many such influences are there? How pervasive are they? How much and what effect do they have? We don't know for sure. These, of course, are the very points many qualitative researchers have been trying to stress to their "we-are-unbiased-and-objective" quantitative colleagues! Just as qualitative researchers look inward to become aware of how their actions and reactions affect data gathering, so must all researchers seek the effect of perceptual and expectancy problems on their findings.

DOES SCIENCE FUNCTION AS INTENDED AT THE PEER LEVEL?

You will recall that peers, usually colleagues, are the first screens in the development of a consensus around the interpretation of data. Colleagues can help considerably by correcting misperceptions, calling attention to expectancy effects, and so forth. Other peers are gatekeepers to journals and convention presentations. And *peer review* of applications for funding, although less prevalent with private foundations, is widespread across government research programs. How well does peer review work? Is it a matter of friends taking care of friends instead of attending to the concerns of science? Do people with famous reputations get by with things that lesser-known researchers cannot? Is there the expected single standard of quality?

Peer Review for Publication

Several studies illuminate these issues. First, are reviews really blind, or do reviewers generally know the authors? Studying perceptions among psychologists, Ceci and

Peters (1984) found their survey respondents believed, on average, that authors were correctly identified about 72% of the time. Using six psychology journals from a broad range of areas, however, Ceci and Peters showed that only about a quarter of reviewers were actually able to identify the author of a sufficiently blinded manuscript, about one-third of the commonly suspected rate. That is at least partially reassuring.

Does concealing the author's identity—*blind review*—make a difference? Tobias and Zibrin (1978) used abstracts submitted for a convention program to examine this question. They compared four evaluations of each proposal—two blind and two with identifying information. They found no differences between these conditions! The researchers also examined the effect of prominence of reviewer, sex of author, and sex of reviewer. Neither prominence of reviewer nor sex of author interacted with the review process comparing blind and nonblind conditions. Female reviewers gave more favorable ratings to the importance of the problem than male reviewers; but that was the only difference.

Judson (2004) describes an experiment in blind reviewing from an interview with Richard Smith, editor of the *British Medical Journal*. He alternately assigned papers to reviewers as usual or to reviewers who were told their names would be made known to the authors. Using an instrument to evaluate the reviews, he found no negative effects. Although reviewers were initially against the practice, "only some 40 of 5000 referees refused to relinquish anonymity" (p. 286). The next year the journal converted to open reviewing entirely. While this lead has not been followed in the social science community, it appears that abandoning blind refereeing has no negative effects. This is good news.

Does the importance of the topic or its being a replication make a difference? Fictitious studies incorporating combinations of flawed and unflawed with important and unimportant topics were judged for publication suitability (Wilson, DePaulo, Mook, & Klaaren, 1993). Even though publishability of flawed and unimportant topics was judged low, about a quarter more of those dealing with important instead of unimportant topics were judged methodologically sound. Neuliep and Crandall (1990a, 1990b) found both editors and reviewers prejudiced against publication of replications. Considering the pressure for publication and the rejection rates of some journals—as high as 4 out of 5 submissions—their conclusion is not surprising.

Lastly, do reviewers agree on the criteria of research excellence, and do they agree in their evaluations of articles? The picture is mixed, but with significant problems (Jefferson, Alderson, Wager, & Davidoff, 2002). For example, in an interesting recounting of the pressures they experienced as editors, Murray and Raths (1996) reported only 36% of their reviewers were in exact agreement, but 79% were within one step of each other's recommendations on a five-point scale. Indeed, in an intensive study of editorial peer review, Weller (2001) found "generally reviewer agreement studies found more agreement among reviewers when there was a recommendation to reject" (p. 199). Fiske and Fogg (1990), in a careful study of 402 reviews of 153 papers submitted to 12 different psychological journals, found that "reviewers did not . . . disagree on particular points; instead, they wrote about different topics, each making points that were appropriate and accurate. As a consequence, their recommendations about editorial decisions showed hardly any agreement" (p. 591). This comment is typical of research in this area.

Robert Rosenthal's experience in publishing his work on expectancy effects (cited on p. 499) presents the problem in its starkest terms:

> I recall an especially "good news–bad news" type of day when a particular piece of work was simultaneously rejected by an APA journal and awarded the American Association for the Advancement of Science (AAAS) Socio-Psychological Prize for 1960. (Shadish & Fuller, 1994, p. 219)

This lack of agreement on what points to critique in a peer review is at least partially understandable, however, when we consider the many possible trade-offs and their combinations. They result in a comparison of apples and oranges when we stretch them along a single dimension of quality.[3] Furthermore, as Weller (2001) points out, not all editors look on disagreement as a bad thing, especially if reviewers have been chosen to look at the article from different points of view. Editors, therefore, generally make their accept-reject judgment not just on reviewer ratings, but also on a considered evaluation of reviewer comments, synthesizing the different aspects of multiple reviewers into a judgment of the whole.

Peer Review for Sponsored Research

Most governmental agencies and some private foundations that fund research use panels of researchers from relevant fields to help determine those most deserving. Although not without its problems, the system has worked to most people's satisfaction. The system requires such satisfaction, as well as a belief that it can work fairly and equitably, because the research community heavily subsidizes it in the form of contributed labor. Peer reviewers typically agree to serve either without remuneration except for travel expenses, or for honorariums considerably less than the going rate. Judson (2004) concretizes the hidden cost. For the National Institutes of Health (NIH) alone, extrapolating from previous research to present-day levels, he estimates that reviewers put in 240,000 days or some 800 *reviewer-years per year* and that these are "for the most part established younger scientists who should be at their peak" (p. 258).

Strains on the system seem to increase. Applications for funding continue to grow; the cutting score for approval continues to rise; funding is inadequate to support all approved proposals; the quality of the applications is so high that discrimination among them is difficult; and Congressional pressures for consideration of geographical, gender, and racial diversity in awards is great. Still, these are all conditions that to a lesser or greater extent have been with us almost from the beginning. They are mitigated when funding is increased and vice versa. It seems likely that unconventional proposals and replications have little chance in such an arena. With so many pressures, one might expect the system to fail; potential researchers might refuse to invest the substantial time required to prepare a proposal. But governments want to know what they are paying for, and government funding is by far the largest pot. Busy individuals might refuse to serve on panels, but what better seminar than panel discussions of the latest ideas and methods with competent people in your field? No alternative has developed substantial support.

One alternative is to fund productive people. Judson (2004) points out this is what Warren Weaver did so successfully with the Rockefeller Foundation's Biology

Program prior to World War II. Though not funding "comers" as Weaver did, the NIH Senior Scientist Awards are an effort in this direction, working within the political realities. They cover research salary and time for mentoring junior colleagues for up to five years.

Langfeldt (2001) found an interesting review alternative used in the Research Council of Norway. Following discussion of the projects, each panel member proposes one study that is then funded. She points out that the practice of funding only those agreed as having the highest scores makes it unlikely that risky, unconventional, creative projects would be funded. Such a project has a chance of being funded under the Norway procedure, even though it might be at the bottom of another panel member's list. When such projects are successful, they encourage risk taking. However, criticisms of failures and political atmospheres typically work to prevent program administrators from maintaining such a course long enough for its value to be accepted.

Another View of Peer Review

Edwards and Schneider (2001) point out, "Most of the criticisms of peer review depend on a particular (and often tacit) view ... [that it] acts as a kind of 'truth machine' automatically separating 'good' science from bad" (p. 231). In contrast:

> We maintain that peer review ought to be regarded as a human process whose primary functions are to improve the quality of scientific work, to maintain accountability both inside and outside the scientific community, and to build a scientific community that shares core principles and beliefs even when it does not agree in detail. . . . Peer review can also be described as an institutionalized form of the "virtual witnessing" process by which science establishes factual knowledge. It ensures that at least a few relatively disinterested parties have carefully scrutinized the . . . procedure and the reasoning and agreed with the conclusions drawn by the authors. It is . . . a way for the community to rehearse (and enforce) its fundamental norms and practices. For some or all of these reasons, nearly every scientist regards peer review as an extremely important mechanism, even though most are aware of its problems. (pp. 232–233)

Such a view makes sense, since there is some evidence that the process improves manuscripts. A study of resubmissions by Goodman, Berlin, Fletcher, and Fletcher (1994) showed that 33 of 34 changes were improvements, and the bottom 50% showed the greatest improvement.

Conditions for Productive Science

Under what conditions are researchers most productive? Every college administrator and director of a research and development center would like to know the answer. There are, however, some useful research results, mostly from the physical and biological sciences, but some of the findings seem likely to apply to the social sciences. For instance, Dunbar (1995) video and audiotaped scientists in immunology and molecular biology laboratories working by themselves. Encountering an inconsistent finding, they

> usually attributed inconsistent evidence to error of some sort, and hoped that the finding would go away. However, when the finding was presented at a laboratory

meeting, the other scientists tended to focus on the inconsistency to dissect it, and either (a) suggested alternate hypotheses, or (b) forced the scientists to think of a new hypothesis. This happened at numerous lab meetings and was one of the main mechanisms for inducing conceptual change in scientists when inconsistent evidence occurred. Often this resulted in the phenomenological experience of insight in which the scientist exclaims that they now know what was going on in their experiment. (p. 11)

Inexperienced researchers were found more likely to resist giving up their original hypothesis than experienced ones.

The social structure of the research group seems to be influential. Reasoning by analogy was common in finding successful solutions except in one laboratory, an unsuccessful one. Why the difference? A critical aspect seemed to be diversity of backgrounds; individuals in this lab all drew on the same knowledge base. "When all the scientists are from the same background it is difficult for them to generate multiple hypotheses, but when the scientists are from different backgrounds many different hypotheses can be generated" (Dunbar, 1999, p. 97). "Findings indicate the groups of individuals must have different pools of knowledge to draw from to make fruitful analogies" (Dunbar, 1995, p. 14). Along the same lines, Dunbar suggests providing "opportunities for the members of the research group to interact and discuss the research by having overlapping research projects and breaking the lab up into smaller groups working on similar problems" (p. 18). Continued research on scientists by Dunbar and others is summarized in Dunbar and Fugelsang (2005).

Examining the size of research groups, Stankiewicz (1979) hypothesized that larger groups would be more fruitful because of the greater opportunities to interact, to pursue alternative research strategies in parallel, and to attack different aspects of a complex problem. Beyond a certain point, size would prove counterproductive because of problems of communication. Examining research groups in Sweden, he found an increase in effectiveness from three to five members and from five to seven, depending on the performance measures used, but a decline in larger groups.

In an excellent comparison of U.S. and Soviet science, Gustafson (1980) observed that the Soviets could concentrate enormous resources on crucial problems in basic research. In that system senior colleagues were oriented more toward theory than toward experimentation, and they provided planning and coordination for young researchers. This method was seen, at best, as producing teamwork; at worst, conservatism, deference to superiors, immobility, and going along for the sake of agreement. Conversely, the American belief in individual initiative, tolerance for risk and conflict, and lack of respect for authority were seen as producing a dynamic and competitive system with a zest for "unplanned opportunity" (p. 58). Highly productive, the American system lacks the predictability of support formerly granted in the Soviet system, and there is considerable lack of coordination of governmental support in this country. Gustafson was careful to note that large, block-funded institutions in the United States experienced many of the same problems as the block-funded institutions of the former Soviet Union.

One of the most interesting omissions is the lack of findings that more resources make a difference. It is clear that in the physical and life sciences expensive equipment is a necessity for certain lines of work, but this is rarely true in the social and behavioral sciences. Indeed, Weick (1984) argues for "small wins," cutting social problems into manageable pieces. "Small wins are like miniature experiments that test implicit theories about resistance and opportunity and uncover both resources and barriers that were invisible before the situation was stirred up" (p. 44). For instance, he notes that the feminist movement failed at the equal rights amendment but found that sex references in speech were more susceptible to change than had been thought. The opponents were "more dispersed, more stuffy, and less formidable than anticipated" (p. 44). Weick provides a number of arguments for "small wins" as a strategy.

Obviously, there are myriad unsolved problems in this area; many are probably context-dependent. In contrast to "hard" science, the "soft" social sciences, as must be clear from this textbook, are still evolving standards and goals and improving their methods—but we are getting closer to the target.

The National Institutes of Health's interest in collaborative interdisciplinary research resulted in considerable research activity in this area and a special issue of the *American Journal of Preventive Medicine* (2008).

THE POTENTIAL OF THE INTERNET

In the past we typically considered peers to be mainly those in nearby offices, or the colleagues we met at annual conventions—contacts governed by geography. Electronic journals, forums, and listservs are building global cross-institutional peer communities through the Internet. Further, as already noted throughout this text, support groups for substantive fields of research, for methodological problems, for software packages (e.g., statistical and qualitative analysis programs), and for specific instruments and measures can bring expert help to the novice from some of the most knowledgeable persons from anywhere in the world—available to all through the use of automated agents that search the Web. Electronic journals facilitate communication in small niches of content with subscriber bases far too small to be viable in conventional published form. Because of the speed and ease of publication, the *APA Review of Books* has switched entirely from print to online form. Will other conventional journals follow? Online publishing can be a mixed blessing, particularly if the site isn't set up for skimming. It is much easier to skim print, especially in a book where access to the full contents is immediately available, than to peer at it through the peephole of a screen at a time.

Particularly facilitating the growth of Internet content is the open-access movement. It was given international momentum by the February 2002 Budapest Open Access Initiative, in which publishers and individuals from all fields pledged to make their research articles freely available on the Internet. Some publishers who charge nonsubscribers for online access have resisted this trend as have some professional associations dependent on journal income. But some archives have been opened, and increasingly individuals are free to put their articles online, following a suitable period after publication. This is particularly true of research subsidized by public money, some funders requiring open availability.

The body of material indexed by search engines continues to increase as search engine companies make arrangements with publishers to gain access to at least abstracts and tables of contents at the time of publication. Google's index currently contains over eight billion entries! Furthermore, in 2004 Google announced agreements with major libraries to digitize all or part of their print collections—millions of volumes. As these are added to Google Books, those published prior to 1922 are considered to be in the public domain, and the full text can be accessed. In response to a search for books published after 1922 (considered still in copyright unless access is granted by copyright holder), searchers receive three snippets of text surrounding their search term—about three lines, the number of times the search term appears in the text, and where to find the book at a local library or buy it.

It is too early to determine the eventual direction and nature of all these influences, but they seem likely to be substantial. Search engines and their indexes have the potential to markedly raise the quality of work in all the sciences, and the number of specialty search engines as well as databases continues to grow. Combined with computer translation services, they place the world's literature at one's fingertips. Add to this the increasingly open access to current literature, the convenience of access by computer, and the subscriptions to databases made available online by most universities, and there is the promise of marked facilitation of the use of past and contemporary literature. Already, because of the breadth of their indexes, search engines are a handy and quick (though incomplete) substitute for citation indexes—tools for locating follow-ups to past publications.

One concern arises from the fact that each of us has only so much discretionary time, and time devoted to the Internet is not available for journals and books. Further, as Van Alstyne and Brynjolfsson (1996) note,

> As quickly as information technology collapses barriers based on geography, it forces us to build new ones based on interest or time. . . . Researchers [may] . . . focus on only those articles and colleagues that really interest them. . . . The same information lens that brings distant colleagues into focus can inadvertently produce tunnel vision and peripheral blindness . . . and narrower scientific interactions. . . . Depending on how this task is managed, the Internet could lead to . . . a balkanization of the global village. (p. 1479)

So far people seem to be tinkering, trying to find the right mix of electronic and print formats, of reading broadly across fields and narrowly to keep up in their own field.

Some individuals have always sought new uses for tools found in other fields, and some have always read widely; those individuals will no doubt transfer those habits to the Web. But with such a deluge of information, they will have to find new ways to explore the margins. It seems likely, however, that those who are slow to use these resources will be left behind. Van Alstyne and Brynjolfsson (1996) already cite one study suggesting that those who use information technology "write more papers, earn greater peer recognition and know more colleagues" (op. cit.).

DOES SCIENCE FUNCTION AS INTENDED AT THE SOCIETAL LEVEL?

The social sciences as disciplines developed relatively late among the arts and sciences. It was an important act of faith for the University of Chicago to erect the first building just for the social sciences in the late 1930s. Although psychology considered itself a discipline and had its own national association, some of its regional societies were still merged with philosophical societies as late as World War II. Emergence of separate departments for each of the social sciences resulted in many changes—for example, better training for new entrants and the development of more sophisticated research methods.

Of course, the literature of social science began centuries before such departments existed. In the past, although they were often the best-educated persons of their period, authors wrote in the ordinary language of their day. Thus, their writing was immediately available to educated persons and was often widely read. As the social sciences matured, however, the useful shorthand—*jargon*—that develops within every field increasingly placed publications beyond the understanding of the common person. Jargon impedes communication to the general public, increases problems of dissemination, expands the social distance between researchers and practitioners who might benefit from their work, and markedly diminishes public support for research.

The use of jargon unique to each social science field leads to the charge that social scientists write mainly for others like themselves. But while that is true of all scientists, when social science findings are translated into the popular press, because of the "obviously true" problem referred to earlier (p. 45), public esteem for the enterprise decreases further. This denies to social scientists the trust freely granted to physical scientists that their work is equally valued.

The distance between professional and practitioner has led to research on the dissemination of findings. As this utilization knowledge has developed, so has a translation industry that explains science for the intelligent layperson. Witness the journals *Scientific American, Popular Sciences, Popular Mechanics, Discover,* the extensive front section in *Science,* and the like. Dissemination and adoption research has facilitated this transition.

Dissemination Research

Dissemination was researched early in the field of agriculture, centered around getting findings adopted by farmers. It created the agricultural extension agent who translated research for the farmer, showed how these new practices applied in a specific situation, and grew demonstration plots to show the results. These techniques proved effective but expensive. Rogers (1995) found it helpful to understand the dissemination process by dividing individuals into five classes: Early adopters, individuals who were ready and eager to try new things, were categorized as (1) *innovators*—2.5%, and (2) *early adopters*—13.5%. A middle group was categorized as (3) *early majority*—34%, and (4) *late majority*—34%. A late group was categorized as the (5) *laggards*—16%. The early adopters are important sources of practices for the middle group, which will tend to follow their lead when innovations are successful.

Rogers (1995) also showed that individuals tend to go through five stages of information use in the adoption process:

1. *Awareness* sensitizes them to pay attention when they encounter a demonstration of an innovation or literature about it.

2. *Interest* encourages them to seek information about it.

3. *Evaluation* lets them estimate the chances of its success in their situation.

4. *Trial* involves making a small commitment to the innovation to determine whether it performs as anticipated.

5. *Adoption* is the result of a successful trial.

In addition, Rogers (1995) studied the characteristics that enable people to predict the probability of successful implementation. A first characteristic is the *relative advantage of the innovation over alternatives*—it fills a need. Thus, cost-effectiveness, especially when it saves time and effort, is important, as is the immediacy of the results. Consider the adoption of wait-time in teaching, which shifts the character of student responses to a much higher level of thinking (Rowe, 1974). It costs the embarrassment of silence following a question and may cause initial discomfort for both teacher and students. However, the resulting greater thoroughness and depth of discussion cost little and are easily perceived as much more satisfying to both parties than the classroom climate produced by a bombardment of simple questions.

A second characteristic is *compatibility with the existing values, needs, standards, and practices of the adopter*. The better the match, the less amount of change needed and the more likely that the innovation will be adopted and integrated into ongoing practice. Wait-time will result in the kinds of responses the teacher values—those much closer to desired standards—and the questioning pattern is not a drastic change from previous practice. Wait-time has a second characteristic leading to ease of adoption.

A third aspect is *lack of complexity—the simpler, the better*. It is a relatively simple matter to extend the time the teacher waits for an answer to a question. But it does require inhibiting the natural propensity to modify the question, substitute another, or call on a student, all routine actions strengthened by habitual practice. Further, it may require some thought on the part of the teacher to pose challenging questions. Wait-time doesn't fare so well on this characteristic.

A fourth property is *trialability*—the extent to which a *small commitment* on the part of the adopter will permit a trial that provides sufficient evidence to determine whether to make a complete commitment to the innovation. Certainly, wait-time can easily be given a trial, but it takes consistent trying for the sense of what is happening to be rewarding.

A final characteristic is *observability*, the degree to which the *results are apparent* to potential adopters. If the research on wait-time is correct, the result should be a change in the quality and level of class discussion, but how quickly this is sensed and appreciated by all the parties may take a bit of time.

Key in all the literature on adoption of innovations is administrative support, involvement of adopters in the adoption decision, adaptation to their situations, and trial of the innovation to obtain evidence firsthand (action research). Administrative support is a necessary but not sufficient condition. Involvement of the adoptee, however, is a sufficient condition if adoption results are sufficiently rewarding in and of themselves. Thus, involvement is stressed in nearly all the literature.

The characteristics that facilitate adoption have implications for how to choose and develop a research idea that will have a practical impact. Let's combine the mentioned principles with the example used earlier, Glass's (1976) development of meta-analysis. Meta-analysis has spread to medicine and many natural science fields and has become widely used in a very short time. Together the characteristics and example suggest a five-step process:

1. *Advantage*. Glass chose the long-standing problem of combining quantitative studies to yield a summary overall result. Meta-analysis had an advantage in expressing in a single metric what several words, sentences, or paragraphs had only clumsily conveyed.

2. *Compatibility*. This means finding a solution that is close to current practice, one that it can be easily grafted onto. Glass found that quantitative results could be translated into something approximating standard scores, familiar to other researchers and many teachers.

3. *Simplicity, Lack of Complexity.* Standard scores are widely used and fairly broadly understood, so the results of meta-analysis were well related to previous experience. Further, using terminology that is self-descriptive, simple, and fits with other terms in the field, Glass called the translated findings *effect sizes*. Similarly, the name given the process, meta-analysis, from the Greek *meta* for comprehensive and *analysis*, is self-descriptive. Both terms fit their other usage in the field and have been widely adopted and used. Choosing a name that is self-descriptive and easily remembered markedly facilitates communication about the new item, reduces complexity, and facilitates trialability.

4. *Trialability*. Demonstrating the effectiveness of what had been developed, Glass forcefully established the power of meta-analysis by showing its effectiveness in an area where previous research summaries had yielded only equivocal results—psychotherapy.

5. *Observability*. Glass demonstrated that instead of another equivocal result, meta-analysis showed some methods to be more effective than others.

Thus, research on dissemination has provided a basis for researchers to be more effective in getting their innovations adopted. A basic problem, however, is that the involvement of the adopter in the adoption process is costly and time consuming. Informational materials seem to go only so far. This same issue emerged in chapter 23 where, to get evaluation findings used, the extent and nature of the stakeholder involvement in an evaluation are at issue—an issue solved by action research where the researcher and stakeholder are one and the same. This same solution, having potential users research solutions, is often employed to get a practice adopted. Research is still needed on decreasing the cost of the adoption process and making it more effective.

The Contributions of Research to Policy

Probably the earliest involvement of the social sciences in U.S. policy was the 1832 grant to the Franklin Institute to study the causes of explosions in steamboat boilers. "Professor Bates . . . reported that 'sometimes there is a little carelessness in stoking the fire.' A bursting steam boiler is not just a matter of chemistry and physics; it is also a matter of operator training and human behavior" (Prewitt, 1980, p. 2). Over the years the government has repeatedly recognized the importance of the human element in its attempt to regulate and plan. (Plan, that is, in terms of averages and tendencies. However, my historian friend, J. B. Van Hise [personal communication, February 21, 1989] wrote: "Social science always leaves out irrationality: the force of fear, panic, faith, and myth in causing things to happen.")

A surge in the utilization of social science knowledge in policy decisions came with the use of social science evidence in the federal courts in such cases as the landmark desegregation decision, *Brown v. Board of Education of Topeka* (347 U.S. 483). It was continued in the development of accurate survey samples that provided information on the public's view of important policy decisions. The increased use of planning, programming, and budgeting techniques under Robert McNamara in the Defense Department spread into management information systems in business and industry as well as across government. Concern over the effectiveness of federal programs by Congress and federal agencies resulted in many large-scale evaluations (see p. 565, note 2). It is only comparatively recently that studies have been undertaken primarily to serve policy purposes. Most past policy decisions based on research findings cited basic research or evaluations done for other purposes.

The increased involvement in policy decisions by researchers resulted in new understandings of themselves. They found that they differed from policy makers in important ways. Their time scales for studies were determined by the problems rather than politics. Rather than selecting them on the basis of societal need, the problems they chose to work on were those of interest to them, or where they thought they could leverage a solution. Scientists preferred to qualify findings, in probabilities. Furthermore, administrators, who had been decision makers long before they were responsible for public policy, have nonscientific as well as scientific ways of identifying policy options.

As a result, researchers have often found themselves and their work at center stage, forced to try to be useful before they were ready. Their research is often used for unintended purposes. They have regularly given equivocal opinions when asked for concrete choices. (Politicians are said to prefer one-armed experts rather than those proclaiming "On the one hand . . .") And, in general, they have behaved in ways that, although consistent with their values, lifestyle, and milieu, did not endear them to policy makers.

Researchers have had to learn that timing is extremely important. If clients are suffering, withholding action until research is complete is not an option. But, because policy development goes through stages, and the role of research and the demands on it differ with each stage, it is difficult for just the right research to be ready at just the right time.

At the earliest stage, when policy makers are trying to articulate policy, research helps define the problem. At the second stage, which involves the deliberation, modification, and aggregation of support for various proposals, research turns desires into concrete alternatives for action. If there is time, it may pilot them to determine implications. In the priority-setting and allocation-of-resource stages that follow, research helps indicate effect sizes relative to costs of alternative or competing programs. Research is probably more powerful in killing proposals than in improving their chances—the Income Maintenance Experiments and its family-breakup side effect, for example (p. 483). At the final stage, that of legislative oversight, summative evaluation studies indicate how well the programs are working, formative evaluations show how they might work better, and comparative evaluations show which programs to emphasize and which to downsize or eliminate.

Thus, different kinds of research are needed at different stages. And timing, so that the results are available when decisions must be made, is crucial. Academic researchers have not been very good at crash research intended to produce results on call. Time demands are most severe in the early stages, when support is being aggregated for a given policy, and in later stages, when budget deadlines must be met for authorization of funding. As a result, the government often has helped establish research centers at or near universities to have the benefit of drawing on their faculty and graduate students. Their staff are expected to survive by obtaining their own funding. The private sector has developed to meet those demands.

Most discouraging to researchers, however, is the apparent politicization as policy makers decide on choices for implementation. It often appears that most policy makers seek out research that fits their point of view and ignore whatever does not. This may be increasingly harder for politicians as meta-analysis and research syntheses are developed on policy topics. However, policy makers used to making decisions in the absence of complete information argue that they must take many more things into account than the usually simplified evidence provided them by research. Even when policy makers lend a listening ear, current practices of academic researchers are not ideally suited to policy making. The private sector will probably be the main supplier of policy research.

WHAT ARE WE TO THINK, THEN, OF SOCIAL SCIENCE RESEARCH?

Is the Goal of Social Science Generalizable or Local Knowledge—Explanation or Use?

Throughout this book, while acknowledging the importance of local knowledge, we have largely concentrated on the creation of generalizable knowledge. And we have argued that strengthening the links in the chains of reasoning, through which findings are advanced as knowledge, will result in the best research, irrespective of method. We have focused on providing the spectrum of methods from which researchers could choose that would enable them to build the strongest chain of reasoning, whatever their skills, interests, and abilities.

But Charles Pierce, an American philosopher writing in 1868, took the chain analogy a step further: "The reasoning should not form a chain which is no stronger than its weakest link, but a cable whose fibers may be so slender, provided they are sufficiently numerous and intimately connected." A good point!

One hundred forty years later, the cable analogy, with its numerous connections, could be thought to refer to meta-analyses that, given sufficient data (lots of slender fibers), can show the relation of cause to effect. The intimate connections refer to theory that integrates knowledge—a higher goal to be sought, as, it is hoped, this textbook has made clear. But how strong are our theories? Consider the fact that two psychological theories as different as cognitive psychology (which focuses on the inner intentional control of behavior) and behaviorist psychology (which focuses on external control) can both coexist and be useful at the same time. This dichotomy says something about the present state of our knowledge.

So, is generalizable theory the goal to be sought? Schon (1983), in his *The Reflective Practitioner*, argues that practitioners depend on knowledge that is concrete, context rich, and analogous to previous situations—so-called "local knowledge." As generalizable knowledge findings prove practical and useful, they wend their way into local knowledge, so the two are not entirely distinct. But it is clear that there is a substantial gap and lag. We have a long way to go to connect research to practice.

But How Far Is the Journey? What Is the End?

Boulding (1968) is not only hopeful; he sees social science research as essential:

> It is only by the . . . activities of the . . . social sciences that we can hope to understand the social system sufficiently well to be able to control it and to be able to move into a positive image of the future through our own volition and policy. Otherwise we are merely slaves of necessity or victims of chance. (p. 107)

Along the lines of prediction and control, Asimov (1977) tells of inventing *psychohistory*, the mathematical analysis of every kind of sociological trend. We could then predict, with a high degree of accuracy, the social movements of the future. He based his idea on the kinetic theory of gases in which, although trillions and trillions of molecules are moving randomly, we can predict exactly what will happen to a gas if it is heated or compressed. "All the random behavior of the individual molecules ends up by making the gas, as a whole, a completely predictable system" (p. 11). (Does this remind you of Popper's gnats and a cloudlike world, p. 137?) No doubt, this is the dream of many social scientists. Some, particularly those interested in chaos theory, believe that not even that level of predictability can be achieved, let alone that of the individual's behavior—for example, the prisoner seeking parole or the developmental path of a mentally disabled child. Can we find an intermediate level that is usefully predictable?

Do We Seek More Knowledge Than We Should?

Religious persons might ask whether, given God's purposes in the world, a search for behavioral predictability and therefore its potential control is an evil act, whether it is more knowledge than humans should have. Berger (1961) argues that the scientist must assume that the fundamental integrity in a universe ruled by God is meant to be plumbed. It is an act of faith—an exploration that leads us to understand and appreciate ever more the intricate complexities of our being and to wonder how it all came about.

The insatiable drive of science has been to learn enough about everything so that it would be understandable. It is only very recently that scientists have begun to believe that there are phenomena that are inherently unpredictable. They can be predicted only statistically; the odds of a given condition can be stated:

> According to Cronbach, what frustrates a would-be empiricist social scientist are complex interactions that make generalization to causal laws *practically* impossible.... What is interesting about Cronbach's ... views is the sense of *déjà vu* one has. For the argument concerning the complexity of educational and social phenomena is precisely the one invoked by John Stuart Mill nearly 140 years ago to explain the paucity of progress in the social sciences! (Ericson & Ellett, 1982, pp. 505–506, emphasis in original)

But There Really Is Progress in the Social Sciences!

Concerns about the progress of social science clearly are not new. Indeed, the American Psychological Association, concerned that the field's contributions to research were not appreciated, started a Web site, Psychology Matters (http://www.psychologymatters.org), devoted to informing the public of its research applications. Their Web site organizes findings, described in layperson terms, into 19 topics relevant to public concerns.

Similarly, the American Educational Research Association's online quarterly, *Research Points* (http://www.aera.net/publications/?id=314), connects research to policy and "was established to help ensure that decision-makers have accessible sound and important research on timely education topics."

Web sites seem especially relevant, given some evidence that "online research is proving a counterforce to policy makers' reliance on a small number of academic consultants as gatekeepers and sources for research" (Willensky, 2003). Levin (2004), in describing the barriers and possibilities to making research relevant to policy, notes significant efforts in this direction in Canada, the United Kingdom, and the United States.

Gage (1996) makes a strong case for social science research. He cites examples of useful main effects, not just complex, weak, low-generality interactions that were the concern of Cronbach. For instance, he notes that Walberg (1986), in a synthesis of meta-analyses, turned up nine generalizable findings just examining research on teaching, even though he selected only meta-analyses with 90% consistency in the direction of relationship and covering at least 20 studies. Lipsey and Wilson (1993) found 156 meta-analyses of experimental or quasi-experimental studies of mental health treatments, work-setting interventions, and educational methods that met their criteria for lack of bias. They found an average effect size of .47 and about the same results in each of their three categories of interventions. Gage notes:

> Such effect sizes betoken a ... substantial mean-level of effectiveness. ... whatever the moderating or weakening influences of interaction effects may be, many main effects are consistent and strong enough to allay despair for the behavioral sciences. (p. 11)

Furthermore, Gage gives several examples of effect sizes that were considered highly significant findings in the medical field but would have been deemed too small to attract much attention in the social sciences, a point we considered in discussing meta-analysis (p. 522).

And findings are reasonably consistent. Many persons believe that social science findings are less consistent than those in the physical sciences. Hedges (1987) notes that "essentially identical methods are used to test the consistency of research results in physics and psychology" (p. 443). He compared 13 exemplary reviews from each domain and found that the results of physical experiments are not strikingly more consistent than those of social or behavioral experiments. This welcome news contradicts a stereotype about the "softness" of behavioral science results. The social sciences hold their own, better than many would have thought.

Furthermore, We Do Make Progress on Social Issues.

The author was struck by a 1992 publication of the Developmental Disabilities Planning Council of New York that compared being a parent of a developmentally disabled child in successive recent decades. In 1942, the parent believes the doctor knows best and is told to put their child in an institution even though it is 150 miles away. Ashamed of their child, parents try to keep the disability secret from coworkers and friends. Rarely is anyone with a disability seen in public, and parents don't know other parents in similar situations.

By 1962, the child is attending a day-care program, but the doctor says he will never be able to function in society. The child has no friends and mainly sits in the living room. The parents are considering purchasing a television to entertain him. The parents are too ashamed to attend a parent group started by the day-care center.

By 1982, a congressional act has been passed giving such children the right to attend public school. There is an emphasis on deinstitutionalization and normalization. Nevertheless, preschool children attend segregated programs operated by specialized agencies. Some children have been returned from institutions to community residential settings.

By 1992, preschool programs are mandated by the state with an emphasis on programs integrated with nondisabled children. Families are getting support and have an influential role in policy planning, program development, and evaluation of services for people with developmental disabilities.

How many of these changes are due to research? It is difficult to tell. Certainly, parents were central to bringing about change, yet it is clear that research played an important role in decisions to deinstitutionalize and normalize the education of children with developmental disabilities. Furthermore, the earlier discussions on dissemination as well as on evaluation and action research emphasized the importance of involving stakeholders to get findings used. This point is well illustrated by those working in the developmental disabilities fields, where professional societies reporting and discussing research meet simultaneously with the organizations of parents and others concerned with bringing about change. As a result, stakeholders and researchers are aware of each other's work and reinforce each other's efforts. It is a model that is worth considering for other fields.

However, marshalling research users—parents, educators, etc.—to advocate for their research is an uncomfortable role for many scientists. They prefer to work at "building a better mousetrap" so that the world will beat a path to their door. Researchers striving hard to keep their work objective wonder:

> How can we move from gathering facts to telling society how to use them without crossing the line that separates knowledge from values? Once crossed, we find

ourselves on the proverbial slippery slope—the one where our more activist colleagues slide as fast and as far as they can in their zeal to cure society's ills. (Howell, 1995, p. 28)

But many other researchers argue that all knowledge is value tinged; the choice of
what problem to research—for example, the normalization of education for disabled
children—is a value choice in itself. Values determine what we study and may determine how we study it, what we focus on, what we find surprising or significant in the
studying, and what we think is important enough to report as a finding. Which brings
us to the need of the social sciences for the humanities.

The Role of the Humanities in the Social Sciences

Ultimately, the answer to the question of how—and how rapidly—the social sciences will develop is an empirical one that will be increasingly uncovered by you, the
future researcher! Whatever your route, however, you can be certain that science
alone does not hold all the answers.

Frye (1981) notes that there are three different ways in which language can be
used. One is the language of science, which seeks to convey information about the
world. A second is the language of transcendence, used in philosophy and religion, an
"abstract, analogical language that expresses what by definition is really beyond verbal
expression" (p. 129). Third is the language of immanence, of poetry, where "natural
objects can become images of human emotions" (p. 129). It is in the language of transcendence and immanence that the goals of science are found. As Frye (1981) puts it:

> The arts and sciences, . . . for all their obvious differences, have a common origin
> in social concern. . . . When we think . . . of a world to be remade, we find we need
> a model or imaginative vision of what we are trying to achieve. . . . The world of
> dream and fantasy can be a source of models . . . and models are the first product
> of the chaos of hunch and intuition and guesswork and free association out of
> which the realities of art and science are made. (pp. 130–131)

We have been studying the processes of science with the intent of improving the
quality of our journey through life—but it is to the humanities that we must turn to
understand our goals, what "quality" means, and where the journey leads.

Dr. Clifford Erickson, then dean of the College of Education of Michigan State
University, closed his address to the college's faculty in 1961 with this still relevant
statement, which seems a fitting way to close this book:

> We are grateful for this opportunity to serve mankind. . . . Grant us the courage and
> the wisdom to play our parts effectively. Forgive us if we falter and seem to hesitate,
> for the problems are very complex. Strengthen us in our resolve to join hands with
> our colleagues in doing together what we cannot do alone. Provide us the stimulation
> needed to venture into the unknown. Keep us from being divisive, trivial, or lacking
> in faith in each other. For the only things we have to fear are timidity and mediocrity.

ADDITIONAL READING

See Collins and Pinch's (1993) discussion of physical science as produced by social factors
and on public understanding of science (see a review of the book by Segerstråle, 1994). On

654   Chapter Twenty-Eight

public understanding of science, see Tuomey (1996). On defense of the behavioral sciences, see Gage (1996), particularly against Gergen (1994); also see Medawar (1984). On editorial peer review, see Weller (2001). On the complexities of educational research, see Berliner (2002). On making research matter more in policy, see Levin (2004).

Notes

[1] Wouldn't packaging distort the process of how findings become knowledge? If at all, only in the short run, not in the long. Things get evaluated for what they really are over time, and the self-correcting process of science will be at work on "packaged" as well as "unpackaged" ideas. Where packaging is perceived, it will likely receive more intense scrutiny.

[2] Just as hardly anybody remembers vice presidents of the United States, so those who come in second serve the purpose of validating the discovery but are not usually associated with it. This phenomenon may contribute to the lack of replication of research in the social sciences, although the costs in time, energy, and the forgone opportunity to pioneer are the main reasons.

[3] Buchmann and Floden (1989) note that "in trying to determine how many different ways for doing work in a discipline actually exist—reasoning inductively from some [assumptions] . . .—Schwab (1978) arrived at 2^{20} or 1,048,576 as the number of possible alternative schemes an individual investigator might choose from, on a conservative estimate" (pp. 245–246).

Appendix A
Writing a Research Proposal

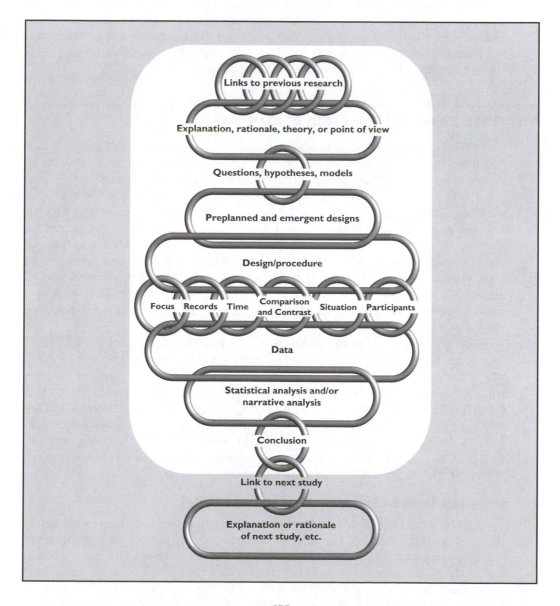

Links to previous research

Explanation, rationale, theory, or point of view

Questions, hypotheses, models

Preplanned and emergent designs

Design/procedure

Focus   Records   Time   Comparison and Contrast   Situation   Participants

Data

Statistical analysis and/or narrative analysis

Conclusion

Link to next study

Explanation or rationale of next study, etc.

OVERVIEW

This appendix, building on the material covered in the text, will assist you in developing a proposal such as that usually required for a doctoral dissertation or, in some instances, for a master's thesis. It begins with an unusual definition of a proposal, the implications of which are important to bear in mind as you prepare your own. Discussing the sections of the proposal in sequence, it describes their ideal characteristics and offers tips for writing their subsections. Because certain kinds of proposals with emergent problems pose unique challenges, a section discusses these aspects. The chapter closes with a description and illustration of some writing conventions you will be expected to follow in this and other academic writing. This appendix is adapted from Krathwohl and Smith (2005).

DEFINITION OF A RESEARCH PROPOSAL

What is a proposal? It is an opportunity for you to present your idea and proposed actions for consideration in a shared decision-making situation. You, with all the integrity at your command, are helping those responsible for approving your proposal to see how you view the situation, how the idea fills a need, how it builds on what has been done before, how you will proceed, how you will avoid pitfalls, why pitfalls you have not avoided are not a serious threat, what the study's consequences are likely to be, and what significance they are likely to have. It is not a sales job but rather a carefully prepared, enthusiastic, interestingly written, skilled presentation. Your presentation displays your ability to assemble the foregoing materials into an internally consistent chain of reasoning. The write-up of the proposal follows a logical, deductive sequence of presentation. The process of doing the research, however, may or may not also follow a similar sequence.

This differentiation of work sequence from presentation format is particularly true of qualitative or exploratory research, what we call emergent research projects, where the nature of the research problem is not known at the outset—it emerges from the research work. The discussion of the proposal in the following sections is directly relevant to all researchers who think they know their problem focus and are seeking some kind of generalization. Preparation of proposals for qualitative, emergent, or descriptive research also will markedly benefit from the following material, though it may require some adaptation. A discussion devoted to unique aspects of emergent studies appears later in a separate section.

Relation to the Chain-of-Reasoning Model

Insofar as you can anticipate the nature of the study before beginning the actual dissertation data collection, the proposal encompasses the upper part of the chain of reasoning (see pp. 62–68), all the way down through the six rings of the study's design and analysis, as shown in the inset illustration. Build the problem statement so that the project's hypotheses, questions, or models flow logically from it. The statement of objectives and method of attack should build upon and move beyond the review of past research, showing how this study will add to prior accomplishments and remedy past failures. These, in turn, will suggest the population and sample and the rest of the research design. The data gathered will determine what analysis—statistical, qualitative, or other—is appropriate.

A strong proposal intended to demonstrate or validate a generalization reflects this chain by the plan of its structure, by its internal logical consistency, and by the appropriate development of each section. Each section reflects the previous material and carries it, in a consistent way, a step further. Always make sure that ends are not dropped, objectives slighted, data collected but not included in the analysis plan, and the like. Allocate resources properly to strengthen weak aspects, and make appropriate design trade-offs.

Proposal Format

If you plan a career in research or higher education, prepare your proposal in typical proposal sequence, as outlined in the following sections. Preparing a proposal is excellent practice, since part of such a role is seeking resources and a proposal is the usual method of requesting them. The sequence of sections described in this material is typical of that used by most funding organizations or expected by foundations. To submit for funding, in addition to what is described here, the proposal requires a budget, a description of any other needed resources, a vita for yourself and for those working with you, and other indications of competence and institutional support.

If you are not planning to enter academia or a research institution and do not expect to do research again, you may wish to consider a proposal that is basically the first three chapters of a conventional dissertation. Some faculty request this format. It consists of:

- chapter 1—Introduction and statement of the problem, placing it in perspective to its field,

- chapter 2—Review of literature bearing on the problems, and

- chapter 3—Description of the design of the study and the procedure to be followed, together with a justification for the choices made.

With this structure, if the findings of the research do not call for a reformulation of the problem, you may be able to use the proposal as the first three chapters of your dissertation with little more than a change of verb tense from future to past and such touch-ups as are required by modifications you made as the plan was implemented. This format will save considerable time and effort.

We will start the discussion of proposal preparation with the description of the problem, its basis in the literature, how it relates to theory, and the objectives of the study. We then move to the operationalization of the problem and objectives, describing the study's design and procedure.

STATEMENT OF THE PROBLEM

Your first task is to describe your problem in terms so enticing as to make the reviewer eager to examine the rest of the proposal. This job falls especially to the introduction or problem statement, but it is also shared with the literature review and objectives sections.

The introductory section typically develops an understanding of the problem by describing its significance in relation to the large, important problems already of concern to your readers and by showing the problem in the perspective of the field in which it is embedded.

The introduction leads into a section on related research, which further develops problem understanding and appreciation by showing specifically how the problem is solidly grounded in the previous work of the field and how this project will take a significant step beyond that.

Thus, it is possible for you, at the end of the literature review, to restate your problem in a more precise and detailed fashion with greater understanding. And from that problem statement you can tease out the research questions and hypotheses, or—if you know enough of the causal factors—describe a model of how the phenomenon occurs. This will lead to the development of the objectives and goals of the study. You can then describe the problem statement and goals in such a way that their translation into the procedure, the topic of the second part of the proposal, is natural and easy.

Introduction and Initial Problem Statement

First impressions are important! Your opening sentences suggest to the reader whether your proposal will be creative and interesting or just routine. Return to your opening after you have a complete draft and rework it so that it invites the reviewer to read further.

Tips on Developing the Introductory Statement

- *Show the problem's importance.* The opening statement should convince the reviewer that the project is important. For example:

   Just as Japanese adaptations of the United States' social-psychological discoveries have contributed to their industrial success, so our failure to use that knowledge has compounded our problems in competing with them. This project seeks modifications in Japanese uses of this knowledge that will be effective in our culture. The modifications . . .

- *Show the problem in the perspective of the larger field in which it is embedded.* For example, "show our management practices as a part of our lagging in international economic competition, accounting procedures as a facet of making government intervention effective."

- *Show the problem's generality.* For many, the dissertation's place in the graduate program has become primarily that of a learning experience. As originally conceived, it is at the same time a contribution to knowledge. Many dissertations are still expected to be. Therefore, indicate the generality of the problem and the generalizability of the research. A good way of doing this is to point to the project's contribution to theory and new knowledge. Indicate how the project builds on previous theory or contributes to new theory. Relate it to the large, important problems of the field. If you can, describe the value of some concrete applications of the knowledge as well as the potential importance of these applications.

- *Foreshadow what is to come.* Save details for the procedure section, but provide enough in the introduction that the reader can see where the project leads. For example, a generalizable project does not necessarily require a national sample. Therefore, very briefly outline here the basic characteristics of the intended sample, situation, and procedure so it will be possible to infer to whom findings might transfer.

- *Limit the problem.* Learning to focus a study is a skill. Novices often believe that only by encompassing large pieces of a problem can they avoid triviality. Dissertation proposals are often rejected three or four times as a project is successively reduced in scope. However, it is only by focusing on the manageable, on the critically important aspects of problems, that you can successfully complete a project.

- *Don't dwell on the obvious.* The author recently read a proposal that used its first eight pages to convince the reviewer that research in the field was necessary. If reviewers were not already aware of this, they would not have been asked to be reviewers or should not have agreed to be when asked. Assume interest in research in the area.

- *Find the balance between completeness and brevity.* Some researchers are too brief, taking too much for granted concerning the reviewer's knowledge of the topic (e.g., knowledge of a new complex statistical procedure). Conversely, some may make this section extra long on the assumption that if they can sell the reviewer on the importance of the project, the reviewer may overlook flaws in the remainder of the proposal in order to get something going in this field. This is not likely. In this section, as in others, find the balance between completeness and brevity; adjust the length of this section to correspond to the way the rest of the proposal is developed.

- *Give the reader perspective on the whole proposal.* As part of the foreshadowing in the introduction, describe the approach you are planning to use with a two- or three-sentence sketch. Also briefly point out the merit of this approach.

- *Set the frame of reference.* The problem section establishes the frame of reference and the set of expectations that the reviewer will carry throughout the proposal; be sure it is the correct one.

Related Research

This section builds further understanding of the problem by showing that it is solidly anchored in past work yet moves beyond it in important ways. *It is an excellent place for you to give an indication of your scholarly competence.* Writing this section well is a sign of professional maturity; it indicates your grasp of the field, your methodolog-

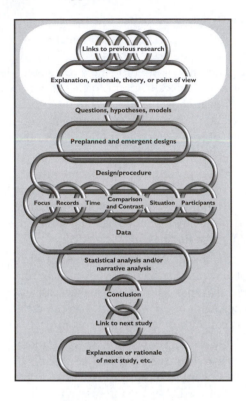

ical sophistication in critiquing others' research, and the breadth and depth of your reading. In the chain of reasoning, this section links the rings representing the findings of prior research to the statement of the rationale or explanation for whatever phenomenon you are examining.

Qualitative dissertations may differ in the way they handle the literature review from what is described here, particularly if of the orientation: "I don't want to be contaminated by the past literature until I know what is of significance in the situation I want to study." Although you may be approaching your dissertation from this point of view, you will still find the discussion below of value, since you will do a review of the literature for your research report—if not for your proposal—and the same rules will apply.

No project starts de novo. A conscientious researcher shows the proposed project as building upon what has already been done and as contributing to the forward movement of the field in some significant manner. The section on related research provides such an opportunity. Use the many library indexing, abstracting, and reference tools described in Chapter 6 to find the most appropriate literature. Don't forget to include the Internet and the access that it provides to expert help and resources beyond those provided by your faculty and library.

Survey a select group of studies that provide a foundation for the proposed project. Discuss these studies in detail sufficient to provide an understanding of their relevance, how they contribute to this study, and how this study moves beyond them. Obviously, the review should encompass the most recent literature in both content and method; an outdated review hardly adds to the impression of scholarship. Similarly, consulting secondary sources (such as other literature reviews) is quite appropriate, but as a scholar you will usually want to *check some of the original literature* yourself.

Too often this section is an afterthought. Some researchers develop the "fresh, new idea" into a project, then go to the library to complete the sole remaining section—that on related research. This often makes it difficult to reconcile past research with the "new" project. If you take past studies into account during the planning stage, the project is much stronger.

Tips for the Related-Research Section

- *Point out any technical flaws in the studies you discuss*. Show how you will avoid these pitfalls. If possible, revise the findings of studies that were incorrectly interpreted by the authors and show how the findings of those studies should be viewed to fit the study proposed.

- *Describe the theoretical base for your study*. Science is a systematically accumulated body of knowledge. Theories interrelate individual findings and permit greater generalization. This section is an excellent place to convey your grasp of how theory is currently being developed and tested in your area and to critique the solidity of the structure your field is erecting.

  If yours is an emergent study, you may not initially have such a base, but, with the completion of pilot studies that indicate future directions, developing such a foundation for your study not only becomes possible but also is important to determining how best to shape its directions.

- *Be highly selective, citing only those studies that form the base from which your study is building*. More is not necessarily better. The most common error is including too many references and commenting too little on them. Proposals are often submitted with lengthy bibliographies on the research topic. Such a comprehensive list does little to convince the reader that the researcher has anything other than the ability to use indexes. It is what you do with the references that is the basis for judging this section. The things that will impress readers are the skill shown in selection, the technical competence used in evaluating contributions, and, above all, the originality displayed in realistically and constructively synthesizing the conceptual bases of past work and those of the proposed problem.

- *Become aware of literature bearing on your problem from disciplines other than your own*. Review research in related disciplines using bibliographic sources that extend broadly, such as the *Social Science Citation Index*. Discuss your proposal with colleagues from related disciplines to provide a broader perspective on it as well as to provide a fresh point of view. By alerting you to the jargon these fields use to discuss your problem, such contacts can help you use the journal indexes much more successfully.

- *Include studies currently underway that are likely to overlap your project*. Knowing what is currently being investigated in your field is another sign of competence. Show how this project differs from such studies or meshes with them in a constructive way. Many government agencies have Web sites on which they list newly funded projects. Large foundation grants are listed in *The Chronicle of Philanthropy*. Skim the most recent convention programs of professional associations in your area for related work (often posted on their Web sites) and contact their authors for a copy of their papers or more information. Use forums, bulletin boards, and listservs to find the invisible college of individuals who are working in your area and determine how their work parallels or reinforces yours.

- *If you state that "no prior research bearing on the problem exists," cite the closest research you found and show how it falls short*. Also indicate under what headings and in which references you made checks.

  Researchers naturally want to claim their ideas as original, unrelated to what others have done. All too often when readers encounter the statement that "nothing has been written that bears on the problem," it becomes a challenge! They know that few projects start from scratch, and they are challenged to search their memories for relevant studies. If they find some, they are inclined to question the thoroughness of your scholarship and, perhaps, your technical competence as an investigator. Your description of your search shows your efforts and may result in suggestions of untried sources from reviewers.

- *Conclude your literature review with a restatement of the problem as it is informed by past work and indicate how your attack on the problem avoids the mistakes of the past and benefits from prior advances.*

Questions, Hypotheses, Models, and the Goals of the Study

Thus far in the problem statement you have described the problem in general terms, shown its importance, and set it in a larger context. In the related-research section you have described what previous work has been done and alluded to how

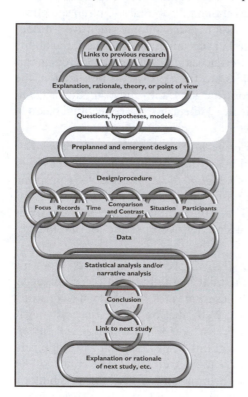

you are going to build on it: going beyond previous accomplishments, opening new territory, redoing a study in a new and better way, possibly replicating a study to show the generality of its findings, and so forth. The section that follows shows the study emerging further from the background of previous thinking and theory. In the chain of reasoning it is the link that joins the problem statement to the design.

Like each successive link in the chain of reasoning, this section forms a basis for judging the remainder of the proposal. It sets the stage for showing how you intend to solve or contribute to the solution of the problem sketched out in the first sections. Just how specific this section can be depends on what you have said in the previous sections, and what turned up in your review of literature:

- The less you have found out about the area, the more likely you are to devote this section to questions.

- If you have a good idea about how at least certain aspects work, you may have hunches to test to see if they are true. This section will set forth those hunches as hypotheses.

- If you have a good idea about how things work, you may be able to construct a model of how various variables are related to each other. This section will describe the model you would like to test.

Because this section comes early in the proposal, you may, still in an expansive "I'm-going-to-show-the-world!" frame of mind, claim more in this section than you find possible once you flesh out the details of the procedure section. Therefore, once the proposal is completed, one of the first things to do is to reread it to make sure that this section flows neatly from the problem statement and that the procedure section that follows adequately encompasses all that you cover in this section.

The most frequent error made in writing this section is that it becomes a set of vague generalities rather than clear-cut criteria against which the rest of the project can be judged.

Another error is that, instead of having a section in which the research objectives are clearly set forth, they are embedded in a running description of the project, and usually by implication rather than explicit statement. Your readers must then tease out the objectives as best they can, trying to infer what you have implied and placing such emphasis on different objectives as they can "guesstimate" from the contextual clues. Obviously, the readers' accuracy in doing this is critical. Rather than run the risk of misinterpretation, most writers will fare better by making the objectives clear and explicit.

The final common error, as already noted, is to include material that is not developed in the procedure section. If the proposal is to be an integrated chain of reasoning, everything should be appropriately followed up in successive sections.

Tips for a Questions Section

- *Use questions instead of hypotheses where the problem is emergent, the research is exploratory, or a descriptive study or a survey seeks certain facts.* The specificity of the questions shows how carefully you have thought through the problem. For example, consider a study of the effects of female teachers on male students. Instead of merely asking, "What is the effect of the female teacher on male students?" a researcher will much more convincingly demonstrate competence by rephrasing the question to, "Which of these is the dominant effect of female teachers on male students?" If a listing of the possible dominant effects and explanations follows, it is clear that the researcher has thought through the possible alternatives and is prepared to investigate at least these particular ones.

  Where such specific questions might be expected, and you prefer to look at the phenomenon with a fresh eye rather than possibly bias your search with prior expectations, be sure to explain your approach. If you are eschewing reading previous research, as do some qualitative researchers in order to come to their own conclusions about what is significant, then you will mainly state questions in this section. You will indicate what kinds of questions will initially guide your observations or your inquiries, and why you are starting with these instead of other possibilities. If you are a "purist" about starting de novo in the situation, this will be a very short section.

- *Indicate why your questions are the important ones to ask.*

- *Develop the implications for the field of addressing and possibly answering these particular questions.*

- *Explain why other reasonable questions that might be asked in the situation are not of interest and will not be addressed.*

Tips for a Hypotheses Section

- *Relate hypotheses to their theoretical base if at all possible.* If you have not introduced the theoretical base in the previous sections, state it succinctly (showing how the objectives are derived from it), refine it, and extend it—carefully building the bridge from theory to study so that the relation is clear. For instance, a study of the effects of a vocational education program would be strengthened if the choices that the student must make in the program were related to developing theory on why and how students go through stages of vocational choice.

- *State hypotheses as objectives in such a way that they are testable*—that they can be translated into research operations that will give supporting or disconfirming evidence.

- *Do not state objectives as value judgments* (e.g., "All sixth-grade boys should learn to play a musical instrument"). Research can indicate the extent of popular support for such a value statement (such as, "Seventy-five percent of our town believes that all sixth-grade boys . . ."); or it can indicate the consequences of an action (such as, "If all sixth-grade boys play musical instruments . . ."); but humans must judge how much value to attach to these consequences or to the extent of popular support.

- *Use directional hypotheses wherever there is a basis for prediction*. There will be a basis for predicted outcomes and findings if the study has a theoretical underpinning. (Remember, if you are looking for statistical significance, this is an easy way to increase the sensitivity of a study—see p. 454.)

- *State hypotheses as succinct predictions of the expected outcomes rather than in the null form*. For instance: "Students who receive the experimental treatment will show greater and more differentiated interests than those who do not," rather than, "There will be no difference in interest patterns between the experimental and control groups." The latter statement is a part of the logic of the statistical test, but it does not belong in the objectives section and will likely make an amateurish impression on experienced researchers.

Tips for a Models Section

- *Construct a model when you are concerned with a picture larger than the relationship between two variables, and you can reasonably hypothesize the interrelationships among a set of variables.* Using previous research and synthesizing disparate pieces of a larger picture, construct an illustration of how each variable influences or is influenced by other variables. Usually, this step results in the construction of a diagram with arrows indicating the direction of influence.

- *Show how the study will provide evidence that the relationships exist, confirm the directions of influence, and estimate their size.* Most such diagrams are relatively simple, since our knowledge of phenomena is in its infancy. Our ability to confirm complex ones requires the kind of large-scale studies unlikely to be undertaken in a dissertation.

- *Include the basis in previous research for the proposed model in the literature review section of the proposal.* If not done previously, indicate where you will have gone beyond previous work and how this study contributes new knowledge to the field.

- *Describe the model both graphically and verbally, and indicate the parts of it that are well confirmed by previous research as well as those that are more tenuous.* If there are alternative conceptualizations of the relationships, indicate them and give the basis for each. If you believe that one is more likely than others to be supported by the data, indicate that as well.

Design and Procedure: General Considerations

The design and procedure section is concerned with translating the just discussed problem section into project activities. *This is usually the most carefully read section of the proposal.* Up to this point you may have told, in glowing terms and appealing generalities, what you hope to do and what this will mean to your field. The section on procedure brings your problem down to earth in operational terms. Proposals that sound as though they will revolutionize a field frequently appear much more mundane in the procedure section; the techniques proposed for attacking the problem may fall far short of earlier claims.

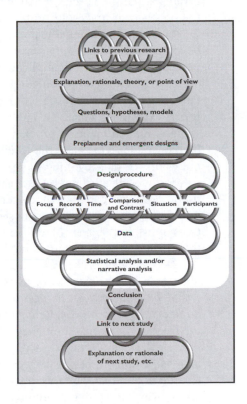

This discussion of the procedure section first covers general points to take into consideration in developing and describing procedures. Following these are detailed discussions of each of the subsections that, together, usually make up the procedure: population and sample, design, instrumentation and data collection, analysis, and work plan (charts showing the sequence of events and the time required for their completion). Adapt this section to fit your study and show it in the best light possible. Most proposals cover all these topics—if not in this order, then in an order that gives priority to what is important.

An Iterative Process

As you operationalize the terms with which you described your problem, you often come to a different understanding of the study than you had when you initially conceived it. Terms take on new meaning, and often you have to sharpen and modify your initial conceptualization as you better understand the problem.

Suppose that you start out to study the relation of per-pupil expenditures to achievement across a set of public school districts. In operationally defining—that is, determining the dollar value of per-pupil expenditures—you find that different districts include different costs. In an effort to get comparable data across districts, you adjust each district to include a common set of costs. But at that point, the study begins changing. There is not much variability in these costs across districts—the variability is in the amount of discretionary money available to the school's principal to improve instruction. Thus, that becomes the focus of the study, forcing you to change the whole front end of the proposal to fit this new conceptualization of the problem. Some researchers argue that you come to a real understanding of the problem only when undertaking operationalization of the study.

Operationalization may never be completely satisfactory, especially when you are dealing with constructs that you cannot concretize in a way that satisfies everyone (e.g., certain personality characteristics such as likableness, or monetary estimates of the value of good health). Remember this limitation if you are dissatisfied with your study or if the redevelopment of the procedure section seems never-ending. A compromise operationalization may be the source of your dissatisfaction, but it may be the only way to study your problem.

Sometimes, when the hypotheses of a study are given operational translations, it becomes immediately apparent that the problem is too large or too complex. In the per-pupil expenditure example above, an attempt to estimate all the resources available in a given classroom might put the project beyond the realm of feasibility (parent volunteer time, unusual equipment brought into the class by students, and so forth). Yet these might be important inputs to the classroom in certain circumstances. First attempts at problem definition are particularly susceptible to having to be reduced in scope when the researcher does not want to just go through an exercise but wants to "do something significant" and starts too ambitiously.

Refocusing and limiting the problem to restore feasibility are the answers. Sometimes, however, certain requirements may still be too great. Consider whether these may be handled by alternative design choices. For example, if there are too few cases to establish both a control and an experimental group, you might use the subjects as their own control, with pre- and posttests.

Development of the procedures and design of a study is an iterative process. The researcher sets an initial set of pieces in place; then, finding that one must be changed, sets off an entire cycle of changes that may in turn result in a further reconceptualization, further changes, and so on, until all the pieces fit together and are feasible. (For example, the treatment becomes unmanageable, so it must be cut down. This step requires the size of the sample to be increased in order to detect a weaker treatment. The increase results in having to use subjects with characteristics that interact with the treatment and that therefore must be controlled. And so it goes.) Often you must go all the way back to the beginning and plan the procedure and design on a different basis. Many cycles may take place before you reach a satisfactory solution. (You don't realize how typical such iterations are because they don't appear in the write-ups.)

Key Sections for Your Research Method

A reader's judgment of the adequacy of a particular procedure is often dependent on how well certain subsections are developed. Some examples:

- For a sample survey, carefully develop the population and sample, the instrumentation sections, and the handling of the nonrespondent problem.

- For an experimental study, carefully develop the experimental design section and identify what rival explanations it will and will not control.

- For a study using new analytic techniques, carefully develop the analysis section.

- For a longitudinal study, carefully describe the population and sample, data and instrumentation, and work plan. Depending on the kind of longitudinal sample (see p. 573), describe plans for replacing lost cases.

Because choice of design is still part art, persons may reasonably differ about the best design for a given problem. Your initial choice of design may not be that which springs to the mind of your readers and reviewers. However, they may be thinking in stereotypes, and your approach may indeed be the best. To minimize the impact of such differences of opinion, help them to follow your line of reasoning so that they, too, can see your rationale. *Carefully describe your design choices, your reasons for so choosing, and why you preferred this choice over alternatives*. There is more on this point in the material that follows.

Limits and Constraints

With your first consideration of the procedure section, you must make tentative decisions:

- What level of resource use is both possible and practical, including your own time?
- What ethical considerations are involved?
- What access and cooperation can you expect from your own institution, from other institutions, from participants, and so forth?

These estimates are important for making methodological decisions: the possible number of participants, location of study settings, and so on. Indeed, the limits may rule out certain methods that take too long, such as a longitudinal study. The most desirable and cooperative institutions may be far too distant. Some of the limits are easy to estimate, others more difficult; but you must make some reasonable determination for all of them if development of procedures is to proceed realistically. Further, just as you iteratively develop other parts of the design, so you may have to successively reexamine initial limits and adjust them as your plan develops.

Resource limits.   As soon as you begin to translate the study into operational terms, the question immediately arises, "How big shall I make it?" Although you need not answer this precisely at the outset, you must set some working limits. Include the sensitivity analysis mentioned on page 452 for inferential statistics if you plan on the use of such statistics.

Ethical limits.   Recall that every institution receiving federal moneys is required to have a Committee for the Protection of Human Subjects (i.e., an IRB), which is concerned with the ethical implications of your research plan. Nearly every university extends the federal requirement to all research carried on at the institution, including dissertations. Most institutions have procedures for expeditious approval, but you will do well to look into this aspect early so it will not be a barrier to your collecting data when you are ready.

Institutional limits.   When other institutions or agencies are involved (as collaborators, as sources of data collection, and so forth), be sure you consider your requests to them from their perspective to ensure they are reasonable. Most institutions have not only limited funds but also limited availability of participants, facilities, equipment, and personnel. Institutions tend to resist changes in their routines that interfere with "business as usual." It is important to ensure that the sites you expect to use are amenable to your plans. It is good practice to append letters to your proposal from the sites you plan to use, indicating that access will be granted. Funding agencies often require them.

Time limits on proposal development.   Although it seems that you ought to be able to control your timetable, pressures to get your degree in a reasonable time, to gather data before certain natural breaks in institutional calendars, faculty sabbaticals and trips, or other scheduling difficulties may impinge on it. These problems may, for example, shorten the time you have to get your proposal developed and approved, enforce a particular schedule on data collection, require data collection before you are comfortably ready or at inconvenient times, necessitate the use of nonpreferred sites, or inadequately involve personnel vital to the study in proposal development. It is important to delineate those things that you can do satisfactorily in the time available for proposal development from those that are unwise to attempt or, perhaps, you cannot do even if you try.

Consider the trade-offs involved in rushing to meet an immediate deadline versus waiting until a later time when you could more successfully resolve these problems. A several-month delay in proposal approval might pay handsome dividends in more cooperative site conditions, as the staff of institutions and agencies are given a chance to contribute to the research plan and feel it is partly theirs. Considering that this delay may provide better and more convenient working conditions over the period of the study as well as better data, it may be worthwhile. But other considerations, such as the availability of your own or a key person's time, may be overriding factors.

One thing is certain, however: Trying to do too much in the available proposal development period usually results in a proposal that shows it, as does similar haste in data collection and analysis in the research report. As in sewing, "find a pattern that fits the cloth available" or, as in sports, "find a league in which you can comfortably play."

Organization and Adaptation of the Design and Procedure Section

The organization described below, though different from that of the chain of reasoning, was chosen because it is typical of the outline requested by many funding agencies and is one commonly followed in dissertations. As in many things, there are established conventions you may be expected to follow. However, except when your chair, committee, or a prospective funding agency decrees that a certain outline must be followed (and many do) if your study is better fit otherwise, *organize this section to fit your study*. The only problem you encounter when you challenge convention is disturbing expectations, and if your presentation is better for having done so, there is no problem. On the other hand, if it isn't, your advisor may ask you to rewrite it in conventional form; that is the risk you take.

The topics in the design and procedure sections differ from the six rings forming design in the chain of reasoning. Established as convention long before the chain of reasoning was described, the topic headings confusingly use the term design both in the title for the section (Design and Procedure) and as a subsection heading under it. Similarly, *procedure* appears on multiple occasions: in the title for the section, as a topic under the design subsection, and as the major focus of the work plan subsection.

However, the six design procedure rings of the chain of reasoning easily translate into this pattern, which simply repackages the material. Each of the six rings is discussed in its own subsection and is indicated by italics in parentheses below:

1. population and sample (*participants* and, sometimes, *situation*)
2. design/procedure (*situation, focus, comparison and contrast*)
3. data and instrumentation (*records*)
4. analysis (*records, comparison and contrast*)
5. work plan (*time*)

SUBSECTIONS DESCRIBING DESIGN AND PROCEDURE

Begin the write-up of the design and procedure section with a one-paragraph foreshadowing summary or overview. The discussion that follows describes each subsection, provides suggestions for writing each, and descriptions of some of the common, or most serious, errors.

Population and Sample (*Participants* and, sometimes, *Situation*)

The description of population, and the sample of participants and possibly situations, determine the generality of the findings. Obviously, this generality should be consistent with the generality claimed in the problem statement and objectives sections.

The characteristics of the population define the group to whom the study's results may be expected to transfer. The more representative the sample(s), the more confidently you can generalize from the sample to the population. However, see p. 179 on reusing convenience samples for universal propositions.

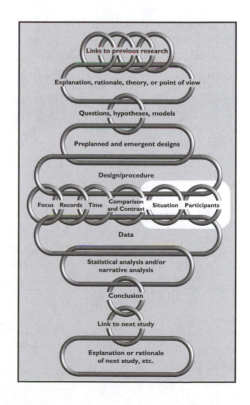

Tips for the Population and Sample Section

- *Describe the sampling plan in detail.* Give a rationale for why that plan is the best of those available.

- *Indicate the variables that will be used as the basis for ensuring representativeness— for example, the basis of stratified and cluster sampling. Show the significance of those variables for the study and why you chose them over others.* Also describe where you will obtain these data. If there is any reason to think some of the units might be misclassified into strata or clusters, give an indication of the anticipated error's extent, size, and likely impact.

• *Give a worthy rationale for the sample size. For studies with inferential statistics, this step clearly calls for a power or sensitivity analysis to ensure that a real difference is not mistaken for a chance one.* If, because of insufficient sample size, you write "the results are in the predicted direction, but there is no significant difference," reviewers will suspect that the hypothesis should have been supported. You can—and should—avoid this situation with a power analysis.

Design/Procedure (*Situation, Focus, Comparison and Contrast*)

The term *design* in most proposals is used to describe the structure of the study: how subjects or situations will be studied; how groups will be organized; if there is a

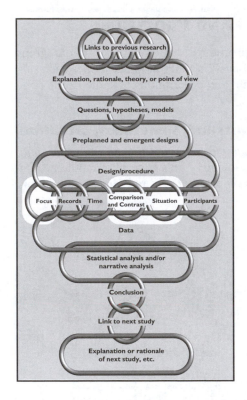

treatment, when and how it will be administered; when observations will be made—of whom, when, and, if known, of what; and how rival explanations will be eliminated. Of all the subsections of procedure, the design subsection varies most with the methodology. Although we will cover the procedure here, we will also see it in time perspective later in the work plan.

A major purpose of the design subsection is to show how you will structure the situation so that you can gather data with the least contamination by factors providing rival explanations. Whether experimental, qualitative, survey, or other, if the design does not ensure the integrity of the study's chain of reasoning against rival explanations, you will have compromised the case for whatever finding you may be advancing.

What is an example of a rival explanation such as we are considering here? For example, in a study of the effect of two different curricula, the researcher should be concerned with any initial differences in the groups that might be reflected in their after-treatment performance. The researcher should control such potentially contaminating factors as the beginning level of competence or achievement, general academic ability, or motivation.

The term *design* seems to go with *experimental*, as in *experimental design*. Accordingly, you might be tempted to assume this section is of little importance to other than experimental studies—to a qualitative study, for example. Nothing could be further from the truth! A qualitative study observer, for example, must protect against a variety of potential rival explanations: the effect of prevailing attitudes and values on observation, the choice of individuals and times to observe as "typical" samples, the effect of "dropouts" (persons present at the start of the observations but not as they progress), and the impact of going "native" and perceiving things differently as observations progress—to name just a few. Describing how such problems will be avoided both strengthens your proposal and shows your competence with your chosen method.

Tips for the Design/Procedure Section

- *Ask questions such as: How likely is each of these sources of contamination to occur? As you consider confounding variables one at a time, how likely is each to have its expected effect?* In your estimation, therefore, how critical is it that you control for each rival explanation? How would you prioritize them? Are your reviewers and intended audience likely to agree with your priorities? Will they see these as "long shots" or real possibilities?

- *Having determined the possible rival explanations, you must decide which ones are the most serious threats to the study.* Taking your own and these other opinions into account, how will you prioritize their claim on resources? Then determine the ways you can control each, combining them into a design that controls the set of most serious threats. Finally, you must determine whether that design is feasible, given the other claims on resources. If not, redesign it until it is.

- *Convincingly indicate the nature and basis of the particular compromise being proposed and the reasons for accepting it.* Unfortunately, not all judges will weight the desirability of controlling possible contaminating factors the same way. Their "most acceptable compromise" may differ from yours. Once again, this is a place to demonstrate your mastery of the problem. If you have wrestled with the focus of your study and done pilot studies, nobody knows better than you the multiple sources of contamination that might affect it and how best to control them.

- *State clearly the reasons for choosing to control the variables you have selected and for ignoring certain others.*

- *Show how the design realistically controls the critical variables without sacrificing the integrity of the study.*

Data and Instrumentation (*Records*)

Many studies go awry in the leap from describing what is intended to what is actually done. The congruence of data and what it is intended to represent is at issue. This is usually less of a problem with qualitative studies, although it can be if the examples the researcher pulls from the data to represent the concept are not what the reviewers and audiences consider the concept to be. It is in the translation into instrumentation, however, that so many quantitative studies fail. Therefore, this section needs to provide satisfactory evidence that instrumentation is not a problem.

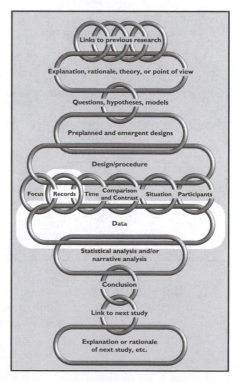

Tips for the Data and Instrumentation Section

- Provide the best possible evidence of *validity and reliability of all instruments* with which your audience is likely to be *unfamiliar.*

- Where you have used observation scales, *choose low-inference scales* or, *if high inference, provide evidence for the greater appropriateness* of the ones you have chosen.

- *Observe unobtrusively.* If you cannot, indicate the *steps you have taken to allow for accommodation* to being observed.

- Provide *evidence of appropriate self-analysis* of your observation processes, possibly from pilot studies or prior similar work.

Analysis (*Records, Comparison and Contrast*)

It is not always possible to completely anticipate the nature of the analysis that you will use; it may depend on the data you have collected. This is especially true of qualitative analysis procedures, but it may also be true of statistical methods.

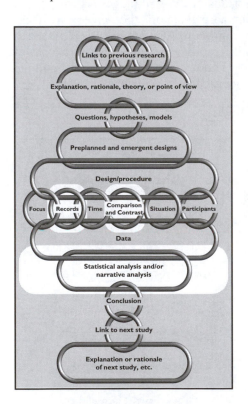

Tips for the Analysis Section

- *Reveal the depths to which you have anticipated analysis problems by describing projected solutions in sufficient detail to clearly convey their nature.* At the same time, show awareness of where departures from plan are more likely to occur. As you must realize by now, *anticipating the concerns of the audience and answering their questions even before they think of them are consistent strategies throughout the proposal!*

- *Keep the method of analysis consistent with the objectives and design.* For instance, in a study with quantitative data, when the study calls for finding the extent of a relationship, some kind of correlation coefficient is in order instead of a comparison of high and low groups with a difference statistic such as a t test. A statistically significant t test indicates the true correlation is greater than zero, but it could be so low as to be practically insignificant.

- *Statistics should match the level of data* (e.g., nonparametric statistics for categorical data) or a rationale for the exception provided.

- *Assumptions of the statistics should fit the data.* If they seem not to do so, tell what corrections you made. For instance, analysis of variance assumes normally distributed populations, but you can make corrections in the level of significance for nonnormal data.

- *Carefully describe new statistical techniques, computer programs, or other unfamiliar analytic tools and indicate their advantages over current methods* so that the reader is assured of their appropriateness.

- In complex multifactor designs involving analysis of variance, show awareness of the appropriate error term and describe how missing data or unequal cell frequencies are to be handled.

- With enough qualitative pilot studies to have identified the focus of an emergent problem, you should be able to *project the future direction of the analysis, and describe what analytic progress has been made.* While not necessarily held to these projections, as in so much of the proposal, they indicate your competence to handle divergence from anticipated directions as necessary.

Work Plan (*Time*)

The work plan, or time schedule, basically translates the procedure into a time scale showing what events precede what others, which events can be concomitant, and how they progressively result in the study's findings. The plan can take different forms depending on the complexity of the study.

The work plan is another sign of how carefully and realistically you have developed the project. Some readers turn to it first to get an overall perspective on the activities. In other instances, a reader who is having difficulty understanding the flow of the procedure turns to the time schedule for the first real understanding of what the researcher intends to do. These uses at critical points in understanding the project indicate the importance of the work schedule as a clear, sequential statement of the operations to be performed.

It follows, of course, that the work schedule should present *a consistent and comprehensive representation of the material preceding it.* Omission of segments of the study makes projections of its length unreliable at best and indicates carelessness, sloppiness, or disorganization. None of these is conducive to a favorable impression.

Depending on the complexity of the project, the plan may take different forms. A simple time schedule, with a list of dates for completion of various activities in the order in which you will do them, often suffices. A more complete plan lists the dates on which activities will begin and end. You can show the latter thermometer-style, using a calendar scale (often called a Gantt chart). Figure A.1 is such a chart.

Links to previous research

Explanation, rationale, theory, or point of view

Questions, hypotheses, models

Preplanned and emergent designs

Design/procedure

Focus   Records   Time   Comparison and Contrast   Situation   Participants

Data

Statistical analysis and/or narrative analysis

Conclusion

Link to next study

Explanation or rationale of next study, etc.

Figure A.1   A thermometer (Gantt) chart showing the work plan and milestones.

ID	Task Name	Duration
1	**Questionnaire Preparation**	24
2	Hire staff	10
3	Write questionnaire	5
4	Pretest questionnaire	5
5	Develop sampling plan	3
6	Procure mailing lists	2
7	Selection of the sample	1
8	Revise questions and prepare for mailing	3
9	Prepare mailing envelopes	2
10	**Prepare Interim Report — Feb 12, '09**	5
11	**Questionnaire Mailing**	11
12	Duplicate questionnaire and stuff envelopes	4
13	Request questionnaire clearance with interim report	3
14	Receive clearance from sponsor	7
15	**Send Questionnaires — Feb 20, '09**	0
16	**Questionnaire Followup**	27
17	Wait for returns	19
18	Interview sample of nonrespondents	5
19	**Questionnaire Analysis**	33
20	Analyze initial returns	7
21	Analyze returns to date, integrate with interview data	10
22	Prepare final report	15
23	**Submit Final Report — May 5, '09**	0

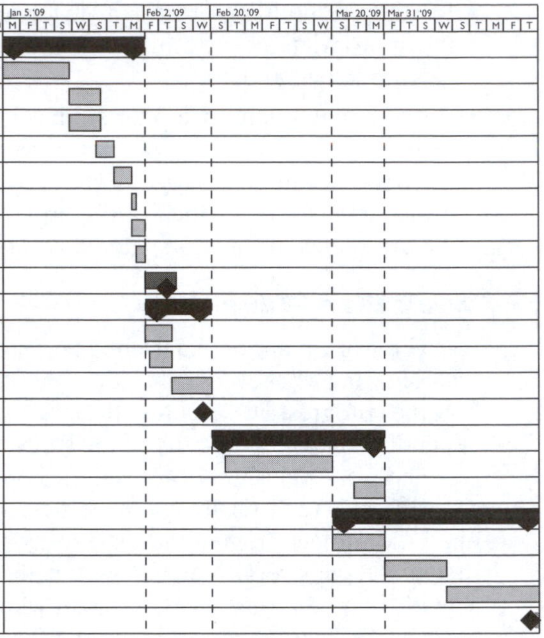

The lines indicate both when and for how long the activity will take place. The diamonds mark what are called *milestones*, events marking the completion of a phase or the production of some product. The black bars indicate the length of a phase with points at start and end. The details of the phases are in gray.

More often, however, researchers lay out the work plan graphically in flowcharts or diagrams, which work better for more complex projects. Figure A.2 is such a flowchart, as can be created by software.

Note that the flowchart shows instances where two or more activities can be carried on at the same time, making it possible to shorten the total length of the project. The figures at the top of each box indicate the number of days that activity is expected to require; the dates below it are its actual time period. In place of the diamonds of Figure A.1, dark rounded boxes indicate milestones.

Such detailed flowcharts make it possible to show the interrelationships among the different parts of the study, to reveal activities that can be carried on concomitantly, and to demonstrate more clearly the relative length of various phases. Their advantages are these:

- They require an estimate of the time required to meet all criteria appropriate for each activity (e.g., how long it should take to get a 65% questionnaire return).
- They force an exploration of the interrelationships between activities.

Figure A.2   A flowchart showing the work plan for a questionnaire study.

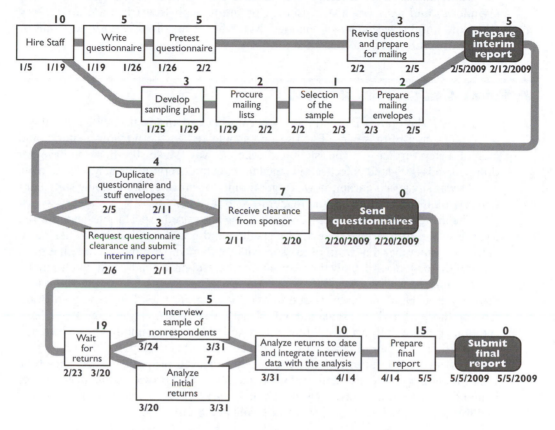

- They require that each step be analyzed in sufficient detail so that difficulties are uncovered that might have remained hidden in a less clearly specified proposal (only to arise later and bedevil the researcher when the proposal is approved).

- They serve as a basis for resource allocation of personnel time to various parts of the proposal.

- They provide a basis for administrative control of the project.

- By maintaining the overall perspective that promotes accurate inferences regarding the implications for the total operation, they provide a better foundation for making informed change decisions.

- If you decide to seek funding, the work plan gives a big boost toward realistic budget preparation. It is more accurate to estimate the cost of the items in each step and sum them than to estimate larger chunks.

    If the work schedule is laid out well, the reader will have little question about what is planned, and the major concerns will be problem significance and strength of design.

Computer programs are now available that markedly facilitate preparation of the work plan such as *Microsoft Project*. Two free programs are *OpenWorkbench* (Windows) and *OpenProj* (Mac, Linux); programs with free trials are *SmartDraw* (Windows) and *ConceptDraw* (Windows, Mac). See a list of Macintosh programs at http://www.pure-mac.com/charts.html.

A FINAL CHECK AND REVIEW

At last! The draft is finished! Now you can check to ensure that the proposal is a consistent chain of reasoning. Each section should reflect the previous material and carry it a step further in a consistent and coherent way. Make sure that you have not dropped ends—slighted objectives, planned for data but overlooked analysis, and so on.

As was suggested earlier, now is a good time to return to the opening statement and rework it so that it invites the reader to read further.

The universal availability of word processing has raised expectations and lowered tolerance of poorly prepared text. Use spelling and grammar checkers to get rid of gaffs, but remember that word processors will not flag typographical errors that form a correctly spelled word. Only time-consuming, careful proofreading eliminates them.

Even the best writers benefit from the criticism of someone who is not familiar with their problem. Don't be embarrassed to ask one or more friends to read your draft. Choose those who will be frank, but only if that is what you *honestly* want. If you have the time, put the draft aside and then return to it after a long enough period to look at it afresh, in a different perspective. You'll be amazed at what you will find.

It is always helpful to examine previously approved proposals. There may be a file of them in your department, or faculty members may provide some from former students. Four specimen proposals appear in Locke, Spirduso, and Silverman (2007), and three annotated ones appear in Krathwohl and Smith (2005).

Preparing the Final Copy

How important is the appearance of the proposal? Some researchers do a very careful and complete job of preparing the proposal in especially attractive form. This may very well impress readers. Notwithstanding, your major effort should be on lucidity and clarity of presentation. If it is a long or complex proposal, it may help to use tabs or colored paper to convey the structure and make sections accessible; tabs more readily convey the organization. When using colored paper to distinguish sections, place the coding key in a prominent and accessible place (front cover, table of contents, or first pages). Don't put text on dark-colored paper that makes reading difficult.

Other than the time required for assurances, clearances, and letters of support, the place where the writer is most likely to underbudget time is that required for careful, accurate, final review. Though word processing and rapid duplication services have cut the required time for many preparation steps, careful proofreading is extremely time consuming. Most of us who read a lot are so used to skipping past errors, particularly in familiar material like our own writing, that we are terrible proofreaders. If possible, find someone who is good at it and treasure that person. In fact, the less familiar the proofreader is with the proposal, the better.

QUALITATIVE METHOD AND
OTHER EMERGENT PROBLEM PROPOSALS

It may seem a contradiction in terms to suppose that a study, the focus of which is expected to emerge from data collection, could be the subject of a proposal. Preparing a proposal for qualitative methods studies (including participant observation and ethnographic studies) requires more than just describing the method you will use. However, if you want to begin your entry into the study situation with a clean slate, a proposal anticipating your objectives seems to violate a basic premise of the method. However, to satisfy reviewers that you have a viable dissertation topic and the know-how to do it, for need-to-know gatekeepers who control your entry to their institutions, for funders in case you seek subsidy, and for yourself (to get clear in your own mind what you are talking about), a proposal is indeed in order.

As Miles and Huberman (1994) note:

> At the proposal stage: many design decisions are being made—some explicitly and precisely, some implicitly, some unknowingly and some by default. . . . Design decisions can . . . be seen as . . . a sort of *anticipatory data reduction*—because they constrain later analysis by ruling out certain variables and relationships and attending to others. Design decisions also permit and support later analysis; they prefigure your analytic moves. (p. 16, emphasis in original)

Qualitative proposals can range from the lightly structured proposal that is basically a hunting license, to the structured and detailed proposal that matches a quantitative study in its anticipatory nature. Just how much structure is required depends on a variety of factors:

- the caliber of the proposer's previous qualitative research experience,
- the trust the reviewers have in the proposer,
- the persuasiveness of the rationale for the study, and
- the case that can be made that pilot studies are unnecessary or impossible. (For those with little qualitative research experience, a pilot study is essential.)

Although it is possible to discuss the rationale and related literature sections of the proposal without having considered the findings of pilot studies, the remaining sections of the proposal usually require a pilot study for their accurate formulation. As well, the rationale and related literature sections also benefit from prior pilot work. Pilot studies help define the dimensions of the problem, the sample of persons and sites to be used, the instruments (if any) beside the observer(s) to be involved, the behaviors to be targeted, the sources and availability of records or others' data, the protections against reasonable rival explanations, and the likely ethical problems to be encountered. Once the pilot study is complete, writing the proposal is markedly simplified.

As we discussed in chapter 16, one of the criteria of a good study is provision for an *audit trail*, a record of the study's methods and procedures detailed enough that someone else can follow it. Such a trail for a pilot study will be of help to those who must approve your study. Make sure to include provision for such a trail in your proposal.

Fully aside from the fact that you will need to clear the ethical aspects of your study with whatever human-subjects protection apparatus exists in your institution, you will also have to deal with ethical problems that occur in the field. True, you will not be able to anticipate many of these situations, but some you can. When you foresee such situations, describe them in your proposal and indicate your proposed solutions. Here again, a pilot study is of special value, since the ethical problems you are likely to encounter are often apparent from events occurring during the pilot stage, even if they don't appear full-blown.

We have already discussed the necessity of providing for the elimination of rival explanations in general or justifying why you could not eliminate them. Because, as the researcher, you are the data-collection instrument, qualitative studies have the additional burden of ensuring that your need to have the study come out in a certain way was not the reason that it did so. Providing some assurance that predilections, biases, attitudes, likes, and dislikes will minimally affect data collection (or, where they are expected to do so, indicating and anticipating the consequences) is important. Try to provide "neutrality and reasonable freedom from unacknowledged researcher biases—at the minimum, explicitness about the inevitable biases that exist" (Miles & Huberman, 1994, p. 278). As Lillian Rubin (1981) puts it, "The quest should not be for the fool's gold of objectivity but for the real gold of self-awareness" (p. 101).

WRITING FORMATS

As long ago as 1660, the Royal Society of London discouraged authors of scientific literature from reports full of emotion and colorful adjectives that were advertisements for their findings, and encouraged them to seek an unbiased and unemotional tone. Such advice continues to be the convention today. That does not mean that your proposal has to be dull, but it does mean that it should be, as indicated by the initial definition of a proposal, "a carefully prepared, enthusiastic, interestingly written, professional presentation." For example, omit personal details of your travails that are irrelevant to process or result. Use of the first person is still discouraged in most quarters but is increasingly tolerated.

Ideally, writers expect that reviewers will give their proposals as much time as necessary to adequately comprehend and evaluate them as, for that matter, do those responsible for reviewing them. But it is always safest to assume that your proposal might have to be reviewed under time pressures or when there are distractions (e.g., reading during committee meetings, or at the end of the semester when everything and everyone clamors for attention).

Depending on the field, the conventions used in writing will typically follow the APA style (American Psychological Association, 2001), the University of Chicago style, or the MLA style (Modern Language Association). Use of the APA style appears to be increasing and is the basic style used in this book.

Format of Headings

We note here only two of the stylistic conventions: headings and references. Headings are important because they convey the organization of your writing. APA style consists of five levels for complex, long articles. For shorter articles, use the lower levels: two levels, use 2 and 4; three levels, add level 5; four levels, add level 3. The five levels are:

LEVEL 1: CENTERED, ALL UPPERCASE

Level 2: Centered, Upper- and Lowercase

Level 3: Centered, Italicized, Upper- and Lowercase

Level 4: Flush left, Italicized, Upper- and Lowercase

Level 5: Indented, Italicized, Upper- and Lowercase that Ends with a Period.

Underlining may be substituted for *italics*.

Format of References

Reference format varies by type of reference. Following are illustrations of APA style for many of the reference types you are likely to encounter. Again, underlining may be substituted for italics.

Bogdan, R., & Biklen, S. K. (2006). *Introduction to qualitative research methods: The search for meanings* (5th ed.). New York: Wiley.

Baker, G., & Chapman, D. (Eds.). (1962). *Man and society in disaster*. New York: Basic Books.

Atkin, J. M. (1994). Teacher research to change policy: An illustration. In S. Hollingsworth & H. Sokett (Eds.), *Teacher research and educational reform* (pp. 103–120). Ninety-third Yearbook of the National Society for the Study of Education, Part I. Chicago: University of Chicago Press.

Adair, J. D., Sharpe, D., & Huynh, C. (1989). Hawthorne control procedures in education experiments: A reconsideration of their use and effectiveness. *Review of Educational Research, 59*, 215–228.

Florio, S. E. (1978). Learning how to go to school: An ethnography of interaction in a kindergarten/first grade classroom. *Dissertation Abstracts International, 39*, 3239A (University Microfilms No. 78-23, 676).

Guba, E. G., & Lincoln, Y. S. (1982). *Causality vs. plausibility: Alternative stances for inquiry into human behavior*. Unpublished paper presented at the Annual Meeting of the American Educational Research Association, New York.

Milne, C. (2005, January). Overseeing research: Ethics and the institutional review board [33 paragraphs]. *Forum Qualitative Sozialforschung / Forum: Qualitative Social Research* [Online Journal], *6*(1), Art. 41. Retrieved September 2, 2007, from http://www.qualitative-research.net/fqs-texte/1-05/05-1-41-e.htm

SPSS for Windows, Rel. 17.0 2007. Chicago: SPSS Inc.

You can find style reference manuals at almost any library reference desk. Also search "APA reference style" and "bibliographic software" in a browser. Software like *Writers Workbench*, and for references, *Endnote* and *Zotero*, improve products as well as facilitate production.

Tips on Good Writing

- Good writing, like good acting, uses both verbal emphases and nonverbal gestures to facilitate communication.

- *Be generous in your use of headings to help the reader sense the organization of the material*. Use headings to break up long sections, to signal the important points, to pilot the reader conceptually through the structure, and, through assigning heading levels appropriately, to provide a continuous sense of where in the structure the piece being read fits.

- *Signal upcoming content with topic sentences at the beginning of paragraphs.*

- *Use foreshadowing of what is to come throughout the proposal to integrate it.*

- *Use diagrams, flowcharts, tables, and other graphic devices.* Employ them to present overviews of content, to put details into perspective, to provide a succinct summary of important aspects, to show the sequence of a process, and to provide a road map of the important concepts and their relationships.

In sections that tend to be lengthy and unbroken by headings or subsections, it is especially important to:

- *Help the reader to easily find essential substance within certain parts of the proposal.* For example, place a succinct statement of the purpose of the research in an obvious position in the problem section. Similarly, list the objectives in order of importance in the objectives section. Summarize the points being made. Underlining, paragraphing, and summary boxes are especially useful.

- *Use punctuation, underlining, bullets, listings, indenting, spacing, paragraphing, and the like to indicate to the reader what is important.*

- Adopt the circular pattern that newspapers use. *Paint in broad strokes; then go over it again, filling in the details. Finally, summarize and pull it together.*

- *Work the definitions of unfamiliar terms (or words used in unusual ways) into the presentation early and prominently.* The reader learns them from the beginning, and they cease to be a continual stumbling block to understanding. Better still, find a way to avoid their use!

- *Test your structure by skimming your proposal.* Read it very rapidly, jumping from topic sentence to topic sentence. Does it convey what you intend?

Avoid "jazzing up" the copy with jargon or with more gesture than sense. Remember, research is essentially a scholarly activity.

ADDITIONAL READING

For how to write a qualitative dissertation proposal: Kilbourne (2006) and Biklen and Casella (2007). For a general treatment and sample proposals see Locke, Spirduso, and Silverman (2007). For a variety of additional proposal types and annotated examples see Krathwohl and Smith (2005).

Appendix B

Greater Understanding of the Frontispiece through Alternative Graphics

Some people learn best from words, others like to see how something can be pictured, and many want both. Pictures show the relationships that may be more quickly and intuitively grasped in a graphic than in words. Intending to cover a range of learning styles, this appendix consists of three different ways of portraying the frontispice graphic. The first one puts the frontispiece in a larger perspective and combines the graphic with its verbal explanation. The second graphically embeds a fleshing out of the questions implicit in the framework's titles to provide the best of both worlds. The third uses a logic tree to show how the parts fit together to form larger wholes. It is hoped that one of the three versions will so fit your learning style so that it makredly eases your comprehension of the framework.

THE FRONTISPIECE PLACED IN THE CONTEXT OF THE POPULATION OF STUDIES

The first graphic adds information to the frontispiece by placing a study in the larger research context of which it is a part. Accompanied by a one-page explanation of its various parts, the graphic portrays the population of all research studies as the background of the graphic. Then it selects for attention that part of the population that consists of studies of the same phenomenon—the widest circle. Within that, from the next circle on to the center, it concentrates on the one study chosen as the focus of attention. Within that study are placed the various parts of the criteria of a good study, much as they appear in the frontispiece. The circled numbers indicate the chapter in which the topic is discussed.

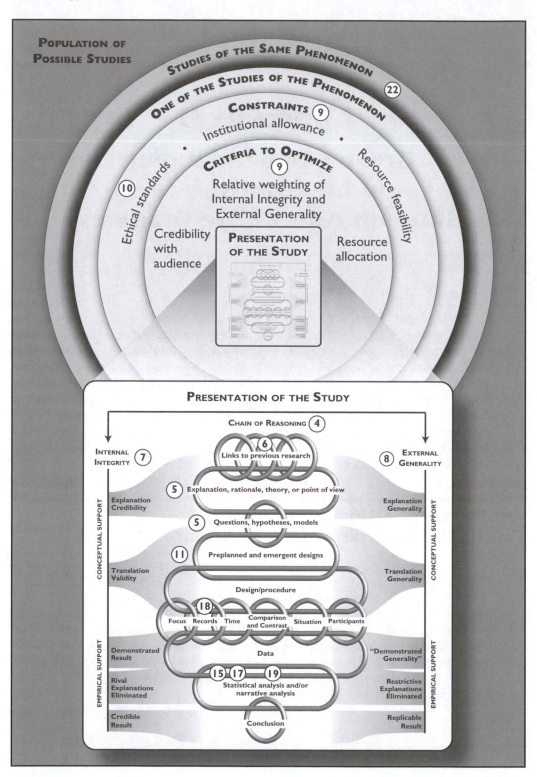

EXPLANATION OF ALTERNATIVE FRONTISPIECE GRAPHIC

Out of the population of possible studies (the background), we find all the other studies (if any) of the chosen phenomenon (the outermost ring ㉒). Whatever studies exist, if they include quantitative data, can be combined in a synthesis or meta-analysis to show the present understanding of the phenomenon. If there are qualitative data, they can be appropriately added to make a best-evidence synthesis.

A researcher has chosen to do a new study of the phenomenon, which is represented by those rings at the top of the figure which are inside the outermost ring and have lighter shading. They represent the choices we encounter in planning and carrying out a study. The first of these rings—the third ring in ⑨—represents the choices made within the three constraints that every study must observe: what can be done within ethical standards ⑩, what the institutions responsible for the intended research site(s) will allow, and what is feasible within the resources available for the study.

The choices in the next ring focus on optimizing: Internal Integrity's ⑦ weight with that of External Generality ⑧ within the study's resource limits in order to build credibility with the audience ⑨. The best case must be made for the hypothesized relation(s) among the variables (or for the process being studied) at the same time showing the intended generality and keeping in mind both building credibility with one's audience and the limits of one's resources.

A break-out analysis of the completed study's write-up or publication is shown below its miniature representation. Any study intended to have generality includes the information shown in the chain of reasoning ④, although it may not be presented in the chain's order (e.g., emergent studies). Preplanned studies present this information as shown in the graphic—logically linked. The chain starts by showing the study's base in previous research ⑥. Out of this emerges the explanation, rationale, theory, or point of view taken by the study ⑤ and the question, hypothesis, or model that informs its design ⑪. The focus of the design is described as well as the records or measures ⑱, the schedule or procedure (time), the way we will be able to sense what change occurred or how the process was modified (comparison and contrast), where the study will take place (situation), and who will be involved (participants). Analyzed data ⑮ ⑰ ⑲ support appropriate conclusions.

Judgments of the justifiability of the conclusions and of their generality are the province of, respectively, their Internal Integrity ⑦ and External Generality ⑧. They are displayed on either side of the chain of reasoning alongside appropriate parts of the chain that contribute to their conceptual and empirical support.

For Internal Integrity ⑦, conceptual support starts with the credibility of the explanation, rationale, theory, or point of view (*explanation credibility*). It extends to a judgment of how well that explanation is translated in the study's design (*translation validity*). Empirical support is a judgment of how well the data support the case (*demonstrated result*) as well as how well the design protects against rival explanations of the phenomenon (*rival explanations eliminated*). Given prior positive judgments and no studies with contrary findings, appropriate conclusions are presented (*credible result*).

Parallel judgments support External Generality ⑧ with conceptual evidence: The explanation lends itself to generality (*explanation generality*). The choices of the design in terms of the persons, situation(s), measures, and so on support an appropriate level of generality (*translation generality*). There is empirical evidence as well: The data support the explanation, rationale, etc. (*"demonstrated generality"*), and the design choices were not too unique to plausibly have generality (*restrictive explanations eliminated*).

The above judgments being positive, the results seem likely to replicate with different choices of persons, places, measures, and designs; appropriate conclusions regarding generality are presented (*replicable result*).

THE JUDGMENTS OF INTERNAL INTEGRITY AND EXTERNAL GENERALITY SUMMARIZED

The second graphic is an expanded version of the Internal Integrity and External Generality portions of the frontispiece. It inserts the questions to be answered for each of their judgments, thus summarizing them in a single useful graphic. (See the following page.)

THE FRONTISPIECE AS A FAMILY TREE OR FLOW-CHART

The third graphic is a family tree that shows the relationships of the various parts of the logic supporting the findings of a study. It answers such questions as "What is this part derived from? Is a part of? Or belongs to?" Each successive level expands the contents of the terms above it to reveal its meaning more completely.

Alternatively, it may be thought of as a flowchart where the judgments made of the various aspects of the study are successively combined into increasingly encompassing criteria that determine the quality of the study in terms of how firmly we can assert a causal relationship and how broadly we can generalize it. (See pp. 686–687.)

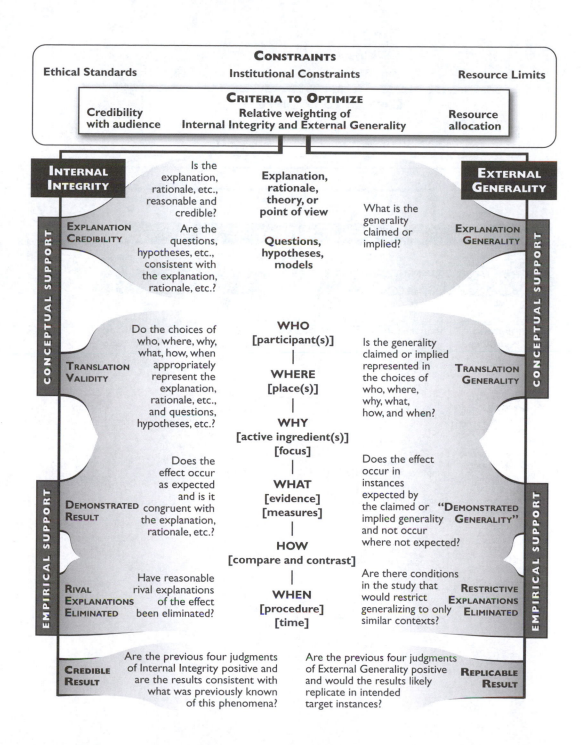

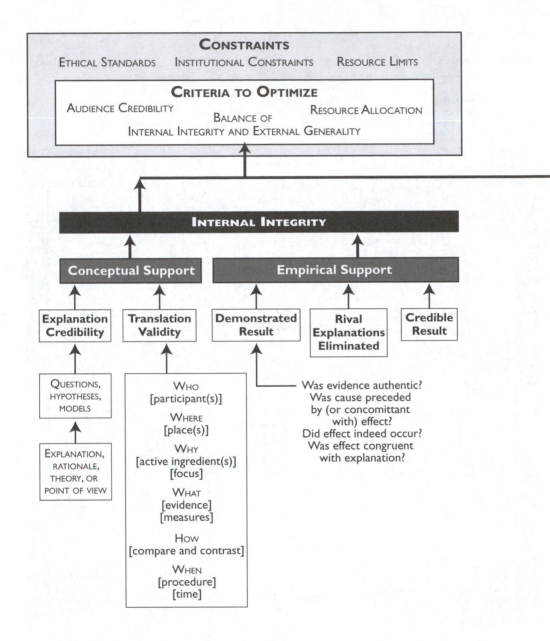

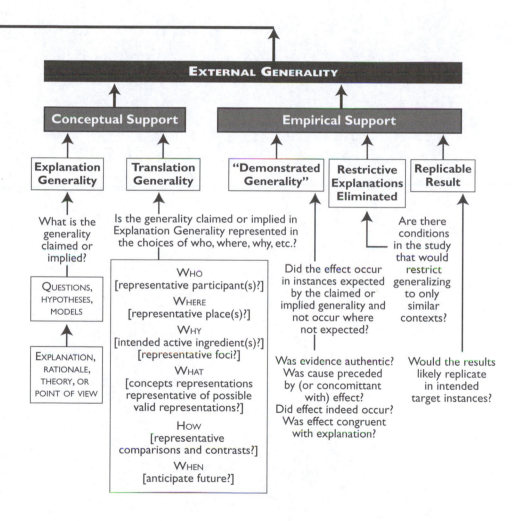

Glossary

The number following each entry indicates the page in the text where the term is discussed. You are encouraged to consult the glossary regarding the meaning of key terms when reviewing material as well as when studying. The necessarily succinct statements in the glossary may pull together the material in ways that are helpful. Use the index to find additional places in the book where the term is discussed.

ABA design A time-series design in which a control phase called the baseline (A) usually precedes a treatment phase (B), which is followed by the baseline remeasures (A). (chapter 21, p. 504)

After-the-fact natural experiments Studies in which the data are assembled after the presumed cause and effect occurred in an attempt to demonstrate a causal relationship. Also called *ex post facto studies* and causal comparative studies. (chapter 21, p. 507)

Alpha coefficient A measure of internal consistency reliability. (chapter 18, p. 415)

Alpha error *See* Type I error.

Alpha level The percentage of instances, on average, that a researcher will conclude that a value is atypical (there is a statistically significant difference) when in fact it is not (there is none). (chapter 19, p. 435)

Alternative explanations *See* Rival explanations.

Analysis of covariance A statistical technique for adjusting the means of groups for the effect of an unwanted variable. (chapter 21, p. 485)

Analysis of variance (ANOVA) Estimates of the population variance are made from the variability between groups (which is presumed to be affected by the intervention or independent variable of interest) and from the within-group variability (which is not so influenced). Comparison of estimates from these two sources shows whether the former is larger than the latter by a ratio (F ratio) greater than would be expected by the influences of random sampling and chance error. (chapter 20, p. 466)

Audience credibility Judgment by the audience of the credibility they grant the researcher for having made good judgments in the design and implementation of the study, especially for aspects not directly described in the report. (chapter 9, p. 192)

Audit trail A trail left by a qualitative researcher so that others can see for themselves how the researcher arrived at the findings. (chapter 15, p. 331)

Authenticity of evidence Assurance that the evidence is what it purports to be—for example, that a test score represents a sample of a particular individual's behavior and not someone else's. (chapter 7, p. 145)

Base rate The rate at which an event occurs naturally. When not taken into account, the base rate may affect study outcomes in ways that are confounded with treatment. (chapter 21, p. 488)

Baseline phase The phase of a time-series design during which the natural state of the subject is determined before the intervention is applied. (chapter 21, p. 504)

Behavioral objectives Objectives stated in terms of the behavior to be learned or acquired with respect to specified content. (chapter 23, p. 544)

Beta error *See* Type II error.

Bias In sampling, an influence that systematically prevents obtaining a representative sample. (chapter 8, p. 165)

Blocking Grouping individuals with a similar level on a characteristic perceived to be related to the effect. *See also* Stratified sampling. (chapter 21, p. 486)

Borderline examples Cases used in conceptual analysis to help define the boundaries of the term being analyzed. (chapter 13, p. 279)

Buckley Amendment The nickname of the U.S. Family Educational Rights and Privacy Act that is intended to safeguard the privacy of personal information in school records. (chapter 10, p. 213)

Case study A careful, in-depth study of an individual or a situation, usually using qualitative research methods; in quantitative research, an application of treatment followed by observation and measurement. (chapter 4, p. 68)

Causal chain The sequence of events that results in an effect. (chapter 7, p. 135)

Chain of reasoning The steps in the presentation of a logical argument in support of a knowledge claim. (chapter 4, p. 62)

Chain-referral sampling The identification of the members of a group by asking individuals, who would be expected to know who the members are, to identify them. Those named are similarly contacted, continuing until no new information is being obtained. Also called *snowball sampling*. (chapter 8, p. 172)

Chi-square A statistic that helps determine whether the pattern of frequencies found in categorical data is likely due to chance or is atypical. Also used to compare data with a model to determine whether the data's fit is within the typical range of sampling and chance error. Also used to combine the results of independently conducted studies to determine overall statistical significance. (chapter 20, p. 469)

Citation indexing Indexing of all references during a given time period that cited a given journal article, including when and where cited. (chapter 6, p. 123)

Clocklike world A conception of causation as resulting from tightly coupled events, such as the meshing of a train of gears. (chapter 7, p. 136)

Cloudlike world A conception of causation as resulting from loosely coupled events, such as a swarm of gnats always maintaining a cloud rather than dispersing. (chapter 7, p. 137)

Cluster sampling Random samples of cells in a geographic grid placed over a map, or random samples of units organized on some prior basis such as schoolrooms. (chapter 8, p. 170)

Code of ethics A set of rules for ethical behavior to be observed in dealing with humans or animals. Most are written and approved by the relevant professional society. (chapter 10, p. 211)

Coding Categories of recurring facts, themes, comments, and the like selected for attention because they are likely to help explain a situation of interest. Once established, new material is coded into these categories. (chapter 15, p. 314)

Cohort studies Studies of change over time using a constant population but taking new samples during each data-gathering period. (chapter 24, p. 573)

Comparison and contrast One of the six design rings in the chain of reasoning: the basis on which we can determine whether an attribute is present or there was a change in the dependent variable as a result of the independent variable or treatment. (chapter 4, p. 67; chapter 7, p. 142)

Computer searches Search of the index of a search service such as Google or Yahoo for that part of the Internet of interest; most indexes have been constructed by bots (robots) that continuously search for new or changed entries. (chapter 6, p. 114)

Computer-assisted personal interviewing (CAPI) Like CATI, except that it is an in-person interview that is then uploaded to a central computer on completion. (chapter 24, p. 585)

Computer-assisted telephone interviewing (CATI) Random-digit dialing is used to select a sample randomly from a list of the population to be sampled who are then queried to determine whether the respondent fits the sample, what questions to ask, and in what order. Responses immediately entered directly into the computer are checked for consistency and errors. (chapter 24, p. 583)

Concept *See* Construct.

Conceptual analysis A process for finding the characteristics that define a term. Especially useful for defining constructs and concepts. (chapter 13, p. 279)

Concurrent validity A test that correlates with a criterion measure obtained at the same time as the test was administered. (chapter 18, p. 411)

Confidence interval An interval constructed around an observed value such as a test score or a mean within which the true value is believed to lie with a confidence expressed by certain odds. The greater the odds and the less reliable the test, the wider the confidence interval. (chapter 19, p. 436)

Confidence level The odds we are willing to accept that express our confidence that the population value is contained with the confidence interval. (chapter 19, p. 437)

Confidence limit One end of a confidence interval. (chapter 19, p. 436)

Confidentiality Control of access to information. (chapter 10, p. 213)

Confounding Two or more variables that might have caused an effect were simultaneously present, so that we do not know to which to attribute the effect. (chapter 21, p. 487)

Constant comparison method Fieldnotes are coded as the study progresses, and new instances of a dimension or a concept of interest are sought until saturation. These concepts are linked with others to develop a theory or an explanation that is constantly compared with new data from the field. Discrepancies call for modification or additions to fit the new data. *See also* Saturation. (chapter 13, p. 287)

Construct An idea formed from specific instances of which we have a mental image but that has no direct physical referents; an abstract noun. (chapter 13, p. 279)

Construct validity Evidence from potentially relevant sources—content, internal structure, and so on—indicating the validity of the measure. (chapter 7, p. 141)

Content validity Comparison of the items of the test with a table of specifications or test blueprint to determine if the items representatively sample the behaviors and content of the subject matter the test is intended to cover. Also called *curricular validity*. (chapter 18, pp. 407 and 423)

Contrary examples Cases that are far enough beyond the boundaries of a term that they help delineate its boundary; used in conceptual analysis to help establish defining characteristics of a term. (chapter 13, p. 279)

Contributing conditions Conditions that make an effect more likely to occur but are neither necessary nor sufficient to cause it to appear. (chapter 25, p. 607)

Controlled vocabulary The dictionary or thesaurus that lists the stable set of subject-matter terms used as keywords or index entries. (chapter 6, p. 119)

Correction for attenuation A formula for correcting a correlation coefficient for unreliability in the measures to estimate the size of the relationship if the reliability were perfect. (chapter 18, p. 431)

Correlation *See* Pearson product-moment correlation.

Cost-benefit analysis Weighs the costs of a program against its benefits, usually in monetary terms. (chapter 23, p. 545)

Cost-effectiveness analysis Determination of the costs of achieving certain levels of benefits. (chapter 23, p. 545)

Counterbalanced designs Studies designed such that if two or more treatments are administered in sequence, the treatments are administered in all possible sequences so as to reveal and eliminate the effect of ordering. (chapter 21, p. 501)

Credibility The closest equivalent term to Internal Integrity in qualitative research except that in such research, it usually refers to the credible linking of the steps in a process rather than to the establishment of causality. (chapter 16, p. 344)

Credible result The prior four judgments in Internal Integrity are positive, the expected result occurred, and there is not prior evidence that gives reason to question the finding. (chapter 7, p. 147)

Criterion A measure generally accepted as valid; a measure to be predicted; a standard to be attained. (chapter 18, p. 431)

Criterion-referenced tests Tests whose interpretation is based on meeting the mastery requirements of a content area rather than interpreting the score in the context of a reference group, such as with norm-referenced tests. (chapter 18, p. 417)

Criterion-related validity *See* Concurrent validity; Predictive validity.

Cronbach's alpha *See* Alpha coefficient.

Cross-break *See* Cross-tabulation.

Cross-sectional studies Studies of change that compare current individuals at different stages on the variable of interest (e.g., age, experience) rather than doing a longitudinal study over time. (chapter 24, p. 572)

Cross-tabulation Tabulation of data in terms of two or more variables. For example, respondents' choices of each of five possible answers to a question are tabulated by gender, and results are displayed in a table with two rows (one for males and one for females) and five columns (for each of the five responses). As a result, each cell shows the frequency of persons choosing a particular response, by gender. (chapter 24, p. 589)

Curricular validity *See* Content validity.

Debriefing Informing an individual who has been deceived in an experiment of that fact and assuaging any unfortunate consequences. (chapter 10, p. 213)

Degrees of freedom The number of data entries free to vary when their total is fixed. (chapter 20, p. 470)

Demand characteristics Responses that subjects perceive are required by the study. (chapter 21, p. 500)

"Demonstrated generality" Evidence that the effect appeared in instances where it was expected within the limits of generality provided by the study and did not show where it should not have. (chapter 8, p. 174)

Dependent variable A variable presumed to be affected by a treatment or by an independent variable. (chapter 2, p. 27)

Derived score A standard score in which the mean and the standard deviation have been changed to numbers chosen for ease of interpretation or computation. Also called *scaled score*. (chapter 17, p. 384)

Diffusion Spread of a treatment to the control group; spread of a finding to the people who can make use of it. (chapter 21, p. 498)

Disconfirmation The process of trying to invalidate a proposition. Causal relations can never be proved; there may always be some as yet untested circumstances under which the relationship does not hold. With each successful test, the proposition is said to have escaped disconfirmation. (chapter 7, p. 136)

Disinterestedness Ignoring personal advantage when interpreting data. (chapter 3, p. 51)

Double-barreled questions Two questions rolled into one, making it impossible to determine to which the respondent formulated her answer. (chapter 24, p. 579)

Double-blind procedures Neither the subject nor the treatment administrator knows whether the treatment being given is a placebo or the actual treatment. (chapter 21, p. 499)

Effect size The average size of an effect, usually in standard deviation units. (chapter 22, p. 521)

Elite bias Overrepresenting in a study the views of those in power or with authority, or in the upper class, better educated, or higher in the social structure. (chapter 13, p. 270)

Emergent study An investigation in which the aspect to be studied inductively emerges as the inquiry proceeds. (chapter 2, p. 30)

Emic perspective An individual's perception of how things are viewed by another person—the view from the inside. (chapter 12, p. 243)

Empirical keying Responses are collected on a broad, multi-item instrument over sizable samples of individuals, each sample having certain group characteristics (e.g., normal personality, schizoid tendencies, paranoid tendencies). Items answered similarly by members of a group but differently from members of the other groups (differentiating responses) are assembled into a key for each group. Each key's score shows how closely a new individual's responses resemble those of the original group members. (chapter 18, p. 419)

Epistemology The branch of philosophy that studies the nature of knowledge, its assumptions, and its validity. (chapter 12, p. 242)

Equivalence reliability Evidence that a test measures consistently across different but equivalent forms. (chapter 18, p. 415)

Estimation The process in statistical inference whereby a confidence interval is constructed around an observed value within which the population value is presumed to lie with a confidence expressed by odds (such as 19 to 1). (chapter 19, p. 436)

Etic perspective The person as viewed from the outside by another person—the view that person presents to the world. (chapter 12, p. 243)

Ex post facto studies *See* After-the-fact natural experiments.

Explanation credibility The plausibility of the explanation advanced for a phenomenon. (chapter 7, p. 139)

Explanation generality The generality that is claimed, implied, or must be inferred from the study's problem statement. (chapter 8, p. 176)

Explanatory variable *See* Independent variable.

External Generality The power of a study to support inferences regarding the generality of the findings to other persons, situations, measures, and times. (chapter 8, p. 174)

Face validity The appearance of being a valid test. (chapter 18, p. 407)

Factor analysis Clustering the variables most highly correlated with each other into homogeneous groups called "factors" and making inferences of the constructs measured by the factors from the nature of the variables most highly correlated with the factors. (chapter 18, p. 409)

Factorial design A study design in which data on the effect of every combination of variables in the study are provided. (chapter 21, p. 505)

Fieldnotes The observer's records of what has been observed. (chapter 13, p. 260)

Fish-scale analogy Knowing judgments made by each person in sequence, extending from the researcher to laypersons. Each, being less expert than the previous person, looks at the evidence presented by previous judges and determines whether to accept their judgment. (chapter 3, p. 41)

Focus One of the six design rings in the chain of reasoning: the variables that are the target of the investigation, e.g., the independent and dependent variables, treatments, effects, parts of a process. (chapter 4, p. 67; chapter 7, p. 140)

Focus group A panel, selected to be representative of a population, interviewed on a topic of interest. Probes determine the popularity of various comments and points of view and the depth of feeling toward them. There may also be trials of material to determine the panel's reactions to it and how it could be changed. (chapter 24, p. 581)

Focused interview An interview in which the respondent is allowed to set the initial course but is increasingly guided by the interviewer to narrow and/or refocus the course of the interview as it progresses. (chapter 14, p. 299)

Formative evaluation An evaluation intended to provide information that can be used to guide the progress of a project toward its goals. (chapter 23, p. 540)

Framing of questions The context in which the questions are put. (chapter 24, p. 579)

Frequency distribution A graphic portraying the frequency with which each score occurred in a set of data, the scores being arranged in order from low to high. (chapter 17, p. 373)

Functionally equivalent groups Groups that function as though they were identical to each other in every way that is relevant to the experiment. (chapter 21, p. 478)

Funnel-sequenced questionnaire A questionnaire that, like the focused interview, begins broadly and narrows to the target of interest. (chapter 24, p. 578)

Gatekeeper A person from whom one must get permission to proceed to the next step, as in gaining access to participants or in getting a study published. (chapter 13, p. 263)

Generalization A statement of the relationship between two or more variables that holds across a variety of persons, places, times, measures, and/or procedures. (chapter 7, p. 137)

Goal-free evaluation Inferring the goals of a project from observations by an evaluator unfamiliar with the intended goals, and measures of what has occurred as a result of the project. These goals, and the success with which they have been achieved, are compared with the intended goals. (chapter 23, p. 549)

Grounded theory An explanation of phenomena based on (grounded in) observations of it and accounting for those events. (chapter 13, p. 281)

Hawthorne effect The subject's perceived feeling of being special as a result of being part of an experiment and the resulting impact on the effectiveness of treatment. (chapter 21, p. 497)

Hypothesis A tentative explanation of a phenomenon that can be subjected to verification. (chapter 1, p. 3)

Hypothesis guessing Subjects' guessing what the researcher has in mind and reacting accordingly. (chapter 21, p. 497)

Hypothesis testing The process in statistical inference whereby the likelihood that an observed value, such as a difference between means, is typical of what might be expected as a result of random sampling variation and chance error (at certain odds, such as 19 to 1, the Type I error we allow) or is atypically larger and therefore the result of some other influence such as a treatment or rival explanation. (chapter 19, p. 439)

Independent variable A variable believed to be a cause, usually used to designate a variable that cannot be manipulated through treatment. (chapter 2, p. 27)

Inferential statistics Statistics that infer the value of a characteristic of a population from the information in a sample from that population. (chapter 19, p. 433)

Informants Persons selected for their sensitivity, knowledge, and insights into their situation, their willingness to talk about it, and their ability to provide access to new situations. (chapter 13, p. 270)

Institutional constraints Limitations imposed on a research study by institutions to minimize the impact of the study on their regular program or otherwise protect their clients. (chapter 9, p. 198)

Institutional review boards (IRBs) Boards established by institutions receiving federal research funds that are responsible for ensuring that research participants do not suffer any harmful consequences or if there is a possibility of some risk, that the benefits outweigh the risks. (chapter 10, p. 207)

Instrument decay A change in the way a measure or observation schedule is used over the course of a study that might provide an explanation for a phenomenon other than the one proposed; in qualitative studies, a change over time in observational point of view or attitude toward the people observed that affects the nature of one's observation in ways one would be concerned about if aware of it. Should be noted in memos when suspected. (chapter 16, p. 348)

Instrumentation decay by treatment interaction Treatment-induced change in the way an instrument, measure, or observation schedule is used over the course of a study. (chapter 21, p. 496)

Interaction Potentiation or weakening of the effect of an independent variable or treatment due to the presence of another variable or condition. (chapter 2, p. 32)

Internal consistency reliability Evidence that the items of a test are homogeneous, measure a single construct, and correlate highly with one another. (chapter 18, pp. 409 and 413)

Internal Integrity The power of a study to link variables in a causal relationship or in a process. (chapter 7, p. 138)

Interval scale A scale whose units are presumed to be equal (e.g., the difference between a score of 10 and 20 is the same as that between 30 and 40). (chapter 17, p. 371)

Invented cases These are cases in conceptual analysis in which all constraints are released as a last test to the concept formulation to see whether there are additional conditions not yet found. (chapter 13, p. 279)

Invisible college A group of researchers interested in the same problem who communicate with one another by exchanging drafts of articles, corresponding or phoning regarding problems, or trading messages through blogs, forums, listservs, e-mails, and Internet services like *Facebook*. (chapter 3, p. 37)

Item analysis A method of improving a test by correlating the items with either the total score or a criterion measure. Reliability is improved by correlating with the total score, keeping only items that correlate highly with it and changing others to be like those kept. Validity is improved by a similar process, except that a valid measure (criterion) is used rather than a total score. (chapter 18, p. 418)

Item difficulty index An index indicating how hard a test item is; usually the percentage of students passing a test item. (chapter 18, p. 418)

Item discrimination index An index indicating the correlation between the item score and some criterion. To improve validity, the criterion is some measure already accepted as valid; to improve internal consistency reliability, the total test score is used. (chapter 18, p. 418)

Item response theory Also called *modern test theory* (as opposed to classical), it extends classical test theory by modeling the information in the item characteristic curve—the plot of each response to the item in relation to levels of the construct being measured. (chapter 18, p. 416)

Judgmental sampling Persons are chosen by the researcher to fulfill some research goal such as showing the generality of a construct, finding the limits of a characteristic, etc. (chapter 8, p. 171)

Keyword indexing Indexing with a controlled vocabulary descriptive of a field. An article is found by determining the intersection of two or more keywords descriptive of it. (chapter 6, p. 120)

Knowing in action The spontaneous, off-the-cuff reaction to new situations by professionals, demonstrating that they know more than they thought they did. (chapter 27, p. 627)

Kuder-Richardson reliability (KR21) A measure of internal consistency reliability. (chapter 18, p. 414)

Letter of transmittal The letter accompanying a questionnaire that, besides explaining what to do, is intended to motivate the respondent to complete and return the instrument. (chapter 24, p. 585)

Linear relationship A relationship between two variables best described by a straight line; that is, as one variable increases, the other consistently either increases or decreases proportionately. Also called a *straight-line relationship*. (chapter 17, p. 391)

Local history An event that occurs during the course of a treatment that could have the same effect as the treatment. (chapter 21, p. 489)

Longitudinal studies Studies of change in a particular individual or group over time. (chapter 24, p. 573)

Mann-Whitney *U* test A measure of the relationship between two ordinal variables over a group of persons. (chapter 20, p. 465)

Masking A form of control whereby an unwanted variable's effect is mitigated by a stronger variable that blocks the unwanted one from perception by subjects. (chapter 21, p. 484)

Maturation Changes that occur in subjects over the course of a study that, because they could also have caused the effect, are confounded with it; includes such changes as growing tired or bored. (chapter 21, p. 490)

Mean The arithmetic average of a set of scores. (chapter 17, p. 378)

Median The middle score of a set of scores; also, the second quartile. (chapter 17, p. 377)

Member checking The researcher presents the report and findings to those studied for their review and comment. (chapter 16, p. 346)

Memos Notes written by a qualitative method observer to record some insight or some aspect of a process that may be helpful in the interpretation of the data. (chapter 13, p. 276)

Meta-analysis Combining the statistical results of studies of the same question into a single result to enhance statistical power, to find the average size of the effect, to determine the nature of the relationship, and to find how the relationship is affected by other variables. (chapter 22, p. 520)

Method of agreement If two situations of a phenomenon under investigation have only one circumstance in common, the instance in which they agree is presumed to be causally related to the phenomenon. (chapter 11, p. 223)

Method of concomitant variation Phenomena that consistently vary together are presumed to be connected to one another, directly or indirectly, through a causal relationship. (chapter 11, p. 226)

Method of differences A situation in which a phenomenon occurs and one in which it does not occur are exactly alike save for one circumstance in the former. The circumstance in which they differ is presumed to be causally related to the phenomenon. (chapter 11, p. 224)

Method of residuals Subtract from any situation all aspects known to be the cause only of phenomena other than the one of interest, and the cause of the phenomenon of interest is in the residual. (chapter 11, p. 227)

Mode The most frequently occurring score in a set of scores. (chapter 17, p. 377)

Model examples Perfectly clear and unquestioned examples of a construct; used in conceptual analysis to help define a term. (chapter 13, p. 279)

Mortality Changes in the composition of the sample due to individuals dropping out of the study before its completion that could have caused the effect and are confounded with it. (chapter 16, p. 348)

Mortality by treatment interaction Similar to mortality, but changes in the sample result from dropouts who react negatively to the treatment. (chapter 21, p. 501)

Multimeasure-multimethod procedure Multiple measurement or observation of the same phenomenon or attribute with different methods. This triangulation ensures that the researcher knows if characteristics of the measure or the method of measuring or observation are affecting the result. (chapter 7, p. 141)

Multiple-treatment interaction The effect of earlier treatments on later ones. (chapter 21, p. 500)

Necessary condition A condition that must be present for an effect to occur or for a term to apply. (chapter 13, p. 279)

Nested designs Factorial designs that reduce the number of groups to the combinations in which one is particularly interested and allow confounding of variables in the remainder. (chapter 21, p. 506)

Nominal level (of measurement) The grouping of like individuals or units (such as institutions) into categories. (chapter 17, p. 371)

Nondirective interviewing An approach in which the interviewer rephrases and reflects the interviewee's responses, especially to draw out the underlying feelings and central significance of their responses. (chapter 14, p. 301)

Nonequivalent control group design Experimental design in which individuals are not randomly assigned to control and treatment groups so there is no assurance that they are equivalent. Usually involves preformed groups such as schoolrooms. (chapter 21, p. 502)

Nonlinear relationship A relationship between two variables best described by other than a straight line; as one variable increases, the other does not consistently either increase or decrease, or if it does, it does not do so proportionately (for example, a distribution best described by a U or J). (chapter 17, p. 391)

Nonparametric statistics Inferential statistics that assume random assignment or random categorization as a basis for determining probabilities rather than random sampling. (chapter 20, p. 471)

Nonprobability sampling Any sampling procedure that does not involve random sampling at some stage. (chapter 8, p. 163)

Nonrespondents Persons who do not return questionnaires or other instruments and must be recontacted to obtain a large enough sample to determine whether their responses differ from those whose responses have been received. (chapter 24, p. 572)

Normal frequency distribution A frequency distribution with a particular shape produced by the action of probability in a chance event over an infinite number of trials. Often used as an approximation or model for test score distributions. (chapter 17, p. 377)

Norm-referenced tests Tests on which performance is interpreted in the context of the performance of a group with whom it is reasonable to compare the individual (for example, achieving at a certain grade level). (chapter 18, p. 416)

Null hypothesis The observed value is the result of randomness and chance error; that is, there is a null (no) difference between the value and what typically results from chance error; the value derived from a sample is typical of those in its chance sampling distribution for samples of that size. (chapter 19, p. 433)

Objectivity The similarity with which two or more judges would evaluate a performance or record an observation. (chapter 16, p. 347; chapter 18, p. 419)

Obtrusiveness The change in the pattern of events, schedule, or situation resulting when an intrusion is perceived as sufficiently significant by participants to affect their typical actions (e.g., an unfamiliar adult visiting a kindergarten class). (chapter 21, p. 497)

One-group pretest-posttest design Experimental design in which a group is measured, treated, and then remeasured to determine change. (chapter 21, p. 502)

One-tailed test A test in which all Type I error is assumed to be in one tail of the sampling distribution; a directional hypothesis forecasts the direction of the expected change (for example, experimental group mean greater than control group mean). (chapter 19, p. 443)

Operational definition The definition of a construct formed by the operations of measurement or the actual behavior. (chapter 7, p. 141)

Ordinal level (of measurement) The ranking of individuals or units (e.g., rank order of ten best colleges). (chapter 17, p. 371)

Organized skepticism The process whereby new knowledge claims in science are routinely challenged by other researchers to determine their validity. (chapter 3, p. 51)

Original sources The original sources of data, facts, findings, theory; the publications of the original authors rather than quotation, summary, or paraphrase of the material by other authors. (chapter 6, p. 127)

Oversampling Taking more samples from a stratum than its proportional share of the sample. (chapter 8, p. 167)

Panel sample A panel chosen so as to be representative of a population; usually used in order to study change over time. (chapter 24, p. 574)

Parametric statistics Statistics that assume random sampling as the basis for calculating probabilities. (chapter 20, p. 471)

Participant observation Circumstances wherein individuals are aware that they are being observed, but the observer, by participating in the situation as normally as he or she can, is as unobtrusive as possible. (chapter 13, p. 260)

Participants One of the six facets in the chain of reasoning: the persons chosen to be involved in a study of a process or those in the treatment or control groups in an experiment. (chapter 4, pp. 67 and 143)

Pearson product-moment correlation A number between zero and ± 1.00 indicative of the strength of relationship between two variables where zero indicates no relation. Positive correlations indicate that they vary directly; negative ones, inversely. At ±1.00 they vary perfectly proportionally; between ±1.00 and zero, they vary increasingly imperfectly as zero is approached. (chapter 17, p. 387)

Peer review Material submitted for publication is sent to peers in the same field for review and approval before being approved for publishing. (chapter 13, p. 287)

Percentile The percentage of cases in a frequency distribution that fall below any given score (e.g., the median is the 50th percentile because 50% of cases have lower scores than the median). (chapter 17, p. 386)

Phenomenological point of view A point of view in which we see reality in terms of the meaning we attach to things; reality is in the eye of the beholder. Also called *symbolic interactionism*. (chapter 12, p. 242)

Pilot testing Trying out an instrument or a procedure to determine problems before it is employed in its intended use. (chapter 24, p. 588)

Placebo A treatment that is just like the actual treatment but lacks the active ingredient. (chapter 21, p. 480)

Population The total group to whom a researcher expects to be able to generalize and which is to be represented in a sample. (chapter 8, p. 160)

Positivism/positivist epistemology In contrast to phenomenology, there is a reality to be sensed and discovered; conjectures are confirmed by actually sensing them. (chapter 12, p. 242)

Posttest-only control group design Experimental design in which individuals are randomly assigned to experimental and control groups, given experimental and control treatments, and then measured to determine effects. (chapter 21, p. 503)

Power of a statistical test The capacity of a statistical test to avoid a Type II error. (chapter 19, p. 452)

Predictive validity Evidence that a test correlates with a criterion obtained before a selection decision or choice was made. (chapter 18, p. 411)

Preplanned study An investigation that is deductively developed to answer a question or test a hypothesis or theory before the study is begun. (chapter 2, p. 29)

Pretest-posttest control group design Experimental design in which individuals are randomly assigned to experimental and control groups, measured before treatment, treated, and remeasured. (chapter 21, p. 503)

Primary sources *See* Original sources.

Privacy The ability to control information about oneself. (chapter 10, p. 213)

Probability sampling A sampling procedure that involves random sampling at some stage. (chapter 8, p. 163)

Probe An interviewing technique designed to cause the respondent to amplify a response or to jog the respondent's memory. (chapter 14, p. 308)

Projective techniques Techniques used to indirectly assess responses to presented stimuli; what is being measured is not apparent to the subject. For instance, individuals may merely be asked to respond to a stimulus by telling what is seen, telling a story about it, or giving the first response that comes to mind. (chapter 24, p. 577)

Proportional stratified sampling The percentage of cases randomly selected from strata is the same as the percentage the strata represent in the population. (chapter 8, p. 167)

Purposive sampling Samples assembled by intentionally seeking individuals or situations likely to yield new instances and greater understanding of a dimension or concept of interest. Also used to test the generality of a coding category, finding, or principle. (chapter 8, p. 172)

Quartile The point below which one-quarter of a set of scores fall (first quartile), half the scores fall (second quartile, median), or three-quarters of the scores fall (third quartile). (chapter 17, p. 375)

Quota sampling Interviewer chooses units for the sample such that their characteristics fill certain quotas. The quotas may insure diversity, representation of extremes, proportional representation, etc. (chapter 8, p. 172)

Random assignment Assigning treatment by some chance method to individuals or groups in such a way the each has an equal probability of receiving the treatment. (chapter 21, p. 486)

Random sampling Choosing samples by chance in such a way that every sample has an equal chance of being selected each time a sample is drawn. (chapter 8, p. 164)

Range The distance from the lowest to the highest score. (chapter 17, p. 380)

Ratio scale An interval scale with a true zero point (in contrast to one set for convenience) that represents the complete lack of what is being measured. (chapter 17, p. 371)

Reactivity Change in individuals' behavior due to their perception that they are part of an experimental study or are being observed. (chapter 21, p. 497)

Records One of the six design rings in the chain of reasoning: the observations, measures, or other records that provide operationalization to the constructs of a study. (chapter 4, p. 67)

Referential sampling *See* Chain-referral sampling.

Reflexivity The self interview by a qualitative researcher to determine possible bias, unconscious tendencies, preferences, and the like that could affect observations, interpretations or findings. (chapter 13, p. 277)

Regression The prediction of one variable from another variable. Alternatively, scores of individuals selected as low or high on a characteristic with a less than perfectly reliable measure and placed in separate groups will move closer to the mean of their original group on retesting. Also, a phenomenon measured at a peak will appear to have improved if remeasured at more typical levels. (chapter 21, p. 491)

Related cases Cases that are almost but not quite the same as the term being examined in a conceptual analysis. They help distinguish the term's boundary. (chapter 13, p. 279)

Relative weighting of Internal Integrity and External Generality Balancing the study's capacity to link cause and effect with its capacity to show the generality of the relationship. Internal Integrity can be strengthened by tight controls and/or using a laboratory. These characteristics decrease External Generality. (chapter 9, p. 195)

Reliability Evidence that a test measures consistently in some respect. (chapter 18, p. 412)

Replicable result A final judgment based on the fact that the prior four judgments in External Generality are positive and whether or not the result would be replicable with new choices of any or all the facets of the study design. (chapter 8, p. 181)

Researcher expectancy effect Researchers or judges, knowing what to expect, believe they perceive it. (chapter 21, p. 498)

Resource allocation The allocation of resources to achieve the purposes of a study, especially to achieve the appropriate balance of Internal Integrity to External Generality and to build a strong chain of reasoning. (chapter 9, p. 196)

Resource limits The limits on resources available for a study, especially limits on the researchers' time and energy—a constraint. (chapter 9, p. 200)

Respondent The interviewee or the participant who completes and returns a questionnaire or poll. (chapter 13, p. 270)

Response sets Tendency of respondents to answer questions in certain directions (such as "yes" or "true") regardless of the actual question. (chapter 24, p. 591)

Restriction of range The extremes of the range were omitted thereby usually lowering a correlation over what it would have been had the full range been present. (chapter 17, p. 389)

Restrictive explanations (conditions) eliminated Conditions of the study that restrict the generality that may be inferred from the evidence. In the interests of greater generality, it is desirable these be eliminated in the study's design. (chapter 8, p. 180)

Rival explanations Explanations other than the intended one proposed to explain the phenomenon or effect under study. A major purpose of experimental design is their elimination. (chapter 7, p. 146)

Robust Describes a statistical test that can be accurately interpreted even when the conditions of its use violate certain of its assumptions. (chapter 20, p. 472)

Sample A means by which cases are taken from a population in such a way as to accurately represent the variables of interest in that population; thus a study of a sample may economically be substituted for a study of the entire population. (chapter 8, p. 159)

Sampling frame The frame from which the sample is to be drawn. An enumeration of all the units in the population or in a cluster. (chapter 8, p. 164)

Sampling unit The units that make up the population and are chosen in a sampling procedure. (chapter 8, p. 165)

Saturation Describes a situation in qualitative research where enough examples of a dimension or concept of interest have been gathered that nothing new is being learned. (chapter 13, p. 278)

Scaled score *See* Derived score.

Scatterplot The plot of scores developed when one variable is measured on the vertical axis (usually the dependent variable) and the other on the horizontal axis. Also known as a *scatter diagram* or *scattergram*. (chapter 17, p. 387)

Secondary sources Quotation, paraphrase, or summary of data, facts, findings, or theory by other than the original authors. (chapter 3, p. 39; chapter 6, p. 118)

Selection A rival explanation; assignment of individuals to groups in such a way that any characteristic that could have caused the effect is not equated between the groups and is therefore confounded with treatment. (chapter 21, p. 494)

Selection-maturation interaction A selection factor creates groups of differing maturation levels. (chapter 21, p. 496)

Selection by treatment interaction The rival explanation of selection resulting from the attractiveness or repulsiveness of the treatment (often self-selection). (chapter 21, p. 496)

Semi-interquartile range Half the distance from the first quartile to the third quartile. (chapter 17, p. 380)

Seminal minds Groundbreaking researchers whose influence provides a foundation upon which further development of the researched topic can occur. (chapter 5, p. 90)

Sensitivity of a statistical test *See* Statistical sensitivity.

Sequential sampling Taking successive samples until the required precision of measurement and stability of the data across samples is attained. (chapter 8, p. 173)

Significance level The frequency or probability (e.g., 1 time in 20, or 5%) with which one is willing to be wrong in saying that a value is atypical and not due to chance error (i.e., statistically significant) when it *is* the result of chance error. (chapter 19, p. 441)

Situation One of the six design rings in the chain of reasoning: the circumstances, location, and milieu in which a study is done. (chapter 4, p. 67)

Skewness A deviation of the frequency distribution from symmetry. Positive skewness has a long tail to the right toward the high scores; negative skewness, the opposite. (chapter 17, p. 377)

Solomon four-group design A combination of the pretest-posttest experimental and control group design with the posttest-only experimental and control group design. (chapter 21, p. 503)

Spearman-Brown formula A formula that allows one to estimate the effect on the test's reliability by changing the length of a test. Also called the *Spearman-Brown Prophecy Formula*. (chapter 18, p. 430)

Stability reliability Evidence that a test measures consistently over time. (chapter 18, p. 415)

Stakeholders Individuals who are affected by the outcome of a project and who therefore have a stake in how it is developed, implemented, and evaluated. (chapter 23, p. 541)

Standard deviation A measure of the variability or spread of scores; the square root of the average of the squared deviations of the scores from the mean of the data set. (chapter 17, p. 381)

Standard error of measurement A measure of the reliability or consistency of measurement; used to construct confidence intervals. (chapter 18, p. 427)

Standard error of the mean The standard deviation of a distribution of the means of an infinite number of random samples from a data set. (chapter 19, p. 436)

Standard score A raw score divided by its standard deviation. Also known as the *z-score*. *See also* Derived scores; it and scaled scores are forms of standard scores. (chapter 17, p. 384)

Stanine score A score in one of nine categories formed by dividing the score range into nine scores, each half a standard deviation wide, with the top and bottom scores open-ended. (chapter 17, p. 386)

Statistical sensitivity The probability that a statistic will yield a positive result when a statistically significant situation truly exists at or above the significance level set. Also one minus the beta or Type II error. (chapter 19, p. 443)

Statistical significance A value is atypical in a sampling distribution; a value that would not typically result from the operation of random sampling variation and chance error and would appear with a rarity expressed by long odds such as 19 to 1 or 99 to 1. (chapter 19, pp. 443 and 452)

Stimulated recall Audio- or videotaping the respondent during a session and later playing back the tape, stopping it, and asking the respondent to explain his or her thoughts and feelings at that time. (chapter 12, p. 248)

Stratified sampling Dividing a population into groups (strata) on the basis of some variable such that the groups are more homogeneous on the variable of interest than in a simple random sample. Units are randomly sampled from within strata, usually proportionally to the size of a stratum in relation to the total sample. (chapter 8, p. 166)

Structural equation modeling The prediction of a complex phenomenon by statistical equations. Also called *linear modeling*. (chapter 21, p. 512)

Structured interview An interview in which the questions and their order are predetermined. (chapter 14, p. 297)

Sufficient conditions (In relation to causation) all those conditions, in the presence of which the effect occurs; (in relation to conceptual analysis) conditions which are sufficient to distinguish all examples from non-examples of a term. (chapter 13, p. 279)

Summative evaluation Evaluation intended to determine the value or worth of something. (chapter 23, p. 540)

Systematic sampling Choosing every nth unit (for example, every tenth person) from the sampling frame. (chapter 8, p. 168)

t **test** A parametric test of statistical significance, often of the difference between two means. (chapter 20, p. 464)

Table of specifications A table displaying the curriculum of a unit in which the knowledge to be learned is specified across the rows, and the behaviors the student should be able to display with respect to that knowledge is specified down the columns. Each cell describes a behavior as indicated by the entry at the head of the column; that behavior coincides with the knowledge described in the intersecting row. If the table displays the content of a questionnaire, the topic being queried takes the place of knowledge in the rows, and the verb in the query takes the place of behaviors in the columns. (chapter 18, p. 407; chapter 24, p. 576)

Tailored (adaptive) tests Tests that are adjusted to the appropriate level of difficulty for each subject by having each subject who passes an item branched to a more difficult item and each who fails branched to an easier one. (chapter 18, p. 421)

Tandem interviewing Two persons conduct the interview, one recording the other engaging the respondent. (chapter 14, p. 304)

Testing A rival explanation; changes in the scores of individuals resulting from familiarity with a test taken two or more times; the resulting higher scores are confounded with treatment. (chapter 21, p. 495)

Testing-treatment interaction The rival explanation of testing resulting from individuals having been sensitized to aspects of treatment by a pretest and subsequently paying greater attention to those aspects during treatment than they otherwise would. (chapter 21, p. 501)

Threats to validity *See* Rival explanations.

Time One of the six design rings in the chain of reasoning, which could also be called procedure; it is the scheme of who does what to whom when and for what reason. (chapter 4, p. 67)

Time-series designs Experimental designs that follow subjects through time, treating and remeasuring them to determine changes. (chapter 21, p. 504)

Trade-off A gain in one aspect of a study with loss in another (e.g., breadth vs. depth—a good general achievement test in a particular area does a poor job of diagnosing specific weaknesses in that area). (chapter 4, p. 74)

Translation generality A judgment of the extent to which the translation of the question, hypothesis, or model into the six design facets supports the generality claimed or implied by the problem statement. (chapter 8, p. 177)

Translation validity The validity with which the terms in the question, hypothesis, or model are translated into the six facets of design. (chapter 7, p. 140)

Treatment A potential cause controlled by the investigator. (chapter 2, p. 28)

Treatment fidelity The faithfulness with which the operational definition of a treatment represents it. (chapter 21, p. 481)

Trend studies A time-series design intended to show a trend. (chapter 24, p. 573)

Triangulation Determining the consistency of evidence gathered from different sources of data across time, space, and/or persons, by different investigators, times, measures, observations, and/or different research methods. (chapter 7, p. 141; chapter 13, p. 285)

Trustworthiness The qualitative equivalent of scientific rigor; building credibility with the audience. (chapter 16, p. 344)

Two-tailed test A test in which Type I error may be found in either tails of the distribution; we do not have a directional hypothesis; we expect an effect but do not know its direction. (chapter 19, p. 443)

Type I (alpha) error The error of erroneously indicating that an effect is statistically significant when in fact it is the result of random sampling variation and chance error. (chapter 19, p. 443)

Type II (beta) error The error of indicating that a given value is due to sampling variation and chance error when it is not. (chapter 19, p. 435)

Uncertainty reduction Whenever we find new evidence to support the validity of a proposition, we do not say that the proposition is true, because there may always be some additional finding that refutes or changes it. Instead we say that our uncertainty regarding the truth of the proposition is reduced. Usually we reach some point where we act on it as if it were true, even though all uncertainty has not been eliminated. (chapter 3, p. 44)

Unobtrusiveness Administration of treatment or measures in such a way that they appear to be part of the situation normally expected by the participants. (chapter 21, p. 498)

Unstructured interview Interview in which interviewers, taking their cue from previous responses, formulate, and order questions on the spot to obtain the desired information. (chapter 14, p. 297)

Validation Checking an explanation or a hypothesis to determine whether predictions made from it are accurate or that replications confirm the original result. (chapter 1, p. 4)

Validity Evidence that a test measures what it is intended to measure. (chapter 18, p. 401)

Variance A measure of the variability of the scores in a frequency distribution; more specifically, the square of its standard deviation. (chapter 17, p. 381)

Z-score *See* Standard score.

References

Abelson, R. P. (1995). *Statistics as principled argument.* Hillsdale, NJ: Erlbaum.

Adair, J. D., Sharpe, D., & Huynh, C. (1989). Hawthorne control procedures in education experiments: A reconsideration of their use and effectiveness. *Review of Educational Research, 59*, 215–228.

Alberts, B., & Shine, K. (1994). Scientists and the integrity of research. *Science, 266*, 1660–1661.

Allen, J. R., & St. George, S. A. (2001, September). What couples say works in domestic violence therapy. *The Qualitative Report, 6*(3). Retrieved from http://www.nova.ed/ssss/QR/QR6-3/allen.html

Allen, M. J., & Yen, W. M. (2002). *Introduction to measurement theory.* Long Grove, IL: Waveland Press.

Allen, M. S. (1962). *Allen morphologizer.* Englewood Cliffs, NJ: Prentice-Hall.

Altrichter, H., Posch, P., & Somekh, B. (1993). *Teachers investigate their work.* London: Routledge.

American Council on Education. (1995). *Guidelines for computerized-adaptive test development and use in education.* Washington, DC: Author.

American Educational Research Association (AERA). (2002). *Ethical standards of the American Educational Research Association.* Washington, DC: Author.

American Journal of Preventive Medicine. (2008). The science of team science—Assessing the value of transdisciplinary research. Retrieved from http://dccps.nci.nih.gov/brp/scienceteam/ajpm.html

American Psychological Association. (2001). *Publication manual of the American Psychological Association* (5th ed.). Washington, DC: Author.

Anastasi, A., & Urbina, S. (1997). *Psychological testing* (7th ed.). Upper Saddle River, NJ: Prentice-Hall.

Anderson, J. R. (1987). Methodologies for studying human knowledge (with discussion). *Behavior and Brain Sciences, 10,* 467–505.

Anfara, V. A., Jr., Brown, K. M., & Mangione, T. L. (2002). Qualitative analysis on stage: Making the research process more public. *Educational Researcher, 31*(7), 28–38.

Anscombe, F. J. (1973). Graphs in statistical analysis. *American Statistician, 27*(1), 17–21.

Aronow, E. Reznikoff, M., & Moreland, K. (1994). *The Rorschach technique: Perceptual basics, content interpretation, and applications.* Des Moines, IA: Longwood.

Asimov, I. (1977). The future of futurism. *American Way, 10*(4), 11–12.

Atkin, J. M. (1994). Teacher research to change policy: An illustration. In S. Hollingsworth & H. Sockett (Eds.), *Teacher research and educational reform* (pp. 103–120). Ninety-third yearbook of the National Society for the Study of Education, Part I. Chicago: University of Chicago Press.

Aydelotte, W. O., Bogue, A. G., & Fogel, R. W. (1972). *The dimensions of quantitative research in history.* Princeton, NJ: Princeton University Press.

Babbie, E. R. (1992). *The practice of social research* (6th ed.). Belmont, CA: Wadsworth.

Baker, F. & Kim, S. H. (2004). *Item response theory: Parameter estimation techniques* (2nd ed., revised and expanded). New York: Marcel Dekker

Baker, G., & Chapman, D. (Eds.). (1962). *Man and society in disaster.* New York: Basic Books.

Balay, R. (Ed.) (1992). *Guide to reference books* (supplement to 10th ed.). Chicago: American Library Association.

Bampton, R., & Cowton, C. J. (2002, May). The E-interview. *Forum Qualitative Sozialforschung / Forum: Qualitative Social Research, 3*(2). Retrieved from http://www.qualitative-research.net/index.php/fqs/article/view/848/842

Bandura, A. (1978). The self system in reciprocal determinism. *American Psychologist, 33,* 344–358.

Barlow, D. H., Nock, M. K., & Hersen, M. (2008). Single case experimental designs: Strategies for studying behavior change (3rd ed.). Boston: Allyn & Bacon.

Barnett, J. E., & Johnson, W. B. (2008). *Ethics desk reference for psychologists.* Washington, DC: American Psychological Association.

Baron, R. A., & Ransberger, V. M. (1978). Ambient temperature and the occurrence of collective violence: The long hot summer revisited. *Journal of Personality and Social Psychology, 36,* 351–360.

Barzun, J., & Graff, H. F. (1992). *The modern researcher* (5th ed.). New York: Harcourt Brace Jovanovich.

Barzun, J., & Graff, H. F. (2003). *The modern researcher* (6th ed.). Belmont, CA: Wadsworth.

Baumrind, D. (1985). Research using intentional deception: Ethical issues revisited. *American Psychologist, 40,* 165–174.

Becker, H. S. (1961). *Boys in white.* Chicago: University of Chicago Press.

Becker, H. S. (1963). *Outsiders: Studies in the sociology of deviance.* New York: Free Press.

Becker, H. S. (2007). *Writing for social scientists: How to start and finish your thesis, book, or article* (2nd ed.). Chicago: University of Chicago Press.

Becker, H. S., Geer, B., & Hughes, E. C. (1968). *Making the grade: The academic side of college life.* New York: Wiley.

Begley, S. (1997, April 21). The science wars. *Newsweek,* 54–57.

Behrens, J. T. (1997). Principles and procedures of exploratory data analysis. *Psychological Methods, 2,* 131–160.

Behrens, J. T., & Smith, M. L. (1996). Data and data analysis. In D. C. Berliner & R. C. Calfee (Eds.), *Handbook of educational psychology* (pp. 945–989). New York: Macmillan.

Behrens, J. T., & Yu, C. H. (2003). Exploratory data analysis. In J. A. Schinka & W. F. Velicer (Eds.), *Handbook of psychology: Vol. II. Research methods in psychology* (pp. 33–64). New York: Wiley & Sons.

Bellak, L. (1993). *The TAT, CAT, and SAT in clinical use* (5th ed.). Des Moines, IA: Longwood.

Bereiter, C. (1994). Implications of postmodernism for science, or science as progressive discourse. *Educational Psychologist, 29,* 3–12.

Berger, P. (1961). *The voice of solemn assemblies.* Garden City, NY: Doubleday.

Berk, R. A. (Ed.). (1986). *A guide to criterion-referenced test construction.* Baltimore, MD: Johns Hopkins University Press.

Berk, R. A., Lenihan, K. J., & Rossi, P. H. (1980). Crime and poverty: Some experimental evidence from ex-offenders. *American Sociological Review, 45,* 766–786.

Berk, R. A., & Rossi, P. H. (1976). Doing good or worse: Evaluation research politically re-examined. *Social Problems, 23*(February), 337–349.

Berkowitz, L., & Donnerstein, E. (1982). External validity is more than skin deep. *American Psychologist, 37*(3), 245–257.

Berliner, D. (2002). Educational research: The hardest science of all. *Educational Researcher 31*(8), 18–20.

Bernstein, R. J. (1986). *Philosophical profiles.* Philadelphia: University of Pennsylvania Press.

Berrueta-Clement, J. R., Barnett, W. S., & Weikart, D. P. (1985). Changed lives—The effects of the Perry Preschool Program on youths through age 19. In L. H. Aiken & B. H. Kehrer (Eds.), *Evaluation studies review annual* (Vol. 10, pp. 257–279). Beverly Hills, CA: Sage.

Bersoff, D. N. (2003). *Ethical conflicts in psychology* (3rd ed). Washington, DC: American Psychological Association.

Biernacki, P., & Waldorf, D. (1981). Snowball sampling: Problem and technique of chain referral sampling. *Sociological Method and Research, 10*(12), 141–163.

Biklen, S. K., & Casella, R. (2007). *A practical guide to the qualitative dissertation.* New York: Teachers College Press.

Billington, R. A. (1975). *Allen Nevins on history.* New York: Scribner.

Blair, R. C., & Higgins, J. J. (1980). A comparison of the power of Wilcoxon's rank-sum statistic to that of student's t statistic under various nonnormal distributions. *Journal of Educational Statistics, 5*(4), 309–335.

Blair, R. C., & Higgins, J. J. (1985). Comparison of the power of the paired samples t test to that of Wilcoxon's signed-rank test under various population shapes. *Psychological Bulletin, 97*(1), 119–128.

Blee, K. M. (2002). *Inside organized racism: Women in the hate movement.* Berkeley: University of California Press.

Bloom, B. S. (1954). The thought processes of students in discussion. In S. French (Ed.), *Accent on teaching: Experiments in general education* (pp. 23–46). New York: Harper.

Bloom, B. S. (1976). *Human characteristics and school learning.* New York: McGraw-Hill.

Bloor, M. (1997). Techniques of validation in qualitative research: A critical commentary. In G. Dingwall & R. Miller (Eds.), *Context and method in qualitative research* (pp. 37–50). Thousand Oaks, CA: Sage.

Bluebond-Langer, M. (1980). *The private worlds of dying children.* Princeton, NJ: Princeton University Press.

Bogdan, R. C., & Biklen, S. K. (1992). *Qualitative research for education: An introduction to theory and methods* (2nd ed.). Boston: Allyn & Bacon.

Bogdan, R. C., & Biklen, S. K. (2007). *Qualitative research for education: An introduction to theory and methods* (5th ed.). Boston: Allyn & Bacon.

Bogdan, R., Brown, M. A., & Foster, S. B. (1982). Be honest, but not cruel: Staff-parent conversation on a neonatal unit. *Human Organization, 4*(1), 6–16.

Bogdewic, S. P. (1999). Participant observation. In B. F. Crabtree & W. L. Miller (Eds.), *Doing qualitative research* (2nd ed., pp. 47–70). Thousand Oaks, CA: Sage.

Bond, T. G., & Fox, C. M. (2007). *Applying the Rasch Model: Fundamental measurement in the human sciences* (2nd ed.). Mahwah, NJ: Erlbaum.

BonJour, L. (2001). Epistemological problems of perception. Archives of the *Stanford encyclopedia of philosophy.* Retrieved from http://plato.stanford.edu/archives/fall2001/entries/perception-episprob/

Boote, D. N. (2005). Scholars before researchers: On the centrality of the dissertation literature review in research preparation. *Educational Researcher, 34*(6), 3–15.

Borenstein, M. T., & Rothstein, H. (1999). *Comprehensive meta-analysis: A computer program for research synthesis* (1.0.23) [Computer software]. Englewood Cliffs, NJ: Biostat. Retrieved from http://www.meta-analysis.com/

Borman, K. M., & O'Reilly, P. (1987). Learning gender roles in three urban U.S. kindergarten classrooms. *Child and Youth Services, 8,* 43–66.

Boruch, R. F. (1997). *Randomized experiments for planning and evaluation: A practical guide.* Thousand Oaks, CA: Sage.

Boruch, R. F., McSweeney, A. J., & Soderstrom, E. J. (1978). Bibliography: Illustrative randomized field experiments for program planning, development, and evaluation: An illustrative bibliography. *Evaluation Quarterly, 2*(4), 655–695.

Boruch, R. F., & Wothke, W. (Eds.). (1985). *Randomization and field experimentation.* New directions for program evaluation, No. 28, Appendix 1. San Francisco: Jossey-Bass.

Bosk, C. L. (1979). *Forgive and remember: Managing medical failure.* Chicago: University of Chicago Press.

Bouchard, T. J., Jr. (1976). Field research methods: Interviewing, questionnaires, participant observation, systematic observation, unobtrusive measures. In M. D. Dunnette (Ed.), *Handbook of industrial and organizational psychology* (pp. 363–413). Chicago: Rand McNally.

Boulding, K. E. (1968). *Beyond economics.* Ann Arbor: University of Michigan Press.

Bowen, W., & Bok, D. (1998). *The shape of the river: Long-term consequences of considering race in college and university admissions.* Princeton, NJ: Princeton University Press.

Bracht, G. H., & Glass, G. V. (1968). The external validity of experiments. *American Educational Research Journal, 5*(4), 437–474.

Bradburn, N. M., Sudman, S., & Wansink, B. (2006). *Asking questions: The definitive guide to questionnaire design—For market research, political polls, and social and health questionnaires* (Rev. Ed.). San Francisco: Jossey-Bass.

Bradbury, K. L., & Downs, A. (Eds.). (1981). *Do housing allowances work?* Washington, DC: Brookings Institution.

Brandt, P. T., & Williams, J. T. (2007). *Multiple time series models*. Thousand Oaks, CA: Sage.

Brannen, J. (2005). *Mixed methods research: A discussion paper*. Retrieved from http://www.bournemouth.ac.uk/cap/documents/MethodsReviewPaperNCRM-005.pdf

Bratlinger, E., Jimenez, R., Klingman, J., Pugach, M., & Richardson, V. (2005). Qualitative studies in special education. *Exceptional Children, 71*(2), 195–207.

Breland, H. (1987). *Assessing writing skill.* New York: College Board Publications, College Entrance Examination Board.

Brennan, R. L. (2001). *Generalizability theory.* New York: Springer.

Brennan, R. L. (Ed.). (2006). *Educational measurement* (4th ed). Westport, CT: Greenwood.

Brewer, J., & Hunter, A. (2005). *Multimethod research: Synthesizing styles.* Thousand Oaks, CA: Sage.

Brickell, H. M. (1978). The influence of external political factors on the role and methodology of evaluation. In T. P. Cook, M. L. Del Rosario, K. M. Hennigan, M. M. Mark, & W. M. Trochim (Eds.), *Evaluation studies review annual* (Vol. 3, pp. 94–98). Beverly Hills, CA: Sage.

Briggs, J. W. (1978). *An Italian passage: Immigrants to three American cities, 1890–1930.* New Haven, CT: Yale University Press.

Brinberg, D., & McGrath, J. E. (1985). *Validity and the research process.* Beverly Hills, CA: Sage.

Broad, W. (1983). Frauds from 1960 to the present. In B. K. Kilbourne (Ed.), *The dark side of science. Proceedings of the annual meeting of the Pacific Division, American Association for the Advancement of Science, Vol. 1, Part 2* (pp. 26–33). San Francisco: American Association for the Advancement of Science.

Bronfenbrenner, U. (1977). Toward an experimental ecology of human development. *American Psychologist, 32,* 513–531.

Bronowski, J. (2002). *The identity of man.* New York: Prometheus Books.

Brophy, G. W. (2006). *Reading education research: How to avoid getting statistically snookered.* Portsmouth, NH: Heinemann.

Brown, C. L. (2000). Sociolinguistic dynamics of gender in focus groups. In R. Hopson (Ed.), *How and why language matters in evaluation* (pp. 55–68). New directions in evaluation, No. 86. San Francisco: Jossey-Bass.

Buchmann, M., & Floden, R. E. (1989). Research traditions, diversity and progress. *Review of Educational Research, 59,* 241–248.

Burks, B. S., Jensen, D. W., & Terman, L. M. (1930). *The promise of youth: Follow-up studies of 1000 gifted children* (Vol. 3). Stanford, CA: Stanford University Press.

Burton, M. A. B. (1988). *School discipline: Have we lost our sense of purpose in our search for good method?* ERIC Document Reproduction Service No. ED 291 686.

Cahalan, D. T. (1968–69). Correlates of respondent accuracy in the Denver validity survey. *Public Opinion Quarterly, 32,* 607–721.

Cahnmann, M. (2003). The craft, practice and possibility of poetry in educational research. *Educational Researcher, 32*(3), 29–36.

Calishain, T. (2005). *Web search garage*. Upper Saddle River, NJ: Prentice-Hall.

Campbell, D. T. (1969). Definitional versus multiple operationism. In E. S. Overman (Ed.), *Methodology and epistemology for social science: Selected papers* (1988, pp. 31–36). Chicago: University of Chicago Press.

Campbell, D. T. (1988). Descriptive epistemology: Psychological, sociological and evolutionary. In E. S. Overman (Ed.), *Methodology and epistemology for social science: Selected papers of Donald T. Campbell* (pp. 435–486). Chicago: University of Chicago Press.

Campbell, D. T., & Stanley, J. C. (1963). Experimental designs for research on teaching. In N. L. Gage (Ed.), *Handbook of research on teaching* (pp. 171–246). Chicago: Rand McNally.

Cannell, C. F. (1985). Overview: Response bias and interviewer variability in surveys. In T. W. Beed & R. J. Stimson (Eds.), *Survey interviewing: Theory and techniques* (pp. 1–23). North Sydney, Australia: George Allen and Unwin.

Caracelli, V. J., & Greene, J. C. (1993). Data analysis strategies for mixed-method evaluation designs. *Educational Evaluation and Policy Analysis, 15,* 195–207.

Carifio, J., & Biron, R. (1982). Collecting data anonymously: Further findings on the CDRGP technique. *Journal of Alcohol and Drug Education, 27*(2), 38–70.

Carlsmith, L., Merrill, J., & Anderson, C. A. (1979). Ambient temperature and the occurrence of collective violence: A new perspective. *Journal of Personality and Social Psychology, 37,* 337–344.

Carney, T. F. (1990). *Collaborative inquiry methodology.* Windsor, Ontario, Canada: University of Windsor, Department of Instructional Technology.

Carr, E. H. (1962). *What is history?* New York: Knopf.

Carr, W., & Kemmis, S. (1986). *Becoming critical: Education, knowledge and action research.* London: Falmer.

Casey, K. (1995). The new narrative research in education. In M. J. Apple (Ed.), *Review of research in education* (Vol. 21, pp. 211–253). Washington, DC: American Educational Research Association.

Ceci, S. J., & Peters, D. (1984). How blind is blind review? *American Psychologist, 39,* 1491–1494.

Centra, J. A. (1977). *How universities evaluate faculty performance: A survey of department heads (Report BRED–75–5bR).* Princeton, NJ: Graduate Record Examinations Board.

Charmaz, K. (2002). Qualitative interviewing and grounded theory analysis. In J. F. Gubrium & J. A. Holstein (Eds.), *Handbook of interview research: Context and method* (pp. 675–694). Thousand Oaks, CA: Sage.

Charmaz, K. C. (2006). *Constructing grounded theory: A practical guide through qualitative analysis.* Thousand Oaks, CA: Sage.

Chase, W. G., & Simon, H. A. (1973). Perception in chess. *Cognitive Psychology, 4,* 55–81.

Chelimsky, E. (1998). The role of experience in formulating theories of evaluation practice. *American Journal of Evaluation, 19*(1), 35–56.

Chen, P. T. (2005). Conducting telephone surveys. In F. T. L. Leong & J. T. Austin (Eds.), *The psychology research handbook: A guide for graduate students and research assistants.* (2nd ed., pp. 210–226). Thousand Oaks, CA: Sage.

Cialdini, R. B., Borden, R. J., Thorne, A., Walker, M. R., Freeman, S., & Sloan, L. R. (1976). Basking in reflected glory: Three (football) field studies. *Journal of Personality and Social Psychology, 34*, 335–359.

Clausen, J. A. (1993). *American lives: Looking back at the children of the Great Depression.* New York: Free Press (Macmillan).

Cohen, J. (1990). Things I have learned (so far). *American Psychologist, 45,* 1304–1312.

Cohen, M. R., & Nagel, E. (1934). *An introduction to logic and scientific method.* New York: Harcourt Brace.

Coleman, J. S. (1972). *Policy research in the social sciences.* Morristown, NJ: General Learning Press.

Coleman, J. S., Hoffer, T., & Kilgore, S. (1982). *High school achievement: Public, Catholic and private schools compared.* New York: Basic Books.

Collins, H., & Pinch, T. (1993). *The golem: What everyone should know about science.* New York: Cambridge University Press.

Collins, L. M., & Horn, J. L. (1991). *Best methods for analysis of change: Recent advances, unanswered questions, future directions.* Washington, DC: American Psychological Association.

Collins, L. M., & Sayer, A. G. (2001). *New methods for the analysis of change.* Washington, DC: American Psychological Association.

Cook, C., Heath, F., & Thompson, R. L. (2002). A meta-analysis of response rates in Web-or Internet-based surveys. *Educational and Psychological Measurement, 60*(6), 821–836.

Cook, T. D., & Campbell, D. T. (1979). *Quasi-experimentation: Design and analysis issues for field settings.* Chicago: Rand McNally.

Cook, T. D., Cooper, H., & Cordray, D. S. (1992). *Meta-analysis for explanation: A casebook.* New York: Russell Sage Foundation.

Coombs, C. H., Dawes, R. M., & Tversky, A. (1981). *Mathematical psychology: An elementary introduction.* Englewood Cliffs, NJ: Prentice-Hall.

Cooper, H., & Hedges, L. V. (Eds.). (1994a). *The handbook of research synthesis.* New York: Russell Sage Foundation.

Cooper, H., & Hedges, L. V. (1994b). Research synthesis as a scientific enterprise. In H. Cooper & L. V. Hedges (Eds.), *The handbook of research synthesis* (pp. 3–14). New York: Russell Sage Foundation.

Cooper, H., & Rosenthal, R. (1980). Statistical versus traditional procedures for summarizing research findings. *Psychological Bulletin, 87*(3), 442–449.

Cooper, H., Nye, B., Charlton, K., Lindsay, J., & Greathouse, S. (1996). The effects of summer vacation on achievement test scores: A narrative and meta-analytic review. *Review of Educational Research, 66,* 227–268.

Cooper, H., Robinson, J. C., & Patall, E. A. (2006). Does homework improve academic achievement? A synthesis of research, 1987–2003. *Review of Educational Research, 76,* 1–62.

Cooper, H. M. (1985). Literature searching strategies of integrative research reviews. *American Psychologist, 40*(11), 1267–1269.

Cooper, H. M. (2006). *The battle over homework: Common ground for administrators, teachers, and parents.* Thousand Oaks, CA: Corwin.

Cordray, D. S. (1993). Strengthening causal interpretations of nonexperimental data: The role of meta-analysis. In L. Sechrest (Ed.), *Program evaluation: A pluralistic enterprise* (pp. 59–96). New directions for program evaluation, No. 60. San Francisco: Jossey-Bass.

Corno, L., Cronbach, L. J., Kupermintz, H., Lohman, D., Mandinach, E. B., Porteus, A. W., & Talbert, J. E. for The Stanford Aptitude Seminar. (2002). *Remaking the concept of aptitude: Extending the legacy of Richard E. Snow.* Mahwah, NJ: Erlbaum.

Coscarelli, W. C., & Stonewater, J. K. (1979). Understanding psychological styles in instructional development consultation. *Journal of Instructional Development, 3*(2), 16–22.

Cosper, R. (1972). Interviewer effect in a survey of drinking practices. *Sociological Quarterly, 13*(2), 228–236.

Cox, C. M. (1926). *The early mental traits of three hundred geniuses* (Vol. 2). Stanford, CA: Stanford University Press.

Crabtree, B. F., & Miller, W. L. (1999a). Clinical research: A multimethod typology and qualitative roadmap. In B. F. Crabtree & W. L. Miller (Eds.), *Doing qualitative research* (2nd ed., pp. 3–30). Thousand Oaks, CA: Sage.

Crabtree, B. F., & Miller, W. L. (Eds.). (1999b). *Doing qualitative research* (2nd ed.). Thousand Oaks, CA: Sage.

Crain, R. L. (1984). *Is nineteen really better than ninety-three?* Washington, DC: National Institute of Education.

Crane, V. R., & Heim, A. W. (1950). The effects of repeatedly testing the same group on the same intelligence test. Part III, further experiments and general conclusions. *Quarterly Journal of Experimental Psychology, 2*, 82–197.

Creswell, J. W., & Plano Clark, V. L. (2007). *Designing and conducting mixed methods research.* Thousand Oaks, CA: Sage.

Cronbach, L. J. (1975). Beyond the two disciplines of scientific psychology. *American Psychologist 30*, 116–127.

Cronbach, L. J. (1982). *Designing evaluations of educational and social programs.* San Francisco: Josscy-Bass.

Cronbach, L. J., Gleser, G. C., Nanda, H., & Rajaratnam, N. (1972). *The dependability of behavioral measurements: Theory of generalizability of scores and profiles.* New York: Wiley.

Cronbach, L. J., & Snow, R. E. (1977). *Aptitudes and instructional methods: A handbook for researchers on interactions.* New York: Irvington.

Cronbach, L. J., & Suppes, P. (1955). Construct validity in psychological tests. *Psychological Bulletin, 52*, 281–302.

Cronbach, L. J., & Suppes, P. (1969). *Research for tomorrow's schools: Disciplined inquiry for education.* New York: Macmillan.

Crotty, M. (1999). *The foundations of social research: Meaning and perspective in the research process.* London: Sage.

Culler, R. E., & Holahan, C. J. (1980). Test anxiety and academic performance: The effects of study related behaviors. *Journal of Educational Psychology, 72*(1), 16–20.

Cusick, P. A. (1980). Personal communication.

Daniels, A. K. (1983). Self-deception and self-discovery in fieldwork. *Qualitative Sociology, 6*(3), 195–214.

Darley, J. M., & Batson, C. D. (1973). From Jerusalem to Jericho: A study of situational and dispositional variables in helping behavior. *Journal of Personality and Social Psychology, 27*, 100–108.

Daves, R., Krosnick, J., Callegaro, M., & De Keulenaer, F. (2006). Interviewer effects in a RDD telephone pre-election poll in Minneapolis 2001. An analysis of the effects of interviewer race and gender. Paper presented at the annual meeting of the American Association for Public Opinion Association, Fontainebleau Resort, Miami Beach, FL (October 5, 2006). Retrieved from http://www.allacademic.com/meta/p17173_index.html

De Chardin, P. T., (1961). *The phenomenon of man.* New York: Harper and Row.

De Groot, E. V. (2002). Learning through interviewing: Students and teachers talk about learning and schooling. *Educational Psychologist, 37*(1), 41–52.

De Vries, R., Anderson, M. S., & Martinson, B. C. (2006). Normal misbehavior: Scientists talk about the ethics of research. *Journal of Empirical Research on Human Research Ethics, 1*, 43–50. Retrieved from http://caliber.ucpress.net/doi/abs/10.1525/jer.2006.1.1.43

DeAngelis, T. (1988). Gerontologists lament practice-research gap. *American Psychological Association Monitor, 19*(2), 9.

DeBack, V., & Mentkowski, M. (1986). Does the baccalaureate make a difference: Differentiating nurse performance by education and experience. *Journal of Nursing Education, 25*(7), 275–285.

DeMarrais, K. B. (Ed.). (1998). *Inside stories: Qualitative research reflections.* Mahwah, NJ: Erlbaum.

Denmark, F. L. (1984). Zeigarnik effect. In R. J. Corsini (Ed.), *Encyclopedia of psychology*, Vol. 3 (pp. 484–485). New York: John Wiley.

Denzin, N. K. (1978). *The research act: A theoretical introduction to sociological methods* (2nd ed.). New York: McGraw-Hill.

Denzin, N. K., & Lincoln, Y. S. (Eds.). (2000). *Handbook of qualitative research* (2nd ed.). Thousand Oaks: Sage.

di Gregorio, S. (2000). Using Nvivo for your literature review. Paper presented at Strategies in Qualitative Research: Issues and Results from Analysis Using QSR NVivo and NUD*IST (Conference at the Institute of Education, London), September 29–30. Retrieved from http://www.sdgassociates.com/mainframe.html (click on Training Tasters)

di Gregorio, S. (2003). Teaching grounded theory with QSR NVivo. *Qualitative Research Journal*, Special Issue 2003, 78–94. Retrieved from http://latrobe.edu.au/aqr (click on Journals)

Dichter, D. N., & Roznowski, M. (2005). Basic statistical analysis. In F. T. L. Leong & J. T. Austin (Eds.), *The psychology research handbook: A guide for graduate students and research assistants* (2nd ed., pp. 293–305). Thousand Oaks, CA: Sage.

Dillman, D. A. (2007). *Mail and internet surveys: The tailored design method* (2nd ed.). San Francisco: Wiley.

Dogpile. (2005). *Different engines, different results: Web researchers not always finding what they're looking for online.* Retrieved from www.dogpile.com/dogpile/ws/metasearch/_iceUrlFlag=11?_IceUrl=true.

Donmoyer, R. (2001). Paradigm talk reconsidered. In V. Richardson (Ed.), *Handbook of research on teaching* (4th ed., pp. 174–250). Washington, DC: American Educational Research Association.

Downing, S. M. & Haladyna, T. M. (Eds.) (2006). *Handbook of test development.* Mahwah, NJ: Earlbaum.

Duffy, G., & Roehler, L. (1990). The tension between information giving and instructional explanation and teacher change. In J. Brophy (Ed.), *Advances in research on teaching: Vol. 1. Teaching for meaningful understanding and self-regulated learning* (pp. 1–33). Greenwich, CT: JAI.

Dunbar, K. (1995). How scientists really reason: Scientific reasoning in real-world laboratories. In R. J. Sternberg & J. Davidson (Eds.), *The nature of insight* (pp. 365–395). Cambridge, MA: MIT Press. Retrieved from http://www.dartmouth.edu/~kndunbar/pubpdfs/DunbarStern.pdf

Dunbar, K. (1999). How scientists build models in vivo science as a window on the scientific mind. In L. Magnani, N. Nersessian, & P. Thagard (Eds.), *Model-based reasoning in scientific discovery* (pp. 85–99). New York: Plenum. Retrieved from http://www.dartmouth.edu/~kndunbar/pubpdfs/KDMBR99.pdf

Dunbar, K., & Fugelsang, J. (2005). Scientific thinking and reasoning. In K. J. Holyoak & R. Morrison (Eds.), *Cambridge handbook of thinking & reasoning* (pp. 705–726). New York: Cambridge University Press. Retrieved from http://www.dartmouth.edu/~kndunbar/pubpdfs/DFholyebk.pdf

Duncan, O. D. (1984). *Notes on social measurement: Historical and critical.* New York: Russell Sage Foundation.

Edwards, J. A., & Lampert, M. D. (Eds.). (1993). *Talking data: Transcription and coding in discourse research.* Hillsdale, NJ: Erlbaum.

Edwards, P. N., & Schneider, S. H. (2001). Self-governance and peer review in science-for-policy: The case of the IPCC second assessment report. In C. A. Miller & P. N. Edwards

(Eds.), *Changing the atmosphere: Expert knowledge and environmental governance* (pp. 219–246). Cambridge, MA: MIT Press.

Einhorn, H. J., & Hogarth, R. M. (1986). Judging probable cause. *American Psychologist, 99*, 3–19.

Einstein, A., & Infeld, L. (1938). *The evolution of physics.* New York: Simon and Schuster.

Eisner, E. W. (1976). Educational connoisseurship and criticism: Their form and function in educational evaluation. *Journal of Aesthetic Education, 10*(3–4), 135–150.

Eisner, E. W. (1981). On the differences between scientific and artistic approaches to qualitative research. *Educational Researcher, 10*, 5–9.

Eisner, E. W. (1991). Taking a second look: Educational connoisseurship revisited. In M. W. McLaughlin & D. C. Phillips (Eds.), *Evaluation and education at quarter century* (pp. 169–187). Ninetieth yearbook of the National Society for the Study of Education, Part II. Chicago: University of Chicago Press.

Elliott, M. (2006). *Internet surveys.* QUARLS-L listserv archives, October 2006, week 2 (Oct. 12, 2006). Retrieved from http://listserv.uga.edu/archives/quarls-1.html

Ellsworth, P. D. (1977). From abstract ideas to concrete instances: Some guidelines for choosing natural research settings. *American Psychologist, 32*(8), 604–615.

Elstein, A. S., Shulman, L. S., & Sprafka, S. A. (1978). *Medical problem solving: An analysis of clinical reasoning.* Cambridge, MA: Harvard University Press.

Elstein, A. S., Shulman, L. S., & Sprafka, S. A. (1990). Medical problem solving: A ten-year retrospective. *Evaluation & the Health Professions, 13*, 5–36.

Ely, M. (1991). *Doing qualitative research: Circles in circles.* Philadelphia: Falmer.

Emerson, R. M., Fretz, R. I., & Shaw, L. L. (1995). *Writing ethnographic fieldnotes.* Chicago: University of Chicago Press.

Ercikan, K., & Roth, W. (2006). What good is polarizing research into qualitative and quantitative? *Educational Researcher 35*(5), 14–23.

Erdos, P. L. (1970). *Professional mail surveys.* New York: McGraw-Hill.

Erickson, F. (1986). Qualitative methods of research on teaching. In M. Wittrock (Ed.), *Handbook of research on teaching* (3rd ed., pp. 119–161). New York: Macmillan.

Ericson, D. P., & Ellett, F. S., Jr. (1982). Interpretation, understanding and educational research. *Teachers College Record, 83,* 497–513.

Ess, C., & the Association of Internet Researchers Ethics Working Committee. (2002). Ethical decision-making and Internet research: Recommendations from the AoIR Ethics Working Committee. Retrieved from http://www.aoir.org/reports/ethics.pdf

Everhart, R. B. (1977). Between stranger and friend: Some consequences of "long term" field work in schools. *American Educational Research Journal, 14*(1), 1–15.

Exner, J. E., Jr. (2003). *The Rorschach: A comprehensive system: Vol. 1. Basic foundations and principles of interpretation* (4th ed.). Hoboken, NJ: Wiley.

Eysenbach, G., & Till, J. E. (2001). Ethical issues in qualitative research on Internet communities. *British Medical Journal, 323*, 1103–1105. Retrieved from http://www.bmj.com/cgi/content/full/323/7321/1103#

Fairweather, G. W., & Tornatzky, L. G. (1977). *Experimental method for social policy research.* New York: Pergamon Press.

Feldman, M. S., Bell, J., & Berger, M. T. (2003). *Gaining access: A practical and theoretical guide for qualitative researchers.* Walnut Creek, CA: AltaMira.

Ferber, R., & Verdoorn, P. J. (1962). *Research methods in economics and business.* New York: Macmillan.

Ferris, T. (1981). The spectral messenger. *Science, 81*(2), 66–71.

Fetterman, D. M. (1989). *Ethnography: Step by step.* Newbury Park, CA: Sage.

Fetterman, D. M., Kaftarian, S. J., & Wandersman, A. (Eds.). (1996) *Empowerment evaluation: Knowledge and tools for self-assessment and accountability.* Thousand Oaks, CA: Sage.

Fielding, N. G., & Fielding, J. L. (1985). *Linking data.* Qualitative research methods series: Vol. 4. Beverly Hills, CA: Sage.

Fillenbaum, S. (1966). Prior deception and subsequent experimental performance: The "faithful" subject. *Journal of Personality and Social Psychology, 4,* 532–537.

Firestone, W. A. (1993). Alternative arguments for generalizing from data as applied to qualitative research. *Educational Researcher, 22*(4), 16–23.

Fischer, C. T. (1999). Designing qualitative research reports for publication. In M. Kopala & L. Suzuki (Eds.), *Using qualitative methods in psychology* (pp. 105–119). Thousand Oaks, CA: Sage.

Fischer, D. H. (1970). *Historian's fallacies: Toward a logic of historical thought.* New York: Harper & Row.

Fisher, R. A. (1959). *Statistical methods and scientific inference* (2nd ed. rev.). Edinburgh: Oliver and Boyd.

Fiske, D. W., & Fogg, L. (1990). But the reviewers are making different criticisms of my paper! *American Psychologist, 45,* 591–598.

Flanders, N. A. (1970). *Analyzing teacher behavior.* Reading, MA: Addison Wesley.

Florio, S. E. (1978). Learning how to go to school: An ethnography of interaction in a kindergarten first grade classroom. *Dissertation Abstracts International, 39,* 3239A. (University Microfilms No. 78–23, 676).

Foddy, W. (1993). *Constructing questions for interviews and questionnaires: Theory and practice in social research.* Cambridge, UK: Cambridge University Press.

Fontana, A. (2002). Postmodern trends in interviewing. In J. F. Gubrium & J. A. Holstein (Eds.), *Handbook of interview research: Context and method* (pp. 161–189). Thousand Oaks, CA: Sage.

Fox, R. J., Crask, M. R., & Kim, J. (1988). Mail survey response rate: A meta-analysis of selected techniques for inducing response. *Public Opinion Quarterly, 52,* 467–491.

Frechtling, J., & Sharp, L. (1997). *User-friendly handbook of mixed method evaluation.* Arlington, VA: National Science Foundation.

Frederiksen, N., Glaser, R., Lesgold, A., & Shafto, M. G. (Eds.). (1990). *Diagnostic monitoring of skill and knowledge acquisition.* Hillsdale, NJ: Erlbaum.

Freed, M. N. (Ed.), Hess, R. K., & Ryan, J. M. (2002). *The educator's desk reference: A sourcebook of educational information and research* (2nd ed.). Westport, CT: Praeger.

Freedman, D., Pisani, R., & Purves, R. (1997). *Statistics* (3rd ed.). New York: Norton.

Freeman, M., deMarrais, K., Preissle, J., Roulston, K., & St. Pierre, E. A. (2007). Standards of evidence in qualitative research: An incitement to discourse. *Educational Researcher, 36*(1), 25–32.

Freire, P. (1970). *Pedagogy of the oppressed.* New York: Seabury.

Frey, J. H., & Oishi, S. M. (1995). *How to conduct interviews by telephone and in person. Survey Kit: Vol 4.* Thousand Oaks, CA: Sage.

Friedman, J., & Weinberg, D. (Eds.). (1983). *The great housing experiment.* Beverly Hills, CA: Sage.

Friedman, V. J., & Rothman, J. (n.d.). *Action evaluation knowledge creation in social-education programs.* Retrieved from http://www.ariagroup.com/libraryC3.html

Frye, N. (1981). The bridge of language. *Science, 112,* 127–132.

Gage, N. L. (1996). Confronting counsels of despair for the behavioral sciences. *Educational Researcher, 25*(April), 5–15, 22.

Gaiser, T. (1997). Conducting online focus groups. *Social Science Computer Review, 15,* 135–144.

Gale Research Company. (1983–present). *Surveys, polls, censuses and forecasts directory.* Detroit, MI: Author.

Gallego, M., Hollingsworth, S., & Whitenack, D. (2001). Relational knowing in the reform of educational cultures. *Teachers College Record, 103*(2), 240–266.

Gans, H. J. (1962). *The urban villagers: Groups and class in the life of Italian-Americans*. New York: Free Press.

Garvey, W. D., Lin, N., & Nelson, C. (1970). Communication in the physical and social sciences. *Science, 170,* 1166–1173.

Geertz, C. (1973). Thick description: Toward an interpretive theory of culture. In *The interpretation of culture: Selected essays* (pp. 3–30). New York: Basic.

Geisinger, K. F., Spies, R. A., Carlson, J. F., & Plake, B. S. (2007). *The seventeenth mental measurements yearbook*. Lincoln: Buros Institute of Mental Measurements, University of Nebraska.

Gerberich, J. R. (1956). *Specimen objective test items: A guide to achievement test construction*. New York: Longman, Green and Co.

Gergen, K. J. (1994). *Toward transformation of social knowledge* (2nd ed.). Thousand Oaks, CA: Sage.

Gergen, K. J., & Gergen, M. M. (2000). Qualitative inquiry: Tensions and transformations. In N. K. Denzin & Y. S. Lincoln (Eds.), *Handbook of qualitative research* (2nd ed., pp. 1025–1046). Thousand Oaks, CA: Sage.

Gerstel, N. (1993). The life voyage. [Review of American lives: Looking back at children of the Great Depression.] *Science, 260,* 1157, 1159–1161.

Getzels, J. W. (1982). The problem of the problem. In R. M. Hogarth (Ed.), *Question framing and response consistency* (pp. 37–49). New directions for methodology of social and behavioral science, No. 11. San Francisco: Jossey-Bass.

Getzels, J. W., & Csikszentmihalyi, M. (1976). *The creative vision: A longitudinal study of problem findings in art*. New York: Wiley.

Gibbs, G. R. (2002). *Qualitative data analysis: Explorations with NVivo*. Birmingham, UK: Open University Press.

Gilbert, L. (2002). *Qual-Software Archives*, 7/26. Retrieved from http://www.jiscmail.ac.uk/cgi-bin/webadmin?A2=ind0207&L=qual-software&T=0&F=&S=&P=5254

Gladwin, C. H. (1989). *Ethnographic decision tree modeling*. Newbury Park, CA: Sage.

Glaser, B., & Strauss, A. (1967). *The discovery of grounded theory: Strategies for qualitative research*. Chicago: Aldine.

Glass, G. V. (1976). Primary, secondary, and meta-analysis research. *Educational Researcher, 5*(10), 3–8.

Glass, G. V. (1995). The next-to-last word on meta-analysis [Review of Handbook of Research Synthesis]. *Contemporary Psychology, 40,* 736–738.

Glass, G. V. (2000). *Meta-analysis at 25*. Retrieved from http://glass.ed.asu.edu/gene/papers/meta25.html

Glass, G. V., McGaw, B., & Smith, M. L. (1981). *Meta-analysis in social research*. Beverly Hills, CA: Sage.

Glass, G. V., & Smith, M. L. (1979). Meta-analysis of research on class size and achievement. *Educational Evaluation and Policy Analysis, 1*(1), 2–16.

Glavin, J., & Quay, H. (1969). Behavior disorders. *Review of Educational Research, 39,* 83–102.

Glesne, C., & Peshkin, A. (1992). *Becoming qualitative researchers: An introduction*. White Plains, NY: Longman.

Goetz, J., & LeCompte, M. (1984). *Ethnography and qualitative design in educational research*. Orlando, FL: Academic.

Goffman, E. (1983). The interaction order. *American Sociological Review, 48,* 1–17.

Goldberger, A. S., & Cain, G. G. (1982). The causal analysis of cognitive outcomes in the Coleman, Hoffer and Kilgore Report. *Sociology of Education, 55*(2–3), 103–122.

Goldstein, J. H., & Arms, R. L. (1971). Effects of observing athletic contests. *Sociometry, 34,* 83–90.

Good, T., & Brophy, J. (1977). *Educational psychology: A realistic approach*. New York: Holt, Rinehart and Winston.

Goodman, S. N., Berlin, J., Fletcher, S. W., & Fletcher, R. H. (1994). Manuscript quality before and after peer review and editing at Annals of Internal Medicine. *Annals of Internal Medicine, 121*(1), 11–21.

Google, Inc. (2004). *Google Print Library Project*. Retrieved from http://print.google.com/googleprint/library.html#1

Gottman, J. M., Murray, J. D., Swanson, C., Tyson, R., & Swanson, K. R. (2002). *The mathematics of marital conflict*. Cambridge, MA: MIT Press.

Gottschalk, L. A. (1956). *Understanding history*. New York: Knopf.

Gouldner, A. W. (1954). *Patterns of industrial bureaucracy*. Glencoe, IL: The Free Press.

Gove, P. P. (Ed.). (1976). *Webster's third new international dictionary of the English language* (unabridged). Springfield, MA: G. & C. Merriam Co.

Grant, G. P. (1979). *On competence: A critical analysis of competence-based reforms in higher education*. San Francisco: Jossey-Bass.

Grant, R. (1986). Advice to dissertation writers. *Political Science, 19*(1), 64–65.

Green, T. F. (1971). *The activities of teaching*. New York: McGraw-Hill.

Greene, J. C. (2001). Mixing social inquiries. In V. Richardson (Ed.), *Handbook of research on teaching* (4th ed., pp. 251–258). Washington, DC: American Educational Research Association.

Greene, J. C., & Caracelli, V. J. (1997). *Advances in mixed-method evaluation: The challenges and benefits of integrating diverse paradigms*. New directions for evaluation, Number 74. San Francisco: Jossey-Bass.

Greene, J. C., & Caracelli, V. J. (2003). Making paradigmatic sense of mixed methods practice. In A. Tashakkori & C. Teddlie (Eds.), *Handbook of mixed methods in social and behavioral research* (pp. 91–110). Thousand Oaks, CA: Sage.

Griffin, L., & Ragin, C. C. (1994). Some observations on formal methods of qualitative analysis. *Sociological Methods and Research, 23*, 4–21.

Groenewald, T. (2004). A phenomenological research design illustrated. *International Journal of Qualitative Methods, 3*(1) April, 2004. Retrieved from http://www.ualberta.ca/~iiqm/backissues/3_1/pdf/groenewals.pdf

Groves, R. M. (1990). Theories and methods of telephone surveys. In W. R. Scott (Ed.), *Annual Review of Sociology*, 16, 221–240. Palo Alto: Annual Reviews.

Groves, R. M., Fowler, F. J., Jr., Couper, M. P., Lepkowski, J. M., Singer, E., & Tourangeau, R. (2004). *Survey methodology*. Hoboken, NJ: Wiley.

Groves, R. M., & Magilavy, L. J. (1981). Increasing response rates to telephone surveys: A door in the face or foot-in-the-door? *Public Opinion Quarterly, 45*(3), 346–358.

Grunder, T. M. (1983). DHHS Human subjects protection: The new regulations revisited. *Health Matrix, 1*(2), 37–41.

Grunder, T. M. (1986). *Informed consent: A tutorial*. Owings Mills, MD: National Health Publishing.

Guba, E. G., & Lincoln, Y. S. (1982a, April). *Causality vs. plausibility: Alternative stances for inquiry into human behavior*. Unpublished paper presented at the Annual Meeting of the American Educational Research Association, 1982.

Guba, E. G., & Lincoln, Y. S. (1982b). Epistemological and methodological bases of naturalistic inquiry. *Educational Communications and Technology Journal, 30*, 233–252.

Guba, E. G., & Lincoln, Y. S. (1985). *Naturalistic inquiry*. Beverly Hills, CA: Sage.

Guba, E. G., & Lincoln, Y. S. (1986). The countenances of fourth-generation evaluation: Description, judgment, and negotiation. In D. S. Cordray & M. W. Lipsey (Eds.), *Evaluation studies review annual* (Vol. 11, pp. 70–88). Newbury Park, CA: Sage.

Guba, E. G., & Lincoln, Y. S. (1989). *Fourth generation evaluation*. Newbury Park, CA: Sage.

Gubrium, J. F., & Holstein, J. A. (Eds.). (2002). *Handbook of interview research: Context and method*. Thousand Oaks, CA: Sage.

Guenzel, P. J., Berckmans, T. R., & Cannell, C. F. (1983). *General interviewing techniques: A self-instructional workbook for telephone and personal interviewer training.* Ann Arbor: Survey Research Center, Institute for Social Research, University of Michigan.

Guilford, J. P., & Fruchter, B. (1978). *Fundamental statistics in psychology and education* (6th ed.). New York: McGraw-Hill.

Gulliksen, H. (1986). Perspective on educational measurement. *Applied Psychological Measurement, 10,* 109–132.

Gustafson, T. (1980). Why doesn't Soviet science do better than it does? In L. L. Lubrano & S. G. Grossman (Eds.), *The social context of Soviet science* (pp. 31–68). Boulder, CO: Westview.

Guy, W., Gross, M., & Dennis, H. (1967). An alternative to double-blind procedure. *American Journal of Psychiatry, 123*(12), 1505–1512.

Gwartney, P. (2007) *The telephone interviewer's handbook.* Thousand Oaks, CA: Sage.

Haack, S. (2001, April). An epistemologist in the bramble-bush: At the supreme court with Mr. Joiner. *Journal of Health Politics, Policy and Law, 26*(2). Retrieved from http://www.ahrq.gov/clinic/jhppl/haack1.htm

Habermas, J. (1984). *Theory of communicative action: Vol. 1. Reason and the rationalization of society.* Boston: Beacon.

Hage, J., & Meeker, B. F. (1988). *Social causality.* Contemporary social research series, No. 16. Boston: Unwin Hyman.

Haladyna, T. M. (2004). *Developing and validating multiple-choice items* (3rd ed.). Hillsdale, NJ: Erlbaum.

Hall, J. A., Rosenthal, R., Tickle-Degnen, L., & Mosteller, F. (1994). Hypotheses and problems in research synthesis. In H. Cooper & L. Hedges (Eds.), *The handbook of research synthesis* (pp. 17–28). New York: Russell Sage Foundation.

Hamilton, W. L. (1979). *A social experiment in program administration: The housing allowance administrative agency experiment.* Cambridge, MA: Abt Books.

Hammersley, M., & Atkinson, P. (1983, 1995). *Ethnography: Principles in practice* (1st & 2nd eds.). London: Tavistock.

Hancock, G. R., & Klockars, A. J. (1996). The quest for (alpha); Developments in multiple comparison procedures in the quarter century since Games (1971). *Review of Educational Research, 66,* 269–306.

Hansen, R. A., & Robinson, L. M. (1980). Testing the effectiveness of alternative foot-in-the-door manipulations. *Journal of Marketing Research, 17*(3), 359–364.

Hanson, N. R. (1958). *Patterns of discovery.* Cambridge, UK: Cambridge University Press.

Hargreaves, A. (1996). Transforming knowledge: Blurring the boundaries between research, policy and practice. *Educational Evaluation and Policy Analysis, 18,* 105–122.

Harrington, B. (2002). Obtrusiveness as strategy in ethnographic research. *Qualitative Sociology, 25*(1), 49–61.

Harris, R. J. (1973). Answering questions containing marked and unmarked adjectives and adverbs. *Journal of Experimental Psychology, 97,* 399–401.

Hart, C. (2001). *Doing a literature review: A comprehensive guide for the social sciences.* London: Sage.

Hays, W. L. (1994). *Statistics* (5th ed.). Fort Worth, TX: Harcourt Brace College Publishers.

Heath, A. W. (1997). The proposal in qualitative research. *The Qualitative Report, 3*(1). Retrieved from http://www.nova.edu/ssss/QR/QR3-1/heath.html

Hedges, L. V. (1982). Estimation of effect size from a series of independent experiments. *Psychological Bulletin, 92*(2), 490–499.

Hedges, L. V. (1987). How hard is hard science, how soft is soft science? *American Psychologist, 42,* 443–455.

Hedges, L. V., & Olkin, I. (1985). *Statistical methods for meta-analysis.* Orlando, FL: Academic.

Hedges, L. V., & Vevea, J. L. (1996a). Estimating effect size under publication bias: Small sample properties and robustness of a random effects selection model. *Journal of Educational and Behavioral Statistics, 21,* 299–332.

Hedges, L. V., & Vevea, J. L. (1996b). Fixed- and random-effects models in meta-analysis. *Psychological Methods, 3,* 486–504.

Hendricks, M., & Papagiannis, M. (1990). Do's and don'ts for offering effective recommendations. *Evaluation Practice, 11,* 121–125.

Henry, G. T. (Ed.). (1997). *Creating effective graphs: Solutions for a variety of evaluation data.* New directions for evaluation, No. 73. San Francisco: Jossey-Bass.

Henshel, R. L. (1980a). Seeking inoperative laws: Toward the deliberate use of unnatural experimentation. In L. Freese (Ed.), *Theoretical methods in sociology: Seven essays* (pp. 175–199). Pittsburgh: University of Pittsburgh Press.

Henshel, R. L. (1980b). The purposes of laboratory experimentation and the virtues of deliberate artificiality. *Journal of Experimental Social Psychology, 16,* 406–478.

Hewett, F., & Blake, P. (1973). Teaching the emotionally disturbed. In R. M. W. Travers (Ed.), *Handbook of research on teaching* (2nd ed., pp. 657–688). New York: Macmillan.

Hillard, J. M. & Easter, B. J. (2000). *Where to find what: A handbook to reference service* (5th ed.). Lanham, MD: Scarecrow Press.

Himmelfarb, S., & Edgell, S. E. (1980). Additive constants model: A randomized response technique for eliminating evasiveness to quantitative response questions. *Psychological Bulletin, 87*(3), 525–530.

Hoaglin, D. C., Light, R. J., McPeek, B., Mosteller, F., & Stoto, M. A. (1982). *Data for decisions: Information strategies for policymakers.* Cambridge, MA: Abt Books.

Hodkinson, P. (2000). *The Goth scene as trans-level culture.* Unpublished PhD Thesis. Centre for Urban and Regional Studies, University of Birmingham, UK.

Hoffmann-Riem, C. (1986). Adoptive parenting and the norm of family emotionality. *Qualitative Sociology, 9,* 162–177.

Hollingsworth, S., & Sockett, H. (Eds.). (1994). *Teacher research and educational reform.* Ninety-third yearbook of the National Society for the Study of Education, Part I. Chicago: University of Chicago Press.

Hollowood, T. M., Salisbury, C. L., & Rainforth, B. (1995). Use of instructional time in classrooms serving students with and without severe disabilities. *Exceptional Children, 61,* 242–252.

House, E. R. (1976). Justice in evaluation. In G. V. Glass (Ed.), *Evaluation studies review annual* (Vol. 1, pp. 75–100). Beverly Hills, CA: Sage.

House, E. R. (1980). *Evaluating with validity.* Beverly Hills, CA: Sage.

House, E. R. (1990). Trends in evaluation. *Educational Researcher, 19*(3), 24–27.

House, E. R. (2001). Unfinished business: Causes and values. *The American Journal of Evaluation, 22*(3), 309–315.

Hovland, C. I., Lumsdaine, A. A., & Sheffield, F. D. (1949). *Experiments on mass communication.* Princeton, NJ: Princeton University Press.

Howe, K. R. (2005). The education science question: A symposium. *Education Theory, 55*(3), 235.

Howell, W. (1995). We can "build" data but will they come? *American Psychological Association Monitor, 26,* 28.

Huehls, F. (2005). An evening of grounded theory: Teaching process through demonstration and simulation. *The Qualitative Report, 10*(2), 328–338. Retrieved from http://www.nova.edu/ssss/QR/QR10-2/huehls.pdf

Huff, D. (1954). *How to lie with statistics.* New York: Norton.

Hughes, E. C. (1971). *The sociological eye.* Chicago: Aldine.

Hume, D. (1902). *Enquiry concerning human understanding.* (L. A. Selby-Bigge, Ed., 2nd ed.) Oxford, England: Clarendon Press. (Originally published in 1748.)

Humphreys, L. (1975). *The tearoom trade: Impersonal sex in public places* (2nd ed.). Chicago: Aldine.

Hunt, M. (1982, September 12). Research through deception. *New York Times Magazine, 66,* 138–144.

Hunter, J. E. & Schmidt, F. L. (2004). *Methods of meta-analysis: Correcting error and bias in research findings* (2nd ed.). Thousand Oaks, CA: Sage.

Huxley, E. (1982). *The flame trees of Thika: Memories of an African childhood.* London: Chatto and Windus.

Hyman, H. H. (1954). *Interviewing in social research.* Chicago: University of Chicago Press.

Idea Works. (2008). *Qualrus: The intelligent qualitative analysis program.* Retrieved from http://www.ideaworks.com/qualrus/example.html

Isreal, P. (1998). *Edison: A life of invention.* New York: Wiley.

Jaeger, R. M. (1984). *Sampling in education and the social sciences.* New York: Longman.

Jaeger, R. M. (1990). *Statistics: A spectator sport* (2nd ed.). Beverly Hills, CA: Sage.

Jaffe, E. (2007). How we reflect on behavior. *Observer, 20*(5), 20–23, 25.

Jahoda, M., Deutsch, M., & Cook, S. W. (1951). *Research methods in social relations with especial reference to prejudice.* New York: Dryden.

Jefferson, T., Alderson, P., Wager, E., & Davidoff, F. (2002). Effects of editorial peer review: A systematic review. *Journal of the American Medical Association, 287,* 2784–2786.

Johnson, J. M. (1975). *Doing field research.* New York: Free Press.

Johnson, R. H. (1978). Individual styles of decision-making: A theoretical model for counseling. *Personnel and Guidance Journal, 56*(9), 530–536.

Johnson, T. H. (1966). *Oxford companion to American history.* New York: Oxford University Press.

Joint Committee on Standards for Educational and Psychological Testing [U.S.]; American Educational Research Association; American Psychological Association; National Council on Measurement in Education. (1999). *Standards for educational and psychological testing.* Washington, DC: American Educational Research Association.

Jonassen, D. H. (1987). Assessing cognitive structure: Verifying a method using pattern notes. *Journal of Research and Development in Education, 20*(3), 1–14.

Jones, L. V., & Appelbaum, M. I. (1990). Psychometric methods. In M. R. Rosenzweig & L. W. Porter (Eds.), *Annual review of psychology*, *40* (pp. 23–44). Palo Alto, CA: Annual Reviews.

Judson, H. F. (1980). *The search for solutions.* New York: Holt, Rinehart and Winston.

Judson, H. F. (2004). *The great betrayal: Fraud in science.* Orlando, FL: Harcourt.

Jung, C. G. (1976). Psychological types (1923). In Appendix of *Collected works of C. G. Jung* (2nd ed., Vol. 6, pp. 510–523). Princeton, NJ: Princeton University Press.

Kagan, N., Krathwohl, D. R., & Farquhar, W. (1965). *IPR-interpersonal process recall by videotape in exploratory studies of counseling and teaching-learning.* East Lansing: College of Education, Michigan State University.

Kagen, J., Rosman, B. L., Kay, D., Albert, J., & Phillips, W. (1964). Information processing in the child: Significance of analytic and reflective attitudes. *Psychological Monographs: General and Applied, 78* (1, Whole No. 578).

Kamin, L. J. (1976). Heredity, intelligence, politics and science. In N. Block & G. Dworkin (Eds.), *The IQ controversy: Critical readings* (pp. 374–382). London: Quartet Books.

Kaplan, A. (1964). *The conduct of inquiry: Methodology for behavioral science.* San Francisco: Chandler.

Katayama, A. D., Shambaugh, R. N., & Edmonds, T. (2004). *Inadequacies of the copy-and-paste method of on-line notetaking: Why keying-in the notes may lead to higher knowledge transfer.* Poster Session presentation at the meeting of the American Educational Research Association, San Diego, CA.

Katz, J. (1973). A new conception of service: Principles and strategies. In J. Katz (Ed.), *Services for students* (pp. 127–139). New directions for higher education, No. 3. San Francisco: Jossey-Bass.

Kazdin, A. E. (1980). *Research design in clinical psychology*. New York: Harper and Row.

Kelling, G. L., Pate, T., Dieckman, D., & Brown, C. E. (1974). *The Kansas City preventive patrol experiment: A technical report*. Washington, DC: Police Foundation.

Kennedy, M. M. (2007). Defining a literature. *Educational Researcher, 36*(3), 139–147.

Kerlinger, F. N. (1986). *Foundations of behavioral research* (3rd ed). New York: Holt, Rinehart and Winston.

Keyser, D., & Sweetland, R. (2004). *Test critiques* (Vols. I–II). Austin, TX: Pro-Ed.

Khosrow-Pour, M. (2002). *Issues and trends of information technology management in contemporary organizations, Vol. 1*. Toronto, Canada: Idea Group Publishing.

Kidder, L. H. (1981). Qualitative research and quasi-experimental frameworks. In M. B. Brewer & Barry E. Collins (Eds.), *Scientific inquiry and the social sciences* (pp. 226–256). San Francisco: Jossey-Bass.

Kilbourne, B. (2006). The qualitative doctoral dissertation proposal. *Teachers College Record 108*(4), 529–576.

Kincaid, H. V., & Bright, M. (1957). The tandem interview. *Public Opinion Quarterly, 21*(2), 304–312.

Kish, L. (1965). *Survey sampling*. New York: Wiley.

Klahr, D. (2002). *Exploring science: The cognition and development of discovery processes*. Cambridge, MA: MIT Press.

Klein, J. D., Voss, D. R., Reiser, R. A., & Gardner, G. N. (1987). The effect of age of viewer and gender of the narrator on children's visual attention and recall of story ideas. *Educational Communication and Technology Journal, 35,* 231–238.

Knapp, T. R. (1990). Treating ordinal scales as interval scales: An attempt to resolve the controversy. *Nursing Research, 39,* 121–123.

Köbben, A. J. F. (1973). Cause and intention. In R. Naroll & R. Cohen (Eds.), *A handbook of method in cultural anthropology* (pp. 89–98). New York: Columbia University Press.

Koshland, D. E., Jr. (1990). To see ourselves as others see us. *Science, 247*(4938), 9.

Kounin, J. S. (1970). *Discipline and group management in classrooms*. New York: Holt, Rinehart and Winston.

Kounin, J. S., Friesen, W. V., & Norton, A. E. (1966). Managing emotionally disturbed children in regular classrooms. *Journal of Educational Psychology, 57*(1), 1–13.

Kounin, J. S., & Obradovic, S. (1968). Managing emotionally disturbed children in regular classrooms: A replication and extension. *Journal of Special Education, 2*(2), 129–135.

Krathwohl, D. R. (1985). *Social and behavioral science research: A new framework for conceptualizing, implementing, and evaluating research studies*. San Francisco: Jossey-Bass.

Krathwohl, D. R. (1988). *How to prepare a research proposal: Suggestions for funding and dissertations in the social and behavioral sciences* (3rd ed.). Syracuse, NY: Syracuse University Press.

Krathwohl, D. R., & Smith, N. L. (2005). *How to prepare a dissertation proposal*. Syracuse, NY: Syracuse University Press.

Kreps, G. A. (Ed.). (1989). *Social structure and disaster*. Newark: University of Delaware Press.

Krueger, R. A. (1994). *Focus groups: A practical guide to applied research* (2nd ed.). Thousand Oaks, CA: Sage.

Krueger, R. A., & Casey, M. A. (2000). *Focus groups: A practical guide for applied research* (3rd ed.). Thousand Oaks, CA: Sage.

Kruglanski, A. W. (1976). On the paradigmatic objections to experimental psychology. *American Psychologist, 31,* 655–663.

Kruglanski, A. W., & Kroy, M. (1976). Outcome validity in experimental research: A reconceptualization. *Representative Research in Social Psychology, 7,* 166–178.

Kuusela, V., & Simpanen, M. (2002). *Effects of mobile phones on telephone surveys and results*. Retrieved from http://www.icis.dk/ICIS_papers/A_2_3.pdf

Kvale, S. (2002). The social construction of validity. In N. K. Denzin & Y. S. Lincoln (Eds.), *The qualitative inquiry reader* (pp. 299–325). Thousand Oaks, CA: Sage.

LaMura, L. M. (1987). *Whole vs. part practice for the acquisition of gross motor skills: A meta-analysis.* Unpublished manuscript, Syracuse University, School of Education, Syracuse, New York.

Lancy, D. F. (1993). *Qualitative research in education: An introduction to the major traditions.* New York: Longman.

Lancy, D. F., & Zupsic, A. B. (1991, May). *A case study of running start.* Paper presented at a conference on Family and School Support for Early Literacy, Toledo, Ohio.

Lane, S. (1991). Implications of cognitive psychology for measurement and testing: Assessing students' knowledge structures. *Educational Measurement: Issues and Practice, 10*, 31–33, 36.

Lang, K., & Lang, G. E. (1960). Decisions for Christ: Billy Graham in New York City. In M. Stein, A. J. Vidich, & D. M. White (Eds.), *Identity and anxiety: Survival of the person in mass society* (pp. 415–434). Glencoe, IL: Free Press.

Langfeldt, L. (2001). The decision-making constraints and processes of grant peer review, and their effects on review outcome. *Social Studies of Science, 31*(6), 820–841.

Lansing, J., Withey, S., & Wolfe, A. (1971). *Working papers on survey research in poverty areas.* Ann Arbor: Survey Research Center, University of Michigan.

Laslett, B. (1978). Family membership, past and present. *Social Problems, 25*, 476–490.

Laslett, B. (1980). Beyond methodology: The place of theory in quantitative historical research. *American Sociological Review, 45*(2), 214–228.

Lather, L. (2001). Validity as an incitement to discourse: Qualitative research and the crisis of legitimization. In V. Richardson (Ed.), *Handbook of research on teaching* (4th ed., pp. 241–200). Washington, DC: American Educational Research Association.

Lavrakas, P. J. (1993). *Telephone survey methods: Sampling, selection, and supervision* (2nd ed.). Applied social research methods series, Vol. 7. Newbury Park, CA: Sage.

LeCompte, M. D., Millroy, W. L., & Preissle, J. (Eds.). (1992). *Handbook of qualitative research in education.* San Diego: Academic.

LeCompte, M. D., & Preissle, J. (1994). *Ethnography and qualitative design in educational research* (2nd ed.). Thousand Oaks, CA: Sage.

Lee, R. M. (1993). *Doing research on sensitive topics.* Newbury Park, CA: Sage.

Lee, R. M. (2000). *Unobtrusive methods in social research.* Buckingham, UK: Open University Press.

Lee-Treweek, G., & Linkogle, S. (Eds.). (2000). *Danger in the field: Risk and ethics in social research.* London: Routledge.

Legeiwe, H. (1998). How to use computers in qualitative analysis. In A. Strauss & J. Corbin (Eds.), *Basics of qualitative research* (pp. 276–279). Thousand Oaks, CA: Sage.

Leinhardt, G. (1989). Math lessons: A contrast of novice and expert competence. *Journal of Research in Mathematics Education, 20*(1), 52–75.

Leinhardt, G., & Leinhardt, S. (1980). Exploratory data analysis: New tools for the analysis of empirical data. In D. C. Berliner (Ed.), *Review of research in education* (pp. 85–157). Washington, DC: American Educational Research Association.

Leong, F. T. L., & Pfaltzgraff, R. E. (2005). Finding a research topic. In F. T. L. Leong & J. T. Austin (Eds.), *The psychology research handbook: A guide for graduate students and research assistants* (2nd ed., pp. 23–40). Thousand Oaks, CA: Sage.

Levin, B. (2004, October 17). Making research matter more. *Education Policy Analysis Archives, 12*(56). Retrieved from http://epaa.asu.edu/epaa/v12n56/

Levine, H. G. (1985). Principles of data storage and retrieval for use in qualitative evaluations. *Educational Evaluation and Policy Analysis, 7*(2), 169–186.

Lewis, D. (1983). Causal explanation. In D. Lewis (Ed.), *Philosophical Papers* (Vol. 2, pp. 214–240). Oxford, UK: Oxford University Press.

Liebow, E. (1967). *Talley's corner: A study of Negro street corner men*. Boston: Little, Brown.

Light, R. J. (1984). Six evaluation issues that synthesis can resolve better than single studies. In W. H. Yeaton & P. M. Wortman (Eds.), *Issues in data synthesis* (pp. 57–73). New directions for program evaluation, No. 24. San Francisco: Jossey-Bass.

Light, R. J., & Pillemer, D. (1984). *Summing up: The science of reviewing research*. Cambridge, MA: Harvard University Press.

Lincoln, Y. S. (1995). Emerging criteria for quality in qualitative and interpretive research. *Qualitative Inquiry 1*(3), 275–289.

Lincoln, Y. S. (2001). Varieties of validity: Quality in qualitative research. In J. C. Smart & W. G. Tierney (Eds.), *Higher education: Handbook of theory and research* (Vol. XVI, pp. 25–72). New York: Agathon.

Lincoln, Y. S. (2002). Emerging criteria for quality in qualitative and interpretive research. In N. K. Denzin & Y. S. Lincoln (Eds.), *The qualitative inquiry reader* (pp. 327–345). Thousand Oaks, CA: Sage.

Lincoln, Y. S., & Guba, E. G. (1986). But is it rigorous? Trustworthiness and authenticity in naturalistic evaluation. In D. D. Williams (Ed.), *Naturalistic evaluation* (pp. 73–84). New directions for program evaluation, No. 30. San Francisco: Jossey-Bass.

Linn, R. L. (Ed.). (1989). *Educational measurement* (3rd ed.). New York: American Council on Education/Macmillan.

Lipsey, M. W., & Wilson, D. B. (1993). The efficacy of psychological, educational, and behavioral treatment: Confirmation from meta-analysis. *American Psychologist, 48*, 1181–1209.

Lipsey, M. W., & Wilson, D. B. (2001). *Practical meta-analysis*. Applied social research methods series (Vol. 49). Thousand Oaks, CA: Sage.

Locke, L. F., Spirduso, W., & Silverman, S. J. (2005). *Proposals that work: A guide for planning dissertations and grant proposals*. Thousand Oaks, CA: Sage.

Lofland, J. (1971). *Analyzing social settings: A guide to qualitative observation and analysis*. Belmont, CA: Wadsworth.

Lofland, J. (1995). Analytic ethnography: Features, failings, and futures. *Journal of Contemporary Ethnography, 24*, 30–67.

Lynd, R. S., & Lynd, H. M. (1929). *Middletown: A study in contemporary American culture*. New York: Harcourt Brace.

Machado, A., & Silva, F. J. (2007). Scientific method and conceptual analysis. *American Psychologist, 63*(7), 671–681.

Mackintosh, N. J. (Ed.). (1995). *Cyril Burt: Fraud or framed?* Oxford, England: Oxford University Press.

Madaus, G. F. (1981). NIE clarification hearing: The negative team's case. *Phi Delta Kappan, 63*(2), 92–94.

Madaus, G. F., & Stufflebeam, D. (1989). *Educational evaluation: Classic works of Ralph W. Tyler*. Boston: Kluwer.

Madigan, R., Linton, P., & Johnson, S. (1996). APA style: Quo vadis? *American Psychologist, 51*, 653–655.

Madill, A., & Gough, B. (2008). Qualitative research and its place in psychological science. *Psychological Methods, 13*(3), 254–271.

Maher, M. (1999), Relationship based change: A feminist qualitative research case. In M. Kopala & L. A. Suzuki (Eds.), *Using qualitative methods in psychology* (pp. 187–198). Thousand Oaks, CA: Sage.

Mann, C., & Stewart, F. (2000). *Internet communication and qualitative research: A handbook for researching online*. Thousand Oaks, CA: Sage.

Mann, C., & Stewart, F. (2002). Internet interviewing. In J. F. Gubrium & J. A. Holstein (Eds.), *Handbook of interview research: Context and method* (pp. 603–627). Thousand Oaks, CA: Sage.

Mark, M. M., & Shotland, R. L. (1987). Alternative models for the use of multiple methods. In M. M. Mark & R. L. Shotland (Eds.), *Multiple methods in program evaluation* (pp. 95–100). New directions for program evaluation, No. 35. San Francisco: Jossey-Bass.

Marshall, H. (2002). *Qual-Software Archives,* 7/26. Retrieved from http://www.jiscmail.ac.uk/cgi-bin/webadmin?A2=ind0207&L=qual-software&T=0&F=&S=&P=5030

Marshall, S. P. (1990). Generating good items for diagnostic tests. In N. Frederiksen, R. Glaser, A. Lesgold, & M. G. Shafto (Eds.), *Diagnostic monitoring of skill and knowledge acquisition* (pp. 433–452). Hillsdale, NJ: Erlbaum.

Mathison, S. (1988). Why triangulate? *Educational Researcher, 17*(2), 13–17.

Mathison, S. (2005). *Encyclopedia of evaluation.* Thousand Oaks, CA: Sage.

Maxcy, S. J. (2003). Pragmatic threads in mixed methods research in the social sciences. In A. Tashakkori & C. Teddlie (Eds.), *Handbook of mixed methods in social and behavioral research* (pp. 51–89). Thousand Oaks, CA: Sage.

May, R. B., Masson, M. E. J., & Hunter, M. A. (1990). *Application of statistics in behavioral research.* New York: Harper & Row.

Maydeu-Olivares, A., Coffman, D. L., & Hartmann, W. M. (2007). Asymptotically distribution-free (ADF) interval estimation of coefficient alpha. *Psychological Methods, 12,* 157–176.

Mazur, D. J. (2007). *Evaluating the science and ethics of research on humans: A guide for IRB members.* Baltimore, MD: Johns Hopkins University Press.

McCall, W. A. (1923). *How to experiment in education.* New York: Macmillan.

McCleary, R., Gordon, A. C., McDowall, D., & Maltz, M. D. (1979). How a regression effect can make any delinquency intervention look effective. In L. Sechrest, S. G. West, M. A. Phillips, R. Redner, & W. Yeaton (Eds.), *Evaluation studies review annual* (Vol. 4, pp. 626–652). Beverly Hills, CA: Sage.

McKim, B. J., & Cowen, E. L. (1987). Multiperspective assessment of young children's school adjustment. *School Psychology Review, 16*(3), 370–381.

Mead, M. (1928). *Coming of age in Samoa: A psychological study of primitive youth for western civilization.* New York: W. Morrow & Company.

Medawar, P. B. (1984). *The limits of science.* New York: Harper & Row.

Meehl, P. E. (1974). The place of theory in educational research. *Educational Researcher, 3*(6), 3–10.

Mertens, D. M. (2003). Mixed methods and the politics of human research: The transformative-emancipatory perspective. In A. Tashakkori & C. Teddlie (Eds.), *Handbook of mixed methods in social and behavioral research* (pp. 135–164). Thousand Oaks, CA: Sage.

Merton, R. K. (1959). Notes on problem-finding in sociology. In R. K. Merton, L. Broom, & L. Cotrell (Eds.), *Sociology today: Problems and prospects* (pp. ix–xxxiv). New York: Basic Books.

Merton, R. K. (1968). *Social theory and social structure.* New York: Free Press.

Merton, R. K., Fiske, J., & Kendall, P. O. (1956, 1990). *The focused interview: A manual of problems and procedures* (2nd ed.). New York: Free Press.

Messick, S. (1989). Validity. In R. L. Linn (Ed.), *Educational measurement* (3rd ed., pp. 13–104). New York: American Council on Education/Macmillan.

Messick, S. (1995). Validity of psychological assessment: Validation of inferences from persons' responses and performances as scientific inquiry into score meaning. *American Psychologist, 50,* 741–749.

Miles, M. B., & Huberman, A. M. (1984). *Qualitative data analysis: A sourcebook of new methods.* Beverly Hills, CA: Sage.

Miles, M. B., & Huberman, A. M. (1994). *Qualitative data analysis: An expanded sourcebook* (2nd ed.). Thousand Oaks, CA: Sage.

Milgram, S. (1963). Behavioral study of obedience. *Journal of Abnormal and Social Psychology, 67,* 371–378.

Milgram, S. (1974). *Obedience to authority: An experimental viewpoint.* New York: Harper & Row.

Milgram, S. (1977). Ethical issues in the study of obedience. In S. Milgram (Ed.), *The individual in a social world* (pp. 188–199). Reading, MA: Addison-Wesley.

Milgram, S., Sabini, J., & Silver, M. (Eds.). (1992). *The individual in the social world: Essays and experiments* (2nd ed.). New York: McGraw-Hill.

Mill, J. S. (1898). A *system of logic: Ratiocinative and inductive: Being a connected view of evidence and the methods of scientific investigation* (People's ed.). London: Longman, Green and Co.

Miller, J. D. (1984). A new survey technique for studying deviant behavior. *Dissertation Abstracts International, 45,* 319A (University Microfilms No. DA84–10–488).

Miller, S. (2003). Impact of mixed methods and design on inference quality. In A. Tashakkori & C. Teddlie (Eds.), *Handbook of mixed methods in social and behavioral research* (pp. 423–455). Thousand Oaks, CA: Sage.

Milne, C. (2005). Overseeing research: Ethics and the institutional review board *Forum Qualitative Sozialforschung / Forum: Qualitative Social Research 6*(1), Art. 41. Retrieved from http://www.qualitative-research.net/fqs-texte/1-05/05-1-41-e.htm

Mitchell, R. G., Jr. (1994). *Secrecy and fieldwork.* Qualitative Research Methods, No. 29. Newbury Park, CA: Sage.

Moffitt, R. A. (1979). The labor supply response in the Gary experiment. *Journal of Human Resources, 14*(4), 477–487.

Moreland, R. L., & Zajonc, R. B. (1977). Is stimulus recognition a necessary condition for the occurrence of exposure effects? *Journal of Personality and Social Psychology, 35,* 191–199.

Morgan, D. L. (1997a). *Focus groups as qualitative research* (2nd ed.). Qualitative research methods, Vol. 16. Thousand Oaks, CA: Sage.

Morgan, D. L. (1997b). *The focus group guidebook.* Focus group kit, Vol. 1. Thousand Oaks, CA: Sage.

Morgan, D. L. (2002). Focus group interviewing. In J. F. Gubrium & J. A. Holstein (Eds.), *Handbook of interview research: Context and method* (pp. 141–159). Thousand Oaks, CA: Sage.

Moss, P. A. (1996). Enlarging the dialogue in educational measurement: Voices from interpretive research traditions. *Educational Researcher, 25*(Jan.–Feb.), 20–28, 43.

Mosteller, F. (1981). Innovation and evaluation. *Science, 211,* 881–886.

Mosteller, F. K., & Wallace, D. L. (1984). *Applied Bayesian and classical inference: The case of the Federalist papers* (2nd ed.). New York: Springer-Verlag.

Murphy, L. L., Spies, R. A., & Plake, B. S. (2006). *Tests in print VII.* Lincoln: Buros Institute of Mental Measurements, University of Nebraska.

Murray, F. B., & Raths, J. (1996). Factors in the peer review of reviews. *Review of Educational Research, 66,* 417–421.

Nelkin, D. (1984). *Science as intellectual property: Who controls research?* New York: Macmillan.

Nesbit, J. C., & Adesope, O. O. (2006). Learning with concept and knowledge maps: A meta-analysis. *Review of Educational Research, 76,* 413–448.

Neuliep, J. W., & Crandall, R. (1990a). Editorial bias against replication research. *Journal of Social Behavior and Personality, 5,* 5–90.

Neuliep, J. W., & Crandall, R. (1990b). Reviewer bias against replication research. *Journal of Social Behavior and Personality, 8,* 22–29.

New Zealand Ministry of Education (2004). *Iterative best evidence synthesis programme.* Retrieved from Iterative Best Evidence Synthesis Web site: http://educationcounts.edcentre.govt.nz/research/Bes/index.html (see also commentary on BES highlights).

Newhouse, J. P., Rolph, J. E., Mori, B., & Murphy, M. (1980). The effects of deductibles on the demand for medical care services. *Journal of the American Statistical Association, 75*(371), 525–533.

Neyman, J., & Pearson, E. (1933). On the problem of the most efficient tests of statistical hypotheses. *Philosophical Transactions of the Royal Society of London, Series A, Containing Papers of a Mathematical or Physical Character, 231*, 289–337.

Nideröst, B. (2002) Computer-aided qualitative data analysis with Word. *Forum Qualitative Sozialforschung / Forum: Qualitative Social Research 3*(2). Art 22. Retrieved from http://www.qualitative-research.net/index.php/fqs/article/view/861

Nolan, K. L. (1983–present). *Gale directory of online databases.* New York: Gale Research.

Norman, K. L. (n.d.). *Online survey design guide.* Retrieved from http://lap.umd.edu/survey_design/guidelines.html

Norris, J. (1995). *QualPage: Resources for qualitative research.* Retrieved from http://www.qualitativeresearch.uga.edu/QualPage/

O'Donnell, C. L. (2008). Defining, conceptualizing and measuring fidelity of implementation and its relation to outcomes in K–12 curriculum intervention research. *Review of Educational Research, 78* (1), 33–84.

Opdenakker, R. (2006). Advantages and disadvantages of four interview techniques in qualitative research. *Forum Qualitative Sozialforschung / Forum: Qualitative Social Research 7*(4), Art. 11. Retrieved from http://www.qualitative-research.net/fqs-texte/4-06/06-4-11-e.htm

Oppenheim, A. N. (1966). *Questionnaire design and attitude measurement.* New York: Basic Books.

Ornstein, A., & Phillips, W. R. (1978). *Understanding social research: An introduction.* Boston: Allyn & Bacon.

Osborn, A. (1959). *Creative imagination: Applied imagination principles and procedures of creative thinking.* New York: Charles Scribner.

Page, M. M. (1973). On detecting demand awareness by post-experimental questionnaire. *Journal of Social Psychology, 91,* 305–323.

Parnes, H. S. (1967). *Creative behavior workbook.* New York: Scribner.

Patrick, H., & Middleton, M. J. (2002). Turning the kaleidoscope: What we see when self-regulated learning is viewed with a qualitative lens. *Educational Psychologist, 37*(1), 27–39.

Patten, S. C. (1977). Milgram's shocking experiments. *Philosophy, 52,* 425–440.

Patton, M. Q. (1980). *Qualitative evaluation methods.* Beverly Hills, CA: Sage.

Patton, M. Q. (1987). *How to use qualitative methods in evaluation.* Newbury Park, CA: Sage.

Patton, M. Q. (2002). *Qualitative research and evaluation methods* (3rd ed.). Thousand Oaks: Sage.

Patton, M. Q. (2003/2004). On evaluation use: Evaluative thinking and process use. In "Where we've been and where we're going: Experts reflect and look ahead," *Evaluation Exchange, 9*(4). Retrieved from http://www.hfrp.org/evaluation/the-evaluation-exchange/issue-archive/reflecting-on-the-past-and-future-of-evaluation

Payne, D., Krathwohl, D. R., & Gordon, J. (1967). The effect of sequence on programmed instruction. *American Educational Research Journal, 7,* 125–132.

Payne, S. L. (1951). *The art of asking questions.* Princeton, NJ: Princeton University Press.

Penslar, R. L. (2001). *The IRB guidebook.* Washington, DC: Office of Human Research Protections, U.S. Department of Health and Human Services. Retrieved from http://www.hhs.gov/ohrp/irb/irb_guidebook.htm

Peterson, R. A. (2000). *Constructing effective questionnaires.* Thousand Oaks, CA: Sage.

Phelan, P. (1987). Compatibility of qualitative and quantitative methods: Studying child abuse in America. *Education and Urban Society, 29*(1), 35–41.

Phillips, D. C. (1987). *Philosophy, science and social inquiry.* Oxford, UK: Pergamon Press.

Phillips, D. C. (1992). *The social scientists' bestiary.* Oxford, UK: Pergamon Press.

Phillips, D. C. (Ed.). (1994). Epistemological perspectives on educational psychology. *Educational Psychologist, 29,* 1–55.

Phillips, D. C., & Burbules, N. C. (2000). *Post-positivism and educational research.* Lanham, MD: Rowan and Littlefield.

Piantanida, M., & Garman, N. B. (1999). *The qualitative dissertation.* Thousand Oaks, CA: Corwin.

Piel, G. (1986). The social process of science. *Science, 231*, 201.

Pifer, D. (2000, May). Getting in trouble: The meaning of school for "problem" students. *The Qualitative Report, 5*(1/2). Retrieved from http://www.nova.edu/ssss/QR/QR5-1/pifer.html

Piliavin, J. A., & Piliavin, I. M. (1972). Effect of blood on reactions to a victim. *Journal of Personality and Social Psychology, 23*, 353–361.

Pletz, A. (1965). Psychology of the scientist: XI Lotka's law and research visibility. *Psychological Reports, 16*(2), 566–568.

Poincaré, H. (1913). *The foundations of science: Sciences and hypothesis, the value of science, science and method.* New York: Science Press.

Polkinghorn, D. (1983). *Methodology for the human sciences: Systems of inquiry.* Albany: State University of New York Press.

Popham, W. J. (1981). The case for minimum competency testing. *Phi Delta Kappan, 63*(2), 89–91.

Popper, K. R. (1959). *The logic of scientific discovery.* New York: Basic Books.

Popper, K. R. (1972). Of clouds and clocks: An approach to the problem of rationality and the freedom of man. In K. R. Popper (Ed.), *Objective knowledge: An evolutionary approach* (pp. 206–255). Oxford, UK: Clarendon Press.

Potter, D. M. (1954). *People of plenty: Economic abundance and the American character.* Chicago: University of Chicago Press.

Powers, D. E., Fowles, M. E., Farnum, M., & Ramsey, P. (1994). Will they think less of my handwritten essay if others word-process theirs? Effects on essay scores of intermingling handwritten and word-processed essays. *Journal of Educational Measurement, 31*, 220–233.

Prewitt, K. (1980). *Kenneth Prewitt, Frederick Mosteller, and Herbert A. Simon testify at National Science Foundation hearings.* Social Science Research Council Newsletter *Items, 34*, 1–7. (Available from Social Science Research Council, 810 Seventh Avenue, New York, NY 10019.)

Prewitt, K. (1981). Usefulness of the social sciences. *Science, 211*, 659.

Price, D. J. D. (1963). *Little science, big science.* New York: Columbia University Press.

Price, D. J. D. (1975). *Science since Babylon* (enl. ed.). New Haven, CT: Yale University Press.

Price, D. J. (1976). A general theory of bibliometric and other cumulative advantage processes. *Science, 27*, 292–306.

Pritchard, I. A. (2002). Travelers and trolls: Practitioner research and institutional review boards. *Educational Researcher, 31*(3), 3–13.

Radnofsky, M. L. (1995). *CHROMACODE: A conceptual and pedagogical tool in qualitative data analysis.* ERIC Document Reproduction Service No. ED 390 936. Retrieved from http://www.eric.ed.gov/ERICDocs/data/ericdocs2sql/content_storage_01/0000019b/80/14/55/c4.pdf

Ragin, C. C. (1987). *The comparative method: Moving beyond qualitative and quantitative strategies.* Berkeley: University of California Press.

Ragin, C. C. (1993). An introduction to qualitative comparative analysis. In T. Janowski & A. Hicks (Eds.), *The comparative political economy of the welfare state* (pp. 299–314). New York: Cambridge University Press.

RAND Corporation. (1969). *A million random digits with 100,000 normal deviates.* Santa Monica, CA: The RAND Corporation.

Raphael, B. (1986). *When disaster strikes: How individuals and communities cope with catastrophe.* New York: Basic Books.

Raudenbusch, S. W. (1984). Magnitude of teacher expectancy's effects on pupil IQ as a function of credibility of expectancy induction: A synthesis of findings from 18 experiments. *Journal of Educational Psychology, 76*(1), 85–97.

Raudsepp, E. (1977). Daydream a little. *American Way, 10*(April), 27.

Reason, P., & Bradbury, H. (Eds.). (2006). *Handbook of Action Research.* Thousand Oaks, CA: Sage.

Redfield, R. (1955). *The little community.* Chicago: University of Chicago Press.

Reed, J. G., & Baxter, P. M. (2003). *Library use: A handbook for psychology* (3rd ed.). Washington, DC: American Psychology Association.

Reichardt, C. S. (2006). The principle of parallelism in the design of studies to estimate treatment effects. *Psychological Methods, 11,* 1–18.

Rippey, R. M. (Ed.). (1973). *Studies in transactional evaluation.* Berkeley, CA: McCutcheon.

Rist, R. (1977). *The invisible children: School instruction in American society.* Cambridge, MA: Harvard University Press.

Robins, P. K., Spiegelman, R. G., Weiner, S., & Bell, J. G. (Eds.). (1980). *A guaranteed annual income: Evidence from a social experiment.* New York: Academic.

Roethlisberger, F. J., & Dickson, W. J. (1939). *Management and the worker.* Cambridge, MA: Harvard University Press.

Rogers, E. M. (1995). *Diffusion of innovations* (4th ed.). New York: Free Press.

Rosengarten, T. (1981). Stepping over cockleburs: Conversations with Ned Cobb. In M. Pachter (Ed.), *Telling lives: The biographer's art* (pp. 104–131). Philadelphia: University of Pennsylvania Press.

Rosenthal, R. (1969). Interpersonal expectations: Effects on experimenters' hypothesis. In R. Rosenthal & R. L. Rosnow (Eds.), *Artifact in behavioral research* (pp. 181–277). New York: Academic.

Rosenthal, R. (1979). The "file drawer" problem and tolerance for negative results. *Psychological Bulletin, 86*(3), 638–641.

Rosenthal, R. (1994). Parametric measures of effect size. In H. Cooper & L. Hedges (Eds.), *The handbook of research synthesis* (pp. 231–244). New York: Russell Sage Foundation.

Rosenthal, R., & Rosnow, R. L. (1975). *The volunteer subject.* New York: John Wiley.

Rosenthal, R., & Rubin, D. (1980). Summarizing 345 studies of interpersonal expectancy effects. In R. Rosenthal (Ed.), *Quantitative assessment of research domains* (pp. 79–94). New directions for methodology of social and behavioral science, No. 5. San Francisco: Jossey-Bass.

Rosenthal, R., & Rubin, D. (1982). Comparing effect sizes of independent studies. *Psychological Bulletin, 92*(2), 500–504.

Rosner, S., & Abt, L. (1970). *The creative experience.* New York: Grossman.

Rossi, P. H., Berk, R. A., & Lenihan, K. J. (1980). *Money, work and crime: Experimental evidence.* New York: Academic Press.

Rossi, P. H., Lipsey, H. E., & Freeman, M. W. (2003). *Evaluation: A systematic approach* (7th ed.). Thousand Oaks, CA: Sage.

Rossi, P. H., & Lyall, K. (1976). *Reforming public welfare: A critique of the negative income tax experiments.* New York: Russell Sage Foundation.

Rossi, P. H., & Wright, J. D. (1986). Evaluation research: An assessment. In D. S. Cordray & M. W. Lipsey (Eds.), *Evaluation studies review annual* (Vol. 11, pp. 48–69). Beverly Hills, CA: Sage.

Rothman, B. K. (1986). Reflection: On hard work. *Qualitative Sociology, 9,* 48–53.

Rowe, M. B. (1974). Relation of wait-time and rewards to the development of language, logic and fate control: Part I, wait-time. *Journal of Research in Science Teaching, 11,* 81–94.

Rowley, Sir Walter (1751). Quotation #45915. In R. Andrews, M. Biggs, & M. Seidel (Eds.), *The Columbia world of quotations* (1996). New York: Columbia University Press.

Royce, J. M., Lazar, I., & Darlington, R. B. (1983). Minority families, early education, and later life chance. *American Journal of Orthopsychiatry, 53*(4), 706–720.

Rubin, L. B. (1976). *Worlds of pain: Life in the working class family.* New York: Basic Books.

Rubin, L. B. (1981). Sociological research: The subjective dimension. *Symbolic Interaction, 4*(1), 97–112.

Ryan, G. W., & Bernard, H. R. (2000). Data management and analysis methods. In N. K. Denzin & Y. S. Lincoln (Eds.), *Handbook of qualitative research* (2nd ed., pp. 769–778). Thousand Oaks, CA: Sage.

Ryan, G. W., & Bernard, H. R. (2003). Techniques to identify themes. *Field Methods, 15*(1), 85–109.

Sadler, D. R. (1981). Intuitive data processing as a potential source of bias in naturalistic evaluations. *Educational Evaluation and Policy Analysis, 3*(4), 25–31.

Saldaña, J. (2003). *Longitudinal qualitative research: Analyzing change through time.* Walnut Creek, CA: AltaMira.

Salomon, G. (1981). *Communication and education: Social and psychological interactions.* Beverly Hills, CA: Sage.

Sandelowski, M. (2003). Tables or tableaux? The challenges of writing and reading mixed methods studies. In A. Tashakkori & C. Teddlie (Eds.), *Handbook of mixed methods in social and behavioral research* (pp. 321–350). Thousand Oaks, CA: Sage.

Sanjek, R. (Ed.). (1990). *Fieldnotes: The makings of anthropology.* Ithaca, NY: Cornell University Press.

Sasz, T. S. (1974). *Ceremonial chemistry: The ritual persecution of drugs, addicts, and the pushers.* Garden City, NY: Doubleday.

Schaefer, D. R., & Dillman, D. A. (1998). Development of a standard e-mail methodology: Results of an experiment. *Public Opinion Quarterly, 62,* 378–398.

Scheerer, M. (1963). Problem solving. *Scientific American, 208*(4), 118–128.

Schmidt, F. (2008). Meta-analysis: A constantly evolving research integration tool. *Organizational Research Methods, 11* (1), 96-113.

Schmidt, F. L. (1996). Statistical significance testing and cumulative knowledge in psychology: Implications for training of researchers. *Psychological Methods, 1,* 115–129.

Schmidt, F. L., Oh, I. S., & Hayes, T. L. (2007, November 13). Fixed versus random effects models in meta-analysis: Model properties and an empirical comparison of differences in results. *British Journal of Mathematical and Statistical Psychology.* Retrieved from http://www.ncbi.nlm.nih.gov/pubmed/18001516

Schneider, B., Carnoy, M., Kilpatrick, J., Schmidt, W. H., & Shavelson, R. J. (2007). *Estimating causal effects using experimental and observational designs.* Washington, DC: American Educational Research Association.

Schneider, J. W., & Conrad, P. (1985). *Having epilepsy: The experience and control of illness.* Philadelphia, PA: Temple University Press.

Schon, D. A. (1983). *The reflective practitioner: How professionals think in action.* New York: Basic Books.

Schon, D. A. (1987). *Educating the reflective practitioner.* Presentation to the 1987 meeting of the American Educational Research Association, Washington, DC. Transcribed by Jan Carrick, January, 1998; posted by Tom Russell, Queen's University, January, 1998. Retrieved from http://educ.queensu.ca/~ar/schon87.htm

Schonlau, M., Fricker, R. D., & Elliott, M. N. (2002). *Conducting research surveys via e-mail and the web.* Santa Monica, CA: RAND Corporation. Retrieved from http://www.rand.org/pubs/monograph_reports/MR1480/index.html

Schuman, H., & Converse, J. (1971). The effects of black and white interviewers on black responses in 1968. *Public Opinion Quarterly, 35*(1), 44–68.

Schuman, H., & Kalton, G. (1985). Survey methods. In G. Lindzey & E. Aronson (Eds.), *The handbook of social psychology* (3rd ed., pp. 635–698). New York: Random House.

Schwab, J. J. (1978). Education and the structure of disciplines. In I. Westbury & N. J. Wilkof (Eds.), *Joseph J. Schwab: Science, curriculum and liberal education* (pp. 229–274). Chicago: University of Chicago Press.

Schwalbe, M. (1996) *Unlocking the iron cage: The men's movement, gender politics, and American culture.* New York: Oxford University Press.

Schwandt, T. A. (2001). *Dictionary of qualitative inquiry terms.* Thousand Oaks, CA: Sage.

Schwarz, N., & Sudman, S. (Eds.). (1996). *Answering questions: Methodology for determining cognitive and communicative processes in survey research.* San Francisco: Jossey-Bass.

Schweinhart, L. J., & Weikart, D. P. (1985). Evidence that early childhood programs work. *Phi Delta Kappan, 66,* 545–551.

Schweitzer, A. (1990). *Out of my life and thought: An autobiography* (A. B. Lemke, Trans.). New York: Holt, Rinehart and Winston. (Original work published 1933.)

Scriven, M. (1967). The methodology of evaluation. In R. W. Tyler, R. M. Gagné, & M. Scriven (Eds.), *Perspectives of curriculum evaluation* (pp. 39–83). Chicago: Rand McNally.

Scriven, M. (1972). Prose and cons about goal-free evaluation. *Evaluation Comment, 3,* 1–4. Reprinted in *Evaluation Practice, 12,* 55–62.

Scriven, M. (1991). Beyond formative and summative evaluation. In M. W. McLaughlin & D. C. Phillips (Eds.), *Evaluation and education: At quarter century* (pp. 19–64). Ninetieth yearbook of the National Society for the Study of Education, part II. Chicago: University of Chicago Press.

Scriven, M. (2007). Key evaluation checklist. Retrieved from http://www.wmich.edu/evalctr/checklists/kec_feb07.pdf

Scriven, M. (2008). A summative evaluation of RCT methodology: An alternative approach to causal research. *Journal of MultiDisciplinary Evaluation, 5*(9), 11–24. Retrieved from http://survey.ate.wmich.edu/jmde/index.php/jmde_1/article/view/160/186

Secrist, C., de Koeyer, I., Bell, H., & Fogel, A. (2002). Combining digital video technology and narrative methods for understanding infant development. *Forum Qualitative Sozialforschung / Forum: Qualitative Social Research 3*(2), Art. 24, Retrieved from http://www.qualitative-research.net/fqs-texte/2-02/2-02secristetal-e.htm

Segerstråle, U. (1994). Science by worst cases. *Science, 263,* 837–838.

Seidman, I. E. (1991). *Interviewing as qualitative research.* Thousand Oaks, CA: Sage.

Seligman, E. P. (1995). The effectiveness of psychotherapy. *American Psychologist, 50,* 965–974.

Shadish, W. R. (1993). Critical multiplism: A research strategy and its attendant tactics. In L. Sechrest (Ed.), *Program evaluation: A pluralistic enterprise* (pp. 13–57). New directions for program evaluation, No. 60. San Francisco: Jossey-Bass.

Shadish, W. R. (1996). Meta-analysis and the exploration of causal processes: A primer of examples, methods and issues. *Psychological Methods, 1,* 47–65.

Shadish, W. R., Cook, T. D., & Campbell, D. T. (2002). *Experimental and quasi-experimental designs for generalized causal inference.* Boston: Houghton Mifflin.

Shadish, W. R., & Fuller, S. (Eds.) (1994). *The social psychology of science.* New York: Guilford.

Shavelson, R. J. (1996). *Statistical reasoning for the behavioral sciences* (3rd ed.). Boston: Allyn & Bacon.

Shavelson, R. J., Webb, N. M., & Rowley, G. L. (1989). Generalizability theory. *American Psychologist, 44,* 922–932.

Sheehan, K. B., & Hoy, M. G. (1999). Using e-mail to survey internet users in the United States: Methodology and assessment. *Journal of Computer Mediated Communication, 4 (3).* Retrieved from http://jcmc.indiana.edu/vol4/issue3/sheehan.html

Sheehan, K. B., & McMillan, S. J. (1999). Response variation in e-mail surveys: An exploration. *Journal of Advertising Research, 39*(4), 45–54.

Sherman, C. (2005). Searching for a good searching book. Retrieved from http//:searchenginewatch.com/3557326

Sieber, J. E., & Stanley, B. (1988). Ethical and professional dimensions of socially sensitive research. *American Psychologist, 43,* 49–55.

Sieber, S. D. (1973). The integration of fieldwork and survey methods. *American Journal of Sociology, 78*(6), 1335–1359.

Siegel, S., & Castellan, N. J. (1988). *Nonparametric statistics for the behavioral sciences* (2nd ed.). New York: McGraw-Hill.

Simon, A., & Boyer, G. E. (1974). *Mirrors for behavior.* Philadelphia: Communication Materials Center.

Simon, H. A. (1992). What is an explanation of behavior? *Psychological Science, 3,* 150–161.

Skinner, B. F. (1957). *Verbal behavior.* New York: Appleton-Century Crofts.

Skinner, B. F. (1959). A case history in scientific method. In S. Koch (Ed.), *Psychology: A study of a science, Vol. 2, General systematic formulations, learning, and special processes* (pp. 359–379). New York: McGraw-Hill.

Skipper, J. K., & McCaghy, C. H. (1972). Respondents' intrusion upon the situation: The problem of interviewing subjects with special qualities. *Sociological Quarterly, 13,* 237–243.

Slavin, R. E. (1986). Best-evidence synthesis: An alternative to meta-analytic and traditional reviews. *Educational Researcher, 15*(9), 5–11.

Slavin, R. E. (1987). Best-evidence synthesis: Why less is more. *Educational Researcher, 16*(4), 15–16.

Slovic, P., Fischhoff, B., & Lichtenstein, S. (1982). Response mode, framing, and information-processing effects in risk assessment. In R. M. Hogarth (Ed.), *Question framing and response consistency.* New directions for methodology of social and behavioral science, No. 11. San Francisco: Jossey-Bass.

Smith, M. L., Gabriel, R., Schott, J., & Padia, W. L. (1976). Evaluation effects of outward bound. In G. V. Glass (Ed.), *Evaluation studies review annual* (Vol. 1, pp. 400–421). Beverly Hills, CA: Sage.

Smith, M. L., & Glass, G. V. (1977). Meta-analysis of psychotherapy outcome studies. *American Psychologist, 32,* 752–760.

Smith, M. L., Glass, G. V., & Miller, T. I. (1980). *Benefits of psychotherapy.* Baltimore, MD: Johns Hopkins University Press.

Snyder, M., & Cunningham, M. R. (1975). To comply or not comply: Testing the self-perception explanation of the "foot-in-the-door" phenomenon. *Journal of Personality and Social Psychology, 31*(1), 64–67.

Soffer, E. (1995). The principal as action researcher: A study of disciplinary practice. In S. E. Noffke & R. B. Stevenson (Eds.), *Educational action research: Becoming practically critical* (pp. 115–126). New York: Teachers College.

Spalding, W. B., & Krathwohl, D. R. (1959). *A report of the evaluation of the Arkansas Experiment in Teacher Education.* Unpublished manuscript available at University of Illinois at Urbana-Champaign Library.

Spradley, J. P. (1980). *Participant observation.* New York: Holt, Rinehart and Winston.

Stabb, S. D. (1999). Teaching qualitative research in psychology. In M. Kopala & L. Suzuki (Eds.), *Using qualitative methods in psychology* (pp. 89–99). Thousand Oaks, CA: Sage.

Stack, C. (1974). *All our kin: Strategies for survival in a black community.* New York: Harper & Row.

Stake, R. E. (1975). *Evaluating the arts in education: A responsive approach.* Columbus, OH: Charles Merrill.

Stake, R. E. (1991). Excerpts from: "Program evaluation, particularly responsive evaluations." *Evaluation Practice, 12,* 63–77.

Stake, R. E. (1995). *The art of case study research.* Thousand Oaks, CA: Sage.

Stankiewicz, R. (1979). The size and age of Swedish academic research groups and their scientific performance. In F. M. Andrews (Ed.), *Scientific productivity: The effectiveness of research groups in six countries* (pp. 191–222). Cambridge: Cambridge University Press.

Stanley, B., Sieber, J. E., & Melton, G. B. (1987). Empirical studies of ethical issues in research: A research agenda. *American Psychologist, 42,* 735–741.

Steiner, J. (1984). *Notebooks of the mind.* Albuquerque: University of New Mexico Press.

Stevens, S. S. (1946). On the theory of scales of measurement. *Science, 103,* 677–680.

Stevens, S. S. (1951). Mathematics, measurement, and psychophysics. In S. S. Stevens (Ed.), *Handbook of experimental psychology* (pp. 1–49). New York: Wiley.

Strauss, A. (1987). *Qualitative analysis for social scientists.* Cambridge: Cambridge University Press.

Strauss, A., & Corbin, J. (1998). *Basics of qualitative research: Techniques and procedures for developing grounded theory* (2nd ed.). Thousand Oaks, CA: Sage.

Struyk, R. J., & Bendick, M., Jr. (1981). *Housing vouchers for the poor: Lessons from a national experiment.* Washington, DC: Urban Institute.

Stufflebeam, D. L., & Shinkfield, A. J. (1985). *Systematic evaluation: A self-instruction guide to theory and practice.* Boston: Kluwer Nijhoff.

Stufflebeam, D. L., & Shinkfield, A. J. (2007). *Evaluation theory, models, and applications.* San Francisco: Jossey-Bass/Wiley.

Subkoviak, M. J. (1988). A practitioner's guide to computation and interpretation of reliability indices for mastery tests. *Journal of Educational Measurement, 25*(1), 47–56.

Sudman, S., & Bradburn, N. M. (1982). *Asking questions: a practical guide to questionnaire design.* San Francisco: Jossey-Bass.

Sullivan, M. A., Queen, S. A., & Patrick, R. C., Jr. (1958). Participant observation as employed in a study of a military training program. *American Sociological Review, 23,* 660–667.

Sulloway, F. (1979). *Freud, biologist of the mind: Beyond the psychoanalytic legend.* London: Burnett Books.

Survey Research Center, Institute for Social Research. (1976). *Interviewer's manual* (rev. ed.). Ann Arbor: Institute for Social Research, University of Michigan.

Swazey, J. P., Anderson, M. S., & Louis, K. S. (1994). Ethical problems in academic research. *American Scientist, 81*(6), 542–553.

Symon, G. (2002). Positioning qualitative research: Meaning and value. *APA Review of Books, 47,* 176–178.

Tashakkori, A., & Teddlie, C. (Eds.). (2003). *Handbook of mixed methods in social and behavioral research.* Thousand Oaks, CA: Sage.

Taylor, S. J. (1977). The custodians: Attendants and their work at state institutions for the mentally retarded. *International Dissertation Abstracts, 39,* 1145–1146.

Taylor, S. J., & Bogdan, R. (1998). *Introduction to qualitative research methods* (3rd ed.). New York: Wiley.

Terman, L. M., & Bird, T. B. (1926). *The mental and physical traits of a thousand gifted children* (Vol. 1). Stanford, CA: Stanford University Press.

Terman, L. M., & Oden, M. M. (1947). *The gifted child grows up. Twenty-five year follow-up of a superior group* (Vol. 4). Stanford, CA: Stanford University Press.

Terman, L. M., & Oden, M. M. (1959). *The gifted group at midlife* (Vol. 5). Stanford, CA: Stanford University Press.

Tesser, A. (1990) *Interesting models in social psychology: A personal view.* Invited address presented at the meeting of the American Psychological Association, Boston.

Test Collection, Educational Testing Service. (1986–1991). *The ETS test collection catalog, Volume 1: Achievement tests and measurement devices; Volume 2: Vocational tests and measurement devices; Volume 3: Tests for special population; Volume 4: Cognitive aptitude and intelligence tests.* Phoenix, AZ: Oryx.

Thorndike, R. L. (1947). *Research problems and techniques.* AAF Aviation Psychology Research Program Reports, No. 3. Washington, DC: U.S. Government Printing Office.

Thurstone, L. L. (1935). *Vectors of the mind.* Chicago: University of Chicago Press.

Thurstone, L. L. (1947). *A development and expansion of the vectors of the mind: Multiple factor analysis.* Chicago: University of Chicago Press.

Tinto, V. (1987). *Leaving college: Rethinking the causes and cures of student attrition.* Chicago: University of Chicago Press.

Tobias, S., & Zibrin, M. (1978). Does blind reviewing make a difference? *Educational Researcher, 7*(Jan.), 14–16.

Toynbee, A. J. (1948). *A study of history.* London: Oxford University Press.

Travers, R. M. W. (1961). *Measured needs of teachers and behavior in the classroom.* Salt Lake City: University of Utah, Department of Educational Psychology.

Tripp-Reimer, T. (1983). Retention of a folk-healing practice (matiasma) among four generations of urban Greek immigrants. *Nursing Research, 32*(2), 97–101.

Tuchman, B. (1962). *The guns of August.* New York: Macmillan.

Tuckman, H. P. (1976). *Publication, teaching and the academic reward structure.* Lexington, MA: D. C. Heath.

Tufte, E. R. (1983). *The visual display of quantitative information.* Cheshire, CT: Graphics Press.

Tukey, J. W. (1997). *Exploratory data analysis.* Reading, MA: Addison Wesley.

Tuomey, C. P. (1996). *Conjuring science: Scientific symbols and cultural meanings in American life.* New Brunswick, NJ: Rutgers University Press.

Turner, C. F., & Martin, E. (Eds.). (1984). *Surveying subjective phenomena, Vol. 1.* New York: Russell Sage Foundation.

Tversky, A., & Kahneman, D. (1981). The framing of decisions and the psychology of choice. *Science, 211*, 453–458.

Tyack, D. (1976). Ways of seeing: An essay on the history of compulsory schooling. *Harvard Educational Review, 46*(3), 355–389.

Tyler, L. L., Klein, M. F., & Associates. (1976). *Evaluating and choosing curriculum and instructional materials.* Los Angeles: Educational Resource Associates.

Tyler, R. W., & Waples, D. (1930). *Research methods and teacher's problems: A manual for systematic studies of classroom procedure.* New York: Macmillan.

Umesh, U. N., & Peterson, R. A. (1991). A critical evaluation of the randomized response method: Applications, validation, and research agenda. *Sociological Methods & Research, 20*(1), 104–138.

Valenstein, E. S. (1994). Neuroscience: Paths, detours, and hazards. [Review of *The Neurosciences: Paths of Discovery*, 1]. *Contemporary Psychology, 39,* 140–143.

Van Alystyne, M., & Brynjolfsson, E. (1996). Could the Internet balkanize science? *Science, 274*, 1479–1480.

Van den Hoonaard, W. C. (Ed.). (2002). *Walking the tightrope: Ethical issues for qualitative researchers.* Toronto: University of Toronto Press.

Van Maanen, J. (2002). The fact of fiction in organizational ethnography. In M. Huberman & M. B. Miles (Eds.), *The qualitative researcher's companion* (101–117). Thousand Oaks, CA: Sage.

Venkatesh, S. (2008). *Gang leader for a day: A rogue sociologist takes to the streets.* New York: Penguin Press.

Wade, N. (1978). Guillemin and Schally: A race spurred by rivalry. *Science, 200*, 510–513.

Walberg, H. J. (1986). Syntheses of research on teaching. In M. C. Wittrock (Ed.), *Handbook of research on teaching* (3rd ed., pp. 214–229). New York: Macmillan.

Walker, D. F., & Schaffarzick, J. (1974). Comparing curricula. *Review of Educational Research, 44*, 83–111.

Wanner, E. (1995). Foreword. In T. D. Cook et al., *Meta-analysis for explanation: A casebook.* New York: Russell Sage Foundation.

Warner, S. L. (1965). Randomized response: A survey technique for eliminating evasive answer bias. *Journal of the American Statistical Association, 60,* 63–69.

Watson, J. D. (1968). *The double helix: A personal account of the discovery of the structure of DNA.* New York: Atheneum.

Watt, J. H. (1999). Internet systems for evaluation research. In G. Gay & T. Bennington (Eds.), *Information technologies in evaluation: Social, moral, epistemological and practical implications* (pp. 23–44). New directions in evaluation, No. 84. San Francisco: Jossey-Bass.

Watts, H. W., & Rees, A. (Eds.). (1976). *The New Jersey income maintenance experiment* (Vol. 2). New York: Academic.

Wax, M. L., & Wax, R. H. (1980). Fieldwork and the research process. *Anthropology and Education Quarterly, 11*(1), 29–37.

Wax, R. H. (1971). *Doing fieldwork: Warnings and advice.* Chicago: University of Chicago Press.

Weaver, L., & Cousins, J. B. (2004). Unpacking the participatory process. *Journal of Multidisciplinary Evaluation, Vol. 1.* An online peer-reviewed journal. Retrieved from http://www.wmich.edu/evalctr/jmde/content/JMDE_Num_001_Part_I.htm

Webb, E. J., Campbell, D. T., Schwartz, R. C., & Sechrest, L. (1981). *Nonreactive measures in the social sciences* (2nd ed.). Boston: Houghton Mifflin.

Weick, K. E. (1984). Small wins: Redefining the scale of social problems. *American Psychologist, 39*, 40–49.

Weiner, B. (1972). *Theories of motivation from mechanism to cognition.* Chicago: Markham.

Weiss, C. H. (1991). Evaluation research on political context: Sixteen years and four administrations later. In M. W. McLaughlin & D. Phillips (Eds.), *Evaluation and education at quarter century* (pp. 211–231). Ninetieth Yearbook of the National Society for the Study of Education, Part II. Chicago: University of Chicago Press.

Weiss, D., & Davison, M. (1981). Test theory and method. In L. E. Tyler (Ed.), *Annual review of psychology,* Vol. 32 (pp. 629–658). Palo Alto, CA: Annual Reviews

Weiss, R. S. (1994). *Learning from strangers: The art and method of qualitative interview studies.* New York: Free Press.

Weitzman, E. A., & Miles, M. B. (1995). *Computer programs for qualitative data analysis.* Thousand Oaks, CA: Sage.

Weller, A. C. (2001). *Editorial peer review: Its strengths and weaknesses.* Medford, NJ: Information Today.

Welsh, E. (2002). Dealing with data: Using NVivo in the qualitative data analysis process. *Forum Qualitative Sozialforschung / Forum: Qualitative Social Research, 3*(2). Art. 26, Retrieved from http//www.qualitative-research.net/index.php/fqs/article/view/865/1880

Wentland, E. J. (1993). *Survey responses: An evaluation of their validity.* San Diego, CA: Academic.

Wertheimer, M. (1945). *Productive thinking.* New York: Harper.

Wharton, C. S. (1996). Making people feel good: Workers' constructions of meaning in interactive service jobs. *Qualitative Sociology, 19*, 217–233.

White, H. D. (1994). Scientific communication and literature retrieval. In H. Cooper & L. V. Hedges (Eds.), *The handbook of research synthesis* (pp. 41–56). New York: Russell Sage Foundation.

Whyte, W. F. (1953). Interviewing for organizational research. *Human Organization, 12,* 15–22.

Whyte, W. F. (1957). On asking indirect questions. *Human Organization, 15,* 21–23.

Whyte, W. F. (1984). *Learning from the field.* Beverly Hills, CA: Sage.

Whyte, W. F. (1993). *Street corner society: The social structure of an Italian slum* (2nd ed.). Chicago: University of Chicago Press.

Willensky, J. (2003, January 11). Policymakers' online use of academic research. *Educational Policy Analysis Archives, 11*(2). Retrieved from http://epaa.asu.edu/epaa/v11n2/

Wilson, J. (1971). *Thinking with concepts.* Cambridge, UK: University Press.

Wilson, J., & Musick, M. (1997). Who cares? Toward an integrated theory of volunteer work. *American Sociological Review, 62*(5), 694–713.

Wilson, T. D., DePaulo, B. M., Mook, D. G., & Klaaren, K. J. (1993). Scientists' evaluations of research: The biasing effects of the importance of the topic. *Psychological Science, 4*, 322–325.

Windle, C. (1954). Test-retest effect on personality questionnaires. *Educational and Psychological Measurement, 14*, 617–633.

Winne, P. H. (1995). Inherent details in self-regulated learning. *Educational Psychologist, 30*, 173–187.

Wolcott, H. (1973). *The man in the principal's office: An ethnography.* New York: Holt, Rinehart and Winston.

Wolcott, H. F. (1995) *The art of fieldwork.* Walnut Creek, CA: AltaMira.

Wolcott, H. J. (2001). *Writing up qualitative research.* Thousand Oaks, CA: Sage.

Wolf, R. L. (1975). Trial by jury: A new evaluation method. *Phi Delta Kappan, 57*(3), 185–187.

Wolf, R. L. (1979). The use of judicial evaluation methods in the formulation of educational policy. *Evaluation and Policy Analysis, 1*(3), 19–28.

Wong, L. Y. (1995). Research on teaching: Process-product research findings and the feelings of obviousness. *Journal of Educational Psychology, 87*, 504–511.

Worthen, B. R., & Sanders, J. R. (1987). *Educational evaluation: Alternative approaches and practical guidelines.* White Plains, NY: Longman.

Worthen, B. R., Sanders, J. R., & Kirkpatrick, J. L. (2004). *Program evaluation: Alternative approaches and practical guidelines* (2nd ed.). White Plains, NY: Longman.

Wurman, R. S. (1989). *Information anxiety: What to do when information doesn't tell you what you need to know.* New York: Doubleday.

Wylie, R. C. (1979). *The self-concept* (rev. ed.). Lincoln: University of Nebraska Press.

Yin, R. K. (2002). *Case study research: Design and methods* (3rd ed.).Thousand Oaks, CA: Sage.

Youngstrom, N. (1990). Psychologist receives NAMI science award. *Monitor on Psychology, 21*(September), 7.

Zdep, S. M., & Irvine, S. H. (1970). A reverse Hawthorne effect in educational evaluations. *Journal of School Psychology, 8*(2), 89–95.

Zeigarnik, B. (1927). Untersuchungen sur handlungs und affektpsychologie, herausgegeben von K. Lewin. 3, Das behaten erledigter und unerledigter handlunger. Von Psychologisches Forschung. *Psychological Research, 9*, 1–85.

Zimbardo, P. G., Anderson, S. M., & Kabat, L. G. (1981). Induced hearing deficit generates experimental paranoia. *Science, 212*(June), 1529–1531.

Zwicky, F. (1969). *Discovery invention & research through the morphological approach.* New York: Macmillan.

Name Index

The abbreviations *t*, *f,* and *n* stand for table, figure, and reference notes, respectively.

Subject Index

The abbreviations *t, f,* and *n* stand for table, figure, and reference notes, respectively.